THE SOVIET SIXTIES

THE SOVIET SIXTIES

ROBERT HORNSBY

YALE UNIVERSITY PRESS
NEW HAVEN AND LONDON

For information about this and other Yale University Press publications, please contact:
U.S. Office: sales.press@yale.edu   yalebooks.com
Europe Office: sales@yaleup.co.uk   yalebooks.co.uk

Set in Adobe Garamond Pro by IDSUK (DataConnection) Ltd
Printed in Great Britain by TJ Books, Padstow, Cornwall

Library of Congress Control Number: 2023940054

ISBN 978-0-300-25052-7

A catalogue record for this book is available from the British Library.

10 9 8 7 6 5 4 3 2 1

MIX
Paper from
responsible sources
FSC
www.fsc.org   FSC® C013056

For Ella and Nina

CONTENTS

ILLUSTRATIONS

1. Stalin lying in state, 1953. National Archives – Stills / Getty Images.
2. Jawaharlal Nehru and Indira Gandhi with Nikita Khrushchev and Nikolai Bulganin, June 1955. Bettmann / Getty Images.
3. Ilya Ehrenburg in Geneva, 1955. ullstein bild Dtl. / Getty Images.
4. *Carnival Night*, directed by Eldar Ryazanov, 1956. TCD / Prod.DB / Alamy.
5. Students in Moscow for the sixth World Youth Festival, 1957. Sovfoto / Getty Images.
6. Sergei Korolev and Igor Kurchatov, date unknown. Sovfoto / Getty Images.
7. Nikita Khrushchev and Che Guevara, 1960. Bettmann / Getty Images.
8. Soviet space dogs Belka and Strelka, 1960. Bettmann / Getty Images.
9. Andrei Sakharov, early 1960s. Heritage Images / Getty Images.
10. May Day parade in Kiev (Kyiv), 1961. FPG / Getty Images.
11. 'Glory to women: active builders of communism' propaganda poster, unrecorded artist, 1962. © Wright Museum of Art Collection, Beloit College. Women's Industries, Lithograph (Museum Purchase 2010.5.1).
12. Anastas Mikoyan, Nikita Khrushchev and Leonid Brezhnev speak to Valentina Tereshkova on the telephone, 1963. Keystone-France / Getty Images.
13. Maya Plisetskaya performing in the United Kingdom, 1963. Evening Standard / Getty Images.
14. Poet Yevgeny Yevtushenko, Moscow, 1964. ullstein bild Dtl. / Getty Images.
15. The Soviet Union's cosmonaut team, 1964. Bettmann / Getty Images.

SPELLING AND NAMING CONVENTIONS

In transliterating words and names into English from Russian (the standard language of Soviet officialdom), I have largely employed a simplified version of the British Standard System. There are, however, exceptions to this trend: primarily in regard to people and terms that already have an 'accepted' spelling in English. In the footnotes and bibliography I have been more rigorous in applying the rules of transliteration.

As for Soviet towns and cities, I have used the names and spellings that were used by the authorities at the time, for purposes of historical accuracy. For those places that have since changed their spelling, I have included the contemporary form in parentheses at first mention. The text thus refers to Kiev and Lvov, for example, rather than today's correct spelling of Kyiv and Lviv. Where the name of a place changed entirely either during the period (such as Stalingrad to Volgograd and Stalino to Donetsk) or after (such as Frunze to Bishkek and Leningrad to St Petersburg), that is reflected in the same way.

ACKNOWLEDGEMENTS

I have had the good fortune to work in archives and libraries in Belarus, Estonia, Georgia, Latvia, Lithuania, Russia, Ukraine, the UK and the US. I have been treated kindly and with patience everywhere, for which I am grateful.

At Yale University Press, Heather McCallum has been an insightful and supportive editor during what has been a demanding project, much of which has taken place during a global pandemic. Many of my fellow scholars working in Soviet history have offered perceptive thoughts, pointed me towards useful readings and shared materials over the years, and I am grateful to all of them for this. I am especially indebted to those who have read and offered valuable comments on draft material, including anonymous reviewers at Yale University Press, Thetis Abela, James Glossop, John Hornsby, Yoram Gorlizki, Philip Boobbyer, Siobhán Hearne, Melanie Ilic, Pia Koivunen, Joshua Rubenstein and Tomas Sniegon.

NORTH Sea

NORWAY

WEST
GERMANY

EAST
GERMANY

SWEDEN

LATVIAN
SSR

LITHUANIAN SSR

*Baltic
Sea*

FINLAND

Kaliningrad

POLAND

Tallinn

Murmansk

Riga

Leningrad

Vilnius

Minsk

ESTONIAN
SSR

Arkhangel

MOLDAVIAN
SSR

Kiev

BELORUSSIAN SSR

Chişinău

UKRAINIAN SSR

Moscow

Odessa

Kharkov

Gorky

Crimea

R U S S I A N   S O V I E T

*Black
Sea*

Rostov-on-Don

S O C I A L I S T

Volgograd

Kuybyshev

GEORGIAN
SSR

Sverdlovsk

Chelyabinsk

TURKEY

Tbilisi

ARMENIAN SSR

Yerevan

Omsk

Nagorny Karabagh

Novosibirsk

Baku

*Caspian
Sea*

Aral Sea

K A Z A K H
S S R

AZERBAIJAN
SSR

UZBEK SSR

TURKMEN SSR

Lake Balkash

Ashkhabad

Tashkent

Alma-Ata

I R A N

Bishkek

Dushanbe

TAJIK SSR

AFGHANISTAN

KIRGHIZ
SSR

C H I N A

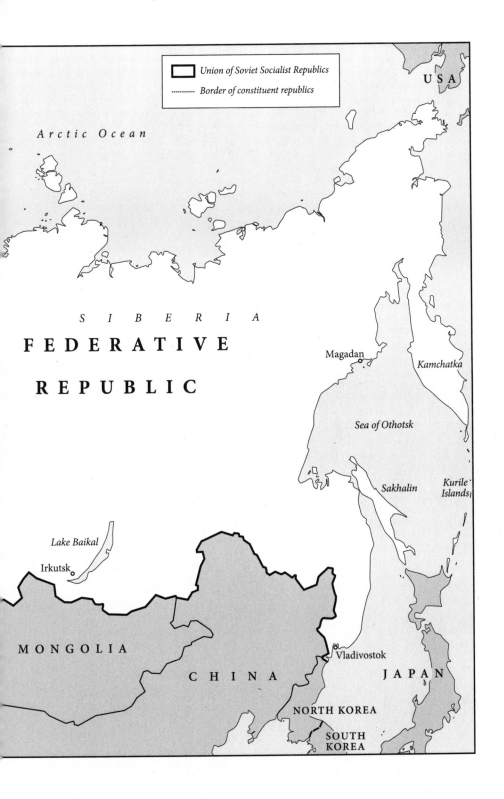

Union of Soviet Socialist Republics
Border of constituent republics

Arctic Ocean

USA

S I B E R I A

FEDERATIVE

REPUBLIC

Magadan

Kamchatka

Sea of Othotsk

Sakhalin

Kurile Islands

Lake Baikal

Irkutsk

MONGOLIA

CHINA

Vladivostok

JAPAN

NORTH KOREA

SOUTH KOREA

INTRODUCTION

An increasingly lonely and capricious old man in physical decline, on the evening of 28 February 1953 Stalin once again summoned a handful of key underlings for one of his regular night-time get-togethers. First, they watched a movie together at the Kremlin before heading off to Stalin's country house, a few miles from central Moscow. There, they ate, drank and talked until the early hours, as usual. Among the select few present that night, Nikita Khrushchev later recalled that Stalin had been in good spirits and the evening had passed without incident, adding that 'not all these dinners ended well'.[1] A little while before morning broke, the guests all headed home to their families and Stalin went to bed. The following day, Khrushchev waited again for Stalin's call to dinner, but it never came.

The next fifteen years would be among the most eventful and transformative periods in the Soviet Union's history. Stalin had been dead for less than a month when more than a million prisoners were released from the gulag. Ideals and goals from the revolutionary era that had largely faded from view since the 1930s returned to the forefront of regime rhetoric. A great vibrancy burst forth in literature, cinema and more, while new heroes and fashions were embraced. Tens of millions of Soviet citizens moved out of dingy communal flats (or worse) and into new apartments, while consumer goods like refrigerators and radios finally started to become accessible for the masses. Education levels and living standards rose, new opportunities for recreation appeared, and there were improvements to welfare and infrastructure.

Mass shootings of protesters at Tbilisi and Novocherkassk also demonstrated a much darker side to the period, as did intermittent but swingeing clampdowns in the cultural sphere. Religious believers of all faiths were

1

subjected to renewed discrimination, KGB penetration of everyday life grew steadily deeper, and even in the absence of Stalin-era mass repression, regime critics were still liable to be persecuted and imprisoned.

International affairs would be no less dynamic. Stalin's notion of inevitable war between the capitalist and communist camps was replaced by the concept of 'peaceful co-existence'; but there were nonetheless still dangerous flashpoints with the US in particular, even before the Cuban Missile Crisis brought nuclear apocalypse closer than it had ever been before. Huge effort was poured into winning new allies and gaining influence across Africa, Asia and Latin America as decolonisation reshaped the global system. Relations with communist China shifted from declarations of eternal friendship to a bitter enmity that seemingly threatened war, and Soviet troops invaded both Hungary and Czechoslovakia when the Kremlin feared that its grip over East European allies was threatened. In the arms race, the USSR proved itself a more than capable rival to the US; and in space it forged ahead with gusto, winning a series of victories in the cosmos that dazzled the world. In fact, around the end of the 1950s and the start of the 1960s especially, it was not at all clear which side would come out on top in the Cold War. Following a trip around the USSR in summer 1958, Adlai Stevenson – the defeated candidate for the US presidency in both 1952 and 1956 – fretted that his homeland was 'losing ground everywhere' against its great rival, both at home and abroad.[2]

In some important senses, the USSR remained fundamentally 'closed' to the outside world, and deep suspicion of everything foreign remained prevalent among more conservative officials especially. However, these were also years in which all manner of international interactions – from cultural exchanges and business deals to tourism and education – proliferated and could be felt in the biggest cities especially. Cinemas showed Italian neo-realist films and Bollywood movies, while student dormitories housed Iraqis, Angolans, Poles, Americans, Cubans and many other nationalities. Foreign film stars, musicians and writers attracted growing attention, entering the mainstream of youth culture as the period progressed. This was in part a result of successful 'penetration' from outside, through broadcasts by the likes of Radio Liberty and the BBC. It was also a result of decisions made at the very top of the Soviet system, as the authorities sought to gain a variety of benefits from 'opening up' and worked to construct a more attractive image of the USSR for audiences abroad.

The period under discussion here is really an era rather than a decade: it runs not from January 1960 to December 1969, but from 1953 to 1968. Put briefly, this book presents the death of Stalin in March 1953 as the beginning of a new era, and the Soviet-led invasion of Czechoslovakia in August 1968 as the endpoint of that era. Of course, almost any attempt at periodisation is open to debate. There are, for example, compelling arguments to say that it was not Stalin's death in 1953, but the end of the war in 1945 that really marked the start of a different age in the USSR. A range of social and political developments that would help characterise the post-Stalin years, such as the emergence of new youth subcultures and political mechanisms, can certainly be traced back to before 1953.[3] Key structures that defined the Soviet system, from the centrally planned economy through to the Communist Party's monopoly on power, remained largely unchanged by Stalin's death. Similarly, the vast majority of political and cultural figures mentioned in this book – like many millions of ordinary citizens – had already had their lives, mindsets and careers fundamentally shaped by the events of the Stalin years. A quarter-century of Stalinism had left a mark so deep that no kind of clean and total break could ever be possible.

While it is true to say that the late Stalin years offered important precursors of social and political developments yet to come, it is also the case that Stalin himself represented the single greatest impediment to change – during his last years, especially. A host of crucial developments that would go a long way towards defining the Soviet Sixties as an era, from the end of mass repression through to cultural liberalisation and much-expanded interaction with the outside world, became possible only with Stalin's passing. Indeed, at least a few of the figures who went on to shape the period under discussion had previously been considered enemies during the Stalin years. Many contemporaries also described a new atmosphere taking hold among the Soviet public after March 1953. The writer Vasily Aksenov, for example, recalled of the period following Stalin's death that 'the mood was that of an absolutely new country'.[4]

Rather than end with the removal from power of Nikita Khrushchev in autumn 1964, this book presents the year 1968 as the close of the era in question. It argues that the later part of the Khrushchev period and the early part of the subsequent Brezhnev years were not nearly so different as has typically been understood through established notions of a (relatively) liberal and reform-minded Nikita Khrushchev and a much more conservative Leonid Brezhnev. Although it had always ebbed and flowed, much of the liberalising agenda typically associated with Khrushchev's years was already in abeyance some time before his ouster. Similarly, the conservatism (sometimes even described as 're-Stalinisation') that has always been associated with the Brezhnev era was not so clearly in evidence during its opening stages. In fact, even some seasoned regime insiders thought at first that the new leadership team might represent further progress in the direction of liberalisation, after reform had gone awry towards the end of Khrushchev's rule. As the end of the 1960s approached, though, a broad conservative turn was becoming more and more apparent, with the August 1968 invasion of Czechoslovakia serving as the pivotal moment in this process.

What then followed was an increasingly conservative 'long 1970s' (sometimes referred to as an 'era of stagnation') that lasted until Mikhail Gorbachev began the reform programme that would eventually bring the whole Soviet system crashing down in 1991. By no means was this long 1970s a return to unfettered Stalinism, and nor was it a period that can be painted only in dark colours: it brought rising living standards, greater stability and a growing sense of international prestige, which were all much valued. Actually, there is still considerable affection for the 'long 1970s' among some citizens of the former Soviet Union; but it was unmistakably an age without the kind of vibrancy, optimism and engagement which characterised much of the decade and a half that had followed Stalin's death.

In the historical literature, the term most commonly used to describe the post-Stalin era has always been the 'thaw': a reference to Ilya Ehrenburg's seminal 1954 novella about changing times, and 'spring' arriving after a harsh winter. The present work, however, instead adopts the term 'Soviet Sixties' for a number of reasons. In part, this is because the notion of 'thaw' is so closely associated with the Khrushchev years (and with developments in the cultural sphere especially), while this book extends through that period and into the early part of the Brezhnev era. It is also because 'thaw' is a term overwhelmingly associated with a sense of liberalisation, and there are significant passages herein where this notion would be jarring at best.

The term 'Soviet Sixties' also references what has often been seen as a quite distinct generation of the communist period: the *shestidesyatniki* (often rendered in English as 'sixtiers' or 'people of the sixties'). This was a cohort of citizens who reached maturity in the 1950s and 1960s, who were often characterised by relatively reform-minded political views, with a rejuvenated sense of humanism and internationalism, and who are sometimes seen as the last Soviet generation that really believed communist utopia would be achieved in the USSR. Writing his memoirs many years later, for example, the author Anatoly Gladilin insisted that he had been a typical *shestidesyatnik* by virtue of his clear conviction at that time that a better world was being built in the Soviet Union.[5] Even the KGB career man Oleg Kalugin recalled that the desire to make the Soviet system 'human again' marked out him and his peers in the security organs as the 'Generation of the Sixties'.[6]

The title *The Soviet Sixties* is also intended to draw parallels with the distinctive 'Sixties' era that happened across other parts of the world. In summarising key dynamics of that age as it played out in North America and Western Europe, Arthur Marwick emphasised a new prominence of youth and a spirit of change; an unprecedented audacity in books and media; a surging importance of popular culture; better material conditions for ordinary people; changes in personal relationships and sexual behaviour; acts of protest against the status quo; and a sense of optimism for the dawning of a better world.[7] Each of these was also a defining feature of the period inside the USSR.

The Soviet Union did not witness the prominent counterculture that characterised the Sixties in the West, but there were clear and sharp battles being fought over the past, present and future, as well as emerging divisions about art, sex, fashion, ideology and much more. Anyway, plenty of figures iconic to Western counterculture, such as Che Guevara, the Beatles and the Rolling Stones, were little less resonant inside the Soviet Union. Further, with the passing of Stalin – whose judgement on any given matter, from music to linguistics, was both decisive and enduring – new spaces did open for plurality of opinion, albeit these remained limited and policed. Conservative and liberal-minded figures within the establishment not only showed sharply differing viewpoints at times, but they also laid into one another publicly on occasion, this being especially clear in their conviction that the socio-political order of Stalinism would have to be fundamentally changed if communism was to be achieved.[8]

No less than in the West, the developments of the Sixties era were also divisive domestically. Some people felt that the key social, political and cultural trends of the age – from ending the Stalin cult through to proliferating cultural exchange with the outside world – represented steps towards a badly needed renewal of the system, and thus promised great things for a more progressive future. Many others perceived that new reformist tides and apparent 'rubbishing' of the recent past threatened chaos and the breakdown of the proper order of things, with young people in particular in danger of losing their way; such people would rejoice in the eventual close of an unwelcome age of upheaval, and the timely reassertion of proper authority.[9] Plenty of people naturally stood somewhere between these positions; but it is important to note that during much of the Sixties era especially, the key debate was fundamentally still about the best way of reaching the promised land of communism, rather than any kind of pro- and anti-communist divide.

Lastly on this theme, the title *The Soviet Sixties* is also aimed at connecting the Soviet experience of the age with a wider literature that has begun to emerge in the last couple of decades on the 'Global Sixties', taking in developments across not just Europe and North America, but also Africa, Asia and Latin America. In the first instance, Khrushchev made his country part of the wider 'Global Sixties' when he explicitly declared Soviet support for those fighting to free themselves from colonialism, backing this up with aid and arms for almost anyone who asked, and seeking to proffer a compelling non-capitalist and non-Western vision of modernity. Key social and political phenomena that were influential in shaping the experience of 'the Sixties' in the developing world – such as widening access to higher education, increasing urbanisation and evolving patterns (and expectations) of consumption – were also crucial in changing the dynamics of the Soviet system. The embrace of modernity, development, science and technology that was seen across the developing world, as countries sought to redefine themselves for the new age after colonialism, was very much in evidence in the USSR, which also proved a particularly eager exporter of such ideas. Furthermore, proliferating interactions with the outside world – including capitalist, communist and developing countries – not only saw Soviet influences spreading abroad, but also brought for the first time foreign ideas, information and goods into the USSR.

None of the above is to suggest that the Soviet Union experienced the same 'Sixties' as did other countries. Indeed, experiences of the period varied hugely within the USSR itself, not least by geographic location and social constituency. The Sixties that happened in the USSR were distinctly Soviet in some key ways. While fears of the younger generation 'going soft' or of rising consumer appetites feeding a harmful obsession with material goods emerged in many countries, these could be perceived as existential threats under Soviet conditions. Similarly, plenty of countries saw the reach of the state apparatus expanding throughout the post-war years; but the extent to which the authorities sought to observe and shape daily life for Soviet citizens was clearly an important marker of difference.

In a number of important senses, a new version of the Soviet system was taking shape across the period in question. The lives of citizens became much more secure, both from groundless repression and from the most extreme material deprivation – both of which had left a massive impact on the preceding quarter-century and more. Improved provision of not just essentials like foodstuffs, but also items like radios, televisions and refrigerators all spoke of a social order in which consumption (and incentives more broadly) came to play an increasingly important social role as the authorities' use of mass repression ebbed. This not only helped sustain stability after the move away from Stalinist terror, but it also drove up citizens' expectations and generated challenging new social dynamics. Further, the end of mass terror did not signal any kind of retreat from regime aspirations to reshape citizens' behaviours and attitudes; but there was now a recognition that there were more effective ways of achieving such a transformation. In fact, while naked repression declined, the forms that policing and social control took actually proliferated: mobilising peer pressure against offenders, getting members of the public patrolling city streets, utilising new technologies, harnessing the latest sociological research and more.

From cinema and literature through to nuclear energy and space travel, there was a huge appetite for all things 'modern', and scientists, in particular, were frequently held up as the heroes of the age. It was, however, frequently a reckless and damaging modernity at the ground level, destroying irreplaceable cultural heritage, doing untold ecological harm and sometimes also deeply offending citizens' sensibilities. Partly in response to this, by the end of the Soviet Sixties there was a growing nostalgic impulse to look backwards in time, rather than forwards, and to seek to protect that which seemed threatened with destruction by the onward march of modernity. Similarly, the authorities yearned to reap the benefits of opening up to the outside world – from foreign currency income to reputational gains – but dreaded the challenges such a move posed to the existing order of things inside the country.

Not unrelated to the above, another key feature of the age domestically was its ambiguity and inconsistency of messaging.[10] Citizens were encouraged to be internationalist in outlook, while the authorities placed tight restrictions on interactions with the outside world and fretted about the spread of foreign influences. Officials boasted of increases in the availability of consumer goods, but complained about citizens becoming overly materialistic. Propaganda aimed to mobilise public idealism and initiative, but often found the results unpalatable and either ignored them or else clamped down hard. Imbued with the idealism that Khrushchev had summoned up in his appeals to both the revolutionary past and the utopian future, some felt the best service they could perform for the communist project was to expose its failings, so that they might be corrected. In fact, this sentiment would soon prove dangerous.

Importantly, there was also far greater scope for inclusion and participation in the Soviet project after Stalin. Key regime structures like the Communist Party and Komsomol (the party's youth wing) more than doubled in size, with new members flocking to join as the opportunity arose. This anchored them ever more securely in the country's social structure, with both organisations becoming less and less of an ideological vanguard, as those with an eye on the associated perks sought and gained membership. Recognition, rewards and incentives – such as improved access to goods, tourist travel and other tokens of official esteem – grew in importance as a facet of governance. Ordinary citizens were increasingly mobilised for everything from opening up new land for agriculture, to building hydroelectric dams in the Siberian wilderness and policing city streets – though the results proved variable. More than ever before, the notions of 'state' and 'society' were less and less distinct from one another, and in a number of important respects seemed to fuse together, or at least to accommodate one another's prerogatives. Even so, ordinary citizens in factories and farms, and even plenty of high officials, continued to bend and break the rules as they saw fit – from contracting fake marriages in order to acquire residence permits and holding secret baptisms for children, through to cases of massive financial malfeasance.

The Soviet system also became more authentically 'Soviet', as opposed to Russian, with expanded (although still far from limitless) scope for celebration of everything from Georgian and Uzbek food, to Estonian art and Ukrainian dance. Accoutrements of nationhood, such as republican film studios and political leaders of the local nationality, increased in the non-Russian republics. As with rising levels of consumption though, this was to prove a change that helped to generate problematic dynamics further down the line, as non-Russians and Russians alike grew steadily more interested in their social and cultural heritage, and as nationalist sentiment quietly began rising in several parts of the country. New investment from Moscow and new narratives on matters like the Second World War and decolonisation in the developing world also helped to weave previously neglected regions – and especially the Central Asian republics of Turkmenistan, Tajikistan, Kyrgyzstan, Uzbekistan and Kazakhstan – more closely into the wider Soviet tapestry.

In some ways, the story of the era is also one of avenues not taken and of projects that never worked out: when thoroughgoing reform appeared imminent, but failed to materialise, or when the stage seemed set for a resurgence of Stalinism that never quite happened. Some of the most remarkable developments of the era – such as the publication of Alexander Solzhenitsyn's ground-breaking novella *One Day in the Life of Ivan Denisovich* – happened not because the system had changed fundamentally, but because regular structures and practices had been temporarily bypassed by Khrushchev. This could mean that events which had seemed to be major breakthroughs on the path to liberalisation – including even Khrushchev's famous denunciation of Stalin in 1956 – actually proved to be surprisingly fleeting or narrow in scope, with momentum for change easily stalled and conservative impulses quickly resurgent. No less important, for all that liberalisation has always been regarded as a defining theme of the age, there were some – religious believers in particular – for whom things largely got worse after 1953. Anyway, one would be wholly mistaken to assume that the forces for conservatism and against reform amounted to only a few Stalinist holdovers among the political and cultural elite.

There has been a tremendous flowering of truly excellent scholarship on the post-Stalin Soviet Union since about the turn of the millennium, and without this the present book would never have been possible. Of course, there are still many important events, groups and processes around which knowledge remains patchy. There are, for example, valuable KGB materials now available to researchers in the likes of Lithuania and Ukraine, but a far greater mass of such documents remains inaccessible inside Russia. Similarly, innovative studies have been undertaken in recent years on subjects that were previously (at best) peripheral in mainstream histories of the USSR, such as works on the Central Asian republics or on the experiences of various marginalised groups, though much naturally still waits to be done on many fronts.

From nuclear energy and the space race, through the inner workings of Soviet officialdom, evolving notions of masculinity and femininity, developments in Soviet media, the experiences of gulag returnees and more, the present book attempts to bring together much of the excellent research of recent years in order to give as wide a view as possible of a remarkably dynamic age. Of course, I make no claim to have achieved anything like comprehensive coverage.

I have tried to ensure that the key political, social and cultural developments of the period not only all receive coverage, but are also organised in such a way that they stand alongside and interact with one another. This means, for example, that the deeds of political and cultural elites, along with major international flashpoints, are to be found cheek by jowl with accounts of ordinary citizens' living conditions, sexual proclivities and musical tastes. There are thus far more detailed works on offer if the reader is only interested in, say, the Cuban Missile Crisis or the Secret Speech, though few of them will better establish the broad context in which those events played out. I have also attempted to ensure that groups and themes which have at times been overlooked in mainstream histories of the USSR occupy a place here. There is thus a conscious effort to include the stories of Soviet women and the many non-Russian peoples of the Soviet Union, and to weave into the narrative everything from tourism and shopping through to sex and sci-fi.

The book proceeds in broadly chronological order, opening with the end of the Stalin era and closing with the onset of the increasingly sclerotic 'long 1970s'. Chapter 1 starts with an exploration of post-war Stalinism, then centres on the remarkable sequence of events that took place between the spring and summer of 1953, as Stalin's death plunged much of the country into profound grief and fear for the future, while his successors quickly began to enact far-reaching and tumultuous reforms. This initial, frenetic phase of upheaval then culminated in June with the arrest of one of the most prominent and notorious members of the new leadership team – Lavrenty Beria.

Chapter 2 traces key developments in Nikita Khrushchev's unexpected emergence as the predominant figure among the political elite, and explores a series of wide-ranging changes to the country's social, political and cultural life over the next couple of years, as the contours of the new era started to take on a clearer form. Focusing on one of the epochal moments in the Soviet regime's history, Chapter 3 opens with the Twentieth Party Congress in February 1956, at which Stalin's cruelty and vanity were denounced and Khrushchev promised a return to the 'true path' towards communism that had been set out by Lenin. As the year progressed, the authorities wrestled clumsily with the resulting fallout, as both anti-Stalin and pro-Stalin dissent flared on a scale not seen for many years.

Chapter 4 centres on another hugely transformative year, 1957. It starts with the Soviet invasion of Hungary in autumn 1956 and the reverberations that ensued over the following months, which prompted a domestic crack-down that saw thousands jailed. Then, an attempt to oust Khrushchev as leader was only narrowly defeated in summer 1957, before thousands of young people from all over the world transformed Moscow into a riot of colour and fun during the 1957 World Youth Festival, and a gargantuan construction drive saw millions of citizens moving into new homes from Tallinn to Tashkent. At the heart of Chapter 5 is the Soviet Union's tremendous success in the space race across the second half of the 1950s and the first half of the 1960s, along with the wider cult of science and technology that characterised the age and saw both era-defining achievements and cata-strophic environmental and human disasters.

Chapter 6 focuses primarily on international affairs during the same period, exploring Soviet interactions with the capitalist world, with allies of the communist camp and the developing world. It ends by looking at the impact that new flows of foreign visitors and cultural imports had inside the

USSR. Also spanning the late 1950s and early 1960s, Chapter 7 explores a number of fields in which new boundaries of acceptable behaviour were established, tested and enforced: from the scandal surrounding Boris Pasternak's epic novel *Dr Zhivago* and evolving attitudes towards sex, religion and alcohol, through to questions of national sentiment, hooligan behaviour and illicit economic activity. Chapter 8 begins with perhaps the high point of the era's optimism, as Khrushchev redoubled his earlier attack on Stalin at the Twenty-Second Party Congress in October 1961 and declared that the final construction of the communist utopia was already appearing on the horizon. In reality, problems were mounting – not least as economic struggles led to price rises, which triggered a mass protest that ended in a massacre at Novocherkassk. Soon after that, events in Cuba threatened global nuclear apocalypse, and the already strained relationship with communist China snapped once and for all.

At the centre of Chapter 9 is the audacious coup that removed Nikita Khrushchev from power in October 1964 and the initial attempts by the new leadership team around Leonid Brezhnev to make their mark on the country. Chapter 10 first examines the non-conformist milieu that emerged in Moscow towards the middle of the 1960s. It then moves on to address the origins of the subsequent human rights movement, before broadening out to highlight other struggles that were starting to gather pace elsewhere at around the same time – among Ukrainian nationalists, Soviet Jews seeking to emigrate and more.

The final chapter makes a case for the late 1960s as the point at which we see a distinctive era coming to a close. People and themes that had defined the Soviet Sixties exited the stage, and a deepening conservatism took hold in both cultural and political life: a process both encapsulated and accelerated by the invasion of reformist Czechoslovakia in 1968.

I

nEw BEGInnInGS

Neither the raising of the hammer and sickle over the Reichstag on 2 May 1945 nor the formal German surrender days later really brought peace to the Soviet Union. Fighting in western Ukraine by partisans resisting forced incorporation into the USSR saw Soviet armed forces kill over 110,000 people in 1944–46 alone, with a further 250,000 jailed. Both Soviet troops and the opposition Ukrainian Insurgent Army (UPA) terrorised the civilian population to varying degrees – including through executions, followed by public displays of mutilated corpses.[1] Similarly, perhaps 50–60,000 people across the Baltic republics of Latvia, Lithuania and Estonia also took to partisan warfare against Soviet occupation. These 'forest brothers' managed to keep their desperate fight going on for several years, though they were hopelessly outgunned. Mass deportations eventually drained away vital rural support, with estimates suggesting that around 370,000 people were forcibly despatched to the Soviet east from across the Baltics in only the first three years following the war.[2] The last embers of armed resistance in the region were finally snuffed out only in early 1953, though deep resentment would endure there for many years to come.[3]

Even away from the fighting in the USSR's western borderlands, the socio-political situation across the country by 1945 was horribly strained. Added to the millions of citizens killed during the war were many more left wounded or disabled, orphaned or widowed, scrabbling to survive in an often-unforgiving environment. Around a third of Soviet national wealth had been lost in the war, including perhaps a quarter of the country's total housing stock (of which there was already a serious shortage before the war). Major cities like Leningrad (St Petersburg), Kiev (Kyiv), Riga and Minsk were left in varying degrees of advanced ruination. In Stalingrad (Volgograd),

13

only a little over 12 per cent of the city's pre-war housing remained standing, with all of its hospitals, theatres and schools destroyed.[4] On being sent to work in the Ukrainian capital a whole five years after the war was over, Petro Shelest found that even Kiev's beautiful central boulevard, Khreshchatik, remained practically in ruins; the provision of water, electricity and living space was either non-existent or wholly inadequate in what was the USSR's third-biggest city.[5] Even in parts of the country that had been thousands of kilometres from the front line of the fighting, like the Uzbek capital Tashkent, the flow of incoming refugees and the pressures of the war economy had seen infrastructure such as hospitals, houses, police stations, schools and universities stretched to breaking point, with little prospect of repair on the horizon.[6] Problems with street crime, juvenile delinquency and more were commonplace in urban areas especially and testified to a regime whose powers of control had been badly weakened by the war, if only temporarily.[7]

Post-war Stalinism

The end of the war also presented little chance for the country to stop and catch its breath. Millions were immediately mobilised for work in huge campaigns to rebuild mines, bridges, power plants and factories, or to gather up human remains and unexploded war materiel left in the rubble.[8] This desperate scramble to rebuild after the war – the results of which were hugely impressive, but by no means completed at the time of Stalin's death – also took place against the backdrop of escalating tensions with the West. This meant that reconstruction of the country's industrial and military capacity (including a hugely expensive push to break the Americans' monopoly on the atomic bomb) was accorded priority over all else, with the whole gamut of human wants and needs largely overlooked: some estimates suggest that almost half of the Soviet population was suffering from malnutrition during the initial post-war years.[9] A failed harvest in 1946 saw even the most basic foodstuffs, such as potatoes, disappear from the shops. As famine struck, perhaps a million and a half people starved to death. One Russian recalled being so hungry as a child in 1947 that he 'used to lick the cupboard shelf where we had always kept bread'.[10] In Soviet Central Asia, thousands also died and much infrastructure was ruined as a series of powerful earthquakes struck the region during the second half of the 1940s.

14

The writer Lyudmila Petrushevskaya described joining lines of beggars who waited by the cash desk in shops, hoping for customers to leave them some spare change.[11] Wartime rationing was abolished at the end of 1947, but there was anyway little to buy, and concurrent economic reform wiped out most people's savings. Many essential items, like soap, were almost entirely absent from the shops, which drove up health problems that stemmed from unhygienic conditions.[12] In urban areas, the average Soviet citizen occupied less than 5 square metres of living space (much less in some places). Returning to Moscow after military service, one demobilised soldier found that the single-room apartment he had previously shared with his mother had been requisitioned; instead, as living space they were allocated a storeroom with space for only a single bed and a bedside table, underneath a low ceiling covered with mould from the damp.[13] Some had it worse still. In his account of a 1947 visit to Stalingrad, John Steinbeck described witnessing people there still living in holes in the ground – a whole four years after the Battle of Stalingrad had been won. He wrote of watching from his hotel window in amazement as locals literally emerged from piles of rubble to go off to work in the morning.[14]

Remarkable as it might seem in light of the above, people were still heading for the country's battered cities with alacrity whenever they got the chance. The rural economy was in a state of steadily deepening crisis, and the authorities in Moscow typically responded not by easing the demands they placed on the countryside, but by pressing even harder. Denied the right to internal passports (necessary in order to change one's place of residence and work) peasants had very limited legal ability to leave the village. Laying the blame for agricultural failings not on the badly flawed collective farm system, but on peasants' perceived thieving and work avoidance, new crackdowns despatched thousands of collective farmers to labour camps and prisons for the tiniest of infractions. Anyway, those still officially at liberty in the countryside were often basically trapped in servitude. In the Tatarstan region of Russia, for example, more than half of all collective farms paid their workers nothing at all for their labour for several consecutive years after the war, with farm members surviving only thanks to the vegetables grown on their meagre private plots.[15] State taxes on produce that peasants sold from these private plots rose repeatedly, and the prices that the central authorities paid collective farms for their compulsory deliveries of grain, milk and meat

15

were close to derisory. Many war veterans, in particular, initially returned to their collective farms, as instructed after demobilisation, but promptly 'looked around, and left again', heading for the cities to take up unskilled labour or even simply to beg, rather than remain in the village.[16]

Much of the progressive action and discourse on equality of the sexes that followed the revolution had already fallen by the wayside through the 1930s, as Stalinism became increasingly socially conservative. Having become the first country in the world to legalise abortion in 1920, the procedure was again banned in 1936. A new 'family law' in 1944 (behind which Nikita Khrushchev was a notable driving force) then took things further in loading fresh hardships onto women, as the authorities strove desperately to raise the birth rate and plug the massive demographic hole left by the war.[17] In a move that was essentially intended to encourage Soviet men to get as many women pregnant as possible, unmarried mothers were forbidden to seek child maintenance support from their child's father, and were even banned from including the father's name on the child's birth certificate. The state promised to provide financial support in place of absent fathers, but in practice it often failed to do so. Regardless of their contribution to the war effort – and many of them had fought heroically – women were quickly demobilised and then banned from re-enlisting in the military.[18] Rural life, in particular, was often deeply patriarchal. Scholars have, for example, cited cases of farm chairwomen (already a rarity) being beaten and having their party cards burned by their husbands, and of leading female workers having their houses smashed and even torched on occasion.[19]

The picture in the late Stalinist cultural sphere was similarly bleak. With the potential cost of any ideological misstep dangerously high – in the late 1940s, the composer Dmitry Shostakovich expected to be arrested at any moment, after a new production was attacked in the press – the vibrant innovation and experimentation that had characterised the early years of the revolution were over. Instead came grandiose hymns to Stalin, formulaic stories of jolly collective farm workers and stodgy novels about heroic production deeds (what one commentator has called 'a vast, dull literature of make-believe').[20] Things were little better in the art world. With the avantgarde of the 1920s long since crushed, the country was left with an artistic sphere that has been described as 'cliché-ridden, vapid and uninteresting'.[21] The Soviet cinema industry, for which Stalin liked to serve as the ultimate censor, was barely a shadow of its former self, turning out a mere nine movies for the whole of 1951, compared to an annual total of almost 130 two decades previously.[22] Growing regime xenophobia also demanded an aggressive rejection of foreign cultural influences. Almost any kind of links to or interaction with the outside world could arouse suspicions of disloyalty, and the media demanded citizens' constant vigilance against Western subversion. When jazz music came under fierce attack for its American origins, groups were forcibly dissolved and bandleaders jailed. In 1949, the authorities even seized saxophones.[23]

Nonetheless, for all that hardship and coercion justifiably occupy a place close to the centre of the picture of late Stalinism, there was also optimism and a huge amount of public pride following victory in the war. Determined to have fun after the prolonged and intense struggle, young people flocked to cinemas and public spaces to dance, make friends and find love.[24] As in other parts of post-war Europe, the country's big cities also began to witness the emergence of new youth subcultures. Most famous of these were the *stilyagi*: a small but growing body of young people (often, but not invariably, from privileged backgrounds) who scandalised public opinion as they clumsily appropriated Western fashions and slang, wearing lurid shirts, loud ties, short skirts or narrow trousers, calling each other 'baby' and dancing the jitterbug, to the rising consternation of Soviet officialdom.

Both the war victory and the successes of post-war reconstruction aroused popular expectations that better days surely lay ahead. A student at Moscow State University at the time, Alexei Adzhubei recalled young people in particular as being eager to do their bit for the motherland and prove themselves in the new struggle.[25] For many, this post-war optimism was fused with a sense that the general public had demonstrated its loyalty to the Soviet regime during a time of great crisis, and in return should now be entitled to a more secure and comfortable life.[26] Similarly, emboldened by their wartime heroics, many veterans were unafraid to speak up when the rewards they had been promised for their service – such as better housing and jobs – were not forthcoming, or when they felt shabbily treated by officials, who – as many former soldiers often saw it – had hidden away from the fighting.[27] In fact, there was to be no post-war liberalisation at all for the Soviet masses, though these aspirations for better days were stifled, rather than eradicated.

The domestic political repression of the post-war years never again reached the dizzying peaks of the late 1930s, but it nonetheless remained frightening in scale: 1946, the first full year of post-war Stalinism, saw almost 130,000 people convicted under the notorious article 58 for 'counter-revolutionary crimes'.[28] An even greater number (almost 700,000 in 1947) were also being jailed for 'regular' crimes like theft. The state security organs fabricated massive conspiracies as they both fulfilled and fed Stalin's demands to uncover enemies. One Kremlin insider recalled of the late 1940s and early 1950s that 'All night long the Black Marias prowled the streets and courtyards. People who had only recently been released from concentration camps . . . were arrested all over again . . . others were arrested for no apparent cause.'[29] Needless to say, an unknowable (but undoubtedly very large) proportion of these convictions was based on either flimsy or wholly fabricated evidence, often backed up with denunciations and confessions gained through torture.

Accordingly, by the early 1950s, around 2.5 million people were detained in the country's myriad corrective labour camps, about 150,000 more were in prisons, and a further 2.75 million were held in places of internal exile.[30] This last group, in particular, was growing all the time, since it had become common practice for those reaching the end of a sentence to be immediately despatched into perpetual exile, rather than actually being freed. Many of these victims of repression, of course, also had families, whose fates were blighted not only by the loss of their loved ones, but also by the fact of their personal connections to 'enemies', since applications for jobs, housing, university places and more routinely required information about family members, and news of 'undesirable elements' frequently closed doors.

In contrast to Lenin's early warnings about the dangers of 'Russian chauvinism' as a force liable to destabilise the multi-national Soviet Union, the Russian nationalist sentiment had been one of the most consistently tapped emotional resources of the war years. It continued to enjoy considerable official sanction thereafter, too, giving the system a distinctly 'imperial' feel beyond its Russian heartland. Allied to this was sharpening regime suspicion at any hint of nationalism among the many different non-Russian peoples of the country. Whether in Ukraine, Azerbaijan, Lithuania or elsewhere, attempts to celebrate native writers, costumes, historical figures, and more could open up dangerous accusations of subversive intent. The Estonian

Communist Party leadership especially was purged extensively, with many of its members jailed or killed, following groundless denunciations of bourgeois nationalism.[31] Allied regimes across Eastern Europe were also kept on a particularly tight leash, with extensive purging demanded in the likes of Czechoslovakia, Bulgaria and Hungary, and with Tito's Yugoslavia vilified and ostracised from 1948 onwards after proving too independent-minded for Moscow's liking.

An increasingly martial atmosphere enveloped the country. For veterans, service in the war became the central point of one's biography, and there was an increased emphasis on military-style toughness and decisiveness in political discourse and behaviour.[32] The great Russian ballerina Maya Plisetskaya recalled that there were men in uniform everywhere and 'being a civilian was somewhat shameful'.[33] From its beginnings in 1950, the war in Korea then brought Soviet relations with the US to an especially dangerous pitch as the two superpowers heavily backed opposing sides. One of those who saw the decision making process at first hand later likened the febrile Soviet diplomatic situation of the time to a feverish human body on the point of hallucination.[34] Serious war scares were confidentially reported in several parts of the USSR, with people stockpiling basic supplies like kerosene, salt and matches, withdrawing money from banks and making preparations for imminent evacuation.[35] Writing in March 1949, *New York Times* correspondent Harrison Salisbury overheard Moscow housewives discussing world affairs as they stood in queues to buy groceries. He surmised that 'Russia is a preoccupied land today – preoccupied with concern lest a new war break out while the scars of the old are not yet healed.'[36]

The rampant xenophobia of late Stalinism was perhaps best encapsulated in the era's burgeoning anti-Semitism. Of his own childhood in post-war Leningrad, Joseph Brodsky recalled that open anti-Semitism from his schoolteachers 'had to be coped with like low marks'.[37] More than ever before, discrimination came not just from below, but also from above – and from Stalin in particular. The celebrated Jewish actor Solomon Mikhoels was murdered in 1948, with his death then framed as the result of a motor accident. Meanwhile, more than a hundred of his fellow members of the Jewish Anti-Fascist Committee (a wartime propaganda organisation, set up by the Soviet regime) were groundlessly arrested as traitors.

Most ominously, what would become known as the 'Doctors' Plot' was first announced in the newspaper *Pravda* (*Truth*) on 13 January 1953. An initial group of nine doctors to the Kremlin elite – most of whom had recognisably Jewish surnames – were accused of having murdered one of Stalin's closest lieutenants, Andrei Zhdanov, in 1948 on the orders of Israeli and Western intelligence services. In reality, Zhdanov's death can largely be attributed to his heavy drinking and demanding work regime having exacerbated an existing heart condition. Even so, Khrushchev later claimed to have personally overheard Stalin demanding that the arrested suspects be beaten mercilessly.

Prominent Soviet Jews were coerced into signing public letters decrying Zionism, begging the Russian people's forgiveness and calling for ruthless punishment of the guilty doctors. These cues from the Kremlin were quickly picked up and acted upon elsewhere, as Jews faced visceral hostility in the street and in their places of work. Many patients refused to be treated by Jewish doctors and lashed out viciously. The physicist Yuri Orlov wrote of being jostled and spat at in the street as people mistook his curly red hair as an indication of Jewishness.[38] On firing a Jewish member of academic staff, officials at Molotov State University (Perm) 'had seen the Doctors' Plot as the start of the hunt for Jews . . . and quickly considered it necessary to join in', according to one witness to events.[39] Some accounts have suggested that all this hysteria was intended to serve as the pretext for a much bigger plan: to deport over 2 million Soviet Jews to the east 'for their own safety', though the evidence for such a scheme – which was by no means beyond the realms of the possible under Stalin – is not entirely conclusive.[40]

The post-war years were, in the main, a much more positive time for bureaucrats and party officials. The scramble to re-establish administrative control after the shattering damage done to political structures during the war meant that top-level authorities granted a wealth of new privileges (such as higher wages and special access to hard-to-find goods) to their representatives on the ground. In places, corrupt officials ran riot, claiming precious supplies of food and clothing for themselves, embezzling state funds, protecting friends and clients from the law and persecuting any who sought to expose them.[41] Myriad certificates, stamps and documents needed to obtain medical treatment, explain work absences or prove qualifications were all the subject of illegal payments to corrupt bureaucrats.[42] Party and state officials, factory directors, military officers and members of the cultural establishment also came to enjoy a lifestyle with an increasingly bourgeois sheen to it, as egalitarianism gave way to stratification and elite privilege. While the country's housing crisis saw many ordinary citizens living in ruins, members of the elite moved into grand new apartments in columned buildings on wide boulevards and stuffed their homes with the trappings of privilege and glamour, like ball gowns, porcelain statuettes and expensive rugs.[43]

The Stalin cult flourished as never before. One member of the party apparatus recalled an unwritten rule of the time which instructed authors that Stalin should be mentioned at least two or three times more frequently than Lenin and five or six times more often than Marx and Engels.[44] In December 1949, the Great Leader's seventieth birthday was marked with a series of staggeringly grandiose events and gestures, including mountaineers scaling peaks to deposit busts of Stalin at the top, the country's most prestigious learned association, the Academy of Sciences, labelling him 'the greatest genius of humanity' and Politburo members vying to outdo one another in their praise for his humanity wisdom and modesty.[45] Afterwards, an exhibition opened at Moscow's Pushkin Museum of Fine Arts, displaying the beautiful and expensive gifts sent from across the globe in homage to Stalin.

The day-to-day lives of Stalin's top lieutenants were in many senses enviable. While the rest of the country faced intense material hardship, they had no such worries: as malnutrition ran rampant, Georgy Malenkov, Lavrenty Beria and Khrushchev were severely overweight by the early 1950s. They all had access to top-quality accommodation (Beria even lived in a mansion), domestic staff and the best healthcare available. Nonetheless, the price for this great material comfort was an incredibly demanding working life that was conducted in frightening proximity to existential danger, especially as Stalin's suspicions grew increasingly unchecked with age, and came to centre more frequently on those closest to him. Khrushchev would later insist that each time they were summoned to see Stalin, even his closest comrades did not know if they would make it home again. Almost all of them had their own brushes with disaster.

In 1951, the so-called Mingrelian Affair saw many of Beria's closest allies across the Caucasus region arrested; but then it suddenly ended before reaching Beria himself. In late 1952, Stalin also directed the security organs to begin formal investigations into two of his very closest acolytes, Vyacheslav Molotov and Anastas Mikoyan, questioning openly whether they were working for foreign powers (Molotov's wife had already been in jail since 1948). Both men were soon cut out of Stalin's social circle and looked to be in very serious trouble. Most notable in scope, though, was the Leningrad Affair that began in 1949. This affair was, it seems, driven primarily by intra-elite jostling for position among Stalin's subordinates.[46] After Leningrad party boss Andrei Zhdanov had died the previous year, his old rivals for Stalin's favour, Malenkov and Beria, went after the remaining members of Zhdanov's 'team', fabricating a plot in which Leningrad officials were suppos-edly seeking to subvert the Soviet system. Almost the entire upper echelon of the Leningrad Communist Party organisation was removed from office, with forced confessions and denunciations culminating in the arrest and impris-onment or execution of thousands across the city and beyond. Most notably, those executed included Politburo member Nikolai Voznesensky and Central Committee secretary Alexei Kuznetsov, both of whom had been regarded as rising stars up to that point.

Importantly, by the early 1950s Stalin's key lieutenants were becoming increasingly unnerved by his capriciousness, and were also aware that reform was badly needed in a variety of fields, from penal policy and foreign affairs through to agriculture and industry. They likewise knew full well that Stalin was the key obstacle to reform; and to propose any substantial change of direction could easily prove ruinous for the individual who did so.[47] The Politburo – the inner circle of the Communist Party's ruling Central Committee, whose members represented the elite of the elite – had long since ceased to function in any but a tokenistic manner.[48] Decisions were mostly reached at informal gatherings between Stalin and his closest associ-ates, before being passed on for rubber-stamping. It was also telling of Stalin's attitude towards established party procedures that not a single Communist Party congress – officially the party's supreme ruling organ – was convened in the period between 1939 and 1952. When the Nineteenth Party Congress was finally held in October 1952 – an event at which the Politburo was renamed the Presidium, and the party name was changed from the 'All-Union Communist Party' (Bolshevik) to the 'Communist Party of the Soviet Union'

(CPSU) – the aged Stalin declined to give the keynote address (which typically lasted for several hours) and passed the duty on to Malenkov, a clear sign that he was the heir apparent. Stalin did not speak publicly until the very end of the congress – and even then did so for only a few minutes. Soon afterwards, though, he addressed Central Committee members at length in private, suggesting at one point that the time had come for him to retire. Those present all knew exactly what was expected of them, however, and clamoured for him to continue. When, earlier that same year, Stalin's personal doctor had urged him to consider retirement on health grounds, he had been sacked and later arrested.

The death of Stalin

From about 06:00 Moscow time on 6 March 1953, Soviet radio began reporting that Stalin had died the previous evening. For two days, people had been avidly following official updates on his condition – it had been announced on 4 March that Stalin had suffered a stroke and was seriously ill – with media reports calling for the population to show unity and vigilance. Rabbis, priests, mullahs and their respective flocks had prayed in vain for him to recover. Even if it was not a complete surprise, the news of Stalin's passing unsettled the country in a way that few other events ever would. As one recent historian has argued, probably no leader of the twentieth century amassed greater power over citizens' hearts and minds than Stalin had inside the Soviet Union.[49] At once, there began a period that one eyewitness likened to the first weeks and months that had followed the revolution back in 1917, when people were in 'constant child-like expectation of miracles and horrors'.[50]

Many people simply could not digest at first the fact that Stalin had proven mortal after so many years of god-like status. Even *Pravda* editor Dmitry Shepilov, who spent plenty of time around Stalin and had thus observed the tell-tale signs of arteriosclerosis and hypertension, later wrote how the news was so incredible that he could not fully grasp it.[51] Countless Soviet citizens described the feeling of bereavement (Stalin had long been depicted as the benevolent father of the Soviet family) and of genuine heartbreak. One recounted how, on hearing the news at school in Kyrgyzstan, 'all

23

the children, all the teachers – everyone – cried'.[52] Alongside grief, though, there was also worry. Evgeniya Ginzburg wrote of how 'everyone's head was spinning with the expectation of imminent change', fearing war and potentially even greater repression.[53] In Kiev, from where he was despatched to Moscow in a plane packed with flowers and mourning wreaths, Petro Shelest recalled that the question 'what happens now' was on everyone's lips.[54]

Torrents of mournful telegrams, telephone calls and letters of condolence flowed into newspapers from ordinary citizens and major public figures. Alexei Adzhubei, then a journalist on the communist youth newspaper *Komsomolskaya pravda*, recalled the inordinate amount of time he had to devote to selecting which of the countless declarations of profound grief to publish.[55] On 7 March, four days of official mourning began across the USSR, with all performances, concerts, movie screenings and other entertainments suspended. An official resolution declared that Stalin's body would lie in state at the House of Unions in central Moscow until the funeral, and would thereafter be housed alongside that of Lenin in the mausoleum on Red Square, with initial plans announced for the construction of a vast new pantheon to supersede the existing mausoleum. Soviet citizens (including a youthful Mikhail Gorbachev) responded eagerly to the news of Stalin's lying in state and headed in droves to see the body. Also among those who went along, the poet Andrei Voznesensky later recalled banners, wreaths and uniforms everywhere and Stalin 'lying on his back like a beetle'.[56]

Of course, not quite everyone felt bereft. At the Dalstroi labour camp complex in the far north of Russia, some prisoners hugged and kissed one another on hearing the news.[57] Elsewhere in the gulag, though, Karlo Štajner wrote that one of his fellow inmates requested permission to spend the pitifully little money he had on a bouquet of flowers to send to the funeral.[58] In Moscow, Igor Golomstock quietly opined to friends that Stalin had 'deserved to die a dog's death', and he was not alone in such sentiments.[59] The painter Oskar Rabin later wrote of celebrating the initial news of Stalin's stroke by drinking a toast with a friend.[60] Not many people even noticed that one of the country's most iconic cultural figures – the composer Sergei Prokofiev – had also died in the Soviet capital that same day.

Members of the leadership in Moscow were well enough apprised about the realities of daily life to know that public moods could change quickly in such a febrile environment. Indeed, one leading scholar has argued that the country was already 'on the verge of social explosion' in 1953.[61] It was for this reason that so many of the official pronouncements relating to Stalin's stroke and subsequent death were accompanied by exhortations for 'steel-like unity and monolithic cohesion in the party ranks' and for the wider Soviet public to stand firm behind the party and its leadership, with the police, army and security services all put on high alert. The CIA-funded station Radio Liberation informed Soviet listeners that an uprising against the state was 'inevitable'. Similarly, in Washington, DC, the news of Stalin's death prompted urgent discussions about turning President Eisenhower's recent campaign rhetoric of 'rolling back' communism into concrete action, with John Foster Dulles urging US embassies around the globe to begin psychological warfare against the new Soviet leadership, sowing doubt and confusion as widely as possible.[62]

On 9 March, the day of the funeral, media reports revelled in the news that mourning wreaths had long since filled the hall where Stalin lay, and were now flowing up the surrounding streets; that mourners were continually arriving in Moscow from the furthest reaches of the country; and that an 'endless human river' was snaking around the capital, with the elderly, mothers with infants, young workers and others withstanding freezing temperatures in order to pay their last respects. By then, though, tragedy had already struck. The sheer size of the crowds, combined with policing that showed minimal concern for public safety, made the situation potentially dangerous from the outset. One of those present when the queue turned into a deadly crush at Trubnaya Square in central Moscow, the poet Yevgeny Yevtushenko, later wrote of being swept off his feet by a relentless wave of movement, watching young children suffocating, seeing eyes bulging and feeling the bones of those around him cracking, as people were trampled underfoot or smashed against walls and barricades.[63] Khrushchev apparently later stated in private that 109 people had been killed that day.[64] As with almost all such disasters, the country's media carried no news of what had transpired.

Late in the morning on 9 March, Presidium members Malenkov, Beria, Molotov, Kliment Voroshilov, Khrushchev, Nikolai Bulganin, Lazar Kaganovich, Mikoyan and China's Zhou Enlai carried Stalin's coffin out of the House of the Unions. It was then rested on a gun carriage and taken the short distance to Red Square. As chairman of the committee charged with organising the funeral, Khrushchev spoke first to declare the event open, but the principal orations came from Malenkov, Beria and Molotov. Malenkov, in particular, took the opportunity to begin pitching for public approval, stating that the domestic priority now was to raise living standards for the Soviet masses, while the key foreign policy goal was to prevent conflict with the West. Beria warned darkly of the need to be more vigilant than ever before, as the country's opponents probed for weaknesses. Visibly upset, Molotov's speech was filled almost exclusively with warnings about enemies and effusive praise for the 'exceptionally gifted comrade' that the country had lost.

Just before midday, the casket was carried into the Red Square mausoleum – which already had the name 'Stalin' inscribed on its façade, beneath that of Lenin – and Khrushchev declared the ceremony closed. At 12:00 Moscow time, work stopped at enterprises throughout the country: trams, cars and buses halted; factories, trains and boats sounded their hooters and klaxons for a three-minute show of respect. Artillery salutes were fired in all fifteen republican capitals, as well as in major cities from Lvov (Lviv) and Kaliningrad in the far west to Khabarovsk and Vladivostok over 7,000 kilometres away to the east.

Alongside the public displays of grief, these were also days of frenetic decision making behind closed doors. The very first decision, though, had taken far longer than it probably ought to have done. After household staff had discovered Stalin on the floor of his bedroom on the evening of 1 March – already several hours after his stroke – Beria, Malenkov, Khrushchev and Bulganin were called out to the dacha at around midnight. Seemingly at the insistence of Beria, they agreed that he was sleeping, rather than unconscious, and so did not seek medical help. Stalin's aversion to doctors was well known to all of them, but such inaction was clearly striking. Prompted by another worried call from staff at the dacha several hours later, the group eventually returned at around 07:00 with doctors in tow. While suggestions that Stalin was somehow murdered remain unconvincing, his closest associates were evidently in no great rush to save his life. Indeed, some reputable sources argue that the quartet had deliberately failed to provide timely assistance once they realised the seriousness of his situation.[65]

When they did swing into action, Malenkov, Khrushchev and the others summoned to the dacha a team of the very best doctors, along with Stalin's children Vasily and Svetlana, and took turns to hold a round-the-clock vigil. While they watched on in pairs – Beria and Malenkov; Khrushchev and Bulganin; Kaganovich and Voroshilov (Molotov and Mikoyan were still in disgrace with Stalin at the time and were thus absent) – conversations naturally turned to the question of what was to come next.

On the evening of 5 March, the most important regime officials present in Moscow gathered at the Kremlin. In the forty minutes that the meeting lasted, the roughly two hundred members of the country's political elite present were first told that Stalin would hardly be able to work again, even in the unlikely event that he survived. Then a highly efficient power grab, which had been worked out over the course of the previous few days, was successfully pushed through, as Stalin's closest associates looked to shore up their pre-eminence. Key government roles were doled out between themselves first as the Soviet Union began a period of 'collective leadership'.

Beria proposed Malenkov as the new head of government (effectively, prime minister), and Malenkov in turn proposed Beria, Molotov, Bulganin and Kaganovich as his principal deputies. Also at Malenkov's proposal, Beria was put back in charge of the country's security organs after several years away, spent overseeing the nascent nuclear weapons programme. This time, though, his power base was much expanded, as the security services were combined with the regular police in a hugely powerful institution called the MVD (Ministry of Internal Affairs). Molotov was reinstated as head of the Ministry of Foreign Affairs and Mikoyan was returned to his preferred field, dealing with foreign and domestic trade.

The most senior roles in the Communist Party leadership were now allotted to Malenkov, Beria and Khrushchev. However, with the other two occupied primarily with government duties (Beria with the new MVD; Malenkov overseeing the work of all the ministries, as prime minister), Khrushchev was by default the man in charge of party affairs on a practical level. Nonetheless, as both the head of government and officially one of the heads of the party, Malenkov enjoyed a clear position of pre-eminence within the leadership. None of those present in the audience offered comments or raised questions, passively accepting the news they were presented with.[66] By 21:00 the meeting in the Kremlin had ended and by 22:00 Stalin was dead.

The British ambassador in Moscow, Sir William Hayter, later provided some brief pen portraits following his encounters with key figures in the new collective leadership. Like other members of the foreign diplomatic corps, he saw Malenkov as clearly the strongest candidate to succeed Stalin, finding him polite, 'business-like and clear-headed', as well as 'quick, clever and subtle'. Molotov he described as a genial host who could be both brutal and cold, but had 'the instincts of a gentleman', adding that he and most of the other ambassadors in Moscow 'felt that in dealing with him we were dealing with the real thing'. Voroshilov was depicted only as 'fairly decrepit' and playing no obvious part in affairs, while Kaganovich was noted as both the only Jew and the principal anti-Semite in the leadership group. The Armenian Mikoyan he portrayed as both a 'court jester' and 'highly intelligent and subtle, perhaps the best politician of them all'. Bulganin cropped up in Hayter's depictions mainly in the context of his frequently being drunk.[67]

Often inclined to play up to his reputation as something of a country bumpkin, Khrushchev did not impress the ambassador at first. Hayter described how a formal dinner for the visiting British politician Aneurin Bevan in August 1954 saw Khrushchev come across as 'impulsive, blundering and ignorant of foreign affairs', adding that Bevan repeatedly tried to explain a basic point about the UN that Khrushchev continually failed to grasp until 'it was explained to him in words of one syllable by Malenkov'. At the American embassy, Charles Bohlen was of much the same opinion, viewing Malenkov as the clearest and most nuanced thinker and initially describing Khrushchev to his boss, John Foster Dulles, as 'not especially bright'.[68] As time went on, though, both Hayter and Bohlen would come to consider Khrushchev as an increasingly effective political operator.

Malenkov was the one formally in charge; but to a large extent he was operating in an unofficial duet with Beria. Aware that it would be politically very difficult for another Georgian to follow Stalin as Soviet leader, and confident that he could manipulate the pliable Malenkov, the notorious secret policeman had quickly fastened himself to the heir apparent and rapidly became increasingly self-assertive within the new collective leadership. His colleagues, though, had by no means forgotten or forgiven the years during which Beria had revelled in holding the power of life and death over them, as head of the security organs. Stalin's daughter recalled that all the others in the collective leadership feared Beria, who was habitually rude and constantly used foul language.[69]

The first amnesty

Whether in a bid to win Molotov's allegiance or else to demonstrate the extent of his own powers, the day after Stalin's funeral Beria presented the foreign minister with the most remarkable gift for his sixty-fourth birthday: his wife Polina, who had been jailed on Stalin's direct orders four years previously. Like Molotov, though, she remained steadfastly devoted to Stalin's memory and had apparently even collapsed with grief on hearing the news of his death. Soon enough, dozens of repressed generals and admirals were being quietly released and rehabilitated.[70] In a number of cases, the widows and children of repressed members of the elite also received relatively generous financial support.

On 26 March 1953, Beria reported to colleagues with his initial assessment of the security organs' work during the years he had been away from the Lubyanka, heading up the bomb programme: he warned bluntly that there were too many people serving sentences that were too long.[71] The very next day, the process of draining the vast gulag network began in earnest: those with sentences of less than five years' duration, pregnant women and women with children under the age of ten, juvenile prisoners under the age of eighteen, prisoners with incurable illnesses, men over fifty-five and women over fifty were all released at a stroke. Although not yet freed, many others also had their sentences halved. In total, over a third of all those imprisoned were now set free.

Notably, this first amnesty explicitly did not apply to those serving more than five years on charges of 'counter-revolutionary activity'. This was the part of the criminal code under which most Stalin-era political repression had taken place, so those classified as 'politicals' mostly remained incarcerated for the time being. Those amnestied in March 1953, then, were typically people serving a sentence for an 'ordinary' crime, such as theft, assault or murder. The official rationale for the amnesty was that the Soviet system had now reached a sufficiently high level of development that it could – and should – allow those who had previously erred to correct themselves through reintegration into society. The amnesty was thus presented to the public primarily as a mark of the regime's achievements and its humane approach, not as an acknowledgement of errors or abuses previously committed by the authorities.

The speed with which the amnesty was introduced – a mere three weeks after Stalin's death – reflected the fact that there was little argument among the collective leadership that the gulag had to change. Nonetheless, that rapidity of action surely also contributed to the chaotic nature of what followed. Indeed, later on there would be talk in certain quarters that this initial amnesty had really been a cynical provocation by Beria – an attempt to sow public discord and panic, which his MVD would then resolve through a new crackdown that would power him to pre-eminence. Proving such a hypothesis seems impossible, but one can understand why its logic might have appealed, in light of what transpired. Despite the official narratives about redemption and reintegration of those released, the spring and early summer of 1953 saw a frightening crime wave – part real, part imagined – sweep over the country, as more than a million prisoners emerged from places of confinement. The number of crimes registered in 1953 was more than double the figure for the previous year, and police repeatedly found themselves outnumbered and overpowered in the face of rampaging groups of returnees.[72]

Even in Moscow, Dmitry Shepilov wrote of how people were afraid to go out in the evenings and 'with the coming of night, shutters were secured with heavy bolts, and residents waited anxiously and fearfully for dawn'.[73] There were myriad drunken fights on trains and station platforms, instances of shops and buffets being looted and gangs of prisoners engaging in pitched battles with police. In one notorious incident, a group of released prisoners entered a female-only train carriage and raped almost all of the forty women inside.[74] In the remote city of Magadan – for years a major gulag centre – released prisoners were everywhere, living underground or around heating pipes, gathering in the city's Park of Culture to drink and fight, terrorising the city at will.[75] A complaint sent from the city of Molotov (Perm) in the Urals during April 1953 to the Supreme Soviet in Moscow gave an almost apocalyptic vision of the situation there. Purporting to be a collective letter from eighty-five residents of the city, it told of a dramatic rise in banditry, which made it impossible to walk the streets after 22:00, and reported that every night there were killings, violence and debauchery.[76] When officials investigated the matters set out in that letter (and other documents like it), they found that there had indeed been a notable rise in crime, but that some of the more shocking details were based on rumour and hearsay. In short, the crime wave was real, but it was also being exaggerated by mass panic. This panic fed growing public anger aimed both at the criminals involved and at the authorities that had released them. There were soon calls for the police to be allowed to shoot bandits in the streets and to send them straight back to the camps.[77]

Crucially, the country's leadership had no intention of setting out an honest explanation for how so many people had come to be imprisoned and were now being released. That would clearly prove far too explosive on the whole; but it did happen in regard to one specific case. Still building towards a climax when Stalin died, the on-going Doctors' Plot also had to be dealt with by the new leadership. It seems that few among them were ever truly convinced about the veracity of the plot (several knew some of the accused doctors personally), but Beria really hammered that point home now, distributing to Central Committee members harrowing excerpts from his investigations into the case, including testimonies about the use of torture against the defendants. At the start of April, the denouncer whose claims had created the basis for the whole affair, Lidiya Timashuk, was declared a liar and the Order of Lenin medal that she had been awarded in January was rescinded.

Thirty-seven suspects in the Doctors' Plot were released from custody. Remarkably, the end of the affair was even made public. In early April, both *Pravda* and *Izvestiya* (*News*) carried the news (albeit on their inside pages) that an investigation had been carried out and the doctors' arrests had been found to have been based on false accusations and fabricated evidence, with the accused subjected to means of interrogation that were strictly forbidden under Soviet law. Those who had overseen the investigation had, in turn, been arrested and would face criminal charges. At least some among the public remained unconvinced by this turn of events, though, and numerous citizens wrote to officials in fury that the 'poisoners' had been allowed to go free, alleging that treasonous intent was the only possible reason behind

31

such a reckless decision. For many Soviet Jews, of course, the abandonment of the Doctors' Plot was the close of an especially dark and frightening chapter. It by no means marked a complete end to the discrimination they faced, but synagogues in Moscow, Leningrad and Kishinev (Chişinău) were again filled to overflowing for Passover, as a new sense of optimism for better times ahead emerged.[78]

Changes begin

While it ultimately took another three years for anyone to tackle the Stalin cult head-on, subtle changes at the top began almost immediately. As early as 10 March, Malenkov informed fellow Presidium members that there had been 'great abnormalities' in the country as a result of the cult of the individual, and that ending it was now deemed obligatory.[79] As heir apparent, he also took a distinctly collegial approach to leadership from the outset, encouraging others to contribute and trying to smooth over differences of opinion (although a doctored photo of him alongside Stalin and Chinese leader Mao Zedong that appeared in *Pravda* – clearly intended to underline his status as Stalin's successor – seriously alarmed colleagues, who took him to task for it). Malenkov summoned the editors of major newspapers to the Kremlin and informed them that the days of cults were over, both for Stalin and for those who succeeded him; he ordered that members of the collective leadership should now receive an equal amount of attention in the press.[80] Newspapers were also instructed to list the names of Presidium members alphabetically, rather than by any order of seniority. Even so, other members of the leadership remained concerned by the episode of the faked photograph, and by 14 March had pressured Malenkov to give up his top-ranking party post as a Central Committee secretary.[81] Stalin had accumulated tremendous power by being both head of the government and head of the party, and it was decided that nobody should again combine those two posts, in order to prevent any such concentration of power in one pair of hands from ever happening again.

Already in early April, the *New York Times* Moscow correspondent Harrison Salisbury noted that Stalin was being cited less and less frequently in the Soviet media. By 6 April, he could find only one mention in that day's

Pravda; a year previously, it might easily have been more than a hundred.[82] Soon enough, the publication of Stalin's collected works quietly drew to a close, ahead of schedule. Draft designs for the grand pantheon that had been promised when Stalin died did eventually appear in the press; but that project, too, was discreetly shelved. In the middle of April, the Stalinist 'command style' of leadership also came under attack, as *Pravda* lambasted officials who rejected criticism and bullied colleagues, insisting that there was no place in the party for one-man leadership (ironically, offering a quotation from Stalin to support that assertion). On 10 June 1953, the term 'cult of personality' appeared in the pages of *Pravda*; it insisted that Lenin, Marx and Engels had warned against such a phenomenon, but it still shied away from levelling any explicit accusation against Stalin. Towards the end of that month, *Pravda* also carried a major speech given by the editor of the journal *Voprosy filosofii* (*Questions of Philosophy*) which rejected as ideologically unsound any emphasis on 'outstanding personalities' as the makers of history. In what was presumably an indirect reference to the galloping anti-Semitism and Russian chauvinism of recent years, another editorial in *Pravda* also emphasised the impropriety of any attempt to stir up national and ethnic tensions between different Soviet peoples, or to impose advantages or disadvantages on any group based on race or nationality.

Beria quickly appointed (or reappointed) his own allies throughout the security apparatus and continued to investigate and expose the repressions undertaken during the years while he was away from the security organs. On 4 April, he announced that there had been serious breaches of legality in recent years – including the arrest of innocent people, falsified evidence and the use of torture – and signed an order banning the use of violence in interrogations. He soon went even further, putting an end to the widespread use of prisoner labour for major construction projects like railways and canals.[83] Then, on 8 April, Beria informed colleagues that the so-called Mingrelian Affair (which had seen many of his own allies across the Caucasus republics imprisoned) had also been fabricated. On 10 April, this too was announced to the Soviet public.[84]

Nobody (apart from his son Sergo) has given much credence to the notion that Beria led the way in exposing and tackling such abuses either for reasons of conscience or out of a sense of the public good. The most common theory for why he proved such an active proponent of reform during this period is that he was trying to present himself as the 'liberal' (in relative terms) candidate for power, in a bid to outflank his rivals as Stalin's successor. Doubtless there is some considerable truth in this notion. However, the exposure of the Doctors' Plot and the Mingrelian Affair also helped Beria strengthen his grip on the two institutional power bases that he had cultivated for years: the security organs and the political elite of the three Caucasus republics (Georgia, Azerbaijan and Armenia). Both re-investigations had concluded not only with the removal of officials whom Stalin had put in place to disrupt Beria's client network, but also with the appointment to important posts of people fundamentally loyal to Beria himself.[85]

Beria saw officials in the non-Russian republics as a key constituency to win over to his side, and, with Khrushchev's support, he ensured that nationalities questions moved to the centre of the political arena that spring.[86] In particular, he highlighted the continuing prevalence of hostile nationalist sentiment in several non-Russian republics, and then pinned the blame for this on the overt Russian dominance and chauvinism that Stalin had encouraged both during and after the war. The result of this trend, he showed, was that in the Baltics, Ukraine and elsewhere, party officials and those people who held all manner of responsible posts – from factory directors to police chiefs – were not locals, but Russians despatched from Moscow. Of the 600 officials in the government ministries of Kyrgyzstan at the time of Stalin's death, for example, only forty were Kyrgyz by ethnicity.[87] All this gave an unambiguously 'imperial' dimension to post-war Stalinism in the non-Russian republics, driving up resentment and animosity among the many millions of citizens outside the Soviet system's Russian heartland.

The first announcement, about the state of affairs in western Ukraine, came on 26 May 1953. It began by acknowledging that the political situation there remained unsatisfactory and stating that poor leadership was a root cause of dissatisfaction among the local population. Of the 311 leading party officials in western Ukraine at that point, it said, only eighteen were actually from western Ukraine. Of the fifty-six academic disciplines taught at one Lvov university, all were taught in the Russian language (although prevalent in eastern Ukraine, knowledge of Russian was not nearly so widespread in the west of the republic). Within a couple of weeks, the Russian head of the

Ukrainian Communist Party in Kiev, Leonid Melnikov, was removed and replaced with an actual Ukrainian communist, Alexei Kirichenko (though it would not be until the 1960s that Ukraine had a party boss who consistently spoke Ukrainian in public).[88]

An analogous decree on Lithuania was also issued. It complained that Lithuania was largely being run by people who did not know the Lithuanian language or understand the republic's culture and way of life; it stated that this divide ensured the party and the masses remained distant from one another, while anti-Russian propaganda flourished. The party was thus ordered to find suitable Lithuanians to promote to important posts in the republic (never one to miss an opportunity, Beria fought – albeit in vain – to ensure that these new openings went to people loyal to him).[89] The fundamental message of these decrees – reining in Russian dominance – was to be acted upon across the USSR, quickly giving rise to a new self-assertiveness where Stalinist 'imperialism' had been felt most keenly. In June 1953, the Latvian Communist Party Central Committee held a plenary session in the Latvian language for the first time in its history, an event at which the recent Russification was loudly denounced.[90] In some places, this radical shake-up of nationalities policy apparently even fostered perceptions of fatal regime weakness and a belief that the whole union was ready to collapse.[91]

Stalinist positions were soon being revised in international affairs, too. Official rhetoric on the USA, in particular, was more aggressive and paranoid than ever at the start of 1953. Since 1950, the on-going war in Korea had brought the two superpowers into dangerously close quarters, as American troops fought North Koreans and Chinese armed with Soviet weaponry and supported by Soviet training and advisers. Less than two weeks after Stalin's death, on 15 March, Malenkov stated publicly that all points of conflict with the US could be resolved by peaceful negotiation, and the Soviet media began to rein in its shrill anti-Americanism for the first time in a long while. Even more striking, after Stalin had for months blocked any real progress towards peace on the Korean Peninsula, by the end of March 1953 the new Soviet leadership encouraged its North Korean allies to engage in more meaningful ceasefire negotiations, with a lasting truce finally agreed on 27 July.

Soviet territorial claims against Turkey and Iran, which had already prompted both countries to strengthen their bonds with the US, were also dropped. Diplomatic ties with Israel were re-established in July, having been broken off in the course of the Doctors' Plot. In the middle of April, President Eisenhower's famous 'Chance for Peace' speech – emphasising the mutual benefits of reducing international tensions and increasing co-operation – was published in Soviet newspapers. When the official May Day slogans for 1953 were carried in the press towards the end of April, peace was the dominant theme, including one slogan that declared 'Long live the friendship of the people of Great Britain, the USA and the Soviet Union in their struggle to prevent war and to ensure world peace'. Of the forty-seven slogans announced, Stalin's name featured in only the forty-third and the forty-seventh.

Reports reaching Moscow during the late 1940s and early 1950s had also made it clear that economic crisis and social discontent were threatening to boil over throughout Soviet-dominated Eastern Europe, though Stalin was again the key impediment to any change in direction. By the summer of 1953, the situation was clearly very serious: East Germans were continuing to flee across the open border to West Berlin in ever greater numbers; strikes had broken out among Bulgarian tobacco workers at Plovdiv in May; and growing tensions in Czechoslovakia had flickered throughout April and May, before bursting into flame at the start of June in Plzeň, when angry crowds burned Soviet flags, occupied government buildings and smashed busts of Lenin and Stalin before the authorities were eventually able to restore order.[92]

The new Soviet leadership summoned to Moscow allied communist leaders from across Eastern Europe and demanded that they undertake substantial reform before even greater explosions of discontent struck. With Beria taking the lead, East Germany's Walter Ulbricht was told in no uncertain terms to ease the 'intensified building of socialism' (including forced collectivisation and heightened political persecution) that had been ordered by Stalin but was proving to be a source of rapidly swelling discontent within the German Democratic Republic (GDR). Mátyás Rákosi of Hungary was subjected to a particularly fierce dressing-down when his turn came to visit Moscow in mid-June. Ordered to vacate the post of prime minister (like Stalin, Rákosi was both head of the ruling party and head of the Hungarian government), he too was directed to begin enacting measures to ease public ferment inside Hungary. Moscow also imposed upon Rákosi its own choice of prime minister: the reform-minded Imre Nagy.

Although they publicly admitted to having 'made mistakes', the East German leadership floundered over the change of direction now expected of them, and protest broke out among construction workers in East Berlin on 16 June. The authorities there initially vacillated, and by the next day the East German regime was in a state of outright crisis, as demonstrations spread to more than 450 towns around the country. Alarmed at seeing a key ally seemingly teetering on the brink, the Soviet leadership deployed tanks and troops onto the streets of East Germany, imposing martial law and arresting thousands of 'troublemakers', with Beria despatched to oversee the pacification process. Order was restored soon enough, with perhaps forty protesters killed and another 200 wounded; but the men in the Kremlin were nonetheless shaken by the volatility that had arisen, and optimistic notions of enhancing stability through broad liberalisation measures were soon scaled back.[93]

Stopping Beria

As spring 1953 turned into summer, Beria was more and more obviously asserting himself within the collective leadership. He had made sure to play an active role in diplomatic developments around Korea, Turkey and Iran, and also tried to begin mending fences with Yugoslavia (with which Stalin had initiated an especially acrimonious split in 1948) – although this latter move in particular prompted Molotov to fury and was soon abandoned. Beria was also treating colleagues in a manner that aroused resentment and suspicion. According to Mikoyan, soon after a disagreement in the Presidium over policy towards East Germany, Beria had telephoned Bulganin in a furious mood, hurling abuse and threatening to have him sacked as minister of defence.[94] Colleagues were also wary of the vast scale of Beria's policing operation and feared that he was secretly spying on them. This was subsequently proved to be correct when investigators found his tapes of their private conversations after his arrest. Malenkov's son wrote of how neither his parents nor he and his siblings could leave the house or even make a telephone call without Beria's men knowing about it.[95] Possibly apocryphal, one story also recounts that Bulganin lost a winning ticket for the state lottery in early 1953, only for it to be discovered in Beria's personal safe, when it was broken open after his arrest.[96]

As MVD boss, Beria had access to mountains of records that incriminated his colleagues for their role in earlier repressions, and his recent investigations into abuses showed him willing and able to weaponise such material. Further, he commanded not only the country's intelligence apparatus, but also the security organs' elite military detachments and units that protected both the Kremlin and members of the leadership. In short, Presidium members were all hugely vulnerable if he decided to act against them, and they felt it keenly.[97] Nonetheless, they were seemingly also unsettled by the scope and speed of the reforms set out above. As one biographer has convincingly argued, taken together these were measures that promised to change the very nature of the Soviet system and potentially even bring down the wider socialist bloc.[98]

Although some of the details remain contested (since accounts contradict each other on a number of important points), it is clear that Khrushchev was key to initiating the plot against Beria. He approached Malenkov in the middle of June 1953 to share his concerns about what lay ahead if Beria were left unchecked. Malenkov proved surprisingly easy to convince, presumably because he, too, was wary of Beria's designs on power and was perhaps also concerned that the exposure of historic abuses might soon come to include the Leningrad Affair, in which he had been a key actor behind the extensive blood-letting. Molotov's personal disdain for the 'unprincipled careerist' Beria made him an easy convert, once he knew that Malenkov was on board. Bulganin had not forgotten the threat to have him fired, and was also quick to sign up. Meanwhile, Kaganovich and Voroshilov were similarly content to go along with the majority when approached.[99] Nobody doubted how dangerous the fallout might be if the plan failed or if news of it reached the security organs ahead of time. Crucial in this regard were two of Beria's seemingly loyal lieutenants at the MVD, Ivan Serov and Sergei Kruglov. As it transpired, the former had pre-existing ties to Khrushchev and the latter to Malenkov, and both of them proved willing to turn against their boss. Enticed by the rewards on offer and driven by frustration at affairs within the MVD, they prevented information about suspicious activity among plotting Presidium members from reaching the Lubyanka, and ensured that troops loyal to Beria could be side-stepped when the big day came.[100]

Returning from Berlin with the uprising there decisively smashed, on 25 June Beria updated Presidium members on his investigation into the crimes of one of his predecessors at the security organs, Mikhail Ryumin, who had just confessed to fabricating a plethora of anti-regime conspiracies.[101] At the end of their day's work, Khrushchev, Malenkov and Beria all shared a ride home as usual. That evening, Bulganin, as minister of defence, moved to secure the support of senior military figures. Thanks largely to Beria's leading role in the vicious purging of the Soviet armed forces years earlier, the plot proved an easy sell, and head of the Moscow Military District Kirill Moskalenko readily agreed to participate. Next morning, the great war hero Marshal Georgy Zhukov was also signed up, having long blamed Beria's scheming for the fact that Stalin turned against him after the end of the war. Being in charge of political affairs in the army, Leonid Brezhnev was also with the party of high-ranking officers that arrived at the Kremlin on the morning of 26 June, in government cars full of hidden guns. The group gained entry through a side door that had been left open for them by the plotters – thus evading Beria's Kremlin security guards – and were then briefed by Malenkov on the details of the plan, before retiring to an adjoining room to wait.

Once the unwitting Beria joined his colleagues at the Kremlin, Malenkov declared the morning's meeting open. He immediately proposed that the ensuing discussion focus on Beria. Over the next two hours, each of those present laid into their stunned and increasingly panicked target over both his political activity and his personal conduct. Once everyone had spoken, Malenkov pressed a secret button that alerted Moskalenko, Zhukov and the others to burst in and arrest Beria. While Presidium members figured out exactly what to do with him next, the military men hurriedly bundled Beria out of the room, with strict orders to execute him instantly in the event of any rescue attempt. With his security personnel everywhere inside the Kremlin and around the capital, this was a particularly tricky part of the operation, and it ultimately ended with Beria being smuggled out of the Kremlin wrapped in a blanket in the back of a car once it got dark. He was then taken to a top-secret military facility and held there under armed guard, lest forces loyal to him in the security organs sought to force his release. Many of Beria's closest allies, as well as various members of his family, were quickly tracked down and arrested, both in Moscow and in the Caucasus. Telephone calls were placed to editors of the country's major newspapers, warning that there was to be no mention of Beria's name in the next day's editions. Republican and regional party organisations were also instructed to assert control over local MVD branches throughout the country. In a calculated show of unity, the remaining members of the leadership went to the Bolshoi Ballet together that evening.

The day after Beria's arrest, Presidium members informed the wider Central Committee that their presence was required in Moscow for a meeting that would commence on 2 July, and Ukrainian Procurator General Roman Rudenko (a Khrushchev ally) was instructed to put together a legal team to investigate and prosecute Beria's 'harmful anti-Party and anti-state activity'. Soon, images of Beria were being removed from public display and destroyed; literature by or about him was being taken off library shelves; and researchers were at work in the archives, digging up whatever incriminating evidence they could find. Shortly after that, those formerly close to Beria offered up names of mistresses and victims, told of his deviousness and cited cases of his slandering Stalin and members of the collective leadership. Some gave testimony claiming that he was plotting to seize power, others that he had secretly been an agent of British intelligence. Numerous victims also spoke of being viciously beaten in Beria's Lubyanka office as he looked on. On 8 July, Rudenko began to interrogate Beria personally, building a case against him that went all the way back to 1917.[102]

The Central Committee plenum convened on 2 July, and over the course of the next five days, meeting both day and night, members fell over one another to denounce Beria. The charges that speakers hurled at him included both accurate recollections of real crimes and wild fabrications. His bid to rein in the dominance of Russian cadres in the non-Russian republics was now presented as a cynical attempt to undermine the friendship of Soviet peoples. He was also blamed for recent agricultural failings, accused of fostering his own personality cult and of misleading Stalin with intrigues against rivals. Malenkov claimed that the March amnesty had been enacted for Beria's own ends, and that he had previously conspired to discredit both Molotov and Mikoyan in Stalin's eyes. Khrushchev insisted that Beria was not a communist, but an agent of imperialism, while others swore that a bid to seize power by force had been imminent. His moral dissoluteness and brutality were made plain, and his luxurious lifestyle was offered as proof of his lack of communist ideological convictions. One Central Committee member, Andrei Andreev, got the wrong end of the stick at the plenum and started to attack Beria for trying to discredit Stalin through his reforms; but Malenkov quickly made it clear that this was not part of the issue at hand.[103]

Beria's lieutenants across the country came into the firing line, too, as his former power base was dismantled (including the removal of party bosses in both Armenia and Georgia by the end of 1953) and his henchmen were made to pay by members of the political elite whom they had previously been able to intimidate and abuse with virtual impunity. In Georgia, eight of Beria's closest allies were ultimately put on trial, with six of them executed for treason.[104] The ruthless party boss of Azerbaijan, Dzhafar Bagirov, quickly tried to distance himself from his long-time patron, describing the arrest as 'a weight being lifted from me' and expressing gratitude to Khrushchev and the others for dealing with Beria. For Bagirov, though, there was little hope of salvaging a career so closely associated with the fallen Georgian, and he was subsequently removed from all posts, before being arrested in March 1954. On trial, witnesses claimed that he had not just sanctioned the arrest of innocent people, but had personally executed some of them.[105] The Azeri press later described how the republic had suffered 'a most repulsive manifestation of the cult' thanks to Bagirov, who had surrounded himself with flatterers and had committed persecutions and lawless acts at will. Once found guilty, he and three of his closest collaborators were executed by firing squad.

News of Beria's arrest was finally announced to the public in *Pravda* on 10 July. Far less graphic than the remarks at the Central Committee plenum, the fairly brief report stated that he had been trying to undermine the Soviet state in the interests of foreign capital and to place the MVD above the party and government for his own ends. It announced that he had been expelled from the Central Committee as an enemy of the Communist Party and the Soviet people. Countless very real crimes – such as his personal involvement in the arrest and torture of innocent citizens, as well as an unknown number of rapes – passed virtually without mention, in favour of wholly invented offences like espionage. By 11 July, the affair was the subject of party meetings across the country, with newspapers thereafter relaying furious condemnations of Beria by ordinary citizens and party officials alike. As with the show trials of previous years, many demanded his execution.

As he awaited trial, Beria wrote increasingly desperate letters to his former comrades. He reminded Malenkov, in particular, of their previously friendly relations and their achievements working together during the war. He wrote to Khrushchev that he was 'an excellent Bolshevik and a marvellous friend', adding 'I always cherished your friendship.' He not only apologised profusely for instances of rudeness to colleagues – writing of his recent tirade against Bulganin, for example, that 'I am guilty without question and have to be denounced thoroughly' – but also reminded of times when he had helped shield each of them from Stalin's suspicions. As he sought to avoid execution, Beria wrote that he was willing to go off and work on a farm or construction site, where he could 'improve my behaviour and will still be of some use to you'.[106] Eventually, Presidium members had his pencil taken away, and the letters stopped.

By early December 1953, Rudenko's investigation was complete and a military tribunal headed by Marshal Ivan Konev heard the case. Tried alongside Beria from 18 December were half a dozen of his closest associates. The verdict was, of course, preordained; but witnesses were summoned and evidence presented. Perhaps most notably, the Old Bolshevik Alexei Snegov was brought to Moscow all the way from the Kolyma camp complex in the far east to give testimony at the trial, after he had heard of Beria's disgrace and managed to smuggle a letter about his own case out to Mikoyan, with whom he had worked many years previously. On 23 December, Beria and the rest of the accused were sentenced to death; Colonel-General Pavel Batitsky duly carried out the sentence soon after. The following day, the country's newspapers told their readers how Beria had been found guilty of aiming to seize power for himself, had been working for British intelligence and plotting to restore capitalism in the USSR.

In the sense that Beria was jailed and executed on charges that were clearly fabricated, his case paradoxically represented a continuation of the illegalities that had characterised Stalinism, even though he undoubtedly was guilty of myriad horrific offences. In several important senses – most notably in its use of a simplistic person-centred narrative on Beria's crimes, rather than any genuinely thoroughgoing explanation for the mass abuses conducted on his watch – this was also a forerunner of the attack on Stalin that was eventually to follow. Indeed, Beria's arrest and denunciation in summer 1953 helped to slow the initial burst of reforms that he had spearheaded following Stalin's death.[107] The public disgrace after his arrest in June 1953 made it clear that Beria had been the one to blame for almost all the country's past and present ills. This represented an excellent holding position for a leadership that was not yet ready to tackle the far more sensitive question of Stalin's record in power.[108] Nonetheless, Beria's removal from the political scene clearly also had epoch-shaping social resonance. Many of those who lived through the period later remembered this as a key moment when the sense of fear about what the future held finally began to dissipate inside the USSR.[109]

Virtually unimaginable at the end of February, a series of incredibly powerful shocks rocked the Soviet Union between the start of March and the middle of July 1953. The death of a seemingly omnipotent and infallible leader was followed in short order by the release of around a million inmates from the gulag, abrupt changes in both domestic and foreign policy and then the news that one of the most prominent men in the country was really a usurper and an agent of imperialism. For all that Stalin had not yet been publicly singled out for blame – he was still officially celebrated at this point, albeit rather more mutedly – key pillars of Stalinism were already crumbling with remarkable rapidity. Even so, the omens for a genuinely compelling and constructive reckoning with its causes and legacy were ambiguous at best.

2

POWER STRUGGLES, SOCIAL CHANGE AND LIBERALISATION

The two and half years that ensued after Beria's arrest would be less dramatic than the months immediately following Stalin's death, but they were none-theless still full of important changes that were crucial to the re-forging of the Soviet system. At the apex of power, Nikita Khrushchev was emerging first as an increasingly serious contender for power, and then as the domi-nant figure in the Soviet leadership. For ordinary people, and for peasants in particular, living standards would begin to rise appreciably and a host of key restrictions were eased or removed, covering everything from rein-stating women's access to abortion through to the publication of challenging new literary works. Former prisoners fought to salvage what they could of their lives after returning from the gulag, while hundreds of thousands of young people headed out to Siberia and Kazakhstan to make their own contribution to the construction of communism as the new era got under way.

Social and political change begins

For all that there was a struggle for supremacy going on inside the Kremlin, it mostly happened in a relatively restrained manner now, only rarely erupting into open antagonism. Of the three principal candidates for power after Beria's removal – Malenkov, Khrushchev and Molotov – only the latter remained an unflinching Stalinist in political outlook. Khrushchev and Malenkov were mostly on friendly terms and were broadly aligned on the need for reform in a number of key fields. Indeed, it seems likely that Malenkov for a time enter-tained a notion that he and Khrushchev might even rule together; but the latter clearly had no interest in such an arrangement.[1]

In early August 1953, Malenkov brought the question of raising living standards back to the centre of public discourse. He spoke first of his pride at Soviet industrial achievements, but then called for a new balance to be struck between investment in heavy industry and investment in light industry, insisting again that the time had come to prioritise a rapid rise in the material and cultural level of the Soviet people.[2] A couple of months later, Mikoyan joined in, declaring that production of consumer goods would be increased by nearly 50 per cent between 1954 and 1956, with items like refrigerators, radios, sewing machines and vacuum cleaners soon to be owned by the majority of Soviet families.

Khrushchev took up the topic of better times ahead with regard to food provision, first of all lamenting that the country had fewer head of cattle in 1953 than in 1916. The blame for this state of affairs, he insisted, lay with harsh policies towards the peasantry: setting overly high quotas for delivery of produce from collective farms; paying far too little for the grain and meat that were demanded; and taxing too heavily any income that peasants made by selling produce from private plots. Put briefly, the Stalinist model of squeezing the countryside ever harder was not working, and a raft of new measures was hurriedly announced. More investment in agricultural machinery was promised, along with the despatch to rural areas of over 100,000 specialists and 50,000 Communist Party activists. Key from the peasants' point of view, though, was the fact that the reform included a major drop in taxes, a cancelling of tax arrears and significant rises in the prices that the state paid for collective farms' produce. Even so, this was very much 'a salve but not a cure', staving off immediate crisis rather than fixing a deeply flawed system.[3]

Already doing the job in practice, by the end of September 1953, Khrushchev was formally recognised as head of the Communist Party (taking the title First Secretary instead of General Secretary, as Stalin had been). This now brought into focus the question of where real power lay within the Soviet system: with control of the government ministries and their vast resources or with the Communist Party and its ideological power. Malenkov clearly believed that the former would prove decisive, but he was wrong. Khrushchev was soon putting officials loyal to him into important party jobs throughout the Russian regions and non-Russian republics. On relinquishing his role as Moscow party chief in March 1953, he ensured that this key post passed to one of his own protégés – Ekaterina Furtseva. By the end of 1953, Khrushchev had also appointed new republican party leaders in Georgia and Armenia, as well as in Leningrad, Bashkiria, North Ossetia and Tula. The following year brought the appointment of new party heads for Kazakhstan, Azerbaijan and Moldavia, as well as important Russian regions such as Voronezh and Khabarovsk.[4] Khrushchev's network of loyal clients remained stronger in Ukraine and Moscow, where he had worked for many years under Stalin, but it was fast spreading across the country.[5]

In sharp contrast to Stalin and other Presidium members (who rarely left the capital, except perhaps to holidays in the south), Khrushchev was always keen to get out beyond the Kremlin, regularly travelling around the country and meeting regional officials, who much appreciated both the chance to lobby on local issues and the raised profile that came with a visit from the party boss. Khrushchev also met and seemingly connected well with ordinary members of the public. Even Molotov later conceded that on his travels 'people would treat him [Khrushchev] as one of their own and they would be absolutely at ease with him'.[6] Of course, popularity among the general public alone was hardly a decisive issue in a system without democratic institutions, but it certainly did no harm to his credibility as a candidate to lead the country.

Khrushchev was also winning favour among the large and hugely influential army of bureaucrats that remained off-stage but nonetheless oversaw vital party tasks – from drafting speeches and reviewing complaints through to passing information up and down the ladder.[7] In what was presumably a moment of populism, Malenkov had criticised corruption and abuses of power among officials, but Khrushchev sprang to their defence, insisting that they were a vital pillar of the system. He also reined in the gruelling working hours that they had previously been subjected to. Party workers, ministerial staff and others had typically remained in their offices for a huge number of hours per week, often sleeping there, essentially to accommodate Stalin's personal timetable as an avowed night owl. Anatoly Dobrynin, for example, wrote that he regularly worked until 03:00 or 04:00 at the Ministry of Foreign Affairs during the late Stalin years, adding 'God forbid if someone was not on the job when Stalin phoned him after midnight.'[8] One joke from the time told of an official who eventually returned home from work early one day, only to find an unknown young man in the house with his startled wife. On being asked what was going on, the wife duly explained that the young man was, in fact, his son.[9] Preferring to be home with his family by evening, Khrushchev ordered that something more like a normal working day be re-established.

Malenkov's standing took a serious hit in April 1954, when the Leningrad Affair was officially recognised as a fabrication and its victims were rehabilitated, albeit posthumously in many cases. His name was not explicitly mentioned in the decision, but it was widely known that he had been both the main instigator and the prime beneficiary of that particular purge. Khrushchev then landed another blow when the long-term future of the security apparatus was finally settled. The vast MVD that had been created for Beria in March 1953 was deemed too powerful for any one individual to control, and it was now broken in two. One part retained the name MVD and took responsibility for matters like day-to-day policing and control of residence permits. The other part, tasked with carrying out both intelligence and counter-intelligence work, was named the Committee for State Security, or KGB.

While still a hugely powerful organisation within the Soviet system, the new KGB was not quite the indomitable behemoth that its Stalin-era predecessors had been. Even the change of institutional title from a ministry to a committee represented something of a downgrade in status.[10] It no longer had the economic power of previous security organs, its control over the camp and prison network was handed to the MVD, and special functions like supervision of nuclear weapons work were also hived off to other ministries. Domestically, its jurisdiction was mainly pared back to investigating espionage, treason and terrorism (admittedly, each of these could be broadly conceived). New rules prohibited the use of torture, demanded hard evidence be presented in court when seeking prosecution, and gave legal officials at the procuracy the right to evaluate the legality of KGB investigations and to intervene to prevent or overturn abuses where deemed necessary (though they rarely did so in practice).[11]

Of the two deputies who had betrayed Beria in June 1953 – Ivan Serov and Sergei Kruglov – it was Khrushchev's ally, Serov, who was named head of the newly constituted KGB. Without question, it was Serov's personal loyalty that prompted Khrushchev to push hard for his appointment to head up the new security organs, even in the face of resistance from other Presidium members who loathed Serov. Some even suggest that Khrushchev supported Serov for the job precisely because his career under Stalin had been so blood-stained: that he, more than anyone else, had to show supreme loyalty to his new political patron if he wanted to keep a lid on questions about his own record of involvement in past abuses.[12] Nonetheless, Khrushchev was still set on bringing the security organs to heel, soon instituting cuts to staffing numbers and salaries, and (according to Serov) at one point referring to the KGB as 'our eyes and ears', but warning that if the KGB were to betray the party's trust 'we will prick out the eyes and tear off the ears'.[13]

Subtle changes continued to take place close to the heart of the Soviet system. At the end of August 1953, the Pushkin Museum of Fine Arts finally closed the sumptuous exhibition of gifts that had been sent to Stalin from around the globe to mark his seventieth birthday (though Stalin Prizes continued to be handed out for a range of notable achievements, and a Stalin exhibition was also opened at Moscow's Lenin Library). Having been off limits to the general public since the end of the 1920s, the grandiose State Department Store (GUM) abutting Red Square was reopened in December 1953. The famous Praga (Prague) restaurant at the tip of Moscow's Arbat district reopened to the public after years of being closed to all but the country's top elite.[14] At the end of 1954, the Kremlin also hosted a New Year's Eve party for the capital's young communists, with Presidium members in attendance. Previously unthinkable, in 1955 the Kremlin complex was even opened for locals and tourists alike to visit.

The material situation was beginning to improve for most already from 1953, but it did so only haltingly and from a very low base. On visiting the Podol district of central Kiev in 1956, the American Marvin Kalb was astounded at the 'Dickensian' filth and poverty he encountered there.[15] Even some quite large towns still had no central water supply or sewerage. A seasoned traveller around the Russian provinces of the mid-1950s, Igor Golomstock described how most towns had a couple of grandiose Stalin-style buildings in the centre, but the outskirts were packed with 'squalid hovels' and endless seas of mud instead of footpaths and roads.[16] In the republican capitals of Central Asia – like Tashkent and Alma-Ata (Almaty) – roadways were as likely to feature laden donkeys as motor cars or trucks. Visiting villages around the provincial town of Stavropol in the mid-1950s, and seeing dirty, smoke-filled peasant huts dotted across the horizon, Mikhail Gorbachev later wrote that 'I wondered, "How is it possible, how can anyone live like that?"'[17]

Rather than promising a US-style consumerism – as the Soviet regime presented it – of unrestrained and unnecessary acquisition, driven by manipulative corporations seeking profit, the authorities promised a distinctively socialist approach to consumption. At its heart, this was to be rooted in 'self-restraint, moderation, and the satisfaction of "rational" needs' and seeking to avoid the fetishisation of goods.[18] In 1953, work began on building the giant Detsky mir (Children's World) department store in Moscow, with branches in provincial cities to follow further down the line, making available items like children's clothes and prams that had for years been all but impossible to find in shops. A Ministry of Consumer Goods was formed to improve the country's supply network. In Alexei Kosygin it was headed by one of the most capable officials around, but this would always remain a realm that was riddled with failings – not least because Soviet consumers never proved to be quite as 'rational' as planners envisioned. This was itself largely a result of habitually unpredictable supply, meaning that many people grabbed even items they did not really need as soon as they went on sale – either in case they did not appear again, or else to sell or swap for what they did need but could not find. Substantially more investment was put into the production of consumer goods, but this was still dwarfed by spending on heavy industry and the military, and progress was to prove slow. Despite Mikoyan's confident assertion that such items would soon be commonplace, only around one in every thousand citizens owned a washing machine or a vacuum cleaner by 1955, and a mere four per thousand owned a refrigerator.[19]

A new minimum wage was introduced in 1955, which constituted a pay rise for millions of the country's lowest earners. In Moscow, by the mid-1950s shelves were also growing notably less bare, with shops often stocking several different kinds of sausage and cheese, *smetana* (soured cream) and preserves; meanwhile, bread was cheap and abundant.[20] Chocolate and ice cream were also increasingly available and popular among the public, while items like canned tomatoes, peppers and peas improved nutrition.[21] This improvement, though, must be offset by data which showed that Soviet citizens on average still ate only around a quarter as much meat and eggs as did Americans, and less than half as much dairy produce.[22] Anyway, in terms of the availability of goods, the picture was always less rosy away from the Soviet capital. In the provincial Russian city of Voronezh, for example, residents still complained that there was sugar in the state shops for only three or four months per year, and rarely any meat or butter available to buy.[23]

All manner of new interactions with the outside world were also starting to proliferate, after years of deep Stalinist insularity. In 1954, there was a successful visit to the USSR from the Comédie-Française, followed in 1955 by a British production of *Hamlet* that played thirteen packed-out shows at Moscow Arts Theatre, and then by a touring US production of *Porgy and Bess* that quickly sold out in both Leningrad and Moscow (present for the Leningrad shows, Truman Capote noticed how shocked Soviet audiences were by the sex scenes in particular).[24] Vasily Aksenov recalled that the appeal of the show was such that he queued a full week to get tickets.[25] There were exhibitions of French arts and furniture (and the singer Yves Montand would soon tour the USSR, gaining huge popularity among Soviet youth), a visit from the English football club Arsenal (which played an exhibition match against Dinamo Moscow and found itself on the receiving end of a 5–0 thrashing) and festivals of Italian, Hungarian and Chinese films held in Moscow, Leningrad and republican capitals.[26] The Global South was also starting to become more of a presence in Soviet life. One of the big hits of 1954 in cinemas was the Indian movie *The Vagabond* starring Raj Kapoor, while the Argentine film *The Age of Love* led to Soviet girls aping the outfits and mannerisms of leading lady Lolita Torres.[27]

Although Beria's drive to empower local officials in the non-Russian republics had since been denounced as a perfidious attempt to sow discord, its basic principle of reducing overt Russian predominance survived intact. Russia was still presented as the 'elder brother' of the Soviet family, nurturing and inspiring the other 'less advanced' peoples of the country; but there was new room to celebrate the non-Russian peoples without arousing accusations of bourgeois nationalism. Conferences were held and academic works published on the national cultures and histories – albeit in appropriately sovietised form – of the Central Asian republics, the Baltic republics and others. At the end of 1953, all-union newspapers (that is, those sold across the USSR) publicised the 150th anniversary celebrations of the great Estonian writer Friedrich Kreutzwald, and in March 1954 Moscow hosted a ten-day festival of Soviet Lithuanian art and literature. That same month, Anastas Mikoyan spoke in Yerevan in praise of the beloved Armenian poet Yeghishe Charents, who had been jailed as a counter-revolutionary and died soon after, in 1937.[28] Khrushchev's personal and professional ties to Ukraine saw that republic, in particular, grow in prominence. In one November 1960 speech, for example, he drew a metaphor of the Soviet Union as an orchestra, in which 'the first violin is played by Russians and Ukrainians'.[29]

Most significant in terms of its longer-term repercussions, in January 1954 the 300th anniversary of the Pereyaslav Agreement (which the Soviet press presented as a historic treaty of Russian–Ukrainian unity, although some Ukrainians viewed it more as a tragic betrayal of their country's independence) was celebrated with great fanfare and declarations of eternal brotherhood between Russians and Ukrainians. This culminated in the legal transfer of Crimea from Russian to Ukrainian control. Although official emphasis was placed on Crimea's economic ties to Ukraine as the reason for the transfer, there was also a clear sense that this was a 'gift', intended to demonstrate and to strengthen the historic friendship between Russian and Ukrainian peoples. Of course, for as long as both Russia and Ukraine remained part of the same country, the switch of jurisdiction was essentially a symbolic one.

This was the start of an age when it became safe again for citizens to gather together socially in private. For many years such behaviour had been largely avoided, since participants risked being accused of conspiratorial activity. Now came the emergence of a type of social group known as a *kompaniya*. Lyudmila Alexeyeva – a regular participant in Moscow's blossoming new social scene – described the various *kompaniya* groups that she belonged to as being all about 'dancing to jazz, drinking vodka and talking until dawn'.[30] On his return to the capital at the end of 1954, after being released from the gulag, Lev Kopelev also fell into a previously unthinkably open circle, where people danced, flirted, talked about books and exhibitions, debated political ideas and more. Raisa Orlova, Kopelev's wife, remembered this above all else as a time of laughter with friends.[31] Soon, the pair would be hosting 'salons' in their own home, featuring freewheeling discussions of new literary works and with up-and-coming writers such as Boris Slutsky reading poetry. There was no surer sign of the changing public atmosphere than apartments crammed full of people talking without fear of being branded anti-Soviet plotters.

Still a small minority, the *stilyagi* were also growing in number and visibility, wearing gaudy clothing that they assumed looked 'Western' as they spent evenings dancing to jazz or promenading around city centres in the likes of Moscow, Leningrad and Baku.[32] Though they were generally not jailed, tales abounded of Komsomol patrols forcibly cutting their hair and clothes, and media attacks on them could be especially shrill at times: one piece in the newspaper *Komsomolskaya pravda*, for example, called them 'worthless, empty souls in gaudy foreign rags'.[33] Other youth subcultures also began to emerge as the 1950s wore on, perhaps most notably the *shtatniki* (a name derived from the word 'States') who similarly aped Western fashions and slang, albeit with a little more insouciance than the determinedly garish *stilyagi*.

New ideas about personal relations, sexuality and dress codes were also developing, in the big cities at least. At the end of 1953, students at Moscow State University demanded an end to the strict separation of male and female living quarters, which meant that even married couples within the student body were not allowed to cohabit (there had already been notable student protests about teaching quality and execrable canteen food at the university earlier that year). On visiting Tashkent in early autumn 1953, Harrison Salisbury noticed signs of changing tides there, too. Where previous generations of husbands and wives in Uzbekistan had not infrequently met for the first time only at their wedding, he wrote, now young men and women were recognisably dating first: going to the movies and taking walks together (though plenty of families did still use matchmakers for their offspring, or else had future marriages arranged even from childhood).[34] Gender-segregated education was then abolished in Soviet schools in 1954. Originally introduced during the war years, this was a measure that had, according to one recent account, done a great deal to prolong contemptuous attitudes towards female participation in public life.[35]

Official pronouncements rejuvenated regime discourse on the equality of the sexes in the USSR. Marking International Women's Day in March 1954, a Central Committee decree boasted of the female scientists, engineers, writers and cinematographers enriching the life of the country, along with a combined total of almost 2,500 female deputies in the republican and all-union parliaments.[36] The same decree also insisted that the USSR had the most far-reaching legislation in the world to protect working women: a claim that was not wholly misleading on paper, though in reality such laws often went un-enforced on the ground. Conferences and workshops on drawing women more fully into social and political activity were held, perhaps most notably in the Central Asian and Caucasus republics, where female participation was typically most limited. The newspaper *Pravda vostoka* (*Eastern Truth*) stated at the end of 1954 that the number of Uzbek women in higher education had already doubled since 1952 (to reach 7,500), though it also warned that many young girls were still being withdrawn from education early on by their parents.[37] Nonetheless, almost a decade later, *Pravda* was complaining about 'backwards' attitudes which meant that Uzbek women were still not being trusted to work with machinery.[38]

In contrast to his predecessor, Khrushchev repeatedly spoke of the need to drive up female involvement in political affairs. Examined from various angles, though, this was a discourse with limited underlying substance. Most notably, the Communist Party was – from top to bottom – a heavily male-dominated organisation, and change on this front was glacial: the proportion of female party members climbed from a little over 18 per cent in the late 1940s to almost 20 per cent by 1957 and to just shy of 21 per cent by 1967.[39] The Komsomol (the party's youth wing) did rather better on this front, with slightly more female than male members in total. That said, its upper ranks were always heavily masculine, and women at the top level were typically only put in charge of Komsomol work with young children. Similarly, the renewed discourse on equality did not prevent the continuing widespread use of tropes around women as the weaker sex or narratives about child-rearing being fundamental to female nature, and nor did it prompt attempts to tackle problems like domestic violence or sexual harassment.[40] Books on cookery, homemaking and the like were almost exclusively addressed to a female audience, while smutty jokes about promiscuous girls and sharply differing public attitudes towards (fairly widespread) extramarital affairs conducted by men and those pursued by women also told their own story of limited change on the ground.[41]

Female participation in the labour market was the most commonly cited testament to equality of the sexes in the USSR. The country did have some of the highest rates of female employment in the developed world, with women consistently making up almost half of the overall labour force, and practically all adult women working by the end of the 1960s. Bald data on the number of women in work, though, can obscure crucial details. Studies suggest that working women typically received only about 60 per cent of what their male counterparts earned, for example.[42] While there was always a good number of women who enjoyed successful careers in prestigious fields such as journalism, the arts and sciences, the overall picture shows that female workers were far more likely to be employed in low-skilled and low-paying work.[43] In the case of rural women, this usually meant physically demanding and dirty jobs, like working with animals, while men undertook cleaner and less physical work, such as operating machinery. Even in those industries where women predominated numerically, such as medicine and education, they tended not to occupy positions at the very top of the hierarchy. Of all ministerial posts throughout the country – both at all-union and republican level – only around 10 per cent were filled by women.[44]

At home, pressure on women to take up paid work was in large part rooted in the fact that a single salary often proved inadequate to keep a family afloat. However, there was also a clear political push in this direction, largely because there were jobs that needed to be filled (worker shortages were a particularly acute problem in some regions and industries) and women represented the largest source of labour that was not yet fully tapped. Being without a job was soon stigmatised. Importantly, though, encouragement to enter the workplace did not counteract the other key expectation placed on Soviet women: to have children (Khrushchev repeatedly spoke of three children per woman as an ideal to aim for). There was also no accompanying realignment of who was supposed to perform domestic work: Soviet men generally expected to undertake very few household chores. During the early years especially, childcare was widely regarded as an almost exclusively female duty.[45] Even women's publications like *Rabotnitsa* (*Woman Worker*) only called on men to offer their wives some help, not to take on an equal share.[46] It is worth stressing, though, that the hollowness of official rhetoric on equality still tells only part of the story in this respect. Large numbers of ordinary citizens simply did not embrace the message coming from above. As Marina Goldovskaya recalled, the notion of equality between men and women 'never was accepted in everyday life' by millions of people.[47]

Wider availability of domestic labour-saving devices such as washing machines and vacuum cleaners was presented as the solution to the increased burden on women, along with the greater provision of public canteens for family dining and expanded childcare facilities. However, the reality was that washing machines and other household appliances only became common very slowly and unevenly, and such discourse anyway perpetuated the notion of housework as a woman's duty (as one scholar has pointed out, the discourse of the era sometimes inadvertently reinforced, rather than dismantled gender hierarchies).[48] Similarly, many people simply did not want to dine regularly in public canteens, which were hardly renowned for the quality of their food or service; and even though state childcare provision grew markedly, it often still proved either hard to find or else not of a standard that parents wanted for their children. Thus, as and when women became wives and mothers, many were hit by an intense 'time poverty' that all but defined their lives.

Sociological studies carried out from the early 1960s onwards made it clear that free time was one of the most fundamental imbalances between the sexes: almost 45 per cent of women polled spent over three hours per day on housework, while less than 10 per cent of men said the same. The myriad inefficiencies of the Soviet system – not least the organisation of shopping, which required customers (who were typically female) to endure three successive queues: first to order, then to pay for and finally to collect even the most basic items – could burden women especially. This then reinforced other inequalities, with women's careers frequently stunted even before they had got going, as the demands of housekeeping and child-rearing left mothers unable to access the kinds of study and training opportunities that were often needed for promotion at work.

Published in the journal *Novy mir* (*New World*) at the end of the 1960s, Natalya Baranskaya's novella *A Week Like Any Other* offered a particularly authentic image of the perpetually unchanging strains on a Soviet working mother. Baranskaya's heroine, Olga Nikolaevna, enjoyed strong and broadly positive relationships with colleagues and with her husband, had a professional career and a reasonable standard of living; but she also faced an

existence of continual exhaustion and stress, juggling her duties at the laboratory where she worked with raising two small children. Mending clothes,
queueing for groceries during her lunch break, taking the children to and
from school, childcare responsibilities (as well as repeatedly missing work
when the children fell ill), cooking and cleaning – all this left her perpetually
late, stressed and on the point of emotional collapse. Indeed, part of the
story's power lay in the understated point that the protagonist was considerably luckier than plenty of her peers, who had all the same problems to
worry about – plus drunk and abusive husbands, dead-end jobs, health
problems and poverty.[49]

Although such domestic strains still persisted, key planks of Stalin-era
legislation on family matters were being dismantled by the mid-1950s. The
expectation that fathers should contribute both materially and emotionally
towards their children's upbringing was again being pushed in literature, art
and more.[50] Films targeted distant and absent fathers for criticism, emphasising the importance of fatherhood and family life for parent and child
alike.[51] Most notably, Soviet women were again granted legal access to abortions (after the procedure had been banned on all but very narrow medical
grounds in 1936). Because this was often the default form of contraception
for many couples, especially in rural areas, the ban had resulted in a shocking
rise in dangerous and unsanitary 'homemade' abortions. These had killed an
average of 4,000 women a year in the late 1940s and early 1950s, and left
many others permanently injured.[52]

With Minister of Health Maria Kovrigina at the forefront, concerned
health professionals had seized upon the change of power in the Kremlin as
a chance to raise again their concerns about the damage being done by the
abortion ban. Kovrigina showed considerable political acumen: while recognising the issue as one on which women ought to have the right to make
their own decisions about pregnancy and motherhood, she presented it to
higher authorities in a more pragmatic form, arguing that the existing ban
was actually harming women's reproductive health and thus undermining
wider attempts to raise the birth rate.[53] This argument proved effective,
and in November 1955 Presidium members approved universal access to
abortion. The decree that followed then framed the decision primarily in
progressive terms, as a reform centred on empowering women to make their

own choices. Although far from flawless in its implementation, this measure surely saved thousands of women's lives each year, as the number of dangerous backstreet abortions declined sharply.[54] Nonetheless, the regime remained avowedly pro-natalist, with discourse presenting motherhood as both a patriotic duty and a source of personal fulfilment for all women, and abortion as a potentially dangerous procedure that was not to be undertaken lightly.[55] Even so, huge numbers of Soviet women steadfastly resisted such messaging, and more than 5 million registered abortions were carried out during 1957.[56] By 1965, a little over 8.5 million abortions were being performed across the USSR; and by 1970, research showed that the average Russian woman had two to four abortions in her lifetime, with some having several each year.[57]

After the Gulag

Some of the most draconian legal provisions of the Stalin period were also being withdrawn from use. These included laws that threatened jail for absence from work or for changing one's place of employment without permission. Prosecutions already in progress for these offences were dropped and prior convictions annulled. The minimum age for prosecution was also raised – from fourteen to sixteen years. Perhaps most telling, new convictions for counter-revolutionary crimes declined especially sharply after spring 1953: from an average of over 40,000 per year in 1950–52 (and more than 100,000 annually in the immediate post-war years), the figure plummeted to just over 2,000 in 1954, and then to about 1,000 in 1955.[58]

Rhetoric on the penal system began to emphasise the 'correction' of wrongdoers and 'second chances', rather than the merciless punishment of enemies.[59] Conditions started to improve somewhat inside labour camps, too. Alexander Solzhenitsyn described the period 1953–56 as 'the mildest three years in the history of the archipelago' – though this mildness was, of course, relative to the horrors that had gone before.[60] Nonetheless, after he was arrested for anti-Soviet activity in 1957, Boris Vail was kept alone in a cell that had formerly held twenty men, and even wrote that he was fed three times a day.[61] Detained as another member of the same underground group, Revolt Pimenov later wrote that his KGB interrogators mostly treated him 'with ostentatious politeness'.[62] This was by no means the experience of all those arrested and jailed, but efforts were made to crack down on guards' violence against prisoners, with mortality rates declining notably. Inmates' heads were no longer shaved by default, they were allowed to send and receive more letters and parcels, and popular recreation activities – such as occasional film screenings, sports and chess – were reintroduced.[63] In 1954, a parole system was brought back, granting prisoners freedom after two-thirds of their sentence, provided certain conditions were met with regard to good conduct and corrective labour performed.[64] Nonetheless, individual camp bosses often retained considerable leeway to oversee their respective fiefdoms as they saw fit, and many still demanded especially strenuous labour, such as mining and logging, in order to meet economic targets dictated from above.[65] So, while an improvement in conditions was real on the whole, it was nonetheless uneven, and limited in places.[66]

Following the initial amnesty in March 1953, a further 1.3 million inmates would be released in a series of smaller amnesties over the next couple of years. Categories of prisoners such as juveniles, the elderly and the seriously ill were successively freed en masse.[67] Additionally, once the crimes of Beria and his 'gang' had been announced to the public, a torrent of appeals calling for individual cases to be re-examined quickly overwhelmed officials. As letters from the outposts of the gulag piled up in Moscow, the likes of Khrushchev and Mikoyan, in particular, began intervening directly to help old comrades as they resurfaced. Meanwhile, a number of high-profile writers and Old Bolsheviks made it their business to support repressed friends and peers to gain their freedom and recover what they could of their former lives and reputations.

Olga Shatunovskaya was one such individual who threw herself into the fray. Having joined the party at the age of fifteen, prior to the revolution, she had been an early fighter for the Bolshevik cause in Azerbaijan, later working alongside Khrushchev during his tenure as Moscow party boss, but she had been pulled into the meat grinder in 1937. The publicity around Beria's arrest energised Shatunovskaya to press for a reconsideration of her case, and in early 1954 the Central Committee ordered her release and full rehabilitation. By that summer, she was back in Moscow and not only readmitted to party membership, but again employed in party work.[68] Along with Alexei

Snegov, who was freed after giving evidence at Beria's trial in December 1953, Shatunovskaya revived former friendships with Khrushchev and Mikoyan, talking at length about her experiences in the camps and pressing them to accelerate the process of releasing political prisoners.[69] Mikoyan later acknowledged that Snegov and Shatunovskaya had together played a major role in 'educating' both him and Khrushchev about the realities of the gulag.[70]

In September 1953, the USSR Supreme Court was granted the right to reassess various types of convictions from the Stalin era that had featured the most egregious abuses of legality, such as those conducted by the notorious troikas and special boards by which countless individuals had been executed or jailed for twenty-five years following the merest pretence of a trial, lasting only a few minutes in some cases. That same month, efforts also got under way to improve the training and 'cultural level' of the militia (the regular Soviet police), in order to eradicate old habits and reinforce what officials termed 'socialist legality'.[71] Basic but important legal principles were also re-established, such as giving defendants in court the right to a lawyer, not allowing the authorities to hold suspects indefinitely before trial and not punishing citizens for the actions of their relatives.[72]

In May 1954, a commission chaired by Procurator General Roman Rudenko (with subsidiary commissions in the regions) began working to investigate and adjudicate on incoming prisoner appeals. The mechanism was badly flawed from the outset, though. While Rudenko, at the head of the whole process, was seemingly committed to ensuring that the innocent were released, others were less supportive. There were, for example, plenty of camp bosses who proved adept at ignoring or obstructing moves to reconsider cases and release prisoners: giving negative assessments of inmates' behaviour and failing to hand over vital documents.[73] Furthermore, KGB representatives were prominent – or even predominant – in many commissions, and they were very often being asked to evaluate the merits of cases that they had been wholly complicit in fabricating, sometimes very recently. As head of the KGB, Serov was a key figure in the process; but he repeatedly expressed doubt and outright opposition to any substantial re-examination of Stalin-era repression, lest it accidentally facilitate the release of 'genuine enemies'.[74] One of those who certainly was committed to seeing the process through, Olga

Shatunovskaya alleged that Serov still considered her a counter-revolutionary, had her followed by KGB agents and had her telephone bugged and her mail read because of her advocacy on behalf of prisoners.[75]

Re-evaluating convictions could be deeply harrowing work for those involved, as they came face to face with the gruesome details of Stalinist repression. Years later, the film director Elem Klimov described how his father, who examined dossiers of evidence from Stalin-era investigations as part of the rehabilitation process, had been deeply troubled by his work, coming home at the end of the day and locking himself away in a darkened room.[76] The offices dealing with incoming appeals were often badly under-staffed, and the need to track down records relating to original convictions, and sometimes also to re-interrogate old witnesses and denouncers, slowed things down even further. By the end of 1955, an underwhelming total of 42,796 prisoners had been released following legal review of their cases.[77] Furthermore, the process at this stage most often still released prisoners without granting them rehabilitation, simply by reducing sentences to the period of time already served. This meant that the bulk of those released were, in the eyes of the law, freed criminals rather than exonerated victims.[78]

The experiences and attitudes of those returning from camps naturally varied a great deal. In not wanting to acknowledge how so many had come to be unjustly imprisoned, the political authorities could hardly explain to the public why prisoners had been released on such a scale, thus creating consid-erable confusion and uncertainty.[79] Quite a few of those now freed were anyway barred from returning to their home regions or to prestigious cities such as Moscow, Leningrad and republican capitals like Tbilisi or Minsk. Many who did make it home discovered that their apartments had since been claimed by others, or that neighbours had divided up their belongings between them and now had no intention of returning their bounty. As of September 1955, legislation promised that returnees cleared of any wrong-doing should receive payment equivalent to two months of their former salary to help get them back on their feet, along with restitution of lost housing and jobs; in practice, though, this support often did not materialise.[80]

Some of those people whom friends and relatives now expected to see again had, in fact, been secretly executed or had died in custody many years previously. By contrast, Vasily Aksenov – both of whose parents had been jailed back in 1937 – recalled witnessing his aunt answer the door one day in 1955, only to scream in shock at the sight of her brother (his father) standing before her. Vasily's father had been assumed long dead and his mother had remarried. He in turn did not recognise his son, who had been only a small child when they had last seen one another, eighteen years earlier.[81] Other former prisoners whose children had been sent to orphanages when they were arrested never managed to track them down again. Many got home to find that their husbands or wives had since died or had divorced them and moved on. Some left the camps with their health utterly ruined, and there was, of course, no kind of counselling available for the many who returned with deep trauma at what they had experienced. A few people did slip straight back into their former lives, but many either faced huge difficulties returning to the status quo ante, or else chose not to try.

Some returnees were forever embittered and alienated by their experiences, but others remained committed to the Soviet project. And plenty stood somewhere between those two positions.[82] In the Baltics and parts of Ukraine, some returning nationalists sought to resume their former struggle against Soviet power, and many released priests, mullahs and others similarly looked to resume their religious work.[83] While a great many former prisoners either did not seek or did not manage to obtain 'satisfaction' from those whose denunciations had landed them in jail (or had consigned loved ones to the grave), there were some who did. By the end of 1956, the head of the Belorussian Communist Party wrote to the Kremlin warning of the prevalence in his republic of returnees threatening their former denouncers with violence or murder.[84] One widowed Muscovite tracked down the man whose claims had seen her imprisoned and her husband executed. She turned up at his door and spat in his face. Another incident saw a returned prisoner apprehend his denouncer in a Moscow underpass and beat him mercilessly, as witnesses walked on by.[85]

The poet Anna Akhmatova wrote that this period saw two countries come eyeball to eyeball with one another: those who had been jailed and those who had jailed them. More prosaically, another poet, Margarita Aliger, described the sense of deep personal shame at meeting an old friend who had returned from the camps whom she had been unable to defend when he was arrested.[86] The writer Vasily Grossman, who discreetly observed and

61

interviewed numerous returnees around this time, later put this difficult process at the centre of his novel *Everything Flows* (which would only be published in the late 1980s, long after Grossman's death). On preparing to receive his cousin as he returned to Moscow after many years in the camps, the prosperous and respectable Nikolai Andreevich not only worried intensely about the unspoken moral judgement on his having – out of a sense of self-preservation – never sent even a single letter or parcel to his formerly close relative, but also fretted that he would be expected to offer the dishevelled returnee a place to stay or at least the chance to have a bath. By way of rationalising his conduct, Nikolai Andreevich ultimately deceived himself that his own complicity in voting for the arrest and execution of innocent colleagues was a torture for his soul that was no less excruciating than the hardships suffered by those in the camps.

Often unable to find social acceptance, jobs and living quarters in what they sardonically called 'the big zone' (which implied that the whole country was essentially a labour camp), many released inmates drifted back towards their former places of confinement. Of the more than 100,000 prisoners released from the Vorkuta camp complex inside the Arctic Circle, for example, almost a quarter were soon back in the city voluntarily.[87] Struggling to attract sufficient workers once the formerly rich supply of gulag labour came to an end, bosses in the region's coal-mining industry were often keen to employ former inmates. In Vorkuta and other former gulag centres, released prisoners were soon commonplace in public, helping one another to find work, lodgings and companionship in the face of indifference or hostility from the authorities and other citizens.[88] Among such communities of released prisoners, a rich gulag subculture survived and steadily leaked into the outside world, as camp legends, slang, songs and codes of conduct were shared and preserved. Worryingly for the authorities, elements of that subculture soon enough gained a kind of fashionable 'rebel' status among Soviet youth, in particular.[89]

Inside what remained of the camp system, the run of events that followed Stalin's death had also created a febrile 'demobilisation atmosphere'.[90] A gulag veteran of seventeen years by that point, Karlo Štajner noted a distinct slackening of discipline, along with an increased sense of assertiveness among the inmates still incarcerated.[91] A rash of prisoner work refusals and protests duly broke out, including major disturbances at Norilsk in May 1953 (which involved around 16,000 prisoners) and at Vorkuta in July–August of that year. The most storied of these disturbances, though, took place at Kengir, in central Kazakhstan, during May and June 1954.

Inmates at Kengir had already undertaken a three-day work stoppage during 1953 in response to guards shooting prisoners who were purportedly trying to escape (Solzhenitsyn later claimed that foiling faked or manipulated escape attempts was the guards' way of showing higher authorities that they were still needed, as the camp system contracted sharply).[92] Further unrest in May 1954 saw guards open fire again, killing at least seventeen prisoners, as running battles continued for several days. This time, though, the violence ended not with the guards reasserting their dominance, but with the prisoners seizing control inside the camp compound.[93] The authorities were driven out and now patrolled only the outside edge of the camp. They then cut off both the electricity and the water and erected loudspeakers around the perimeter. These they used to blast out regime propaganda and promises of harsh retribution for those who did not submit, along with offers to accommodate prisoners' demands if matters were resolved peacefully. Officials on the outside also worked hard to turn inmates against one another, broadcasting messages that sought to pit 'political' against 'criminal' prisoners and Russians against Ukrainian nationalists, insisting that the latter were fascists of exactly the kind that the former had fought against during the war. Despite the authorities' best efforts though, the prisoners did not break ranks.

Barricades went up inside the camp, entrance points were secured with barbed wire and weapons were improvised. Inmates ensured that there was neither looting nor sexual violence against the women prisoners once the wall separating the male and the female parts of the camp was taken down. Keen to show that they were not against the Soviet system in general, but rather against Kengir camp officialdom specifically, protesters erected banners saluting the party leadership and declaring support for Soviet power. They demanded a shorter working day, the punishment of those responsible for recent shootings, free interaction between male and female prisoners and an end to the practice of sending prisoners into indefinite exile on completion of their sentence. Lastly, they wanted someone from the leadership in Moscow to come and hear their grievances about camp officials.

Having initially refused to sanction the storming of the camp, after several weeks without progress the Soviet leadership finally ran out of patience. On 23 June, Malenkov directed the MVD to see that the affair was rapidly brought to an end. Decisive action began in the early hours of 26 June: snipers picked off the prisoners on guard and tanks crashed through the camp walls on all sides, with armed soldiers rushing in behind shooting, letting off tear gas and using their bayonets. The prisoners' attempts to fight back were quickly quelled by indiscriminate and overwhelming force. Estimates of the number of dead have ranged from forty-six (in classified official documents) to seven hundred (according to Solzhenitsyn). Of the survivors, at least five were sentenced to death for their role in the uprising and two others were jailed for a further twenty-five years.[94]

The Virgin Lands

By January 1954, it was becoming apparent that grain reserves were far lower than expected and that another potentially disastrous year for agriculture was in prospect, raising the spectre of a further deadly famine.[95] In contrast to the Stalin years, this was something that the country's new leaders were no longer willing to countenance. Firmly convinced that, provided there was sufficient energy and enthusiasm, any task could be accomplished, and always attracted by the prospect of a panacea, Khrushchev settled on a solution that would become known as the Virgin Lands scheme. This was an attempt to solve the country's agricultural problems not by improving on the existing (and hugely inefficient) collective farm system, but by opening up millions more hectares of unused land for cultivation, primarily in northern Kazakhstan and south-west Siberia. In theory, this would resolve at a stroke the intermittent food shortages that had dogged the USSR from the very start and that had seen millions starve to death in previous years.

With reliance on mass gulag labour no longer an option, the authorities had to look elsewhere for the necessary workforce. In February 1954, Khrushchev issued a radio appeal for young people to volunteer their services – to head out to the new lands, under the direction of the Komsomol, to perform heroic deeds for the good of their country. This was presented as an opportunity for a post-war generation that was sometimes portrayed as having 'gone soft' to make its own contribution to the great project of building communism, just as their parents and grandparents had contributed in the course of revolution, industrialisation and war. Working at a district Komsomol branch in Moscow at the time, Sergei Pavlov arrived at his office the morning after Khrushchev's appeal, to be greeted by long lines of young people waiting in the snow to sign up.[96] That first year, around 300,000 volunteers headed east from all across the USSR, with thousands of others turned away once that target had been reached.

Many of the volunteers went out of a sense of patriotism and ideological conviction. For others, it was a chance for adventure away from the drudgery of dead-end jobs, or else an opportunity to earn wages, low as they were for work in the Virgin Lands. With the passing years, the 'voluntary' aspect of the project became rather more ambiguous, and people who refused outright to go might well find themselves expelled from university and from the Komsomol.[97] In 1954, though, the sense of pioneer spirit and ideological enthusiasm was strong, and even some formally rejected volunteers stowed away on trains heading east in order to join their comrades.[98] The first tranche of volunteers departed with great public fanfare from Moscow's Kazan station late at night on 22 February, directly from a Kremlin celebration with Khrushchev and other Presidium members.

The long train ride that followed, sometimes in excess of ten days' duration, was often the first indicator of problems to come. Volunteers typically set off in the highest of spirits, singing Komsomol songs and holding impromptu talks about agricultural developments; but logistical problems soon began to take a toll on morale. Organisations assigned to provide fresh water and food for the volunteers as trains passed through their territory frequently failed to do so, and locomotives sometimes spent hours stuck in sidings. It also became apparent that some of those travelling were not really youthful enthusiasts at all, but 'criminal elements with Komsomol passes'.[99] Indeed, one historian has written that some of the parties which headed east were 'essentially drunken hordes', who caused uproar along the way: singing obscene songs in public places, picking fights with locals and stealing from train station cafeterias.[100]

Already tired, dirty and often hungry, for some the chaos only worsened on arrival. The bulk of volunteers were supposed to be set to work either constructing new collective farms or extending existing ones, with the opening stages of the project in particular dominated by hard physical labour, as land was cleared and prepared for cultivation, then sown and later harvested. In many cases, though, there was simply nobody to meet the arrivals, either from the collective farms they had been assigned to or from the local Komsomol and party organisations that were meant to be organising affairs on their behalf. Others arrived and found either that no work had been arranged for them (and not working meant not earning wages, with which to pay for one's upkeep), or that the work they had been assigned to was wholly inappropriate to their skills and abilities. In short, disorganisation and inefficiency often reigned. A few volunteers quickly fled home, though this was soon made a punishable offence.

The above notwithstanding, some volunteers found the experience little short of life-affirming. The author Lyudmila Petrushevskaya participated as a young woman and later aptly captured the duality of the experience: she described back-breaking labour, being able to shower only twice in two months, finding herself covered in lice and living off a daily diet of brown rice and boiled lamb fat; but she also insisted that 'It was a fantastic life. Freedom. Endless spaces . . . For the rest of my life, I will remember the sunrise over the steppe.'[101] Others wrote home to say how bonds of friendship were being forged between different Soviet nationalities there, and how they were living happily despite the absence of modern amenities.[102] There was even a spate of impromptu marriages among volunteers, although often these were quickly regretted and annulled.[103] Those left back at home were invited to participate vicariously by sending warm clothes, books and musical instruments. Restarting his stalled political career in Kazakhstan, after incumbent Kazakh party boss Zhumabai Shayakhmetov was sacked for questioning the hugely ambitious scale of Khrushchev's plan, Leonid Brezhnev later likened the campaign to a great and heroic battle, working morning to evening every day and travelling constantly from place to place as he monitored progress and sought to spur participants on to ever greater feats.[104]

From Khrushchev's initial plan to open up 18 million hectares of new land, within a few months the scope was extended to more than 30 million. The year 1954 saw the best harvest for a long time in the USSR, comfortably averting any danger of famine, with more than four hundred new collective farms brought into operation. The ensuing rhetoric was deeply triumphal, with Khrushchev in particular declaring his plan a huge success – and being awarded the honorific title Hero of the Soviet Union in recognition. Nonetheless, anyone who looked close enough could see serious flaws from the start. In a number of places, the harvest was ready before there was any real means of transport or storage, and so masses of grain simply rotted. Anyway, the pouring of vast resources into Khrushchev's pet project meant that long-established agricultural regions in other parts of the country were left short of what they needed for their own sowing and harvesting. In 1954, for example, somewhere around 90 per cent of all new tractors produced were sent to the Virgin Lands, meeting the needs of the new campaign but leaving shortages elsewhere.[105]

Life was often hard on the ground in the Virgin Lands. The tents that many volunteers lived in were supposed to be a stop-gap solution until suitable accommodation could be built, but they often ended up becoming long-term fixtures. This made life hard in 1955 especially, when a prolonged drought and a succession of big storms hit the region (which also made for a far weaker harvest that year). Supplies of basic necessities, such as drinking water, soap and food, also proved precarious or else simply failed, prompting rising frustration among volunteers in some places. Officials on the ground in Kazakhstan, however, could prove indifferent (at best) to the hardships that volunteers faced. One of the leading Komsomol organisers on the project, Sergei Pavlov, recalled visiting a collective farm where volunteers had complained bitterly of prolonged food shortages; on breaking down the locked door of a warehouse, he found stockpiles of rice and pasta that had been siphoned off by farm bosses.[106]

During a brief visit to review progress in Kazakhstan, Khrushchev spoke at length to volunteers about the problems they faced, returning to Moscow with one major directive: to send more girls.[107] The key rationale in expanding the number of women in the Virgin Lands seemingly centred on the notion that an increased female presence would have a calming influence on the occasionally volatile young men. It was also hoped that the measure would help bring long-term settlement to the region, as couples got together and put down roots.[108] The Virgin Lands, then, was not just about producing grain, but was also about 'sovietising' rural Kazakhstan – a region where there was still much work to be done in embedding communism culturally.

67

Soon enough, the Komsomol was specifically urging its millions of female members to throw themselves into the cause. As in most Soviet workplaces, there was plenty for women to do, but mostly that involved low-skilled and low-paid labour, such as looking after livestock, while the men undertook better-paid construction work or drove tractors. Like the men, those women who travelled to the Virgin Lands faced myriad shortages of basic necessities, harsh living conditions and callous attitudes towards their welfare. Unlike the men, though, they faced a much-elevated threat of rape and sexual assault, with terrifying night-time struggles to keep drunken and aggressive males away from their tents, a seemingly regular occurrence for some.[109] Local officials could also be even more dismissive or openly hostile in their dealings with female workers, while outfits and modes of behaviour that were entirely uncontroversial back home were deemed scandalous in rural Kazakhstan. Inter-ethnic violence broke out repeatedly in the wake of flash-points between Kazakh men and Slavic women, in particular.[110]

As the 1950s progressed, the situation in the Virgin Lands turned more volatile at times. Numerous officials were physically attacked by angry volunteers, and many farm directors took to carrying guns.[111] The biggest confrontation of them all came at Temirtau in August 1959. Conditions there were especially hard for the volunteers: they lived in ripped tents, were provided with only rotten food and were subject to continuing theft and intimidation by local criminal elements, but their complaints were repeatedly ignored and disparaged by officials. Frustration at the persistent lack of water for drinking and washing eventually boiled over and volunteers began looting storehouses and a local cafeteria. The police arrived and managed to disperse the crowds, but the vigour with which they did this only intensified their sense of resentment. Over the next few days, the army had to be called in as mobs attacked the town's police station, trashing equipment and files inside; they also pillaged the main department store and engaged in pitched battles with troops (a few rioters had by this point acquired guns of their own). By the time the dust had settled, more than a hundred police had been wounded, 190 people had been arrested, 11 rioters were dead and a further 5 would die of their wounds.[112]

It would not be too long before the impressive grain output from the Virgin Lands declined precipitously, as soil quality deteriorated. Lasting ecological damage had also been done in places, leaving a decades-long legacy of soil erosion. Nonetheless, there were significant gains, too. The arrival of doctors, dentists, agronomists and others, along with increased electrification and the construction of roads, schools and more, brought far better living conditions than the region had ever seen before. The central town of the Virgin Lands project, Tselinograd (now the city of Astana, the capital of Kazakhstan), received huge investment. Over the course of several years, it gained new housing, an airport, sports facilities, factories and education institutes, becoming a 'vibrant young student city'.[113] Furthermore, from its inception in 1954 the project struck an important ideological chord that would do much to define the era that followed: that of youthful romanticism and mass public mobilisation in the name of a rejuvenated commitment to building a communist utopia.

Cultural thaw

The fact that the Khrushchev era as a whole gained the epithet 'the thaw' (from the title of a 1954 novella) is surely indicative of the extent to which cultural developments represented a key barometer of the age. Well looked after materially and afforded considerable prestige, writers, musicians, actors and other cultural elites were very much part of the system, not outside it. Liberals and conservatives alike generally accepted and embraced the basic premise that culture must play an ideological role, helping Soviet citizens to understand the world around them and developing attitudes and tastes suitable for the coming communist future. Nonetheless, there were important cleavages opening up, and there was considerable accumulated frustration in the cultural sphere. The boundaries of ideologically acceptable work had grown so narrow under late Stalinism that even many conservative-minded figures acknowledged that Soviet culture had fallen into a parlous state by 1953. For the political authorities, then, cultural liberalisation was primarily aimed at bringing a degree of vitality and colour back to the arts, so that they could contribute more effectively to the task of building communism.[114]

After years in which dreary novels and films had centred on clear-cut heroes performing great feats in the name of communism and the motherland, there was a widespread yearning for culture that was simply more 'human' and true to life. As early as April 1953, the poet Olga Berggolts called for a return of literature about real people and their emotional lives, and about love in particular. Vera Panova's 1953 novel *Seasons of the Year* was one of the first to eschew the usual focus on industry and agriculture, exploring instead personal relations and the minutiae of family life. After initially positive reviews, though, Panova's work came under attack for lacking 'ideological substance'. Three more important pieces then appeared in quick succession at the end of 1953. In October, the journal *Novy mir* published Ilya Ehrenburg's essay 'On the Work of the Writer', in which the famous author lambasted the ideological guardians of Soviet literature as people who 'examine a novel almost as if they are investigating a crime'.[115] If literature was to help educate the reader, make him live better and be more considerate towards fellow citizens, Ehrenburg argued, novels, stories and poems had to show real people and real lives, with their merits, defects and complexities, rather than sanitised and idealised images that nobody could believe in.

Writing the following month in the journal *Sovetskaya muzyka* (*Soviet Music*) the Armenian composer Aram Khachaturian posed the question of whether contemporary Soviet music was satisfying the spiritual requirements of the masses. He answered bluntly in the negative, stating that 'the creative achievements of Soviet composers of recent years are far from corresponding to the high expectations of the people'.[116] Like Ehrenburg, Khachaturian insisted that for music to help educate and uplift the masses, it needed to be 'fresh, beautiful . . . and inspired' – unlike the formulaic anthems about love for the motherland that were the stock in trade of the Stalin years. Perhaps most strikingly, he called for officials in the cultural establishment to 'abandon the rotten practice of interfering in the composer's work', since artists themselves, and not the bureaucrats who hovered over them, were those best qualified to decide how to meet the lofty social responsibility of helping to instil in the masses the values and tastes of communism.

The most famous of these early cultural critiques came at the end of 1953, with Vladimir Pomerantsev's strident essay 'On Sincerity in Literature', published in the December edition of *Novy mir*. The 'insincerity' that Pomerantsev railed against was not just outright lying and 'varnishing of reality', but also artificiality and a hackneyed approach to character and plot that he insisted left readers indifferent and distrustful. He declared that an author 'can and should check whether he has in his book evaded any hidden evils of life', asserting that the true communist duty of a writer lay not in trying to embellish Soviet reality, but in exposing problems, discussing failings openly and thus helping to overcome the 'difficult questions' that the country faced.[117] What Pomerantsev's piece encapsulated most effectively was that many of those who spoke or wrote with critical remarks around this time did so not as political opponents of communism, but as people with a passionate belief in rendering a service to the Soviet system, moved by the notion that they now could and should help 'fix' its failings.

That same month, the journal *Teatr* (*Theatre*) carried a piece by the playwright Leonid Zorin, entitled *The Guests*, which clearly alluded to the fading dedication to 'true' Bolshevik values that had occurred under Stalin. Soon enough, though, both Zorin and Pomerantsev met with increasingly shrill criticism from outraged conservatives within the cultural establishment. *The Guests* was branded an artistic failure, with 'gross ideological and political errors', and was even dubbed 'a libel on our life' in *Izvestiya*.[118] In *Literaturnaya gazeta* (*Literary Gazette*), the official organ of the Soviet Writers' Union, Pomerantsev's arguments were branded 'naïve, theoretically unfounded, unproveable and simply wrong' in January 1954.[119] It was indicative of the way in which times had changed, though, that readers still sprang to his defence. In mid-March, *Komsomolskaya pravda* carried a collective letter from several Moscow students, first accepting that there were valid grounds on which to criticise Pomerantsev's essay, but nonetheless insisting that his ideas must be explored, not silenced.[120]

Ilya Ehrenburg's October 1953 essay was followed several months later by his seminal novella *The Thaw*. Although hardly a classic in purely literary terms, this was perhaps the boldest political commentary yet to emerge in fiction. Two separate storylines drew obvious allusions to changes emerging since Stalin's death, of spring following harsh winter. The first centred on two artists: after years of success, the one who painted only formulaic and state-mandated pieces now saw his fortunes decline; the other, whose talent had previously been suppressed because he followed his conscience and refused such work, finally won acclaim. The second plot line focused mainly on a brutish factory director and his wife. The man's bullying behaviour first led him to power and career success; but then came the onset of 'the thaw', when his abuses were eventually condemned and his long-unhappy wife abandoned him. The story was a huge success with the public, instantly selling out and ensuring that

Ehrenburg would remain one of the most prominent and influential voices of the era.

Very quickly, though, this initial wave of cultural liberalisation ran into trouble. There were still plenty in the upper ranks of the Soviet cultural establishment who would not entertain any reassessment of the Stalin period, and who did not agree that the way forward lay in open and honest discussion of 'shortcomings'. For most of the next decade, the intermittent emergence of new liberal-minded works and cultural trends would quickly prompt conservatives to fight back hard. Often they did so with a degree of success, too. At the end of May 1954, *Pravda* carried a piece by Writers' Union official Alexei Surkov, in which he insisted that, in publishing 'On Sincerity in Literature', *Novy mir* had not only 'contributed nothing of any use' to on-going discussions about cultural direction, but also had actually 'damaged the development of literature by the deep-seated errors of its contentions'. The article added that Pomerantsev had, in essence, made 'an attempt to give our literature a good beating instead of helping writers'.[121] In August 1954, the top officials of the Writers' Union met and condemned those members calling for greater artistic freedom and 'sincerity'; this was followed soon after by open criticism of *Novy mir* in the party's Central Committee. The journal's editor, the poet Alexander Tvardovsky, was fired and the first phase of cultural thaw effectively drew to a close.

Khrushchev in the ascendancy

In keeping with Malenkov's remarks on international affairs at Stalin's funeral, both he and Khrushchev quickly threw their weight behind a new rhetoric on peaceful co-existence with the US. After years of being shunned by Soviet officialdom, one Western diplomat in Moscow described the Soviet leadership at this point as being 'ruthlessly friendly'.[122] Presidium members even turned up unexpectedly at the American embassy in Moscow to join their celebrations on 4 July 1954. No less remarkable, after Soviet fighter pilots erroneously shot at an American naval patrol plane over the Bering Strait in June 1955, Khrushchev and Bulganin offered to pay towards the cost of the damage.[123] In July 1955, came the first of several major military cuts, when the Soviet army was reduced by 640,000 personnel. Geneva then became the centre of Cold War diplomacy later in summer 1955, when the leaders of Britain, France, the US and USSR convened a summit aimed at lowering global tensions. The concrete results of the meeting were few, but all sides made clear their desire for peace and their deep concern about the danger of nuclear war, creating a sense that the superpowers in particular were now able to talk and to co-operate with one another. For Khrushchev personally, the summit also helped to dispel Stalin's repeated warnings that the West would quickly outfox and then crush the remainder of the Soviet leadership once he was no longer around.

The Soviet bid to project a more co-operative image to the outside world, coupled with a desire to shed the considerable cost of maintaining 40,000 occupation troops there, brought change to Austria next. For years, Stalin had insisted that any ending of the post-war occupation regime in Austria had to be accompanied by international agreement over the future of divided Germany. The Kremlin leadership now decided that the two issues should be decoupled, and Khrushchev contacted Austrian Chancellor Julius Raab in February 1955, expressing a willingness to make a deal that would, in effect, re-establish Austria as a sovereign state. Agreement was reached relatively easily, hinging mainly on the conditions that Austria should remain militarily neutral in future, should not host any foreign bases and should not unite with Germany again. When West German Chancellor Konrad Adenauer went to Moscow that autumn to reopen diplomatic relations between the two countries, he also secured agreement on the repatriation of those German POWs still held in the USSR since the Second World War.

More surprising still, in June 1954 Khrushchev unexpectedly initiated a private exchange of written correspondence with Yugoslav leader Josip Broz Tito, as he sought to heal the bitter feud between the two communist countries.[124] By the autumn of 1954, the regular Soviet press attacks on Yugoslavia had ended. Then, on the tenth anniversary of Victory Day, an article by Marshal Georgy Zhukov in *Pravda* acknowledged the valuable contribution that Yugoslavia had made in the defeat of fascism, and expressed hope that the two countries could put their differences behind them and move forward as friends once again. In fact, the initial version of Zhukov's article that was circulated to Central Committee members for approval did not contain any mention of Yugoslavia: the crucial passage was included only at the very last moment, on Khrushchev's orders.[125] Not long after that, Khrushchev, Bulganin and Mikoyan headed to Belgrade in person. Touring Yugoslav factories and farms, the Soviet delegation was soon satisfied that the regime there was not, as the unbending Molotov had warned them, either bourgeois or fascistic.

Before long, Khrushchev was becoming a globetrotting statesman. After leading a delegation to China in August 1954, he and Bulganin undertook a three-week-long South Asian tour, visiting Afghanistan, Burma (Myanmar) and India during October and November 1955. The last of these made a particularly powerful impression on Khrushchev, as he travelled to Delhi, Bombay (Mumbai), Calcutta (Kolkata), Kashmir and elsewhere. He was horrified by the poverty that he witnessed, and he struggled badly with the heat and humidity, but marvelled at local customs, nature and architecture; he gamely took an elephant ride and briefly picked up a scythe to join in with the harvesting (though he turned down the opportunity to go tiger hunting).[126] The reception from locals, he recalled, was 'the warmest, friendliest, most benevolent' he had experienced. Everywhere he expressed a desire for peace and a willingness to share Soviet experience and expertise in building industry and developing agriculture, proclaimed his admiration for local achievements and cultures and professed indignation at Western colonialism and racism.

By the end of 1954, Khrushchev was sufficiently on top within the leadership struggle that he was 'openly pushing Malenkov around', according to William Taubman.[127] In January 1955, Khrushchev and Molotov together attacked Malenkov over his call for more investment in the production of consumer goods, which they dismissed as an ideologically flawed attempt to win 'cheap popularity'. Malenkov's former ties to Beria were also cited against him, despite his having played a crucial part in the plot to remove the Georgian. Some Khrushchev allies even spoke quietly of having Malenkov put on trial for his role in the discredited Leningrad Affair. Colleagues also lined up to criticise his work as chairman of the Council of Ministers, insisting that he did not prepare properly for meetings, proved indecisive on major issues and had failed to show himself 'a politically mature and steadfast Bolshevik'.[128] Perhaps seeking to salvage what he could of a career that was clearly starting to flounder, Malenkov meekly accepted the essence of the criticism that poured down on him. Though he remained a member of the party's Presidium, on 8 February 1955 he resigned from the post of chairman of the Council of Ministers, to be replaced in the role by Khrushchev's (far less able) ally Nikolai Bulganin.

Molotov was never one to kowtow to his colleagues in the collective leadership, and an increasingly clear split between him and the others was opening up, especially following disagreements over the 1955 treaty with Austria (which Khrushchev initiated and Molotov abhorred). Fully invested in Stalinist notions of an outside world utterly implacable in its hostility towards the USSR (Churchill claimed that Molotov had slept with a loaded revolver beside him when he stayed at Chequers in 1950), Molotov had no truck with the notion of peaceful co-existence with the West, continuing to insist in private that 'as long as imperialism exists, war is inevitable'.[129] While other members of the leadership felt reassured by declining international tensions, Molotov fretted that the West would see the new Soviet diplomacy as evidence of weakness.[130] Just as Khrushchev had encroached on Molotov's institutional prerogatives as foreign minister in formulating the deal with Austria, so the invitation for West German Chancellor Adenauer to visit Moscow had also been deliberately issued while Molotov was away at the UN. Adenauer's resulting visit to Moscow duly saw Molotov in combative form. It ended in a moment of political humiliation for him, though: after considerable rhetorical provocation from Molotov about contemporary West Germany's 'fascistic' policies, and an outright refusal to shake Adenauer's hand, the chancellor pointedly reminded those present that it was Molotov, not he, who had once shaken hands with Hitler.

Soviet rapprochement with Yugoslavia proved an even greater blow for Molotov. He steadfastly refused to participate in any reconciliation with Tito, insisting that anything more than basic diplomatic relations would be 'un-Leninist', and he stuck to the Stalinist line that Yugoslavia's leaders were fascists. He also lectured colleagues that the Yugoslavs had as recently as 1952 called the Soviet regime a global force for aggression. The others then reminded Molotov of the far sharper accusations they had all thrown at Belgrade during the course of the split, going on to insist that Molotov and Stalin had needlessly created the whole schism in the first place.[131] In July 1955, Molotov was subjected to a formal dressing-down by other members of the leadership, with colleagues lining up to condemn his attitude and errors of judgement. Mikoyan insisted that Molotov was both living and working in the past. To disagree with colleagues was fine, he said, but to insist that those one disagreed with were 'un-Leninist' was not acceptable. Typically pugnacious, Khrushchev concluded by warning Molotov that if his conduct did not change, it would soon be time for him to retire.

On what would have been Stalin's seventy-fifth birthday, in December 1953, the Soviet press was once again effusive in its praise for his achievements. When it marked the first anniversary of his death in March 1954, *Pravda* used most of the old formulations about Stalin being the great continuer of Lenin's work.[132] On the anniversary of the revolution in November 1955, the front page of *Pravda* featured a line-up of Presidium members standing beneath a giant flag bearing the faces of Stalin and Lenin. When the question arose within the Presidium about how the upcoming anniversary of Stalin's birthday ought to be marked the following month, Molotov, Kaganovich and Voroshilov still wanted to continue the public commemorations of previous years, but they were opposed by Khrushchev, Mikoyan, Bulganin and others.[133] By way of compromise, when the day came around on 18 December 1955, Stalin's likeness was again plastered across the front page of Soviet newspapers, but without the official celebratory events of old.[134] It was also telling of changing political winds that when Voroshilov was awarded the honorific title Hero of Socialist Labour at the start of February 1956, the official citation described him as a 'faithful pupil of Lenin', but made no reference at all to Stalin, with whom Voroshilov's career had been far more closely linked.[135]

By this time, the country was on the verge of a new party congress. Compared to the eve of the previous congress, which had taken place as recently as October 1952, the Soviet Union was in several senses a country transformed. Its leaders spoke not of inevitable war with the West, but of a desire for peace; the gulag still existed, but was already a shadow of its former size; and new connections with the outside world were proliferating at a previously unimaginable rate. The overall direction of travel was proving far from straight, though, and there would be distinctly turbulent times ahead.

Two letters that reached the Central Committee at the start of 1956 aptly characterised the fork in the road that lay ahead: either continuing to avoid any real reckoning with the Stalin issue, or finally addressing it. On 10 January, the director of the Central Lenin Museum wrote to inform party bosses that work on a Stalin memorial museum – the dacha outside Moscow where he had died – was almost complete. He suggested that the new museum might be used as an official excursion for delegates to the upcoming Twentieth Party Congress in February, and as a venue for events to commemorate the third anniversary of Stalin's death the month after that. Around the same time, the Old Bolshevik and gulag returnee Alexei Snegov wrote to the Central Committee, requesting a pass to attend the same congress. In his letter, Snegov noted that he had attended each and every party congress from the tenth in 1921 to the seventeenth in 1934, adding that he had been absent from the eighteenth and nineteenth 'for reasons that are known to you'.[136]

3

TIME TO TALK ABOUT STALIN

It was at party congress that recent achievements were celebrated, plans for the future presented and the official ideological line on any given matter definitely set. It was also there that the party's key bodies – most notably its Central Committee – were elected by delegates to run things until the next congress. In practice, these elections returned candidates who had been pre-selected from above, while the reports and discussions that took place were always carefully choreographed well in advance. Nonetheless, this remained the political showpiece event of Soviet socialism, dominating the media agenda for weeks before the opening day. Afterwards, congress resolutions and speeches were typically presented as key moments not just in the life of the USSR, but of 'all progressive humanity'. The Twentieth Party Congress, in February 1956, would be one of few that unquestionably did have such global significance. For many, both inside and outside the USSR, it seemed as though a more liberal-minded and authentically progressive Soviet system might be emerging.

On 14 February, around 1,300 delegates, along with journalists and invited guests from around the world, filed into the Kremlin for the start of a party congress that would continue to reshape the Soviet system and the wider socialist bloc. This time it was Khrushchev who opened proceedings as party boss. In accordance with tradition, he called on delegates to stand in memory of leading communists lost since the last congress. The noteworthy part of this lay in the fact that there was no special recognition of Stalin's passing. His death was merely mentioned, alongside those of the late Czechoslovak leader Klement Gottwald and Japanese Communist Party leader Kyuichi Tokuda. The lack of a more specific and substantial tribute to Stalin immediately struck a somewhat discordant tone, but this was actually to prove one of the few instances when his name was even mentioned from the rostrum over the next ten days.

Even without open discussion of Stalin, the congress either produced or codified as party policy some remarkable new developments. The credo of peaceful co-existence with the US was approved, representing a decisive revision of Stalin's line on inevitable war between capitalism and communism. There was also renewed emphasis on improving relationships with other countries of the socialist camp, and with foreign leftist parties outside Moscow's control. The importance of bolstering friendship between the different national groups inside the USSR was underlined, and the emerging struggles against colonialism in the developing world were celebrated (with the new notion put forward that countries no longer had to go through capitalism to reach socialism, as Marx had originally written). Khrushchev promised to reduce the working day to seven hours for millions of citizens, and he announced the scrapping of tuition fees for higher education and the last three years of high school (which had been introduced under Stalin). Maternity leave was extended, with mothers granted eight weeks' paid leave both before and after the birth. Soon, new legislation introduced a regular pension system for urban residents, reducing (if not eradicating) the virtual penury that had previously faced the elderly and those unable to work through disability.[1] A new focus on the development of Siberia and better exploitation of the country's natural resources was also announced, including a move to develop the oil and gas industries that would, in time, prove critical for the Soviet economy.[2]

Most speakers at congress sidestepped the Stalin issue by simply not mentioning his name, though even arch-Stalinists like Molotov reaffirmed the line that any kind of 'cult of personality' (albeit without naming a specific personality) was 'alien to Marxism-Leninism'. Anna Pankratova, the editor of the leading history journal *Voprosy istorii* (*Questions of History*), was rather more explicit than most, stating that the cult of personality had for years served as a brake on the development of the social sciences, since it had so distorted the truth about the country's past and present. Mikoyan was the only figure among the very top-ranking party men to criticise Stalin explicitly during the regular congress. He declared that both the principle of collective leadership and 'Leninist norms of Party life' had now been restored after a long interval, stating that for twenty years the Stalin cult had had a deleterious impact on the party and its work. Such comments were not universally well received, though. Soon after his speech was finished, Mikoyan's brother tracked him down and warned that there had been real hostility over his remarks among the audience, with a group of delegates soon afterwards sending an angry letter to Presidium members opposing Mikoyan's 'slanderous attack' on Stalin.[3]

The secret speech

As congress approached its scheduled close on 24 February, delegates were informed that an additional sitting had been organised for that evening. Foreign participants, however, were not invited. The events that followed marked the climax of a process that had begun at the very end of 1955, when Presidium members discussed a letter from Olga Shatunovskaya. In it, she asserted that the security organs had been behind the 1934 murder of Sergei Kirov, which had subsequently provided the catalyst for the Great Terror of 1936–38.[4] During the deliberations that ensued, it was decided to form a commission, under former *Pravda* editor Petr Pospelov, to look into her claim and to establish the reasons for the mass repression of party members that had followed in the wake of the Seventeenth Party Congress of 1934. A little over a month later, Pospelov's team had its report ready and presented it to Presidium members on 9 February – just a week before the congress opened.

Mikoyan later wrote of this meeting that Pospelov had struggled to read the report in places and at one point had burst into tears, such was the harrowing nature of its content.[5] It began with some bald figures. The number of arrests for 'counter-revolutionary crimes' had hit an incredible peak of 918,671 in 1937, followed by 629,695 the following year. Across the five years from 1935 to 1940, almost 2 million citizens had been jailed for political crimes, and the number of those subsequently executed approached 700,000. Pospelov's report then told of how all manner of conspiracies had been fabricated throughout the country, driven by Stalin's insatiable demands to uncover enemies, and how those arrested had faced brutal torture, as established rules of policing and justice disintegrated. He said that an incredible 98 of the 139 members and candidate members of the Central Committee elected at the Seventeenth Party

Congress in 1934 had been subsequently arrested and shot, while over half of the 1,966 delegates to that congress had also been branded enemies of the people and jailed or executed. Khrushchev, Bulganin, Kaganovich, Mikoyan, Molotov and Voroshilov were among the minority of delegates who had remained alive.

Many whose stories Pospelov outlined had at one time been friends and colleagues of those now in the Presidium. The fates of former party elites, such as Pavel Postyshev, Stanislav Kosior, Robert Eikhe, Karl Bauman and Yan Rudzutak, were singled out for individual attention in the report. Each had been a party member since before the revolution and had played a distinguished role in building the fledgling Soviet regime, but had then faced groundless arrest, torture and execution.[6] Along with exposing the scale and ferocity of the repressions that had taken place, the report unambiguously situated Stalin at the heart of events. Documents provided by Pospelov showed that Stalin had personally sanctioned both the groundless arrest and the execution of Postyshev, for example; the documents also included a January 1939 telegram from Stalin to regional party bosses and security officials encouraging the use of violence in investigations against those arrested as counter-revolutionaries, in order to help speed up their 'unmasking'.[7]

In outline at least, much of this did not constitute wholly new information to Presidium members. Back in 1953, Beria had directed colleagues to examine confidential materials outlining the true events of the Doctors' Plot. In any case, all the top leaders had had some degree of involvement in the repressions, and several of them were especially deeply implicated. Nonetheless, Khrushchev's subsequent claim that they (or at least he) had only grasped the full scale of the matter once Pospelov presented his report does not feel wildly unrealistic, since this was not a field of activity that anyone wished to know more about than they absolutely had to. Pospelov's findings, though, now invited the question of what should be done next with this information.

Khrushchev wanted to raise the matter at congress. Molotov insisted that any discussion of Stalin must be leavened with talk of his achievements. Kaganovich acknowledged Stalin's shortcomings, but protested both that they (his former subordinates) had been powerless to prevent the abuses and that not all the violence had been unjustified. Like Molotov, he wanted further time to consider the issue, essentially hoping to avoid raising the matter at congress. Bulganin argued that party members could already see that the attitude towards Stalin had changed and warned that it would look cowardly not to raise the issue at congress. Voroshilov feared reprisals and urged caution, while Mikoyan argued that it was now simply impossible not to discuss Stalin at congress.[8] Malenkov, too, considered that presenting the issue to congress was the right thing to do. Summing up, Khrushchev proclaimed that the meeting had supported his proposal to take the matter to congress. By way of reassurance to the waverers, he reminded everyone that all those present had worked alongside Stalin, adding that the events in question were 'not connected to us' and 'we can say that we are not ashamed'.[9] In reality, Khrushchev would go on to make extensive use of his rivals' involvement in Stalinist repressions over the years that followed.[10]

Talk of reading Pospelov's report as part of the formal congress schedule was soon dismissed as too risky a step, since the response could hardly be predicted. Similarly, a suggestion by Khrushchev to have some rehabilitated party members address congress was also shot down, though around a hundred of them were at least invited to attend.[11] When Presidium members met again on 13 February – the day before the grand opening of congress – a compromise solution was reached: it was agreed that the report would be discussed at a closed session. Mikoyan suggested that Pospelov read his own report, but Khrushchev insisted that it was his responsibility as party boss to take the lead on such an important party issue. Once congress was already under way, Pospelov began drafting and re-drafting a speech based on his report, taking suggestions for additional material from the likes of Mikoyan, Bulganin and Khrushchev.[12]

Barely mentioned from the rostrum over the previous ten days, on the evening of 24 February the name of Stalin filled the air in the meeting hall of the Grand Kremlin Palace. Bulganin declared the session open and immediately handed the floor to Khrushchev, who informed those in attendance that his aim was not to provide a thoroughgoing evaluation of Stalin's life and work, but to set out how the Stalin cult had developed and triggered all manner of negative phenomena. Actually, as one recent scholar has noted, what followed was 'less an objective analysis of Stalinism than an ad hominem attack on Stalin'.[13]

Present in the hall at the time, Nikolai Baibakov later recalled that even though they were all aware of people returning from the camps, the entire audience remained transfixed throughout.[14] Drawing on the canon of works by Marx, Engels and Lenin, Khrushchev began by recapitulating the point that it had been ideologically improper to set a single individual above the rest, insisting that Lenin never forced his opinions on colleagues. He also revealed that Lenin had early on perceived in Stalin the negative traits that would later underpin the cult. Proof of Lenin's rejection of Stalin was furnished in the form of his 'testament', dictated by the ailing Bolshevik leader shortly before his death, but concealed from the wider public: in it he had criticised Stalin's character and urged that he be removed from the post of party general secretary. In presenting this, Khrushchev constructed a platform on which the rest of the speech would be built: he split Stalin off from Lenin, both ideologically and personally, and he put Stalin's character at the centre of his narrative.

Khrushchev then arrived at the Great Terror of 1936–38, asserting that the campaign against Trotskyists and other 'anti-Leninists' (which he framed as a perfectly legitimate and necessary struggle) had been turned into something much darker by Stalin. The term 'enemy of the people', he said, began to sweep away all need for evidence of wrongdoing, with any who disagreed with Stalin accused of hostile intent and subject to the harshest consequences, without regard for the principles of revolutionary legality. Stalin's reliance on mass arrests, exiles and executions without proper trials or evidence had created uncertainty, fear and bitterness in the ranks of the party, he insisted. Once he had amassed unlimited personal power, Khrushchev said, Stalin rarely consulted or informed Central Committee members – or even his Politburo colleagues – on the most important party and state questions. 'In dealing with colleagues', said Khrushchev, Stalin had 'shown in a whole series of cases his intolerance, his brutality and his abuse of power'.

Khrushchev made it plain that other members of the leadership had been politically neutered by Stalin – and by implication could hardly be responsible for the events that followed. Then he opened the floodgates and details of the baseless repressions poured out. Time and again, Khrushchev evidenced Stalin's personal involvement in cases, insisting that he had not simply granted permission for key individuals to be arrested, but had issued direct orders. He cited Stalin's letters demanding that the actions of the NKVD (the KGB's notorious forerunner) against 'enemies' be ramped up ever further, and contrasted such remarks with Lenin's 'far more judicious' use of revolutionary violence against 'real enemies'. He read out extracts of interrogation protocols and letters written by the accused to Stalin protesting their innocence, swearing loyalty and begging for a reconsideration of their case. 'Many thousands of innocent and honest communists', he said, 'have died as a result of the falsification of such cases,' adding 'It is clear that these matters were decided by Stalin.'

Turning back to Stalin's character, Khrushchev recounted how he had been perennially suspicious of even those he had worked alongside for years: 'Everywhere and in everything he saw "enemies", "double-dealers" and "spies".' Then he assailed Stalin's reputation as war leader: he made it clear that Stalin had been warned on several occasions (including in a personal message from Winston Churchill) that the Nazis were planning a surprise attack in June 1941. But each of the warnings had been ignored or supressed – ultimately at the cost of huge numbers of Soviet lives and vast swathes of territory. The horrific terror that Stalin had waged against the Soviet military's officer corps in the late 1930s was cited as another reason for the crippling early defeats of the war, along with the claim that Stalin had effectively 'lost his nerve' when the invasion first began, pulling himself together only after other Politburo members insisted that steps had to be taken immediately.

Stalin's supposed genius as a military commander was then ridiculed, with claims that his frequent interference in military operations and his refusal to heed expert advice had caused immense damage. Khrushchev also pointed out that at no time during the war had Stalin ever visited any section of the front – except for one short car ride on the Mozhaisk highway, when the area was already stable. He claimed mockingly that Stalin had planned military operations on a globe (an accusation that Mikoyan and others later rejected as untrue) and had demanded endless suicidal attacks solely for political purposes. Finally on the war, Khrushchev spoke of how Stalin had vainly ensured that credit for victory was to be attributed to himself alone. To audience applause, he corrected this narrative, stating that 'not Stalin, but the party as a whole, the Soviet government, our heroic army, its talented leaders and brave soldiers, the whole Soviet people – these are the ones who provided victory in the Great Patriotic War'.

From the war, the speech turned to what Khrushchev termed Stalin's 'gross violations of Leninist principles of nationalities policy'. Here, he focused on the mass deportations (which, he reminded his audience, had included plenty of communists and young communists) in which whole national minority groups, including the Karachay, Kalmyks, Chechens and Balkars, had been ruthlessly rounded up and deported far from their homelands on the basis of Stalin's groundless suspicions about their loyalty to the Soviet order. He also claimed (albeit without offering any evidence) that 'the Ukrainians avoided this fate only because there was no place to deport them', adding that no healthy-thinking person could have conceived of assigning enemy status to whole national groups and thus condemning them to such suffering and misery.

Coming to the post-war years, he spoke of both the Leningrad Affair and the Mingrelian Affair, at which point he rather injudiciously mocked the fact that many Georgians still fondly referred to Stalin as 'the great son of the Georgian people'. He stated that the Doctors' Plot had centred on no real evidence at all, and also claimed that he had personally seen Stalin order that the accused should be pummelled by their interrogators. Lastly, Khrushchev relayed multiple examples of Stalin's towering vanity: his personal editing of propaganda material to emphasise his own 'genius'; his dedicating badly needed resources to building monuments to himself, even during the desperate struggle for post-war reconstruction; and the naming of endless enterprises and towns in his honour.

As he began to wrap up, Khrushchev told his audience how Stalin had toyed with the idea that Voroshilov might be a British agent and, following the Nineteenth Party Congress, had levelled baseless accusations against Mikoyan and Molotov. He declared that Stalin's death had saved their lives and went on to claim that 'Stalin evidently had plans to finish off the old members of the Politburo.' Even so, in concluding, he reiterated that Stalin had in the past performed great services for the party, the working class and the world workers' movement, albeit these services had since been overstated. Those present were then warned that the legacies of the Stalin cult should be taken seriously, and that the preceding remarks about Stalin must remain for the attention of the party only, since to make such information public would be to provide ammunition for the country's enemies (the report would thus be known abroad as the Secret Speech, since it was not published in the Soviet media or even formally acknowledged by the leadership). It was now necessary, he insisted, to return to the correct path set out by the October

Revolution and to restore properly Leninist principles of Soviet socialist democracy (which he seems to have implicitly understood as meaning something like Stalinism minus the cult, the deep xenophobia, rampant bureaucracy and baseless repression). When Khrushchev had finished, Bulganin asked those present to vote on a resolution that branded the cult of personality 'alien to Marxism-Leninism' and harmful to the party, declaring the need to tackle its consequences in all fields of party and state activity. In true Stalinist fashion, and with no discussion whatsoever, the motion was passed unanimously.

Even at around four hours in length, Khrushchev's speech had nothing to say about a plethora of abominable acts. Of course, he had to avoid undermining the wider Soviet system that he now stood atop as he denounced Stalin. Events like the brutal collectivisation process and the accompanying famine of 1932–33 – which caused a level of human suffering worse even than that of the Great Terror – simply did not come up. Similarly, Khrushchev framed the struggle against Trotskyites and others as fundamentally correct: he was clear that groundless political repression was the problem, rather than political violence per se. In the context of the myriad abuses that were not discussed, though, it is also important to keep in mind that the speech was rooted in a very specific investigation, which centred on party repressions following the Seventeenth Party Congress. Similarly, the lack of attention paid to the suffering of non-communists in the Secret Speech has at times been taken as a sign of Khrushchev's indifference to their fate; in reality, it probably reflected the fact that his remarks were first and foremost intended for a major party occasion. Nonetheless, for all the shocking revelations that were set forth, there was never any intention of providing a thorough and sophisticated reckoning with the recent past.

Exactly why Khrushchev chose to tackle the cult when he did has long been a subject of debate. The most fanciful Western accounts of the time contended that Khrushchev attacked Stalin because he was about to be exposed for his murder and was thus issuing a pre-emptive strike to save his own reputation.[15] Theories naturally abounded inside the Soviet Union, too. Among the most widespread was that Khrushchev had turned on Stalin because of the fate of his own son, Leonid. The claim was that Leonid Khrushchev had not really died when his plane was shot down during the war, but had been captured by the Germans, had co-operated and had some time later found himself in Soviet captivity, at which point he was executed for treachery, despite his father's appeals to Stalin for leniency. Molotov clearly seems to have been among those who believed this story: many years later he remarked that Leonid Khrushchev had been 'a traitor' and that Khrushchev senior's animosity towards Stalin was rooted in the fact that his 'eldest son got himself shot'.[16]

Personal animosity was not the prime reason why Khrushchev delivered the Secret Speech. In fact, he still spoke fondly of Stalin at times, both in public and in private. Fedor Burlatsky – an apparatchik (party functionary) close to Khrushchev throughout his time in power – argued that he gave the speech, at substantial personal risk, because it was morally the right thing to do and was in the best interests of Soviet society.[17] Alexei Adzhubei – married to Khrushchev's daughter Rada and close to his father-in-law – suggested a kind of personal 'exorcism' and described how Khrushchev sought to cleanse the 'shame and horror' in his soul after all he had seen and done during the Stalin years.[18] Khrushchev himself explained his speech both as a moral imperative and as a means of treating the wounds that Stalin had inflicted on the party in the drive to build communism.[19]

Alternatively, some historians have argued that Khrushchev seized on the Stalin issue primarily as a way of wrong-footing and discrediting his rivals for power.[20] Certainly, his utterances and actions regarding Stalin's memory over the previous three years offered limited indication of any burning desire to right historic wrongs. In being the first to tackle the Stalin cult, Khrushchev both distanced his own name from the repressions (in which he had been heavily involved in Ukraine especially) and placed his rivals in a vulnerable position by virtue of the fact that they had not spoken up. He also strengthened his support base among officials by showing that they were now safe from repression. Moreover, by focusing the blame on Stalin as an individual, rather than exploring more systemic roots of the cult, he ensured that they would bear no responsibility for the events he exposed.[21]

Others have adopted a slightly less cynical approach, arguing that the Stalin issue could hardly *not* be tackled at some point, since there were so many areas where reform had either been enacted already or else was urgently needed. In short, silence on the Stalin legacy was hampering the new party leadership as it sought to move forward: the subject simply had to be broached.[22] What makes this line of thinking especially useful is that it best allows for the often-unremarked point that Khrushchev was by no means the sole actor involved in the reforms and discussion that culminated in the Secret Speech. In the background, Olga Shatunovskaya and Alexei Snegov had consistently pushed for some kind of reckoning with Stalin, while Mikoyan had also been an important driving force within the top party elite. Indeed, a majority of the Presidium had been in favour of raising the issue at congress when it was discussed. Asked years later why he had not done more to prevent Khrushchev's attack on Stalin, Molotov insisted that he would have found no support even if he had spoken out.[23]

The wider world responds

Because the USSR, and Stalin in particular, had long been the spearhead of the global workers' movement, this was a moment that had major international ramifications. The political fallout that resulted from Khrushchev's speech would see that movement increasingly fragmented and weakened, while the Soviet position as leader of the communist cause would be brought into question in ways that it never had been before.

Not admitted to the session in which the Secret Speech was read out, the leaders of the ruling Eastern European communist parties – plus Palmiro Togliatti from Italy and Maurice Thorez from France (who unwittingly had spoken approvingly of Stalin at the congress) – were briefed about events on 27 February. Others, though, still had little or no concrete information about what had happened. Rumours that started circulating in Moscow took a while to reach the ears of Western diplomats and journalists (US Ambassador Charles Bohlen first heard of the speech two weeks after the event), but thereafter quickly made it abroad. Knowing full well that Soviet censorship would not allow him to transmit the rumours back home through the regular telegraph system, the British journalist John Rettie made a short trip from Moscow to Stockholm to pass on the news.[24]

Those foreign communist parties still left in the dark were soon bombarding Soviet officials with requests for clarification and advice on what to say, but to little avail.[25] Allied parties abroad were painfully aware that their silence – essentially enforced by Moscow's unwillingness to provide them with either detail or an appropriate political narrative – could only be interpreted negatively in their home countries, and thus brought them under heavy fire from domestic opponents. Plenty of foreign communists, of course, had also been eager participants in the glorification of Stalin, and their own credibility took a hit once he was exposed. Some communist parties witnessed angry schisms between those members who downplayed (or else did not believe) the criticism of Stalin and those who believed it and now expected fundamental change. Many foreign communist party members and officials not unreasonably demanded a more thorough and more genuinely Marxist interpretation of what had gone wrong in the USSR. The Israeli Communist Party split between those for and those against Stalin. The Communist Party leader in Uruguay came under criticism for fostering his own cult of personality (and he anyway chose to defend Stalin's reputation), while Mexico's communists refused to accept news of the Secret Speech as anything other than an American propaganda ploy.[26]

In the Asian part of the socialist camp – where both Kim Il-sung and Mao Zedong were the subject of cults little less grandiose than Stalin's had been – one of the key results of the Secret Speech was a steady loosening of the ideological bonds with the USSR. In Pyongyang, Kim Il-sung barely paid lip service to the new line from Moscow and opted to keep knowledge of the Secret Speech from both the party and the public. China also declined to endorse the speech with any conviction, stating that Stalin had made mistakes, but nonetheless remained a great Marxist-Leninist. Actually, the official greeting that Mao had sent to the Twentieth Party Congress noted how the CPSU had been 'nurtured with care by Stalin and his closest collaborators'. Unsurprisingly, the Chinese leadership privately expressed frustration that the issue had not been discussed with allies beforehand.[27] Mao, in particular, felt that the attack on Stalin endangered his own position within the Chinese leadership. Disagreement between the Chinese and Soviet parties in regard to their assessments of Stalin would, in due course, become a fundamental point of difference in the ideological split that broke the communist world in two only a few years later.[28]

As Soviet leader, Khrushchev held far greater sway in Warsaw, Budapest and Prague than he did in Beijing and Pyongyang, meaning that the USSR's East European underlings could not so easily disregard or disagree with the new line on Stalin. Nonetheless, leaders across the region had until recently revelled in their fealty to Stalin, had built vast monuments in his honour and had zealously purged and persecuted on his orders. As such, the reverberations of the Secret Speech were also powerful in the likes of East Germany, Poland and Hungary, and leaders across the region were themselves hardly enthusiastic about its message. In East Germany, Walter Ulbricht soon found himself under attack from elements within his own party both for his long history of fawning praise for the now discredited Stalin and for fostering his own personality cult. In mid-April, the Soviet consul in Kraków wrote that there were grassroots calls for both the Polish ruling party and parliament to be subjected to re-election in light of the news about Stalin. Further, a troubling cleavage had opened up there between older party members who struggled to accept the veracity of the accusations against Stalin, and younger communists bitterly critical of his criminal activity and seeking stronger action against local perpetrators.

Most portentously, on 3 July 1956 the Soviet ambassador in Budapest, Yuri Andropov, wrote to Moscow warning that Hungarian communist youth, in particular, were growing more antagonistic towards the party leadership there. He added that local officials were no longer confident about how to deal with such critics, since Stalin's repressions were now being condemned in Moscow. Four days later, one of Andropov's colleagues at the Budapest embassy, Vladimir Kryuchkov, also wrote to Moscow about a recent gathering of a young communist group known as the Petőfi Circle. According to Kryuchkov's report, the meeting had proceeded in 'a clearly unhealthy character', with sharp criticism aimed at the Hungarian party leadership, and with demands for the rehabilitation of purge victims and genuine democratisation of political life. All of this, the Petőfi Circle members had asserted, was not hostile, but loyal and was aimed at 'bringing to life' the resolutions of the Twentieth Party Congress.[29] This notion – that support for the new political direction set out in the Secret Speech could and even should entail strident challenges to the existing order of things – would be very much evident inside the Soviet Union. And it would quickly cause problems.

Georgia

While the reforms of 1953–55 showed a party leadership that was broadly apprised of key problems and had consciously, albeit discreetly, begun to move on from the Stalin cult, the same could not necessarily be said of Soviet society more widely. Inside the USSR, the most volatile response to the Secret Speech came in Georgia, Stalin's home republic.

The whole of the Soviet Union went through some abrupt and unsettling changes around Stalin's death, but this was especially true of Georgia. In March 1952, the incumbent republican leadership was removed en masse in the course of the Mingrelian Affair that Stalin had used to weaken Beria's Caucasus client network. Once Stalin was dead, Beria promptly removed the new Georgian leadership and reinstated his team, only for his own arrest in June 1953 to signal yet another clear-out of the Georgian elite. More importantly, while Stalin ruled in the Kremlin – and after that, while Beria retained a place at the top table – Georgia and the political elite in Tbilisi punched well above their weight in terms of prestige and access to power.[30] Problems, such as repeated complaints of official discrimination against the Abkhaz minority inside Georgia, were generally ignored or suppressed in Moscow thanks to these influential connections. With both Beria and Stalin disgraced, though, Georgia lost its informal 'special status' among the non-Russian republics, and its leaders unhappily faced a new reality in the Soviet pecking order.[31]

In 1954, the first anniversary of Stalin's death had seen around ten days of approved mourning events in Georgia. In March 1955, the second anniversary had also been marked with public events, such as meetings, speeches and wreath-laying at Tbilisi's central Stalin monument. At the start of March 1956, without any formal announcement to the contrary, there was no obvious reason for locals to assume that things would be any different to the previous two years. However, the authorities in Moscow had secretly decreed that there was to be no further commemoration of the anniversary.

On 4 March, the first harbingers of trouble were reported, when crowds gathered at Tbilisi's main Stalin monument and grew steadily rowdier by evening, with drinking, shouting and occasional scuffles with police. The following day, processions made up mainly of students and other young people appeared in central Tbilisi carrying wreaths and portraits of Stalin. Accompanied by the sound of cars and lorries blaring their horns in support, they made their way to the monument to pay homage. These processions appeared again the next day – though this time they were bigger, noisier and carried more banners, flags and portraits. In fact, they had all the outward hallmarks of an official mourning event. Soon, a round-the-clock guard of honour had been established at the Stalin monument, and local enterprises sent along food to sustain those on vigil, as sympathisers began to flood into Tbilisi from other Georgian towns like Kutaisi and Borjomi.[32]

Although the wider public did not initially know exactly what had been said about Stalin at the Twentieth Party Congress, top Georgian officials (many of whom had been at the congress in Moscow) mostly did. The Georgian party elite were themselves far from enamoured with the Secret Speech and knew full well that the timing was hardly propitious. For many Georgians, Stalin's name was so closely associated with their republic that any attack on him was understood as an attack on Georgia as a whole. Further, Khrushchev had very specifically made the connection in his speech that both Stalin and Beria were Georgians, and had mocked the fact that the two men were regarded as the pride of their republic. Though investigators seemingly never managed to find a 'smoking gun' that directly linked the Georgian party leadership to the March 1956 disturbances, there certainly were suspicions of complicity. Officials in Tbilisi were, for the first few days, at least willing to turn a blind eye to the swelling protests, even if they did not actively encourage, organise and equip them.[33]

By 7 March, protesters had set up microphones and loudspeakers at the Stalin monument and the crowds there reached an estimated 70,000. Some of those present read poetry about Stalin, some sang songs in his honour and others gave emotional speeches in which they vowed to fight for his cause and defend his name. What started as a demonstration of loyalty to Stalin, though, also began to take on overtly nationalist overtones. Some speakers made unambiguously xenophobic remarks, pointedly boasting of Georgia's past heroics in overcoming foreign invaders, and received wild applause as they did so. All the while, according to one Russian eyewitness, local police looked on impassively.[34]

By the next day, the atmosphere had grown still more volatile, and according to the same Russian witness, 'provocateurs' were becoming prominent in the crowds. Cars, lorries and buses were now being commandeered by protesters, and traffic police were beaten up when they tried to intervene. Non-Georgians, most notably Russians and Armenians, were beginning to face intimidation on the street in Tbilisi. Learning that the Chinese army chief, Marshal Zhu De, was resting up at a nearby sanatorium, a group from the swelling crowd seized vehicles and headed off to enlist his support for the pro-Stalin protest. Soviet troops who tried to stop them were pelted with stones and overcome by sheer weight of numbers. Pleading illness, Zhu De addressed the gathering posse only briefly and rather vaguely, before agreeing to send one of his subordinates to speak at the monument. Back in the centre of Tbilisi, a whole series of demands now emanated from the crowd, among which rumours about the Secret Speech swirled more and more extensively. Some wanted the city's university and its stadium to be again named in honour of Stalin, and there were also calls for the protests to be broadcast in the national media.[35] Demonstrators then demanded that 9 March be designated a day of mourning, with newspapers carrying articles on Stalin, old films about Stalin being screened and the Georgian anthem being performed. One group of protesters even managed to force officials at city hall to fly banners of Marx, Engels, Lenin and Stalin.

With seemingly little option but to make concessions, Georgian party boss Vasil Mzhavanadze promised to defend Stalin's name. He allowed mourning meetings to be held and agreed to publish praise of Stalin in the press. This, though, served to confuse matters further, since the protests now looked a lot like they had official sanction. By 9 March, the authorities in Moscow had been brought up to speed and decided that events in Tbilisi had got out of hand. Ordinary life in the city had ground to a standstill as more and more citizens skipped work or classes to join the protest, closing shops and offices and bringing public transport to a halt. That day, the local newspaper *Zarya vostoka* (*Eastern Dawn*) carried the promised commemoration of Stalin, calling him 'one of the greatest revolutionaries', as well as 'the outstanding disciple of the great Lenin'; commemoration meetings also went ahead in workplaces, schools and elsewhere. The Georgian party and Komsomol put out a joint appeal for calm, warning that provocateurs were trying to play on people's raw emotions to cause harm, and acknowledging the wish to honour Stalin's memory as 'natural and understandable'. At the Stalin monument, though, the increasing radicalism continued as the crowd now called for Beria to be rehabilitated, Khrushchev, Mikoyan and Bulganin to be removed from office, and Molotov to be placed in charge of the country. Further demands insisted that the report on Stalin (the Secret Speech) should be officially rejected. By this time, leaflets were also circulating, calling for Georgia to declare its independence from the Soviet Union.[36]

Moscow officials ordered the army onto the streets of Tbilisi, but this caused the mood to deteriorate further. People climbed onto tanks and scrawled swastikas on them. Around midnight, some protesters surged past soldiers into the city's communications ministry, but were detained there by security. This prompted a much larger crowd to arrive in a bid to free them. Troops first discharged warning shots and then fired on the crowd. Elsewhere, barricades went up on Rustaveli Prospekt (Tbilisi's main thoroughfare) and there were attempts by protesters to disarm police in their own headquarters. Fights broke out and more shots were fired. According to a Russian eyewitness account, a crowd of around 5,000 people at the Stalin monument continued to ignore police warnings and refused to disperse, with soldiers forced to defend themselves when physically attacked. One Georgian witness, however, painted a very different picture of events in a subsequent letter. She described first hearing shots from the communications building, then shooting 'everywhere' – she herself was shot in the leg. She added that Russian troops surrounded the crowd and would not let them leave, destroying the portraits and busts of Stalin that they carried, as well as calling them 'Georgian pigs' and 'dogs'.[37]

Around 200 people were arrested that night and a further 160 the next day, but tensions remained high in the city. Rumours circulated that Mao would come to Tbilisi to meet protesters, and that Stalin's children would also arrive.[38] The Georgian MVD reported in secret that fifteen people had been killed and fifty-four wounded (seven of whom subsequently died of their wounds). The ensuing funerals were severely restricted, while the families of the dead – most of whom were students and school pupils – were placed under special KGB scrutiny for the next forty days.[39] The central authorities in Moscow investigated the chain of events, but – rather than confront the possibility of widespread grievance or systemic problems in the republic – fell back on the simplistic narrative that weak political work with young people by the local Komsomol in particular, and the actions of a few dangerous provocateurs, had been to blame for the troubles in Georgia.

The use of force on the night of 9 March not only succeeded in reimposing order in Tbilisi, but also served as a rallying point around which a much wider Georgian radicalism would emerge. Previously, Georgian national sentiment had largely existed within a wider framework of Soviet patriotism. After March 1956, it increasingly became a nationalism in which growing numbers spoke of the need for independence from the Soviet Union.[40] Most immediately, in April 1957 an underground group consisting of seven people, all aged between sixteen and eighteen, was uncovered and its members convicted of anti-Soviet activity after they handed out leaflets calling on Georgians never to forget the bloody events of 9 March.[41] The group's leader, Zviad Gamsakhurdia, would go on to become Georgia's first democratically elected president, as the Soviet Union approached its collapse in 1991.

Difficult questions and slanderous remarks

Judging it the best way to tackle the legacies of the Stalin cult, on 5 March the Central Committee in Moscow passed a resolution calling for party members, Komsomol members and non-party activists to be acquainted with the content of Khrushchev's speech. The first two of these groups combined to represent a total of almost 25 million citizens. The third group was sufficiently vaguely defined that one individual recalled 'in reality, practically anyone who wanted to do so could go and hear the speech'.[42] The only real attempt at enforcing 'secrecy', aside from not publishing the speech in the press or officially acknowledging that it had happened, was that people who attended these meetings were forbidden from taking notes.

Actually, the original session at which the Secret Speech had been delivered took place without a stenographer present, and so the report that was subsequently sent out around the country was actually a recreation based on earlier draft material, rather than the exact speech given at the congress. As one author has noted, since Khrushchev's speeches were often characterised by his adding 'spicy' details and personal anecdotes, the report that party and Komsomol members and others were familiarised with in March and April

1956 was more than likely somewhat 'toned down' from the original.[43] Nonetheless, the responses that followed were more diverse, and sometimes also more volatile, than anything that had been seen for many years in Soviet political life.

The meetings at which the Secret Speech were read out around the country varied from place to place. Some officials were content for the report to be read in full and then opened up for discussion; others kept the session as brief as they possibly could, doing the absolute minimum, in order to stifle the issue without disobeying party orders.[44] Some attendees applauded the main thrust of the speech and wanted to go further and faster in tackling the problems of past and present; some refused to believe its veracity or else insisted that Stalin's achievements anyway outweighed any mistakes he might have made; others declared that they failed to understand what purpose it served to wash such dirty linen in public. A young Mikhail Gorbachev was one of those who had to read out the report to party members in his native Stavropol, and later recalled both his own wholehearted support for its message and the decidedly mixed response it generated, with younger and better-educated audience members applauding, while others refused to believe it.[45]

By not publishing the speech openly, the party passed up the chance to frame its contents as it saw fit. As one commentator has argued, by failing to provide a clear public narrative on what the Secret Speech said about the Soviet past, present and future, the authorities unintentionally forced citizens to work such things out for themselves. This was all but unprecedented for a regime that had always taken so much care to shape and to control the forms and themes of public discourse.[46] Khrushchev had no intention of starting any kind of public debate: his aim was to 'set' the new line and then quickly move on. This, though, was wildly unrealistic. Interest in studying the country's recent history boomed.[47] People both demanded to be told 'the truth' and insisted on their right to speak 'the truth' after so many years of lies. There was anyway no considered plan of action on what was to come next. Indeed, Georgy Arbatov, a party apparatchik soon to establish himself close to the top of the Soviet bureaucracy, later wrote that Khrushchev 'neither saw nor understood the fundamental tasks ahead'.[48] As then Moscow party boss Ekaterina Furtseva later acknowledged, officials were not at all prepared to give the answers that were now being demanded of them.[49]

The questions that did come ranged across all aspects of the Soviet experience. Some people now wanted to know whether earlier condemnations of the likes of Trotsky and Bukharin were still valid (Trotsky's widow Natalya Sedova wrote, unsuccessfully, asking for her husband and son to have their convictions as counter-revolutionaries overturned). Others asked why Stalin's portraits continued to hang all around the country, why this vital news had not been broken earlier and why Stalin's body remained in the mausoleum on Red Square. Anna Pankratova read the speech to audiences of hundreds of people at a time in Leningrad in March and recorded over eight hundred questions and comments submitted by those in attendance. Some angrily insisted that the Soviet system was not socialist in nature, but a dictatorship of the bureaucracy; they demanded greater openness from the party and lower wages for its officials. Plenty wanted to know the 'real truth' about everything from October 1917 onwards.[50] Many expressed confusion about how to view Stalin's achievements and contributions to the construction of socialism in light of the news about his crimes, and others wanted to know whether the liquidation of the kulaks was still regarded as correct. According to internal reports from the Department of Party Organs (a key body that supervised all manner of affairs within the party), members who spoke up most frequently asked why the report was so limited in its content; why there was no self-criticism from the party elite; whether there was also a cult surrounding Lenin; and what guarantees there were that another cult would not emerge in the future.[51] Clearly, there were no simple and convincing answers to give to such questions.

At a meeting on Sakhalin island, in the far east, there were calls to reconsider the positions of the entire leadership, and for Stalin to be posthumously expelled from the party as an enemy of the people. In Latvia, two KGB officers were reprimanded after placing the blame for the cult at the feet of the entire Central Committee and its Presidium. In Uzbekistan, there were declarations of lost faith in the party, while one speaker mockingly recalled the idea of building a great pantheon for Stalin's remains, suggesting that it should be surrounded by the corpses of his innocent victims. At a party meeting, at the Armenian Academy of Sciences in Yerevan, speakers assailed the Soviet Union's bogus election process and the lack of press freedom.[52] Some likened members of the elite who had survived the Stalin years to deserters who had fled under fire during the war.[53] Fawning remarks about Stalin that had been uttered by members of the leadership at the Nineteenth Party Congress were now held up for ridicule. In a combustible session at Moscow's Gorky Institute of World Literature, speakers railed against Khrushchev's narrow conception of the cult, stating that thousands were actively responsible for the crimes of the era and thousands more knew what was happening but did nothing, insisting that the guilty must be punished and warning that the struggle with the cult was 'being led by those who had created it'.[54] One (unpublished) letter to *Pravda* put the issue bluntly, stating 'This is not a party of communists but a bunch of hypocrites and cowards.'[55]

The political authorities were often inclined to look upon those who spoke up with the most strident remarks as 'anti-Soviet', but this description rarely reflected the way that those in question understood their actions. The majority clearly saw themselves as loyal critics, to whom the Secret Speech had given a sense that they now had the opportunity to help 'correct' the flaws in a system that they believed in. Many felt that, as loyal communists, they were duty-bound to speak up and identify problems and weaknesses, much as Pomerantsev had argued in his essay 'On Sincerity in Literature'. This naturally worried many in Soviet officialdom, who had no such inclination for a root-and-branch examination of the past or present.

Many young and educated people, in particular, were hugely energised by Khrushchev's idealistic promise of a 'return to Leninism' as the antidote to the cynicism and crimes of the Stalin years. This concept was never elaborated in any concrete way, and people seemingly took it to mean whatever they wanted, though the basic notion shared by many was one of a more idealistic and humanitarian approach towards building communism, shorn of the brutality, obsequious leader veneration and the intense assault on the place of the individual within the Soviet system that had been so characteristic of Stalinism. Fedor Burlatsky recalled there being a 'rush of young blood' into the Communist Party, as youth especially took Khrushchev's remarks at face value and sought to participate in the remaking of the Soviet system.[56] Ivan Svitlichnyi – a future Ukrainian nationalist dissident – recalled that it seemed for a time like the country's nationalities problems would now 'resolve themselves at one blow' with this apparently more enlightened approach at the top.[57] Students at Moscow's Mining Institute enthusiastically took it upon themselves to find and expose 'careerists' and 'self-servers', clearly assuming that this was now the right thing to do.[58] Reform-minded journalists increasingly talked about the importance of getting at 'the truth', and of the civic role that journalism should play in creating a better country, expressing hopes that soon nothing would be off limits for them to discuss.[59]

Such sentiment met strong and entrenched resistance elsewhere in the party ranks, though. As one Soviet citizen who embraced the reformist cause at this point later recalled: 'I considered the system to be my own, but my opponents also considered it theirs.'[60] Some foreign commentators began to talk of a dangerous generational divide opening up inside the USSR. Soviet political authorities vehemently denied the existence of such a phenomenon, though they did not always do so convincingly. Valery Ronkin, at the time still a dedicated Komsomol member, later wrote that he was appalled that his parents' generation had either participated in or silently watched on as the mass abuses of Stalinism were perpetrated.[61] Similarly, numerous Soviet universities heard calls for the Komsomol to be freed from the apparently corrupting influence of the Communist Party.[62]

Angry and confused responses to Khrushchev's denunciation of Stalin by no means came solely from a liberal-minded or reformist perspective. There were also those of a far more conservative bent, who felt certain that they were the ones defending the Soviet system's best interests. Indeed, the historian Yuri Aksyutin has surmised that 'most people neither understood nor approved of the change of policy on Stalin' – though such an assertion can hardly be proven definitively.[63] Many party stalwarts, from the likes of Molotov on down, clearly did not approve. Responses among the student body at the likes of Moscow State University were very much divided between those for and those against the attack on Stalin.[64] After a delay of several weeks, the Secret Speech was eventually read out at meetings of party and Komsomol members across Georgia, where it met with a mostly frosty response. In Gori (Stalin's birthplace), around twenty people walked out of one meeting, on 24 April, which had to be abandoned; eight Komsomol members were subsequently expelled for 'hooligan behaviour' at the session. At another meeting, only a third of Komsomol members bothered to turn up to hear the speech, and there were reports of scuffles between Russians – who vandalised portraits of Stalin – and Georgians, who tried to stop them.[65]

Elsewhere, some infuriated party members declared that Khrushchev had slandered Stalin simply in order to build his own reputation as leader. A report from Vladimir oblast described the 'anti-Party slanders' of G.M. Vozzhanikov, who categorically rejected any criticism of Stalin at a party meeting, insisting 'I am for Stalin and fought alongside him for 30 years, but Khrushchev I do not know', before storming out and slamming the door. Claiming to speak in the name of her fellow war veterans, one Old Bolshevik wrote that 'these attacks do not sit well . . . his name should be restored . . . we *frontoviki* [front-line veterans] will never forget him'.[66] A furious letter from Yerevan bitterly rejected Khrushchev's attempt 'to humiliate Stalin' and insisted that 'Stalin will live eternally in history, in the hearts of progressive humanity'.[67] Quite how many others disliked the attack on Stalin but chose not to speak up, we can never know. Anyway, a curious paradox did not take long to emerge. By virtue of the depth of scrutiny and the extent of reform that they demanded, those who most fervently supported Khrushchev's denunciation of Stalin were soon viewed by wary officials as more dangerous than those who rejected the new line and stuck loyally by his memory, wanting only to keep things much as they already were.

Stalin after the secret speech

Stalin's portrait still hung everywhere across the USSR, his body remained on display next to Lenin's in the mausoleum on Red Square, and there were towns, factories, farms, streets and scholarships named in his honour in every corner of the country. In his birthplace of Gori, work was already under way on a Stalin museum (which opened a year later and remains open today). Almost all of the Komsomol's 'upbringing work' with young people centred on the study of Stalin's biography and his written works (substituting one cult for another, Komsomol boss Alexander Shelepin wanted Lenin monuments to be foregrounded again, and places where Lenin visited and worked preserved and made special).[68] Similarly, a new official history of the party was now needed, since the previous one, Stalin's *Short Course* (mandatory reading for young people especially), had become fundamentally unusable.

A number of tangential decisions were made in quick succession following the Secret Speech, though they were not all publicised. Following advice from

KGB chief Serov and Chief Prosecutor Rudenko that the arrests had been groundless and the confessions extracted by torture, on 6 March a Presidium resolution granted posthumous rehabilitation to thirty-six of those who were repressed after being elected to the Central Committee at the Seventeenth Party Congress. On 10 March, Presidium members also rescinded Stalin's February 1948 decree that had codified the practice of sending political prisoners into perpetual exile once their formal sentences had been completed, duly releasing many thousands who had suffered this fate.

During spring 1956, legal restrictions on deported national groups including Balkars, Kalmyks, Ingush and Chechens who had been condemned to internal exile in 1944 were eased, and they were then allowed to return home from January 1957 (though others, like the Crimean Tatars and the Meskhetian Turks, remained in limbo).[69] This was a process that could prompt volatility, however. The return to the North Caucasus of expelled Chechens, for example, eventually culminated in a major riot in Grozny between returnees and those who had since settled in their place, leaving thirty-two dead.[70] On 13 April, the Presidium established a commission to look into the 1930s show trials against Bukharin, Zinoviev and Kamenev.[71] The senior members of that commission, however, were Molotov, Kaganovich and Voroshilov – the most unapologetic Stalinists of them all. Unsurprisingly, the investigation ultimately went nowhere, with Mikoyan complaining years later that Molotov had deliberately killed off any chance of progress.[72]

Another commission was set up in April under Marshal Zhukov to discuss the often abysmal post-war treatment of returning Soviet POWs. In June, its report made it clear that Soviet soldiers in Nazi captivity had behaved honourably, and many had risked their lives escaping to join partisan bands. The huge numbers of POWs who returned home only to face imprisonment, Zhukov wrote, 'broke both laws and Leninist principles'. Some had been jailed as collaborators simply for the fact that they had worked cleaning the barracks in which they were held, or had provided medical care to their fellow prisoners. Many had, for years after the war, faced serious discrimination when they searched for jobs and housing, tried to claim welfare or applied to study.

Recognising that there were still upwards of 100,000 Soviet citizens languishing in camps, prisons and places of exile on account of Stalin-era

101

convictions for counter-revolutionary crimes, the process of the release and rehabilitation of political prisoners was given new impetus. Following the advice of a new commission headed by Mikoyan, on 19 March a revised process was set up, in which a total of ninety-seven sub-commissions were ordered to travel around the country's penal institutions reviewing appeals on site and releasing prisoners or shortening their sentences, as they saw fit.[73] Still including representatives from the KGB, the Procurator's Office and the Ministry of Justice, these travelling commissions now also featured released prisoners. Their inclusion was a clear sign that the central authorities were eager to get the process moving and to counterbalance the influence of those less inclined to support release.[74]

From almost 114,000 political prisoners at the start of 1956, a total of just over 18,000 remained incarcerated in January 1957. By the end of 1956, even the term 'gulag' had been abandoned in the official lexicon. Of course, the network of camps and prisons still contained 'politicals' who were not deemed suitable for release, and the Soviet regime did continue to jail citizens for political crimes after the Secret Speech, though on a completely different scale from the Stalin years. Nonetheless, many 'politicals', including religious believers and clerics of different faiths, and thousands of people who had been jailed or exiled for nationalist activity, were finally also allowed to return home.

A large part of the authorities' work following the Twentieth Party Congress consisted of trying to bring clarity to the new political situation. In particular, this meant reeling in those who were 'going too far' in embracing the denunciation of Stalin. The extent to which the late spring and summer of 1956 saw the party seeking to damp down the social impact of the attack on Stalin could also be seen in the case of a speech that never was. Having just been elected a candidate member of the Presidium, Zhukov was directed to prepare his own account of Stalin's blunders as war leader. On 19 May, he forwarded a draft of his report, which featured a litany of criticisms. He complained that the cult had ensured that proper credit for victory was not given to the military; that Stalin's suspicions towards his commanders had harmed their ability to act; and that Stalin had at numerous points directly intervened in plans, at great human cost. Coming from such a respected figure, this report would undoubtedly have carried a great charge. By the time it was ready, though, the political ground had shifted again, and it was shelved.[75]

As the weeks passed and debates still roiled, the party leadership fought to wrest back control of the narrative on Stalin. The attempt to clarify the situation for the Soviet public made it onto the pages of *Pravda* on 28 March. The piece in question, which had been drafted by a team of the Central Committee's top ideological experts, informed readers that Stalin had performed great services in a range of fields: before and during the revolution; in the civil war; in the industrialisation drive; and in the fight against Trotskyites, Zinovievites and bourgeois nationalists. While such measures were rightly acclaimed, said *Pravda*, Stalin's lack of personal modesty ensured that he encouraged praise to keep on growing until it reached wholly damaging levels. The article then criticised Stalin's growing disregard for genuinely collective leadership and pointed out that the cult had stifled initiative from below, had made possible the covering up of all kinds of shortcomings and had had a debilitating influence on the arts, with books and films focusing first of all on celebrating Stalin.[76] In a subtle redirecting of focus, concrete details on victims and their suffering were almost entirely absent, touched upon only in a passing mention of the fact that a lack of collective leadership had facilitated unjustified repression.

It was not just ordinary citizens who remained unclear where the new boundaries of permissible and impermissible comment lay after the exposure of Stalin. A series of party letters and resolutions emerged across the summer of 1956 in an attempt to bring an end to officials' uncertainty about what was and was not now acceptable comment in light of the speech, as well as to re-establish the fact that punishment should follow for those who breached the new expectations.[77] A party resolution on 30 June, entitled 'On the cult of personality and the overcoming of its consequences', offered further clarification. After the standard boasts about how progressive humanity had cheered the congress while the capitalist world trembled, slandered and plotted away, it insisted that tackling the cult and its associated problems was a necessary and brave step towards the restoration of party democracy and the building of communism. Then, after briefly restating Stalin's achievements and some of his shortcomings, it emphasised that although the consequences of the Stalin cult were serious, the harm done had not changed the fundamental nature of the Soviet system that was born of the October Revolution. In other words, no fundamental surgery was required.

By the summer of 1956, though, the authorities in Moscow were also becoming rattled by on-going public ferment in Poland, which was itself clearly influenced by the Secret Speech, and attitudes at the top again hardened. A further letter sent from the Central Committee to party organisations on 16 July demanded that all levels of the party structure take an active role in tackling what it referred to as 'anti-Party speeches', nationalist outbursts that undermined the friendship of Soviet peoples, and attempts to sow lack of faith in the party. Too many communists, it insisted, still did not understand (or did not want to understand) that problems were not rooted in the nature of the Soviet system and that the character of that system and its adherence to the principles of Marxism-Leninism was sound. It was important to remember, the letter asserted, that the advent of peaceful co-existence with the West did not mean that the ideological struggle with capitalism had weakened, but that Western attempts at sowing subversion and disharmony in the USSR would in fact become ever sharper. The party could not remain passive in the face of so-called communists questioning the democratic nature of the Soviet system and praising the false freedoms of capitalism. Individual communists had 'no right to remain silent' in the face of such attacks, it declared, insisting that there could be no tolerance of communists who stood apart from the party line.[78]

New cultural battles

As summer 1956 turned into autumn, the cultural sphere again emerged as a key battleground on which attitudes for and against reform played out. Writing in the journal *Voprosy filosofii* about the harm that the cult of personality had done in their own sphere, the playwrights V. Nazarov and O. Grudneva called for the theatrical arts to be granted extensive powers of self-government, effectively ending direct party guidance over their work. Their remarks were almost immediately rejected in *Izvestiya* as 'deeply erroneous', but this nonetheless fed into on-going debates about how the effects of the cult were to be excised from the arts. Minister of Culture Nikolai Mikhailov met leading figures from the fine art world and announced that rule by fiat was now deemed inadmissible, offering artists both more state funding and greater input into affairs in their own industry, though he, too, pinpointed the *Voprosy filosofii* piece as an example of incorrect thinking.[79]

The *Izvestiya* article in question had at least accepted that there were real problems in cultural production, but it insisted that guidance from above (from the party) remained absolutely necessary. It accepted that writers should take risks, but reasserted that there could be no 'anything goes' approach to literature. What had now changed – and being published in *Izvestiya*, this was something close to the definitive line – was that artists no longer 'risked their reputation as citizens': essentially this meant that 'ideological errors' in one's work would not be regarded as evidence of political hostility towards the Soviet order of things (with all that could entail). One could now be 'wrong' without being an enemy. This was clearly an advance of sorts, in that it not only promised the basic safety net of not being destroyed on account of one's artistic output, but also reflected the limited nature of the reforms that transpired. Anyway, there would be instances still to come when writers and others would be fiercely berated, traduced and persecuted for such 'mistakes'.

Nonetheless, change clearly was happening. Moscow's new Sovremennik (Contemporary) theatre opened in 1956, foregrounding young writers and directors, as well as new plays, and rapidly becoming a 'flagship of efforts to rejuvenate Soviet culture'.[80] Hardly less significant were the new films of the age, featuring complicated and sometimes troubled protagonists, private struggles and grittier and more lifelike depictions of Soviet reality – and sometimes even love and fun. After domestic film production had dwindled badly during Stalin's last years, it now burst back into life, both in Moscow and republican studios. Studying at the USSR's main film school (VGIK) in the late 1950s and early 1960s, Marina Goldovskaya recalled that 'the atmosphere at the institute was alive, creative and filled with beautiful, talented and radiant people'.[81] There was also a particularly eager audience. With an annual total of around 4 billion tickets sold by the late 1960s, few countries in the world saw cinema-going on such a scale as in the USSR.[82] With tickets kept cheap, it was not wholly uncommon for some people to watch almost every film that was released, sometimes more than once (one 1963 survey, for example, found that almost 45 per cent of respondents went to the cinema several times a week).[83]

Notable already by virtue of being a love story, *Spring on Zarechnaya Street* in 1956 was also the first film for many years to show the overcrowded housing and dirty streets of a Soviet workers' suburb.[84] A huge success both at home and abroad was the 1957 film *The Cranes Are Flying*. Played by Tatyana Samoilova, the protagonist was Soviet cinema's 'most complex female lead', in turns playful, despondent and vulnerable, and with no obvious interest in politics.[85] On first watching it, Goldovskaya recalled that 'suddenly from the screen, life, passion and fresh air burst into the world'; adding that, like the rest of the audience, she clapped until her hands hurt at the end of the film.[86]

Among the most enduring of all in its popularity among Soviet citizens was the musical comedy *Carnival Night*. This marked the arrival of the director Eldar Ryazanov, whose comedies would be among the most popular with Soviet audiences for many years to come. As he seeks to enforce a deadly dull and formulaic New Year's Eve event at the House of Culture to which he has been posted, the pompous, ignorant and transparently Stalinist bureaucrat Ogurtsov runs up against the energy and enthusiasm of young people eager for fun and determined to prevent him from ruining their special night. As the New Year eventually arrives, Ogurtsov has been comprehensively outfoxed and his plans left in tatters: the young volunteers put on a fun stage show of their own, featuring singing, dancing and more, with everyone present (except Ogurtsov) having a great time.

As before, literature remained a key barometer of change. For all that the Soviet era saw numerous great works produced, few of them prompted the kind of immediate and powerful public response that was generated by Vladimir Dudintsev's novel *Not by Bread Alone* when it was published in instalments in *Novy mir* from September 1956. For what was in many respects a typically Soviet production novel – its central character is an inventor who has devised a new machine for casting pipes – this was no mean feat. In late 1956, though, the name of Dudintsev, and especially that of the key villain of his work, Drozdov, was everywhere.

Already that year, writers, including Daniil Granin and Vladimir Tendryakov, had published works with cynical, careerist and corrupt bureaucrats close to the centre of the plot, but none hit the mark quite like Dudintsev. The central storyline of his novel features a talented young inventor named Lopatkin, who is continually and cynically rebuffed by a whole swathe of repellent officials as he tries to get his new machine into production. Much of what made *Not by Bread Alone* stand out was the fact that the villain of the piece is not a rogue individual (as was usually the case), but practically every representative of the bureaucracy that Lopatkin encounters. Time and again, the hero finds his path blocked by venal and cynical officials, interested only in their own betterment. Further, when Lopatkin does eventually win out over his tormentors, it is largely down to good fortune. Most importantly, those who have stood in Lopatkin's way or have tried to steal his ideas for their own benefit are not presented to the reader as having seen the error of their ways, do not emerge as reformed individuals (as Socialist Realist convention dictated) and are not even punished: they walk away largely unscathed and unrepentant.[87] Biting analogies with Stalin-era officialdom abound, and the novel's ending, in which Lopatkin 'declares war' on his chief abuser, Drozdov, proved especially resonant.

Soon enough, all manner of officials and bureaucrats found themselves labelled 'Drozdovs' in real life, as readers enthusiastically embraced Lopatkin's struggle against bureaucratic tyranny. A review in the trade union newspaper *Trud* (*Labour*) at the end of October hailed the work as 'a banner of our times' and a 'useful weapon' in the struggle to re-establish Leninist principles in party life, explicitly linking the emergence of 'Drozdovs' with the atmosphere created by the Stalin cult, and noting that the work described 'the fierce struggle between progressive and conservative forces in our society'.[88] As one scholar has pointed out, the public reception of *Not by Bread Alone* 'quickly developed into a collective examination of the economic and administrative problems, political challenges, past legacies and ethical dilemmas that confronted the country at the time'.[89] Such things naturally unnerved political and cultural authorities.

As before, those who wrote or spoke out in support of Dudintsev's work tended to do so not as enemies of Soviet power, but as loyal critics seeking to defend the system from the damage caused by cynical and careerist 'Drozdovs'. Nonetheless, it was also telling that so much of the language that people now used to criticise the 'bad' bureaucrats, against whom they vented their anger, was characterised by Stalin-era patterns of thought and vocabulary, with talk of 'Drozdovs' as 'enemies', 'rats' and 'insects' that threatened healthy Soviet society.[90] Clearly, neither the death of Stalin nor his subsequent denunciation had the power to immediately erase Stalinist ways of thinking and talking about the world that had been baked into Soviet citizens for decades by this point.

At an uproarious meeting held to discuss Dudintsev's novel in Leningrad on 10 November, a young mathematician named Revolt Pimenov (who had already produced and circulated a biting commentary on the inclusions and omissions of the Secret Speech) lambasted what he called the 'reign of the Drozdovs' in the country, receiving a stern rebuke from the university rector and drawing wild applause from the rest of the audience.[91] At one such meeting in Moscow, the room was so packed that crowds climbed up the side of the building to hear the speeches and mounted police were brought in to keep order.[92] The partisan crowd booed loudly when the writer Valentin Ovechkin offered even mildly critical remarks on Dudintsev's story. Most pointedly, Konstantin Paustovsky, one of the grand old men of the Soviet cultural world, and a writer widely admired both at home and abroad, spoke of witnessing at first hand the venal and self-regarding conduct of officialdom, asserting that Drozdovs were to be found everywhere and were 'acquisitive carnivores . . . encouraged to satisfy their lowest instincts. Their weapons are betrayal, calumny, character assassination and just plain murder.' He went on to insist that the people would soon 'mercilessly sweep away such Drozdovs'.[93] Within days, a concerned Presidium got word of the events and again began to shorten the reins on the country's cultural elite.[94]

With the maelstrom around *Not by Bread Alone* still growing, a groundbreaking Picasso exhibition opened on 26 October at Moscow's Pushkin Museum of Fine Arts, before later moving on to the Hermitage in Leningrad. The exhibition was officially sanctioned and had come about largely through the efforts of the author Ilya Ehrenburg, who was a personal friend of Picasso; but it was nonetheless awkward for the authorities. Picasso was hailed politically, since he was one of the world's most famous communists; but his later work, in particular, represented exactly the kind of 'bourgeois abstractionism' that officials in the Soviet cultural sphere had declared war on in the late 1940s.[95] Officials' hopes of keeping the exhibition limited to Picasso's more conventional early work fell apart when the artist himself insisted on choosing which of his pieces should be shown. Ultimately, it was decided that the benefits of hosting a Picasso exhibition – such as public support from Picasso himself and credit for advancing cultural liberalisation – could be made to outweigh the negatives. The key drawback in the minds of the authorities was the potential for the public to embrace ways of making and thinking about art that fell outside the bounds of approved Socialist Realism.

In both Moscow and Leningrad there were long and lively queues to enter the exhibition, and animated discussions among those inside quickly expanded beyond the works on show (which included exactly the kind of art that Soviet authorities abhorred), as new cultural vistas beyond tired Socialist Realism opened up. One attendee recalled that 'we felt a rapture in those Picasso-ed halls. It softened the pain of understanding how, and for how many years, we had been sitting in a cave, seeing only with the minimum light allowed us.'[96] As with literary works by the likes of Pomerantsev and Dudintsev, all this created what one expert has called 'a forum for public discussion of contemporary culture and political issues of freedom and truth'.[97] Talking about Picasso's work became a way of discussing the past and the future, and of raising questions that the authorities did not want to discuss, such as that of creative freedom inside the Soviet Union.[98] Crowds in Moscow grew so lively that the police were ultimately called in. The ensuing debates on art and politics continued in student dorms and elsewhere long after the galleries had closed for the night.

As the autumn of 1956 progressed, there was little room for doubt that the tide was again beginning to turn against cultural liberalisation. At the start of December, a review of *Not by Bread Alone* in *Izvestiya* showed a much harder attitude. The novel's hero, Lopatkin, was now assailed as an 'individualist' who was indifferent to public life around him, and Dudintsev was criticised for failing to show the collective spirit and unity of Soviet life.[99] When Ukrainian writers met for an official discussion of the novel in Kiev that month, participants declared that Dudintsev's plot failed to reflect Soviet reality and insisted that there was no widespread stifling of creative energies 'from above'. Perhaps most succinct was the speaker who asserted that instead of the 'varnishing of reality' that had happened in literary works under Stalin, Dudintsev was now applying 'tar' to Soviet life – a practice no less dangerous.[100]

When several hundred Leningrad students tried to hold a public meeting at Arts Square in the city to discuss the Picasso exhibition, they were forcibly dispersed by police. When they nonetheless held an unsanctioned meeting elsewhere in the city, participants soon raised inflammatory remarks, disavowing regime control over art and condemning collectivisation, before police forced their way in and made a number of arrests. By the end of December, a Writers' Union meeting saw some conservatives brand *Novy mir* a Trotskyite journal and dub Paustovsky a counter-revolutionary for his remarks about 'Drozdovs'. Such foreboding rhetoric still met with a determined response, though, when the novelist Konstantin Fedin shot back that 'to educate writers by the cudgel is forbidden'.[101]

The story of 1956, then, is not simply one of liberalisation flowing from the exposure of (some of) Stalin's crimes: it is also one of contestation, uncertainty and alarm. As the next chapter shows, by the end of the year, events in neighbouring Hungary would also change the political tone quite sharply inside the Soviet Union. Nonetheless, the Secret Speech, in particular, left an indelible mark both at home and abroad, facilitating unprecedented fractures in the global workers' movement and effectively making impossible – or at least deeply unpalatable – the idea of any full rehabilitation of Stalin further down the line. It had also helped to make visible a political fissure that had largely remained submerged or unarticulated until this point: that of pro- and anti-Stalin currents within the party, both at the top and at the grassroots level.

4

CRISES, CHALLENGES AND TRIUMPHS: 1957

The Secret Speech has always played a major role in the way that commentators have understood the Khrushchev era; but the following year did at least as much to define the post-Stalin years. Events in Poland and Hungary told of limits to reform and of a changing Soviet relationship with Eastern Europe. Most of Stalin's remaining lieutenants exited the political stage. Social ferment inside the USSR showed a rejuvenated but febrile communist idealism, while regime responses to that turmoil spoke of attitudes and practices in some ways consistent with 'the old days' and in other ways fundamentally new. Two key social themes that characterised the post-Stalin years also gained powerful new impetus: a massive housing programme that improved the daily lives of millions of citizens got under way, and an unprecedented influx of foreigners arrived in the country for the 1957 youth festival, driving rapidly expanding interest in and interaction with the outside world.

Poland and Hungary

As with the mass protests that hit East Germany in June 1953, the crises in Poland and Hungary in 1956 had several root causes. What they had in common, though, was frustration at low living standards, anger at overt Soviet interference in local affairs and painful scars from the enforced 'Stalinisation' of the late 1940s and early 1950s. In Hungary, the situation was complicated further by a burgeoning power struggle at the top of the regime, between Stalinist party boss Mátyás Rákosi and reformist Prime Minister Imre Nagy (with whom the Soviet leaders had ordered him to share power). Thanks in part to the scare provided by the 1953 disorders in East Germany, Soviet plans for

111

more wide-ranging reform in the region were soon watered down and the Stalinist Rákosi managed steadily to win back his former good standing in Moscow.[1] Within a couple of years, he had successfully sidelined Nagy, seemingly killing reformist hopes in Hungary. Once news of the Secret Speech began to reverberate across the socialist bloc, though, the situation changed again.

Naturally, discussion of Stalinist repression inside the USSR soon transposed into questions about Stalinist repressions elsewhere. Rákosi's previous glorying in his role as Stalin's loyal Hungarian apprentice now looked deeply problematic. As spring turned into summer 1956, growing sections of both his own ruling party and the wider Hungarian public were openly turning against him. Soviet embassy officials in Budapest were, by the start of July 1956, reporting to Moscow their growing concerns about meetings of the communist youth group the Petőfi Circle in particular, whose members were calling for punishment of those responsible for recent repressions. Mikoyan was sent to Budapest to see things for himself. He came back warning that Rákosi's position was eroding rapidly and insisting that all kinds of 'enemy activity' were going on without any proper response, while the Hungarian regime stood bitterly divided. In mid-July, the Soviet leadership pressured Rákosi to step down entirely. However, while the popular mood in Budapest was calling for a return of the reformist Nagy, Moscow opted instead to back Ernő Gerő, whose personal and political ties to Rákosi ensured that few in Hungary greeted the change with jubilation.

At the height of summer 1956, the situation in Poland then surged to the forefront of the Soviet leaders' attention. Like the USSR, Poland had seen clear elements of 'thaw' following Stalin's death, with repression easing and many prisoners being released. After the Secret Speech, questions about past repressions and other crimes were, for weeks, the subject of lively debate across the country. This unsettled political climate then collided with escalating economic problems . In the end, on 28 June, when a demonstration of about 100,000 finally people broke out in Poznań, with protesters calling for both political reform and improvements to living standards. The crowd on the street soon turned violent, tearing down symbols of communist power and attacking the city's party headquarters. The Polish authorities responded with force, and subsequent clashes left over seventy protesters dead and many more wounded, ultimately making the situation across the country much more volatile.

What most Poles now demanded was to see the return to power of Władysław Gomułka, a former party leader who had fallen victim to Stalinist purging in 1948. He was widely perceived to be a reformist and a patriot keen to pursue a 'Polish' path to socialism. Pro-Gomułka rallies began to take place in a number of cities. Soviet leaders were far less convinced about Gomułka, though, viewing him as rather too independent-minded and perhaps not wholly trustworthy. In mid-October, the Polish leadership was on the verge of installing Gomułka in power without prior agreement from Moscow, prompting an infuriated Khrushchev to threaten direct Soviet intervention to bring the rebellious Poles to heel. Then, on 19 October, Khrushchev arrived unexpectedly in Warsaw with Molotov, Mikoyan and Kaganovich, shaking his fist and bellowing about treason, even as the Soviet and Polish delegations met at the airport. Gomułka worked determinedly to convince Khrushchev that Soviet military action would prove disastrous and that his own reform plans posed no threat to Soviet interests. Having eventually been persuaded that the situation remained under Gomułka's control, and that Gomułka was loyal to Moscow, on 21 October the Soviet delegation agreed to support him, and even acceded to his proposals for a reduction in the extent of overt Soviet influence inside Poland. This looked like a major Polish victory, and it would certainly have been unthinkable under Stalin.

By then, though, the situation in Hungary had grown more dangerous, partly under the influence of events in Poland. At the end of August, Ambassador Andropov warned Moscow of emboldened reactionary elements on the streets of Budapest, raising the spectre of outside powers attempting to destabilise Hungary and the wider socialist camp. Andropov then reported to Moscow on 10 October that oppositionists had grown 'especially arrogant', adding that sources within the Hungarian military indicated an 'unhealthy mood' taking hold there, too.[2] The point at which swelling unrest morphed into outright revolution was reached when hundreds of thousands took to the streets of Budapest on 23 October. Some protesters voiced demands broadly in line with notions of reform communism – greater press freedom, the reinstatement of Imre Nagy and punishment for Rákosi; but there were additional calls for the withdrawal from Hungary of all Soviet influence. That night, the city's giant Stalin monument was torn from its pedestal, while surging crowds occupied telephone exchanges and arms depots.

In Moscow, Presidium members soon decided that Nagy should be restored to power, in order to help defuse the situation, and that Soviet troops already based inside Hungary should be deployed to restore order. By about 02:00 on 24 October, those troops were entering Budapest. In the Kremlin, they were convinced that events in Hungary represented the start of a concerted Western drive to undermine the socialist camp. Even two decades later, the KGB's own reading of events was unambiguous on this issue, stating bluntly that 'in 1956 NATO organised a counter-revolutionary rising in Hungary'.[3] US President Eisenhower's rhetoric on 'rolling back communism' and continual rumours of massive US spending on subversive activity in the region doubtless made it easy for Soviet leaders to reach such a conclusion. Khrushchev felt he could not afford to look weak, either to his country's enemies or to his own rivals in the Soviet leadership. He also believed that 'losing' Hungary could prove the beginning of the end for Soviet power and influence across the region. Hardliners in the Soviet leadership and allied party bosses in the likes of Romania and East Germany pushed him to act decisively, lest events in Hungary spill over its borders.

Bolstered by mass defections of troops from the regular army, the Hungarian rebels proved organised, determined and skilled opponents on their own territory, and Soviet forces struggled to impose themselves during the brutal street fighting that followed.[4] For a short while on 25 October, it seemed that calm might be established; but the situation deteriorated rapidly once firing broke out in the midst of a peaceful demonstration at Kossuth Square that afternoon. Hungarian sources point to the shooting coming from Soviet troops, while the Soviet troops in turn blamed Hungarian protesters. Whoever started the shooting, it left perhaps a hundred locals dead, and soon all of Hungary was consumed with fighting. The CIA-funded Radio Free Europe stoked the flames, broadcasting encouragement to the rebels, offering advice on methods of guerrilla struggle and inciting anti-communist sentiment.

Once they agreed to reinstall Nagy in power, the Soviet side hoped and expected that he would quickly bring the situation back under control. Confident that Nagy was 'their' man (not least because he had spent many years in Moscow), the Soviet leadership was prepared to grant him considerable leeway to achieve this. Trying (but failing) to serve both his patrons in the Kremlin and his public in Hungary, as October drew to a close, Nagy made ever greater concessions to the protesters: one-party rule was to be abolished, as was censorship; political prisoners were to be released; and key hardline officials were to be removed. The situation still did not stabilise, though. Khrushchev vacillated, torn between a wish to avoid mass blood-shed and global opprobrium, and fear of the consequences for the whole socialist bloc if events in Hungary continued.[5]

The moderate course initially won the day. On the evening of 29 October, Soviet leaders agreed to a ceasefire and their troops started to pull back from Budapest. Even so, the men in the Kremlin were deeply frustrated that Nagy was still giving ground to the protesters, without any notable restoration of control. Indeed, in towns and villages all over Hungary, the rebels seemed to be entrenching their power ever more firmly. On 31 October, *Pravda* announced that the Soviet leadership officially recognised both the sovereignty and equality of all countries of the socialist camp, and the inad-missibility of any kind of unwanted intervention. This looked a lot like a Hungarian victory; but by the time it was published, the decree was already obsolete and Khrushchev had decided to send in the troops again.

When Nagy learned of fresh Soviet troop movements inside Hungary, he went fully over to the side of the rebels, renouncing Hungary's membership of the Warsaw Pact and calling on the UN to help protect against Soviet aggression. With official negotiations about the Soviet military withdrawal still in progress, on the evening of 3 November KGB Chairman Serov and his team struck the first blow by arresting their Hungarian negotiating partners, including the minister of defence and his chief of staff. A devastating military assault named Operation Whirlwind then began at 04:15 on 4 November. The Hungarian rebels had done all they could to prepare – including planting mines and acquiring anti-tank weaponry – but the invaders had also taken advantage of the intervening period to resupply and draw up new plans, and they were now better prepared in all senses.

Around 150,000 Soviet troops attacked in a coordinated movement, quickly getting on top of the rebels. Fighting in Budapest lasted for almost a week before all the main strongholds were destroyed; but it was not until the end of November that all the remaining pockets of resistance in villages and forests were decisively quashed. The figures are naturally subject to debate, but most sources suggest somewhere in the region of 2,700 Hungarian dead, with up to 500 more subsequently executed for their part in the rising, and more than 20,000 jailed afterwards. On the Soviet side, 640 troops were killed, with a further 1,251 wounded and another 67 who disappeared without trace.[6] Imre Nagy and his closest associates sought asylum in Budapest's Yugoslav embassy, but with Romanian help they were lured out and arrested after only a couple of weeks. Nagy was then spirited out of the country, put on trial and, after refusing to declare his support for the new regime in Hungary, executed for treason.

Almost everywhere abroad, public opinion was hostile towards Khrushchev and the USSR following the invasion. In Western Europe especially, allied communist parties in the likes of Britain, France and Italy saw their members walk away in droves out of disgust. Warming diplomatic relations and cultural interactions also took a major hit, though British, French and Israeli attack on Egypt in the Suez Crisis – which ran almost concurrently with Hungarian events – ensured that the global political agenda was not fixed on Soviet aggression for very long.

Echoes of the Hungarian revolution

To the extent that we can say anything much about what 'the people' felt on any given issue in the USSR, it seems clear that many accepted the official narratives on 'counter-revolution' in Hungary and supported the invasion with conviction. Some were uncomfortable at Soviet violence in Hungary, but ultimately felt that any threat to the survival of the socialist camp simply had to be defeated.[7] Many also felt that Hungary was in no position to make demands, or else that the price paid for Soviet victory during the war had been too high to let it go now. It was, after all, barely a decade since Hungary had been a staunch Nazi ally, and a great many Soviet troops had perished in fighting there. Playing to such sentiments, *Pravda* described the desecration of Soviet war graves and instances of communists being hunted down and beaten to death 'by Gestapo methods', hanged from lamp-posts and dragged from hospital to be strung up by their feet and killed.

Soviet citizens who actually protested over the invasion of Hungary were definitely in a minority, but their behaviour was nonetheless noteworthy. In fact, they illustrated a great deal about what the year 1956 had signified inside the USSR. Not quite twenty years of age at that point, Veniamin Iofe later wrote that the Twentieth Party Congress had offered a basis for hope that socialism and the Soviet regime could develop in a more liberal direction. The invasion of Hungary that same autumn, he added, had a sobering effect.[8] In other words, it was in many cases precisely those to whom the Twentieth Congress had given a renewed sense of optimism and purpose about the Soviet project who felt at best deflated or at worst betrayed by the invasion. Lev Krasnopevtsev later recalled that 'the suppression of the Hungarian rising made it absolutely clear that any rehabilitation of Leninist Party norms meant tanks and machine guns, gallows and shootings'.[9]

KGB reports in late 1956 indicated a substantial growth in what they termed 'anti-Soviet phenomena' inside the USSR. Students, in particular, tended to be at the forefront of such activity. By autumn 1956, classrooms and dormitories had for months been abuzz with debates about reinvigorating the Soviet system in accordance with the promised 'return to Leninism'. Some now picked out Yugoslavia as the model to emulate, admiring Tito especially for his more humane approach and refusal to bow down to Stalin.[10] Valery Ronkin, who was still a dedicated Komsomol member at this point, recalled of his group of friends that 'we decided that if there was a revolution in Hungary, that was a good thing, because Stalinists were the counter-revolutionaries'.[11] Cities, including Leningrad, Kiev and Moscow, also saw instances of Polish and Hungarian students joining together to 'educate' their hosts about the true events taking place back home. KGB records show that a crowd of over a hundred gathered around a Pole named Stefan Trojanowski in Moscow as he denounced the invasion of Hungary and the lies printed in the Soviet media about Poland.[12] Foreign radio stations like the BBC and Radio Liberty were also broadcasting a very different version of Hungarian events from that put forward by Soviet officialdom, and students were in some places open in stating that the Soviet media were hiding the truth.[13]

There were demonstrations of varying sizes at universities in Leningrad, Sverdlovsk (Ekaterinburg), Gorky (Nizhny Novgorod), Kuibyshev (Samara) and elsewhere, with riot police drafted in to disperse protesters in Yaroslavl. There the annual 7 November parade to mark the Bolshevik revolution was disrupted by a youth with a banner calling for the withdrawal of Soviet troops from Hungary.[14] In the Philology Faculty of Moscow State University, a group calling itself *sensus* (Latin for 'sense') distributed leaflets around university buildings and on buses to protest the invasion.[15] The militia in Leningrad reported finding leaflets on the walls of the city's Geophysics Research Institute calling on students to mount an uprising; soon after leaflets were also uncovered in Tuva, urging students to 'start an uprising like the one in Hungary'. During a social event at Moscow's State Historical Archive Institute, several students raised toasts to the Polish uprising, the Hungarian revolution and 'the impending fourth Russian revolution'.[16]

Perhaps the most striking about protest activity inside the USSR around the time of the Hungarian rising was the proliferation of underground groups. Although a particularly risky form of dissenting behaviour (since it was so clearly subversive), many of these groups were not just ideologically rooted in communism, but inspired by the regime's own propaganda about both the heroic deeds of the pre-revolutionary Bolshevik underground and the legendary partisan bands during the war. Accordingly, some who now ventured into underground activity (plenty of whom were Komsomol or Communist Party members) fancied themselves as the true continuers of heroic Soviet traditions, as neo-Bolsheviks. The Yugoslav politician and thinker Milovan Djilas's work *The New Class* gained much traction in some quarters, embracing as it did the communist cause, but lambasting the way in which bureaucrats and elites had corrupted the system for their own ends. Valery Ronkin recalled concluding that the USSR was neither socialist nor communist, but a dictatorship of bureaucrats, whose privileges were an affront to the revolution.[17] With some considerable justification, the historian Vladimir Kozlov has written of this as 'probably the last burst of revolutionary idealism in Russia', energised by both the promise of a 'return to Leninism' and the apparent betrayal of that promise in Hungary.[18]

Sometimes underground groups adopted fiery rhetoric about launching uprisings and revolution. Their actual deeds were usually far more limited, however, not least since most were quickly uncovered by the KGB. Many of the participants studied and debated afresh the history of the revolution, of Bolshevism, Lenin and the world communist movement. A Leningrad group formed around Revolt Pimenov and Boris Vail. The pair recruited several of Vail's student friends and Pimenov's common-law wife, held discussion meetings and put together a compendium of officially censored information about events inside the USSR. They also produced several political tracts on the country's past and present, asserting that the Soviet system was no longer a dictatorship of the proletariat, but a dictatorship of the Communist Party, reliant on terror in all spheres of life.[19] Like other groups, though, their impact on wider society can hardly be described as significant. Pimenov conceded years later that in essence they 'boiled with desire for action . . . but did not know how best to act'.[20]

The unsettled situation around late 1956 and early 1957 was perhaps most acute in the far west of the country. In Moldavia, rumours of coming war with the West led to people panic-buying in shops and prompted some Komsomol members to throw away their membership cards, so as not to be caught with them by some invading power.[21] By October 1956, Ukrainian officials had already registered the return to the republic of almost 45,000 people previously jailed for nationalist activity. Local authorities' concerns about these returnees were seemingly supported by the fact that thirty-nine attacks and murders of officials had already taken place during 1955–56, while multiple caches of illegal weapons had also been discovered.[22] On 3 November, KGB chief Serov warned party bosses of danger in the Baltics and Ukraine, especially among returned prisoners, and claimed that the situation was sufficiently pressing for the KGB to consider sending mobile detachments to the region.[23] At the start of December, the Soviet minister of internal affairs also reported on a significant growth in anti-Soviet phenomena in Ukraine's Transcarpathian oblast (which bordered Hungary and featured a sizeable Hungarian minority), including threats of violence against communists, and against Russians in particular.[24] In Estonia, university students demanded an end to teaching carried out in the Russian language and made clear their support for the Hungarian and Polish causes with toasts, banners and songs.[25] In the Lithuanian city of Kaunas, perhaps 40,000 young people congregated in cemeteries to mark All Souls' Day in November 1956, before taking to city centre streets that evening, flying the old Lithuanian tricolour, singing the country's independence-era anthem, calling for an end to compulsory study of the Russian language, expressing their support for the Hungarian uprising and ultimately attacking shops and Communist Party buildings.

A new clampdown

A junior KGB officer at the time, Filipp Bobkov recalled that the security organs came under growing pressure from party officials for not taking decisive measures against student protests at Moscow State University during the autumn of 1956.[26] November and December also saw a flurry of articles in the press angrily denouncing students' supposedly 'bourgeois' and 'undisciplined' behaviour. Komsomol bosses sent political agitators and war veterans to give talks in classrooms and dorms. Directors of universities and other education institutes were given new powers to expel troublesome students and to withhold stipends from those involved in protests.[27] There were also moves to ease some less overtly political sources of friction, such as increasing stipends, improving dilapidated study facilities, reducing students' workloads and removing some of the most hated faculty members.[28]

After Khrushchev had so recently railed against Stalinist abuses, however, there was some considerable uncertainty at all levels about how to respond to the tumult. On 6 December 1956, Presidium members formally discussed the question of what to do about the rising tide of dissent. They decided to put together a commission to produce a letter to be sent out to all party branches offering directions on tackling what they now called 'hostile attacks'. After some considerable editing (a first draft was deemed too hardline), by 19 December a text establishing a new and definitive position had been approved by Presidium members and was sent out to party organisations, courts, security organs and police throughout the USSR. Internal KGB documents later spoke of the importance of this letter in prompting a 'merciless struggle' against enemy elements inside the country.[29] Indeed, up to the end of 1956, convictions for political crimes had been dwindling since Stalin's death; but the eighteen months that now followed saw a more than five-fold rise in the number of people sentenced for counter-revolutionary activity.

The letter in question explicitly linked the 'present harmful atmosphere' in the country with Western attempts to subvert the socialist camp, and insisted that opponents were trying to hijack the struggle with the cult of personality for their own hostile purposes. Drawing particular attention to the so-called 'neo-Bolsheviks', the letter warned that such people must not be mistaken for allies. To avoid any ambiguity, it concluded by asserting that 'in the struggle with anti-Soviet elements we must be strong and unrelenting', adding that it was the duty of every single communist to fight actively in defence of the party line. On seeing the letter at a party meeting in Ukraine, an outraged collective farm chairman, A.I. Zemsha, declared that the CPSU was 'no longer a party of communists but one of fascists' (for which outburst he was subsequently jailed).[30] More succinctly, a party member in Kirov oblast summed up the new situation by noting that 'we are now being told either to shut up or face jail'.[31] One noted expert has written of the events which followed that 'the call was heard. All the links of the Party and state apparatus began to move and to respond, just like in the old days'.[32]

The clampdown that followed was, by some considerable margin, the most aggressive of the post-Stalin years in terms of arrests and convictions for political offences – a point that sits awkwardly with traditional notions of the Khrushchev era as a time of liberalisation – but it was not really like 'the old days'. In the first instance, the number of victims was still of a different order entirely to that of the Stalin era. After dropping to fewer than 400 in 1956, annual convictions for anti-Soviet activity hit a total of 1,964 during 1957.[33] The comparable figure from two decades earlier was in excess of 900,000, with several hundred thousand of those people executed. In 1957, a little over half of all those jailed for anti-Soviet activity received sentences of up to five years; less than 2 per cent were jailed for ten years or more; and nobody was executed.[34]

Similarly, an unknown (but unquestionably massive) number of those arrested in Stalin's terror were victims of wholly fabricated conspiracies, invented to fulfil demand from above for convictions. There is little sign that such fabrications were a major feature of the 1957–58 clampdown. Doubtless, many of the convictions came at the end of deeply unfair investigations and biased trials, and many of those jailed for anti-Soviet activity did not see themselves as enemies of Soviet power; but the convictions were seemingly rooted in concrete events that had actually happened, rather than in invented conspiracies. Even so, in the provinces especially, local officials took the clampdown as a chance to demonstrate both their dedication and their usefulness, and were duly prepared to find anti-Soviet activity almost anywhere.[35] This was the key continuity with Stalin-era justice: knowing that they were expected to act on these latest directives from above, officials took the behaviour of citizens – behaviour which at any other time might have been either ignored entirely or else classified as some less serious offence – and 'fitted' it into the campaign of the day, to be punished as 'anti-Soviet'.

Most of the sentences handed down for anti-Soviet activity were for isolated outbursts, rather than persistent and planned acts of protest and dissent.[36] Quite often these involved drunken confrontations between members of the public and the police (such as calling members of the militia 'fascists') or crude jokes and abusive remarks aimed at Khrushchev, in particular. In Rostov, for example, an electrician was jailed after turning up to work drunk and declaring that communists were corrupt and should be 'strung up and shot, like in Hungary'. In Astrakhan, an invalid was initially apprehended by police for robbing a man who had passed out in the street, at which point he declared that Khrushchev and Bulganin were 'strangling the working class' and shouted 'Down with the Soviet Union, long live Eisenhower', and was subsequently jailed for anti-Soviet activity.[37]

Plenty of others who were convicted during the clampdown were actually already in prison. In many cases, these were criminals acting on the mistaken assumption that being reclassified as a 'political' prisoner would see their living conditions improve. They thus drew swastikas on walls and etched their bodies with politically offensive tattoos, such as 'Slave of the CPSU' and 'Lenin's whore'. For this they received the desired reclassification as political, but not the anticipated benefits.[38]

When it eventually came, the end of the crackdown was also indicative of post-Stalin change. Legal officials, from both the Procurator's Office and the Supreme Court, had already begun to express concerns about the legality of the clampdown during 1957, and in early 1958 they produced a confidential evaluation of some recent cases.[39] This concluded that many of the people being convicted as anti-Soviet should be dealt with in some more suitable manner, since there was little to no evidence that they actually were opposed to Soviet power. A summer 1958 review then added that complaints about shortages of goods and about personal problems, drunken cursing and jokes about political leaders should not necessarily be considered anti-Soviet, if they betrayed no real sign of political hostility. The ultimate directive from the Supreme Court was for officials in the legal system to take greater care before deciding whether a citizen was 'genuinely anti-Soviet', rather than simply someone who had 'a faulty attitude towards certain events or policies'.[40] This decision would be significant for two principal reasons. First, it showed that while the results to date were far from perfect, the discourse on re-establishing socialist legality and preventing a return to Stalinist 'excesses' had taken root to some considerable extent. Secondly, it underpinned what was to become a rather more effective approach to thinking about and tackling manifestations of discontent among the public throughout the late Soviet period.

The Anti-Party Affair

Events in Hungary did not do Khrushchev's standing any good among his colleagues, most of whom felt he was largely to blame for the unrest. But even before 1956 drew to a close, he had clearly emerged as the dominant member of the Soviet political elite. However, he was still surrounded at the very top by powerful rivals, and relations within the Presidium were becoming increasingly fractious. The breaking point came in June 1957. Known subsequently as the 'Anti-Party Affair', this attempt by Molotov, Malenkov and others to have Khrushchev removed from office very nearly succeeded – and it would undoubtedly have changed the path of Soviet history substantially if it had. But its ultimate failure instead marked a decisive end for the collective leadership.

Although the 1957 coup attempt has generally been understood as one in which the leadership's Stalinists flailed against Khrushchev's liberalising reform, that was by no means the full picture. Whether or not it was because of the events in Hungary, there was little question that Khrushchev's political positions were again stiffening by late 1956. Most infamously, he gave a speech at the Chinese embassy in Moscow during January 1957 in which he declared 'being a communist is inseparable from being a Stalinist' and added 'may God grant that every communist will be able to fight for the interest of the working class as Stalin fought'.[41] Not unreasonably, one citizen from Tuapse wrote to the Central Committee sarcastically noting that there now seemed to be two Khrushchevs – 'one who defends Stalin and one who attacks him'. The correspondent added that his speeches were both 'causing disorder in our minds' and raising doubt that the consequences of the cult would be overcome.[42]

123

Conservative voices in the cultural sphere were also asserting themselves more forcefully by the end of 1956, with Vsevolod Kochetov, the editor of the *Literaturnaya gazeta*, declaring that control over literary affairs was slipping from the party's hands, as liberal writers sought to create their own version of Hungary's Petőfi Circle.[43] After swingeing changes to its editorial board – a direct consequence of its 'vilification of Stalin' – the journal *Voprosy istorii* recanted some of its criticisms as ideologically improper.[44] Although only founded in November 1956, the liberal-minded journal *Literaturnaya Moskva* (*Literary Moscow*) was shut down after its second issue, with Khrushchev condemning its content on ideological grounds and viciously attacking its editorial board (despite clearly never having read the publication).[45] When, soon after, he encountered one of the defunct journal's editors the poet Margarita Aliger, Khrushchev threatened to 'grind her into dust'.[46]

Khrushchev was clearly not always an easy person for other members of the leadership to work alongside, and this trait became more pronounced as his power increased. Mikoyan, for example, later wrote that both Malenkov and Bulganin participated in the 1957 plot not because they were opposed to reform, but primarily because of growing personal animosity towards Khrushchev.[47] The British ambassador, William Hayter, recalled a visit to a Moscow air show in June 1956 at which Khrushchev became increasingly drunk and verbally aggressive in front of both Soviet and foreign visitors. He openly berated the equally drunk Bulganin and insulted 'literally every country in the world', as Molotov, Malenkov and Kaganovich all looked on 'pursing their lips and drumming their fingers on the arms of their chairs', before they eventually managed to bring proceedings to a close and usher him away.[48]

The first half of 1957 saw tensions within the Presidium growing steadily more acute. In February, Khrushchev began pushing a major economic reform, which aimed to drastically reduce the power of big government ministries in Moscow and to devolve their functions to more than a hundred new regional economic councils (to be called *sovnarkhozy*) in the non-Russian republics and Russian regions. Molotov and Kaganovich objected vigorously – partly on ideological grounds, but also simply because the idea was poorly conceived and was rushed through without careful planning.

On 22 May, Khrushchev brought his colleagues to fury again with a speech in Leningrad in which he impetuously declared that the USSR would overtake the USA in per capita output of meat, milk and butter by 1960. This was well beyond the realms of the possible, and when Molotov subsequently declared as much in a Presidium meeting (armed with a battery of figures to prove it), Khrushchev laid into him. He then repeated the same claim in a subsequent interview for an American news channel.[49]

Personal relations within the Presidium were becoming so strained that almost any single issue could have triggered confrontation.[50] Secret discussions about removing Khrushchev got under way in May 1957 and gained fresh impetus at the start of June, when he and Bulganin left the country on an official visit to Finland (during the course of which Khrushchev took a sauna with Finnish President Urho Kekkonen, provoking some controversy over the appropriateness of his being undressed in front of a foreign head of state). Back from Helsinki and having lunch at his Moscow residence on 18 June, Khrushchev took an unexpected call from the Kremlin requesting that he head there right away for an important meeting.

As with the plot that had snared Beria four years previously, once Malenkov declared the meeting open, he promptly announced that the only item on the agenda was Khrushchev's behaviour. Malenkov accused him of breaching the principle of collective leadership and of seeking to build a 'Khrushchev cult'; attacked his fanciful promises about catching up and overtaking the US; and blamed him for creating division and rancour within the Presidium. Kaganovich decried Khrushchev's greed for power and his penchant for deciding important matters all on his own: he proposed that Khrushchev be relieved of the post of party first secretary. Molotov criticised his 'un-Leninist' political decisions and seconded Kaganovich's call for him to be removed as party boss.[51] With a total of eight Presidium members in on the plot, Khrushchev was heavily outnumbered. The plan was for Presidium members to vote in support of Kaganovich's motion to strip Khrushchev of his post, and for that decision then to be passed to the wider Central Committee for rubber-stamping.

Deeply wary of a potential return to Stalinism, Mikoyan was the only one of the former collective leadership to take Khrushchev's side from the outset. Newer Presidium members (and Khrushchev appointees) Alexei

Kirichenko and Mikhail Suslov supported Khrushchev, too, though they were still clearly outmatched. He also had valuable support among candidate members of the Presidium (who could participate in Presidium discussions, but were not allowed to vote on its decisions). Here, Leonid Brezhnev and Ekaterina Furtseva defended Khrushchev as best they were able. More importantly, both played a crucial role in hurriedly rounding up whomever they could find in Moscow to come to Khrushchev's aid in the Kremlin, most notably getting Minister of Defence Zhukov and KGB Chairman Serov involved in proceedings.[52] While not entitled to a formal vote on Presidium business, and at first seemingly uncertain which way he might lean in the dispute, Zhukov was able to give the plotters pause for thought by making it plain that he, and by extension the Soviet military under his command, did not support the effort to oust Khrushchev.

Officially at least, the Presidium's role was to conduct affairs between meetings of the full Central Committee, whose members were too numerous and spread too wide across the country to oversee day-to-day governance. In practice, key leaders in the Presidium had, for years, taken decisions among themselves and then passed them to the Central Committee for formal approval, which always came. What turned the situation in Khrushchev's favour was a procedural argument: that the removal of a party first secretary should be decided not by a vote in the Presidium, but by a vote in the full Central Committee, many of whose members were by now Khrushchev appointees and allies. Serov and Zhukov went into overdrive, using the vast resources of the KGB and the military to track down Central Committee members loyal to Khrushchev and fly them to Moscow from distant Russian regions and non-Russian republics. As the confrontation between Presidium members continued to rage behind closed doors, by 20 June almost ninety Central Committee members had arrived at the Kremlin and were demanding to have their say. Pressure for the matter to be decided by the full Central Committee, rather than the Presidium, had grown too great to resist.

The plotters lost the initiative entirely as the fight shifted onto unfamiliar and unfavourable terrain. On 22 June, the emergency Central Committee plenum opened, with 121 out of 130 full members and 94 out of 117 candidate members in attendance. Those present were all aware that Molotov and the other plotters had not wanted to consult them on this critical issue and

126

had only agreed to do so under considerable pressure. Even many of the Central Committee members who had not been appointed by Khrushchev appreciated the fact that he had consistently been willing to allocate resources beyond the capital and to meet leaders in the regions, unlike Molotov, Malenkov and Kaganovich. A last important dynamic – subtle, but not to be underestimated – was the fact that the backstage party apparatus also took Khrushchev's side, controlling key details like the running order of speakers and the provision of documents. The dice were now loaded in his favour.

The first session of the plenum was opened by Khrushchev, now serving as chair. He gave the floor to his ally Suslov, who recapped the events that had transpired so far since 18 June – a narrative that steadily morphed into stinging condemnation of Molotov, Malenkov and the other plotters. Taking the floor after Suslov's opening remarks, Zhukov spoke at length about each of the plotters' roles in mass repressions under Stalin, brandishing official records that showed Molotov and Kaganovich (alongside Stalin) sanctioning the execution of almost 40,000 military personnel, and demanding that they be made to answer for both their past abuses of power and their present anti-party actions. By the time they even got a chance to say anything at the session, the plotters had taken a sustained political battering from a procession of speakers. Just when Malenkov was finally scheduled to speak, Minister of Internal Affairs Dudorov was moved up into his slot. He provided a lengthy condemnation of Malenkov's roles in the post-war repression of fellow party elites, in particular – and especially the Leningrad Affair – telling his audience of cases where party workers were arrested even as they left Malenkov's office.[53] When Malenkov was finally given the floor, he asked to see the documents used against him by Dudorov, but was refused permission. As Malenkov spoke, Zhukov, Khrushchev and others in the audience continually interjected, mocking his claims and hurling fresh accusations.

Over four days, a total of sixty different speakers lined up to condemn the plotters for their roles in Stalinist repression, for factionalism, for opposing and obstructing reform, for being out of touch with party members and more besides. Bulganin was the first to try to distance himself from the crumbling coup attempt. When he was eventually allowed to take the floor, Molotov was, as always, combative: he refuted claims about his supposedly 'anti-Party' activity and continued to attack Khrushchev and his policies with vehemence.

As he spoke, audience members heckled and jeered, while Khrushchev repeatedly interrupted him, misrepresented his remarks and branded him a dogmatist seeking to re-establish Stalinism. After he had finished, Marshal Ivan Konev told those present how Molotov had repeatedly threatened military commanders during the war and had helped turn Stalin against Zhukov.[54]

By the time the plenum drew to a close on 28 June, the plotters had been utterly routed. Notably, though, the final resolution of the session steered clear of the explicit details of the repressions that had been weaponised and wielded so extensively at the plenum; instead, it foregrounded claims that the plotters had obstructed reform aimed at tackling the cult of personality, had engaged in dangerous factionalism and had become 'divorced from reality'. Molotov, Malenkov and Kaganovich were expelled from the Presidium and the Central Committee, and several others were formally reprimanded. Of all the participants in the plenum, including the plotters themselves, only Molotov refused to vote in support of the resolution.[55]

This enforced exodus from the Presidium meant that Khrushchev was finally able to assemble something like his own 'team' at the apex of power. As the defeated plotters departed, Brezhnev, Zhukov, Furtseva and others became full Presidium members, joining existing Khrushchev appointees and the more long-standing Mikoyan. Several others who had not yet reached the very top table – including Komsomol boss Alexander Shelepin – also saw their career trajectory climb steeply as Khrushchev rewarded their loyalty. The scale of the defeated coup attempt was such that it had to be concealed from the public, lest it give rise to tricky questions about the legitimacy of Khrushchev's victory. As such, several participants in the plot, most notably Bulganin and Voroshilov, had their involvement hushed up and were for a time allowed to remain in prominent posts. They were, though, stripped of any real authority and ultimately fired in due course. In fact, Zhukov was also to be unceremoniously dumped in autumn 1957 when Khrushchev grew suspicious that he had his own designs on power.

Although not reported in the media, the archival record makes it clear that there were at least some members of the public who utterly rejected the ensuing attacks on Molotov and the other conspirators. One anonymous author (later tracked down by the KGB) wrote to *Pravda* describing the plotters' sacking as 'disgraceful' and insisting that public sympathy was with them, rather than Khrushchev.[56] In Kuibyshev a meeting held to condemn the plotters had to be abandoned, because so many of those who spoke up supported them.[57] Numerous others expressed serious doubts that Molotov and the others – almost all of whom had been in the front rank of party officials for decades – were really enemies, and demanded that the accused men be allowed to address the Soviet public on the radio or in the press, so that the people could hear them out.[58]

If there were elements of the old Stalinist approach to political struggle in the way that the plotters were publicly traduced, the final outcome was distinctly post-Stalin. Molotov was sent to Ulan Bator as ambassador to Mongolia; Malenkov was appointed director of a power station in eastern Kazakhstan; and Kaganovich went to manage a potash plant in the Urals. Their fates would undoubtedly have been far grislier a few years previously, and in choosing not to act too vengefully at this point, Khrushchev set down a significant marker on how the Soviet political elite now conducted its internecine struggles.

For all that the defeat of the plot was presented as a victory over irredeemable Stalinists, of the new leadership team only Otto Kuusinen and Mikoyan could be described as authentically reform minded. Brezhnev and Furtseva tended to hew pretty close to whichever line the unpredictable Khrushchev took, while Frol Kozlov and Suslov, in particular, consistently exerted a strong conservative influence at the top. The fall of the Stalinist old guard, then, did not see the reformist cause sweep all before it. Anyway, even though Khrushchev was now more dominant than ever before, he still did not hold anything like the kind of prestige or unfettered power that Stalin had enjoyed, either within the party elite or beyond it. Nonetheless, when Bulganin got his delayed comeuppance for participating in the plot and was sacked as chairman of the Council of Ministers in March 1958, Khrushchev took the post for himself (after some encouragement from Brezhnev and others). In combining the roles of head of party and head of government, he broke perhaps the key principle that the collective leadership had established following Stalin's death: that no one person should again simultaneously occupy the two most powerful posts in the country.

129

New places to live

Even as the dust was still settling on the Anti-Party Affair, one of Khrushchev's most impactful undertakings as Soviet leader began in earnest. What was to prove perhaps the defining feature of the era, at least as it was experienced by many millions of ordinary Soviet citizens, started with a July 1957 decree that promised to overcome the country's terrible housing shortage within the next ten to twelve years. As ever, this promise proved hugely overambitious; but vast numbers of people were indeed soon moving out of crowded and dilapidated communal flats and barracks and into newly built single-family apartments, changing lives for the better right across the USSR.

The country's housing crisis was, in part, a result of wartime damage (in some extreme cases like the Belorussian capital Minsk, around 90 per cent of the housing stock had been destroyed), but it was also rooted in two long-standing trends in Soviet life. First, the urban population had been growing rapidly for decades – from 21.6 million in 1923 to 99.8 million in 1958 – as a continual flow of people left the countryside for the cities. Second, during the Stalin years in particular, the living conditions of ordinary Soviet citizens were simply not a high priority for the regime, when it came to investment of scarce resources. In most of the big Soviet cities, including republican capitals such as Moscow, Kiev, Minsk, Tbilisi, Alma-Ata (Almaty) and Stalinabad (Dushanbe), on average each citizen had less living space in 1956 than they had three decades previously. In many cities, that meant less than 5 square metres per person, and in some places less than 4 square metres. The scientist Yakov Alpert was hardly exaggerating when he recalled that space and privacy were the country's 'greatest scarcity and luxury'.[59]

Somewhere around half of all families in Soviet towns and cities occupied a single room or part of a room, usually sharing a bathroom and kitchen with multiple neighbours. The smells, sounds and detritus of serious human overcrowding were for many constant and harrowing features of life: one former resident of a *kommunalka* (communal flat), for example, recalled a neighbouring family of fifteen that lived in just two rooms; others remembered endless queues for the toilet or telephone, and noise of all kinds at all hours. One source described regularly hearing an alcoholic neighbour who 'beat his wife with such violence that we would plug up our ears'; and another recalled that, as a young woman on her own, she was frequently harassed by a lecherous and drunken neighbour at night.[60] Communal kitchens especially were where simmering tensions and feuds between neighbours could boil over into blazing rows (between women usually, since they were the ones who did most of the cooking), and the general lack of privacy offered fertile ground for informers and gossips. Of his own formative years spent in a Leningrad *kommunalka*, the poet Joseph Brodsky described how the forced intimacy among residents was such that 'you knew who was farting in the toilet, when all the women had their periods'; nonetheless, he added that real warmth and mutual reliance could also characterise relationships in these settings for those fortunate enough to be living among people they could trust and get along with.[61]

Anyway, the *kommunalka* was not the very worst type of accommodation. In 1957, for example, the Latvian Komsomol Central Committee reported that one of its staff members (along with his elderly parents) was occupying a room above the garage of a Riga cement factory, where the fumes were making them all seriously ill. Another was living with her two children in a damp cellar that had no natural light whatsoever.[62] When the writer Vladimir Voinovich moved to Moscow from the provinces in 1956, he initially spent nights sleeping on the platforms and concourses of the city's Kursk train station. He then took a job (as a railway worker) primarily because it came with accommodation – in a disused rail wagon: each unheated carriage was divided in half, and each half slept four people.[63]

A review into the living conditions of young workers revealed swathes of dilapidated dorms, in which sometimes hundreds of people lived without even any facilities for cleaning or cooking. One case cited was a building which provided shelter for six hundred people in a filthy and wet hall with no canteen, no cooking facilities, broken windows and no shops nearby for purchasing even basic necessities, while residents often had to sleep two to a bed.[64] Some children's homes were even worse: not only were staff found to be beating (and in some cases sexually abusing) the children, but it was also discovered that they were selling off the allotted rations for personal profit, while their negligence was allowing contagious diseases to thrive.[65] Such bleak living conditions were not unjustifiably seen as a likely breeding ground for pernicious social problems, where hard drinking, fighting, thieving, sexual promiscuity and more were liable to take hold. There was little question, then, that creating the communist man and woman of the future was, in large part, dependent on solving the country's housing crisis.

Thinking about a concerted drive to tackle the housing problem had actually begun as the war drew to a close; but citizens' wellbeing was not considered a high enough priority at that time for resources to be diverted from the new military build-up and the reconstruction of heavy industry.[66] In fact, much of the building work that had taken place in the late Stalin years centred instead on Moscow's imposing skyscrapers and neo-classical apartment blocks on grand boulevards for members of the elite.[67] With Stalin gone, Khrushchev pursued a much more egalitarian line. In December 1954, he demanded an end to the 'architectural excesses' that had characterised this late-Stalinist construction. Delegations of experts then began travelling to countries such as Britain, Sweden and Finland to study their efforts at constructing mass housing with the latest materials and methods.

From the outset, the July 1957 decree on housing construction announced that raising the people's living standards was the key goal, establishing this point as a clear regime priority. As to the question of how to make rapid prog-ress, the answer lay in prefabricated and heavily standardised apartments and apartment blocks. The decree announced a huge expansion in the production of everything – from cement and glass, through to wallpaper and bathtubs – in order to 'produce the greatest possible amount of living space in the shortest possible period' in the form of single-family apartments. The decree also made it plain that new housing was to come to rural areas, too, since Khrushchev had long been convinced that raising the woeful levels of agricultural produc-tivity demanded extensive rural modernisation – not least in the form of new housing blocks, but also by creating facilities like cinemas, libraries, bath-houses and schools.[68]

Of course, this modernisation drive demanded a vast amount of work, especially in some parts of the country. In Tajikistan, Dagestan and numerous other places, for example, there were still plenty of people living in the mountains with only limited interaction with the nearest towns and their modern cultural facilities.[69] Similarly, by the end of the 1950s still only about one in every four collective farms in the Irkutsk region was connected to electricity.[70]

Very soon, though, per capita housing construction in the USSR was far outstripping everywhere else in Europe, as teams of builders raced one another to erect block after block. Informally known as *khrushchevki* ('Khrushchev houses'), from Uzbekistan and Turkmenistan in Central Asia, to Russia's Arctic north and the westernmost parts of Ukraine, these five-storey housing blocks made from prefabricated concrete panels all looked virtually identical. It was never intended that there should be anything particularly spacious or luxurious about the new homes. Actually, one scholar has suggested that the designers deliberately kept them small, so as not to tempt unscrupulous officials to put more than one family into a new apartment.[71] Nonetheless, there was a tremendous scramble of people, as war veterans, young families, gulag returnees, skilled workers and others all desperately tried to prove that they deserved priority access to one of these flats.

New novels, plays and movies centred on optimistic families starting new and happy lives in their private apartments, with the latest appliances and furnishings serving to bring modernity into the everyday lives of citizens.[72] The great composer Dmitry Shostakovich was commissioned to write an operetta celebrating the new housing construction site in the Moscow suburb of Cheremushki, and one of the era's most famous paintings was Yuri Pimenov's *Wedding on Tomorrow Street*, depicting a just-married couple picking their way across building-site duckboards to reach their new apartment. For many Soviet families, the chance to move into their own apartment, with the security and peace that brought, was truly a dream come true. It was also vital to an emerging sense of private life, of creating spaces where families and friends could open up and relax in relative comfort, escaping from the world beyond their front door, increasingly eschewing the collective activity and experience on which communism was supposed to be built. Previously a notorious battleground in the *kommunalka*, the kitchen now became a place where friends and family could gather to debate, rant, sing and joke to their hearts' content about politics, culture and daily life, in a way that few would have dared previously.

Among those lucky ones who did move into a new home, things did not always go smoothly, however. For some people, another nickname for these new apartment blocks emerged. A sardonic twist on *khrushchevki*, the punning *khrushcheby* was rooted in the Russian word for slums (*trushcheby*):

this made the new flats not 'Khrushchev houses' but 'Khrushchev slums'. Vital construction materials such as concrete and glass often varied greatly in quality and would sometimes fail within months. The wildly ambitious promise to fix the country's housing shortage in only a few years also under-pinned crucial failings.[73] The temptation to cut corners in order to meet demanding plan targets was simply too great, as both builders and building inspectors were pushed into signing off new blocks as satisfactory and complete before they actually were: new residents were sometimes left with windows that did not close, wires that were exposed and wallpaper that was already peeling when they moved in. Similarly, measuring success in terms of living space erected meant that key infrastructure – like roads, paths or public transport links – could be overlooked, since it did not contribute to plan fulfilment. New blocks could be left without any connections to power or water supplies, and standing in a sea of mud.[74] The new consumer goods with which people filled their apartments (or at least tried to) were sometimes little better in terms of quality. In 1961, for example, a quarter of all refrigerators produced at one Leningrad factory broke down within a month.[75]

The massive housing campaign clearly helped to start solving one of the country's most pressing social problems, but it was not without significant socio-political legacies in the longer term. Once told they had a right to an apartment, people expected that right to be fulfilled; but for all that Khrushchev, and later also Brezhnev, invested considerable resources in improving the situation, the shortage of housing was an issue that continued to plague the Soviet regime to its very end.[76] The average amount of living space never came close to the recommended minimum of 9 square metres per person; and it was far more likely that a newly married couple would live for months (or years) with one set of parents, than that they would be allocated a new apartment straight away. Nonetheless, the sheer number of Soviet citizens who moved into the new single-family apartments during this period (possibly as many as 70 million by the mid-1960s) probably has to be the yardstick of success. One Muscovite who did just that in the mid-1960s later stated simply: 'All my life I will be thankful to Khrushchev for understanding that communal apartments had to end.'[77]

It was not just housing that was being built. After years in which the central authorities had been deeply reluctant to allocate any money at all to the provinces for 'non-productive infrastructure', that picture also began to change, as investment in sports and cultural facilities expanded rapidly. The Russian city of Kazan, for example, gained a new opera house in 1956, and would soon also boast new cinemas, swimming pools, a sports stadium, art gallery, a circus, television centre and more.[78] In the south, holiday resorts and sanatoria for the masses (rather than just the elite) were being expanded or built from scratch.[79] In the Arctic north, new homes and boarding schools, as well as roads, power stations and telephone connections, were being built for the indigenous peoples there.[80] Similarly, data from Magadan show spending on health infrastructure in the region trebling from 1953 to 1959, with the number of hospitals almost doubling and new centres being established for the treatment of tuberculosis, cancer and venereal disease, and for psychiatry and paediatrics.[81]

There was also growth in previously neglected facilities, such as residential homes for citizens with disabilities. The authorities presented this as evidence of Soviet humanitarianism, though it could also result in those people ending up even more isolated from society and wholly reliant on welfare.[82] In Moscow, there were new boarding schools for deaf children, as well as a deaf theatre with a café and a library. Efforts were made to add subtitles to films and to create new employment opportunities for deaf people.[83] Children's summer camps were extended or built from scratch as never before, as were new schools and clubs in rural areas. In June 1962, a massive new central Pioneer Palace was opened in Moscow, with a library, swimming pools, a theatre, laboratories, a performance stage and more – all available for use by the city's children free of charge.

From about the mid-1950s, real effort was also being put into the provision of recreation opportunities for young people, to help prevent them from being lured in other, politically and socially 'inappropriate', directions. Huge numbers thus participated eagerly in everything from photography clubs and choirs to dance troupes and ham radio societies and more.[84] Perhaps most notable in this respect was the introduction of youth cafés around the start of the 1960s. These served as places where young people could socialise and as venues for talks, performances, movie screenings and concerts. The most popular events at the new youth cafés frequently had queues around the block, and the trendiest of them quickly became real social and cultural hubs. The Sinyaya ptitsa (Blue bird) café became an unofficial jazz venue, with nightly jam sessions that attracted all manner of Soviet celebrities.[85] The Molodezhnoe (Youth) in central Moscow also became tremendously popular and was regularly presented to foreign visitors as a showpiece of the good life on offer for young people in the USSR. One of those who played there regularly with his jazz ensemble, the saxophonist Alexei Kozlov, wrote years later of how he remembered 'an atmosphere of elation, lightness and freedom' in the very walls of the place.[86]

New things to buy and do

In his fanciful promises to catch up and overtake the US economically, Khrushchev had made it plain that the Cold War rivalry was not just about military prowess, but also about goods and living standards. As one expert has argued, the Khrushchev regime 'staked its legitimacy at home and its credibility abroad on consumption'.[87] Fighting on what was essentially the Americans' own turf, though, would prove deeply problematic. Put simply, neither the Soviet Union's economy – which remained fundamentally unreformed since Stalin's death – nor its political system offered any real chance of competing with the West in this field.

Most notably, the Soviet economy was absolutely shot through with a multitude of inefficiencies that proved virtually impervious to reform. The central planning process, which calculated how much of what items needed to be produced by industry, was hugely cumbersome and clumsy. At the factory level, managers frequently resisted changes (such as the introduction of new product lines) that might make it harder for them to meet their targets or that could cause those targets to be raised further down the line (such as if new machinery was introduced to increase productivity). Regular delays in receiving orders from above and components from other factories meant that workers and machines were frequently idle for long spells. Then, around the end of the month, the quarter or the year, they made up for lost time by 'storming': a frantic rush to meet production targets, with workers sometimes barely leaving the factory for days on end. Of course, this was bad for worker morale, for factory machinery and for the quality of the items produced. The reliance on 'storming' also meant that managers routinely hoarded more labour and resources than they actually needed for efficient working, in order to make swifter progress once the pressure was on for quick results.[88] This overmanning also fed into a much wider shortage of workers, which hampered economic growth and contributed to poor labour discipline: some employees would frequently start late, leave early, arrive hungover, drink at work and take unsanctioned breaks to run personal errands. Managers were generally loath to fire even the least productive staff, lest they be needed for 'storming' further down the line.

Inefficiency in the rural economy could be even more severe. First, it was especially hard to attract qualified people from the cities to the countryside. New graduates, in particular, strongly resisted rural assignments, and some-times simply failed to turn up. Corrupt and tyrannical collective farm bosses, often imposed from outside, were a widespread source of resentment. Collective farm members privileged cultivation of their own private plots over other duties (a problem that led to the imposition of hugely unpopular restrictions on the size of such plots in 1955) and theft of farm property and produce was rife. Regime attempts at driving agricultural modernisation repeatedly foundered when they encountered the realities of rural life and labour. In Tajikistan, for example, bids to mechanise cotton production collided with the fact that farm bosses were reluctant to expend their meagre budgets on expensive new equipment, which often broke down and was difficult to repair (spare parts being scarce). In order to be sure of meeting demanding plan targets, then, they often stuck with the tried-and-tested method of drawing on the cheapest labour available: women and children. Despite endless regime boasts about mechanisation opening the way to the future, even in the mid-1960s a mere 14 per cent of all cotton grown in Tajikistan was harvested mechanically.[89]

Factories and farms were not the only weak links in the attempt to satisfy Soviet consumers. The number of people working in the retail sector almost doubled between 1959 and 1970 (from 1.1 million to 2.1 million), but economic managers had only a limited understanding of what customers actu-ally wanted or when they wanted it. The result was warehouses full of unsold goods, and citizens who preferred to save rather than spend their money (the amount of cash held in savings accounts more than quadrupled between 1958 and 1965, and then doubled again between 1965 and 1968).[90] In so doing, they held back economic growth.[91] Customer service remained notoriously surly and unhelpful – and was consistently mocked in satirical publications like *Krokodil* (*Crocodile*) – despite continual attempts to bring about cultural change. This was in large part because work in this sector, which had a heavily feminised labour force, was often badly paid. Employees tended to have limited education or training, and their labour was commonly denigrated as 'not real work', since jobs in the service sector were viewed as somehow inferior or undignified (though in time, retail work would become much more desirable, thanks largely to the enhanced access to goods that it could provide).[92]

All the above notwithstanding, living standards certainly did start to rise appreciably for most. This rise brought social stability, especially once mass terror had been eschewed; but it also drove types of behaviour and expectations that would prove problematic in the longer term. Increased contact with the outside world also made it clear that even the recent gains still left Soviet citizens lagging far behind people in many other countries in terms of living standards. Furthermore, even when apparently 'socialist' in form, this new consumerism raised some uncomfortable issues from an ideological perspective, as the authorities worried that people (and women in particular) were becoming excessively materialistic and acquisitive, or else were devoting themselves to the selfish pursuit of private pleasure, rather than public good.[93]

Where the late Stalin period had seen elites gain increased access to a plethora of bourgeois-style luxuries, the Khrushchev years witnessed a return to a more egalitarian rhetoric. Some still benefited far more than others, of course, as clear social hierarchies remained across countless fields. Party members often received better access to prestigious goods and jobs, and enjoyed greater social prestige, than their non-party compatriots. It is important to note in this context that the Communist Party was not just an organisation of the ruling elite, but also one that included a vast number of ordinary citizens at the grassroots level, right across the country. At the time of Stalin's death, there were just over 6 million members. By the early 1960s, that figure had climbed past 9 million; and by 1967 the total was over 12 million – about one in twelve of the adult population. Although the trend had first started to emerge during the war, this massive expansion in party membership (and the accompanying expansion of Komsomol membership was even more pronounced) was to be one of the socio-political hallmarks of the post-Stalin era. In short, it was becoming easier (and also more attractive) for more citizens to participate in the basic structures of the Soviet system, and to draw the associated benefits. In fact, until well into the 1980s there were always more people seeking to join the party than it was willing to enrol. Nonetheless, as its membership base expanded so substantially, the party also diluted its ideological vigour. Bringing more and more people 'inside' the system helped maintain socio-political stability in the same way as rising consumption did, but it did not bode well for the long-term viability of the communist project.

At the very top of the food chain in all things consumption-related was the *nomenklatura*. Clearly stratified within its own ranks (the higher up the *nomenklatura* ladder, the better chauffeur-driven car one had, the higher standard of hospital one was treated at and the better resorts one holidayed at), this was a group that had already begun to emerge as a distinct entity under Stalin; but by now it had grown to perhaps a million people across the country, occupying all manner of 'responsible posts' that required political approval, like party and Komsomol professionals, ministers and officials, newspaper editors, military officers and factory directors. A former member of that group himself, Michael Voslensky presented the *nomenklatura* as a secretive and self-perpetuating managerial caste, essentially only interested in maintaining its own power and privilege, while also pretending that it did not even exist.[94] This last crucial point was driven by the fact that *nomenklatura* privileges – which again grew steadily more unabashed from the late 1960s especially – clashed too egregiously with the regime rhetoric of egalitarianism, generating popular resentment among ordinary citizens.[95]

At the GUM department store in Moscow there were private appointments for *nomenklatura* members to browse the finest foreign clothes and Soviet furs that never even went on sale to the masses.[96] Tourist travel to the West and places for one's children at the best universities could usually be arranged, too. Indeed, education was a key means of passing on privilege to one's offspring, with access to the best schools and most prestigious universities – such as Moscow State University and Moscow State Institute of International Relations – often favouring the children of elites and officials. Of course, graduation from these esteemed institutions opened up a range of attractive career opportunities that were effectively unavailable to others. A particularly telling example of this social stratification is offered by the figures for the student body of Moscow State University during the period under consideration: through the late 1950s and early 1960s, around 5 per cent of newly matriculated students were from peasant families and 25–30 per cent were from working-class backgrounds; the remainder – up to 70 per cent in some years – were the children of professionals and members of the intelligentsia.[97]

Nomenklatura dacha complexes, which were typically sheltered from public view by high fences and guarded by security, could be especially plush. At the very apex of the system, Presidium members received dachas that boasted fruit trees, tennis courts, billiard tables, cinemas, fine dining, libraries, saunas and more.[98] Where ordinary citizens might on special occasions shop at peasant markets (where produce was not just markedly more expensive, but also of better quality), members of the *nomenklatura* regularly had their chauffeurs obtain provisions this way.[99] Similarly, for the ordinary Soviet citizen, works canteens tended to be notorious for rude staff, undersize portions, dirty crockery and tasteless food. The pinnacle of the *nomenklatura* catering system was the 'canteen of curative food' that belonged to the Central Committee apparatus in Moscow, where the highest rungs of Soviet officialdom enjoyed an array of food and drink that ordinary citizens barely knew existed. Joining the top capital *nomenklatura* as a Central Committee adviser in 1964 (a job that also came with a new apartment), Georgy Arbatov later recalled that the main perk was access to the cafeterias and food supplies on offer. He described how, 'when I brought home my four-day allotment of groceries for the first time, my mother-in-law, who lived with us, could not believe her eyes'.[100]

While not living nearly so richly as members of the *nomenklatura*, for many ordinary citizens the domestic trappings of modernity were beginning to proliferate. By the late 1950s, modern furniture, plastics, ornaments, rugs (often hung on the wall, according to the style of the time) and radio sets were becoming more accessible and affordable. Credit was made available to buy items like refrigerators and washing machines, which were duly held up to citizens as powerful symbols of the new consumer modernity (as was the case in many other countries around this time).[101] More well-to-do urbanites (rather than just the very top political and cultural elites) also began to gain access to dachas, as somewhere to escape the city for a short while.[102] The notion of changing fashions was still derided by officialdom as a waste of scarce resources, but there were clear acknowledgements in the press that Soviet citizens deserved better when it came to clothing – that too many stores stocked only badly made and unattractive goods that fell short of popular expectations. Most famously, Presidium member Ekaterina Furtseva declared that every Soviet woman had the right to a good bra. This kind of discourse, about improved consumption as a right, would in time prove tricky to navigate for the authorities, since demand for good-quality clothing – and footwear especially – always outstripped supply, with citizens less and less inclined to accept meekly the shoddy items that accumulated in the shops.[103]

While male fashions stayed broadly the same as before, for Soviet women, and young women especially, the changes would be rather more pronounced and contested. The authorities' new tone on femininity was exemplified by a September 1962 newspaper article that declared 'it is impossible to deny a woman the yearning to be attractive' and acknowledged that myriad problems – from shops that sold only ugly underwear and misshapen gloves, through to indifferent salespeople and long queues at hair salons – frustrated women's legitimate aspirations on this front.[104] The focus fell on what official discourse termed 'socialist good taste', which one scholar has recently described as meaning 'modest prettiness' or 'feminine but not vulgar'.[105] It did not take long for changes in taste to start taking root. On noting a young woman in Moscow wearing blue slacks and a sweater during his 1959 trip, an amazed Harrison Salisbury (a regular visitor to the USSR over many years) recorded that such an outfit would, until recently, have drawn 'indignant remarks from women and rude wisecracks from men'.[106]

Soviet designers headed out to European fashion houses to learn what they could, while the likes of Christian Dior also came to Moscow to exhibit the latest products. During 1959–61, there were ninety different exhibitions by foreign fashion designers in the USSR, with tickets in incredibly high demand (and frequently snapped up by members of the *nomenklatura*).[107] Most high-end outfits, such as those displayed at fashion shows by designers like Dior, generally did not make it onto sale in regular shops, but were accessible only to the best connected and most privileged. Nonetheless, they were quickly imitated by those who knew how to sew or who could engage the services of someone who did. For ordinary citizens, this usually meant turning to a relative or friend, but actresses, ballerinas and other members of the social elite secured (and then jealously guarded) highly prized and highly skilled seamstresses to meet their fashion needs.

Progress in the development of modern synthetics was by no means plain sailing – some new fabrics smelled bad in hot weather; others were easily damaged and hard to repair – but new kinds of shoes and boots, skirts, shirts and coats were appearing in the shops and on the streets by the early 1960s (and in 1961 a specialist shop, called 'Sintetika', opened in Moscow). As with everything from child rearing to home décor, women in particular were flooded with official advice on how to dress appropriately in every situation, from a day at work to a theatre trip or a meal in a restaurant.[108] Items previously disdained as bourgeois fripperies, like cosmetics, skin creams and perfumes – with names like 'Red Moscow' – were now being produced domestically and started to become more widely available in shops, though they were not always of very high quality, and those with connections often bought foreign brands instead. Nonetheless, it was telling that more genuinely essential products like sanitary towels and tampons were still not commercially available for women, leaving them to fashion their own means of handling menstruation.

Keen to tap the benefits it seemed to offer – both as a powerful new means of communicating with the masses and as a symbol of modernity and the dawn of the promised good life – the state also invested heavily in perhaps the supreme consumer item of the post-war decades: the television. A state-of-the-art the television centre went under construction in Moscow's Ostankino district and TV sets steadily began to appear on sale in shops. Television ownership grew from around 1 million sets in 1955 to 5 million in 1960, 10 million in 1963 and then 25 million by the end of the decade.[109] Actually, television would prove to be a distinctly underwhelming medium for overt ideological purposes, as political figures struggled to master it as a form of communication.[110] The authorities also came to fret that people were watching too much television and that instead of pursuing a suitably collective and activist lifestyle, they were binging on the war movies, sports and documentary films that were served up to them. One cartoon in the satirical journal Krokodil, for example, depicted a clearly exhausted and dishevelled man rapt in front of his screen, wearing pyjamas and sitting next to an over-flowing ashtray, being told by the television set to 'shave, wash and get some fresh air'.

It was really only from the late 1960s, as the number of sets proliferated, that television truly established itself at the top of the Soviet media pyramid. Up until then, the radio had been a much more era-defining item. As in the capitalist world, the arrival of radio sets that were both portable and afford-able (the most common 'Spidola' set cost around seventy roubles) helped to free up listening from parental oversight and facilitated the arrival of a more distinct youth culture. Especially important in the Soviet case was the fact that the new radios appearing on the market from the 1950s were usually able to pick up short wave (or else could be illicitly adapted to do so, for a small fee) – a decision rooted in the sheer extent of the territory across which Soviet radio signals needed to broadcast. This would prove a serious miscal-culation, though. One 1958 report stated that 85 per cent of short-wave radio sets were to be found in the European part of the USSR – a region to which Soviet radio did not even broadcast on short wave, but to which an increasing number of Western stations were transmitting.[111]

It would not be long before large swathes of the country received a stronger signal for some foreign stations than for domestic ones. By 1956, there were 25 million short-wave radio sets in private ownership; and that figure was expected to rise to around 70 million by 1960.[112] That year, the Central Committee learned that as many as 50–60 different radio stations were broadcasting to Soviet audiences from outside the USSR. Although by no means the only crack opening up in the regime's control over the public sphere, this was a large and perpetually widening aperture, through which poured all manner of information and ideas that the Soviet authorities had wanted to keep out of the country: from suppressed details of Stalin's terror through to the truth about events in Hungary and the privileges of the polit-ical elite. Alexander Podrabinek – who would later become a prominent dissident – wrote that when he was only thirteen years of age he had decided that the only place to get 'real' information was from such broadcasts.[113]

Perhaps the most important of the foreign stations, in the sense that it was genuinely popular, and also very much a facet of the US Cold War struggle against communism, was Radio Liberty. Most listeners, it seems, tuned in for the latest Western music – a hook that Radio Liberty very consciously employed to draw in its audience; but this usually came alongside more explicitly politicised content critical of the Soviet system. Occasional speakers on Radio Liberty did call for the overthrow of the Soviet system, but the majority typically emphasised the lack of democracy in the USSR and the better living standards on offer abroad. Listeners were also introduced to banned literary works and provided with religious readings on Sundays. The extent of Soviet officialdom's irritation over Western broadcasting can be gauged from the fact that vast resources were thrown at costly jamming operations, which often (if not always) proved ineffective, sometimes rendering Soviet broadcasts just as inaudible as foreign ones. More darkly, at least two Radio Liberty staff members in Munich were murdered, seemingly by the KGB, and many more were threatened.[114]

It was also telling of the age, however, that one of the ways in which Soviet officialdom sought to combat the lure of Western radio among Soviet youth was by making regime-approved offerings more attractive. Radio shows became less tightly scripted and formulaic, as broadcasters strove to introduce a more 'human' feel to their work, and shows such as 'Cheery Companion' provided a popular mix of music and comedy (though overall, listeners still complained that official offerings were dreary).[115] Similarly, a new station, Radio Mayak (Lighthouse), was established specifically for a youth audience in August 1964, offering more new music and a livelier style of communication. Many people tuned in – and Radio Mayak became one of the iconic Soviet institutions of the 1960s and 1970s – though it seems that many listened to the new station in addition to foreign radio, not instead of it.

The World Youth Festival

While news of the momentous new housing decree was still being carried in Soviet newspapers, an event of no less symbolic power and cultural consequence was also getting under way in the capital. The three weeks from the end of July through to the middle of August 1957 saw more than 30,000 foreigners arrive in Moscow from Africa, Asia, Latin America, both halves of Europe and elsewhere to participate in the Sixth World Festival of Youth and Students, giving Soviet citizens a degree of interaction with the outside world – in person for some and vicarious for others – that was wholly unprecedented. Few events would leave a more powerful impact on the post-Stalin Soviet Union.

Held previously in Prague, Budapest, East Berlin and Bucharest, the festival had, during the Stalin years, essentially been a biennial gathering of the communist youth movements of the socialist world. Featuring tightly drilled parades of young people carrying giant portraits of Stalin and other bloc leaders, earlier iterations of the festival had been distinctly martial and militant in tone. Even in that context, though, Stalin showed no appetite to have the USSR serve as host. Fears of the domestic impacts of hosting the festival remained after Stalin's death, but they were also supplemented – and even supplanted – by a growing attraction to the possible gains to be accrued from such an event, especially as decolonisation opened up new possibilities to extend Soviet influence in the developing world. After first turning down a Komsomol proposal to host the 1955 festival, the Soviet leadership agreed to take the vacant slot for summer 1957.

From the outset, the authorities were determined that the festival should help to create a more positive image of the USSR abroad. That goal was, of course, made harder by the international furore surrounding the invasion of Hungary, which prompted a number of delegations to pull out in protest. Nonetheless, the plan was for the festival to be more open and exciting than ever before, and much less overtly 'communist' in content. Invitations went out not just to foreign youth movements under Moscow's sway, but also to the politically unaligned and even to some religious youth organisations. The lure of the festival and the opportunity to visit the USSR (costs were largely to be met by the Soviet hosts) was sufficiently appealing to cause real alarm in parts of the capitalist world. Some countries, such as Greece and Argentina, simply banned their citizens from attending, while the US applied considerable pressure to dissuade people from going (a small group of Americans did manage to go anyway). Most strident was Pope Pius XII, who organised an alternative festival for Catholic youth in Rome, warning that 'those who are with the anti-Christ travel to the festival in Moscow'.[116]

Months ahead of time, armies of young people were mobilised to prettify Moscow: planting trees and flowers, tidying up parks, painting buildings and putting up peace slogans. Infrastructure as basic as hotels and places to eat had to be built from scratch or refurbished, city maps were produced and legions of guides and translators trained. For all these reasons, and because the number and diversity of participants was to be much greater than ever before, the final bill for the 1957 festival was perhaps a hundred times greater than for its immediate predecessor, in Warsaw.[117] Efforts to impress included work aimed at raising the 'service culture' of the capital's notoriously surly and inattentive shop workers and waiters, while thousands of thieves, beggars, prostitutes and assorted 'troublemakers' deemed detrimental to the desired image were detained in advance or temporarily exiled from Moscow.[118] Newspapers, radio and television shows taught young people about the history and culture of the countries from which visitors would be coming, also offering warnings about the dangers posed by 'enemies' who disguised themselves as friends. Answers to potentially difficult lines of questioning from guests (especially on the Secret Speech or events in Hungary), as well as appropriate and inappropriate forms of socialising – greeting visitors warmly, but not too warmly – were explained at training sessions for those partici-pating directly and were also addressed more broadly across the youth media.

As they entered the USSR at train stations, airports and docks, foreign guests were mobbed by Soviet youth offering flowers, souvenirs and joyful embraces. For all that such displays of affection were to some extent choreo-graphed – Komsomol members were, for example, instructed that guests should 'feel themselves to be in a genuinely friendly and amiable situation' from the moment they arrive – there is no suggestion that the enthusiasm was in any way feigned.[119] A few overcautious parents took their children out of the capital for fear of what might follow if the political winds changed again later on, but most young people were desperate to engage. All over the country, millions of people had for months been participating in contests and competitions to win tickets for festival events. One recent scholar has written of how 'Muscovites felt overwhelmed and over excited, intoxicated as if by an excess of oxygen' and expressed 'spontaneous and boundless joy'.[120] Most of their visitors quickly embraced that infectious spirit. Participating as a member of an unofficial American delegation, Sally Belfrage wrote of the days following her arrival that 'In the next three weeks there was no choice but to forget about sleep,' adding that the whole time 'passed in a blur of activity, exhibitions, mass celebrations, excursions, concerts, seminars, parties, shows and *mir i druzhba* [peace and friendship: the festival's principal slogan]'.[121]

The opening ceremony on 28 July set the tone for what was to follow, with participants carrying banners adorned with peace slogans and declarations of international friendship, rather than portraits of Stalin, Lenin or Khrushchev. Delegations from all across the world clambered onto the back of open trucks and were paraded through Moscow's inner ring road as they headed towards the newly built Central Lenin Stadium, where an opening ceremony featuring fireworks, white doves and mass gymnastics awaited. Virtual pandemonium ensued as millions of ecstatic onlookers lined the parade route, many of them perched on rooftops and in trees, reaching out, cheering and blowing kisses as the exotic procession slowly passed by. Such was the frenzied reception that the Komsomol organising committee had to call ahead and warn members of the Presidium (who were waiting at the stadium for the opening ceremony) that they were running as much as three hours late. Khrushchev told them not to worry, but to make sure that television and radio crews recorded the warm welcome with which Muscovites were meeting their guests.[122]

The Soviet authorities boasted (with only a little creative accounting) that there were delegations from an impressive 131 different countries at the festival. Among the guests were almost 1,500 Africans from 40 different countries, more than 1,000 Latin Americans and more than 4,700 people from Asia. Such a number and array of foreigners on the streets was an especially arresting sight for Soviet citizens. Even aside from those in distinctive national costume, such as Scots wearing kilts and Arabs in robes, foreigners were immediately noticeable and quickly drew curious and welcoming crowds. Press photographs and television pictures showed clutches of Soviet citizens gathered round guests from Africa, Asia and Latin America in parks and public squares, swapping contact details, gesticulating friendship, playing the guitar and singing the festival anthem, 'Moscow Nights' (which would become a staple of international events for many years to come in the socialist camp).

The scheduled events of the festival included sports contests, film screenings, poetry recitals, seminars on the struggle for global peace, concerts and much more. In Gorky Park there was an exhibition of over four thousand works of art by artists from forty different countries – including surrealist, abstractionist and expressionist pieces normally forbidden inside the USSR. Marginalised Soviet artists, such as the painter Oskar Rabin, got the chance to show off their skills in public for the first time, as the rules of what was and was not culturally acceptable softened markedly during the festival (for Rabin, this would be the first and last time his work was officially displayed). Jazz was also embraced by officialdom as never before, with foreign artists from Eastern Europe and the US performing and competing for the title of best jazz group. Accordingly, Soviet jazz musicians like Alexei Kozlov were granted cherished opportunities to play in public and sometimes also to jam with their international brethren. For those like Rabin, who had long been 'on the outside' culturally and would soon find themselves on the outside once again, this experience was hugely uplifting, and did much to shape his subsequent career, even if official acceptance proved fleeting.[123]

With Western propaganda often dealing in overblown Orwellian images of life inside the USSR, and with many of the foreign participants at least broadly sympathetic towards socialism, many guests soon found Soviet reality – as it was presented during the festival – a pleasant surprise. Media reports eagerly transmitted to Soviet audiences visitors' positive remarks about their experience, and boasted how the festival showed that the 'so-called iron curtain' was merely a myth of Western propaganda. Some visitors, of course, proved ideologically troublesome, but not so much so as to throw the wider festival out of kilter. Belfrage wrote that there were one or two among her group who went intending to serve as 'crusaders for America', including one who spent his days standing in Red Square reading aloud from the recent UN report on the events of the Hungarian revolution.[124] Poles, too, proved an awkward presence at times, with some openly taking pride in their 'revolution' the previous year (Hungarian delegates to the festival were more carefully vetted).[125] During the international seminars on cultural developments (among the participants of which were a young Gabriel García Márquez and a not-so-young Pablo Neruda), the hosts always ensured that Soviet participants were 'politically reliable', but Poles in the audience repeatedly returned to the harmful role of politics in Soviet culture.[126]

Not quite all voices of Soviet officialdom were united in praise of the festival. Representatives of the USSR Composers' Union, for example, complained bitterly about the tide of jazz music sweeping the country. Similarly, *Literaturnaya gazeta* accepted that all of the art on display in Gorky Park was 'equal before the court of public opinion', but nonetheless ridiculed a swathe of works by French, Swedish, Italian and Japanese artists for their apparently gruesome and tasteless subject matter (including an image of a child with a dead dog) and apparent lack of substance (deriding one work as 'a newspaper clipping and a toothpaste label on a canvas'), and asserted that such art ultimately served to 'divert people from the bright path of human progress'.[127]

The authorities wanted to retain as much control over events as they could, while simultaneously seeking to create the impression that they were taking a 'hands off' approach to the festival politically.[128] In reality, there was simply too much interaction for it all to be controlled or monitored. Parks and public squares (including Red Square) hummed with life into the early hours. Young people learned new, unsanctioned dances and songs, and had frank discussions about the 'true' state of the outside world, in some cases learning along the way that they had been systematically lied to on a whole range of issues, and sometimes feeling deeply embarrassed that foreigners knew more about key events inside the USSR than they did. The arrival of an Israeli delegation aroused great interest and enthusiasm among parts of the USSR's Jewish community (some of whom travelled thousands of miles just to see their co-religionists in the flesh), and Soviet officials were soon concerned that both the delegation and the Israeli embassy were helping to reanimate flagging Jewish cultural and religious life.

It was also at this point that one of the staple characters of late Soviet youth culture first appeared in a major way: the *fartsovshchik*. Either male or female, this was an illicit entrepreneur who approached visitors to buy up foreign items like clothing, books and make-up, in order to sell them on to Soviet youth at a significant mark-up. The festival offered myriad opportunities for such people, and a roaring trade in anything and everything soon developed, much to the chagrin of the police. Generally disdained by fellow citizens for their money-grubbing (but nonetheless widely utilised), the *fartsovshchik* would become one of the principal avenues through which both the appearance and cultural tastes of young people in the USSR became ever more westernised across the decades that followed.

The saxophonist Alexei Kozlov, in particular, provided a somewhat lurid account of what he described as a mini 'sexual revolution' taking place during the festival. Although insisting that he had not been a direct participant in this 'revolution' himself, Kozlov described how young Soviet women

149

especially descended on foreigners' hotels at night and waited for them to come out, before quickly pairing up and heading off to nearby bushes for sex.[129] One Russian source has claimed that five hundred 'festival babies' were later born to Soviet mothers, though hard evidence for such a figure remains elusive.[130] Certainly, the phenomenon of sexual liaisons between Soviet and foreign youth existed and troubled the political authorities, with more than a hundred girls temporarily detained for 'dishonourable behaviour'. Leonid Plyushch recalled how he and his team of Komsomol police volunteers in Odessa (Odesa) – where some of the foreign delegates visited after the festival's end – were given the 'embarrassing' task of scouring the city's parks and looking in bushes to find couples. Those apprehended were taken to local officials and hectored about the 'honour' and 'responsibilities' of Soviet girls, before being warned about their future conduct. Plyushch recalled one girl, though, who stood resolute, insisting that her sexual organs belonged only to her and were none of the Komsomol's business; only when threatened with prison did she back down and accept her mistake.[131] As Kristin Roth-Ey points out, in reality the panic was specifically about Soviet girls and foreign men, and more broadly about fears surrounding adolescent female sexuality, since instances of Soviet men getting together with foreign women tended to be brushed off with a nod and a wink.[132]

While the main events of the festival all took place in Moscow, echoes of it resonated right across the USSR. In the first instance, youth newspapers, in particular, were packed with festival updates, and hundreds of hours of radio and television coverage were beamed around the country. Further, many of the foreign visitors stayed on for a while after the festival to travel beyond the capital. The extent to which this post-festival tourism was part of a wider project of reshaping the Soviet image abroad could be seen from the fact that, while most westerners went to recognisably European cities such as Leningrad and Kiev, guests from the likes of Sudan, Iraq and Libya went instead to more clearly Islamic-influenced parts of the country, such as Tashkent and Samarkand, in order to glimpse what the Soviet model of socialism might look like in their home countries.

Days after the festival officially ended, Komsomol boss Shelepin boasted in *Komsomolskya pravda* on 11 August that, in spite of Western slanders, not only had it been the most outstanding youth festival ever, but also that 'there has been nothing like it before anywhere at any time'.[133] In the sense that many visitors went home with broadly positive impressions of their time in the USSR, the festival probably did represent a success. Of course, this was in part predicated on festival participants seeing a distinctly atypical snapshot of Soviet life, and that mirage could hardly be sustained indefinitely. Anyway, the domestic price to be paid for that foreign success would reveal itself over years to come, since the festival did a great deal to advance popular interest in foreign music, art and fashions, with Western cultural influence on Soviet youth soon becoming a much bigger and more complex problem for the regime than anyone could have supposed in the summer of 1957.

Although largely overshadowed by the events of 1956 in terms of the interest it has attracted, 1957 was a similarly transformational year domestically. It brought closer and more varied contact with the outside world that would, over time, exert a major impact on popular culture inside the USSR, and – in the massive new housing programme especially – it made plain that citizens' welfare had become a much bigger regime priority. In removing the anti-party plotters from active involvement in political life, it not only disempowered some of the most hardline Stalinists of the political elite (others would replace them in time), but also set a precedent for how struggles among the leadership would play out thereafter: ending in demotion and disgrace rather than blood-letting. In terms of its global impact, however, the biggest event of 1957 was still to come.

5

THE SOVIET SPACE AGE

Like cultural and political change, one of the absolutely core themes that made the Soviet Sixties distinctive lay in the enthusiastic embrace of science and technology as the route to the utopian future of communism. While the likes of Lev Landau and Igor Tamm claimed Nobel Prize wins, millions of ordinary citizens watched sci-fi movies at the cinema, went to public lectures on the cosmos and read voraciously about everything from computing to nuclear physics. Science and scientists were the new heroes, held up as dedicated and selfless 'truth-seekers', striving for the good of humankind.[1] Given substantially increased autonomy and funding, for scientists themselves the era could be hugely empowering: one recalled years later that 'there was a wide-spread feeling in the mid-1950s and early 1960s that we could achieve and do anything'.[2] In the space race especially, this was a time when a series of great Soviet victories firmly established the country as a technological superpower, generating tremendous self-confidence, earning admiration abroad and suggesting that the shining future might indeed be approaching.

Sputnik: dawn of the space age

Even before 1917, there had been a handful of Russian writers – most notably Konstantin Tsiolkovsky – whose works had built popular interest in the theme of space travel. From the start of the Soviet period, extensive effort was undertaken to spread scientific knowledge through public lectures and pamphlets, and the 1920s also saw a first blossoming of science fiction literature and cinema. The wartime drive to tap all the country's scientific expertise for the struggle with Nazi Germany then proved to be the saviour of a little-known rocket designer named Sergei Korolev. After being swept up in Stalin's terror during the summer of 1938, Korolev was tortured until he confessed and then despatched to the deadly Kolyma labour camps of the far east, where he developed scurvy and lost most of his teeth, before being moved first to a special scientists' labour camp (*sharashka*) and eventually freed in June 1944 to return to his work on ballistic missiles. In years to come, Korolev would become the single most important figure of the Soviet space programme, though for security purposes he was kept entirely out of the public eye and referred to only as 'the chief designer'.

A keen admirer of Tsiolkovsky's writing, as Korolev oversaw the development of the Soviet ballistic missile programme in the mid-1950s, he also lobbied hard to get party bosses interested in the prospects for space exploration. Permission and funds to conduct initial research into launching an artificial satellite – on the strict condition that this did not interfere with Korolev's work on missile development – were eventually granted in the second half of 1954. Seeking additional resources for his work, in summer 1955 Korolev put his name to a letter that dangled two tempting carrots before the party leadership. First, he said that the USSR could perhaps still win a major propaganda victory by beating the Americans into space. Second, he reminded that there was considerable military potential in this sphere, citing possibilities for future satellite reconnaissance of US territory from space as an example.[3] He even buttonholed Khrushchev personally to press the issue when he came to check up on progress with Korolev's new R7 missiles in January 1956; the leading historian on this theme considers this encounter to have been the effective start of the Soviet space programme.[4] Korolev got the funds he wanted, and he got the ball rolling on the design and production of a suitable satellite.

However, after three successive failed tests of his R7 rocket during summer 1957, both the satellite programme and Korolev's position looked decidedly precarious. Finally, August brought a successful test and, with the Americans openly talking of their plans to launch the first satellite in the near future, Korolev pushed to get his own model on top of the R7 and onto the launchpad as soon as possible.

Remarkably, most of the initial calculations for the flight were done entirely by hand, before the team was granted access to a computer (possibly the only one in the country at that point) about the size of a room.[5] At the end of September, Korolev informed party bosses that preparations were almost complete and that the launch could take place in October. Always concerned that the US might unexpectedly seize victory in the race to be first – he even checked with the KGB to see if they knew of any possible plans for an imminent American mission – at the last moment, Korolev brought forward the planned launch date from 6 October to 4 October.

The R7 was brought out to the launchpad at the new Tyuratam testing site in the Kazakh desert early on 3 August for final preparations (the amount of time it took to get the rocket ready for launch always made it a deeply imperfect option militarily). At almost 22:30 Moscow time, on 4 August, Korolev's vast rocket fired and then surged into the sky, heading off over the horizon and into orbit. Weighing a little under 84 kilograms, and only 58 centimetres in diameter, Sputnik was tucked inside a nose cone and perched on the top of the 30-metre-high missile. About five minutes after take-off, the nose cone detached itself and Sputnik emerged and began to circle the planet below.

Listening stations confirmed that the satellite had completed its first full orbit of the Earth around ninety-six minutes later, and the call was put through to an expectant Khrushchev.[6] Having dinner with party officials in Kiev at the time, the Soviet leader excused himself to take the call, then returned to the table in jubilant mood and explained that a great scientific feat had just been achieved. He had a radio receiver brought into the room, so that everyone present could listen to the distinctive 'beep beep' sound that Sputnik emitted every few seconds.[7] The following day's edition of *Pravda* carried a brief announcement by the Soviet press agency TASS, providing some bare factual data about Sputnik's physical dimensions and its orbit, and telling people how to pick up its signal and how to observe its passage across the sky.[8] The initial statement justifiably declared the launch a major advance for world science, yet the whole report came in at only a little over 500 words and was not even the lead story for the day. Nonetheless, a new era of human history – the space age – had now begun.

While the Soviet media's initial coverage of Sputnik was rather modest, the international response was straightaway fulsome, with experts everywhere acknowledging the launch as one of history's great scientific achievements. Right across the world, millions of people gathered to stare into the sky and marvel as Sputnik passed overhead, while others listened in on ham radio sets to pick up its signal (the Soviet authorities had chosen to transmit it on a wavelength that could easily be picked up by the public). Wholly unexpected as it was, this Soviet triumph hit the US especially hard. There was both widespread fear of what might come next (such as a possible military attack from space or use of Sputnik's signal for mind-control purposes) and a broiling fury that they had been unexpectedly beaten to the punch by their great adversary, with some even likening the psychological blow to that of Pearl Harbor.[9] Massachusetts Senator John F. Kennedy, in particular, was a notable participant in a spate of scare-mongering which accused President Eisenhower of allowing the USSR to gain strategic superiority.

Soon, the Soviet media also went into Sputnik overdrive, working to generate public interest and pride. Before long, commentators were speaking about potential flights to the moon, to Mars and to Venus. The notion of the USSR catching up with and overtaking the US now had a rather more substantial feel to it. By 8 October, the newspaper *Trud* informed readers that the British media were practically unanimous in recognising that Soviet scientists had 'opened a new page in the history of mankind'.[10] Newspaper reports, editorials and radio broadcasts made it clear that Sputnik was not only a historic achievement on an international scale, but also very much a product of the socialist system and the value it placed on science. In Moscow, an ecstatic Khrushchev admitted to Korolev that members of the leadership had assumed he was merely fantasising when he first wrote to them about putting a satellite into space.[11] Key figures behind the launch were rewarded with titles, cash prizes, dachas and new apartments. A decree was also issued moving the most outstanding contributors to the front of the waiting list to buy a car (though they still had to pay for the car).[12] By that time, Korolev had already received perhaps his most important recognition: the appeal to have his Stalin-era conviction expunged was finally approved in April 1957 (almost two years after it had first been submitted). Rumours persist, though, that he missed out on a deserved Nobel Prize win after members of the Swedish Academy of Sciences enquired who was responsible for the Sputnik mission, and Khrushchev insisted that it was a feat of 'the whole Soviet people'.[13]

Sputnik immediately became a global beacon of Soviet soft power. Soon, a growing part of the image that the USSR sought to project to the developing world, especially, centred more than ever on scientific and technological progress, rather than militant communism.[14] Officials had for some time been puzzling over how best to present the Soviet pavilion at the upcoming 1958 Brussels Expo, but that debate was ended at a stroke with Sputnik. A duplicate was despatched to the Belgian capital (the one that flew had burned up on re-entry), where it was seen by approximately 40 million people and ensured that the USSR took home the prize for best pavilion.[15]

After 23 days and a total of almost 1,500 orbits of Earth, Sputnik's battery finally died and its signal stopped. Nonetheless, the next blow in the space race was already about to be struck.

Once Sputnik had proved such a global hit, Khrushchev's interest in all things space-related grew dramatically. He requested that Korolev quickly send up another satellite, at precious little notice, to mark the upcoming fortieth anniversary of the revolution. Mikoyan suggested that instead of emitting a simple 'beep beep', the next satellite might play 'The Internationale', but Korolev had a better idea. On 3 November, Sputnik 2 blasted off carrying the first ever living creature to leave the planet: a stray dog from the streets of Moscow named Laika.[16] This was a clear scientific advance on Sputnik 1 both in terms of the weight and complexity of the object being propelled into space, and in terms of the scientific data it generated. Laika was doomed from the outset, though. Despite official claims that she survived for as much as a week, and was then painlessly euthanised, she actually died from the heat within a few hours of the launch.[17] Western protests over Laika's welfare made little impact inside the exultant USSR, where she immediately became an iconic figure of the dawning space age.

The Americans responded to the first two Sputniks with the launch of their own Vanguard TV3 on 6 December 1957. But as news cameras from across the world rolled, it climbed a little more than a metre off the ground, fell back onto the launchpad and exploded.

After a failed Soviet mission in April 1958 was successfully covered up, the following month saw the launch of Sputnik 3. Then, timed to coincide with Khrushchev's maiden visit to the US, in September 1959 the Soviet Union became the first country to reach the moon, when the Luna 2 probe landed on its surface. Later that month the Soviet space effort also attracted huge global interest and acclaim when it published the first ever photographs of the reverse side of the moon.

There was another major breakthrough in August 1960, as two more dogs, Belka and Strelka (along with a plethora of less celebrated mice, insects and fungi), were not only fired into space, but also brought back to Earth alive. Television audiences were captivated by footage of the cute dogs in space, especially of Belka doing somersaults in zero gravity (though less telegenically, Belka also vomited during the mission). What was not made known to the public was that Belka and Strelka had originally been backups and were sent into space only after the two first-choice dogs, Chaika and Lisichka, were killed when their rocket exploded on the launchpad.

Along with the less fortunate Laika, Belka and Strelka's likenesses were soon to be found everywhere: on matchboxes, postage stamps, cigarette packets and propaganda posters. One author has even dubbed the pair 'the first Soviet pop stars', with all manner of merchandise produced, fictional stories written about them for children and huge amounts of fawning media coverage focused on them.[18] Photographed in space suits and drawn as cuddly cartoons, these dogs (like the martyred Laika) became powerful images that linked great technological achievement to a softer and friendlier image of the USSR, for both domestic and foreign audiences. Indeed, when Strelka gave birth to puppies in 1961, Khrushchev had one delivered to US First Lady Jacqueline Kennedy at the White House (where it promptly soiled the floor shortly after being handed over).[19]

The cult of science and technology

One product of both the space successes and the wider cult of technological progress was a surging public appetite for science fiction. Coinciding closely with the launch of Sputnik, Ivan Efremov's 1957 novel *The Andromeda Nebula* marked the start of a second golden age for Soviet sci-fi (the first was in the 1920s). Published in the popular science journal *Tekhnika molodezhi* (*Technology for Youth*) and set around a utopian communist society of the future, *Andromeda Nebula* featured everything from intergalactic travel and a robot spaceship through to battles with aliens. It sold millions of copies and was translated into twenty-three languages, before later being made into a hit movie. Similarly, the space film *Road to the Stars* came out in cinemas soon after Sputnik; at the insistence of officialdom, it actually included some real footage from the launch, which proved a huge hit with audiences.[20]

The most internationally acclaimed exponents of Soviet science fiction literature, the brothers Boris and Arkady Strugatsky, were also getting started around this time. While their most famous works, such as *Roadside Picnic* (on which the Tarkovsky movie *Stalker* was later based), were still some years off, their initial breakthrough came in 1958 with the story *From Beyond*, about the alien abduction of a team of geologists at Stalinabad.[21] Movies like the 1961 *Planet of Storms* (about cosmonauts on Venus) and the 1963 film *A Dream Comes True* (about a Martian invasion of Earth) also drew huge audiences to Soviet cinemas.

Thousands of books and pamphlets on science and great scientists were produced in vast print runs each year. Radio programmes discussed the latest scientific developments, mainstream newspapers interviewed scientists and described some of the latest research being done around the country, while there was a constantly expanding stream of public lectures across a whole spectrum of scientific matters. There were monthly journals for young people, such as *Znanie – sila* (*Knowledge is Strength*) and *Yuny tekhnik* (*Young Technician*), that offered a mix of factual scientific information, sci-fi stories and fantastical depictions of future moon bases and space stations. Publications for adults covered even quite advanced scientific subjects, but were nonetheless hugely popular, and one scholar has argued that the likes of *Nauka i zhizn* (*Science and Life*, which sold around 1.75 million copies each month) were no less important to their readers than the widely heralded literary journals of the age, such as *Novy mir*.[22]

Scientists gained new levels of prestige and prominence in public life. At Moscow's Exhibition of Achievements of the National Economy, a new pavilion celebrating nuclear energy was opened in 1956 and considerably expanded in 1959. Alongside the famous statue of the worker and peasant girl, there now stood a scientist in a lab coat; where they had held a hammer and sickle, he held a nucleus. Around 1.5 million people each year visited the pavilion and learned about nuclear fission and chain reactions, peered at uranium ores and models of power plants under construction around the country. For a time, the pavilion also included a scaled-down working reactor, which proved hugely successful in drawing fascinated crowds, though this disappeared without explanation in 1962.[23]

Still highly regarded by many cineastes today, Mikhail Romm's 1962 movie *Nine Days of One Year*, about work at a secret scientific installation, offered viewers a new kind of hero. Where Stalin-era protagonists were tough and unflinching, the nuclear physicist Dmitry Gusev – an iconic film character of the age – is mild-mannered, humanitarian and occasionally wracked with doubt, but is nonetheless so committed to his ground-breaking scientific research as to knowingly risk and then tragically develop fatal radiation poisoning in the course of his work.[24] Both of the film's leading men, Alexei Batalov and Innokenty Smoktunovsky, were among the very biggest stars of the age.

Like the new scientist heroes of the time, Soviet citizens were encouraged to be both 'cultured' and 'modern' in their behaviour and tastes – going to the theatre, visiting museums, dressing smartly and more. Education was continually championed in propaganda messages, and it became a staple of the age to speak of the Soviet population as 'the most given to reading in the whole world'.[25] The number of citizens with secondary education trebled between the late 1930s and the end of the 1950s. The size of the country's student body grew quickly, as new higher education institutions were founded and old ones extended. The network of night-schools, correspondence classes, public lecture programmes and study groups expanded considerably. One Soviet researcher claimed that by 1967 over two-thirds of workers were engaged in either evening school or self-study programmes.[26] There were regular public talks and media discussions on subjects such as 'what is a cultured person', 'what is good taste' and 'how to behave properly', emphasising the importance of cleanliness, not chewing one's nails and 'not making horrible noises whilst eating'.[27]

After being banned as a 'bourgeois pseudo-science' under Stalin, sociology regained its legitimacy and found a new prominence from the second half of the 1950s, with experts seeking to build a genuinely scientific understanding of the lives and needs of social groups like collective farmers (a young Raisa Gorbacheva conducted her doctoral research on the lives of Russian peasant women around this time) and religious believers. In May 1960, a new Institute of Public Opinion began its work, surveying young people about their attitudes and aspirations.[28] In fact, by summer 1964 there were fifty different sociological research groups around the country studying youth, mostly attached to universities and Komsomol branches.[29]

The focus on modernity and science suffused multiple facets of daily life from the 1950s. Domestic devices like vacuum cleaner models now carried names such as 'Rocket' and 'Saturn'. Magazines like *Ogonek* (*Little Flame*) raved about the Soviet Union's first jet plane, the TU-104, which made its maiden flight in 1956: they offered photographs of its sleek, modern design and boasted of how a new age of air travel meant that trips which formerly took days would now last only a matter of hours.[30]

New synthetic fabrics were hailed as the future of clothing, and Khrushchev took particular pride in the fact that people were unable to recognise that his own favourite hat was made of fake fur.[31] Coin-operated machines that dispensed carbonated drinks on the street became an iconic 'modern' artefact of the age. As in the West, the scientific technical revolution touched upon diet, too. Khrushchev pushed hard to expand the production of canned food, pre-prepared meals and new snack foods like popcorn and crisps (known as 'crunchy fried potatoes'), though his ambitious plans tended not to be realised in practice.[32]

Nowhere was Soviet modernity better showcased than in the architecture of the period. The authors of one recent volume have argued, with some justification, that new buildings were crucial signifiers of the break with Stalinist totalitarianism and were just as telling symbols of the age as the Secret Speech.[33] Although not necessarily to everyone's taste (and not always well constructed), the way in which constructivist glass and steel buildings increasingly replaced the 'grand style' ornamentalism of late Stalinism aped the ambitious rethinking of the urban environment that had initially followed the revolution. Visiting Moscow in 1963, Alan Sillitoe wrote of seeing cranes and construction work everywhere, adding that 'they are ripping out the past like rotten teeth'.[34] However, the way in which this modernising impulse was clumsily forced through could also arouse resentment at valuable heritage being lost. Perhaps most egregious was the destruction of a substantial part of Moscow's historic Arbat district, with its centuries-old buildings and alleyways, from the early 1960s onwards.[35] In their place arose a six-lane highway, lined on either side with modernist skyscrapers that could hardly have been less fitting for a city district that dated back four hundred years or more in places. Little less jarring was the new Kremlin Palace of Congresses (known today as the State Kremlin Palace), which opened in 1961: a modernist construction of glass, concrete and marble that stood uncomfortably alongside other buildings in the Kremlin grounds that dated back to the fifteenth century.

Offered considerable public status, and often also an array of highly desirable material privileges, many scientists enthusiastically embraced the chance to play their part in the Soviet project. At the same time as many outposts of the gulag were falling into disuse as the camp population dwindled, a new and very different kind of archipelago was appearing. Dozens of towns were being established around scientific research institutes and plants. The most famous of all – and still today a key centre of Russian research across a range of fields – was Akademgorodok. Thanks to the persistent lobbying of the mathematician Mikhail Lavrentev, and to Khrushchev's eagerness to tap Siberia's great economic potential, in May 1957 authorities approved the construction (at tremendous cost) of a new scientific centre for Siberia, not far from Novosibirsk. By the following year, as the first homes and research institutes were still being erected, an initial tranche of scientists and students was already setting up camp. From the outset, an excited Soviet press relayed to readers a great vision of pioneering heroes, of hardy spirits facing down the harsh Siberian wilderness in the noble pursuit of science.

While the story of Akademgorodok is primarily one of elite-level academic endeavour – leading institutes were established there for the study of physics, biology, economics, computing, cytology and much more – a large part of what made the town special lay in its unique atmosphere. Populated mostly by up-and-coming researchers and students (few established experts could be persuaded to leave their comfortable lives in Moscow, Kiev and Leningrad for Siberia), Akademgorodok was youthful in its demographic make-up and vibrant in its social scene, with the tight-knit community that developed there holding a lively programme of debates, dances, movie screenings and seminars. Though the autonomy on offer was by no means total, the fact that the city was located thousands of kilometres away from the centre of political power did ensure rather more academic freedom, especially for those working in politically sensitive fields. Tatyana Zaslavskaya, who would become prominent during Gorbachev's reforms in the late 1980s, was one of those who headed out to Akademgorodok in 1961 to undertake sociological research, later recalling that the move gave her 'a scope and freedom to work that I could not have had in Moscow'.[36]

In time, Akademgorodok would become a site of considerable privilege for its celebrated residents, with more housing space and better-stocked shops than those on offer in regular towns and cities.[37] Visits from Khrushchev, Richard Nixon, Charles de Gaulle and others over the years were also testament to its prestige, and there was a steady flow of interaction with the outside world. Some academics were able to travel to international conferences; scholars from other countries visited fairly frequently; and researchers enjoyed much wider access to the latest foreign literature than did other citizens. All this made for a pretty cosmopolitan environment and a community with a clear appreciation of its own importance.[38]

Afforded so much public prestige, many scientists felt not just a right, but an obligation to play a role in tackling what they understood as their country's ills. As a result, the 'ideological discipline' that was demanded of ordinary citizens could at times prove rather more lax in Akademgorodok and the other scientific towns like it. When the Komsomol Central Committee sent a team to investigate the mood at Akademgorodok in the mid-1960s, its members left deeply unimpressed, complaining that negative assessments of socio-political affairs were being shared openly in meetings; doubts were being expressed about the truthfulness of official information; the practice of listening to foreign radio stations was widespread; and there were public talks on inappropriate subjects like Western art and Freudianism. They also noted pointedly that party officials in nearby Novosibirsk referred to Akademgorodok as 'a stronghold of demagogues'.[39]

Official rhetoric about the crucial place of science and scientists in the march to communism proved to be no guarantee against the intrusion of political prerogatives, however. When Abel Aganbegyan's research at Akademgorodok showed that the Soviet economy was soon headed for serious trouble unless substantial reform was undertaken, it was ignored. Similarly, Tatyana Zaslavskaya recalled spending two years on a sociological research project, only to see the final report suppressed and destroyed when Khrushchev contradicted one of its findings in a speech.

Especially vexing to much of the scientific community was the continued official favour enjoyed by Trofim Lysenko. During the 1930s especially, many

geneticists who refuted Lysenko's research had been fired, jailed and sometimes even executed. After he had seemed to be falling out of official favour
just before Stalin's death, Lysenko's fraudulent claims about Lamarckian
genetic inheritance (in which he essentially promised rapid increases in crop
yields by 'training' new genetic characteristics into plants) suddenly gained
more traction than ever before, with Khrushchev an enthusiastic advocate of
his sham research.[40] In the decade that followed Stalin's death, though, resistance from inside the scientific community grew steadily more widespread, as
undergraduate students and Nobel Prize-winning scientists alike discreetly
held seminars at which the work of Lysenko and his followers was debunked.
In fact, quite a few of Lysenko's persecuted critics now found refuge and
employment at out-of-the-way places like Akademgorodok.[41]

Perhaps most notable in the longer term, political wrangles also derailed
important progress that was being made on computer research. In the
mid-1950s, cybernetics re-emerged as a legitimate field of academic study
(like sociology, it was denounced as a bourgeois pseudo-science under Stalin),
and by the end of the decade was attracting both growing research funding
and substantial public interest. The Soviet media were hugely enthused (and
Western intelligence apparently alarmed) about the great potential for what
they called 'machines of communism'.[42] Articles in major newspapers like
Izvestiya spoke of the vast promise that computers held for improving the
Soviet economy by streamlining cumbersome planning and management
processes, and assimilating the latest information to make the whole system
more responsive to changing wants and needs.

In May 1962, *Pravda* promised readers that it would not be long before
the Soviet Union pulled ahead of the US in the development of computers.
Things were indeed progressing. Specialists at the Academy of Sciences were
pushing for the development of a series of connected computer centres
around the country, which they saw as the key stage that would allow the
USSR to forge ahead in 'computerisation'. Concerns about the eventual cost,
however, collided with staunch bureaucratic resistance from officials at the
state planning agency Gosplan (who presumably feared losing their whole
raison d'être to the new 'machines of communism'). The plan for a network
of computer centres was repeatedly delayed and then watered down to the
point where the drive for computerisation lost much of its former coherence,

leaving Soviet research and development to fall ever further behind that of the West.[43] One of those involved in the field later recalled that the USSR was at about the same level as the US in its development of computers during this initial phase; however, he then went on to lament that 'we made our last good computer in 1962'. The poor decisions taken at the top around this time (not least, opting to copy Western blueprints, rather than producing home-grown designs) would still be weighing heavily on the country's crippled computer development a quarter of a century later.[44]

Atoms for peace and for war

Public rhetoric around achievements in the cosmos always foregrounded peaceful intentions and purposes; but this was nonetheless a field with obvious military ramifications (and the Soviet air force continually sought to gain control over space research and development for this reason).[45] The R7 rocket that powered successive space missions was in fact the world's first ICBM (intercontinental ballistic missile), meaning that the ability to launch a satellite into space and the capacity to fire a nuclear weapon across the Atlantic were almost one and the same thing. While Stalin's notion of war between capitalist and communist camps as inevitable had been formally abandoned at the Twentieth Party Congress, nobody suggested for a moment that such a confrontation had become impossible. Keen to portray the US and its allies as the global aggressors, the Soviet side continually played to the international gallery, with calls for full nuclear disarmament even as it pumped untold resources into honing more powerful bombs, insisting that these were only ever a defensive shield for self-protection. The central tenet of Soviet thinking on preventing war, then, was to be visibly as strong as one's enemy, in order to keep others' aggressive intentions in check.

With almost 6 million citizens in the armed forces at the time of Stalin's death, the USSR's conventional military power was unmistakably immense. Even so, it was rapidly becoming clear that modern war would demand more than just huge numbers of soldiers, tanks and guns. By 1958, Khrushchev had already cut the military by more than 2 million personnel, with another 1.2 million to be cut in 1960. Such troop reductions fitted well with the desired narrative of the USSR as a global force for peace, but they really

THE SOVIET SPACE AGE

reflected the fact that bigger priorities had come along when it came to military spending. Khrushchev summed up the state of Soviet military thinking when he asserted that any major conflict between the superpowers would quickly become a nuclear war, and that this would be vastly destructive for all concerned, but would ultimately prove fatal for the West.[46]

Just as Sergei Korolev proved the totemic figure in the Soviet space programme, so his counterpart (and friend) in the world of nuclear physics was Igor Kurchatov. Paradoxically, the identity of Korolev (whose work yielded results that the entire world marvelled at) was assiduously hidden from sight, whereas Kurchatov (the fruits of whose labours induced terror, rather than wonderment) delivered speeches at party congresses and on occasion even travelled abroad with Khrushchev.

Across the country, graduates in science and engineering were pouring out of universities and straight into secretive new research institutes. As he prepared to graduate from the Physics Faculty at Moscow State University in the mid-1950s, Roald Sagdeev recalled that one after the other his student colleagues dropped out of contact as they were despatched to work on secret projects at unknown locations. Some of them were at sites scrubbed from maps and identified only by a postbox number, or else at institutions with deliberately misleading names (the ministry in charge of the nuclear weapons programme, for example, was the Ministry of Medium Machine Building). Sagdeev himself was sent to work at Kurchatov's 'Laboratory of Measuring Instruments' (which he described as a kind of Soviet Los Alamos) to the northwest of the capital.[47] Andrei Sakharov was another whose life would be tied up with the arms race from the late 1940s, when Kurchatov directed him and Igor Tamm to explore the theoretical potential for the construction of a thermonuclear bomb to supersede the as-yet-uncompleted nuclear bomb. The pair soon enough decided that such a weapon could be created in practice, and Sakharov then spent years working on the project at the top-secret Arzamas-16 research installation.

At around 06:30 on 12 August 1955, Sakharov found himself lying on the ground in the Kazakh desert, wearing dark goggles. When the countdown from a nearby loudspeaker reached zero, there was a flash of light twenty miles away and a white ball lit up the whole horizon. The shock wave that followed, he wrote, 'blasted my ears and struck a sharp blow to my entire body; then there was a prolonged, ominous rumble that slowly died away after thirty seconds or so' as a giant blue-black mushroom cloud filled the sky.[48] Soon after the explosion, Sakharov and the minister in charge drove over to ground zero and walked on a 'fused black crust that crunched underfoot like glass'. Within a few years, the minister, Vyacheslav Malyshev, had died of radiation sickness. The situation could have been much worse, though. According to Sakharov, nobody in authority had even considered the danger to local residents of nuclear fallout until just days earlier, when thousands were hurriedly evacuated.[49]

Now with the unofficial soubriquet 'father of the Soviet hydrogen bomb', Sakharov was elected to the Soviet Academy of Sciences at the remarkably young age of thirty-two years. He was also assigned two personal 'secretaries', who were in fact armed KGB bodyguards, and he was no longer permitted to travel by aeroplane in order to minimise risks to his safety. He was given the title Hero of Socialist Labour, won a Stalin Prize (which came with a tremendous amount of money) and was awarded a dacha. While in the end such tokens did not keep Sakharov forever in hock to Soviet officialdom, such acknowledgements, honours and rewards were a vitally important part of the system, not just at the level of elite scientists but right down to workers in factories and pupils in schools. Even if they did not get to have meaningful input, it was increasingly possible for ordinary Soviet citizens to get what must have felt like meaningful recognition and reward for their contributions, and to feel themselves part of the system and the drive to build communism.

Just as Sputnik had been followed with improbable alacrity by Sputnik 2, so Sakharov's first device was quickly followed by his second, in November 1955: the USSR's first official thermonuclear explosion (many scientists do not regard the August device as a 'true' hydrogen bomb). This one, he wrote, produced a shock wave that knocked people off their feet dozens of miles away; even at that distance, the heat it generated was 'like that from an open furnace'. It left glass broken a hundred miles away from ground zero, and a little girl was killed even far beyond the official danger zone, when the shock wave caused her shelter to collapse. It also caved in the roof of a distant women's hospital, leaving patients with serious injuries. This test was to prove the point around which Sakharov perceived more and more intensely the grave danger to humanity that his work posed. In particular, he was growing increasingly agitated about the long-term effects of nuclear contamination from open-air weapons tests. Like his protégé, by this point Kurchatov was also beginning to feel steadily more uncomfortable at working on military projects.

For all the privileges and prestige accorded him as a member of the scientific elite, Sakharov discovered the limits of his powers in July 1961. At a Kremlin meeting between top party leaders and scientists, Khrushchev informed those present that he would shortly abandon a recent moratorium on atmospheric testing of nuclear weapons. Deeply alarmed by the ecological dangers that such tests posed, Sakharov first responded by asserting in front of the whole group that there was little to be gained from such a resumption of testing. When this remark failed to register, he passed a handwritten note with the same point scribbled on it along the table to Khrushchev, who read it without comment and put it in his pocket. Not long after that, the guests went to lunch. As they all sat, Khrushchev stood ready to make a toast. Instead of the expected remarks, though, he furiously berated and mocked Sakharov for having the temerity to try to interfere in political decisions, ordering the prized physicist to keep his nose out of such matters.[50]

As he turned away from developing weapons, Kurchatov instead threw himself into promoting the non-military applications of nuclear energy. Always keen to emphasise peaceful intent, the key Soviet slogan of the emerging nuclear age was an exhortation to 'let the atom be a worker, not a soldier'. Of course, this was in part disingenuous, since the plutonium of peaceful nuclear energy could be quickly weaponised with relative ease. Even so, such talk was more than just a smokescreen. As Paul Josephson has argued, harnessing the seemingly vast potential of peaceful nuclear energy was 'at the heart of visions of a radiant communist future' that were propounded during the Khrushchev era.[51] From plans for opening up the frozen north of the country through to irrigating the arid south, there was no better example of the promise that science and technology offered in driving progress towards communist utopia.[52]

In the field of peaceful nuclear energy, the USSR quickly pulled ahead. Located around 100 kilometres from Moscow, Obninsk began life the same way as a handful of other towns in the post-war years: as a secret nuclear research facility built by gulag labour and surrounded by barbed wire. In June 1954, though, the reactor at Obninsk went online and began to supply electricity as the world's first nuclear power station. Such was the foreign interest, and also the Soviet desire to revel in this scientific breakthrough, that delegations from seventy countries visited Obninsk between 1954 and 1962, eager to study the ground-breaking work being done there.[53]

The Soviet regime then took another previously unthinkable step and sent large delegations of top physicists to international conferences on peaceful nuclear energy at Geneva during 1955 and 1958. There they won considerable acclaim both for their academic prowess and for their newfound willingness to co-operate in sharing expertise. As the International Atomic Energy Agency (IAEA) emerged out of these meetings, the Soviet side made two bold statements of what it wanted to see in the agency's founding principles: all nuclear weapons should be banned; and all countries should benefit from peaceful nuclear technology, including those in the developing world. Inside the USSR, scientists studied ways of using nuclear research to transform all manner of everyday activities, from keeping food fresh for longer to getting chickens to lay more eggs.[54]

Kurchatov promised that seemingly limitless nuclear energy could power vast irrigation programmes that would enable new cities to grow up in the desert. The town of Shevchenko (Aktau/Aqtau) in Kazakhstan was one such case. Beginning with the discovery of uranium there in the 1950s, a modern town of about 100,000 people grew up around a nuclear-powered desalination plant on the edge of the Caspian Sea. The Soviet authorities were soon speaking of building such plants not just all over the country, but all over the world – wherever a lack of fresh water held back agricultural development.[55]

At the opposite end of the country, the world's first nuclear-powered icebreaker, named after Lenin, went into service in the Arctic north during September 1959. Able to stay at sea for far longer than regular icebreakers, and with greater power to plough through thicker ice, it promised huge dividends in its ability to open up the mineral wealth of the far north and keep the region properly supplied in the face of long and paralysing winters.[56] Hailed as yet another seminal breakthrough, the *Lenin* nuclear icebreaker worked the seas of the Arctic up to the Soviet collapse; however, it proved not to be a harbinger of things to come, remaining for many years the only ship of its kind in the fleet.

It is certainly true to say that few countries in the 1950s showed much concern for the natural environment, as they rushed headlong towards economic development. Since the early days of Soviet communism, nature was first and foremost something to conquer and exploit, rather than protect. As in a number of other countries, though, there were at least some signs of changing attitudes by the start of the 1960s.[57] Most notably, aspirations for the fuller exploitation of Siberia's beautiful Lake Baikal aroused determined resistance from scientists and members of the public, vehemently opposed to plans to construct heavily polluting industrial enterprises on the lake's shore-line. Moreover, there were even alarming proposals to detonate explosives at one of the lake's outlets that would result in the release of a huge flow of water that could be harnessed to generate hydroelectric power (destroying much of the rich flora and fauna in the process). New laws on nature protection followed in 1960, but these were, in reality, frequently ignored by officials with economic priorities in mind.[58]

Baikal was ultimately spared the planned explosions, but not the industrial development. From 1966 onwards, a new factory producing rayon cord for aeroplane tyres tipped vast quantities of waste into Baikal's famously pure waters. Numerous Soviet cities suffered from dreadful air pollution, as industrial plants pumped out all manner of waste. In April 1960, all the country's major rivers were recognised as 'severely polluted'.[59] In Tatarstan, development of the burgeoning oil industry did tremendous environmental damage to the land and to water supplies.[60] There was also eye-watering contamination of the seas around the USSR, as numerous vessels over the years sank with working reactors or nuclear weapons still on board. In some cases, old reactor carcasses and nuclear waste were simply tipped overboard into the Barents Sea, the Arctic Ocean, the White Sea and elsewhere.[61]

Thanks to pervasive Soviet secrecy, though, the most serious nuclear accident of the age – historically worse than any but Chernobyl and Fukushima in terms of its severity – only came fully to light many years later. Located south of Chelyabinsk in the Urals, Kyshtym was the site of a storage facility for nuclear waste produced at the plutonium plant in neighbouring Ozersk. Another secretive and privileged scientific town closed to outsiders, Ozersk's shops were far better supplied with goods than those of normal towns; the city landscape was prettified and equipped with all manner of recreation facilities; average living space far outstripped that available elsewhere; schools were better and crime was lower.[62] As Kate Brown points out, however, even though their material conditions were probably the closest the Soviet regime ever came to constructing functioning communism, residents of Ozersk (and other special towns like it) still did not behave like ideal communists. The young people growing up there dressed, spoke and danced in ways that irritated and alarmed the political authorities. Adults still drank too much and failed to engage with the 'enlightenment' opportunities on offer to them, and some even used the town's enhanced supply of goods to make extra money, by selling on hard-to-find items at considerable profit elsewhere.[63]

Many of those who worked at the Ozersk plant were repeatedly exposed to dangerous levels of radiation, through faulty or missing safety equipment, occasional spills and leaks – or, at times, simply working by hand with highly radioactive substances. (Kurchatov himself had been known to handle radioactive material in this way when trying to detect a problem with a reactor.) Waste was also being pumped into the local environment, stored in the open air at Lake Karachay and poured into the nearby river Techa, which became so dangerously polluted that dozens of villages along its banks (whose inhabitants used the water for drinking, fishing and bathing) had to be abandoned from the mid-1950s, the residents forcibly evacuated, the animals slaughtered and properties flattened and dug into the soil.[64]

At the end of September 1957, an underground tank full of Ozersk's nuclear waste at Kyshtym overheated and exploded, spewing radioactive dust and debris across the area. With no precedent to go on, no plans in place for how to deal with such an accident, and a keen desire to hush the whole thing up, the response was clumsy at best. For months, conscripted soldiers, prisoners and local residents were roped into the clean-up effort, removing radioactive materials with shovels, scrubbing down walls and burying or burning irradiated items like machinery, crops and clothing. While Ozersk itself was eventually cleaned up, nearby settlements were largely left to their own devices, and – for lack of any alternative – many people continued to drink the local water and eat produce from the contaminated ground. Eventually, growing evidence of a new health crisis meant that another cluster of villages along the Techa river was forcibly abandoned and the residents evacuated.

How many people died in the wake of the Kyshtym explosion remains a mystery, since the relevant records have never emerged. But for decades afterwards, the region suffered noticeably elevated rates of a variety of cancers linked to radiation. In a final cruel irony, three decades later at Chernobyl many of the pertinent lessons of how to respond to such a nuclear accident could not be applied, because the whole Kyshtym incident had been so thoroughly covered up that few in authority even knew it had happened.[65]

'The cosmos is ours!'

Towards the end of October 1960 came a stark reminder of just how risky the world of space flight could be, when a rocket malfunction at the Tyuratam complex ended in a catastrophic fireball. An estimated 126 people were killed, many of them top scientists. They included the head of the Soviet Strategic Rocket Forces, Marshal Mitrofan Nedelin, whose remains apparently consisted of only an arm with his wristwatch attached to it.[66]

A month later, a prototype of the new Vostok capsule – which was designed for the manned flights to come – also had major problems, with the ejection mechanism failing and the craft making a hard landing way off target in Siberia. In December 1960, two space dogs were killed when the on-board bomb – designed to destroy the craft, should it malfunction and fall into the wrong hands – was detonated as they headed off course.

In February 1961, it was decided that a manned flight could proceed, once two further test flights (with mannequins on board, rather than humans) had been completed safely. Korolev proposed that the first human flight should take place that coming May Day; Khrushchev demurred, wary of a potential disaster ruining the holiday.[67] That spring saw more technical issues, though, with radio communications and ejector-seat mechanisms still proving problematic. Moreover, the would-be cosmonaut team could not actually train in spacesuits, as these had still not been finished by mid-March. Even so, by that point, Khrushchev himself was publicly hinting that a human space flight was fast approaching. Then, on 23 March, came another reminder of just how high the stakes were for those involved, when the cosmonaut Valentin Bondarenko was burned alive, following a freak accident during a spell in an oxygen-rich isolation chamber.

However many practice flights were mandated and completed, that did not alter the fact that human spaceflight remained a hugely risky undertaking. Any number of things could go wrong, and even the slightest miscalculation could prove fatal. It was clear to all that a cosmonaut would not be able to survive the 10–12 days required for the craft to fall out of orbit naturally, if the capsule's retro-rockets failed to work, for example. And there was still no practical means of retrieving either pilot or craft in the event of a landing at sea. In fact, of the various press releases prepared in advance to cover any eventuality during the flight, one was a request for all countries to help find a lost cosmonaut.[68] A host of technical difficulties with both the R7 rocket and the capsule that sat on top of it remained unresolved almost up to the final moment.

From an initial pool of around 3,500 candidates drawn from the military, all of whom had to be 170–175 centimetres in height and no more than 72 kilograms in weight, twenty men had begun cosmonaut training in January 1960, under the watchful eye of air force legend Nikolai Kamanin. With little certainty about the kind of challenges that awaited them in space, potential cosmonauts faced an extraordinarily demanding preparation process. As well as parachute jumps and advanced physical fitness, they were spun in huge centrifuges until they vomited, put through extended sensory deprivation and isolation, tested in heat chambers and more. What the trainees did not spend a great deal of time on was learning how to operate the Vostok capsule, since virtually everything about it was to be automated. The key purpose of the training, as one expert has argued, was to make the cosmonauts more like machines – predictable and rational, even under great pressure.[69]

By the end of March 1961, with the two required test launches completed, all parties agreed that it was time for the next step.[70] On 3 April, Korolev informed the cosmonaut team that the Central Committee had given final authorisation for a manned mission. Everyone left the training base outside Moscow and headed for the launch site in Kazakhstan, though still with no decision on who would be the first in space. The choice soon came down to Yuri Gagarin or German Titov. The latter was the better-educated and the more intellectually inclined of the two, but Gagarin seems to have triumphed on the basis of both perceived mental toughness and his suitability for the kind of global attention that would inevitably follow a successful mission.[71] Born on a collective farm near the small town of Gzhatsk (now Gagarin) in the west of Russia, Yuri Gagarin also boasted a politically compelling biography that featured a spell living under Nazi occupation as a child (and which included seeing his own brother tortured by the Gestapo), which fed into a strong sense of patriotism. He was also a party member, a family man and a keen sportsman, all of which suited the political authorities perfectly.

With the flight two days away, on 10 April Titov and Gagarin were informed that the latter would go first and the former would be his standby: a decision which apparently left Titov disappointed until the end of his days. So that she would not be worried when the actual day came, Gagarin told his wife that the flight would take place on 14 April, making no mention of whether he would be the pilot. On 11 April, he wrote a final letter to her and their two children, in case the mission ended in tragedy. Then he and Titov ate space food for dinner (meat puree and chocolate sauce from toothpaste tubes) and retired to bed.

Around 06:00 the following day, 12 April, Gagarin was on the bus to the launch pad, telling colleagues that he would see them soon at the landing site in Kuibyshev. Carrying a gun and a hunting knife, in case he landed somewhere inhospitable and had to defend himself, he got in the lift that took him up to the Vostok capsule on top of the R7 rocket. After about two hours of final checks, Korolev gave the order to start just after 09:00 local time. As the enormous rocket fired beneath him, Gagarin famously shouted 'poekhali' (pronounced po-ye-kha-li), meaning 'let's go'.

From his bunker underground, Korolev quickly called an anxious Khrushchev to tell him that the initial launch had been a success. Thirteen minutes later, Gagarin was in orbit. For the next hour or so, he was mostly occupied with performing tests and recording his impressions of space, as well as marvelling at the beauty of the planet below and trying (often unsuccessfully) to communicate with ground teams across the USSR. In the capsule, he displayed the sang-froid for which he had been chosen, remaining calm throughout and occasionally singing patriotic songs.

With a full orbit completed, the Vostok was ready for re-entry. Fears that the craft's braking mechanism (which would allow it to fall out of orbit and back to Earth) might fail thankfully proved groundless. By that stage, news of the launch and the name of the cosmonaut involved had been announced on the radio, and people on the ground were pouring into the streets to celebrate. For both Gagarin's wife and his parents, this was the point at which they found out that he had been the chosen cosmonaut. Their lives quickly changed forever, too, as they were instantly pulled into the scrum that followed. After re-entry, Gagarin ejected from the Vostok 1 capsule and parachuted back down to Earth, landing outside Saratov (the city where he had first learned to fly), around 500 kilometres from his intended destination. Military spotters (and members of the public) saw him coming out of the sky and were soon able to confirm that he was alive, much to the delight of Korolev and Khrushchev.[72] On returning to Soviet soil, he hitched a lift with a peasant lady on a horse and cart to get to the nearest telephone and report his whereabouts.

Records uncovered since the Soviet collapse show that Gagarin's mission did not proceed anywhere near as smoothly as official sources claimed at the time. His orbit was much higher than planned and he had come close to catastrophe on re-entry, as the craft failed to separate into two parts on cue, causing it to spin dangerously and leaving Gagarin to watch flames through the porthole until the cables that had failed to detach burned off.[73] Then, after he ejected, his parachute became dangerously tangled during his descent, which could easily have killed him. Gagarin and his Vostok craft also landed about 2 kilometres apart from each other – though officials would insist that they had touched down in the same place, in order to fulfil the established international criteria for having achieved spaceflight.

By the time the helicopters arrived to pick everything up, crowds of locals were already chatting to the cosmonaut and pilfering souvenirs from his capsule. Having been connected by telephone to an ecstatic Khrushchev, Gagarin ended their brief chat by declaring 'Now let other countries catch up with us!'[74] From Saratov, he was flown to Kuibyshev to be debriefed and examined by a team of doctors, and there he was reunited with his cosmonaut comrades. Two days later, he was flown to Moscow, with a fighter jet escort, flying low over the city's centre and watching the vast crowds waiting to greet him. Touching down at the capital's Vnukovo airport, he was embraced on the red carpet by Khrushchev and driven by open-top car into the city.

While mass public displays of enthusiasm usually required a little cajoling from the authorities, in April 1961 they could barely hold the people back.[75] Streets and rooftops were all packed as the motorcade drove Gagarin and Khrushchev to Red Square for a celebration that was rivalled in scale and enthusiasm only by the victory parade of 1945.[76] The public mood could hardly have been better, as Gagarin spoke of how his love for the motherland and the party had given him strength during the flight. He declared himself a 'loyal son of a people who can accomplish wonders'. One commentator has argued that 'the Soviet people and their government had never been so aligned in their feelings and sense of belonging' since the end of the war.[77] One witness to the events later spoke of Gagarin's flight simply as 'the high-water mark of Soviet communism'.[78]

Naturally, the Soviet authorities rejoiced in this great success. An official statement from the party's Presidium and the Council of Ministers called the flight 'an unprecedented victory . . . the greatest achievement of science and technology'. It declared the triumph one for all mankind and promised to place it in the service not of war, but of peace and security for all peoples of the world. Gagarin was immediately awarded the title Hero of the Soviet Union. Among the gifts bestowed upon him were a car, a television, a new apartment, a washing machine, a vacuum cleaner and a piano, as well as new suits, shoes, raincoats and heaps of other hard-to-acquire items.[79]

The following day, *Izvestiya* started to get a cult of Yuri Gagarin under way, with a special supplement all about the conquering hero. The hagiography would continue for years to come, as Gagarin and his cosmonaut comrades were presented as flawlessly wholesome icons to be emulated and admired by all. Gagarin's image as both a military man and a family man was especially important in this respect. Frequently photographed playing with his children, in military uniform or else exercising shirtless, he was the embodiment of a 'real' Soviet man: not only patriotic, virile and brave, but also responsible and grounded.[80]

From the end of May 1961, Gagarin began to see a lot more of the planet he had just orbited. That summer he went first to Bulgaria, and soon after to

Czechoslovakia, then to Finland, the UK, Iceland, Cuba, Brazil, Canada and France, always smiling as he appeared in public and on television, conveying messages of peace and friendship and receiving tremendous public adoration wherever he went. By the end of the year, he had also undertaken a gruelling tour of India, Sri Lanka and Afghanistan (with as many as nine engagements per day for three weeks). In early 1962, he headed off to Africa, where he made friends with Kwame Nkrumah in Ghana, was paraded again through vast crowds and showered with honours, including the Great Star of Africa in Liberia and the Order of the Nile (along with the keys to the gates of Cairo) in Egypt.

In the UK, he was received by both Prime Minister Harold Macmillan and Queen Elizabeth II, the latter apparently informing Gagarin that British women 'swooned for him'. Indeed, rumours of his apparent romantic success with bourgeois women (most famously, the feted Italian actress Gina Lollobrigida) elicited a certain macho pride back home.[81] In all this globe-trotting, he presented to the world a striking new face of the USSR – a handsome and smiling young man, modern, self-confident, affable and articulate. As Asif Siddiqi has argued, all this helped to reshape the Soviet image abroad, from a country of dreary collective farms to one at the vanguard of a new and dynamic future.[82]

While Gagarin was off touring the world, German Titov became the second human to go into orbit, in August 1961 (American Alan Shepard had, in the meantime, become the second person in space, but he made a much shorter and lower sub-orbital flight). While his predecessor had been in space for less than two hours (and Shepard for only about fifteen minutes), Titov completed a mission of over twenty-five hours as he orbited the Earth seventeen times. In the process, he became both the first person to sleep in space and the first to suffer from space sickness. He also filmed the Earth through the capsule's porthole with a special movie camera. On his return, Titov was hailed with honours and parades like Gagarin had been (he was also promoted from candidate member to full member of the Communist Party). He made all the requisite political remarks – insisting, for example, that he had not felt alone in space, because he knew that Khrushchev and the entire Soviet people were watching his flight – and was duly written into the cosmonaut cult, as reporters gushed about his vigorous, healthy and good-humoured manner.

The promise that such successes the cosmos would, in time, transform everyday life in the Soviet Union was absolutely clear. *Pravda*, for example, declared that space victories promised scientific breakthroughs in everything from ice surveying and weather predicting to radio and television broadcasting (and maybe even contact with other worlds, further down the line).[83] In July 1962, one newspaper report opined that recent scientific advances were giving grounds for optimism about finding a cure for cancer before the century was out. Titov even suggested in a media interview that the day was not far off when ordinary people would spend their holidays and weekends in space. He, too, was quickly despatched on global tours to spread the Soviet message far and wide, even meeting President Kennedy at the White House and upsetting religious believers (as well as delighting Soviet propagandists) later in his US trip by announcing that he had looked carefully while flying through the heavens, but had seen no angels or gods there. However, Titov also gave those above him plenty of headaches. As head of the cosmonaut training team, Nikolai Kamanin received all kinds of reports of his problematic behaviour over the years, including instances of public drunkenness, car crashes (including a drunken crash that killed someone), persistent womanising and leaving classified documents unattended.[84]

After Titov's flight came Andrian Nikolaev in Vostok 3 during August 1962. He again shattered the endurance record by spending almost four whole days in space, orbiting the Earth more than sixty times in the process. The day after Nikolaev was launched, Pavel Popovich also went into orbit. The pair became the first to fly simultaneously in space and to communicate from one space craft to another. Both pilots returned safely to Earth on 15 August 1962. In a nod to rhetoric about the friendship of Soviet peoples, Khrushchev declared that Popovich's fellow Ukrainians were especially proud of him (also on the line, Leonid Brezhnev promised to embrace Popovich 'Ukrainian style' when they met in Moscow).

On each occasion, a return from space was marked by a huge homecoming event, with crowds, speeches, awards, banners and great media fanfare at the latest step forward and successes soon to come. As with several other Soviet cults, it is by no means entirely clear how far the regime was responsible for driving the mass veneration of space victories, and how far it was actually responding to an authentic public mood. Popular magazines like *Ogonek* were regularly full of images and stories of cosmonauts and their daily lives.[85] Gagarin's picture hung on the walls both of bureaucrats' offices and children's bedrooms. Countless thousands penned letters to cosmonauts (or wrote to newspapers about them), musicians sang about their glory, schoolchildren wrote essays about them, while newspapers, television shows, propaganda posters and postage stamps made them virtually inescapable in public life.

Like President Kennedy in the US, Gagarin rapidly became one of the iconic figures of the age, especially at home: a (seemingly) clean-cut, articulate and confident young man who encapsulated perfectly the self-image that his country wanted to project to the outside world. Cosmonauts were heralded not just as ideal role models for Soviet youth to emulate, but also as prototypes of the coming Soviet man and woman. Khrushchev described them as embodying the goals of communism by virtue of their 'high intellectual capacity, moral purity and physical perfection', as well as their 'love for their country and social responsibility'.[86]

Away from the public gaze, the cosmonauts' training base (known as Star City) became the site for the most exclusive parties in the land, replete with heavy drinking and macho excess. Well aware of the political clout he wielded, Gagarin, the self-styled 'mayor of Star City', used his tremendous prestige to lobby for central investment in his hometown and to help out old friends. Contrary to the highly sanitised official image, he also enjoyed fast cars and parties little less than Titov. Indeed, Kamanin noted in his diary instances of both Gagarin and Titov drinking to excess, causing minor public scandals that had to be hushed up, and hanging around with prostitutes. He also recorded one particularly striking incident from October 1961, when Gagarin's wife almost caught him in another woman's apartment late at night, while they were holidaying in Crimea. He evaded her by jumping off a first-floor balcony, but his legs got tangled in the process. He landed face first on the ground and required emergency surgery. The timing could hardly have been worse: he was supposed to be the star guest at the upcoming party congress, but now had to pull out as his face was in no fit state to be seen in public.

Before 1961 was over, cosmonaut trainer Kamanin had begun promoting the idea of a female space mission, though he came up against almost unanimous opposition, until he managed to get Khrushchev on board with the plan.[87] In large part, the motivation for this step centred on the propaganda gains on offer in terms of validating Soviet claims about equality of the sexes in the USSR. The alacrity with which the planning for the mission developed seemingly stemmed from rumours that the US was aiming to put its own female mission in space in the near future (actually, the USSR would beat the Americans to this by a clear twenty years). A female mission also made sense at a scientific level, though, since one key purpose that manned spaceflights served in terms of research was learning about the effect of space travel on the human body.[88]

Kamanin and his team began to whittle down the pool of female applicants in January 1962. The shortlisted women were enrolled in the air force and put through exactly the same intensive training that their male counterparts faced. One of the trainees, Valentina Ponomareva, recalled that all of the initial (male) cosmonaut group were against the idea of a female mission – and Korolev apparently even considered it bad luck for women to be present at the launch site – though they did understand its value and all of them treated the new female cosmonauts well.[89]

Kamanin recorded that Ponomareva was the one who performed best in the tests, but it was another candidate, Valentina Tereshkova, who gave the better responses during interviews: at one point he referred to her as 'Gagarin in a skirt'.[90] In fact, it seems that Gagarin himself objected to Ponomareva's candidacy, on the basis that she was already a mother and thus should not be allowed to take such risks with her own safety. Kamanin also disliked what he saw as her excessive self-confidence, as well as the fact that she both drank and smoked. A textile worker, Komsomol activist and recreational parachutist, Tereshkova would win out in large part because she was closer to the political ideal than her rivals.[91]

On 14 June 1963, Valery Bykovsky went into space in Vostok 5, to be joined in orbit two days later by Tereshkova in Vostok 6 (initial discussions about sending two women up separately had gone nowhere). The biometric data showed that she coped with the terrifying launch process better than several of her male predecessors. Live footage of the pair in their respective crafts was shown on Soviet television, as Tereshkova racked up more hours in orbit than all the US astronauts combined up to that point. When she was put through to Khrushchev for a mid-flight conversation, he confessed that he felt a fatherly pride in her, and that all the women in his family were especially excited by her breakthrough.[92]

Once Tereshkova and Bykovsky returned to Earth and headed for their flight back to Moscow, it was clear that she was the star, as crowds lined their route to the airport, chanting for 'Valya'. On 22 June, she and Bykovsky enjoyed the same lavish homecoming ceremony that had been thrown for their predecessors. Soon enough, the pair would also head out on a world tour that took in Italy, Cuba, Mexico, Ghana, Norway and India. Tereshkova's likeness soon became another mainstay of propaganda imagery, appearing particularly in a host of iconic posters celebrating International Women's Day. For millions of Soviet women especially, her flight was a source of immense pride, and they wrote to her and about her with huge enthusiasm.[93] It was telling, though, that when Khrushchev presented the pair to exultant crowds from atop the Lenin mausoleum, Bykovsky was in military uniform, while Tereshkova was in civilian dress. Similarly, at the Star City training base (apparently on Gagarin's orders), female cosmonauts were obliged to wear dresses, rather than military uniform or tracksuits.[94]

Some of Tereshkova's views on women were hardly progressive – she made no secret of her belief that motherhood was the most important calling for any woman, for example – but her achievements were widely used to encourage girls and young women to dream of careers in science and space exploration, and the next decade did indeed see a notable rise in the number of Soviet women studying and working in the fields of science and technology.[95]

For all that Tereshkova's flight was a powerful symbol of equality, an important theme soon became apparent. On 25 June, she had to leave a meeting with Korolev and other cosmonauts early, as she was the star speaker at the International Women's Committee congress that was being held in Moscow. Soon, such commitments would come to dominate her schedule. Tereshkova's time was increasingly taken up with representing her sex, rather than participating in her profession. Kamanin recorded in his diary that she fought bitterly, but ultimately unsuccessfully, against her appointment to the leadership of the Soviet Women's Committee, with the constant tours, appearances and meetings that the role demanded of her. She complained that all this got in the way of the training and study expected of a cosmonaut.[96] More than any other cosmonaut, her image was shaped and scrutinised from above.

While a certain air of sexiness was a distinctive part of Gagarin's image, there was to be no hint of this with Tereshkova: decisions on whether she should be photographed in military uniform or civilian dress could be taken as high as the party Central Committee.[97]

When rumours of romance between Tereshkova and Andrian Nikolaev (the third cosmonaut to go into space) began to circulate, the pair came under political pressure to marry. When they did so, on 3 November 1963, it was the epitome of Soviet celebrity: at the civil wedding ceremony, Khrushchev gave away the bride (her own father having been killed in the war) and Gagarin led the toasts. The newly-weds then headed off for a honeymoon in India, where they were embraced by Prime Minister Jawaharlal Nehru on arrival. When the pair had a child the following year, Tereshkova would be portrayed as the ideal Soviet mother. Like Gagarin, her propaganda value was such that she could never be allowed to undertake another space mission. And – important as her own achievement had been – it was not followed by more women going into space. As Ponomareva recalled it, even though the female cosmonauts kept on training after Tereshkova's flight – and there were tentative plans for an all-female mission in 1965 or 1966, though these came to nothing – it was soon understood that neither she nor any of the other women would ever go into space.[98]

There is little question that the Soviet Union enjoyed more victories than defeats during the early years of the space race, and that these successes had significant payoffs in terms of the regime's standing abroad and the popular mood at home. The wider cult of science and technology – which the space victories both reflected and reinforced – promised to speed the country towards the construction of communism, though the results on the ground were often patchy at best, and sometimes (in the ecological damage done especially) decidedly regrettable. The embrace of science and technology was a hallmark of Soviet socialism from the outset, and it was also a feature of the Sixties era in many other countries; but at no time would the notion of progress through modernity be championed quite so powerfully as during the second half of the 1950s and the first half of the 1960s in the USSR.

FIRST, SECOND AND THIRD WORLDS

It was not just the Soviet domestic scene that was looking much changed by the end of the 1950s. Soviet dominance over Eastern European allies continued, and also grew rather less overt. Meanwhile, ties with fellow communist giant China initially blossomed, but then went downhill quickly, with a supposedly eternal friendship growing increasingly fractious. This was also the point at which Soviet eyes turned towards the developing world in a major way, as decolonisation reshaped Africa, Asia and Latin America.[1] There, Khrushchev saw untold opportunities for the USSR, investing huge effort and resources in a bid to win new allies in the struggle for the future of humanity, though with decidedly mixed results. Relations with the USA could still turn volatile quickly, not least because of conflicting interests in the developing world; but on the whole, they were notably less hostile than they had been during Stalin's last years.

Peaceful co-existence

The later part of the 1950s continued to see expanding interaction between the USSR and Western Europe. In its message to the likes of the UK, France and Italy, the Soviet leadership often sought to emphasise a sense of shared European identity that looked down on the supposedly soulless materialism and lack of culture in the US, as it aimed to split the capitalist camp. In trade, especially, a web of important relationships and interactions was emerging, as major commercial agreements were signed with West Germany in 1958 and the UK in 1959. Japan, too, was becoming an important trade partner for technology, especially. It was telling, though, that the USSR typically exported raw materials (increasingly meaning gas and oil) and imported technology and light engineering – a trend which pointed to longer-term economic weakness compared to its new partners.

On New Year's Eve 1956, members of the Western diplomatic corps had walked out in unison, as Khrushchev used his speech at the annual Kremlin ball to lambast various countries of the capitalist camp. On New Year's Eve 1957, they found him in much more ebullient form, even offering a toast to President Eisenhower. Then, a series of agreements on mutual exchanges with the US in fields such as the arts, science, tourism and agriculture was finalised in January 1958. American Ambassador Llewellyn Thompson even appeared on Soviet television in April to talk of his hopes for improving relations. Similarly, after meeting Khrushchev during a private visit to the USSR that year, former presidential candidate Adlai Stevenson wrote of how the Soviet leader had kept on bringing their conversation back to the question of how to improve US-Soviet relations. Even so, Stevenson also recalled that when he broached the issue of the uprising in Hungary, Khrushchev 'let me have it', citing recent American interference in Jordan, Lebanon and Guatemala. He also complained about his country being 'surrounded' by American bases, and went on to ask how the US would feel about a Soviet missile base 'in Mexico, or some such place'.[2]

The January 1958 agreements on cultural exchanges included provision for either side to host an exhibition showcasing the other's economic and technological achievements. Although the official rhetoric emphasised the mutual benefits of co-operation and exchange, both sides saw these events as a chance to score a precious propaganda victory.[3] The Soviet exhibition opened in New York in June 1959 and ran for a little over a month. As at the Brussels Expo, they put Sputnik front and centre, along with a model of the new *Lenin* nuclear icebreaker. The media back home boasted proudly of the exhibition's great success, but it seemingly made a fairly limited impression on the Americans who visited, and the organisers faced plenty of difficult encounters with hostile émigrés, as well as accusations of regime anti-Semitism, war-mongering and more.

The second leg of this exchange of exhibitions, staged at Moscow's Sokolniki Park from late July to early September, was to prove much more noteworthy. Even before Khrushchev met the unabashed anti-communist Vice President Richard Nixon for the opening of the exhibition, the omens for their encounter were not good. Eisenhower had chosen that month as the point at which to institute what he called 'Captive Nations Week', which condemned 'the enslavement of a substantial part of the world's population by communist imperialism'. Naming the Baltic states, Armenia and Georgia among the list of victims, the decree insisted that 'these submerged nations look to the United States as the citadel of human freedom'. When he met Nixon, an angry Khrushchev told him that the Captive Nations Week initiative 'stinks like fresh horse shit'. He later took the vice president on an impromptu trip on the Moskva river, repeatedly pulling their boat up to the bank to ask bemused sunbathers whether they were slaves.[4]

Around 3 million Soviet citizens visited the US exhibition, which was no mean feat since local authorities tried to limit the distribution of tickets. While the Soviet exhibition in New York showed off recent scientific achievements that had dazzled the world, the Americans instead foregrounded the tremendous gap in living standards between the two countries. The Soviet authorities vetoed their plans to hand out cosmetics, but huge numbers lined up for free samples of Pepsi (Khrushchev tried it, and declared it 'very refreshing') and went home with all manner of pamphlets and brochures about life in the US. Lists of figures told visitors how much ordinary Americans earned and what they could purchase with that money. Even if they did not necessarily believe that such items were owned by 'ordinary' Americans, visitors were awe-struck by the latest cars, televisions, kitchen appliances, children's toys and other items on show. Oskar Rabin recalled of his own visit to the exhibition that his friend drank fifty cups of Pepsi, while he tore out and took home reproductions of famous American artworks from the books left on display (which was exactly what the Americans wanted people to do).[5] The most memorable part of the exhibition, though, came as Khrushchev and Nixon inspected a mocked-up 'typical' American home: with both politicians and a group of reporters cramped together in a tight space, the two men grew especially vehement in their disagreements about the merits of capitalism and communism, jabbing each other in the chest with their fingers and displaying obvious personal animosity.

The heated clash with Nixon hardly boosted Khrushchev's reputation as a statesman, but it did little real damage to Soviet-US relations. A few months later, he was undertaking the first ever visit to the US by a Soviet leader: a two-week jaunt described by one seasoned reporter as 'undoubtedly the most fascinating story that I covered'.[6] Over the course of ten days, the Soviet delegation was a blur of movement right across the US, visiting New York City, Los Angeles, San Francisco, Pittsburgh, Des Moines and elsewhere. Khrushchev was at perhaps his most maverick during the trip, sometimes engaging in furious shouting matches with critics, sometimes cracking jokes, petting babies, going on television, inspecting everything from livestock to train station lockers and the self-service canteen of the IBM plant (which he was particularly impressed by).[7] Sometimes boisterous and charming, but occasionally outright aggressive, he was followed everywhere by a huge crowd of journalists, who sensed a good story: from the first moment on, he missed few opportunities to play to the gallery. Just two days before he arrived in the US, the Soviet Union had successfully launched the first probe to reach the moon. As soon as he and Eisenhower sat down to talk at the White House, Khrushchev handed over a model of the probe in question. Later on in the trip, he also gave communist red star badges to each of the president's grandchildren.

Convinced that he could get through to ordinary Americans and counter the lies of Western propaganda, Khrushchev spoke whenever and wherever he could, and was also prone to impromptu mingling with crowds of onlookers, much to the chagrin of his security team. In Hollywood, he met the likes of Marilyn Monroe, Judy Garland, Frank Sinatra, Bob Hope and Kirk Douglas among many others, famously planting a kiss on *Vertigo* star Kim Novak for the press. He was bitterly disappointed, though, when plans to visit Disneyland were cancelled on security grounds by the local police. Sensing an underhand insult, Khrushchev complained lengthily and somewhat surreally to an audience full of movie stars about the whole episode.

Khrushchev also caught up with his friend Roswell Garst in Iowa (the pair had first met when Garst visited the USSR selling seeds in 1955) and thoroughly enjoyed himself in the process. One member of the travelling party who seems to have missed most of this was Mikhail Sholokhov, author of the classic novel *Quiet Flows the Don*. Taken along as a symbol of Soviet cultural prestige, but only after a preliminary warning from Khrushchev not to let his drinking become a source of embarrassment, Sholokhov apparently tracked down the American author William Faulkner in San Francisco, where the pair promptly hit the whisky together for several days, despite having no language in common.[8] At the end of the trip, a couple of days at Camp David with the president and his grandchildren also helped Khrushchev and Eisenhower start to build a personal rapport, agreeing to hold a summit in Paris the following year about disarmament and the future of Berlin. Present as an interpreter, Viktor Sukhodrev later wrote that Khrushchev was so keen to make a good impression that he asked to be taught the words 'my friend' in English, so that he could say this to Eisenhower, which he then did repeatedly (even so, he had quickly shut down Eisenhower's earlier attempt to start a conversation about golf).[9] Concrete progress on important issues was to prove minimal, however, with Khrushchev's hopes of improving trade ties, making headway on disarmament and the cancellation of Soviet war debts to the US all going unfulfilled.

Much of the progress that had been made in building a better relationship between the USSR and US was immediately derailed not long after Khrushchev's return home, however. The CIA had already been sending its U2 spy-planes on occasional reconnaissance missions over Soviet territory for several years by this point. The Soviet Union was unable to match the Americans' advanced technology and was apparently incapable of shooting the planes down at their operational altitude of over 20,000 metres. For Khrushchev, the flights had started to become a particular frustration, since they so painfully showed up Soviet vulnerability.[10] Then, in the early hours of 1 May 1960, Francis Gary Powers set off on the latest such flight from an American airbase at Peshawar in Pakistan, flying across Afghanistan and deep into Soviet airspace, photographing the territory below.

As usual, the flight was quickly picked up on radar once Powers entered Soviet territory, and both Khrushchev and Defence Minister Rodion Malinovsky were kept regularly informed of its progress (the former even while he observed the annual May Day parade from the Lenin mausoleum). This time, it was decided that all possible effort should be put into shooting down the offending plane: airspace was closed to civilian air traffic across much of the USSR in order to track and chase it. Around the city of Sverdlovsk in the Urals, two battalions fired new S-75 surface-to-air missiles at Powers' plane: one of them brought it down, though another hit a Soviet plane that was chasing Powers, killing its pilot.[11] Against all expectations,

Powers survived. Furthermore, he neither committed suicide (for which he had been provided with a toxic pin) nor activated the mechanism to destroy his plane's highly advanced camera before he was captured.

After a year in which he had repeatedly emphasised the importance of improving relations with the US, Khrushchev was left in a rather invidious position, feeling personally betrayed by Eisenhower. On 5 May, he publicly announced that the USSR had downed an American U2, asking his audience what would happen if Soviet planes were caught over New York or Chicago; but he deliberately made no mention of the pilot's fate. Assuming that Powers had been killed and his U2 destroyed in the crash, the Americans then claimed that they had actually lost a weather research plane that had accidentally entered Soviet airspace. On 7 May, though, the American lie was exposed, as Khrushchev suddenly revealed that Powers was alive – showing off his gun, poison capsule and other items of kit – and was to be put on trial. (Powers was ultimately released in February 1962, when he was famously swapped for the Soviet spy 'Rudolf Abel' at the Glienicke Bridge in Berlin, since known as 'the Bridge of Spies'.) Public meetings were held to condemn the US, photos from the plane's camera were published in the Soviet media, and the wreckage of the U2 was put on public display at Gorky Park in Moscow. Soon afterwards, that wreckage served as the backdrop for a surreal press conference, at which Khrushchev climbed up on a chair and debated with himself whether or not he ought to abandon the upcoming Paris summit in light of Eisenhower's 'betrayal'.[12]

Days later, as most of the travelling party were on the aeroplane waiting to depart, Khrushchev was still going back and forth over whether to go to Paris in light of the U2 episode, eventually deciding that he would. Once in the French capital, his sense of belligerence erupted again. Seemingly believing that Eisenhower would have to find a way to placate him in order to keep the summit from embarrassing failure, at a preliminary meeting on 16 May Khrushchev demanded a personal apology from the president and a promise of no further spying flights over Soviet territory. When Eisenhower refused to provide either of those things, the Soviet party turned around and headed back to Moscow, even before the summit – which Khrushchev had long sought – formally opened. He then pulled out of disarmament talks planned for June 1960 and withdrew an invitation for Eisenhower to visit

Moscow. Disdaining what he viewed as Khrushchev's 'hysterics' over the whole incident, Mikoyan wrote later that wrecking the talks in Paris had put the work of reducing international tensions back by years.[13] The diplomatic rancour continued for some time, with Minister of Defence Malinovsky warning at the end of May that if the overflights persisted, Soviet forces would not only shoot down the planes, but also bomb the bases they set off from.[14]

Khrushchev's next trip to the US – for the UN General Assembly in 1960 – was an altogether more fraught affair than the first. En route by boat, the Soviet delegation heard the news that its new Congolese ally, Patrice Lumumba, had been overthrown. Arriving at New York on 19 September, local dockers refused to service the Soviet boat and crowds of people gathered at the dockside with signs and megaphones, denouncing Khrushchev and communism. This time, Khrushchev stayed at the Soviet mission on Park Avenue. Directed by security not to go out wandering, he soon grew agitated and 'thrashed about like a tiger in a cage'. Knowing there were journalists waiting outside, at one point he went onto the balcony and gave an impromptu press conference from there, bellowing to be heard over the noise of passing traffic and shaking his fist as motorists booed and honked at him on their way past.[15]

Convinced that the Soviet Union continually got a raw deal at the UN, Khrushchev attended the 1960 General Assembly, intent on making himself heard (giving almost a dozen speeches while he was there). From the outset, he launched a charm offensive with leaders from the developing world in particular, seeking to mobilise them behind a planned condemnation of colonialism. This caused considerable agitation among the major Western powers, since the number of UN members from the developing world was growing at such a pace (sixteen newly independent African countries had joined in 1960 alone) that they could soon constitute a majority, if allied to the countries of the socialist camp.[16]

When he got the chance to speak from the rostrum, on 23 September, Khrushchev poured his energy into personal attacks on Eisenhower and UN Secretary-General Dag Hammarskjöld for the organisation's pro-Western bias. This was a charge which had some considerable foundation in reality, and one that resonated with plenty of delegations from the developing world. Khrushchev demanded reform to ensure that both the socialist and the non-aligned camps were better represented in UN structures and decisions. His calls to reorganise the UN went nowhere, but there was considerable sympathy from developing-world delegations for other parts of Khrushchev's address.[17] Speaking with regard to on-going strife in Congo, he declared 'we have stood, we stand, and always will stand for the rights of the people of Africa'. He lauded the bravery of peoples fighting against colonialism around the world (citing struggles in Algeria, Kenya, Rwanda, Northern Rhodesia and Puerto Rico) and called on the UN to take 'immediate steps towards the complete abolition of the colonial system of government', describing it bluntly as 'barbarism' and 'savagery'.

Totally unaccustomed to handling criticism and genuine debate, Khrushchev's temperament let him down badly at the UN. He heckled and roared his disagreement at numerous delegations as he saw fit, and when a number of speakers attacked Soviet dominance over Eastern Europe in light of his own condemnation of colonialism, he was unable to contain himself. The Soviet leader shouted at the top of his lungs and pounded the table with his fists in fury. When the Filipino delegate, Lorenzo Sumulong, raised the same point again, Khrushchev's patience finally snapped. According to Sukhodrev, Khrushchev had by that stage shouted himself hoarse and broken his wristwatch pounding the table, while stamping his feet had proved useless, since the deep carpet meant his stamps could barely be heard. Taking up a right to reply to Sumulong, Khrushchev launched into another furious tirade from the rostrum, which prompted a further rejoinder from Sumulong. Khrushchev then famously removed a shoe and pounded it on the table in protest, with the session ending in ignominy as the chairman broke his gavel and eventually silenced the apoplectic Khrushchev by turning off his microphone.[18] Whether or not they sympathised with his political message, friends and rivals alike found such behaviour unbecoming and embarrassing on the global stage.

Always close to the heart of US-Soviet relations at this time was the matter of West Berlin. Located almost 200 kilometres inside East German territory, West Berlin had, from the outset, been an awkward presence for the socialist camp, both as a known centre of Western espionage activity (in 1955, for example, a secret tunnel dug under East Berlin allowed the West to listen in on almost 370,000 telephone calls between Berlin and Moscow before it was discovered)[19] and as a showpiece of capitalist economic achievement. It had proved impossible to move beyond the temporary occupation regime put in place by the allies at the end of the war, since neither the US nor the USSR was willing to agree concessions that might strengthen the other's hand in a future united Germany. Most problematic for East German leader Walter Ulbricht was the open border between East and West Berlin. The number of people fleeing to West Berlin, from where they could travel on to West Germany, was large and growing. For 1954, the figure stood at around 173,000; by 1955 it was over 270,000; and in 1956 it reached 316,000. Such losses of people – most often the young and educated – were clearly unsustainable for the East German regime, and Ulbricht made this perfectly clear to the Kremlin. In the first instance, the Soviet side provided East Germany with economic aid and wrote off its debts, all of which was supposed to help raise living standards inside the GDR, so that people would stop wanting to leave, but to no avail. Seeking to get what he wanted, Ulbricht's leverage was not the threat to leave the communist bloc, but the warning that his regime might simply collapse if more help were not forthcoming from Moscow. Both for strategic purposes and for reasons of international prestige, Khrushchev could not countenance the loss of communist East Germany.[20]

By 1958, Ulbricht was pushing harder than ever and insisting that his regime had the right to full control over West Berlin, though the Soviet side still wished to avoid the hugely dangerous fallout that any unilateral action would surely cause. On 10 November 1958, Khrushchev had announced during a speech at the Moscow Palace of Sports that the situation in Berlin had to be dealt with once and for all. On 27 November, he sent a formal ultimatum to Eisenhower, giving six months for a suitable deal to be agreed on Berlin's future. The alternative, Khrushchev warned, was for the Soviet Union to sign a peace treaty with the East Germans, which would mean the USSR giving up formal powers and responsibilities agreed as part of the occupation arrangements for post-war Germany. Since one of these responsibilities involved guaranteeing Western access to West Berlin, a separate peace treaty would almost certainly mean the East Germans cutting off all Western access to West Berlin – and probably also a subsequent attempt to forcibly absorb West Berlin into the GDR. Once Eisenhower agreed to hold a conference of foreign ministers to discuss the Berlin question, though, Khrushchev's first ultimatum on the matter was quietly shelved.

The election of John F. Kennedy as US president in November 1960 was a chance to start resetting a US-Soviet relationship that had soured badly since the U2 incident. Khrushchev was delighted to see Kennedy defeat Nixon, whom he had already come to loathe, and he fancied himself able to get the better of the privileged and inexperienced young man entering the White House. Kennedy and Khrushchev were both keen to meet: the former wanted to begin work on a nuclear test ban agreement, while the latter wanted to press again on Berlin. They eventually came face to face over two days in Vienna at the start of June 1961. Again, the initial portents were not great. Only days before travelling to Austria, Kennedy had promised a major boost to American defence spending and a more assertive foreign policy in the developing world, prompting Khrushchev to cancel planned military cuts of his own.

Meeting on the first day at the US embassy in Vienna and on the second day at the Soviet embassy, Khrushchev and Kennedy mostly got along reasonably well, albeit without finding much of substance to agree upon. The part that Kennedy dreaded – the discussion about Berlin – came on the second day. Hectoring and chivvying all the time, Khrushchev insisted that the USSR could wait no longer to solve the question of Berlin. Kennedy worked hard to disabuse the bullish Soviet leader of his conviction that the US would not really be willing to go to war over the city if pushed. In spite of the president's clarity of resolve on this, Khrushchev closed by issuing a new ultimatum: once again, he gave six months for the US to agree terms on Germany's future, or else he would sign a treaty with the GDR, ending Soviet occupation rights and turning over to Ulbricht control of access to West Berlin. By the time they parted ways, each man had explicitly warned the other about the possibility of war breaking out between them over Berlin.[21]

Ulbricht had first floated the idea of building a wall to solve his West Berlin problem back in 1952, but Stalin had not been keen and the plan was soon dropped. Khrushchev had also resisted any such talk at first, insisting instead that improving conditions inside the GDR would be a better solution. By the summer of 1961, though, he was running out of options and Ulbricht was pressing with remarkable persistence, as his emigration crisis again began to accelerate.[22] From around 120,000 refugees in 1959, the figure rose to over 180,000 in 1960. For May 1961 alone, the total was almost 18,000. Following the Vienna summit, by the start of July almost 1,000 people were leaving the GDR every day. Finally, after poring over maps of Berlin while on holiday, on 6 July Khrushchev finally sent word to the Soviet ambassador in East Berlin to tell Ulbricht 'yes'.

Although he urged extreme caution, and insisted that the East German troops should build the wall only on their own territory, Khrushchev was nonetheless wary enough of the potential fallout that he had Soviet military forces put on full alert. At the last minute, the heads of other allied regimes across the region were also warned by Moscow of what was about to come, and were advised to be ready for every eventuality, including economic sanctions and military conflict. Then, in the middle of the night between 12 and 13 August, GDR troops put up the first iteration of what would become the Berlin Wall.

At this stage, the wall consisted of around 140 kilometres of barbed wire and wooden posts, but later it was to be turned into 'bricks and mortar'. The division of Berlin immediately scandalised public opinion around the world, though Soviet media presented the wall as a result of Western aggression and intransigence. Western leaders naturally condemned it, but they did so with no particular vehemence. Although it was politically unacceptable to say so publicly, Georgy Kornienko (an official at the Soviet embassy in Washington at the time) insisted that top US officials 'breathed a sigh of relief' once the wall was up.[23] It showed Kennedy that West Berlin was not going to be grabbed by force, and that it also solved East Germany's refugee problem, and in the process considerably reduced the danger of war breaking out. Accusations still flew on both sides of the divide, but much of the heat was now taken out of the Berlin situation as a facet of the superpower relationship.

Eternal friendship under strain

Relations with East European regimes were also changing considerably by the later part of the 1950s. While the invasion of Hungary had clearly demonstrated Moscow's willingness to intervene as it saw fit in extreme situations, day-to-day dominance over the affairs of Bucharest, Prague, Sofia and elsewhere was much reduced since Stalin's death. In the likes of the Warsaw Pact and Comecon (the Council for Mutual Economic Assistance), a genuine element of multilateralism began to appear in decision making, with Soviet plans sometimes being rejected by allies, and countries of the region gaining a little more latitude to fashion their own policies at home and abroad.[24] Relations with the Asian half of the communist camp, and with China in particular, would prove more problematic.

The middle part of the 1950s had appeared to be something of a golden age for Sino-Soviet relations. In May 1953, Mikoyan had been sent to Beijing to bolster a friendship that Stalin had put under some considerable strain with his exploitative trade deals and demeaning attitude towards Mao. By the time of his return home, Mikoyan had promised Soviet money and technical expertise for the construction (or reconstruction) of more than ninety major projects. Thousands of Soviet technicians and advisers were soon overseeing the construction of Chinese shipyards, petrol refineries and railway lines, as well as helping to train a new officer corps for the Chinese military. A February 1957 report also showed at that point that more than 6,200 Chinese students were studying in Soviet higher education institutions.[25] In 1954, Khrushchev promised to help China develop peaceful nuclear energy, before going further in October 1957 and agreeing to help Mao build his own nuclear bomb. This included training Chinese physicists at top-secret installations in the USSR, providing blueprints and scientific literature, building an experimental reactor and cyclotron near Beijing, and even promising to transfer a working model bomb for study purposes.[26] All told, the Soviet assistance programme to China was not only the biggest that the USSR ever undertook, it was also, in relative terms, the biggest ever undertaken by any country anywhere.[27] As Khrushchev later recalled it, this was a time when the two leaderships talked about everything and 'joked together and laughed a lot'.[28]

One Soviet participant in these interactions recalled great warmth of feeling among ordinary people in both countries, adding that there was a real sense of pride in the USSR at what was being achieved in China.[29] Mao, though, always remained deeply sensitive to any hint of presumed Soviet superiority. Although he publicly reaffirmed the USSR as the leading light of the world socialist camp, Mao was increasingly convinced that role would soon be China's, and it would be they who reached communism first. Not yet visible to the outside world, the months and years that followed the Secret Speech also saw increasing division emerging between the USSR and China around their respective attitudes to Stalin, with each side coming to perceive the other as more and more ideologically wayward. Mao did accept that Stalin had been mistaken on a number of points; though, as one scholar has noted, these mistakes were nearly always instances where Stalin had treated China unkindly.[30] The world's two major communist parties, then, were starting to diverge from one another ideologically, even while their relationship seemed at its strongest.

When the Soviet leadership proposed a plan to build some shared military infrastructure inside China in early 1958, Mao bridled, seeing an attempt at encroachment on Chinese prerogatives and territory. As the Kremlin did not perceive what the problem was, its continued pestering on the matter inflamed Chinese suspicions. Getting under way around the same time, Mao's Great Leap Forward (a bid to transform the Chinese economy and society at breakneck speed) set alarm bells ringing in Moscow, especially once Bulgaria began to talk of emulating the Chinese approach. When Soviet experts inside China and then Soviet leaders cautioned against repeating the kind of mistakes that had been made in the USSR years earlier, the warnings were dismissed as Soviet chauvinism and served only to aggravate Mao. At the Twenty-First Party Congress in 1959, Khrushchev obliquely criticised China's efforts at economic transformation, insisting that they must not be aped inside the USSR. When the Great Leap Forward started to prove a catastrophic failure – with perhaps 13 million dying of famine and the Chinese economy left shattered – Mao intensified his own cult of personality and convinced himself that practically any and all domestic critics were in the pay of Soviet subversion.

By this stage, foreign policy divisions were also growing serious. Khrushchev's emphasis on peaceful co-existence with the US was anathema to Mao's thinking on international affairs, not least since the US stood as the key obstacle to Chinese hopes of bringing Taiwan under the control of Beijing. Refusing to see Chinese territorial ambitions denied in the name of improving relations between the USA and USSR, in the summer of 1958 Mao unexpectedly began shelling Taiwan. Although friendship treaties obliged them to do so, the Chinese had not bothered to forewarn their Soviet partners of the assault. When the US reaffirmed its willingness to defend Taiwan with force if need be – even hinting at preparedness to use nuclear weapons – Moscow had little option but to remind the Americans that China was an ally it had sworn to aid if attacked. This quickly became a point of especially high global tension, and the prospect of being drawn into a nuclear war with the US thanks to Mao's unpredictable foreign policy greatly alarmed the Soviet leadership. The model nuclear bomb that was, by that point, loaded onto a train ready for transportation to China would never leave the USSR, as a wavering Khrushchev first delayed its delivery and then rescinded the promise.

When Khrushchev visited Beijing in October 1959 for the celebrations of the tenth anniversary of the Chinese Communist Party (CCP) taking power, relations deteriorated further. First, he left his Chinese hosts hugely unimpressed by talking positively about his recent US trip and about Eisenhower's desire for peace, even as the Americans still openly supported Mao's nemesis in Taiwan, Chiang Kai-shek.[31] Already strained personal relations with Mao turned to heated arguments during their private talks, and the Soviet leader ultimately cut his visit short and headed home after only three days. When Khrushchev met other Warsaw Pact leaders in February 1960, he again took great pride in his trip to the US and the seeming success of peaceful coexistence. Present at the session as an observer, Mao's ally Kang Sheng warned against such 'revisionism' in thinking about the imperialist camp, and things rapidly descended into a shouting match between him and Khrushchev. At a formal banquet that evening, Khrushchev likened the Chinese leadership to 'a worn-out rubber boot which one can only throw in the corner'.[32]

When an uprising in Chinese-controlled Tibet was put down violently in spring 1959, and the Dalai Lama fled to India, relations between China and India quickly turned volatile, leaving the Soviet leadership struggling to balance two mutually antagonistic allies. When Soviet and Chinese delegations came face to face in Bucharest at a June 1960 meeting of world communist parties, both sides went on the attack, with Khrushchev and Peng Zhen, the head of the Chinese delegation, trading insults. Most dramatically, in August, Khrushchev ran out of patience with perceived displays of Chinese ingratitude and peremptorily withdrew all Soviet technical specialists from

China, removing blueprints for good measure and leaving hundreds of incomplete projects across the country. Both sides still publicly spoke of friendship (and allies begged them to come to terms with one another for the greater good), but the chances of salvaging a positive relationship were rapidly diminishing.

Reaching out to the developing world

Three months after his diatribe against colonialism at the UN, and a mere eleven days before his Congolese ally Patrice Lumumba was murdered, Khrushchev again staked out the Soviet position on the developing world in January 1961. He told his audience in Moscow that the growing wave of decolonisation across former European empires represented a devastating blow to the capitalist camp and was creating 'exceptionally favourable circumstances' for the growth of communist influence. He added that 'Asia, Africa and Latin America are now the most important centres of revolutionary struggle against imperialism.' In order to clarify where all this stood in relation to his rhetoric on peaceful co-existence, he then drew a crucial distinction between different types of wars. Citing on-going struggles in Vietnam and Algeria, as well as the recently victorious revolution in Cuba, he insisted that anti-colonial wars of liberation were different from other wars – he even called the Algerian struggle 'sacred' – stating that communists 'fully support such just wars, and march in the front rank with peoples waging liberation struggles'.[33]

The old notion that countries not already inside the communist bloc were effectively to be regarded as part of the hostile imperialist camp had died with Stalin. The Bandung Conference of April 1955 – at which twenty-nine African and Asian countries came together in Indonesia to declare their opposition to colonialism and to call for solidarity across the developing world – further convinced leaders in Moscow that decolonisation now had a crucial role to play in global affairs. Indian Prime Minister Nehru (accompanied by his daughter, Indira Gandhi) then visited the USSR in June 1955. Over the course of sixteen days, they raced around the country, travelling to Moscow, Stalingrad, Magnitogorsk, Uzbekistan, Turkmenistan and Georgia, visiting collective farms and industrial plants, and attending all manner of civic events along the way. In Samarkand, Nehru addressed a crowd of perhaps 500,000 in the city's historic Registan Square, speaking positively of India's ancient and modern links with Central Asia. One journalist from the *Times of India* offered readers at home a tantalising vision of Tashkent in particular, describing how Soviet power there had 'changed the face of this neglected heart of Asia and brought modern civilisation within the reach of the common man'.[34]

While resolutely set on retaining India's non-aligned status, Nehru praised Soviet anti-colonialism and anti-racism, also insisting that there were plenty of valuable opportunities for co-operation between the two countries. A Soviet gift of 300 tractors and other agricultural machinery for India, as Nehru eventually departed the USSR, helped the trip to finish on a high note.[35] The success of this initial visit apparently also convinced Khrushchev of the value to be had from bringing at least some Soviet Central Asian officials into positions of real influence in Moscow – something that had barely happened at all previously – in order to help the heavily European leadership understand and respond to developments in the decolonising world.[36]

Earlier attempts to grow Soviet influence in the developing world met with serious challenges. Faced with American pressure over its decision to nationalise land owned by the United Fruit Company, the Arbenz regime in Guatemala had negotiated to buy Czechoslovak arms through the USSR in 1954. This apparent embrace of the socialist camp prompted the US to lead a brutal coup in Guatemala, which served as a powerful lesson to others interested in responding to advances from Moscow. Nonetheless, in February 1955 a first batch of co-operation agreements was signed with India, and Soviet specialists were soon at work building a giant steel mill at Bhilai and training officers for the Indian army.[37] By the end of the year, the Soviet Union had agreed a major arms deal (on generous terms) with Nasser's Egypt – a country whose influence across the Arab world made it a very valuable friend. Khrushchev's strident condemnation of Britain and France during the Suez Crisis of 1956 won the USSR many admirers in the Middle East especially, even though he had ultimately provided no military assistance to Nasser when asked.

Soon enough, the Soviet Union had signed trade deals with Burma, Yemen, Syria, Afghanistan and Indonesia, among others. It also began trading with Argentina, Brazil and Chile, swapping oil for items like wool, coffee and copper.[38] At a December 1957 Afro-Asian Peoples' Solidarity Conference in Cairo, the Soviet representative in attendance emphasised his country's willingness to train specialists and build infrastructure in the developing world, adding 'tell us what you need, and we are going to help you'.[39] Before long, Soviet advisers and resources were being despatched all across the Global South, alongside healthcare specialists, builders and teachers, with bodies like the Komsomol and the Soviet Women's Committee also reaching out to their counterpart organisations in an effort to develop friendly ties.[40] The scale of these interactions was soon substantial. One June 1964 report on Soviet aid for educational development noted on-going efforts to build schools, universities and other institutions in India, Burma, Ethiopia, the Republic of Guinea, Cambodia, Mali, Tunisia, Afghanistan, Algeria and elsewhere.[41]

At first somewhat restrained in its criticism of French attempts to stave off Algerian independence (a fact rooted in hopes that France might yet be separated from the Western bloc), after the February 1958 bombing of the town of Sakiet Sidi Youssef, which killed more than sixty Algerian civilians, Moscow's condemnation was swift and powerful, with Khrushchev insisting that the Algerians had the right to self-determination.[42] Following a July 1958 coup in Baghdad, Iraq also became much more amenable to the USSR and was soon signing co-operation agreements. When it looked for a time as though the West might intervene militarily against Iraq's new rulers, Khrushchev threatened to respond robustly to any such move. Soviet experts headed there to open up new oil fields and train a corps of local experts (previously Iraqi oil had been heavily administered by foreigners). By the early 1960s, over 1,300 Iraqis were studying oil production methods in the USSR.[43] Soviet propaganda aimed at Asia, Africa and Latin America also increased dramatically from the late 1950s, with Radio Moscow joining the likes of the BBC and Voice of America among the biggest broadcasters to the developing world.[44] Determined to get to grips with a continent that the authorities in Moscow knew relatively little about at first, the Soviet Africa Institute was founded in 1960 as the country's key site of expertise on Africa, and soon had about 350 scholars studying African law, languages, economics, history and geography.

It was not only doctors, teachers and scientists that the Soviet Union was sending to the developing world. With KGB Chairman and former Head of the Komsomol Alexander Shelepin eager to see US energies and resources depleted wherever possible, the security organs worked hard to stir up trouble for the Americans everywhere they could. Money and training were provided to revolutionary groups like the Sandinistas in Nicaragua, the MPLA in Angola, the ANC in South Africa and to communist parties (both legal and illegal) in places like Chile and Uruguay. Soviet intelligence agents also worked hard to turn governments and public opinion against the US in third countries, planting made-up scandals in the media and forging incriminating documents about CIA interference.[45]

In spite of all this, the Soviet Union – much like the US at the same time – lacked any kind of grand strategy to 'penetrate' or else 'win over' the developing world. In fact, more often than not during the Cold War, it was smaller countries that first approached one, or even both, of the superpowers (sometimes playing them off against one another), seeking to establish relationships of trade, aid and perhaps also some kind of protection from rivals.[46] There was never any shortage of countries in the developing world keen to learn from Soviet achievements in fields like economic planning, prospecting for gas and oil and drives to eradicate illiteracy. For a few years from the late 1950s, flush with optimism for the future and eager to seize the new opportunities that presented themselves, Moscow was particularly receptive to such approaches, barely even making serious analyses of the costs, benefits and risks involved before handing over money and goods.[47]

After years in which the region had been starved of investment and – as in tsarist times – presided over by a succession of Europeans, Soviet Central Asia now gained in status as it became an important facet of Moscow's bid to win friends in the developing world. In the first instance, this meant more funding for the likes of Uzbekistan and Tajikistan, as authorities strove to convey the message that the region was not some kind of colonial backwater, but an important part of the Soviet project.[48] Even so, when Khrushchev addressed a crowd of several hundred thousand people in the Uzbek capital Tashkent during December 1955, he got himself in an unseemly muddle. He opened by mistakenly calling his audience 'Tajiks' and noting how well they were now doing in growing cotton, compared to their neighbours the Uzbeks. An aide eventually managed to tell him that he was, in fact, talking to Uzbeks rather than Tajiks. As was his way, Khrushchev tried to ride out the faux pas in style, telling the audience he had misspoken on purpose, in order to test their reaction, and then expressing his happiness that they had responded correctly to his 'joke'.[49]

Eager to demonstrate the benefits that Soviet socialism could provide in a non-European setting, visitors to the USSR from the developing world were often sent to Central Asia to see the universities, medical facilities, hydroelectric dams and irrigation systems that had been constructed there under Soviet rule.[50] One basic message of all this was that developing countries could now – with Soviet help – reach socialism without first having to go through the capitalist stage of development.[51] Tashkent, in particular, became the showpiece city for demonstrating that Soviet socialism could provide a non-Western vision of modernity, bringing cultural figures from across the developing world to the USSR for the inaugural Afro-Asian Writers' Conference in 1958 (later also holding a festival of Asian and African cinema) and subsequently hosting many thousands of students and tourists from Africa and Asia, especially. Officials from Central Asia were more and more frequently deployed as Soviet representatives to events and embassies across the Global South, in order to bolster the USSR's credentials as a 'non-European' power and to present the Soviet model as one suitable for assimilation outside the industrialised world.[52] Similarly, propaganda publications like *Sovetskaya zhenshchina* (*Soviet Woman*) magazine regularly featured women from Turkmenistan, Kyrgyzstan and other Central Asian republics in order to demonstrate that a balance had been achieved in the USSR between granting women equality and maintaining Islamic customs.[53]

Ethiopian Emperor Haile Selassie toured the USSR in June 1959, leaving with tens of millions of dollars' worth of credit with which to purchase Soviet products. Soon enough, Soviet experts were also to be found in the Horn of Africa, prospecting for valuable minerals, building schools and industrial plants. Feted with praise and awarded the honorific title the Order of Suvorov, Selassie went so far as to call the USSR 'the world's greatest power'. Even so, such flattery did not prevent the development of friendly ties between the USSR and Ethiopia's new regional rival, Somalia. Almost as soon as Somalia gained statehood in 1960, it opened diplomatic relations with Moscow; and within a year, its prime minister, Abdirashid Sharmarke, was visiting the Kremlin, signing agreements that saw Soviet experts travelling to Somalia to build hospitals, a radio station, a deep-water port and more. By the time fighting eventually broke out between Ethiopia and Somalia in 1964 – a conflict that Soviet leaders tried hard to forestall – the USSR had done a great deal to train and equip both sides' armed forces, selling both parties armoured cars, tanks, fighter jets and artillery.[54] Ties with the rebels in Angola also began after a Portuguese crackdown there in February 1961; these were followed by growing links with Guinea-Bissau and Cape Verde, as they, too, struggled for freedom from Lisbon's control. Closer to the forefront of Soviet ambitions for Africa around this time, though, were Ghana and Guinea. In both countries, the Soviet leadership saw great possibilities, perceiving them as potential 'shop windows' of Soviet development to inspire and win over the rest of the region.[55]

The Soviet Union and Ghana began a kind of courtship when the former sent a representative to the Ghanaian independence celebrations in March 1957, but heavy economic pressure from the West initially convinced President Kwame Nkrumah to hold off on establishing full diplomatic ties. Thanks to both persistence and generous terms on offer from Moscow, though, relations developed quickly from 1959. In Guinea, where Sékou Touré explicitly called himself a socialist, independence in October 1958 was soon followed by formal relations being established with the USSR, which stepped in when France extricated itself from the country in a particularly spiteful manner, with former colonial overseers smashing or taking everything they possibly could before leaving. Again, Soviet expertise and resources poured into the country in a bid to establish much-needed infrastructure, such as schools, roads and industry.

Potentially the greatest partner of all – in terms of its location, population size and wealth of natural resources – lay at the very heart of Africa. In Patrice Lumumba, the Congolese independence movement had a charismatic and articulate figurehead. Although no communist, he did have sympathy for key aspects of Soviet thinking and a strong antipathy towards Western imperialism. The country's first democratic elections in June 1960 brought Lumumba to power, and mutual diplomatic recognition with the USSR ensued. This created profound consternation in Washington, where he was viewed as a dangerous radical. Within weeks of Lumumba coming to power, though, things began falling apart in Congo, as Western-backed secessionists rose up in mineral-rich Katanga province. The situation was soon perilous, and the UN sent a mission to the country, ostensibly to help keep the peace. In reality, this mission (made up largely of NATO troops) was far from impartial, with both the US and UN Secretary-General Dag Hammarskjöld eager to get rid of Lumumba before Soviet influence in Congo fully took hold. Before long, Lumumba perceived the true situation and urgently requested Soviet help.

As with Suez in 1956, Khrushchev held forth with fiery rhetoric about Soviet support for Lumumba, implying that military help would be imminent. This time, though, that rhetoric was put to the test and proven hollow. Although hugely powerful within Europe, the Soviet military did not yet have the logistical capacity to handle major operations far away in Africa.[56] With the UN force taking control of Congolese airfields, meaningful supplies could not easily be flown in. Disappointingly for Moscow, Ghana also refused either to help Lumumba or to serve as a conduit through which Soviet aid might have passed. Before long, Lumumba was overthrown and placed under arrest. Then, in January 1961, he was murdered with the connivance of American and Belgian security services.[57] At the UN and elsewhere, Soviet representatives howled their outrage, but with no discernible result. Forces still loyal to Lumumba gathered in Stanleyville province under the leadership of Antoine Gizenga and begged for Soviet help; but again they mostly received only moral support, rather than the troops and ammunition they needed.[58] Before August 1961 was out, Gizenga had given up. Taking power in Leopoldville (Kinshasa), Mobutu Sese Seko gave the embassies of all Soviet-bloc countries forty-eight hours to leave the country.

Things would get worse elsewhere, too. In Ghana, a US offer of funding for the Volta River dam project in spring 1961 saw Nkrumah increasingly turn away from the USSR, as American aid proved more generous. In Guinea, Touré was turning out to be a far from steadfast and predictable ally, as well as a hopeless debtor who was unwilling to meet loan payments and blew extensive Soviet aid on self-glorification and vanity projects. Khrushchev later recalled how the Soviet embassy in Conakry had discreetly warned that Touré and those around him (and especially his brother) were fast enriching themselves at the expense of the public.[59] Ultimately, Touré would bring the country to the verge of economic collapse, before turning against the Soviet Union and expelling its ambassador in December 1961.

Affairs in Congo, Guinea and Ghana had shown that even very extensive investment of energy and resources in the developing world could be lost almost in an instant.[60] Soviet officials also began to learn that even those leaders with whom they built seemingly strong relations were never going to be obedient puppets, doing as Moscow asked, and that Soviet plans could not simply be grafted onto African or Asian realities. In truth, the decision to support almost any anti-colonial movement (rather than just the explicitly pro-socialist ones) was always likely to produce brittle political results. In both Somalia and Ethiopia, for example, the authorities quickly grew wary of Soviet attempts to build soft power, resisting Moscow's efforts at setting up cultural exchanges and keeping the distribution of Soviet publications to a bare minimum, even as they issued more and more requests for support. With regard to India, the USSR's relations with the ruling authorities were, to some extent, predicated on Moscow not supporting the local communist party in its efforts to seek revolution.[61] Egypt, in particular, made grandiose shows of friendship with the Soviet regime and repressed communists at home almost simultaneously.

Allied to the above was a frequent failure to develop the same soft power appeal as that of the West. Where the Americans sent Hollywood movies and consumer goods, Soviet propagandists often came armed with dry economic data and the works of Marx and Lenin. Indeed, Soviet goods sent abroad were sometimes of such poor quality that they were spurned and mocked by shoppers; meanwhile, industrial and military hardware broke down quickly.[62] Sometimes the promised goods simply never arrived, or else came months late. Generous trade terms also backfired at times, such as when it was agreed that a loan to Burma would be repaid in rice: the Burmese subsequently handed over only the very worst of their crop to Moscow, while selling the best on the open market.[63] Furthermore, Khrushchev himself could be distinctly undiplomatic on occasion: he offended the socialist leader of Mali, Modibo Keita, in May 1962 when he visited Moscow to ask for aid, instead receiving a lecture in which he was told that socialism could not be built 'lying in the shade of a tree waiting for everything to arrange itself'.[64]

Inability to make greater headway in the developing world also had its roots in more systemic Soviet failings. With a far weaker economy, the USSR simply did not have the financial power to compete equally with the US when it came to aid. When Mozambican women's organisations asked their Soviet counterparts for items like radio equipment and type-writers, they were typically turned down, receiving instead postcards and badges.[65] A Komsomol plan to send large numbers of youth volunteers to Africa to counter the influence of the Americans' new Peace Corps, building schools and medical facilities, conducting vaccinations and fighting illit-eracy, fell through because of a lack of funding.[66] Nonetheless, the USSR proved an important force in the World Health Organization's struggle to eradicate smallpox in particular, and from 1958 the Ukrainian virologist (and Soviet deputy minister of health) Viktor Zhdanov played a vital role in pushing a mass vaccination drive that has since saved millions of lives across the planet, prompting some recent experts to suggest that he made perhaps the most important contribution to humanity of the whole twentieth century.

As the middle of the 1960s approached, and the reality of wasted resources and embarrassing setbacks mounted, Soviet thinking on the developing world eventually started to become more hard-headed, and fresh requests for aid from the likes of Uganda and Burma were rejected. Not all endeavours in the developing world up to this point had proved fruitless, though. The most resonant of all could be traced back to late summer 1959, when the KGB's key man in Latin America was despatched to Havana to take a look at what was happening there, after Fidel Castro and his band of guerrillas had over-thrown the US-backed dictator Fulgencio Batista. Armed with vodka and caviar, Alexander Alexeev quickly made contact with Che Guevara and the brothers Raúl and Fidel Castro: the former two had already embraced communism, though the latter had not. With American hostility towards the Cuban revolution intensifying all the time – Fidel Castro had initially gone to Washington in summer 1959 to ask for economic help, but a blunt refusal followed and both sides quickly grew spiteful – Alexeev asked his hosts what they might want from the Soviet Union. Knowing that Mikoyan was at that moment in Mexico, they asked that he come for talks. By the time he trav-elled to Cuba in February 1960, Mikoyan had already amassed plenty of information about the island and its new leaders, suggesting to Khrushchev that this might well be a revolution of considerable potential.[67]

The month that he spent on the island, travelling around with Fidel Castro and drawing up initial trade agreements, imbued Mikoyan with a great enthusiasm for the Cubans' revolution. Locals were soon getting their first real look at the USSR, too, with a major Soviet exhibition of science, technology and culture opening in central Havana as Mikoyan arrived, showing off the latest in cars, radios, clothes and books (as well as the obligatory model of Sputnik) to a fascinated Cuban public.[68] On his return to Moscow, Mikoyan's support for Cuba and Castro quickly proved infectious, as he told comrades of how the trip had transported him back to his own youth as a revolutionary in the Caucasus. What then followed between the two countries has been likened to a passionate romance that burned very bright on the Soviet side, in particular.[69]

By July 1960, Raúl Castro was in Moscow to start working out a proper economic relationship between Cuba and the USSR. The Soviet side began to send badly needed aid, bought Cuban sugar and provided Soviet oil, along with thousands of experts to help build up agriculture and industry. In Soviet popular culture, Cuba came to represent an exotic younger brother to the USSR. A sense of nostalgia and rejuvenated idealism soon enough became widespread, as Cuba also became a vicarious link to an idealised Soviet past, even providing a way to 'see the revolution again'.[70] Cinema screens showed viewers Cuban people, landscapes and culture. Journalists and poets visited what they now called 'the island of freedom' and wrote stirring travelogues of their experiences, while photo exhibitions of Cuban life and culture toured the country. The director Mikhail Kalatozov travelled to Havana and produced the propaganda movie *Soy Cuba* (*I am Cuba*), which showed the lives and struggles of the Cuban people, later winning considerable international acclaim. Fidel Castro became an immensely popular figure among young people in the Soviet Union. Young men aped his beard and his hyper-masculinity, while Soviet women lusted after him.[71] At the opening of the Fourteenth Komsomol Congress in spring 1962, delegates briefly applauded as First Secretary Pavlov announced the presence of foreign delegations from the likes of Canada, Israel, Brazil and France; but then they burst into prolonged cheers and chants of 'Cuba, Cuba, Cuba' when visitors from the Caribbean island were introduced.[72] The problem for the Soviet authorities was that all this adulation for Cuba and Castro implicitly under-lined the point that the USSR was now in a very different place as a country, with the romantic days of heroic struggle and the sense of seemingly bound-less possibilities for the future already long gone.[73]

Fidel Castro and Khrushchev finally met in New York towards the end of 1960, as both men attended the UN General Assembly. Spurning the advice of his security team, Khrushchev had his driver take him on an impromptu visit to Castro's Harlem hotel – causing New York traffic chaos along the way – where the two embraced and quickly became friends.[74] On returning to the Soviet embassy that night, an impressed Khrushchev declared that the young and virile Castro was 'like a horse that hadn't been broken yet'.[75] In light of events in Congo, the Soviet leadership was acutely aware of how quickly such promising allies could be lost. After a spate of terrorist bomb-ings on Cuba and attempts to assassinate Castro, Kennedy signed off on a plan that saw up to 1,500 Cuban exiles (picked, trained and transported by the US) attempt to force their way onto the island to launch an anti-Castro uprising at the Bay of Pigs in April 1961. Thanks in part to armaments and military training already provided by the USSR, the attempt was routed within a couple of days, but it left a mark. Moscow was now much more inclined to believe Cuban warnings about American plans to overturn their revolution and thus get rid of another prized Soviet ally.

The outside world inside the USSR

One of the most significant themes running through the Soviet Sixties – and one of the sharpest breaks with late Stalinism – was the expanding presence of the outside world inside the USSR. For years the authorities had carefully curated a socio-political ecosystem which, although never isolationist in its rhetoric, had relied on shutting out as wide a range of foreign influences as possible. While the country remained in some ways fundamentally closed to the outside world after Stalin – and this was especially true beyond the major cities – points of contact with people and information from other countries were proliferating all the time. The foundations for an international tourist industry were established in 1955, driven primarily by the aim of acquiring more foreign currency. This soon started to grow, in time bringing hundreds of thousands of visitors to the USSR every year. Travellers from other parts of the socialist camp always predominated, but there were also plenty from Western Europe and North America keen to take a look. The authorities tried to keep tourists and locals apart, and the KGB watched visitors as closely as it could, including stationing agents to snoop on conversations around tourist hotspots like Red Square and the Tretyakov gallery in Moscow. Even so, the flow of visitors was far too great for such separation and surveillance to be anything like comprehensive, and the authorities were anyway keen to avoid the reputational damage of being too overt in policing incoming tourists.[76]

Even without any subversive intent – and both camps came to make use of tourism for nefarious purposes during the Cold War – visitors made an impact simply by virtue of looking and behaving very differently to Soviet citizens and asking the kinds of questions that locals often could not or would not. Plenty also gave or sold all kinds of items – such as books, magazines and clothing – to the eager Soviet youths who often crowded round their hotels. A 1961 report by the Lithuanian KGB, for example, described locals buying up 'chewing gum, cigarettes, ties and records' from foreign tourists in Vilnius.[77] Police occasionally cracked down and imposed fines for such behaviour, but repeated KGB warnings about the negative impact of foreigners inside the country never proved compelling enough to counteract the regime's desire for the precious foreign currency that visitors brought with them.

As part of the new 'good life' that the Khrushchev regime promised, by the middle of the 1960s over a million Soviet citizens were also going abroad every year for tourist travel (many others were denied permission for travel, of course), mainly to Czechoslovakia, Poland and Bulgaria, but sometimes as far afield as the USA, Japan and Cameroon for those with the right connections.[78] In the name of peaceful co-existence and trust building, a few Soviet students also went to study at prestigious Western universities from the late 1950s (most notably Alexander Yakovlev, one of Gorbachev's chief reformist allies during the late 1980s), though a large number of these people were actually undercover intelligence operatives. Travel abroad became both a marker and an engine of social status, with access to foreign goods of all kinds becoming a real symbol of prestige.[79] It also highlighted the extent to which consumption – of travel in this case – was becoming an ever more important facet of the Soviet social system, as the numbers heading abroad grew year on year. Similarly, we can see the way in which the general public was increasingly being managed not just with the stick (the threat of punishment for transgressions), but also with inducements for compliance and active participation, such as permission for coveted tourist travel abroad.

Expanded grassroots interaction with Eastern Europe, including tourism, cultural exchanges and pen-pal schemes, was meant to help establish a more durable and stable relationship between the USSR and the rest of the socialist bloc, and to give Soviet travellers a reassuring sense of their country's international power and status, but it proved tricky to manage in practice.[80] Often finding shops and markets better stocked than those at home, Soviet visitors to Warsaw, East Berlin and Prague raced to buy whatever they could – from ladies' underwear and men's raincoats, through to cut glass and bed linen. The ballerina Maya Plisetskaya even wrote of eating dog food while on tour in the West in order to save funds for shopping. Because they did not want their tourists undertaking such unseemly consumer rampages, the authorities usually granted only very small per diem allowances, leaving travellers all but impoverished while abroad. This frequently aroused a sense of humiliation, and it invited scorn from hosts in the likes of Romania and Poland, where big-spending Western customers were often openly preferred to their penniless communist brethren.[81] Not only could such experiences undermine Soviet discourse about friendship within the socialist bloc, but they could also sometimes discomfit travellers by showing how far ahead of the USSR living standards were in the GDR and Czechoslovakia, especially.

Proliferating grassroots interaction with Eastern Europe, then, could prove surprisingly problematic. Years before the liberalisation programme that began in Czechoslovakia in 1968, the leaders of Soviet tour parties griped bitterly about the amount of Western music and 'immoral' foreign dancing (the Twist was a particular source of ire) that their charges were exposed to there.[82] Other countries of the bloc were little better in this sense. For a good number of years in the 1960s, for example, Romanian radio was one of the key sources of rock music in parts of Ukraine.[83] For obvious and justifiable reasons, the relationship between the USSR and its Eastern European allies has mostly been considered in terms of the former subjugating the latter, but in light of the greater interaction that followed Stalin's death, we might also start to think in terms of Eastern Europe as an important source of the irrepressible contagion that was cultural westernisation inside the USSR.

By the late 1950s, students from both the West and the developing world began to appear in increasing numbers in Soviet higher education institutions (students from fellow socialist countries had already been coming for a few years by that time). In fact, many of these foreign students appeared at the very best Soviet universities, since the authorities' aim was to impress visitors with the standard of education on offer in the USSR. This meant, of course, that they often studied and lived alongside the party and state elite of the future. Extended interaction with people from the developing world was meant to drive home to local students regime messages about the evils of Western imperialism and the importance of Soviet assistance to its victims, though there is little evidence that this outcome was achieved in practice. What we know for sure is that foreign students - and by no means only those from the West - became an important conduit through which a wide variety of goods, information and ideas from the outside world reached the Soviet student body.

As in the West, Soviet officials viewed higher education as a route by which to build global soft power, by establishing a growing body of professionals and future leaders around the globe sympathetic to the Soviet worldview. Once the USSR joined UNESCO in 1954, Khrushchev loudly touted the accessibility of Soviet universities to students from Africa, Asia and Latin America, offering a steadily growing number of stipends for those wishing to come. By 1960, there were over 1,200 students from capitalist and developing countries studying in the USSR, among them a dozen or more each from Nepal, Sudan, Tunisia, Jordan, Somalia, India, Afghanistan and Indonesia, along with almost three hundred from the United Arab Republic (a short-lived union between Syria and Egypt, created in 1958).[84] Painfully aware of how far ahead the West was at drawing in students from the developing world, in 1961 the Soviet authorities demanded that the number be ramped up to 10–12,000 a year, and soon exceeded that target comfortably.[85]

Around the peak of the first flush of Soviet optimism for engagement with the developing world, during a 1960 visit to Indonesia, Khrushchev announced the creation of the University of People's Friendship (soon renamed in honour of the late Patrice Lumumba) in Moscow, as an institution specifically for students from Africa, Asia and Latin America. When applications for the new university opened, there were a reported 43,000 submissions of interest for the initial 600 places available (demand would always outstrip supply in regard to study places for foreign students). By 1964, there were 33,000 foreign students studying in 76 Soviet cities – over half in Moscow, but with large contingents to be found in Odessa, Tashkent, Baku, Minsk, Kharkov (Kharkiv) and Kiev, too.[86]

With so many students coming and going over the following years, the picture of their experience was naturally very mixed. Lasting friendships and love affairs were not uncommon, and some people left as convinced friends of the USSR, forever grateful for the education they received. Others, though, returned home deeply jaded and sometimes downright hostile. With the Soviet authorities wary of foreigners' potential political impact on the Soviet students around them, integration with locals was often only partial at best, and some foreigners complained that they felt isolated and unable to make Soviet friends, and struggled to cope with the social system, food and climate.[87] Seemingly much more likely to encounter hostility than Arabs or Latin Americans, those from sub-Saharan Africa often had it hardest.[88] Some Africans later spoke of curious locals wanting to touch their hair and skin, or simply staring at them in the street.[89] Interactions and relationships between African men and Soviet women could be a particular point around which controversy and violence broke out in social situations. In spite of a long history of anti-racist propaganda – US racism in particular was a regular target of Soviet attacks – plenty of Africans suffered insults and sometimes also physical violence; and they grew doubly offended when uninterested authorities brushed off their complaints or else sided automatically with Soviet students as and when fights broke out.

Racial prejudice was not the only source of tension between visiting and home students. Plenty of Soviet students resented the fact that international students' stipends (which were pegged to those on offer in the West) could be as much as five times higher than those on offer for locals, or else complained that they did not have to clean their dorms or attend the hated political classes like locals did. Similarly, David Gurevich recalled that instead of building friendly ties with incoming Vietnamese students in his dormitory, he found the extent of their communist zeal alarming.[90] On occasion, confidential reports acknowledged that some Soviet students saw particularly the Africans in their midst as 'parasites and spongers'.[91] Clearly, many Soviet students were far from enthusiastic about embracing their 'internationalist duty' (as regime discourse put it) to the developing world, often proving far more interested in learning new songs and dances from Western dorm-mates than in helping or socialising with the Africans and Asians among whom they lived.[92]

On a number of occasions, frustrations boiled over in an alarming fashion. A big fight broke out between Yemeni and Soviet students in Baku during October 1963, with the Yemeni students subsequently going to their embassy in Moscow to make a formal complaint. In December 1964, a mass brawl at a Leningrad university dorm saw more than twenty Nigerian and Soviet students clash, after months of escalating tensions had gone unaddressed.[93] The death of a Ghanaian student named Edmund Assare-Addo in December 1963 – in circumstances which at least hinted at racist violence, though the evidence was perhaps not conclusive – made international media coverage and was followed by an unsanctioned protest against Soviet racism that saw perhaps five hundred African students gather on Red Square.[94] Confidential reports made it clear that the occasional physical assaults and verbal abuse of foreign students were seen by officials as a problem primarily for the damage they did to propaganda efforts, rather than for the suffering they caused the victims.[95]

Even if citizens did not necessarily embrace the struggles of the developing world, this increased interaction with foreigners and foreign cultures was changing things inside the USSR. Latin American music and literature quickly grew very popular, and ties with India helped yoga, Buddhism and Bollywood movies become a growing part of the Soviet cultural scene. More prominently, though, and more worrying for the Soviet authorities, a growing number of young people, in particular, were coming to embrace an array of Western cultural products.

By the 1960s, Western-inflected youth culture was becoming a mass phenomenon, with even otherwise conformist youth increasingly fascinated by the styles, sounds and brands of the West. Of a late 1961 trip to the Soviet capital, for example, one journalist described how 'the sound of Western

211

rhythms echoed from every restaurant in Moscow', as young people danced the Cha-Cha-Cha, the Mambo and the Rhumba.[96] Both Soviet authorities and some Western observers habitually overstated the extent to which these foreign influences demonstrated either ideological indifference or even opposition on the part of Soviet youth; but they did nonetheless offer challenges to the status quo. Most importantly, one scholar has pointed to the long-term importance of an increasing decoupling of general belief in the Soviet project – which remained strong at this stage – from everyday behaviour in matters like cultural consumption that did not conform to the authorities' expectations.[97]

While there had always been at least a few foreign authors published inside the USSR, in the late 1950s the journal *Inostrannaya literatura* (*Foreign Literature*), in particular, began bringing Soviet readers many more great works of world culture, though sometimes with just a little reworking of political and sexual content, in order to make them acceptable to Soviet officialdom.[98] Erich Maria Remarque became wildly popular for a time: when *All Quiet on the Western Front* appeared in shops, hundreds of thousands of copies were snapped up in only a few days. Halldór Laxness and Heinrich Böll, J.D. Salinger, Jack Kerouac, Gabriel García Márquez, Antoine de Saint-Exupéry and more were all published to major public interest. Soviet officialdom proved decidedly uncertain about the appropriateness of *The Catcher in the Rye*'s Holden Caulfield as a central protagonist, but readers loved the fact that his words were translated into authentic Soviet youth slang.[99] The likes of Jean-Paul Sartre and Albert Camus enjoyed wide popularity, too, as existentialism became fashionable among Soviet intellectuals. The iconic figure for most Soviet readers, though, was Ernest Hemingway.

When a new two-volume collection of Hemingway's works appeared in 1959, huge queues formed outside shops overnight.[100] Kiosks on the street sold copies of his photo, young men took to wearing chunky sweaters, growing beards (up to then largely the preserve of priests and ageing villagers) and smoking a pipe, while aspiring writers aped his staccato literary style. At film school in the 1950s, Andrei Tarkovsky's first directorial project was a production of Hemingway's short story 'The Killers'.[101] No less important was Hemingway's wider impact on changing notions of masculinity – his embrace of adventure and daring, his 'no nonsense' tough-guy image and love of hunting.[102] One recent scholar has gone so far as to assert that Hemingway was for Soviet admirers 'a paragon of machismo and manhood, conscience and courage . . . sincerity and heroism'.[103] This fed into a wider socio-cultural phenomenon of the time that was known as *romantika* – a desire to head off into the wilderness with friends, a tent and perhaps a guitar, looking for adventure, going off on long geological expeditions to the remote north or far east of the country, forsaking modern conveniences and comfort to test one's mettle. Accordingly, activities like mountaineering and cross-country skiing also surged in popularity, among young urbanites especially. In fact, it was in February 1959 that a team of nine student mountaineers from Sverdlovsk were killed in mysterious circumstances in the Ural mountains, in what has since become known as the Dyatlov Pass incident.

Western movies like *The Magnificent Seven* and *The Maltese Falcon* were screened in Soviet cinemas and drew huge audiences, raking in a lot of money and giving citizens intriguing glimpses of worlds far removed from their own.[104] French New Wave and Italian Neo-Realist films were no less important. However tame they might seem by today's standards, scenes from these kinds of movies played an important part in shaping young people's perceptions of life, fashion, romance and love.[105] While young men were trying to look and act like Hemingway, more and more young women aimed for Brigitte Bardot, whose film *Babette Goes to War* reached Soviet cinemas in 1960.[106] The Moscow International Film Festival also became a regular fixture from 1959, drawing large crowds and attracting visiting stars of world cinema, like Elizabeth Taylor and Satyajit Ray. The big winners at the festival mostly still came from the socialist world, but a clear statement of how far things had changed inside the USSR came when the festival's top prize was awarded (albeit only after Khrushchev had personally given his approval) to the Italian director Federico Fellini in 1963 for the movie *8½*. Khrushchev apparently admitted privately that he had not understood the film and therefore assumed others would find it similarly baffling.[107] Nonetheless, it became a cult hit, with one former Soviet citizen recalling that 'anyone who considered themselves intelligent had to know almost every scene by heart'.[108]

Founded in 1958, the International Tchaikovsky Piano Contest was another attempt to show off both the Soviet Union's cultural prowess and its newfound goodwill to the outside world. Still a student at New York's

Juilliard School for performing arts at the time, Van Cliburn was thoughtful, modest and deeply immersed in Russia's rich musical heritage, quickly becoming an American that Soviet citizens were allowed (and wanted) to like. As the gawky newcomer progressed further into the competition, public support for him morphed into a full-fledged mania, with huge crowds fighting to gain entry to his performances and growing audiences watching his recitals on television. When the contest reached its final stages, judges had to check with the minister of culture whether the American could be allowed to win such a prestigious Soviet competition. Unwilling to take such a bold decision, the minister went to check with Khrushchev, who gave his blessing for Cliburn to be crowned champion. By the time that he departed for home, laden with all manner of gifts from members of the public and top officials, Van Cliburn had played a series of sold-out concerts in the likes of Leningrad, Riga and Kiev, becoming genuinely friendly with the Khrushchev and Mikoyan families.[109] He even had the immense good fortune on a later trip to be photographed with the beloved space dogs Belka and Strelka, when they broke free of their handlers and rushed into a television studio where he was being filmed.[110]

By the end of the 1950s, the spread of jazz lovers' clubs and jazz cafés had reached even provincial cities such as Yaroslavl, Petrozavodsk and Voronezh, along with an annual jazz festival in Tallinn that became an enduring fixture on the international scene. The Azeri capital Baku became especially noted for its vibrant jazz scene in the 1950s and 1960s.[111] In 1962, the American bandleader and 'king of swing' Benny Goodman undertook a short Soviet tour, but tentative plans for Louis Armstrong and Dizzy Gillespie to do the same never quite got off the ground. By that time, though, jazz would soon be giving way to rock and roll in terms of popularity among young people. Elvis, Chubby Checker and Bill Haley were starting to become known among Soviet audiences, to be followed from the mid-1960s especially by Beatlemania. Spending a year at Moscow State University in the mid-1960s, William Taubman wrote that he was subjected to more of the Beatles' music in his dormitory there than back home in the US.[112] Fans of the Beatles and other Western groups soon began to ape their hairstyles and to gather in the evenings in the underpass at the bottom of Moscow's Gorky Street – which had long since been unofficially renamed 'Brodvei' (Broadway) by

Western-oriented youth – singing songs and playing the guitar, until police moved them on.[113]

Much as they disliked the raucous new musical genres, the Soviet authorities proved singularly unable either to prevent or to roll back the growing popularity of Western music, with rock and roll followed in due course by disco, heavy metal and more, as the years passed. A black market in Western music quickly thrived, as people swapped taped copies of in-demand albums, or else bought and sold original records (usually obtained from foreign students, sailors at ports like Tallinn and Odessa, or else brought back from trips abroad) for as much as a month's salary in some cases. As cassette players grew more widely available, some made good money taping and selling copy after copy of any given album.[114] One of the most curious facets of this illicit music trade was a phenomenon that would become known as 'rock on ribs': a process by which used X-ray plates were stolen and repurposed by resourceful youths to press recorded music onto; they would display broken bones and chests with tumours and tuberculosis (along with the official stamp of the Ministry of Health) as they revolved on the turntable, playing the latest hits.

This burgeoning interest in Western culture became an important part of a generational identity.[115] That, of course, was a growing source of concern for the political authorities. Most of the young people in question took a fairly nuanced view of things – professing their loyalty to the Soviet cause and insisting that there was nothing subversive in their cultural tastes. It was, as the saying went, possible to love both Lenin and Lennon at the same time. Nonetheless, it was always the political authorities who got to have the final word on what was and was not acceptable, and their tolerance of the fascination with all things Western ebbed and flowed with the passing years.

Soviet youths were not simply passive consumers of Western music; soon they were getting hold of instruments and forming their own bands. Known in official parlance as vocal instrument ensembles, it was not long before every factory and university faculty had its own group. In theory, the vetting of groups' setlists by the Komsomol was supposed to limit the amount of rock and roll that they performed; but songs by the Beatles and other Western acts frequently appeared under alternative titles, or else bands diverged from the pre-agreed running order without warning, in order to keep expectant audiences happy.

215

David Gurevich recalled that the singer in his own band had a picture of John Lennon taped to his guitar, while one of his best friends lived in a room that was basically a shrine to Mick Jagger (and even called his girlfriend Marianne).[116] Bands like The Hawks and The Slavs became well established in Moscow and beyond, playing at parties and private concerts, and modelling much of their sets on Beatles and Rolling Stones hits, respectively.[117]

There was, though, a balance to be struck, which helps us to understand why there was not the same sense of counterculture as in the West, where many writers, musicians and others made great play of their opposition to 'the establishment'. In the West, capitalism gave this counterculture a degree of protection against perturbed officialdom, since it ruffled feathers politically and socially, but also generated a lot of money. There was no such economic cover available in the Soviet Union, and the authorities there anyway wielded far more power to control cultural production. Nonetheless, instead of simply seeking to crush the emergence of Western music, officials often chose instead to exert control through co-opting and taming the new trends that they felt wary of. Many groups relied on the patronage of the Komsomol (or on the management of places where they worked and studied) to obtain instruments and spaces to rehearse, as well as access to youth cafés and venues in which to perform. The basic price of that patronage came in the form of political oversight – pushing rebellious behaviour too far would bring an end to the limited freedom that had been granted.

From Khrushchev hobnobbing with Hollywood royalty through to the growing numbers of foreign students in university dormitories around the USSR, there were few areas in which post-Stalin change was more evident. The strength of its economy and the scope of its soft power appeal gave the US a considerable advantage; but the Soviet Union was nevertheless a potential partner that many in the developing world were strongly attracted to around this time, especially. The renewed emphasis on internationalism was to prove double-edged, however. Determined to draw on the economic and political benefits of 'opening up', the authorities also exposed the country to myriad foreign influences that would prove increasingly difficult to control in the longer term.

7

CHANGE, CONTINUITY AND THE BORDERS OF THE PERMISSIBLE

Returning to Moscow in May 1959, after last visiting five years previously, one Western newspaper correspondent noted how 'the impression of change struck with landslide force'. He described a new gaiety, vibrancy and sense of casualness, as he walked the streets of the Soviet capital.[1] Of course, the reality was that both change and continuity could be found almost everywhere, often at one and the same time. Liberalisation in the cultural sphere, for example, was very real, but it was also uneven and precarious. Much the same could be said in regard to nationalities affairs: the worst excesses of Stalinist nationalities policy were largely reined in, but the authorities in Moscow remained deeply wary of any threat to the status quo and could respond aggressively to any perceived challenge. The security organs found their powers reduced somewhat, but they nonetheless continued to harass and persecute those who stepped out of line. Even so, from religious believers and homosexuals through to would-be entrepreneurs and corrupt officials, many people around the USSR still engaged in a plethora of activities that they knew to be either taboo or outright forbidden. Taken together, these things help to build a composite picture of what had and had not changed in the Soviet Union by the early 1960s.

The new security organs

After inveterate Stalinist Ivan Serov was moved on from the post of KGB chairman in 1958, it was particularly notable that he was succeeded by Alexander Shelepin, who had built his career to date in the Komsomol, not in security work. In fact, Khrushchev had brought in an outsider with no professional background in this sphere, precisely in order to shake things up.

217

Shelepin did just that, clearing out much of the old guard that remained from the Stalin years, with the notorious prison inside the Lubyanka finally being closed down.[2] The new chairman also presided over on-going attempts to decouple the KGB from the mass repression of its Stalin-era predecessors, seeking to rehabilitate the 'good name' and prestige of the security organs, by linking the new KGB back to the revolutionary-era Cheka (the first iteration of the Soviet security organs, widely believed to be markedly less brutal than those of the Stalin era) and to create a new public image as an organisation whose people were cultured and fair-minded, fearless protectors of their country against outside enemies, rather than thugs and torturers of innocent Soviet citizens.[3] The cult around original Cheka head Felix Dzerzhinsky was given new life, and his statue was erected outside the Lubyanka, presenting the Bolsheviks' first head of the security organs as a selfless and sagacious fighter for communism and a saviour of the downtrodden, cut from very different cloth to the brutal security chiefs of the Stalin years.

Like Khrushchev, at the Twenty-First Party Congress in 1959 Shelepin knowingly lied that there were no longer any political prisoners inside the USSR. He also spoke at length about Western powers' attempts to subvert the existing Soviet order and insisted that this demanded a ruthless response. But he also promised that every Soviet citizen should be confident that there would be no return to the shameful phenomenon of past groundless repressions.

Writers and film-makers were urged to produce works with positive KGB protagonists bravely defending their country with intellect and verve, along the lines of a Soviet Sherlock Holmes. Soon, movies such as *The Chekist* (1963) and *A Shot in the Fog* (1964) offered up much more positive and even laudatory portrayals of the security organs' work, not least since KGB 'consultants' were increasingly demanding that scenes be cut and plot lines changed as and when they were deemed undesirable by the image-conscious security organs.[4] Rather than tough guys in leather jackets with pistols at the ready, contemporary security operatives were now depicted in suits, almost as regular civil servants, and they gave a growing number of public talks as they sought to 'correct misperceptions' about their work.[5] In September 1962, for example, the magazine *Nedelya* (*The Week*) held a round-table discussion with some KGB officers, first making it clear that they were all regular people who enjoyed ordinary activities like fishing, reading and playing volleyball. Asked about their work, they spoke of KGB involvement in the rehabilitation of gulag returnees and reassured readers that there were no longer any unwarranted arrests, that all the 'old' people had now gone from the security organs and that the 'traditions of Dzerzhinsky' had been restored. Making it clear that they now knew the enemy was outside the country, rather than inside, they also showed off a range of captured Western spy paraphernalia, including a matchbox spycam, a pen that turned into a pistol and a hunting knife with espionage ciphers in the handle.[6]

The regular police – the militia – did not receive the same kind of 'reputation laundering' as the security organs. They retained a reputation among ordinary people for incompetence, violence and corruption, and were widely scorned by members of the public.[7] Many *militsionery* still had only a few years of schooling, and some were barely literate, while the most promising recruits were typically siphoned off for more prestigious KGB work.[8] Indeed, regular Soviet policing could sometimes be far less efficient than many outsiders imagined. In Estonia, for example, the Procurator's Office complained that the republican militia had almost 160 cases of large-scale fraud left unsolved and that they were letting people off offences in exchange for payment. It also cited instances where wanted criminals had not been tracked down and apprehended, even when they continued to live at their officially registered address.[9]

Denunciations from members of the public still poured into the KGB, but it was generally recognised that these consisted mainly of lies, score settling and rumours, and they were thus often discarded.[10] Instead of torture, various first-hand accounts point to the security organs developing 'a growing mastery of human psychology' that they now used to considerable effect during investigations.[11] The post-Stalin years also saw KGB work bolstered by an increasingly sophisticated knowledge of social trends and public moods. All this was achieved in part by working with more subtlety than before, but also by penetrating deeper into the sites of everyday life, from workplaces to apartment blocks. This was reflected in the appearance of a new and more flexible type of informer – the 'trusted person'. This was an ordinary civilian (rather than an undercover agent) whom the KGB turned to on an ad-hoc basis, to provide information on specific individuals and events of interest, or else to verify tipoffs received from other sources.[12] Declassified KGB reports from Lithuania, for example, showed 'trusted people' among the student body there reporting on classmates singing anti-Soviet songs in their dorms and listening to foreign radio broadcasts.[13]

Details on the scale and forms of KGB surveillance of the public remain somewhat fragmentary, but there are telling scraps of information to be found. One Lithuanian KGB report from 1966, for example, confirmed that there were at that time forty-one agents reporting on the republic's cultural elite (including writers, film-makers, musicians, dancers and others), along with fifteen agents inside the Lithuanian Academy of Sciences and twenty among the 'medical intelligentsia' of the capital.[14] More compelling, an all-union review of KGB work in 1967 reported that 25,000 new agents had been taken on that year (representing about 15 per cent of all KGB agents), while a total of 6,747 persons were presently being 'shadowed' by the security organs.[15]

The change in the ways that the security organs went about their work can be summed up as 'less repression but more policing': a shift perhaps best encapsulated by the emergence in the late 1950s of *profilaktika* (prophylaxis). This was a move towards the wider use of preventive (rather than reactive) measures, defined in Vasily Mitrokhin's KGB lexicon as:

> activity carried out by Soviet state bodies and social organisations, aimed at the prevention of crimes against the state, politically harmful misdemeanours and other acts . . . by identifying and removing the causes which give rise to such crimes, and the circumstances which encourage them to happen.[16]

What this mainly boiled down to was responding to small signs of trouble – such as telling off-colour jokes about party leaders and drunken cursing about political developments – before they went on to become more serious problems further down the line.[17] The use of intimidation from officialdom (rather than outright repression) and social pressure from the wider public were to be at the heart of this new approach to tackling the erring citizen without branding them 'anti-Soviet' at the first sign of trouble.

In its 'open' form, *profilaktika* consisted mainly of public meetings held (in one's workplace, place of study or other suitable setting) at the instigation of the KGB in which individuals deemed to be erring were publicly confronted about their 'harmful' or 'mistaken' actions and faced the censure of their peers, usually promising to mend their ways in the end. This reflected a growing regime expectation that ordinary people should help police, shame and 'guide' those around them – at work and school, in housing blocks, sports teams and more – instead of relying solely on the state for such work.[18] These sessions could be rhetorically brutal at times – more vociferous audiences would still fall back on terms like 'enemy of the people' on occasion and demand severe punishment when confronting wrongdoers – and could see the target sacked from their job and expelled from the party or Komsomol, but they tended to go no further than that.

At the heart of 'private prophylaxis' was the 'prophylactic chat', in which individuals about whom the security organs had cause for concern were summoned to their local KGB offices for a talk about their conduct. In the course of this session, they were informed in no uncertain terms that the KGB was paying close attention to them, before being given a clear warning that more serious consequences would follow if problems persisted. Before long, many thousands of people were being 'subject to prophylactic methods' each year. According to the KGB's own assessment, *profilaktika* was a real success at deterring deviant behaviour, with one early report noting unambiguously that 'the majority of those subjected to prophylactic measures did not offend again'.[19]

While much of its work at home may have lacked the outright ferocity of old, KGB operations overseas showed little sign of mellowing. Nonetheless, from the start of the period there were some very public embarrassments for the Soviet authorities. In April 1954, the KGB assassin Nikolai Khokhlov chose not to murder his target once he had located him in Frankfurt, but instead defected and blew the lid on the whole operation, even holding a press conference to expose the plan to the whole world.[20] That same month, photographs of KGB men manhandling Evdokiya Petrova (whose KGB husband Vladimir Petrov had just defected in Australia) quickly went all round the globe and saw diplomatic relations between the USSR and Australia severed for five years. When KGB agent Anatoly Golitsyn fled to the US at the end of 1961, he exposed a host of different people spying for the USSR in the West (most famously Kim Philby). Personally close to some of the highest-ranking

221

people in the KGB, Yuri Nosenko's decision to defect while in Geneva during 1964 also wrecked entire agent networks abroad. Khokhlov, the Petrovs, Golitsyn and Nosenko were all sentenced to death in absentia and duly included on the list of KGB assassination targets. Others were less fortunate still. Both Oleg Penkovsky and Alexander Cherepanov were caught spying for the West and executed.

Agents were sent abroad in the guise of tourists, exchange students, journalists, diplomats and much more besides. In terms of spying, the KGB never managed to replicate earlier achievements in penetrating the highest levels of officialdom in the West, though this was not for lack of trying. Rudolf Abel (real name William Fisher) was presented in Western media as a kind of Soviet master spy after he was uncovered in 1957, but he had not actually achieved a great deal and was anyway uncovered in large measure thanks to KGB blundering.[21] A few attempts at ensnaring Western diplomats and their spouses in 'honey traps' proved successful – one account suggests KGB counter-intelligence had at least a dozen educated and attractive young women on the payroll for this purpose – and a number of agents were successfully 'dangled' to the West (such as fake defectors used to spread disinformation abroad), though the results tended not to be transformative.[22] Industrial espionage, however, proved rather more positive, as KGB agents sought and acquired information about a wide range of prohibited Western science and technology, such as computers and rocket engines.[23]

KGB agents in New York also worked to confect scandals and stir tensions among various ethnic and religious communities there, secretly defacing synagogues with swastikas and sending racist abuse to African officials at the UN, in order to damage America's reputation globally.[24] CIA Director Allen Dulles was a constant target for smear campaigns, rumours and faked documents, as the KGB attempted to sow confusion and distrust.[25] The Vatican, in particular, was regarded as a dangerous and wily adversary, prompting a steadily rising number of undercover KGB agents to be despatched for supposed theological study at Catholic institutes in Rome, Munich and Vienna.[26] Similarly, émigré groups of practically all Soviet nationalities became targets for penetration, as the KGB bid to compromise, discredit and divide them. With almost 2 million ethnic Ukrainians in North America – a number of whom were openly and implacably hostile to Soviet power – untold KGB resources were expended on attempts to sow political dissension among them, to disrupt flows of information or to uncover and foil plans (which were assumed to be ultimately funded and directed by Western governments) to stir unrest inside Soviet Ukraine.[27]

One particularly notorious case of KGB activity in foreign lands came to light after Joseph Lehmann and his wife Inge furtively crossed from East to West Berlin in August 1961. On seeking asylum in West Germany, Lehmann revealed that he was in reality Bogdan Stashinsky, and that he had, as a KGB operative, assassinated two prominent figures of Ukrainian émigré politics resident in West Germany: Lev Rebet in 1957 and Stepan Bandera in 1959. In both cases, Stashinsky had fired deadly poison at his target from close range to wipe out men whom the Soviet authorities considered dangerous enemies. For carrying out these two murders, Stashinsky had been given the Order of the Red Banner by the KGB boss, Shelepin, but had subsequently grown disillusioned with his work, not least after discovering that his own home was bugged and his mail was being read.[28] Once Stashinsky confessed all to the West German authorities, a host of valuable KGB intelligence networks were exposed, with the Soviet Union quickly embroiled in a major international scandal for conducting assassinations on foreign territory.

Targeting social evils

One of the most striking exceptions to wider trends of post-Stalin liberalisation came in regard to renewed persecution aimed at the country's millions of religious believers. Anti-Semitism excepted, late Stalinism had largely backed away from the anti-religious zeal of earlier years. In fact, with religious faith a widely tapped emotional resource during the country's struggle against Nazism, thousands of formerly closed churches and mosques had been allowed to reopen during and after the war.

This pragmatic accommodation to religion was viewed by some as a facet of Stalin's wider drift away from Leninism, and confrontation soon resumed after his passing. A fresh attack on religion initially got under way in July 1954, seemingly on Khrushchev's personal orders. New books and pamphlets were hurriedly produced, as public lectures, newspaper articles and more all propounded anti-religious themes, ridiculing 'backward' superstitions and rites, and demonising clergy of all faiths as corrupt, immoral and ignorant. Already by November 1954, though, the authorities were publicly conceding that their approach had been heavy-handed and alienating, and they effectively wound down the new campaign.[29] A degree of toleration then returned for a time, with new print runs of both the Bible and the Quran permitted in 1956.

With officials growing concerned about an apparent religious resurgence, the assault then resumed with gusto from summer 1958. Authorities lambasted the failings of anti-religious work around the country and complained that too many in officialdom had simply resigned themselves to expanding church influence.[30] The journal *Voprosy filosofii* unambiguously pinned much of the blame for the survival of religious belief inside the USSR on Western efforts to stall Soviet progress towards communism, by both legal and illegal means. Taxes levied on religious establishments climbed steeply, and laws intended to stymie believers' charitable giving to churches, mosques and other institutions were tightened up.[31] In 1961, the situation intensified further, as the authorities ruled that those who still received religious rites like weddings and baptisms now had to present their passports in order to do so. This meant that their details were formally recorded and the matter could be raised again at a later date.[32]

By summer 1959, it was reported privately to the top party leadership that the clampdown was being enforced with worrying zeal in places. Churches and monasteries were being forcibly closed down, icon screens seized and inhabitants evicted with little or no warning. Cases of vandalism were also being registered, including anti-religious slogans daubed on church walls. In a few instances, the public discontent with all this was visceral. One case from Moldavia saw locals living near one monastery organise a round-the-clock watch armed with pitchforks, sticks and stones, ringing church bells to call hundreds of others to the monastery's defence as and when officials approached.[33] Somewhere between 5,000 and 6,000 previously registered and legally functioning Orthodox churches were closed in Russia between 1956 and 1965, representing around 40 per cent of all those still left open after four decades of Soviet power; meanwhile, the number of functioning monasteries fell to a mere eighteen.[34] From a total of thirty-three mosques in 1957, by 1963 Tajikistan had only eighteen left.[35] Numerous synagogues were also being closed down on often spurious grounds, such as supposed lack of worshippers, buildings declared to be in unsafe condition – or else because they were in city districts slated for redevelopment.[36]

For smaller religious denominations, things were often worse still, as the Soviet authorities fought to stamp out 'unlicensed' religious activity. Propaganda presented groups like the Baptists, Mennonites, Pentecostalists and Seventh Day Adventists as socially dangerous zealots who denied their own children access to medical care, culture and fun, while newspapers occasionally ran lurid stories of child sacrifice. One popular movie of the era included a scene where Pentecostalists attempted (unsuccessfully) to crucify a young Komsomol member. Another depicted Catholic clergy in Ukraine betraying resistance fighters to the Nazis during the war.[37] One piece in the publication *Literatura i zhizn* (*Literature and Life*) referred to Jehovah's Witnesses as 'a filthy sect that receives direct instructions from abroad'. In fact, the regime viewed Jehovah's Witnesses as such a subversive danger (since the movement was headquartered in the US and it operated underground inside the USSR) that the organisation was penetrated from top to bottom by KGB informers seeking to divide members, discredit intransigent leaders and send disinformation back to the US.[38] In some cases, religious believers even had sons and daughters permanently taken away from them by the authorities (purportedly to protect the children in question). Records from the Procurator's Office also show numerous instances in which clusters of participants in underground religious groups such as Jehovah's Witnesses and Adventists were jailed for anti-Soviet activity.[39] When Soviet Baptists organised themselves to campaign against recurrent regime attacks in 1960, around two hundred supporters were arrested over the next three years.[40]

Thanks to on-going efforts aimed at winning friends and allies in the developing world, however, the authorities were keen to show that the USSR was not fundamentally hostile to Islam. A trickle of Soviet Muslims was permitted to undertake the Hajj each year, spreading the word about Soviet religious tolerance as they did so. Some historic mosques were renovated (although mostly for the benefit of tourists rather than worshippers), the famous Mir-i-Arab madrassa at Bukhara was allowed to enrol a small number of students (there were apparently sixteen applicants for each place available) and to undertake exchanges with Islamic universities in Egypt, Syria and

Morocco. Actually, the madrassa served two key purposes for the Soviet authorities: as a prominent symbol for the outside world of accommodation between communism and Islam in the USSR, and as a means of inculcating in its students a progressive and modern form of Islam that was amenable to Soviet values.[41] The Soviet drive to take on Islam, then, was far from whole-hearted, but it did still have important manifestations for the country's millions of Muslims.

Islamic traditions like veiling were presented as evidence of oppression, imposed on subjugated women by husbands, fathers and brothers, though in reality such practices could be an important part of Muslim women's sense of identity.[42] Access to holy places such as shrines could be closed on all sorts of spurious grounds in order to prevent pilgrimages, and in some cases they were simply destroyed by being concreted over. However, in Central Asia and the North Caucasus especially, Islam often also proved more able than other faiths to withstand the state's attacks, since it was less hierarchically structured and centralised, and therefore better able to adapt to changing circumstances.[43] Unofficial mosques sprang up in warehouses and libraries when registered mosques were closed down, for example. Anyway, the political authorities were sufficiently concerned about the potential influence of wandering mullahs that they typically avoided suppression of the registered Islamic clergy, lest that give rise to more radical alternatives.[44]

Presenting science as the counter to religious faith, planetariums sprang up around the country – from just one in the early 1950s, there were more than seventy by the early 1970s; there, popular lectures, question-and-answer sessions and film screenings on science, the universe and space exploration ran alongside anti-religious talks.[45] One such talk at Moscow's 'Krasny bogatyr' factory, with over three hundred people in attendance, addressed questions like 'does fate exist?', 'why do people believe in god?' and 'can one believe in premonitions?'.[46] Stories in the press linked religious weddings to unhappy marriages and to the persistence of inequality between men and women. Others presented cautionary tales of cynical clergy extorting money from believers in order to fund their own lavish lifestyles, and published 'conversion narratives', whereby former believers discussed how they had come to under-stand the error of their ways and embrace science and rationality.[47] More overtly intimidatory, Komsomol members were sometimes deployed to picket outside places of worship, turning away young attendees or else recording their details to be passed upwards for further action. Nonetheless, in rural parts of the country especially, even many rank-and-file communists still had religious icons and other artefacts on display inside their homes.[48] To the continual bafflement and frustration of some officials, many people proved able to embrace the benefits and breakthroughs of science without seeing them as incompatible with their religious faith.[49]

Another important part of the Soviet effort to tackle religion involved creating secular events and ceremonies to supplant the old religious ones. New and more colourful celebrations were instituted to mark key life stages for young people especially, like receipt of one's first passport (for domestic purposes only) at age sixteen and receipt of one's first wages. Most prominently, there was a drive to transform non-religious weddings from a drab and fundamentally administrative exercise – of her own nuptials in October 1958, Maya Plisetskaya recalled that she and her husband-to-be went to the correct government office, filled in the necessary forms, had their passports stamped and left again – into something much more joyful and attractive.[50] Many of the old markers remained – such as the rings, flowers, a wedding march and a ceremonial kiss; but there were also new elements, like Komsomol members in parade dress, and speeches and toasts by party members or work colleagues. The year 1959 marked the opening of Leningrad's first 'Palace of Weddings', replete with decorations and space for guests to celebrate the happy occasion properly; and soon such wedding palaces were appearing all around the country in a bid to tackle the draw of church ceremonies. New wedding shops also appeared for couples booked into a wedding palace, giving privileged access to various items of food and drink for their big day and to otherwise hard-to-find goods, like wedding rings and dresses.[51]

It remains open to debate how much impact these anti-religious campaigns really had, but there were signs of change on the ground. Some accounts have described how educated urbanites, in particular, had practically no interest in God by the early 1960s, with religious faith being viewed by many as 'embarrassing and backward'.[52] Interviewed since the Soviet collapse, Kyrgyz citizens offered contrasting memories on this issue: some recalled that only old people still went to the mosque in those days; others that people were simply too busy even for Friday prayers.[53] Under prolonged Soviet influence, taboos around drinking alcohol and eating pork were also on the wane among many Muslims. Nonetheless, while they might adhere to Soviet norms in many respects, traditional Islamic rites like circumcision remained widespread, festivals like Eid were still celebrated discreetly and practices like female seclusion within the home were not wholly uncommon, even among some officials.[54] Indeed instances of 'bride capture' that were exposed in the press sometimes revealed that party and Komsomol members, as well as police, were involved either as perpetrators or else in trying to shield the guilty parties from punishment. Long depicted as a part of the country in which communism made only quite limited headway, recent scholarship on Central Asia shows that the region ought not to be understood in terms of 'Soviet or Muslim' but 'Soviet and Muslim'.[55]

Another notable shift from Stalin-era toleration to Khrushchev-era clampdown came in regard to alcohol. Although not yet so pervasive as it would become in the 1970s and 1980s, alcoholism was already a substantial social problem. One foreign visitor to the USSR in the mid-1950s described seeing people in restaurants passed out through drink, and noting that they drew almost no attention from fellow diners, since it was such a common sight.[56] Similarly, Joseph Brodsky recalled of his native Leningrad that the main pastime there was 'the bottle', and that on the street at 9:00 one was more likely to encounter a drunk than a taxi.[57] Rural areas were often even worse than the cities when it came to alcoholism, with vodka one of a fairly small handful of products that could practically always be found in shops. The data are naturally incomplete, but studies have suggested that spending on alcohol represented around 6.5 per cent of the average family budget, rising to more than 40 per cent for about one family in ten as the era progressed.[58]

The mass consumption of vodka meant that its sale represented a significant stream of tax revenue for the state. Facing tremendous outlays for developing industry and strengthening the military, authorities in the Stalin era had helped to raise consumption (and tax receipts) by lowering the retail price of vodka.[59] Although no teetotaller himself, Khrushchev approached the situation from a different angle: he viewed excessive drinking as both a powerful brake on economic development and a major impediment to the emergence of the communist man and woman of the future. Workplace drinking – later featured in a number of hair-raising accounts by the great émigré writer Sergei Dovlatov – was a serious problem that affected safety, productivity and the quality of goods. Alcohol abuse was also understood to be at the heart of countless social problems, from domestic violence and negligent parenting through to street crime, traffic accidents and climbing suicide rates. As Khrushchev perceived it, any attempt to reach communism first called for a reckoning with the bottle.

A December 1958 decree demanded a more intensive battle against alcohol abuse: it clamped down on sales to those under age, called for better public education on the dangers of drink, tightened laws against home brewing and instigated compulsory treatment for people repeatedly detained for public drunkenness.[60] Satirical cartoons showed pathetically drunk men being divorced by despairing wives (alcoholism was consistently one of the leading grounds for divorce), hopelessly slumped in front of disappointed children, or being carried away from fields and workshops in a stupor. Some images also recognised that the problem was deeply ingrained in society. One *Krokodil* cartoon depicted a kindly old lady offering glasses of vodka to workmen in the process of decorating her apartment; another showed an angry father pouring himself and his adolescent son a large vodka for a 'man-to-man talk' about the son's hooligan behaviour.[61]

The authorities did experiment with closing stores selling vodka in Ryazan, but that resulted in large queues of angry shoppers, prompting a quick U-turn.[62] Instead, new decrees prohibited the sale of vodka at a range of key sites, like train stations and bus stations, near schools and hospitals, and at sports stadiums. Cinemas showed propaganda about the dangers of alcohol before the start of movies, and posters exhorted citizens to embrace sobriety. The authorities also sought to develop alternative tastes among the public, encouraging people to drink beer instead of vodka, or trying to popularise 'exotic' cocktails (with names like 'the scent of the fields') and Soviet champagne (a sparkling wine). They also raised prices in places where vodka remained on sale, sometimes imposing a low maximum limit (100 grams) that customers were permitted to buy. As always, though, ways were found to get around the new measures: sales of other spirit drinks, like cognac and rum, climbed sharply as vodka was restricted, and growing numbers of people distilled their own *samogon* (moonshine) instead. Cafés and restaurants with financial targets to meet sold customers more alcohol than they were supposed to, and patrons brought their own drinks to serve themselves from under the table. In fact, for all that regime efforts on this front were substantial and prolonged, the picture continued to worsen, rather than improve. In Magadan oblast, for example, annual arrests for drunkenness climbed from a little over 7,400 in 1959 to 14,000 in 1961 and approached 19,000 by 1965.[63]

The struggle against alcohol abuse, in particular, was inherently linked with on-going efforts to tackle 'hooliganism' – a deliberately catch-all term that included everything from gang fights and knife crime through to public drunkenness, spitting and swearing. For years already, many ordinary citizens had been deeply alarmed at an apparent rise in juvenile delinquency, and parts of the country undoubtedly did have serious problems with street crime.[64] David Gurevich, for example, wrote of growing up in provincial Syzran that 'after dark, the town belonged to hoodlums'.[65] In the mid-1950s, hooligans among the student body were reportedly terrorising schools in Sverdlovsk – with one pupil stabbed to death, a deputy head almost killed when someone threw a hammer at him and students swearing in teachers' faces, all apparently without any response from officialdom.[66] Newspapers then used instances like the murder of Otto Grossman – who was stabbed and killed in autumn 1958 after defending two young women against a pair of drunken youths on a trolleybus – to mobilise public indignation, insisting that hooligans were traitors to Soviet society, and decent citizens must be neither indifferent to such people nor afraid of them.

During the mid- to late 1950s, which represented the peak of the clamp-down (though by no means its entire duration), almost half a million people were charged (and either fined or detained for a few days) with hooliganism, and almost 3 million more with the slightly lesser offence of 'petty hooliganism'.[67] As with the 1957 clampdown on dissent, though, the number of people being arrested did not necessarily reflect a country in the throes of a social crisis, but rather one in which a new campaign (deliberately loosely defined) had been decreed at the top, and thus had to be acted upon. With officials keen to show the expected vigilance, actions that might previously have been punished under very different articles of the criminal code, or else not punished at all, were now defined by police as 'hooliganism'.[68] Seeing both a way of saving money in the new struggle and a compelling ideological throwback to revolutionary times, Khrushchev insisted that the protection of public order was not just a job for the state, but also for the masses. In March 1959, the long-abandoned *Druzhina* (People's Patrol) was resurrected. The *druzhinniki* were essentially ordinary citizens mobilised in their factories, construction sites, universities and elsewhere to patrol the streets, as a supplement to the regular police. By summer 1960, there were officially 80,000 of these volunteer patrols around the USSR, with a seemingly impressive 2.5 million participants.

In fact, People's Patrols were just one of many ways in which ordinary citizens were drawn into the work of policing society. Also a throwback to the revolutionary era, 'comrades' courts' were local bodies staffed by volunteers and empowered to pass judgement on a range of minor offences in their district (such as drunken and unruly neighbours, or children who habitually truanted from school), hand out fines and propose evictions. By 1963, there were an estimated 200,000 such comrades' courts functioning around the USSR.[69] The *domkom* (house committee) was another long-redundant body brought back to life in the 1950s. Usually elected by the residents of a housing block – and often (but not always) consisting mainly of pensioners – the *domkom* was used to collect rent, organise the cleaning of communal spaces, prettify the local neighbourhood, handle repairs and sometimes also organise recreation activities for children; but it, too, had involvement in matters like dealing with problem neighbours and cases of child neglect.[70] Similarly, the *zhensovety* (women's councils) that appeared in the late 1950s were primarily a mechanism for getting Soviet women more active in political life and in the affairs of their local communities. Not only were they training women to acquire labour skills, but they also worked on providing parenting advice for new mothers, helped to round up material goods for poorer families and organised volunteer work in their district.[71]

This grassroots participation in policing could be of decidedly variable efficacy, however. The People's Patrols represented a useful example of some key problems. First, the number of recorded participants was too high, in large part because of data inflation: given targets for the number of volunteers to sign up from among their workers, many factories declared the requisite numbers attained when they were barely even close. No less important, because many people 'volunteered' only after some arm twisting, they were not exactly committed to their task, and numerous reports spoke of patrols existing only on paper, or else of instances where volunteers simply fled as and when a dangerous situation reared its head. Receiving little in the way of training, many participants also had limited understanding of good policing practice or of the laws that they were supposed to enforce. Some thus strayed into aggressive vigilantism. An active participant in Komsomol patrols in his native Ukraine, Leonid Plyushch described how those caught engaging in illegal trade were occasionally dragged off to an old bomb shelter for a beating.[72] Lastly, because volunteers were generally not vetted in any meaningful way, it turned out in numerous cases that those participating in patrols were little more than criminals themselves, and a number of groups had to be entirely disbanded as they did more harm than good, spreading fear and resentment on streets where they were supposed to be bringing order.[73]

In summer 1961, another new decree was issued, entitled 'On strengthening the struggle with persons avoiding socially useful labour and leading an anti-social, parasitic, way of life'. This demanded that the masses 'create an atmosphere of implacable condemnation' towards not only the deliberately and habitually unemployed, but also those who made their living through 'unearned income', such as begging, letting out spare living space and buying and selling on the black market. Although not quite so broad as the drive against hooligans, the 'anti-parasite' campaign that followed was again wide in scope, and alarming for Soviet legal professionals in particular, since it was so vaguely defined.[74] During 1961–62 alone, the militia detained almost 240,000 people on charges of parasitism.[75]

Those found guilty under this clampdown could face sentences of up to five years of exile, labouring on remote collective farms. One of those convicted as a parasite, Andrei Amalrik categorised his fellow detainees into four types: chronic alcoholics out of work because of their drunkenness (this was the largest group); people engaged in illegal private trade; professional criminals; and religious believers, intellectuals and others whom the authorities wanted to be rid of without recourse to formal political trials (Amalrik fell into this last group). As he later recalled of his time spent with fellow victims of the clampdown, he never saw any 'real parasites'.[76] Anyway, the clampdown did not solve the issue at hand, so much as move problematic individuals from the city to the countryside. As one *Komsomolskaya pravda* piece complained in August 1962, 'some come good but many just go on acting badly in their new environment'.[77]

Bending the rules

For ordinary citizens, successfully navigating the barriers and inefficiencies of the Soviet system meant that plenty of everyday modes of behaviour and transactions nestled in an ambiguous space between legal and illegal. Sham marriages and fake jobs were arranged by individuals seeking to obtain a residence permit for this or that city, and electricians, plumbers, seamstresses and others regularly took on paid private jobs either after or during regular working hours. In time, the black market would assume vast proportions. Most pervasive and most ambiguous was *blat*: this was an informal process by means of which citizens of any and all positions in society cultivated and used personal connections, gifts and reciprocal favours between family, friends and colleagues to acquire goods, information and services in short supply. A shop worker, for example, might put hard-to-find items – such as meat, nice dresses, or good quality shoes – to one side for contacts who could possibly help in getting hold of in-demand theatre tickets or securing a pass to a prestigious holiday resort. This was a process that not only perpetuated systemic flaws and 'made the Soviet system tolerable but also subverted it', not least as citizens grew increasingly used to evading and ignoring official prescriptions on proper and improper means of conducting their everyday lives.[78]

Citizens sometimes also showed real creativity when it came to illicit money-making schemes. One recent study has described people lending out their apartments for use by prostitutes and their clients, and of taxi drivers doing the same with their cars.[79] Estonian police uncovered a case in the spring of 1960 in which a delivery driver taking bread to canteens around Tallinn was systematically stealing and then selling off his wares. A host of canteen supervisors across the Estonian capital were signing off to say that bread had been delivered as expected, and then taking a cut of the profits when the driver duly resold that same bread through the city's shops.[80] Another criminal case from Tallinn around the same time centred on a man who had persuaded more than a dozen of the city's young women to let him take naked photographs of them, which he then sold on to clients. When his case was uncovered in 1960, almost 3,300 pornographic images were found in his flat, along with over 1,000 negatives and a long list of customers.[81] Theft from the workplace was also particularly widespread. When Estonian investigators looked closely at a range of republican enterprises in 1960, they found signs of malfeasance everywhere: hundreds of kilos of flour missing from bakeries; piles of banknotes unaccounted for in cash registers; and construction sites with tonnes of rubber and brick simply vanished.[82]

Cities frequented by foreign tourists, in particular, saw a rising tide of illicit economic activity. By hanging around hotels and tourist sites, those willing to risk a run-in with the police were often able to buy up all kinds of Western items – clothing especially – to be sold on at a profit to Soviet buyers eager for foreign goods. One young man named Yura Rabinovich developed a system for gaining access to tourist buses on the way into Moscow from the airport, convincing passengers that he worked for the state bank and changing their foreign currency into roubles (thanks to its official monopoly and deeply unfair exchange rates, the Soviet state made a lot of money changing tourists' currency, and was easily undercut). Some enterprising locals also made a good living out of selling 'souvenirs', like religious icons, to visitors: some were real and plundered from abandoned churches; others were fakes made to order in clandestine workshops.[83]

One of the most notable affairs of the shadow economy played out in a Moscow courthouse in June 1961, when Jan Rokotov and eight of his associates were put on trial for buying and selling foreign currency. The trial evidence revealed that Rokotov's gang had acquired perhaps 20 million roubles and had been found with thousands of US dollars, British pounds, French francs, West German marks, gold coins and more. Seeking to stoke popular outrage, the press reported on Rokotov's lavish spending and his scorn for those who followed the rules. Most telling, though, was the authorities' desire to make an example of the group. At the time of arrest, the maximum sentence for their offence was eight years; but by the time the trial came around, a new law had been rushed through that prescribed the death penalty for the most egregious economic crimes. Flouting one of the most basic legal principles, the new rules were applied retroactively and Rokotov was shot.[84]

The rigour with which Moscow pursued such cases in the early 1960s was surely connected to what was the most embarrassing scandal of the age. Back in 1958, self-promoting Ryazan party boss Alexei Larionov had seized on Khrushchev's bullish rhetoric of catching up and overtaking the USA to declare that the farms of his region would triple their annual milk production that year. When it was later announced that this feat had indeed been achieved, Larionov was showered with awards and praise from Khrushchev himself. Desperate to make headway on his own impulsive promises, Khrushchev then urged Larionov to work wonders again the following year, pushing him to triple the region's meat production from 50,000 to 150,000 tonnes. Unable or unwilling to refuse such an obviously impossible assignment, Larionov took the mission on. Towards the end of 1959, he once again declared the target met, and to massive fanfare he even promised to deliver 200,000 tonnes of meat the next year. By the time 1960 drew to a close, though, Ryazan had delivered little more than 30,000 tonnes – and Larionov was dead.

Larionov committed suicide in September 1960, just as the story of his grand deception was being unravelled. Investigators – spurred to action by other regional party bosses' suspicions and by whistle-blowers' claims – found that in 1959 Ryazan had actually delivered 100,000 tonnes of meat, with the missing 50,000 tonnes entirely a product of creative accounting by Larionov. Furthermore, the 100,000 tonnes that was delivered had come thanks to cheating on a ruinous scale. Desperate to secure the expected meat, allies of Larionov across the Ryazan region had been strong-arming citizens into 'lending' or selling their privately owned cattle. Some had been stealing animals from nearby regions or else slaughtering dairy cows for their meat; others had even been buying up meat in Moscow stores and then passing it off as their own farm produce. Of course, such stunts could not work forever, and Larionov's attempt to produce another 'miracle' in 1960 quickly came apart at the seams. It then became apparent that a vast number of officials had been involved in the deception, with numerous attempted whistle-blowers silenced.[85]

The scandal was a huge and infuriating embarrassment for Khrushchev personally, since he had been a vocal cheerleader of Larionov's. It prompted him to launch a wider investigation into economic crimes and the affairs of Soviet officialdom. This revealed deeply worrying results, showing serious cases of fraud taking place – perpetrated by officials – right across the USSR, including Ukraine, Kazakhstan, Tajikistan, Azerbaijan, Armenia, Latvia, Belorussia and myriad Russian regions (one source later described how Georgian Communist Party boss Vasil Mzhavanadze 'set the bar for corruption', going so far as to auction off ministerial roles in his republic and taking bribes in the form of money, jewels, artworks and antiques).[86] A major wave of sackings duly followed, and some scholars have argued that the ensuing fallout – within the party–state establishment, rather than among the public at large – marked one of the critical moments of the age, when Khrushchev's approach to governing began to harden markedly.[87]

The Friendship of Soviet peoples

When Khrushchev spoke to mark the end of a ten-day celebration of Ukrainian culture in Moscow during November 1960, he told his audience that 'our future depends on how strong our union will be, our union of peoples'.[88] The years since Stalin's death had already started to see the multi-national nature of the USSR become more evident. Regime discourse on the subject of nationalities depicted a happy and united Soviet family, in which Russians played the role of benevolent older brother, with the country's different national cultures steadily drawing closer together. In reality, the situation was much more complex. There were clear gestures towards inclusion and celebration of national diversity, though. For example, intermarriage between members of different ethnic groups inside the USSR – which accounted for around one marriage in every ten at this time – was lauded in the media and presented as evidence of progress towards the emergence of a unified Soviet people.[89] Rhetoric around the friendship of different Soviet peoples could carry real meaning for some citizens, and plenty took up the opportunities that the system presented for mobility, studying, working and living far from their native corner of the USSR.[90] Nonetheless, acts of national self-expression in the non-Russian republics could quickly alarm wary officials in Moscow.

To some extent, this was a time of 'nation building' for many non-Russians inside the USSR.[91] Khrushchev's promise of a 'return to Leninism' in nationalities matters, along with increased latitude for cultural expression, facilitated a real blossoming of cultural and political energies in multiple non-Russian republics. Republican film studios in the likes of Georgia, Ukraine, Lithuania and Tajikistan began to revive and then flourish. Economic decentralisation (the *sovnarkhoz* reform) had quickly seen the individual republics prioritise their own economic needs and goals, rather than those of the wider USSR.[92] Numerous writers banned or stifled on grounds of nationalism under Stalinism were published again and were embraced with great enthusiasm. Small markers of nationhood also proliferated, with official sanction. In Kiev, for example, multi-volume encyclopaedias and histories of Ukraine were published, along with a new dictionary of the Ukrainian language.[93]

However, these changes did not simply serve to alleviate the accumulated frustration over the extent of Russian predominance; they also helped to make many non-Russians much more keenly attuned to questions of their own heritage, rights and culture, rendering perceptions of Russian dominance and Russification more acute in the long run.[94] Some drew parallels between Soviet rhetoric in support of countries seeking independence from colonial masters and their own subjugation to what they saw as 'red imperialism'.[95] In Latvia, Ukraine and Kazakhstan, there was frustration over the growing influx of Russians coming to work and live there (an established means of 'sovietising' non-Russian regions). By the 1959 census, Kazakhs accounted for only about 30 per cent of the people in Kazakhstan – behind both Russians and Ukrainians in some regions – with local language and culture accordingly in pronounced decline, prompting calls for protection.[96] In the Tatarstan region of Russia there was a flowering of Islamic cultural forms, following a successful festival of Tatar literature and art in Moscow during 1957, including efforts to push back against the Russification of Tatar musical and literary styles, attempts to revivify the local language after years of decline, and even talk of adopting the Arabic script instead of Cyrillic.[97] Before long, the central authorities were seeking to rein in such aspirations.

Nationalities questions sometimes defied simple formulas. In some republics – such as Georgia after the events of March 1956 – patriotic sentiment was becoming increasingly entwined with anti-Russian resentment and yearning for independence. In neighbouring Armenia, however, local patriotism largely fitted within a wider sense of Soviet patriotism, rather than working against it.[98] Sometimes national tensions did not centre on

Russian dominance and Russification at all. There were, for example, long-standing animosities between Azerbaijanis and Armenians, between Abkhaz and Georgians, and between Uzbeks and Tajiks. Even as the leaders of various non-Russian republics demanded that Moscow observe their constitutional rights in regard to matters like native-language cultural provision, some of them also failed to provide those same rights to smaller ethnic minorities inside their own republics.[99]

Although armed resistance to Soviet rule in the Baltics was finally snuffed out in the early 1950s, there were clearly substantial pockets of resentment that remained. Lithuanian KGB reports from 1957, for example, showed that twenty-four underground groups, representing almost 140 members, were uncovered in the republic that year.[100] The above notwithstanding, by this point the situation in the Baltics was more subtle than simply universal and implacable opposition to the Soviet regime. Much of the period in question saw a new degree of calm and normality in Latvia, Lithuania and Estonia, as Moscow granted a little more latitude to local officials. Realising that communist power would be in place for the foreseeable future, many people began coming to terms with that reality, taking up university places, joining the party and Komsomol and building careers within the Soviet system, if not necessarily embracing it.[101] One scholar has even noted the emergence during these years of a genuine 'Soviet Lithuanian' identity among young people in that republic, with former Stalin-era partisan fighters returning home from the camps to find that society had largely moved on in their absence.[102] In fact, the Baltics gained a rather fashionable status within the USSR as the most westernised and European part of the country, as well as the region with the highest standard of living, where members of the cultural elite went to enjoy the nightlife (the Neringa café in Vilnius was one of the trendiest spots in the whole USSR) and listen to the latest jazz.

Narratives on nationalities affairs that were aimed at the outside world always portrayed an enlightened approach to the rights and freedoms of the USSR's non-Russian republics. The 1959 pamphlet *Tajikistan: Land of Sunshine* informed foreign readers that the republic not only had its own constitution, but also enjoyed the right to secede from the USSR; it insisted that 'the Tajik people decide all of their internal affairs themselves'.[103] Such claims were, of course, fundamentally misleading. Nonetheless, it did at least become standard practice for republican leaders to be of the local nationality, albeit usually with a Russian second-in-command, and some significant powers (especially over spending) did reside in republican capitals like Riga, Baku and Tashkent, and elites there occasionally showed themselves willing and able to exert some genuine agency.[104]

In the post-Stalin era, and especially after Khrushchev's promise of a 'return to Leninism' in nationalities policy, party bosses in Tallinn, Tbilisi and other republican capitals were no longer quite such unquestioning and zealous executors of the centre's will. In Kyrgyzstan, for example, the local leadership pushed hard to ensure that Kyrgyz students were granted preferential quotas for access to universities in the republic and to make sure that the Kyrgyz language was protected against the encroachment of Russian.[105] The likes of Johannes Käbin and Antanas Snieçkus (in Estonia and Lithuania, respectively) became effective exponents of a dual role, in which they strove to demonstrate to their compatriots that they were protecting local interests and advancing republican prerogatives in Moscow, while also showing Moscow officialdom that they were imposing the wishes of the centre in their own republic and were guarantors of stability in a region that might well grow volatile without them.[106] For much of the period in question, this approach worked reasonably well, keeping directives from the Kremlin and local sentiment in a broadly workable balance.

November 1958 then marked the appearance of a series of planned reforms to the country's education system. Along with efforts to extend the provision of schooling in rural areas and to ensure that young people gained work experience in factories or on farms before being allowed to enter university – a measure which aroused considerable disquiet among students and academics alike – the new reforms also worked towards standardising how and what schoolchildren studied around the USSR. At the centre of the melee that followed was the question of language study. Inside Russia, most pupils studied Russian and a foreign language, such as English, French or German, but they tended not to study other Soviet languages. In the non-Russian republics, they studied the local language as well as Russian and an additional foreign language, making for a significantly heavier workload. Republican officials wanted to tackle that problem by adding another year to the school programme – an idea that Moscow rejected.

The 1958 reform proposed instead that pupils would no longer be obliged to study the local language in non-Russian republics, with parents allowed to choose between sending their children to schools that either did or did not teach it. This proposal cut against one of the fundamental principles of Soviet nationalities policy from day one: school instruction in the local tongue, in order to protect the long-term viability of non-Russian languages and cultures. With mastery of Russian often vital to 'get on' professionally in the Soviet system, the clear danger was that parents would send their children to Russian-language schools and local-language teaching would wither.[107]

Outside Russia, few issues carried such resonance as language protection, and when the proposed reform was put to the Soviet public 'for consultation', there was clear and strong opposition in many republics; officials in Vilnius, Kiev, Tbilisi and elsewhere found the disquiet too serious to dismiss. Remarkably, the reform plan was openly opposed in the Supreme Soviet by delegates from the Baltics, Armenia and Georgia, Belorussia and Ukraine.[108] The central authorities still had the power to ensure that the plan was formally driven through in the face of such objections, and Khrushchev was clearly riled by the defiance shown, but practical implementation of the new policy nonetheless lay in the hands of officials in those same non-Russian republics. As such, they typically watered down or ignored key provisions of the reform on their own territory, quietly but effectively killing Khrushchev's plan. This was especially true in Latvia and Azerbaijan, where the furore over schooling fed into a much wider swelling of national sentiment.

In both Riga and Baku, powerful forces were mobilising around national sentiment. In Latvia, a new cohort of 'national communists' had begun to rise up through the ranks of the party as early as summer 1953, made possible by Beria's nationalities reforms. Nonetheless, Latvia's nationally minded communists were not plotting to subvert (or depart from) the Soviet system, but were seeking to make it more amenable to Latvians. This meant bringing more of the local population into the republic's Communist Party, primarily by increasing and emphasising its authentically 'Latvian' character.[109] In Azerbaijan, where the party leadership had been extensively purged and reconstituted over the previous few years, playing to patriotic feeling served as the key device that held together an otherwise divided and unstable political elite.[110] In both republics, local leaders would keep pushing at the ambiguous

240

В Колонном зале Дома Союзов 8 марта 1953 года. На снимке слева направо: В. М. Молотов, К. Е. Ворошилов, Л. П. Берия, Г. М. Маленков, Н. А. Булганин, Н. С. Хрущев, Л. М. Каганович, А. И. Микоян у гроба товарища И. В. Сталина.

ДЕЛО СТАЛИНА БЕССМЕРТНО!

Прощание народов с великим вождем

ГЛУБОКАЯ СКОРБЬ

1. Stalin's death in March 1953 prompted both deep mourning and concern about the future. His principal lieutenants styled themselves as a collective leadership until Nikita Khrushchev emerged as predominant. Left to right: Vyacheslav Molotov, Kliment Voroshilov, Lavrenty Beria, Georgy Malenkov, soldier, Stalin, soldier, Nikolai Bulganin, Nikita Khrushchev, Lazar Kaganovich, Anastas Mikoyan.

2. Unlike Stalin, Khrushchev enthusiastically embraced the possibilities that global decolonisation presented for the Soviet Union. After Prime Minister Jawaharlal Nehru and his daughter Indira Gandhi toured the USSR in June 1955, Khrushchev and Bulganin headed to India at the end of the year; Khrushchev also visited Burma and Afghanistan as part of a tour of Asia. Left to right: Jawaharlal Nehru, Nikita Khrushchev, Indira Gandhi, Nikolai Bulganin.

3. With his 1954 novella *The Thaw*, Ilya Ehrenburg created the most enduring epithet for the Khrushchev years. No less important, he consistently displayed the kind of liberal-minded and internationalist outlook that (intermittently at least) helped to make the era distinctive culturally, and for which he was repeatedly attacked.

4. An enduring classic of Soviet cinema, *Carnival Night* was an instant hit in cinemas upon its release in 1956, but it also served as a testimony of changing times in the cultural sphere, pitting a dogmatic Stalinist official against idealistic and energetic young people determined to have fun on New Year's Eve.

5. Eager to reshape global perceptions of the USSR, Soviet authorities welcomed an unprecedented wave of foreign visitors for the 1957 World Youth Festival in Moscow. After years of international isolation, Muscovites enthusiastically embraced their guests. New points of contact and exchange with the outside world would be one of the defining features of the age.

6. As figureheads of the Soviet space programme and nuclear weapons programme respectively, Sergei Korolev (left) and Igor Kurchatov (right) each played a defining role in the Sixties era. Paradoxically, the identity of Korolev remained a closely guarded secret until his death in 1966, while Kurchatov was known to the public and even travelled abroad with Khrushchev on occasion.

7. Soviet attempts to win new allies in the developing world generated decidedly mixed results, but ties with Fidel Castro's Cuba not only proved enduring, but also resonated deeply among the public. An early visit to the USSR in December 1960 saw Che Guevara strengthening personal bonds between Moscow and Havana.

8. In contrast to Laika – whose pioneering journey into space in 1957 was always going to be a one-way mission – Belka and Strelka returned to Earth in one piece in 1960, opening the road to human space fight. Back home, they would quickly become some of the most celebrated and prominent figures of the age.

9. For much of the Sixties era, Andrei Sakharov was among the regime's most prized scientists and a central figure in the Soviet nuclear weapons programme. By the second half of the period, however, he was increasingly coming into conflict with authority on a variety of matters and would, in time, emerge as perhaps the most influential dissenting voice in the country.

10. May Day parade in Kiev (Kyiv), 1961. Partly thanks to Khrushchev's own links to the republic, Ukraine would become a notably more prominent actor within the Soviet system after Stalin. As in several other republics, though, questions of national identity, cultural heritage and nationalism grew steadily more important in Ukraine during the post-Stalin years.

11. 'Glory to women: active builders of communism'. Revolutionary-era discourse on equality of the sexes had largely faded from view under Stalin but would return to the fore under Khrushchev. Nonetheless, Soviet women continued to face a litany of disadvantages in a system that fundamentally privileged men.

12. While Khrushchev was the central figure of the age, the Armenian Anastas Mikoyan was nonetheless a key influence on events, at times encouraging reform and other times urging caution. Although never much of an independent thinker, Leonid Brezhnev was still a pretty effective political operator during the Sixties era. Here, the three men talk on the telephone to Valentina Tereshkova during her June 1963 space flight. Left to right: Anastas Mikoyan, Nikita Khrushchev, Leonid Brezhnev.

13. Regime control over the performing arts remained tight, with creativity and innovation often stifled, but the Soviet Union nonetheless boasted a wealth of globally admired cultural stars, such as the composer Dmitry Shostakovich, cellist Mstislav Rostropovich, opera singer Galina Vishnevskaya and ballerina Maya Plisetskaya, pictured here during a 1963 performance in the UK.

14. The popularity of poetry soared again during the 1950s and 1960s, and there was no bigger star than Yevgeny Yevtushenko, who was able to fill sports stadiums for his recitals. Not only did he embody much of the era's dynamism and verve, he was also a frequent target for conservatives' ire.

15. For the first decade of the space race, the USSR repeatedly claimed spectacular victories over its American rival. Along with scientists, cosmonauts were the great heroes of the age, hailed as exemplars of the communist man and woman of the future. Back row, left to right: Valery Bykovsky, German Titov, Yuri Gagarin, Andrian Nikolaev, Pavel Popovich. Front row, left to right: Boris Yegorov, Konstantin Feoktistov, Valentina Tereshkova, Vladimir Komarov.

16. A marker of increasing regime conservatism, the trial of writers Yuli Daniel (left) and Andrei Sinyavsky (right) on charges of anti-Soviet activity and propaganda in February 1966 would prove the catalyst for a much wider cycle of protest activity and regime repression across the second half of the 1960s and beyond.

17. From jazz in the 1950s to the Beatles, the Rolling Stones and more in the 1960s, one of the key stories of the Sixties as an age was the rapidly growing popularity of Western music and fashions among Soviet youth. Here, we see young people dancing the Twist at a club in Irkutsk in 1967.

18. By the later 1960s, the new Soviet leadership was growing increasingly overt in its conservatism and resistance to reform. Liberalisation in neighbouring Czechoslovakia would thus be deemed a real threat to the existing order of things inside the USSR. Left to right: Nikolai Podgorny, Alexei Kosygin, Leonid Brezhnev, Petro Shelest, Alexander Dubček and Mikhail Suslov in Bratislava, August 1968.

19. Many liberal-minded Soviet citizens had looked on the reforms of the Prague Spring with hope for their own country's future. When Warsaw Pact troops, led by the Soviet Union, invaded to crush reformist Czechoslovakia in August 1968, it extinguished the hopes of Soviet liberals and led to a fresh crackdown inside the USSR.

border between the acceptable expression of national sentiment and the kind of 'bourgeois nationalism' still regarded by Moscow as intolerable.

Eduards Berklavs had risen rapidly through the Latvian Communist Party ranks during the mid-1950s, bringing with him a number of like-minded associates. Then, the Twentieth Party Congress in February 1956 and its promise of a 'return to Leninism' in nationalities matters (essentially understood in Riga and elsewhere as a political rejection of the overt Russian dominance of late Stalinism) gave the reformist Berklavs the opportunity to pursue a more distinctly Latvian line in the republic, since this seemingly now had Khrushchev's sanction.[111]

Berklavs first resisted further development of heavy industry in Latvia, largely as a means of stemming the flow of Russian workers and specialists moving to the republic (one recent account has described the scale of Russian in-migration around this time as marking a 'profound ethno-national demographic shift' in both Latvia and Estonia).[112] In late 1956, he also pushed through a decree which insisted that anyone holding a public-facing role there – from police and factory officials to schoolteachers – now had two years in which to learn the Latvian language, or else forfeit their post. Berklavs' next target was access to housing – a resource that was in short supply and one to which Russians were widely perceived to be receiving privileged access. The granting of residence permits for Riga, in particular, was tightened up, in order to stem the substantial flow of incoming Russians. Also in the hands of nationally minded communists, elements of the Latvian media openly celebrated news of Russians subsequently departing the republic.[113] All this seemingly not only helped to build local popularity for the Latvian communists, but also provoked a flow of letters to Moscow from angry Russians inside Latvia, complaining that they had become subject to public hostility and nationalist discrimination.[114]

As in Latvia, rising national sentiment in Azerbaijan did not emerge from the Twentieth Party Congress, but it was certainly boosted by it. As in a number of other republics, Azeri writers previously banned as symbols of 'bourgeois nationalism' (such as the sixteenth-century poet Fuzuli) were again published, and long-suppressed folk traditions and historical figures were re-embraced. New decrees also emerged, without Moscow's permission, privileging the use of the Azeri language over Russian in public life. When

241

Khrushchev's proposals for education reform emerged in 1958, officials in Baku unmistakably thumbed their noses at them, and decreed that the study of the local language remained mandatory in Azerbaijan's schools. This naturally went down well with the public, but KGB officials were soon warning Moscow of rising hostility towards Russian and Armenian minorities in Azerbaijan, especially once some Yerevan began to demand the return of the Azeri-administered Karabakh region to Armenian control. Leaflets were found calling for the expulsion of Russians and Armenians from Azerbaijan, as well as for the republic's withdrawal from the Soviet Union, to be replaced instead by closer ties to neighbouring Turkey and Iran.[115]

Construction of a pipeline to transport Azeri natural gas to neighbouring Georgia was soon being decried inside Azerbaijan as theft of the republic's natural riches (official narratives optimistically referred to it as the 'friendship of peoples pipeline'). There was also a more generalised resentment – by no means wholly unjustified – that decision makers in Moscow paid little attention to Azerbaijan's problems, with matters like rising youth unemployment and pollution generating popular discontent, while badly needed infrastructure, like sewage treatment facilities, failed to materialise. Since it served them well, Azeri Communist Party boss Imam Mustafaev and his ally Mirza Ibrahimov left this public mood largely unchecked. In time, KGB reports began to suggest that national minorities were living in fear inside Azerbaijan.[116]

After some considerable lobbying, Berklavs' conservative opponents within the Latvian Communist Party leadership won a hearing with Khrushchev when he visited Riga in June 1959. The Stalinist hardliner Arvīds Pelše successfully convinced him that Berklavs and his allies were not 'embracing the line of the Twentieth Congress' on nationalities affairs, but stirring subversive nationalism in Latvia. As he left the Latvian capital, Khrushchev questioned Berklavs about his loyalty, and warned that he would be 'wiped from the face of the Earth' if he proved to be an enemy.[117] When the full Central Committee assembled in Moscow at the end of the month, Khrushchev's patience had clearly snapped. He told those present of his distaste for the new language laws in Latvia, insisting that such discrimination was harmful to strengthening ties between different Soviet peoples, and likening the policies enacted there to those of the nationalist Ulmanis dictatorship of the inter-war years. Mustafaev was accused of doing much the same kind of damage in Baku and was subjected to a crude tirade of his own from Khrushchev. Within days, both Berklavs and Mustafaev, along with their respective cliques, were reprimanded and removed from office. Over the next three years, around 2,000 members of the Latvian party and state elite were removed from their posts once Pelše became the Kremlin's new man in Riga.[118] Clearly alarmed at forces already unleashed, Moscow imposed a wider tightening of the centre's control over the periphery, and republican party leaderships in Turkmenistan, Uzbekistan, Kyrgyzstan, Tajikistan and Moldavia all faced their own censures and sackings over the next couple of years.

The Khrushchev years also saw the Central Asian republics become steadily more integrated into the Soviet system. The likes of Sharof Rashidov and Nuritdin Mukhitdinov both rose from the Uzbek republican elite to the Soviet elite. The Kyrgyz writer Chingiz Aitmatov did the same in the cultural sphere after his 1958 novella *Jamilia* was published in the journal *Novy mir*, drawing much attention to Kyrgyz culture and customs, as well as arousing some moral indignation at home over the fact that the central character, Jamilia, ultimately took the deeply taboo step of leaving her husband (who was away fighting in the war) for another man.[119] Before long, though, Aitmatov was an established literary star both across the USSR and abroad, continuing to make Kyrgyz women key protagonists in his works and claiming all manner of top awards for many years to come.

Investment in the Central Asian republics was also rising considerably, and the benefits of Soviet power more clearly began to materialise in major cities such as Stalinabad and Frunze (Bishkek), as new roads, schools and hospitals proliferated (one recent author has asserted that improving healthcare provision was 'one of the few real success stories in the Soviet saga').[120] Each republic of the region soon had its own academy of sciences, universities, theatres and film studios. Alongside traditional economic activities like sheep rearing, rug weaving and growing citrus fruits, new factories and industrial plants also appeared. One Western visitor to Tashkent in 1961 marvelled at how swathes of the city had been transformed 'from ancient Asian mud hovels to areas of apartment houses', with new cinemas and street lighting, factories and hotels.[121] The picture was rather patchier outside the major urban centres, though, with attempts to connect collective farms to mains electricity and to establish basic welfare provisions often faltering.[122] Massive infrastructure projects aimed to transform the region for the long term. In 1954, work began on the Karakum Canal in Turkmenistan, in a bid to increase the pitifully small amount of irrigated land for agriculture there (almost 90 per cent of the republic was desert). Similarly, construction of the giant Nurek Dam got under way in Tajikistan in 1961, a project intended to generate sufficient hydroelectric power to transform the surrounding area into a hotbed of industrial development (a plan that ultimately never came close to fruition).[123]

The urban development that took off in Central Asia from the mid-1950s not only brought new opportunities, but was also problematic in some important ways. The skilled jobs that appeared with industry, such as technicians and engineers, were often filled by incoming Slavs, rather than locals. Ancient Islamic cities like Samarkand and Bukhara were rapidly being changed forever, as factories and modern apartment blocks, which were geared to neither the cultural traditions nor the practical realities of life in the region, were erected and old buildings were pulled down. Similarly, the modern parts of the region's large cities tended to be inhabited by Russians, Ukrainians and other European Soviet peoples, often living quite separately from locals in many respects, with incomers at times arousing resentment with their condescending attitudes towards local customs, such as local women wearing the yashmak in public.

Modernisation also brought environmental despoliation. Efforts to improve irrigation for the Uzbek cotton industry triggered the dramatic shrinking of the Aral Sea, which at the start of the 1960s was one of the world's largest lakes, with a thriving fishing industry, but today has almost entirely dried up. Not unrelatedly, the continual expansion of cotton growing across much of the region, dictated by the needs of the wider Soviet economy, not only created jobs (albeit low-skilled and low-paying ones) and income, but also displaced people from their ancestral homes and meant that fertile land which could otherwise have been used for agriculture was lost to the production of raw materials that were then sent elsewhere for processing and sale.

Similarly, while it was certainly possible for Central Asians to climb the ranks of Soviet officialdom, that typically demanded taking on overtly 'European' cultural conventions of dress and behaviour.[124] In this context, it is also worth noting the rapid proliferation of new boarding schools during the 1950s and 1960s. In Central Asia especially, these were frequently places where future generations still studied the local language, culture and history, but did so in an environment deliberately separated from the apparent 'harmful influences' (such as religious traditions) to be found in the parental home and village, as part of on-going attempts to 'sovietise' the region.[125]

Cultural scandals

Perhaps more than ever before, by the end of the 1950s the Soviet Union was garnering considerable international acclaim for its cultural exports. With his hugely popular movie *The Cranes Are Flying*, director Mikhail Kalatozov claimed the Palme D'Or at the 1958 Cannes Film Festival. Two years later, Grigory Chukhrai's *Ballad of a Soldier* took a lesser prize at Cannes, but also won awards at competitions in both the USA and the UK. Two years further down the line, in 1962, came the directorial debut of Andrei Tarkovsky, with *Ivan's Childhood*. Although Tarkovsky's global renown would not peak until the 1970s, with movies like *Solaris* and *Stalker*, *Ivan's Childhood* none-theless won the Golden Lion at the Venice Film Festival and helped establish the director's reputation as an emerging talent well beyond Soviet borders. Successes like these were valued especially highly by the political authorities, since the Soviet regime presented itself to domestic and foreign audiences alike as a bastion of high culture, against the soulless materialism of the capitalist world (and the US in particular).[126]

The contemporary output of most Soviet performing arts was generally regarded abroad as pretty conservative and stale, but the country nonetheless boasted truly iconic talents across a wide range of fields. Towards the end of 1956, the Bolshoi Ballet staged its first foreign performances in two hundred years (in London), and thereafter undertook a major US tour which saw as many as 300,000 people watch appearances in New York, Los Angeles and San Francisco during 1958. Foreign audiences clamoured to see the legendary Galina Ulanova dance *Giselle* and Maya Plisetskaya perform in *Swan Lake*. On tour in the West, Plisetskaya's performances attracted stars like Salvador Dali, Coco Chanel and Audrey Hepburn.[127] Soviet musicians of great international renown, like opera singer Galina Vishnevskaya, cellist Mstislav

Rostropovich (Vishnevskaya's husband), violinist David Oistrakh and pianists Sviatoslav Richter, Vladimir Ashkenazy and Emil Gilels all headed abroad to perform, showcasing the standards of Soviet high culture and raking in much-desired foreign currency.[128] Composer Dmitry Shostakovich also returned to the foreground, producing new work and serving as a powerful advocate for Soviet cultural achievements in the West, where his classic compositions of earlier decades were still lauded.

In sports, too, the USSR now emerged as an international superpower. The year 1960 saw the Soviet team walk away as champions when the first ever European Cup was held in football. The USSR would soon become the dominant force in international ice hockey (the most popular sport after football) and it had long swept all before it in chess, with world champions like the Russian Mikhail Botvinnik, the Latvian Mikhail Tal and the Armenian Tigran Petrosian becoming major celebrities at home. At the 1960 summer Olympics in Rome, the USSR stood comfortably clear of the US at the top of the medals table, also emerging in first place when the Winter Olympics were staged in California that same year.

As well as international acclaim and success, however, the late 1950s and early 1960s were also defined by cultural scandal and clampdown. Already a poet of international renown, by the mid-1950s Boris Pasternak had begun reading to friends extracts of what was to become his first novel. He even had a couple of its poems published in *Pravda*, before eventually submitting the completed manuscript of *Dr Zhivago* for consideration at *Novy mir* at the end of 1955. It would take until September 1956 for the manuscript to be politely but decisively rejected by the then editor, Konstantin Simonov. As the *Novy mir* reviewers saw it, the basic thrust of Pasternak's novel implied that the October Revolution had brought little but human suffering and the destruction of the old intelligentsia.[129]

In fact, the problem essentially lay in the fact that, rather than being the militant anti-communist tract that Pasternak's attackers would later denounce, *Dr Zhivago* was insufficiently pro-communist. Its lead characters' clear sense of ambivalence towards both Red and White forces as the Russian Civil War raged around them were hard to miss: one Western scholar even described the eponymous Yuri Zhivago as the antithesis of the positive Soviet hero.[130] For all that the cultural sphere had already changed significantly in the previous few years, it was still not acceptable to ignore such basic conventions of the Socialist Realist genre. However, by the time it had been turned down at *Novy mir*, Pasternak's manuscript had already made it to Milan.

In May 1956, when the Soviet Union had seemed safely on course for substantial liberalisation, Pasternak sent the manuscript of *Dr Zhivago* to the Italian communist and publisher Giangiacomo Feltrinelli, who was immediately taken by the novel. At the end of June, a contract between author and publisher was agreed. Already in August 1956, the Soviet minister of foreign affairs wrote to Presidium members warning that Pasternak's manuscript (which he described as a 'spiteful slander against the USSR') had been transmitted to Feltrinelli and informing them that attempts were being made through contacts in the Italian Communist Party to prevent its publication.[131] Feltrinelli, though, held firm and insisted that the work was a masterpiece that must be published. Pasternak was no less determined that his magnum opus should appear in print. He did eventually concede in August 1957 to send a telegram urging Feltrinelli not to publish (supposedly on the grounds that the work was not yet finished), but the pair had anyway agreed in advance to disregard any such request that he might make under duress.

In November 1957, *Dr Zhivago* first appeared in Italian bookstores and proved an instant hit. Translations were immediately commissioned for French, English and many more editions. Here, Pasternak's undoubted talent also had some outside help. Keen to embarrass its Cold War rival, the CIA worked hard to have the book published and publicised as widely as possible around the globe, including Russian-language copies produced in a physical form suitable for smuggling into the USSR by tourists and others. Before long, Radio Liberty was broadcasting readings of Pasternak's novel at speeds intentionally slow enough for Soviet listeners to type out their own copy of the book along with the transmission.

Across the world, there was tremendous praise for *Dr Zhivago*, and it quickly topped bestseller lists. When they became aware that it was being considered for the Nobel Prize for Literature, Soviet officials tried to avert further embarrassment by warning the Swedish Academy that such a decision would be deemed an unfriendly act.[132] Nevertheless, on 23 October, to the initial rejoicing of Pasternak and his friends, he was announced the winner for 1958. Out of sensitivity to his predicament with the Soviet authorities, the citation did not specifically mention *Dr Zhivago*, allowing the implication that the award was for his poetry. Inside the Soviet Union, this attempt at subtlety made precious little difference.

A vicious scandal quickly engulfed Pasternak. Privately, party leaders debated launching a criminal case against him. In the Writers' Union, many of his peers – including some he had considered friends – were mobilised for individual and collective denunciations, which at times bordered on the hysterical. In the press, his actions were branded 'against the people, against peace, and against socialism', while Pasternak was attacked for his 'moral and political degradation', as well as his 'self-conceit and poverty of thought'.[133] *Dr Zhivago* was branded 'a political weapon in the hands of reaction' and it was asserted that the Nobel Prize had been awarded solely for political purposes (a claim which sat rather awkwardly with the fact that a trio of Soviet physicists won that year's Nobel Prize for Physics). Conservatives in the Soviet cultural sphere seized the moment and went into full-throated attack against their liberal-minded colleagues.[134] By a unanimous vote, Pasternak was expelled from the Writers' Union, a move that stripped him of the generous material benefits afforded to Soviet authors.

Only a few of his peers, including the writers Alexander Tvardovsky and Konstantin Chukovsky, proved willing to help Pasternak, rather than attack him.[135] The poet Yevgeny Yevtushenko was so appalled at the tone of one anti-Pasternak meeting that he walked out, while a few others, including Pasternak himself, refused to attend sessions clearly lined up as public condemnations. Forums were held around the country to whip up public condemnation of a book that almost nobody had actually read. Angry and threatening letters began to arrive at Pasternak's home, and students from the Literary Institute went out to his home at the writers' colony of Peredelkino to shout abuse and smash bottles of ink on his fence.[136] Most notoriously, in a major public speech at Moscow's Palace of Sports at the end of October, Komsomol boss Vladimir Semichastny tore into Pasternak's supposed disloyalty, saying that he had spat in the face of the Soviet people and insisting that 'even a pig does not shit where it eats'. Semichastny then urged that Pasternak should be thrown out of the country, remarking that 'his departure from our midst would purify the air' (a draft decree to this effect was drawn up, but never formally issued).[137] When he recorded his memoirs years later, though, Semichastny insisted that the remarks in question were not really his own, but had been personally dictated to him by Khrushchev (who was sitting in the audience applauding the vulgar diatribe, with the rest of the Presidium).[138] Although impossible to prove, Semichastny's claim does not feel at all outlandish. Khrushchev, it should be noted, had not actually read *Dr Zhivago*. He had instead been presented with a series of cherry-picked extracts that 'proved' its ideological hostility, and thereafter had thrown his full weight against it.

Rounding on Pasternak in this way did considerable damage to the Soviet Union's international standing as a cultural power. Protests at the orchestrated attacks on the poet were sent to Moscow by the likes of Graham Greene, T.S. Eliot and Aldous Huxley, while Austria, Sweden and Norway spoke of suspending recent agreements on cultural exchanges with the USSR. Pasternak himself certainly took the barrage of abuse seriously and was deeply alarmed at the prospect of being ejected from his homeland, eventually agreeing to suggestions that he write a private note of contrition to Khrushchev. Put under immense pressure to refuse the Nobel Prize, he finally acquiesced, rather unconvincingly insisting that he had done so of his own free will. Aware of the immense harm being done to the country's reputation, and having received Pasternak's letter of repentance (which was then published in the major Soviet newspapers), Khrushchev let the matter drop.

For Boris Pasternak, though, there could be no return to normality. Admirers still sought him out at Peredelkino to pay homage – during a 1959 trip to Moscow, the American conductor Leonard Bernstein even persuaded Pasternak to attend a performance of Stravinsky's *Rite of Spring* with him – but he became steadily more reclusive and was anyway growing ill. He died of cancer at the end of May 1960 and was buried at Peredelkino amid tight security. Despite clear discouragement from attending, perhaps five hundred friends and admirers went to the funeral or sent wreaths – a fact that showed the changed times, of people refusing to be cowed into hiding their sense of solidarity with him.[139] Monitoring events closely, officials from the Department of Culture subsequently reported that 'attempts to use the funeral to stir unhealthy moods were unsuccessful', but they did note that one of those in attendance had openly lambasted the authorities for refusing to publish *Dr Zhivago* and had declared that no other Soviet writer came close to Pasternak as an artist.[140]

A final spiteful kick was then aimed at the dead author later that summer, when his long-time lover Olga Ivinskaya and her daughter were both jailed (for eight years and three years, respectively) for their part in efforts to get foreign royalties accrued by *Dr Zhivago* into the USSR and to its author, as he struggled for money in his final months. The Soviet authorities also worked hard to get their own hands on the sizeable royalties that his book had earned abroad, though without much success.[141] Not until 1988, with *glasnost* in full swing, did *Dr Zhivago* at last appear officially inside the USSR. The following year, Pasternak's son Evgeny finally went to Stockholm to collect his father's Nobel Prize.

Where Pasternak was a living link to the heights of pre-revolutionary Russian culture – his parents had been friendly with Leo Tolstoy – there also emerged during the second half of the 1950s a clutch of vibrant new cultural figures who helped to define the Sixties era. In Ukraine, young writers like Vasyl Symonenko, Ivan Drach and Lina Kostenko, and painters like Alla Horska, became hugely popular among young people, especially. In Russia, poets like Yevgeny Yevtushenko, Andrei Voznesensky (who had been tutored by Pasternak for a time) and Bella Akhmadulina, along with prose writers such as Vasily Aksenov and Anatoly Gladilin, were often bundled together as a group of 'Sixties' writers, in some (but by no means all) senses resembling a Soviet version of America's 'Beat Generation' authors. Actually, when US beat poet Allen Ginsberg visited Moscow in 1964, he made sure to hang out with Aksenov, Yevtushenko and their friends (Ginsberg and Voznesensky, in particular, would subsequently develop a life-long friendship).[142] Although very much inside the system, rather than genuinely countercultural figures, almost all of these new writers had their clashes with authority, and they were regularly targets for attack from cultural conservatives in particular.

Of the poets, Yevtushenko was the biggest star (though Voznesensky was perhaps the more gifted). Embracing the notion that he was the voice of a generation, Yevtushenko's energy and self-confidence and his passion for jazz, fashionable clothes and adventure captured much of what was distinctive about the age. The authors Vail and Genis even refer to him as Khrushchev's 'co-author' of the era.[143] Although his first poetry collection was published in 1952, while he was still a teenager, it was only a few years

250

later that Yevtushenko began to attract major attention, as the popularity of poetry surged again from the mid-1950s. When a national Poetry Day was re-established in 1955, Yevtushenko, Bella Akhmadulina (the pair were married for a time) and others gave readings not just in bookshops and libraries, but also in factories and public halls.[144] Before long, they, like Voznesensky, were giving poetry recitals in packed sports stadiums, with many thousands in attendance. Habitually spied on by the KGB and inter-mittently denounced by cultural and political conservatives, Yevtushenko still idolised Lenin during the 1950s and early 1960s, and bought into the fundamental values that the regime professed, though he later remarked that the Soviet regime did all it could to 'knock the Soviet-ness out of me'.[145]

Works such as Voznesensky's poem 'Antiworlds' pushed hard at the bound-aries of staid Socialist Realism, and his live performances were famously powerful affairs. Various of Yevtushenko's major poems were closely aligned with the political message of the day, but this was not always the case. His 1961 work 'Babii Yar' was written in only a couple of hours, following a visit to the site of a September 1941 Nazi massacre in occupied Kiev – when over 30,000 of the city's Jews had been executed and dumped in a ravine, which the Soviet authorities had since turned into a city rubbish dump, with no memorial to the horrors that had taken place there. Controversially, Yevtushenko used that subject matter to decry contemporary discrimination against Soviet Jews. In the poem's closing lines he declared that:

I am each old man here shot dead,
I am every child here shot dead,
Nothing in me will ever forget . . .
In my blood there is no Jewish blood.
In their callous rage all anti-Semites
must hate me now as a Jew.
For that reason, I am a true Russian!

On arriving back in Moscow from Kiev, Yevtushenko promptly read 'Babii Yar' at a performance that same night, to be met first with dead silence and then a standing ovation that lasted for ten minutes.[146] When the poem was subsequently published in *Literaturnaya gazeta*, though, it aroused both tremendous support and great fury. Within days it was being roundly criticised in other publications, and the editor responsible was soon fired.

Like Yevtushenko (whose maternal and paternal grandfathers had been arrested in the late 1930s), Aksenov had a painful family history of Stalinist repression: both his parents were jailed while he was still a child (his mother Evgeniya Ginzburg would later write the classic gulag memoir *Into the Whirlwind*). First finding popularity with his debut novel, *Colleagues* (1959), and following that up with *Ticket to the Stars* (1961), Aksenov would become the leading exponent of the 'youth novel'. This was a literary genre that typically centred on idealistic but questioning young men and women, frustrated by their elders' conservatism, wracked by doubt about their proper place in the world and full of desire for action and excitement.[147] The character Maxim in *Colleagues*, for example, exclaims early on that 'I want excitement . . . I want to enjoy myself while I'm young, wherever I am,' later stating that 'I love my country and all that it stands for . . . but I don't answer to anyone but myself, my own conscience.'[148] Dotted throughout were discussions about jazz, modern art, Western fashions and more. *Ticket to the Stars* would take this theme of restless youth further, with its frustrated young protagonist declaring 'I'm not going to spend my summer sweating over textbooks, doing the family shopping and listening to moral lectures . . . ah, the hell with everything here. Let's blow!' He then leads his friends off to Tallinn for a summer of free-wheeling and encounters with the underside of Soviet life. This novel outraged conservatives with its depictions of jaded and directionless young people and frequent Western reference points (such as Federico Fellini and Brigitte Bardot).

Socialist Realism remained the mandated genre for official Soviet art, though it was at least safer now for artists to probe the borders of acceptable and unacceptable expression. Influenced in part by visits and exhibitions of foreign artists, things grew rather more diverse away from the studios and exhibitions of the establishment.[149] Guzel Amalrik described how 'at the end of the fifties . . . our young artists entered into a period of unusual ferment . . . throwing off the shackles of Soviet realism'.[150] In Kiev, Tbilisi, Yerevan and elsewhere, non-conformist artists of all kinds held salons and staged unsanctioned exhibitions in private apartments and academic institutes, quietly selling their work as they did so. Unofficial movements were also coming together and experimenting in Moscow, around Eli Belyutin's 'Free Studio of Art' and at the village of Lianozovo, where artists such as Oskar Rabin and Lidiya Masterkova were honing their craft, supporting themselves largely by selling work to foreign journalists and Western diplomats in the Soviet capital.[151] Some, like the great Ilya Kabakov, straddled the world of official and unofficial art. Others, like Anatoly Zverev, enjoyed a burgeoning reputation abroad – in 1960, Zverev's work was featured in *Time* magazine – but faced persecution and impoverishment at home.

Potentially the most explosive literary work of the age was pretty effectively hushed up by the authorities at the time, but it was nonetheless a powerful indicator of the limits to cultural liberalisation. Vasily Grossman had come to prominence as a reporter during the war, providing accounts from seminal battles at Stalingrad and Kursk, and later being one of the first to describe the horrors of the Nazis' concentration camps in his famous reportage 'The Hell of Treblinka'. By the time of Stalin's death, though, Grossman was expecting imminent arrest, like many of his former colleagues in the Jewish Anti-Fascist Committee. Even so, he had already begun work on a novel, which he envisioned from the outset as an epic to stand alongside Tolstoy's *War and Peace*. Of the book that eventually followed, Vladimir Voinovich justifiably wrote that 'had it been published when it was finished, that is in 1960, I have no doubt that it would have been a literary sensation of world importance'.[152] In fact, it was lucky that the novel ever emerged at all.

Set during the war, and with storylines alternating between a Nazi concentration camp full of squabbling Soviet POWs, the front line of the fighting and events in the Soviet rear, *Life and Fate* touched upon a plethora of deeply taboo issues. It drew implicit but strong parallels between Soviet and Nazi camps (and between the holocaust and Stalin's drive to liquidate the kulaks). It depicted violent interrogations in the Lubyanka, explored anti-Semitism inside the USSR, both at the elite level and among ordinary citizens and featured a host of vainglorious, ruthless and perpetually suspicious officials (with one character furiously insisting that such bureaucrats were not really a cancerous growth on the state but 'its very essence'). Perhaps most importantly, the novel also undermined key facets of Khrushchev's narrative on the abuses of the Stalin years, suggesting that intolerance and indifference to human suffering were baked into the system from the start, rather than simply being a product of Stalin's personal malevolence. It also made it plain that many people – from the lowest to the highest level – were not just victims of brutality, but also participants in it.

Before he submitted the manuscript to the journal *Znamya* (*Banner*) in October 1960 (*Novy mir* editor Tvardovsky had read and admired the work, but admitted he would be unable to publish it), one of Grossman's friends apparently made a list for him of twenty separate passages that might land the author in jail.[153] He persisted nonetheless, determined to see his novel published. However, the editorial board at *Znamya* were sufficiently troubled by the manuscript for them to pass it directly to the Central Committee's Cultural Department for its evaluation. In mid-December, Grossman was abruptly informed that his work would not be published, and he was ordered not to circulate it to anybody at all.

Evidently fearing a rerun of the Pasternak affair, but uneasy at the prospect of jailing a reasonably prominent writer, the authorities settled on a new course of action: they arrested the novel. A team of KGB men arrived at Grossman's house and seized sacks full of papers; they then went to the home of his typist to claim typewriter ribbons and carbons; finally, they headed to a number of other locations (including the *Novy mir* office) where the author had confessed to storing copies of his manuscript.

As months passed, Grossman wrote desperately to Khrushchev to complain about the fate of his life's work, insisting that he had not written a political book and pointing out that his novel chimed with Khrushchev's own remarks about the need to tell the truth about the Stalin era. His letters eventually elicited a response, but it was not the one that Grossman hoped for. He was summoned in July 1962 to see Mikhail Suslov, a conservative hardliner in charge of ideological affairs. Suslov admitted from the outset that he had not read the manuscript (he did suggest he might read it while on holiday), but he had seen experts' reviews and some extracts. He then bluntly rejected Grossman's insistence that it was not a political work, telling the author that his book was far more dangerous than even Pasternak's had been and insisting that it could not be published for perhaps three hundred years.[154]

Grossman was left at liberty but in clear disfavour, with the very existence of his great novel remaining virtually unknown. He then fell ill and died of cancer in September 1964. For a long time, it was not clear that even a single copy of the novel had survived. A full decade after his death, though, one of the two remaining copies was finally taken out of hiding by the poet Semyon Lipkin, who had kept the manuscript under a pile of old clothes at his dacha (at Peredelkino, the writers' settlement where Pasternak had lived and been buried). Microfilms and photographs were then secretly produced and smuggled abroad. Eventually published in the West in 1980 – with Grossman long dead, but with the aged Suslov still at the apex of Soviet power – *Life and Fate* soon enough won wide international acclaim and is today widely recognised as one of the great masterpieces of Russian literature. Like *Dr Zhivago*, it eventually appeared in Soviet bookstores in 1988.

While the Grossman affair was still being hushed up, another cultural scandal burst that was from the outset both public and international in its dimensions. Second only to the Bolshoi in terms of its renown, when a troupe from Leningrad's Kirov Ballet headed off on tour to Paris and London in the summer of 1961 it agreed (after some French cajoling) to include in its number an unpredictable, but immensely talented, prodigy named Rudolf Nureyev. In Paris, Nureyev immediately became a sensation with French audiences, drawing comparisons to the great Vaslav Nijinsky. However, he also unnerved the tour's KGB overseers and Kirov management by speaking his mind rather too freely, and frequently breaking away from other members of the tour party and socialising at night with new French friends. For Nureyev himself, the month he spent in Paris was utterly bewitching, blighted only by the fact that he was continually trailed by suspicious KGB operatives.[155] With accumulating reports of his indiscretions, it was decided back in Moscow that he should be returned to the USSR when the opportunity arose. During his short time in Paris, though, Nureyev had already begun to sense the mounting likelihood of such an outcome.[156]

As the Kirov touring party waited at Le Bourget airport to check in for the flight to London on 17 June, Nureyev – who had been out walking the streets of Paris until 06:00 with a friend on his final night – was informed that he would travel to the UK a few days later than the rest of the group, after first making a brief return trip to Moscow.

Nureyev was told that he was needed to perform at the Kremlin, and word had supposedly also come through that his mother had fallen sick back at home. Understanding the trap that awaited (he had spoken to his mother the previous evening and knew she was not ill), Nureyev was mortified and knew right away that he would never be allowed abroad again. As he waited for the next flight to Moscow, sandwiched between three KGB guards, one of Nureyev's new French friends found out what was happening. Seeking help, she approached airport police, who informed her that they could help, but only if Nureyev came to them himself. Once she managed to communicate this to him, he quickly jumped up and, before his guards had time to react, strode across the hall to the waiting policemen to request asylum in France.[157] First, the KGB officers tried to prise him away, but they were forced back by French police; then staff from the Soviet embassy arrived to browbeat him into surrender. All were unsuccessful, as Nureyev steadfastly refused to reconsider his asylum bid.

Nureyev's dramatic defection was immediately a massive story across the globe, and it was deeply embarrassing for the Soviet authorities. With huge demand for his talents in the West, he would become probably the world's most famous ballet dancer for many years to come. He was quickly made a 'non-person' at home, though, with all mention of his achievements and existence scrubbed from public life. Maya Plisetskaya, who secretly met him while on a later tour to the UK, recalled that 'Soviet people were afraid even to say the name Nureyev'.[158]

Sex and sexuality

Although he would insist that his decision to flee the USSR was rooted in considerations of artistic freedom, it can hardly have escaped Nureyev's attention that his sexuality could easily pose problems further down the line, if he remained in his homeland. Evolving attitudes towards sex and notions of sexual liberation have long been considered an important part of 'the Sixties' as a global phenomenon. Although this was not nearly so visible inside the USSR, important changes were under way there, too.

Where it was mentioned at all, sex was overwhelmingly framed as a means for a married couple to produce children. Indeed, the political authorities clearly perceived sexual activity as an area in which all manner of potential threats to the socio-political order could emerge.[159] Official rhetoric denied even the existence of prostitution inside the USSR – a phenomenon blamed squarely on the social impacts of capitalism – though police nonetheless worked to shut down brothels and drive prostitutes out of cities.[160] One 1959 pamphlet warned parents not to show too much affection in front of their children, in order to prevent the onset of moral depravity, also asserting that masturbation was bad for attitudes to work and study: it was presented as a product of capitalist alienation and the boast was that 'under Soviet conditions masturbation is no longer the mass phenomenon it used to be under tsarism'.[161]

Sexual activity was very much an area that the party considered within its purview. Party and Komsomol members were expected to set a positive example of both ideological and moral propriety for others to emulate. As such, they could have their personal affairs held up to scrutiny by peers, in some cases effectively being forced to return to a wife (or more rarely a husband) whom they had tried to leave.[162] Similarly, it was not unheard of for the Komsomol to reprimand members for promiscuous sexual conduct, censuring unmarried girls who had an abortion and pressuring male members to marry girls they had got pregnant. A major drive against venereal disease in the early 1960s took a similarly moralistic approach, criminalising transmission and presenting carriers as immoral and anti-social, though healthcare professionals did work hard to improve both education and treatment facilities.[163] Official discourse on divorce was little better, often portraying separation as an act of great selfishness for those with children especially, regardless of circumstances. Until the mid-1960s, separating couples were still legally obliged both to go through a lengthy court process and to announce their parting of the ways in the local press. As with abortions, though, the public proved largely unperturbed by official prescriptions, and divorce rates climbed by 270 per cent between 1955 and 1965.[164]

With a continuing assumption that 'sexual deviance' was connected to political deviance, there was little sign of the era's famed liberalisation when it came to homosexuals. A 1958 psychiatry textbook asserted that homosexuality was typically acquired from a depraved upbringing, rather than being innate, and it also claimed that the morally healthy environment in which Soviet youth grew up typically prevented such 'perversions'.[165] Some experts suggested treatments like surgery and psychotherapy, in order to correct what they understood to be an illness.[166] While a whole host of draconian laws from the Stalin era were being dropped, as legal codes were updated around the end of the 1950s, the 1934 law that declared sodomy illegal was consciously retained and enforced. Nonetheless, recent research has shown that even rather small provincial towns witnessed 'remarkably widespread and sustained' communities of active homosexual men, albeit existing mostly in secret.[167]

Places where gay men habitually met – such as parks, bathhouses and public toilets – were sometimes monitored by police, with informers and honey traps also used to expose practising homosexuals.[168] The available data remain incomplete, but we know that more than 22,000 men were jailed across the USSR for sodomy over the next two decades. One notable victim of this crackdown was Naum Shtarkman, who had come third in the same piano competition that shot the American Van Cliburn to fame in 1958. Not long after that contest, Shtarkman was arrested in Kharkov for homosexual activity, eventually emerging from jail years later to find his once-promising career in tatters. More famous to Soviet audiences was Vadim Kozin, who was a prominent singer of the 1930s. Kozin was entrapped in a Khabarovsk hotel room by a police informer while on tour in October 1959 and – though he served only a few months when convicted – his career lay similarly destroyed.[169] There was no law explicitly criminalising lesbian sexual activity, but there were efforts to 'cure' gay women through medicine and psychiatry.[170]

While the silence surrounding the subject of sex was not as profound as in the Stalin years – there was at least occasional discussion of the nature of romantic (heterosexual) love in the youth press and debates about the need to provide young people with some basic sex education – the central message was typically still blunt: young men should control their urges and young women should defend their honour.[171] Such rules were not necessarily observed, of course, even among Soviet officialdom. Most notably, Minister of Culture Georgy Alexandrov was quietly fired from his post in 1955, when it came to light that he was essentially keeping a harem of young ballerinas and actresses for himself and his friends.

Attitudes were changing at the ground level, however. Influenced by Alfred Kinsey's seminal studies in the US – but frequently hampered by moralising Soviet officialdom – the first sociological research into sex started to get under way in the early part of the 1960s, and the first sexologist's office opened its doors in Leningrad in 1963. Although the limited public discussion about sex meant that it mostly passed unnoticed, surveys of Leningrad students in 1963 made clear that they were going through much the same sort of generational evolutions as their counterparts in the West. They had started to have sex earlier in life, found sex and intimacy an increasingly important part of a relationship, were less inclined to get married and were more likely to have sex before marriage and to have more sexual partners overall.[172] By the end of the 1960s, surveys also showed that 55 per cent of young women and 62 per cent of young men considered sex before marriage an acceptable practice.[173]

Of course, this picture did not reflect reality everywhere. In villages especially, attitudes often remained deeply traditional, with even rumours of impropriety hugely damaging for a young woman; and indeed, it was widely regarded as inappropriate for an unmarried woman to enter a man's house alone.[174] Growing up in Uzbekistan – in an intelligentsia family in multicultural Tashkent – Dildora Muzafari wrote that her parents considered even Soviet movies (which were never even slightly raunchy by Western standards) to be immoral and banned them at home. Meanwhile, local custom dictated that Uzbek girls dressed with the utmost modesty and had to be kept well away from members of the opposite sex.[175]

What limited advice there was on the subject of reproduction could also be badly flawed at times. Pamphlets from the Ukrainian Ministry of Health advised readers on how to practise the 'rhythm method' and recommended that women insert slices of lemon into the vagina as a spermicidal agent – even as other official materials warned against these practices as effective forms of preventing pregnancy.[176] Contraception methods such as the pill and the diaphragm were starting to become available across the 1960s (condoms were widely disdained by both men and women, and were anyway frequently ineffective), but never came close to meeting demand. Medical professionals pushed hard to improve contraceptive provision, but renewed pro-natalism at the very top (again driven by fears of population decline) meant that progress on this front was deliberately stifled, with oral contraceptives 'practically banned' by the late 1960s.[177] For many women, then, unwanted pregnancies had to be risked. Soviet men could often be remarkably sanguine about this, though the abortion procedure could be both humiliating and agonising, since it was not infrequently performed without anaesthetic.[178]

Clearly, we cannot understand the Sixties era solely in terms of either progressive reform or unchanging despotism. One can hardly conceive of the likes of Grossman, Pasternak and Berklavs remaining at liberty and physically unscathed from their brushes with authority had those occurred a decade previously; but then the experiences of homosexuals and religious believers demonstrate the problems of referring too casually to the period as a time of liberalisation. For all that the Soviet authorities aspired to control even the most intimate areas of citizens' lives, there was never a shortage of people who found ways to bend and break rules that hemmed them in.

8

ZENITH AND NADIR: 1961–62

At the Twenty-Second Party Congress in October 1961, Khrushchev presented a text that he described as '*The Communist Manifesto* of our age'. This was the Third Party Programme, which he likened to the final part of a three-stage rocket. The very first party programme, adopted back in 1903, had been created to blast the country away from capitalism; the second programme, produced in 1919, had been to power it towards socialism; and this third programme, Khrushchev insisted, would now take the USSR on to the promised land of communism. While Stalin asserted in the 1930s that the USSR had reached socialism, the subsequent transition from socialism to communism would be the crowning achievement of the Soviet system – the point at which Marx's egalitarian utopia finally arrived. Confident that recent successes would only continue, Khrushchev boldly declared that the next twenty years would see that task just about completed.

The Third Party Programme

From 1958 onwards, top party officials and around a hundred experts – in everything from Marxism and economics through to law and foreign relations – had been working on the new party programme. Khrushchev insisted from the outset that the final document should be 'both a poem and realistic to life'. Not normally one for poring over the fine detail, he was sufficiently invested in the project to send dozens of pages of comments on draft material as it came to him, on a few occasions personally dictating whole passages of text.[1] Publication of a draft programme in *Pravda* in July 1961 marked the start of wide-ranging public discussion, with somewhere in the region of 73 million people actively involved – attending party, Komsomol and trade union meetings where the text was discussed, as well as writing to newspapers, radio and television with comments and suggestions. Some felt the new plan to be overly ambitious, but others embraced its spirit and were especially radical in the suggestions they offered: completely prohibiting private property, cutting the salaries of top earners and forcing bureaucrats and their wives to undertake physical labour for at least a month each year.[2]

A lengthy opening section of Soviet boilerplate boasted of great achievements since 1917, outlined the accelerating crisis facing global capitalism and painted the present day as 'the springtime of mankind', with the Soviet people 'laying roads on which others would follow later'. The rest of the programme focused mainly on the country's continuing economic transformation and on the drive to shape the Soviet man and woman of the future. Vast new irrigation projects were promised to transform the arid Central Asian steppe, along with more and more energy generated by the raft of new hydroelectric stations and nuclear power plants going up around the country. There was to be increasing mechanisation of both factory and farm work, new research into computers, and accelerated development of the chemicals and plastics industries. Projecting a five-fold increase in labour productivity over the coming twenty years, the programme promised that the USSR would soon become comfortably the world's largest economic power.

The image of the communist utopia that the new programme conveyed centred pretty heavily on living standards and consumption. Within the next ten years, it stated, 'all sections of Soviet society will enjoy plenty', as meat consumption would more than double and there would be abundant fish and vegetables. Meanwhile, Soviet men and women would enjoy the shortest working day in the whole world. By 1980, it promised, meat consumption would have quadrupled, with abundance of everything from milk through to modern furniture, attractive clothes and leather shoes. Higher education enrolment was predicted to expand from 2.6 million students in 1961 to 8 million by 1980. Public transport would become free of charge, each citizen would receive one month of paid vacation per year, school meals and uniforms would be free and taxes would be abolished. The existing infrastructure of nurseries, medical centres, health resorts, sports societies, care for the elderly and infirm, public libraries, recreation clubs and more would all be greatly expanded as both crime and religious belief faded away. Khrushchev also joked later that Soviet gold reserves would be used to prettify the country's public toilets, once full communism arrived and the financial value of the commodity disappeared.[3]

The new programme cast aside the long-standing formulation of the Soviet system as a 'dictatorship of the proletariat', replacing it with the more inclusive notion of an 'all people's state', as a marker of the fact that antagonism and inequality between social classes inside the country were now declared at an end. There were also renewed promises about overcoming the 'vestiges of female inequality', by further extending maternity leave and improving the provision of household appliances, such as washing machines and refrigerators. As for the USSR's different national groups, the programme insisted that they would 'move closer' together, as mutual trust and friendly bonds between them continually strengthened (the original draft had promised a 'fusion' of different Soviet peoples, which many non-Russians had vigorously objected to during consultations, on the not unreasonable basis that it seemed to threaten Russification).

There was also an attempt to codify the very character of the people who would complete and inhabit the communist future. Like a Soviet version of the ten commandments, the Moral Code of the Builder of Communism offered a twelve-point guide to how a Soviet person should live their life. First of all it demanded that citizens show devotion to the communist cause, to the socialist motherland and to fraternal socialist countries. Subsequent clauses veered between the clearly admirable (such as mutual respect within the family, honesty and intolerance of national and racial hatred) and the overtly hardline (like 'intolerance towards enemies of communism'). All but omnipresent in the media and in schools when it first appeared, the Moral Code would in time become more a source of mirth than a template for daily life.

The point was made repeatedly in the new party programme that the coming of communism would not mean that citizens had the right to behave and work as they saw fit, but should be disciplined, tightly organised and civic minded, contributing as well as receiving. Members of public organisations like trade unions and the Komsomol, rather than salaried officials, were scheduled to take on a growing role in everything from policing the streets and prosecuting crimes to running theatres and canteens, as public self-government

saw the role of the state shrink. Importantly, the new programme also stipu-
lated that the party needed to do more to refresh the ranks of its leading cadres.
From the Central Committee downwards, officials at almost all levels would
now be replaced every few years, to keep talent progressing upwards and to
prevent stagnation. This was, as one scholar has argued, 'a tragedy for the
nomenklatura', since they would no longer be able to hang on indefinitely
to the posts that had brought them power and privilege; it also showed that
Khrushchev was no longer their protector.[4] Even at the drafting stage, this part
of the programme had aroused such resistance within officialdom that the
plans were repeatedly watered down.[5]

Many Soviet citizens were greatly enthused by the enticing visions of the
new age to come.[6] The main problem was the issue of credibility. One of
those involved in the drafting process, Anatoly Chernyaev admitted years
later that, even as he worked on the programme, he was not sure that he really
believed it, though he definitely wanted to.[7] KGB man Filipp Bobkov subsequently opined that the extent to which the new programme was detached
from reality on the ground ultimately generated disillusion and detachment
that undermined the party's authority.[8] Like his earlier promises to overtake
the US in meat and milk, Khrushchev's talk of communism in twenty years
was more than just ambitious. When composing his memoirs in retirement,
Mikoyan clearly presented the promise as irresponsible, noting with disdain
that Khrushchev knew full well that he would not see 1980 himself and
simply did not understand that people would want answers when his boasts
were not fulfilled.[9]

The central problem was that the programme's figures on economic
growth were predicated on the notion that recent trends would continue in
the long term. There had indeed been some important economic achievements since the mid-1950s: most notably, vast oil deposits were being identified and exploited, doubling the country's oil production between 1955
and 1960 and placing the USSR second only to the USA in terms of the
volume of oil produced.[10] Citizens' consumption levels had risen markedly,
and Soviet gross domestic product had increased by an estimated 265 per
cent during the decade.[11] However, growth rates were about to decline. The
basic issue was one that the system never resolved: growth was still largely
being achieved through expanding exploitation of resources, meaning more

people working, more land sowed and more minerals extracted from the ground. This kind of growth had natural limits, and they had just about been reached in some key areas. What the economy needed was growth through improved productivity – plans for wider mechanisation, better development of the chemical industry and computerisation all sought to do just that; but success on this front was to prove elusive. Once the economic predictions that underpinned it failed to materialise, the rest of the plan – from increased goods in the shops to better hospitals and kindergartens – inevitably faltered.

The Twenty-Second Party Congress

Of course, delegates to the Twenty-Second Party Congress in October 1961 unanimously approved the formal adoption of the new party programme when it was put to a vote. As usual, a parade of speakers took to the rostrum both to condemn Western imperialism and to laud Soviet victories. The party first secretary from Azerbaijan told of how his republic was outstripping the USA in the number of women in political life, in professional careers and in higher education. The Turkmen first secretary boasted that his republic had achieved universal literacy, had produced more cotton than neighbouring Iran and Afghanistan combined and had more doctors per capita than both the US and the UK. The Armenian party boss similarly told of how his republic had raced ahead of Turkey in industry and education levels, and announced that more and more members of the Armenian diaspora were now seeking to return to their ancestral homeland, as it scaled ever greater heights.

Perhaps most prominently, the Twenty-Second Party Congress was notable for a renewal of the attack on Stalin. This time, there was no gesture towards secrecy, as saturation coverage in the newspapers, on the radio and television conveyed everything that was said. In the keynote address, Khrushchev insisted that his earlier condemnation of the cult had strengthened the party's bond with the masses and ensured that 'our breathing is freer and our vision clearer'. This, he said, had speeded up the march towards communism. Most of the other speakers who touched upon the cult did so mainly to reaffirm Khrushchev's remarks. *Pravda* editor Pavel Satyukov went further, though, telling delegates that for years Stalin 'never went anywhere or spoke to anyone', as he grew more detached from the party and neither knew nor wanted to know how ordinary people lived. The Old Bolshevik Dora Lazurkina spoke at length of her own arrest in 1937, and lamented that the Stalin years had seen honest communists forced to lie and slander one another. Khrushchev even floated the possibility of erecting a public monument to Stalin's victims, though the idea never got off the ground.[12]

Again, there was no real attempt to engage with the systemic roots of the Stalin cult. Furthermore, even as they condemned one cult, multiple speakers at the congress were unmistakably building up another. Ukrainian party boss Nikolai Podgorny praised Khrushchev's 'inseparable bond with the people, his humanity and simplicity', calling him 'an inspiring example for the whole Party and every communist'. Uzbek First Secretary Sharof Rashidov told of how cotton workers in his own republic saw Khrushchev as 'their closest friend, their dear and beloved leader'. When Leonid Brezhnev's turn came to speak, he was no less servile, insisting that Khrushchev's 'indefatigable energy and revolutionary ardour inspire all of us to militant deeds'.[13]

Inextricably tied to the revived attacks on Stalin was a new wave of condemnation aimed at the failed plotters of the 1957 Anti-Party Affair. All were reviled as inveterate dogmatists, knee-deep in the crimes of the Stalin era and opposed to all attempts at reform thereafter. Khrushchev declared that Molotov, Malenkov and Kaganovich had been personally responsible for widespread repressions and abuses of power. Suslov branded them 'a contemptible group of factionalists', while the writer Mikhail Sholokhov was among several who suggested that there should be no place in the party ranks for people who had done such harm. KGB boss Shelepin was perhaps the most brutal rhetorically, insisting that Malenkov and the others should 'be haunted by nightmares, hear the sobs and curses of the mothers, wives and children of those who had perished'. Soon enough, the disgraced plotters were finally expelled from the party altogether.

The vanquished members of the anti-party group were not the only Stalinists to be assailed at the congress. While tensions with China continued to simmer off stage, the growing rift with communist Albania could hardly have been more visible. Khrushchev set the tone in his opening speech, when he told delegates that no country 'has ever gone from vows of eternal loyalty to unbridled anti-Soviet hostility', as Albania had. Others then lined up to pour their own scorn on Enver Hoxha's regime, assailing the growing cult of personality there, along with the baseless repression of communists friendly to Moscow. When China's Zhou Enlai got the chance to address the congress, he offered praise for recent Soviet successes and read a personal message from Mao pledging everlasting Sino-Soviet friendship; but he also showed his distaste for the criticism of Albania and called for it to stop (which it did not). A few days later – after pointedly laying a commemorative wreath for Stalin – Zhou headed home early. Within weeks, the Soviet Union and Albania had formally severed relations.

Unbeknownst to Soviet citizens, one week into the congress, a situation suddenly developed abroad that could easily have come to define the whole event. With the Berlin Wall erected only two months previously, East German leader Ulbricht was still set on applying pressure to push the Americans out of the city entirely, while Kennedy's chief representative in West Berlin, General Lucius Clay, was little less antagonistic in asserting the right of US personnel to enter East Berlin. With both sides spoiling for trouble, for some time already East German border guards had been trying to deny US officials the free access to East Berlin that Moscow had promised them, and the Americans had been testing their resolve by repeatedly and ostentatiously crossing the border in small convoys of armed vehicles and cars, refusing to show official papers as they did so.

On the afternoon of Friday 27 October, things suddenly got much more serious. Another US patrol had already entered East Germany without incident that day, with tanks in support. At the next attempt, though, the East Germans dug their heels in and the encounter ended with an armed standoff that saw Soviet tanks rolling up to the checkpoint, directly opposite the Americans who had been refused entry to East German territory. Before long, both sides had tanks – combat ready and with engines running – facing one another only a couple of hundred metres apart. With tensions high, each party hurriedly rounded up reinforcements in case the standoff turned to fighting.

For sixteen hours, Soviet and American tanks faced one another at Checkpoint Charlie. With no direct means of communication yet available to them, Khrushchev and Kennedy negotiated the situation via a Soviet agent in Washington, DC, named Georgy Bolshakov, whose personal links to the president's brother, Attorney General Robert Kennedy, had, since the previous month, made it possible for messages to flow discreetly between the US president and the Soviet leader. Both leaders were keen to de-escalate the situation before tensions on the ground caused nerves to snap. Overseeing the discussions with Kennedy as the congress went on around him, Khrushchev was in sufficiently accommodating mood to agree to his tanks backing up first. Finally, around 10:30 on Saturday, Soviet armour slowly began to draw back; as agreed, the Americans promptly did the same, bringing the situation to a peaceful end. Khrushchev and Kennedy would have to negotiate their way out of another crisis almost exactly a year later, but next time the stakes would be far higher.

Just before lunchtime in Moscow on 30 October, as the congress approached its close, a new Soviet nuclear bomb test was carried out over the Novaya Zemlya archipelago in the Arctic Circle. Based on a design by Andrei Sakharov (this would be his last real involvement in the arms race), what made this test stand out was its sheer size. Even six decades later, the device exploded that day (known as the 'Tsar Bomb') has never been exceeded in its destructive power. At an estimated 57 megatons, this was an explosion over 3,000 times more powerful than the Hiroshima bomb, producing a fireball 8 kilometres wide, with a mushroom cloud around 70 kilometres in height. One observer recalled feeling the resulting heatwave a staggering 270 kilometres away from the blast; another described how the initial flash had been followed by a heavy blow that sounded 'as if the Earth had been killed'.[14] In practice, the bomb was of limited military value, since it was so big and unwieldy that even the plane carrying it had to be extensively modified. The test was instead a Cold War showpiece, intended primarily as a demonstration of Soviet power, to intimidate enemies and impress friends.[15]

A little later that same day at the congress, Leningrad party boss Ivan Spiridonov raised an unscheduled motion: to have Stalin's remains removed from the mausoleum on Red Square (Molotov later claimed that Georgian First Secretary Mzhavanadze had been scheduled to play Spiridonov's part, but he was so desperate to avoid doing so that he deliberately ate so much ice cream that he lost his voice and could not speak, much to Khrushchev's fury).[16] Spiridonov called on the gulag returnee Dora Lazurkina to speak for the proposal. Approaching eighty years of age and a party member since 1902, Lazurkina movingly recounted to delegates how Lenin had told her in a dream that he was uncomfortable at sharing the mausoleum with Stalin, who 'only did harm to the Party'. Spiridonov's proposal was unanimously approved, and the next night, under cover of darkness and with Red Square closed off to the public, Stalin's body was taken out of the mausoleum and buried instead in the Kremlin wall, in an unmarked plot.

Within days, Stalin's name was removed from the façade of the mausoleum. Soon after that, the city of Stalingrad became Volgograd, Stalinabad reverted to Dushanbe and Stalino became Donetsk. Villages, farms and factories, literary prizes and scholarships still named in honour of Stalin now finally changed, too. Museums purged their exhibitions on both the revolution and the war of any traces of Stalin. The last of his works disappeared from school and university syllabi, with remaining portraits and busts of him removed from open display practically everywhere but Georgia, although many doubtless still remained on display in private homes and offices.[17] Staying in Armenia during the congress, where he was keeping a low profile after the arrest of his novel *Life and Fate*, Vasily Grossman noted that people there were not wholly without a sense of humour about such matters. Of the 17-metre-high statue of Stalin that still overlooked the capital Yerevan, some asked whether they would be given their money back when it was pulled down, since it had been paid for by public subscription. Others suggested that maybe the statue should be buried intact, in case it needed to go up again later.[18]

A new literary hero

One of the most consequential speeches at the congress came from *Novy mir* editor Alexander Tvardovsky. He insisted that the literary world had gone through a spiritual renewal since 1956, and also warned that Stalinist attitudes and officials had not yet vanished. He asserted that if culture was to help in the construction of communism, it still had to do more to expose and address problems, rather than cover them up, and he urged writers to push boundaries and to tackle new and difficult themes. In itself, this was no longer a particularly bold call to arms; but its historical significance lay in the fact that this speech prompted one provincial schoolteacher to take from its hiding place a story (entitled 'Shch-854') that he had finished writing two years previously but had never dared to submit for publication.

The author, Alexander Solzhenitsyn, had been jailed while serving at the front in 1945, on the basis of indiscreet remarks about Stalin in letters to a friend; he had then passed from the camp system to internal exile at Kok Terek in Kazakhstan. Once his conviction was overturned on review in April 1956, he headed back to Russia, and in 1957 became a teacher of physics and astronomy in Ryazan, about 200 kilometres from Moscow. There, he led an austere existence and dedicated practically all his free time to writing. Deeply wary of how politically explosive his work might still prove – he followed the Pasternak scandal closely – Solzhenitsyn always made sure to destroy draft materials and research notes as soon as he was able. He was still doing this in 1959 when, over the course of about six weeks, he worked on an idea for a story that had come to him while labouring as a prisoner in Kazakhstan in 1952.[19]

The chief impetus that pushed Solzhenitsyn towards seeking publication for his story came from a friend he had met in the camps. Lev Kopelev had been freed in late 1954 and, in sharp contrast to the more reclusive Solzhenitsyn, had quickly headed to the capital and become a part of the Moscow literary scene alongside his wife, Raisa Orlova. During a May 1961 visit, Solzhenitsyn shared with them the manuscript for 'Shch-854'. Just as Kopelev had managed to persuade his friend to apply for rehabilitation in 1956, after the Twenty-Second Party Congress he and Orlova pushed Solzhenitsyn to take up Tvardovsky's call and send 'Shch-854' to *Novy mir*. Solzhenitsyn eventually agreed, but remained sufficiently wary that he refused to attach his real name to the manuscript when it was submitted. For all that there had been substantial cultural liberalisation since Stalin's death, publishing a story set in the gulag still seemed almost unthinkable.

Crucially, Raisa Orlova was friendly with a junior member of the *Novy mir* editorial team, named Anna Berzer. She would prove the vital link in reaching the editor, Tvardovsky. After first warning Orlova that works on the camps were still unlikely to be published, Berzer first retyped the manuscript to make it more presentable (Solzhenitsyn's original had been very densely packed, without margins or spacing between lines). Sensibly judging that more cautious members of the *Novy mir* board might try to stop it from reaching their respected but impulsive editor, Berzer manoeuvred carefully to ensure that 'Shch-854' landed on Tvardovsky's desk first, once others had shown no interest in her deliberately underwhelming description of its contents. As he left the office on 7 December 1961, Tvardovsky picked up the manuscript for the 'camp tale' that Berzer had casually mentioned to him, and headed home.[20]

Later that night, Tvardovsky began to read 'Shch-854' in bed. On grasping the magnitude of the work in his hands, he got up, put on a suit and went to the kitchen to make coffee. By morning he had read the whole story twice and was bursting to show it to others and to find out who the mysterious author was. Orlova recalled how the excited Tvardovsky suddenly looked twenty years younger, and was even talking about the story as a moment of spiritual rebirth and the saviour of Russian literature.[21] On 12 December, a shabby-looking Solzhenitsyn found himself in the rarefied environment of Novy mir's editorial offices, in front of an enchanted Tvardovsky and the rest of the board. By the time he left later that day, a contract for the work had been agreed and its title changed to One Day in the Life of Ivan Denisovich (Shch-854 had been the author's own prisoner number in the camps, and Tvardovsky felt that would be politically difficult when it came to seeking publication). Quite a few of those present saw little chance of ever getting the story into print, and Tvardovsky made no secret that it would be difficult, but he promised to try. Vladimir Lakshin, a member of the editorial board, later recalled that 'for the following weeks and months we talked of nothing else but how to publish it'.[22]

Months passed without any obvious sign of progress. Tvardovsky was discreetly sharing Solzhenitsyn's work with a number of liberal-minded literary heavyweights – including Konstantin Chukovsky (who called it 'a literary miracle'), Konstantin Paustovsky and Ilya Ehrenburg – and seeking their endorsement of it to present to those at the very top. Having obtained a sheaf of such testaments, he then decided to follow much the same type of process that Anna Berzer had: getting approval at the highest level, before overly cautious bureaucrats had a chance to wreck things. To this end, in early August 1962 he showed the work to Vladimir Lebedev – one of Khrushchev's most influential personal advisers – and then coaxed Solzhenitsyn into accepting some minor revisions suggested by Lebedev to make the story more palatable to Khrushchev. The following month, while Khrushchev and Mikoyan holi-dayed on the Black Sea coast, Lebedev read aloud from the work as his boss relaxed, deliberately choosing passages that he knew would appeal. Khrushchev immediately grasped the political value of the story for his fight against Stalinism, and Tvardovsky was directed to produce additional copies of the manuscript for all Presidium members to read.

As Khrushchev later recalled it, only Suslov was willing to 'make a squeak of protest' when the question of publication was officially approved by the Presidium on 20 October 1962.[23] This, though, has to be understood in the context of Khrushchev's increasing intolerance of Presidium members disagreeing with him, rather than an indication of widespread support for the story. Two days later, President Kennedy would appear on television in the US to give the speech that marked (for Americans) the start of the Cuban Missile Crisis. Sandwiched in between these two events, on 21 October, *Pravda* published another of the era's iconic works of literature: Yevtushenko's poem 'The Heirs of Stalin'. Like *Ivan Denisovich*, though, this was another breakthrough that emerged not because the cultural world had been fundamentally liberalised, but because the regular channels and processes for publication had been successfully bypassed.

Again, 'The Heirs of Stalin' had been passed to Lebedev, who had picked an opportune moment to present it to Khrushchev (after he and Mikoyan had visited a village in Abkhazia and had heard gruesome tales of Stalin-era repressions from locals there), winning instant approval to publish it in the party newspaper, *Pravda*. In the poem, Yevtushenko declared that unreconstructed Stalinists remained hidden throughout the system. He warned that they hated these more liberal times and expressed the fear that they might yet find a way to bring back 'the old days'. Unaware of exactly who had granted approval for publication, conservative writers and officials flooded *Pravda* with complaints.[24] A month later, Boris Slutsky's anti-Stalin poem 'The Boss' also reached a mainstream audience when it was published in *Izvestiya*.

As the day of publication approached for Solzhenitsyn's debut, a buzz of anticipation arose among those in the know. When the poet Anna Akhmatova first met the still-unknown writer toward the end of October 1962, she told him that within a month he would become the most famous person in the world. When members of the editorial board at *Novy mir* finally held the first printed copies of the new edition, they hugged each other with joy, with Tvardovsky famously exclaiming 'the little bird has taken flight'.[25] Since Khrushchev's personal support for the work was well known in the circles that mattered, the response from the media was almost unanimously positive. The public response was even more compelling, though, with the November 1962 edition of *Novy mir* selling out immediately, and long waiting lists forming in libraries, as groups of friends passed copies from hand to hand. When it was republished as a standalone volume early the following year, close to a million copies were snapped up at once by eager Soviet readers. Foreign translations were also soon under way, as Solzhenitsyn was indeed feted the world over. The long-standing Soviet refusal to sign up to international copyright conventions then created a publishing equivalent of the Wild West, with competing translations emerging almost simultaneously with rival publishers.[26]

The story has neither a dynamic hero nor a thrilling plot. Its lead character, Ivan Denisovich Shukov, is a simple peasant who endures his gulag existence (and groundless conviction) through a combination of guile and acceptance. The authentic details of camp life seen through Shukov's eyes – from the food and clothing to the labour and prisoners' slang – shocked those who had never been inside the gulag, and offered up visceral reminders for the many who had. A tide of correspondence from across the USSR immediately poured into *Novy mir* and to Solzhenitsyn himself, with people recounting their own experiences of the camp system.[27] In time, such correspondence would feed into an even more explosive work – one that would see the author permanently expelled from the USSR. What *Ivan Denisovich* had clearly done was to bring the suppressed subject of Stalinist repressions back to the centre of public discourse across the country, prompting people to talk again about difficult questions of guilt, blame and punishment. In many senses, this was the apogee of the cultural thaw. Tvardovsky even took the chance to suggest to the time was right for an end to all preliminary censorship of literary work, and hopes for lasting cultural change were high. It would soon become apparent, though, that the Stalinists were not yet beaten.

Of course, not everyone admired *Ivan Denisovich*. Some camp guards, for example, wrote in rejecting their portrayal as a group and insisting that they worked for the good of the motherland, above all else.[28] Towards the end of November Konstantin Chukovsky wrote in his diary that he had bumped into the conservative writer Valentin Kataev, whom he described as 'outraged' by the story.[29] In fact, Khrushchev himself soon grew alarmed at the volume of unsolicited camp memoirs and stories that now flooded into publishers for consideration. Before long, he would start to backtrack in panic, warning publicly that Soviet enemies would be swarming around the 'camp theme' 'like great fat flies'. The message was clear: public fascination with *Ivan Denisovich* and the gulag must be kept under close control, and that meant no more stories about the camps. When Solzhenitsyn tried to persuade *Novy mir* to publish some of Varlam Shalamov's *Kolyma Tales* – today recognised as perhaps the most powerful work of all on the gulag – the suggestion was rejected.

Novocherkassk

In the summer of 1961, following the previous mass disorders in Kaunas, Tbilisi and Temirtau, there were two more public disturbances – this time in the Soviet regime's Russian heartland, not too far from the capital. In fact, proximity to Moscow was an important part of the story behind clashes in Murom and Alexandrov. Both were towns on the edge of the capital's 101-kilometre ring, an area inside which the majority of released prisoners were forbidden to settle. Seeking the various benefits that Moscow offered, many former prisoners opted to live in towns just outside that exclusion zone, like Murom and Alexandrov.

Trouble began in Murom after a drunken factory foreman fell out of a moving truck on 16 June, smashing his head on the floor. The injured foreman, named Kostikov, was detained by the police and despatched to a cell, rather than to hospital. He died of a brain haemorrhage the next morning, but word soon spread that he had been killed by a police beating. A hubbub grew, with some people determined to confront the authorities. The opportunity for this came with Kostikov's burial on 30 June.[30] Organisers of the funeral procession ensured that it passed by the town's police station, and soon enough rocks were being hurled and those inside were being called murderers and fascists. As evening fell, the police station was breached, as crowds looted papers and weapons and destroyed furniture, freeing prisoners and attacking officers inside.

A similar outbreak of violence occurred in Alexandrov the following month. This time, a couple of drunken soldiers were arrested by the police, again with some considerable use of force, prompting comrades of the detained men to action. By evening, a crowd of about a hundred people had forcibly freed the men from custody, going on to torch police cars and forcing their way into the station, before again trashing and looting, as well as beating police officers and a few unfortunate bystanders. Order was only restored when armed troops arrived on the scene, with the police station already fully ablaze.[31]

Although distinctions between the two were naturally somewhat blurred, these were events characterised more by generalised anti-police sentiment, rather than overt anti-communism. Testimonies of witnesses repeatedly made reference to protesters' intoxication, and many of those subsequently arrested were found to have pretty extensive criminal records already. All this was essentially taken by the authorities to show that the problems underpinning the trouble in Murom and Alexandrov boiled down to the malign influence of a few bad apples and some incompetent local leadership – a subsequent investigation into events branded numerous officials there 'political ignoramuses' – rather than to anything more fundamentally troubling.[32] Even so, there were also hints of public fractiousness elsewhere around this time. In May 1961, when factory bosses raised work norms (meaning more work was now needed to earn the same pay) workers at a large plant in the town of Tula rebelled and refused to go to work for four days in a row. The situation was only resolved when regional party bosses came to investigate, found local officials at fault and reprimanded or fired those responsible. After some concessions were granted, the workers were prevailed upon to return.[33] Similarly, in January 1962 over a hundred Armenian workers went on strike at a shoe factory for several days when work norms were raised, and another major stoppage occurred at the same plant a few months later.[34]

Contrary to the promises at the Twenty-Second Party Congress, by the early 1960s the Soviet economy was already showing increasing signs of stress. Widely touted plans to abolish income tax and further raise the minimum wage were quietly shelved.[35] Citizens' letters of complaint spoke of butter and meat being absent from shops for months on end in some areas, of people queueing for whole days when goods did arrive in stores, of people having to go from town to town as they shopped for basic items (many in the provinces took occasional train trips to Moscow for shopping purposes) and of many stores having nothing but jam on the shelves.[36]

At the start of June 1962, party bosses in the Penza region wrote to the Central Committee in Moscow about local communists' reactions to news of a series of planned price rises. They reported not just acceptance of the need for such measures, but in some cases even claimed enthusiastic support for the increases, which would see the cost of meat, dairy and other products go up by as much as 30 per cent.[37] Such claims were what Moscow clearly wanted to hear, but they were badly misleading in the picture they presented. In fact, the increases came as a very painful shock to many – in the public mind, prices were supposed to come down in the USSR, not go up – especially after the promises of plenty that were made at the recent party congress.

KGB records showed manifestations of public discontent in Donetsk, Dnepropetrovsk (Dnipro), Leningrad, Tbilisi, Grozny and elsewhere.[38] Ukrainian party boss Petro Shelest later wrote of the KGB providing him with the names even of party activists among those heard complaining in Kiev.[39] Reports from the security organs described 'slanderous documents' being found in Minsk and leaflets uncovered in Perm carried claims about citizens having to make soup out of sawdust; workers in several major cities (including Moscow, Leningrad and Novosibirsk) spoke of organising strikes.[40] Editors of newspapers and journals reported receiving over three hundred anonymous letters with complaints about living standards, along with terrorist threats and calls for protest action.[41]

In Novocherkassk, around 1,000 kilometres to the south of Moscow, the nationwide price rises coincided with an additional local dynamic. Management at the town's largest enterprise – the Novocherkassk Electric Locomotive Works (NEVZ) – had decided to increase work norms, just as prices were rising sharply. This exacerbated already existing frustrations among the plant's staff about workplace safety at NEVZ, about poor provisioning in local shops and especially about a long-term shortage of housing for employees. On the morning of 1 June, some workers left home after learning over the radio of the nationwide price rises; when they got to work they heard of the increased work norms (which essentially represented a pay cut).[42] Even so, it was only once they put their concerns to the plant's senior management that the situation began to turn ugly.

In the classic style of the self-important Soviet bureaucrat, the plant manager Kurochkin did not deign to listen to the workers gathering in the factory yard, but lectured them instead, brusquely dismissing their frustrations and ordering them to get to work. Infuriated by his attitude, those massing outside the factory stormed inside to bring comrades out on strike. Soon the yard was heaving as around half of the plant's 12,000 workers downed tools, and placards began to appear bearing slogans like 'give us milk, butter and a pay rise'. Workers cut the railway line that ran alongside the plant (inscribing the words 'make sausages out of Khrushchev' on the side of a halted train) and seized control of management offices, destroying images of Khrushchev (but not of Lenin). They eventually got hold of one senior factory official and dumped him in a barrel of water.[43] The rest of that day, groups of strikers went to nearby enterprises seeking to drum up support, while others took turns addressing the assembled masses with fiery speeches and organising further protest actions for the following day. That evening, protesters agreed to march from the outlying factory district to the town centre the following morning, where they would present their grievances to party officials. As one participant recalled it, the strikers had 'a feeling of unity, a belief in their own power, and in the justice of their demands'.[44]

KGB agents were from an early stage circulating among the crowds, identifying ringleaders, and an initial wave of arrests followed that first night, as police and troops were also mobilised. Nonetheless, the next morning workers and their families gathered at the plant and set out on the long walk to the town centre, passing through the authorities' attempted roadblocks, past tanks and soldiers, singing communist songs and waving red banners and portraits of Lenin. By this stage, the events in Novocherkassk had come to the Kremlin's attention and Khrushchev had despatched two of his most trusted lieutenants – Mikoyan and Frol Kozlov. The latter seemingly took a particularly aggressive stance: one account speaks of him wanting to arrest thousands and even to shoot every tenth person arrested.[45] Mikoyan later wrote that while he spoke to striking workers (whose grievances he recognised as legitimate), Kozlov rang the Kremlin, sowing panic and asking for permission to use armed force. That permission was granted 'in case of extreme necessity'.[46]

Before the swelling crowd, estimated at around 30,000 people, reached the town at about 10:30 that morning, Mikoyan and Kozlov were evacuated to a nearby military base for their own safety. When nobody else in authority materialised to address the expectant throng, frustration and anger began to build. Eventually, some of those present forced their way into the local party headquarters that overlooked the main town square (where they were further infuriated to see the fine foods set out inside for a banquet) and promptly trashed what they could, going out onto the balcony to give furious speeches that railed against the unfairness of elites' privileges and workers' hardships. At the nearby police station, protesters again forced their way inside, fighting with police and trying to release comrades arrested the previous night, only to find that they had already been spirited out of the town to forestall just such an attempt.

It was at this point that troops opened fire on the crowd with automatic weapons. It remains a subject of dispute how the shooting began: whether warning shots were fired first, whether troops consciously prepared to open fire by first withdrawing undercover agents from the crowds, whether they fired under direct orders from above or panicked (few give credence to the notion that they fired in self-defence, as classified reports would later claim). But the outcome was absolutely clear.[47] Reconstructing events via discussions with fellow participants whom he later met in jail, Peter Siuda (who was involved in the initial unrest at NEVZ but had been arrested that first night) wrote of piles of dead and dying victims, of children falling out of trees in the town square after they were sprayed with gunfire, and of people falling over in huge pools of blood.[48]

Even as the local hospital filled with wounded and dead citizens, the cover-up operation began. Bodies were piled onto trucks and taken away, telephone lines and roads in and out of the town were cut to prevent the spread of information. A 21:00 curfew was imposed and the bloody streets of the main square were hosed clean. Later that day, Mikoyan spoke on the radio in Novocherkassk and subsequently also met a delegation of protesters. He avoided direct mention of the violence that had unfolded, but promised to look into the new work norms at the NEVZ plant. Naturally, many more arrests followed. Bodies were secretly buried at remote sites around the town, in order to avoid potentially volatile funerals. Some people apparently only found out where their lost relatives were buried decades later.[49] The cover-up was ultimately to prove pretty effective: rumours about what had taken place that day did spread, but it was only with *glasnost* in the late 1980s that concrete details emerged.

During the weeks and months after the shooting, extra food was shipped to Novocherkassk's shops, new housing construction got under way, and the increased work norms at NEVZ were cancelled. News of the bloodbath was suppressed in the media, and a slew of party and Komsomol meetings saw the authorities in the town establish an 'official line' on events that demonised protesters and minimised acknowledgement of the violence done. A total of 114 people were convicted in a series of trials, with at least half a dozen of them sentenced to death and many others jailed for ten years or more. Again, classified reports repeated the notion that the unrest could mainly be put down to the work of a few malicious ringleaders (actually, police had been proactive in going around the town rounding up many 'undesirables' in their homes before the protesters even reached the town centre). As happened in the wake of the disturbances at Alexandrov and Murom, though, local officials in Novocherkassk would also be punished. A high-ranking (and highly classified) investigation judged, among other things, that the workers at NEVZ had been justifiably angry and that the plant director Kurochkin had done much to cause the ensuing crisis, while local party and factory bosses had long done nothing to tackle a range of long-term problems underpinning local frustrations.[50]

Solzhenitsyn later wrote that the Novocherkassk massacre marked the end of Soviet citizens' idealistic belief in communism.[51] In reality, there is little hard evidence to suggest that enough people outside the town were fully cognisant of events there for it to have had such a major social impact. Actually, there is a compelling counterpoint to Solzhenitsyn, which suggests that the professed ideals, symbols and rhetoric of the communist regime were so prevalent among protesters at Novocherkassk – in their banners, songs and demands for social justice – that it actually showed a substantial degree of public identification with the purported values of the Soviet system. Nonetheless, perhaps the most notable lesson that authorities seemingly took from this unrest was that the link between consumption and social passivity had become crucial. If it was no longer to terrorise the population into submission, the Soviet system would need to provide an acceptable standard of living for long-term stability to be maintained. No subsequent Soviet leader would entertain the notion of imposing such sweeping price rises until Gorbachev had little alternative, as the entire economy approached collapse at the end of the 1980s. In this connection, what happened when a major drought affected the 1963 harvest feels especially significant. By the summer, rumours were circulating that bread, sugar and fat were soon to be rationed, and dock workers in the Ukrainian city of Nikolaev (Mykolaiv) were sufficiently agitated at the prospect for them to refuse to load ships bound for Cuba with their scheduled cargo of flour, until Ukrainian party boss Shelest quickly had extra reserves despatched to the city from else-where.[52] Most notably, Khrushchev took the step of buying grain from the West – a major humiliation after all his boasts about catching up and over-taking. Aside from draining precious reserves of hard currency, this admission of agricultural failure was a step that earned him much domestic ridicule, but it nonetheless staved off the possibility of widespread hunger. Unlike Stalin, Khrushchev was not prepared to countenance mass starvation, however painful it might be to purchase food from one's rivals.

'Accursed palm trees'

Ever since Mikoyan's initial visit to Cuba in 1960, Soviet attachment to the 'island of freedom' had grown steadily stronger. The April 1961 Bay of Pigs incident was presented in the media as proof that the US intended for Cuba the same kind of violence that had been visited on Guatemala, with the 1954 coup. Although already supplying them with considerable economic and technical assistance, the Soviet Union now 'gave the Cubans all the arms they could absorb', according to Khrushchev.[53] At the Twenty-Second Party Congress, Khrushchev declared that Cuba represented a beacon lighting the way for all Latin American peoples. The Cuban leader also hitched his wagon ever more tightly to the USSR, unambiguously pronouncing his country a part of the socialist camp at the end of 1961. On both sides, these attitudes were shaped by the expectation that the US would soon seek to finish the job. Khrushchev recalled that for about a year after the Bay of Pigs he was preoccupied with the question of how to defend Cuba from attack, having learned in Congo that Soviet protest would have little impact after a successful US operation. China, too, had its eyes on winning Havana's loyalty and possibly replacing Moscow as Castro's chief patron. After so proudly championing the Cuban revolution inside the USSR, domestic morale was also at stake. Doing nothing was not really an option.

Soviet-US relations had also been growing more turbulent since the end of the 1950s. Tensions over Berlin, Congo and the civil war in Laos remained fresh and prompted sharpening rhetoric about war-mongering. Both sides had ended their respective moratoriums on nuclear testing, and Kennedy perhaps unwisely publicised American military intelligence in October 1961, which revealed that the US was not behind the Soviet Union in its missile capabilities, as some had believed, but far ahead, with the USSR in reality having only a few rockets with the range needed to hit US territory (though Western Europe was very much within reach). Indeed, although the Soviet narrative on the ensuing events in Cuba always centred on Moscow's desire to protect the island from American aggression, that was only ever a part of the picture. While the USSR was some considerable way behind the US in the number of long-range missiles it possessed, it did have plenty of shorter-range missiles. What Cuba presented was an opportunity to increase significantly Soviet striking power, since the proximity of the island to the American mainland made even the USSR's shorter-range missiles capable of hitting key targets inside the USA.

Khrushchev's fateful idea on how to protect Cuba apparently came to him during a May 1962 trip to Bulgaria. It was in many senses typical of the way in which he had sought to tackle other seemingly intractable problems: a simple and ambitious gesture, usually thrown together in haste, with sensible doubts ignored. With US military bases and nuclear weapons stationed close to Soviet borders, he also felt morally entitled to follow suit. Almost certainly, he assumed that the American response to Soviet missiles on Cuba would be much like the Soviet response when the US had put its missiles in Turkey and Italy during 1961: an initial hurricane of complaints about war-mongering, and then quietly coming to terms with the new reality.

In May 1962, Khrushchev put his idea to the Presidium: to secretly despatch Soviet nuclear weapons to Cuba, and then to announce their existence to the world as a fait accompli once they were already operational. He was easily able to steamroll the calls for caution that were raised by Mikoyan and Foreign Minister Andrei Gromyko. Once Presidium members agreed to the plan, a party was despatched to Havana to secure Castro's approval to host the missiles and to locate suitable sites where the operation could be undertaken without attracting attention. By the middle of June, Castro's agreement had been obtained (though, like others, he was not entirely convinced that the move was solely for Cuba's benefit) and plans were gathering pace. Even so, when Che Guevara visited Moscow in August 1962, he did so with an important proposal from a wavering Castro: to abandon the secrecy around Soviet missiles in Cuba and simply make public an agreement on mutual defence, in order to deter an American attack. Khrushchev refused.[54]

Having surveyed the island, Marshal Sergei Biryuzov assured Presidium members that Cuba's abundant palm trees would provide the needed cover against US aerial surveillance. Others warned Khrushchev that was nonsense, but without success, leaving a crucial facet of the plan (its secrecy) at clear risk of failure from the outset.[55] Despatching all the necessary people and materiel to Cuba was a vast operation that involved huge numbers of troops and so many ships (eighty-six in total, with some making multiple trips) that the USSR had to borrow additional vessels from friendly states, so that its regular shipping needs could still be met. Even the KGB could hardly hope to cover up this extraordinary volume of traffic heading across the open ocean, and American reconnaissance planes were before long aware of the flotilla. Confined below decks during the daytime, to hide their numbers, Soviet troops sweltered in the baking heat. By the end of August, the Americans had also photographed Soviet surface-to-air missiles being unloaded at Cuban ports, though they had no indication yet that there were also nuclear warheads on the way.

With a number of key voices inside the White House increasingly alarmed at the question of what the Soviet navy might be transporting to Cuba, on 4 September the US announced that any Soviet missiles stationed there would be deemed unacceptable, and days later called up 150,000 military reservists for active duty. The Soviet press agency TASS called this move a 'provocation against peace' and denied the presence of missiles on the island, insisting that any weapons being sent there were purely defensive, and asserting the USSR's right to help Cuba defend itself from both US military aggression and attempts to starve the island into submission by economic blockade. It also warned that an attack on Soviet ships heading to Cuba would be considered an attack on the Soviet Union. Sensing that this was a time to be bold, Khrushchev speeded up and even expanded the flow of troops and materiel crossing the Atlantic, adding extra tactical nuclear warheads and directing the ships involved to ready themselves for potential confrontation.[56]

By early September 1962, parts of Cuba must have resembled a giant anthill when seen from above. Keen to evade American spies, the unloading and transporting of Soviet weaponry was overwhelmingly done under cover of darkness. In fact, much of the work was also performed without the use of vehicles, by people carrying military hardware through forests on foot. In places, they also had to build new roads and reinforce bridges that were unable to handle the very heaviest cargo: all of this happened as the Caribbean hurricane season lashed the island. Soon enough, soldiers' food supplies were rotting and dysentery began to spread. Even the Soviet weaponry struggled with the local climate. According to Sergo Mikoyan, Castro had to requisition air conditioners from Cuban brothels to help maintain the nuclear warheads at a suitable temperature.[57]

The first missiles on the island were soon operational, but there were still many more making their way across the ocean. Then, on 14 October a U2 reconnaissance mission over Cuba hit the jackpot. It photographed what American intelligence experts very quickly determined was key infrastructure – including fuel containers, launchpads and control facilities – for nuclear weapons. By 16 October, the photographs were on Kennedy's desk. Khrushchev's intended fait accompli had been blown. Even years later, though, he could not acknowledge the myriad flaws in his own plan, insisting only that 'those accursed palm trees hadn't concealed anything, and our "scouts" had shamefully disgraced themselves'.[58]

From 16 October, several days of highly charged debate ensued between Kennedy and his advisers. There was no question in the White House that the Soviet missiles in Cuba would have to go. There was a body of opinion which considered war with the USSR to be practically inevitable anyway, and it therefore made sense to start that war now, while the US held the initiative.[59] The most hawkish advisers thus pressed for pre-emptive airstrikes before the missile bases could be made operational (not realising that some already were). Others were drawn to the idea of a conventional invasion of Cuba. All options carried major risk of escalation to nuclear war, and after several days of back and forth, the idea of a naval blockade (Kennedy called it a 'quarantine', since a blockade was officially illegal) became the president's preference as a first line of response to prevent any more Soviet missiles from reaching Cuba.

Early on 22 October, it was announced that Kennedy would address the American people on a matter of great importance that evening. In the Kremlin, this news was the trigger for near panic. They could only guess what Kennedy's announcement would involve, but many suspected it would centre on the missiles in Cuba: some expected news of an imminent US invasion of the island, or worse.[60] Presidium members sat throughout the night in a state of high tension, waiting for Kennedy to make his address on the other side of the Atlantic and discussing their options in case war were to break out.

In the context of a potential clash between nuclear armed powers – in which the advantages of striking hard first are especially compelling – this was a moment when bad decisions could easily have been taken. The key danger, then, was that of miscalculation: of one side misreading the other and deciding the time had come to act before the enemy did so.[61] In fact, only the previous year the Soviet authorities had taken very seriously some rather questionable KGB information that the US was already in the process of planning a surprise nuclear attack on the Soviet Union.[62] That danger was exacerbated by the lack of swift and effective communication. Not only was there no direct telephone line between the Kremlin and the White House, but neither side would allow the other to place on their respective embassy roof the necessary equipment for sending and receiving telegrams. Ambassador Anatoly Dobrynin recalled that even during the height of the crisis that followed, sending urgent messages from his embassy in Washington, DC, to Moscow involved summoning a Western Union employee, who cycled across the city to collect his telegram, before cycling back to base for it to be sent on to Moscow.[63]

As Presidium members waited for news of Kennedy's speech, Mikoyan managed to talk Khrushchev out of several dangerous ideas, including authorising the Soviet commander in Cuba to use tactical nuclear missiles in case of invasion and handing over control of the missiles to the Cubans. When the details of Kennedy's announcement eventually reached the Kremlin, there was a huge sense of relief that the outcome was only a blockade (to commence on 24 October), rather than an invasion. The next day, all Cuba-bound ships not yet nearing the Caribbean were turned around and directed back to Soviet ports; those already close, including some carrying nuclear weapons, speeded up to get there before the blockade began; and those still a few days from Cuba were directed to wait and see, rather than try to run the blockade, since that might well entail the US navy getting its hands on Soviet missile technology if it seized the offending ships.[64] Missiles already in Cuba were hurriedly brought to operational readiness.

The first part of the American plan – to stop more Soviet weaponry getting to Cuba – succeeded without sparking conflict, though there were some near misses at sea, with tensions high and the US navy set on policing the quarantine aggressively.[65] However, that still left unresolved the matter of removing the existing missiles from Cuba – something to which the US remained absolutely committed. By no means had the Americans taken the option of a military assault off the table, though they had seriously underestimated what would await them if they did attack. From counting the ships crossing the ocean, they assumed that only a few thousand Soviet troops would be on the island. Actually, there were more than 40,000 of them on Cuba, and they had tactical nuclear weapons ready for use.[66] Soviet troops were also digging trenches in preparation for an American invasion and anti-aircraft teams stood ready to open fire as American planes continually criss-crossed the skies over Cuba. By 24 October, the US military was moved to its highest level of alert short of open war, and dozens of bombers with nuclear weapons on board were kept in the air at all times, in case of a surprise first strike from Moscow. In such febrile circumstances, it would have been close to impossible to prevent an American invasion of Cuba from turning into a much larger conflict between the USA and USSR.

In the Kremlin, where Presidium members sat in almost permanent session throughout the crisis, tensions were peaking around 26 October. Based on informal chatter picked up by spies in Washington, word was reaching Khrushchev that the US would invade Cuba the next day. Although it proved inaccurate, this was not too far wide of the mark: the American military leadership had both 28 and 29 October pencilled in for possible airstrikes on Cuba, with invasion potentially to follow on 30 October. Infuriated by the constant presence of American planes overhead, Castro gave the order for his troops to open fire on them, though with little effect. That changed when Soviet anti-aircraft forces – suspecting that the American planes were performing final reconnaissance of missile sites before an attack – joined the Cubans and successfully shot down a U2, killing its pilot. Some in the American military establishment now demanded permission to retaliate with force. Little less concerning for Khrushchev, that same night Castro wrote him a note calling for the USSR to unleash pre-emptive nuclear war against the US, regardless of the consequences for Cuba. This convinced the Soviet leader that his ally had cracked under the pressure.

As the whole affair seemed to be reaching its most dangerous point, the Rubicon had actually already been crossed. On 25 October, Khrushchev put to Presidium members a compromise solution, which he rather feebly presented as a Soviet win: the removal of the missiles, in exchange for an American pledge not to invade Cuba. As usual, the desired Presidium support was forthcoming, and the following day Khrushchev's offer was privately put to Kennedy. A little later that day, Khrushchev decided, seemingly as an afterthought, to include an additional clause to the deal, for the removal of American missiles based in Turkey. Kennedy was receptive to the idea, though he had to work to convince some of his advisers. Khrushchev was so keen to begin the process of de-escalating the crisis before it got any worse that he had the new offer broadcast openly over the radio, rather than via the more discreet, but slower, communication channels used previously. Robert Kennedy responded on 27 October that Khrushchev's plan could be the basis for a resolution to the crisis. Later that day, Khrushchev formally agreed to the US demand to remove Soviet missiles from Cuba, though (with imminent congressional elections and relations with NATO allies on his mind) Kennedy warned that the decision on the missiles in Turkey could not be made public, and he would deny it if such information ever emerged.

Some Soviet ships in Cuba had not even been fully unloaded when the order came through on 28 October to start returning the missiles to the USSR. By early November, the missile sites had been dismantled and Khrushchev had even agreed to remove Soviet bombers from the island. Castro, however, was furious at what he considered a betrayal, cursing Khrushchev vehemently. The Chinese also denounced what they perceived as cowardice, proclaiming to all who would listen that Khrushchev had abandoned Cuba in order to protect Soviet relations with the USA. Mao put much the same line to Castro himself and found a receptive audience, since the Cuban leader was vastly under-whelmed at the American non-invasion promise that Khrushchev was so pleased with. It took a hastily arranged visit from Mikoyan, and some addi-tional economic aid, before the Cuban leader could be talked down from his fury.

Years later, Khrushchev insisted that the resolution of the crisis had been a victory for all sides (since there was no war), but especially for the USSR and Cuba, since the Americans' non-invasion pledge held firm.[67] Across the globe, though, there was (and largely still is) a clear perception that events had ended in a humiliating Soviet defeat. Some recent reassessments have been a little kinder to Khrushchev, pointing out that Cuba was ultimately protected and that the removal of US missiles from Turkey did count as a clear strategic gain, while the only real loss was that of prestige.[68] Many members of the Soviet political elite felt much less forgiving towards Khrushchev, however, and they did not forget about the crisis he had created.

In the wider picture of Soviet-US relations, there were actually some positive outcomes following the Cuban crisis. Both Khrushchev and Kennedy soon returned to a more peace-focused rhetoric, and the famous 'hotline' to facilitate direct communication between leaders in Moscow and Washington was established. Having gone practically nowhere in the years since the idea was first raised, negotiations on a nuclear test ban treaty also began to move forward. Signed at the start of August 1963, the Partial Test Ban Treaty was one of the key early agreements aimed at de-escalating the global arms race. Undoubtedly, they had been jolted into action in response to the existential dangers that the Caribbean crisis had created, and negoti-ating their way out of that situation provided a certain momentum for more talks thereafter. For both countries, though, an increasing eagerness to stop Mao's China from becoming the next nuclear power also made compromises on previously intractable stalling points easier to reach.

Much like the rest of the world, on 22 November 1963 the people of the Soviet Union were stunned by news of the assassination of President Kennedy. One former citizen described how 'the entire country mourned, as if he were one of our own'.[69] Some of the funeral was even shown on Soviet television. Khrushchev headed to the US embassy in Moscow to offer his condolences. Alongside seemingly genuine sadness, however, there was also grave concern in the Kremlin. In the first instance, Presidium members had more faith in Kennedy's will to avoid conflict than in that of his successor, Lyndon Johnson, who was viewed in Moscow as something of an aggressive reactionary. Most pressing was the fact that Lee Harvey Oswald had, until quite recently, been living in the USSR, and this naturally raised a very awkward question about Soviet complicity in the murder of the American president.

Visiting Moscow as a tourist in 1959, Oswald had decided that he wanted to stay. After initially being refused the right to remain in the country, an appeal proved successful; but a wary KGB insisted that he be settled somewhere out of the way, in the Belorussian capital Minsk. By 1962, Oswald had changed his mind and decided to return to the US with his Soviet wife. Once this Soviet connection became clear after the Kennedy assassination, key officials in Moscow unsurprisingly expected trouble.[70] Khrushchev called Semichastny to make sure that there was no secret KGB involvement in the affair, and then had him despatch all files pertaining to Oswald to the Kremlin at once.[71] In New York, KGB officer Oleg Kalugin received a stream of cables from Moscow directing him to do 'everything possible' to dispel talk there of Soviet involvement in the assassination.[72] Mikoyan – always the man Khrushchev turned to if there was a need to smooth a crisis abroad – took with him to Kennedy's funeral the originals of all KGB documentation on Oswald's time in the USSR, as proof that he had not at any time been working for Soviet security. Satisfied that everything was as Mikoyan said, the Americans moved on.

From friends to enemies

Around the same time as the missile crisis played out in the Caribbean, China and India were also fighting a short border war. Dashing off to Beijing in a bid to exert some restraining influence, Khrushchev was excoriated by the Chinese leadership for refusing to condemn Indian leader Nehru and for a TASS statement expressing a Soviet desire for peace between the two belligerents. Mao's indignation at the USSR had already been rising that year, after perhaps 60,000 Uighurs managed to flee across the Sino-Soviet border into Kazakhstan. Similarly, the Partial Test Ban Treaty agreed with the US would be perceived in Beijing as another betrayal. The façade of friendship could not hold any longer. By the autumn of 1963, the prospect of conflict with communist China haunted the Soviet leadership little less than did conflict with the US.[73]

China made explicit its shift from Soviet partner to rival in the developing world. In Somalia and Mozambique, Mao began to make inroads into the pro-Soviet camp, pumping resources and fiery rhetoric into places where Soviet efforts were flagging or where its message was deemed insufficiently radical. He painted the USSR as just another white European empire that would sell out the developing world for its own ends without flinching. He also lobbied hard to have the USSR removed from the various Afro-Asian forums in which it was involved, and Chinese delegations travelled around Asia and Africa denigrating Soviet actions and forcing potential partners to choose between Moscow and Beijing. Despite huge Soviet effort to counter such actions, and plenty of accusations of ideological betrayal, some of the USSR's most highly valued ties, including with Vietnam and Algeria, were coming under immense strain.[74]

Most disconcerting from the Soviet perspective was the fact that the Chinese leadership began to make claims on large swathes of Soviet territory, which, it insisted, had been unfairly seized by the tsars while China was weakened in the nineteenth century. China's demands for the 'return' of Vladivostok and parts of Central Asia were quickly dismissed by Khrushchev, but its claims to ownership of a series of islands in the middle of the Ussuri river that served as the border between the two countries proved rather more enduring. Negotiations on the issue began, but quickly collapsed. A number of brief clashes ensued, in which Soviet border forces were, from time to time, confronted by Chinese fishermen and peasants (who, the Soviet side had no doubt, were really soldiers in costume).

For about a year from the spring of 1963, the former allies assailed one another with a string of increasingly public and furious polemics. Put together by a team of specialists under the supervision of Mao himself (and underpinned by his new policy of 'oppose revisionism abroad to prevent revisionism at home'), the Chinese pilloried Soviet criticism of Stalin, the apparent ideological betrayal that was peaceful co-existence with the US, and much more. One Chinese polemic of February 1964 was entitled 'The Leaders of the

CPSU Are the Greatest Splitters of Our Time'; another from July was called 'On Khrushchev's Phoney Communism and Its Historical Lessons for the World'. The CCP newspaper *Renmin Ribao* (*People's Daily*) declared in September 1963 that the Soviet leadership had allied itself with US imperialism and Indian reactionaries against socialist China. Two months later, it insisted that the USSR had become an apologist for neo-colonialism. One Chinese polemic even called on people in the USSR to rise up and fight against the Soviet leadership.

Never one to turn the other cheek, Khrushchev proved only a little less adept at throwing insults and accusations, though he genuinely mourned the burgeoning split, while Mao privately embraced it. A Soviet open letter in July 1963 called Chinese attacks 'groundless and slanderous', reminded everyone of Soviet generosity towards China in the recent past and accused Mao of lying about the reasons behind the two countries falling out. When a high-level Chinese delegation, led by Deng Xiaoping, visited the USSR for talks that same month, both sides spent almost two weeks listing the other's various errors and betrayals, before the Chinese party headed home and the polemics resumed.[75] An official Soviet statement on China in September 1963 declared that the USSR was not willing to 'trade abuse for abuse' in a public slanging match, but nonetheless spoke of Chinese 'treachery and hypocrisy in the eyes of communists, in the eyes of all mankind'. Some Soviet media coverage even went so far as to liken Mao to Hitler, Napoleon and Genghis Khan.[76] In the Asian part of the communist world, China quickly gained the backing of North Korea. In Europe, albeit with the exception of Albania, Khrushchev and later Brezhnev successfully circled the wagons and kept nearby allies in line, though Romania (like Vietnam) staked out a deliberately ambiguous position on the split, as Bucharest took the opportunity to build its own autonomy from Moscow.[77]

In late spring 1963, KGB chief Semichastny reported to the Central Committee that China was sending all manner of hostile propaganda materials into the country, with over 5,000 Chinese anti-Soviet leaflets seized that April alone. Semichastny also reported that the Chinese embassy in Moscow was holding clandestine meetings and seminars, at which speakers attacked Soviet policies and forced the remaining Chinese students inside the country to distribute critical leaflets around the Soviet capital.[78] KGB records do indicate at least a few instances of Soviet citizens pasting up leaflets with phrases like 'Our Leader Is Mao Zedong' and 'Long Live the CCP' during the summer of 1963, in particular. Overall, though, there was not an especially receptive audience for Maoism inside the USSR during the 1960s.[79] Many Soviet citizens shuddered at the violence and suffering that was accompanying the transformation of China, especially once the Cultural Revolution got under way there, and even more resented the perceived ingratitude and betrayal after years of massive Soviet aid.[80] Many simply did not understand what had really happened between the two countries.

Soviet media complained bitterly that Chinese students expelled from the country for unfriendly acts were being paraded as heroes on their return to Beijing. When the last Chinese students eventually departed the USSR, a disgusted Khrushchev recalled, one even offered a final insult by taking down his trousers and defecating on the train station platform at the border.[81]

A new cultural crackdown

In autumn 1962, the publication of *Ivan Denisovich* had raised the prospect of a decisive victory for cultural liberalisation. In literature and cinema, reform-minded communists were not only making their voices heard, but were also gaining leadership roles that promised to entrench their power in the longer term. Within a month, though, the country's cultural conservatives were on the offensive and in the ascendancy. Before long, the thaw for which the era is widely remembered was to all intents and purposes over. As one Western commentator observed at the time, the clampdown which followed, aimed at bringing to heel the country's cultural intelligentsia, was 'waged on a vaster and more threatening scale than anything of its kind since the Stalin era'.[82]

For several years already, the Soviet art world had seen occasionally rancorous division between younger and older generations. The former had been granted increased (albeit still limited) latitude to produce and exhibit more innovative and unorthodox works, but the latter had continually voiced their opposition to any challenges to established cultural codes.[83] Now, the older generation would decisively win out. Key to the events that followed were two exhibitions. The first, entitled 'Thirty Years of Moscow

Art' had opened to much official fanfare in early November 1962 at the large Manezh gallery, a stone's throw from the Kremlin. The other exhibition, far smaller in scale and made up mostly of modernist works by young and unknown artists, had lasted only a few hours and took place at the studio of the abstract painter Eli Belyutin on 26 November. A few days afterwards, works from the smaller exhibition were unexpectedly summoned for display at the Manezh. With the excitement around *Ivan Denisovich* still in the air, the artists in question apparently believed – or at least hoped – that this invitation to exhibit in such a prestigious setting marked the moment at which their work was finally about to receive mainstream acceptability. In fact, someone was setting them up for an almighty fall.

Conservatives in the cultural and political establishment had been lobbying hard against what they saw as destabilising liberalisation and expanding Western influences in the arts, focusing in particular on capitalists' apparent attempts to lead Soviet youth astray both morally and politically.[84] Already appalled by much of the modern art he had seen on display at the 1959 American exhibition in Moscow, Khrushchev was surely receptive to such sentiment. Then, on 1 December, he and his retinue made an unexpected appearance at the newly expanded Manezh exhibition, accompanied most notably by two powerful arch-conservatives from the world of officialdom in the visual arts: Vladimir Serov and Alexander Gerasimov. Eyewitness accounts make it clear that the pair were steadily feeding Khrushchev a stream of remarks intended to rile him – about liberal artists' decadent lifestyles, their political views and their mockery of Soviet cultural conventions.[85] Khrushchev readily took the bait, growing increasingly angry. Stopping first in front of a painting by the late Robert Falk, he bluntly announced that it was 'just a mess'. He also ridiculed a modernist painting that had recently been gifted to a colleague's daughter and which, he said, looked as though a child had defecated on canvas while its mother was away.

As they reached the items from the Belyutin exhibition, Khrushchev's mood darkened further. Those present recalled him darting around in a frenzy when he reached the new works, on the second floor.[86] On viewing one abstract image, Khrushchev ordered that any government money that had been spent on producing the picture would be deducted from the wages of the official who was responsible. Soon enough, he thundered that the works on show were anti-Soviet and amoral, asking of the assembled artists 'are you pederasts or normal people'. If they wanted to leave the country, he insisted, they could all do so tomorrow. Of their artwork, he added that 'we are not going to spend a kopek on this dog shit' and announced to the artists in question 'we are declaring war on you'.[87] One painter he even threatened to send to work at a logging camp until all state money he had received was paid back.[88]

Most famous was Khrushchev's clash with the sculptor Ernst Neizvestny, who was a central figure among Moscow's bohemian intelligentsia (his studio was a noted hangout for their drinking sessions) but had also seen action at the front during the war. Again, Khrushchev rudely abused both the art and the artist, but Neizvestny refused to be intimidated. When Khrushchev suggested that he was a homosexual, the sculptor retorted that he was more than happy to prove this untrue if a woman could be brought to them. According to Neizvestny's own post-Soviet account of what happened, the sculptor told Khrushchev 'both God and the Devil live side by side in you Nikita Sergeevich'; he insisted that the Soviet leader understood nothing at all about art, to which Khrushchev shouted and stamped his feet, and Alexander Shelepin apparently threatened to have Neizvestny 'rot in the uranium mines' for his impudence.[89] In retirement, Khrushchev expressed regret at such rudeness on his part, accepted that Neizvestny was a talented man, and sheepishly recalled of the confrontation that 'somehow his name annoyed me' (Neizvestny translates to English as 'Unknown', though it was not a pseudonym).[90]

A number of cultural heavyweights, including the writer Konstantin Chukovsky, the film director Mikhail Romm and composer Dmitry Shostakovich, all wrote to Khrushchev expressing their concerns over what had happened at the Manezh gallery.[91] Nonetheless, the confrontation soon spread beyond the visual arts and throughout the cultural sphere, as conservatives drove home their chance to turn the tide. On 17 December 1962, things grew more heated still when four hundred members of the country's cultural elite were summoned for a formal meeting with their political masters.[92] When Khrushchev spoke, he again showed off the worst of himself, bellowing angrily and making threats. Most notable was an exchange with Yevtushenko, who defended Neizvestny and tried to assure Khrushchev that

293

under-fire artists would in time overcome the tendencies that had so upset him. In a fury, Khrushchev responded that 'only the grave cures the hunchback'. Yevtushenko quickly retorted, chiding the Soviet leader, that the days in which the grave was seen as a cure were supposed to be over.

Soon enough, the mass poetry readings by the likes of Yevtushenko, Voznesensky and Akhmadulina came to an end. Only a month after it had published Solzhenitsyn's stunning debut novella, *Novy mir*, was in trouble over the serialisation of Viktor Nekrasov's *Both Sides of the Ocean*, an account of visits to Italy and the USA in which the author essentially failed to offer sufficient condemnation of the capitalist world that he saw there. In January 1963, a new scandal began to unfold with *Novy mir*'s serialisation of Ilya Ehrenburg's memoirs, *People, Years, Life*. Particularly problematic in this case was Ehrenburg's assertion that people had known about on-going repressions during the Stalin years, but had essentially looked the other way and kept quiet, out of a sense of self-preservation.[93] This clashed with the notion, put about by Khrushchev from the Secret Speech onwards, that those at the top had been unaware of the scale of Stalinist violence and were thus not complicit, whether by silence or otherwise.

Always a key focus for conservatives' ire, Yevtushenko, in particular, would find himself close to the centre of the whirlwind during the clampdown. This began immediately after he had crossed swords with Khrushchev. The next day, on 18 December, he and Shostakovich were due to premiere a collaboration in which Shostakovich's Thirteenth Symphony was set to a number of Yevtushenko's poems, including the controversial attack on Soviet anti-Semitism, 'Babii Yar'. The pair came under pressure to cancel the performance, but steadfastly refused. Intimidated members of the show's choir resigned en masse, but were eventually talked into returning. In the end, the show opened on schedule, but with neither the television cameras nor the VIPs that had been planned. The debut was met with tremendous applause by those in attendance, but, after one more outing the next day, all future performances were cancelled. Soon after this, Yevtushenko took perhaps his most reckless step.

Unlike the vast majority of Soviet citizens, Yevtushenko was a fairly frequent traveller abroad. He was well liked in the outside world and seen by many in the Kremlin as someone who could project the kind of image of the

USSR – bold, energetic, outward-looking – that they wanted to convey. This became deeply problematic in early 1963, when Yevtushenko took the highly unorthodox step of agreeing a contract and then submitting a manuscript for a short memoir during a trip to France. Known to English readers as *A Precocious Autobiography*, the work was serialised in *L'Express* magazine during February and March of that year. Actually, many foreign communists believed that the account reflected well on the Soviet Union – it was even banned in Francoist Spain as communist propaganda; but it raised the hackles of officials back home. This was largely because of the impudence of publishing abroad without permission, but the memoir did also contain some specific passages (including a visceral account of the deadly crush which preceded Stalin's funeral in March 1953) that the authorities objected to. Writing years later, the poet recalled that he 'hardly expected to be met by an orchestra' on his return to the USSR, but he was nonetheless taken aback by the slander and mockery he was subjected to by his opponents.[94] Newspaper editorials and readers' letters fulminated at his behaviour, demanding apologies and calling for punishment as severe as expulsion from the Writers' Union.

Another summit meeting between political leaders and cultural elites was then held on 7–8 March 1963, almost exactly a decade since Stalin's death. Andrei Voznesensky (who had been out of the country for the December 1962 meeting) recalled that he turned up believing that Khrushchev essentially remained a protector of progressive writers, and still harbouring the hope that he would support further liberalisation. On the first day, though, Khrushchev began with an unsettling demand that any undisclosed foreign agents leave the hall before the meeting began, later launching stinging attacks on Ilya Ehrenburg and the director Mikhail Romm. Marlen Khutsiev's new movie *Ilich's Gate* was also the subject of an astonishing attack on its characters' 'moral sickness', and the cinema journal *Iskusstvo kino* (*Film Art*) was upbraided for championing a succession of 'ideologically weak' productions.[95] Speaking after Khrushchev, Leonid Ilichev made clear the root of the leadership's concerns, as he castigated 'those seeking to sow mistrust in the minds of the young' through spreading culture alien to Soviet society.[96]

Yevtushenko, Neizvestny and all the usual suspects again had their works criticised and their attitudes questioned. Once Voznesensky was summoned to the rostrum to speak, he was continually interrupted by Khrushchev pounding his fists on the table, screaming behind him, calling him 'anti-Soviet' and threatening to have him thrown out of the country (Voznesensky later wondered whether the first secretary might have been drunk). Conservatives in the room hooted their support, calling the poet a beatnik and baying for blood.[97] Khrushchev then caught sight of someone he believed to be Vasily Aksenov. He ordered the man to the front for a dressing-down, and continued to berate him for some time – even after the individual in question had repeatedly insisted he was not Aksenov. When the real Aksenov was found (sitting right next to the man Khrushchev had assumed to be him), he, too, took a battering, with Khrushchev opening up with the remark 'so, you don't like Soviet rule' and asking 'do you think we have forgotten how to make arrests'.[98]

Meeting up with fellow writer Anatoly Gladilin after the session, Aksenov told him simply 'it is over, a complete defeat'.[99] Voznesensky was little less despondent, losing what remained of his faith in the bright future he had believed lay ahead.[100] Yevtushenko quietly slipped out of Moscow for a while, to his hometown in Siberia, and from there headed a little further north to write poetry about the gigantic Bratsk hydroelectric dam being built on the Angara river. This March meeting proved the start of a crackdown against younger artists across the creative industries.[101] Concerted efforts were now made to harangue members of the creative intelligentsia back into line.

Under the watch of hardliner Leonid Ilichev, the Central Committee's Ideological Commission summoned a host of poets, playwrights, sculptors and others to face criticism and to explain themselves, creating what one source has described as 'an atmosphere of witch-hunting' that 'left no place for logic, rationality, dignity or legal rights', and leaving many of those involved waiting for the seemingly inevitable arrests to begin.[102] With little option to do otherwise, Aksenov and others restated their support for the party line in the cultural sphere and promised to act on the justified criticism of their mistakes.[103] The sculptor Neizvestny later claimed that Khrushchev's main adviser on cultural affairs, Vladimir Lebedev, personally dictated the content of his letter of repentance, in which he thanked the Soviet leader for his criticism.[104]

Even though Solzhenitsyn escaped the assault that befell many other writers at this juncture – Khrushchev had proudly introduced the newcomer to his fellow authors as 'our Soviet Tolstoy' at the end of 1962 – his fortunes were also quietly changing. By spring 1963, his new short story 'Matryona's House' had come under open attack for painting too bleak a picture of village life. Strenuous (and ultimately successful) efforts were also being undertaken to prevent American plans for a movie of *Ivan Denisovich*.[105] The new situation then became clearer to all in April 1964, with the awarding of the Lenin Prize for Literature, the strongest conferment of political approval that the regime granted a writer. Having had such an impact both at home and abroad, many assumed that Solzhenitsyn would be a shoo-in, since he remained largely untouched by the waves of criticism washing over the country's liberal writers. He was shortlisted, as expected; but, Tvardovsky aside, the judging panel was overwhelmingly made up of moderate to hardline conservatives.

Following the unanimous praise that it initially attracted, a few critics had now begun to assert that even *Ivan Denisovich* was perhaps more problematic than previously acknowledged, since its protagonist was so passive in the face of his suffering. A properly Socialist Realist hero should have struggled for justice, they reasoned.[106] One of the prize judges – Komsomol boss Sergei Pavlov – even smeared the author by airing wholly untrue rumours of Solzhenitsyn's apparent cowardice during the war, making plain his feeling that such a person could not be rewarded with such a high prize. On the eve of the judges' voting in April 1964, *Pravda* published a series of readers' letters criticising *Ivan Denisovich*, taken as a sure sign of its having fallen into official disfavour.[107] Despite its status as a landmark of modern literature, the novella was excluded from the voting at the first opportunity. From that point, things would only get worse in Solzhenitsyn's relationship with the Soviet regime.

In many senses, the early 1960s represented the high point of not just the era's utopian thinking, but also of liberal-minded hopes for the Soviet future. Even so, events like the Novocherkassk massacre, the crisis in the Caribbean and the new clampdown in the cultural sphere followed soon after and combined to give a clear sense of changing tides. Although no single event can be pinned down as either its prime cause or main manifestation, a new tightening-up could be discerned across multiple spheres as the middle of the decade began to approach.

9

KREMLIN COUP AND THE FATE OF REFORM

On 13 October 1964, *Pravda* again reported on the latest Soviet break-through in space exploration: the world's first three-person mission. After their successful launch, the cosmonauts Komarov, Feoktistov and Egorov were put in two-way radio contact with Khrushchev and Mikoyan, who were both holidaying on the Black Sea coast. The pair offered effusive congratulations as usual and wished the cosmonauts luck in their mission. As he brought their brief conversation towards a close, Khrushchev jovially remarked to Egorov that the trio had better get ready for the welcome that awaited them on their return to Earth.[1] By the time the cosmonauts made it back to the Soviet capital less than a week later, jubilant crowds did indeed turn out on Red Square, but it would be Leonid Brezhnev who presided over the celebrations. Khrushchev had already commenced an enforced retirement that would last until his death seven years later.

The plot against Khrushchev

Khrushchev's removal from power has traditionally been understood in terms of hardliners fighting back against liberalisation. Without doubt, many among the plotters wanted rid of him in order to forestall further reform, and the two decades that followed his ouster were to a great extent character-ised by deepening conservatism at the top. Even so, the move was about more than just opposition to reformism. Khrushchev was becoming increas-ingly boorish in person, some of his policy decisions were growing more erratic and the 'Khrushchev cult' was growing apace. Anyway, there were few real signs of any liberalising policy agenda from Khrushchev as the mid-1960s approached. In fact, the broad trend during his final couple of years in office was for considerable tightening-up across a range of fields, including culture, youth policy and nationalities affairs.

Already by the start of the 1960s, previous reform to the penal system was being pushed back in some important ways. The notion that criminals would be better reformed not through incarceration but through the positive influence of the collective was largely abandoned, after provoking public resentment at the sense that serious crimes were not being punished vigorously enough, with genuinely dangerous offenders remaining at liberty.[2] Striking as it might seem, there was even a public rhetoric likening post-Stalin labour camps to health resorts.[3] Large numbers of prisoners were no longer eligible for parole, sentences grew longer and the population of camps and prisons began to climb again after reaching a low point in 1960.[4] Rations were lowered for all prisoners, and the number of visits and parcels allowed was also reduced, with conditions inside camps becoming notably tougher across the early 1960s.[5] Policing, too, was hardening, with the militia again given truncheons and tear gas. Use of the death penalty was considerably expanded, as was the jurisdiction of the KGB, which now gained the right to handle a growing range of offences, from smuggling and currency speculation through to failures to report crimes to the authorities.[6]

Perhaps most noteworthy in regard to the hardening was the emerging use of psychiatry as a means of punishing 'troublemakers'. Widely associated with the late 1960s and 1970s, the practice had clear roots in the Khrushchev years. Although never formally adopted as policy – the Soviet authorities vehemently denied that psychiatry was used for punitive purposes in the USSR – Khrushchev conceded publicly in May 1959 that there were a few people in the country who were opposed to communism; however, he added, 'their mental state is not normal'.[7] New medical guidelines that were issued in 1961 then made the criteria for forced psychiatric detention vague enough to apply to practically anyone.[8] Procurator files from the early 1960s show numerous criminal investigations, often including political dissenters and religious believers especially, being 'paused' for the accused to undergo a period of psychiatric evaluation to ascertain whether or not they were 'responsible' for their actions – and thus whether they required a trial and detention in the regular penal system or 'treatment' in a secure psychiatric unit.[9]

Moscow's Serbsky Institute for Forensic Psychiatry became especially notorious for the fact that doctors there proved consistently able and willing to diagnose psychiatric problems among those detained for fundamentally political offences, and the veneer of medical rationale could be shockingly thin at times. After being arrested as the founder of an underground political group, Petro Grigorenko's diagnosis found him 'not responsible' on the basis of his 'reformist ideas, in particular for the reorganisation of the state apparatus'.[10] The writer Mikhail Naritsa, who was caught trying to smuggle a manuscript abroad in 1961, also faced such a psychiatric evaluation and later described a room full of doctors leafing through pages of his novel before declaring him insane.[11] Another author, Valery Tarsis, was incarcerated from summer 1962 to spring 1963 in a psychiatric unit after his novel *The Bluebottle* was sneaked out of the country and published abroad. This period of psychiatric detention would then become the subject of his next book, *Ward 7*, in which he described encountering 'neither patients nor doctors but only jailers in charge of inconvenient citizens'.[12]

For those declared 'not responsible' at this stage, a uniquely traumatic and dangerous path could open up. Often they were held practically incommunicado and confined alongside severely mentally ill and potentially dangerous people. Vladimir Bukovsky, for example, wrote of sharing a cell with a man who had killed his entire family and eaten his own ears.[13] Some patients were beaten ferociously by orderlies and forcibly given psychotropic drugs. Pavel Borovik, who was declared insane in 1964 and subjected to forced medication, described years later how 'from the drugs I have completely lost my appetite, my limbs tremble, every bone aches and I can't walk'.[14] Having a diagnosis rather than a custodial sentence effectively made appeal impossible – appealing against a diagnosis could be held as evidence of paranoia – and meant that one might be held indefinitely until 'cured'. For some religious believers especially, release from psychiatric detention could be contingent on renouncing their faith, with those who stood firm sometimes spending twenty years or more incarcerated. Even once released, people who had been diagnosed as mentally unwell were especially vulnerable to being detained again on the spurious grounds that their condition had deteriorated and required further treatment.[15]

All this hardening of regime actions surely reflected wider changes in the atmosphere of the time. One must remain cautious in making claims about the state of public opinion inside the USSR, but there seems little doubt that Khrushchev's star was waning badly by the mid-1960s. Some remained forever grateful for changes he had set in motion, but others had long since run out of patience. His name had been inextricably linked to a range of decisions that aroused deep resentment among large sections of the population. He had reduced the size of peasants' private plots and increased the price of basic foodstuffs, and many also took offence at his attacks on religion and on Stalin. His pronouncements on catching up and overtaking the West, and on the imminent construction of communism, were also much derided in some quarters, while jokes about both his ignorance and his corpulence were widespread. Georgy Arbatov recalled going to the cinema twice in September 1964, and on both occasions newsreel footage shown before the start of the movie saw members of the audience laughing openly at Khrushchev's image up on the screen.[16]

Anonymous letters sent to newspapers and regime officials, like illicit leaflets that were scattered on streets or pasted up on walls, sometimes expressed great animosity towards Khrushchev personally. At the end of December 1962, for example, leaflets were discovered in the Siberian city of Chita with comments including 'windbag Khrushchev, where is your abundance?' and 'down with the Khrushchev dictatorship'.[17] In reference to the 'Khrushchev cult', one set of leaflets discovered in Moscow during 1963 asked 'Isn't it time for Khrushchev to claim his pension before he converts to a god?'[18] Assassination plots were uncovered by the KGB in both Tbilisi (1960) and Dushanbe (1962).[19] Years later, two of the key actors in the insider coup that ensued – Vladimir Semichastny and Alexander Shelepin – claimed that Khrushchev's growing unpopularity with the public was such that he had become a danger to the regime, though this was primarily an exercise in post-hoc self-justification.[20] His declining standing among the general public was important, though, because it seems to have emboldened the would-be plotters, who were mostly a pretty cautious group.

For the creative intelligentsia, attitudes towards Khrushchev had long been conflicted. His simplicity and earthiness were popular with many, and there was little doubt that cultural liberalisation had repeatedly been contingent on his personal support; but all this existed alongside some increasingly unappealing behaviour. His crude outbursts at the Manezh gallery, along with the threatening tirades over the months that followed, clearly helped reshape attitudes towards him. Further, in a country where education levels were rising rapidly, and the drive to be 'cultured' in one's comportment was a central tenet of regime discourse, Khrushchev could come across as an embarrassing oaf. As Lyudmila Alexeyeva wrote in her memoir of the period:

> my friends and I were quite indignant about his idiotic 'kitchen debate' with Vice President Richard Nixon, his shoe incident at the United Nations, his laughable attempts to catch up with and overtake America . . . his illiterate pronouncements on art, his attacks on writers . . .[21]

Like the cultural elite, the scientific community was one that had been granted considerable privilege and prestige since Stalin; but it also experienced growing frustration. Khrushchev's continued personal support for the biologist Trofim Lysenko came to a head in June 1964, when one of Lysenko's associates was put up for election to the prestigious Soviet Academy of Sciences. Along with other prominent members of the Academy, Andrei Sakharov spoke out at the decisive meeting, declaring of the nominee that,

> together with Academician Lysenko, he is responsible for the shameful backwardness of Soviet biology and genetics in particular . . . for the degradation of learning and for the defamation, firing, arrest and even death of many genuine scientists.[22]

Several of the speakers who followed Sakharov were similarly coruscating, and the vote went against Lysenko's man. Outraged on hearing of the scientists' impertinence, the following month Khrushchev called for the 240-year-old Academy of Sciences to be abolished – a remark that appalled both scientists and party colleagues.[23] Not long after that, he publicly berated the country's scientists again over setbacks in the development of the chemical industry – another pet project that he had expected to cure the country's ills – refusing to listen to their concerns and demanding ever faster progress.

Three of the key institutions whose support had helped save Khrushchev during the 1957 coup attempt – the military, the KGB and the party apparatus – were no longer so supportive. Within the military there was considerable anger at the deep funding cuts and job losses that Khrushchev had imposed over the preceding decade. Within the KGB there was resentment at having carried much of the institutional blame (with accompanying loss of prestige) for the Stalin-era atrocities that Khrushchev had exposed. Further, Khrushchev had hardly been a generous patron for the security services, with staff wages and perks steadily declining on his watch. He had for several years steadfastly refused to promote any of the KGB's most senior officers to the rank of general, and when Chairman Semichastny asked him to do so, Khrushchev humiliated him in public for it.[24]

Lastly, the party bureaucracy had become increasingly ill-disposed towards Khrushchev as a result of the chaotic reforms that he imposed as he struggled to tackle the country's economic ills. Most egregious was the decision in September 1962 to bifurcate the party – to divide virtually all its structures in two throughout the USSR, creating an industrial branch of the party and an agricultural branch. In Khrushchev's mind, this would ensure that both fundamental facets of the Soviet economy received equal attention, with the benefit of more efficient oversight through specialisation of focus. In reality, the move immediately led to a huge amount of confusion and resentment among those who had to work out how to implement his latest flight of fancy at the ground level. It also created massive inefficiency by duplicating workloads, and generated all manner of bureaucratic tangles in splitting existing jurisdictions and resources into two parts (right down to dividing up office furniture). Naturally, everyone praised this 'far-sighted' reform at the time, but most were in reality seething at what they justifiably saw as ill-thought-out meddling.

Party bosses across the Russian regions and non-Russian republics (who together constituted much of the Central Committee's membership) were even unhappier about Khrushchev's plan to cut in half their political domains, since it would disrupt or wreck connections and patronage networks that they had spent years cultivating. Some regional potentates also griped that it had been several years since they were granted an audience with the first secretary.[25] Most important for this tier of the Soviet political elite, however, were the strict new rules on term limits for all manner of official posts that were introduced at the Twenty-Second Party Congress. Faced with the future loss of power and privileges under Khrushchev, when plotters from Moscow came looking for support, many high officials in the provinces were willing to listen to their overtures.

Antipathy towards Khrushchev was also becoming rife among Presidium members – almost all of whom were his promotees. When he turned seventy years of age, in April 1964, his comrades were especially ostentatious in their praise. They voted to award him the title Hero of the Soviet Union and a fawning collective letter was carried on the front pages of both *Pravda* and *Izvestiya*, calling him 'a glorious son of the heroic working class' and describing his life as 'a shining example of service to the Leninist Party and Soviet people'.[26] An informal reception was held at the Khrushchev family home in Moscow's Lenin Hills, with abundant gifts and obsequious toasts. This was followed by an official engagement at the Kremlin, where Presidium members were joined by foreign dignitaries (several of whom would bestow awards upon Khrushchev from their home countries), feasted again and watched a celebratory screening of the 1961 propaganda film about Khrushchev *Our Dear Nikita Sergeevich*.[27]

In reality, as much as attitudes towards reform, towards Stalin or any other matter, what united the plotters was that they were sick of Khrushchev's behaviour. While not carrying anything like the degree of menace towards those around him that Stalin once did, Khrushchev had nonetheless offended and humiliated most of his closest comrades by this point. On one occasion, Khrushchev insisted, with Gromyko present, that Gromyko was 'not a Foreign Minister' but 'a piece of shit'.[28] He joked to colleagues that Brezhnev had been known as 'the ballerina' back in his native Dnepropetrovsk, on account of the fact that he 'was so easy to turn around'.[29] Belorussian party boss Kirill Mazurov had been the only one bold enough to express concerns about the party bifurcation plan, for which he was sharply rebuked and very nearly sacked. At a Kremlin lunch held for a visiting Vietnamese delegation, headed by Le Duan, Khrushchev told guests that Nikolai Podgorny had originally trained as a sugar worker and 'should have stayed a sugar worker since life has taught him little since'. He went on to add that he still did not know whether Suslov was for or against the Twentieth Party Congress, since he always avoided giving a direct answer when asked. Both Podgorny and Suslov were present at the time and visibly unhappy, while Brezhnev and Shelepin looked on, clearly embarrassed.[30]

Added to such insults was a continual stream of interference in the work of others. Neither Gromyko nor the battery of genuine experts at the Ministry of Foreign Affairs was able to exert much influence over foreign policy decisions once Khrushchev got involved, which he usually did.[30] Similarly, Khrushchev had begun to use his son-in-law, Alexei Adzhubei, as a personal emissary abroad. This policy backfired badly in July 1964, when he went to West Germany and, in a secretly recorded conversation, made racist remarks about the Chinese and suggested that Khrushchev might be willing to pull down the Berlin Wall, causing some considerable diplomatic turbulence with East Germany. In his role as Moscow party boss, Nikolai Egorychev was subjected to all manner of petty and sometimes irrational directives from Khrushchev around this time, including a dressing-down over the apparently excessive amount of street lighting in the capital at night (upon which Egorychev informed Khrushchev that the roads he spoke of were well lit precisely because they were on the route that Khrushchev took home).[31]

Lastly, by 1964 Khrushchev had for some time been suggesting that he was on the cusp of retirement – raising, but not answering, the question of succession. He had also begun to talk with increasing regularity about bringing new blood into the Presidium, complaining that the ruling group had grown 'too old'. In September 1964, a Central Committee plenum was scheduled for the coming November, seemingly with changes to the membership of the party's Presidium on the agenda. Khrushchev's colleagues at the top, then, were not just sick of his behaviour, and opposed to various of his policies, but also fearful for their own careers.

Brezhnev had effectively been Khrushchev's second-in-command since early 1963. Just below him in the pecking order was Podgorny, who had been moved to Moscow from Kiev after several years as head of the party in Ukraine. Khrushchev, it seems, had expected the two men to become rivals for his approval. In fact, they became allies and started to discuss what to do about him. Soon they were joined in this by another powerful Khrushchev protégé, Alexander Shelepin. Along with Shelepin came his most important ally, KGB Chairman Vladimir Semichastny.

Brezhnev and Podgorny won over the first few sympathisers, while Shelepin brought on board important officials in the security organs, the party apparatus and government ministries. One early convert, Nikolai Ignatov, then travelled the Russian provinces and non-Russian republics winning over party bosses there to the idea of removing Khrushchev.[32] After the new Ukrainian party boss Shelest joined the plotters in summer 1964, he was directed to sign up the rest of the elite in Kiev.[33] This kind of work was made much easier by the fact that the KGB chief was in on events from an early stage, and also by Khrushchev being frequently out of the country: by the middle of October 1964, he had been abroad for 135 days already that year.[34] Even when Khrushchev was within Soviet borders, he was frequently away from the Kremlin, visiting Ukraine, the Russian provinces and Central Asia at length in 1964.

Much of the persuading was done during the late spring and summer of 1964, at dachas, hunting lodges and holiday resorts. For Shelest, the approach came at the start of July. While holidaying in Crimea, he received an unexpected call to say that Brezhnev was coming to visit him, though the pair were not personally close. After making small talk for a while, Brezhnev tentatively probed Shelest's feelings about the state of the party, before asking 'What's your attitude towards Khrushchev?' As Shelest recalled, Brezhnev then spoke principally of Khrushchev's rude and domineering behaviour and his plans to remove older members of the Presidium (at this point, Brezhnev asked Shelest's age and reminded him that, at fifty-five, he was in danger, too).[35] Nikolai Mesyatsev was approached in the late spring, while on a mushroom-picking expedition with friend and colleague Nikolai Mironov. As the pair headed for home, Mironov mentioned that colleagues had been talking about removing Khrushchev, adding 'I hardly need to tell you the reasons why'. When asked how he related to this idea, Mesyatsev answered 'positively'. The conversation ended there, and the subject did not come up again until the middle of October.[36] For Presidium member Gennady Voronov, the key moment came at the end of a hunting trip. As he bade farewell to Brezhnev (his hunting companion for the day), Voronov got in his car to be driven home and found old friend Yuri Andropov already in the back seat waiting to talk to him.

Moscow party boss Nikolai Egorychev, too, was approached by a trusted friend, Petr Demichev, who broached the issue with the words 'you know, Khrushchev has been conducting himself badly . . .' Once in on the plot, Egorychev became another recruiter of officials all over the country, later recalling that only one person unambiguously rejected participation. Lithuanian party boss Antanas Sniečkus, Egorychev recalled, feigned confusion and quickly changed the subject when he was approached in August 1964. An early attempt to raise the issue with the ever cautious Mikhail Suslov while he and Egorychev were in Paris together on business was thwarted by a sudden rain shower that caused the pair to run for cover mid-conversation. Because of this important role in growing the plot, it is worth noting that Egorychev subsequently wrote that he participated in it not out of opposition to liberalisation, but because he felt Khrushchev had become a brake on reform. He emphasised that Brezhnev had 'sold' the plan to him on the basis that the end result would be a genuine strengthening of party democracy, promising to support Egorychev's ideas about introducing election to top party posts by secret ballot.[37]

October 1964

Because members of the political elite across the country had signed up in droves, knowledge of the plot's existence soon grew dangerously widespread. By September 1964, the ringleaders were becoming jittery. Egorychev recalled going to see Brezhnev and finding him white as a sheet and shaking, sure that they had been rumbled and would be shot for it.[38] All were deeply afraid of what Khrushchev might do if they were uncovered, and there was a great deal of mutual suspicion between them. Shelest was developing a growing sense of frustration at Brezhnev for failing to pluck up the courage to move things forward. Semichastny, too, insisted that Brezhnev's indecisiveness was becoming dangerous. The burgeoning plot did indeed prove far from watertight. According to Sergei Khrushchev, his sister Rada was the first to receive a tip-off about the plan to topple their father in an anonymous telephone call during the summer of 1964, though at the time she dismissed it as a provocation. Khrushchev's granddaughter, Yuliya, had her own close scrape with the conspiracy, when she turned up unexpectedly for lunch with a party official in Crimea, just as Brezhnev and Podgorny were there seeking to enlist the same individual.[39]

In early October, Sergei Khrushchev was himself contacted by a concerned KGB agent – the minder of plotter Nikolai Ignatov – who had overheard his boss talking about the plot. Sergei told his father the KGB man's story, correctly naming Brezhnev, Shelepin and Podgorny among those involved. Khrushchev was unconvinced, though, and when he mentioned it to Mikoyan and Podgorny the next day, they laughed it off, with the latter suggesting he ask the KGB to look into it. Khrushchev headed off the next day for working visits to Kiev and Krasnodar, before moving on to Pitsunda in Georgia for a holiday, where he was joined by Mikoyan. Once on the Black Sea coast, he also asked local officials about the plot. They, too, insisted that nothing untoward was going on, but were in reality already signed up to the plan themselves (and the KGB was listening in on Khrushchev at Pitsunda).

On 11 October, Khrushchev's interest in the rumoured conspiracy apparently flared again, and he rang underlings in Moscow, angrily announcing that he would get to the bottom of things on his return.[40] Word quickly spread among the plotters, who were well aware that they were bound to be uncovered if they did not make their move at once. Brezhnev, who was away in Berlin at the time, apparently sank into a blind panic, and contact with him could only be re-established after he was sent the coded message 'the weather in Moscow is good'. At this, he returned to the capital immediately, as did Podgorny (from a visit to Kishinev) and Shelest (from Kiev). Members of the Presidium (minus Khrushchev and Mikoyan) met in the Kremlin and resolved that the Central Committee plenum scheduled for mid-November would instead convene imminently for an urgent discussion of the economic plan for the year ahead.

On the evening of 13 October, all the main plotters gathered at Brezhnev's apartment in central Moscow. At about 21:00 it fell to him to make the call that summoned Khrushchev back to the capital. Semichastny later claimed that Brezhnev was so frightened he literally had to be dragged to the telephone.[41] Nonetheless, in the face of considerable irritation from Khrushchev, who did not want to interrupt his holiday for a meeting which he felt could proceed without him, Brezhnev found his nerve and stood firm, insisting that the first secretary was needed for the session the next day. Eventually, Khrushchev acquiesced. The plotters then had a tense few hours while they waited to find out if he was really coming. Around midnight, word came through that Khrushchev had placed an order for a plane to return him to Moscow.

Late that night, Nikolai Mesyatsev was unexpectedly summoned to meet Brezhnev, Podgorny, Kosygin and a couple of others. At this encounter, he was briefed on events soon to follow and then put in charge of overseeing the country's television and radio output during the next crucial days, since the plotters believed that the incumbent head of Soviet television was loyal to Khrushchev and had thus arranged for him to be out of the country. Mesyatsev was then driven directly to the offices of the State Committee for Television and Radio, where he summoned all senior staff in the early hours of the morning and insisted that anyone who objected to Khrushchev's removal must make their feelings known to him at once. His duty from that point on was to vet all central television and radio broadcasting to ensure that the country's media apparatus could not be used for any kind of bid to save Khrushchev.[42] Much the same process took place at the state news service, TASS, as well as at key newspapers like *Pravda* and *Izvestiya*.

By the time Khrushchev's plane was in the air the next morning, the plot had swung fully into action. Semichastny had placed all of Khrushchev's usual security team on leave and warned the Kremlin guards to do absolutely nothing without his explicit permission. Once they arrived at the Kremlin, Khrushchev and Mikoyan were taken straight to the meeting room of the Central Committee Presidium, and the session then opened at 16:00, with Khrushchev nominally in the chair. A proposal was immediately put forward by Brezhnev to strip Khrushchev of all his party and state posts.

Addressing Khrushchev personally, Brezhnev insisted that he had always been loyal to him, but could be no longer. He criticised his rudeness to colleagues, his interfering in anything and everything, his self-aggrandising and poor decision making. After Brezhnev, Shelest attacked Khrushchev's interference in the affairs of the non-Russian republics, his endless reorganisations and policy failures in agriculture and industry. When Khrushchev interrupted his remarks once too often, Shelest shot back that those present had listened to him plenty, and now it was time for Khrushchev to listen to them. Shelepin criticised Khrushchev's leadership style: his bullying of colleagues and lack of collective decision making, as well as his chaotic administrative reorganisations. Belorussian party chief Mazurov targeted the Khrushchev cult and condemned his decision to combine the posts of party first secretary and chairman of the Council of Ministers. After several bruising hours of criticism, the Presidium meeting was adjourned.[43]

The overnight break naturally had the plotters on edge, but in reality there was little prospect of Khrushchev rallying support. The ring that was thrown around him by the security organs proved tight. Semichastny had ensured that all possible sources of communication and travel were under KGB control. Anyway, Sergei Khrushchev later recounted that his father returned home that evening and announced that he would not try to resist, saying 'I am old and tired. Let them cope by themselves.' He marvelled at the idea of anyone trying to tell Stalin that he was no longer required, remarking 'the fear's gone and we can talk as equals. That's my contribution. I won't put up a fight.'[44] This was, of course, a profoundly disingenuous line of thinking: Khrushchev's colleagues wanted him out in large part because they could not ordinarily talk as equals. They had done things in secret because they were afraid of him: had he known enough about the plot, he would surely have tried to stamp it out.

The meeting resumed at the Kremlin around 10:00 the next day. Dmitry Polyansky quickly brought things back to boiling point with a damning report that accused Khrushchev of recklessness and adventurism in foreign policy, such as his promises of military assistance that the Soviet Union was in no position to deliver and his plans for penetration of Latin America, which, insisted Polyansky, were delusional and dangerous. On Cuba, he accused Khrushchev of bringing the world to the brink of nuclear war, and of then imposing a humiliating climbdown that undermined Soviet prestige and morale, as well as damaging relations with Castro. Polyansky also took exception to his nepotism, pointing to Adzhubei's growing political influence and the recent award of the title Hero of the Soviet Union to Khrushchev's son Sergei. Leaving no stone unturned in cutting Khrushchev down to size, Brezhnev also spoke of the shame that he had brought upon the party through the calamitous affair with Alexei Larionov's fraudulent 'miracle' in Ryazan.

The only one to speak up with any kind of defence of Khrushchev was Mikoyan. He not only accepted key criticisms of his behaviour, but also pointed out that numerous of those present were displaying distinctly selective memories of their own roles in some of the affairs that they now blamed on Khrushchev. These remarks were quickly branded 'incorrect' by Shelepin. Mikoyan, who later wrote that he was warned he 'would be next' if he tried to help save his friend, then proposed that Khrushchev be given some kind of ceremonial role, so that use could still be made of his knowledge and skills. Brezhnev replied that such a suggestion might be acceptable, were it not for Khrushchev's character.[45]

Moving things towards a conclusion, Podgorny insisted that he and the others present used to respect Khrushchev, but no longer could. Khrushchev spoke last. He asked forgiveness from those to whom he had been rude, conceded that he had made mistakes, but also insisted that some of those present had actively encouraged things that they now attacked him for (like his combining the top party and government posts). He then agreed to sign a statement to the effect that he wished to retire on health grounds.

As soon as the Presidium meeting concluded, those present trooped across the Kremlin to a nearby hall, where the full Central Committee had been assembled (minus a few members whose loyalties were not clear to the plotters). Brezhnev and Suslov gave a recap of the Presidium's criticism of Khrushchev and directed Central Committee members to vote on whether to accept his request to retire. To forestall potentially tricky questions or debates, the motion was not opened for discussion and Khrushchev was not granted the right to present his case. Unsurprisingly, the vote was unanimous. Scenting blood, some of those present even called for Khrushchev to be punished for his misdeeds, though such remarks were quickly dismissed.

After the coup

Meetings of party and Komsomol activists were hurriedly called to express public support for Khrushchev's removal from office. As in the spring of 1956, though, people wanted to know much more than they were being told. Records from these meetings show that some participants wanted to see a stenograph of the Presidium session; they also queried on whose initiative it had taken place and whether Khrushchev had acknowledged his errors. Komsomol activists asked where Khrushchev was now, whether official views on the anti-party group would be revised and whether policy towards China would change. In Leningrad, they asked when the negative aspects of his rule had begun, on whose initiative he had been awarded four Hero of Socialist Labour medals, whether Stalin's failings were still to be emphasised and whether the 1962 price rises had been a mistake.[46] All of these questions had important implications in terms of what now lay ahead. There was little sign of support for the deposed leader, but it was clear that few believed he had really asked to retire on health grounds.[47]

311

The reaction to the news among the wider Soviet public was fairly muted. There was no sign in the following days and weeks of public protest at his removal from power (and the KGB was looking closely for such activity). When Semichastny later reported to the Presidium in August 1965 with a longer-term view of public reactions to Khrushchev's ouster, the news was exactly what his bosses wanted to hear: there were no manifestations to report of public unrest relating to Khrushchev's removal from office; the number of anti-Soviet leaflets in circulation had actually dropped by around 50 per cent on the previous year; and – best of all – a large proportion of those leaflets that had been uncovered since October expressed satisfaction at Khrushchev being deposed.[48]

At least some people immediately feared the worst, however. On hearing of Khrushchev's fall, Solzhenitsyn descended into panic. Fearing that a dramatic tightening-up was imminent, as Stalinists reasserted themselves, he had copies of his works in progress either burned or sent to the West. With a draft copy of his next novel, *The First Circle*, held in the safe at the *Novy mir* office, Solzhenitsyn expected that both he and the journal's editor Tvardovsky would be 'cast down into the depths of hell' upon its discovery. However, as Solzhenitsyn recalled it, he soon found the *Novy mir* editor 'as cheerful as I was anxious' at the news.[49] Unquestionably one of the key figures of post-Stalin cultural liberalisation, Tvardovsky had evidently tired of Khrushchev's unpredictable and volatile antics, and now hoped that the change in the Kremlin would mark the start of more consistently tolerant cultural policy.

There were a number of other regime insiders whose initial perception was that the coup perhaps boded well for a rejuvenation of the reform agenda. One former adviser to Yuri Andropov later described his boss announcing that 'now we shall move more firmly and consistently along the road charted by the Twentieth Congress'.[50] Although very much a 'Child of the Twentieth Party Congress' himself, Len Karpinsky recalled that on hearing the news on 14 October, he and a friend 'drank some cognac to celebrate Khrushchev's removal'. He continued: 'we thought his impulsive, half-baked decisions had become a brake on the process of reform, even a threat to the process. He had really gotten on our nerves during the preceding two years or so.'[51] This was to prove a serious misjudgement, though it is worth emphasising that Karpinsky knew the corridors of power intimately.

Several years later, after he had himself been banished from the elite for his reformist sympathies, Karpinsky felt differently, telephoning the ageing and isolated Khrushchev on his birthday to thank him for all he had done and to tell him that his achievements were irreversible.

Mikoyan was left unmolested by the plotters, but he anyway chose to retire from political life the following year, and thereafter was largely kept out of the public eye. Although at the time citing age as his reason for retirement, he later wrote that he had not wanted to work in the new leadership team, adding that the group was 'of a low political level', 'primitive' and 'irresponsible', as well as 'cynical' and 'dull'.[52] Khrushchev's son-in-law, Adzhubei, found himself sacked as editor of *Izvestiya* even before the Central Committee plenum had completed its work. Key advisers like Lebedev – who was vital to the publication of *Ivan Denisovich* in particular – were put out to grass (when Lebedev died in 1966, Tvardovsky was notably the only representative of Soviet officialdom to attend his funeral).

Khrushchev himself was not so much consigned to the 'ash heap of history' as he was ploughed into landfill by being rendered a 'non-person'. As always, the portraits quickly came down, and the volumes of collected speeches disappeared from libraries. Imprisoned in the notorious labour camp at Mordovia at the time, Anatoly Marchenko recalled the desperate scramble by administrators to remove the previously omnipresent name 'Khrushchev' from banners and slogans all over the camp, as prisoners looked on, hooting and whistling.[53] After 15 October, Khrushchev's name was barely mentioned again by the party or press for over twenty years.

Once removed from power, Khrushchev lived mainly at the modest dacha he had been allocated outside Moscow. He became much softer and kinder to those he encountered, but also grew depressed and sometimes said only a few words in the course of a whole day.[54] He began listening to radio broadcasts by the BBC and Voice of America; and after his son procured a *samizdat* copy for him, he finally got around to reading *Doctor Zhivago*, deciding that the decision to ban it had been a mistake. Among the occasional guests who came to visit were Yevgeny Yevtushenko and the artist Boris Zhutovsky, both of whom had endured public dressing-downs from Khrushchev, for which he now apologised. The poet Andrei Voznesensky also received a letter from Khrushchev apologising for the public mauling given him in March 1963 (again, Khrushchev claimed to have been misled about his work), as did Margarita Aliger.[55]

Granted both a Moscow apartment (which he barely used) and a dacha, Khrushchev also retained access to the elite medical facilities of the Kremlin. His material lot was thus considerably better than that of the average Soviet pensioner. Nonetheless, his residence was heavily bugged and his post read, though genuine attempts to intimidate him only came with rumours that he was secretly preparing memoirs. These rumours were entirely true. His son Sergei had managed to acquire a recording device and eventually persuaded his father to start setting down his recollections. When summoned to the Kremlin and ordered to hand over the tapes, Khrushchev refused. Once those tapes were sneaked out of the country and the resulting work appeared in the West under the title *Khrushchev Remembers*, he was made to sign a document falsely labelling the memoir a fabrication. Adzhubei insisted that this hounding by the KGB and party leadership shortened what remained of his father-in-law's life. Khrushchev recovered from a first heart attack in May 1970, and from a second at the end of that year, but succumbed to a third in September 1971.

The cost of the funeral was met by the party, with permission granted for a burial at the capital's second most prestigious cemetery, the Novodevichy monastery, and modest wreaths sent from both the Central Committee and the Council of Ministers. However, news of Khrushchev's death was not made public until the day of the interment, and the cemetery grounds were officially closed for the day to prevent any kind of potential scene. The small crowd that did turn up consisted largely of foreign diplomats and journalists. The few Soviet citizens in attendance were kept at bay by police and photographed by the KGB.[56] The official announcement of his passing that was carried in both *Pravda* and *Izvestiya* was buried in the bottom corner of the page and stated only that 'private pensioner Nikita Sergeevich Khrushchev, former First Secretary of the CPSU Central Committee and Chairman of the USSR Council of Ministers died on 11 September after a serious and prolonged illness'.[57] No other information about his life and career, or any kind of tribute, was provided, though his family received letters of condolence from Jacqueline Kennedy, Tito and Andrei Sakharov, among others. No former colleagues from the political elite either attended the burial or passed on condolences to the family, though at the very last moment a wreath arrived from Anastas Mikoyan. After eventually being granted permission to erect a memorial at the grave, Khrushchev's family had the sculptor Ernst Neizvestny make it for them.

The new leadership team

Once everything had finished at the Kremlin on 15 October, the TASS news service announced to the world that the Central Committee had approved Khrushchev's request to be released from his party and state responsibilities in connection with his advancing age and worsening health. On 16 October, the front pages of the country's newspapers were adorned with one photograph each of the party's new first secretary, Leonid Brezhnev, and the new chairman of the Council of Ministers, Alexei Kosygin.[58] Since almost all of the top leadership had been involved in the plot that removed Khrushchev, immediate personnel changes were limited, barring a handful of promotions. As in March 1953, the men now at the top owed almost their entire career trajectory to the man they had replaced. Indeed, one of Brezhnev's long-term advisers recalled that, on coming to power, the new first secretary was basically in alignment with Khrushchev on most key issues, such as no return to Stalinist repression, the continuation of peaceful relations with the US and better living standards for the masses inside the USSR.[59] Years later, an unimpressed Molotov succinctly dismissed the new leadership group as being full of Khrushchev supporters who 'now behave as if they had nothing to do with him'.[60]

For many, both inside and outside the former Soviet Union, the abiding historical image of Leonid Brezhnev is probably that of the increasingly decrepit and risibly vainglorious character that he was to become from the second half of the 1970s onwards, practically unable even to lift his hand to wave and reliant on notes for even the very briefest public remarks. This, though, was not the Brezhnev who came to power in October 1964. Still in his fifties at the time, he was regarded as reasonably young and had an impressive list of important posts already on his CV. In particular, he had been party boss of a strategically significant union republic (Kazakhstan) as well as a region (Dnepropetrovsk) that was central to both weapons and space technology. In his more recent role as head of the Supreme Soviet during the early 1960s, he had headed up state visits throughout the socialist world, as well as to the likes of India, Iran, Sudan, Afghanistan and Ghana, winning friends and building his profile. Mostly overseeing priority fields such as heavy industry and military provisioning, Brezhnev was, according to numerous of those who worked under him, a remarkably open, friendly and effective manager by Soviet standards.[61] Of his own time as British ambassador to the USSR, William Hayter wrote that Brezhnev had long given off 'an impression of vigour and vitality' among the foreign diplomats in Moscow; he added that by the later part of the 1950s, Brezhnev already often featured on outside observers' lists of possible successors to Khrushchev.[62]

While Brezhnev's myriad failings and weaknesses have been widely recognised – a dismissive Mikoyan, for example, wrote that he was neither bright nor hard-working, and that he had no opinion of his own – he was markedly less abrasive and less volatile than Khrushchev.[63] Important speeches and policy decisions were again the subject of genuine collective input, and colleagues in the leadership were no longer bawled out or humiliated.[64] Working at the time of the coup as a Central Committee speech writer, Georgy Arbatov described how during his early years in power, Brezhnev was willing to take others' opinions on board, tried hard to be unpretentious and approachable, tended to shy away from the media spotlight and avoided expressing opinions on things about which he was not qualified to pass judgement.[65] This must have felt like a major improvement after Khrushchev's last few years at the top.

The new head of government, Alexei Kosygin, was certainly among the most able and experienced of the incoming leadership team. He had already held high government posts in defence, finance, light industry and economic planning. That Kosygin had made it to the 1960s in one piece was itself something of a minor miracle, since he had very nearly been dragged into the post-war Leningrad Affair, which had led to the execution of his close friend Nikolai Voznesensky. Kosygin later told friends that Stalin had deliberately tested his nerves by forwarding to him interrogation reports stating that he was also a member of the (fabricated) plot. Although he retained a certain nostalgic fondness for the Stalin years, Kosygin was by no means an arch-Stalinist in all respects, proving willing to countenance pretty

316

fundamental reform in areas under his purview. His weakness, according to one sympathetic observer, was a certain naivety – in particular, his belief that leadership after Khrushchev was going to be genuinely collective and that real attempts would be made to tackle the litany of serious problems afflicting the country.[66]

It was not without good reason that the Western commentator William Henry Chamberlain wrote of the new Soviet administration towards the end of 1965 that 'there have been substantial changes in style and manner; few if any big changes in substance'; he viewed the new leadership's policy up to that point as a kind of 'Khrushchevism without Khrushchev'.[67] Several policy directions most closely associated with the ousted leader were quickly altered or else reversed entirely, though this was not the kind of sharp reversion to Stalinism that Solzhenitsyn had feared. Some of the clearest changes that initially followed were eminently sensible, repealing impulsive and haphazard policies of recent times. The Khrushchev-era emphasis on volunteer police units like the *druzhiny* was reined in, as a more traditional approach to policing re-emerged. The process of undoing Khrushchev's much-disdained bifurcation of the party into 'industrial' and 'agricultural' branches also began right away, the stated rationale being that Khrushchev's plan had been 'carried out without proper preparation, in an atmosphere of unjustified haste' and had created administrative confusion, duplication of workloads, spiralling costs and damaging services provided to the population.[68]

Once his political patron was gone, the biologist Trofim Lysenko and his followers finally began to suffer the discredit and disgrace that most of the country's scientific community had been urging for many years. By the middle of November 1964, Lysenko's influence was coming under increasingly open attack in the official media. Soon after that, investigators uncovered falsified evidence in his experiments, and by the end of January 1965 his work was disproved and he was stripped of his principal power base as head of the Academy of Sciences' Institute of Genetics.

A degree of vibrancy also returned to Soviet culture for a time. The notorious Ideological Commission that had recently hauled over the coals so many wayward cultural figures was wound down. Writers, including Aksenov, Voznesensky and Solzhenitsyn, had work published again after a pause under Khrushchev.[69] In May 1965, a new collection of Boris Pasternak's poetry was published. Having been 'on the shelf' since Khrushchev publicly lambasted it in 1963, Marlen Khutsiev's movie *Ilich's Gate* was released in 1965, although in much-edited form and with the new name *I am Twenty*. In February of that year, a *Pravda* editorial on the relationship between the party and the cultural intelligentsia renounced recent anti-intellectualism and insisted that no one man would again be allowed to serve as arbiter of good and bad in culture.[70] Around this time, Grigory Baklanov's war novel *July 1941* was published in the journal *Znamya* and constituted, according to a recent historian, 'one of the most emphatic denunciations of Stalin's strategic errors and terror's impact on the war effort ever to appear in Soviet literature'.[71] To much acclaim among the intelligentsia especially, Mikhail Bulgakov's long-suppressed novel *Master and Margarita* was finally published in 1966 (albeit with substantial cuts by the censor), more than a quarter of a century after its author had died.

There were also early signs of the more conservative approach to come, however. Following a growing sense of institutional disenchantment under Khrushchev, soon after his removal from office the KGB was lavishly celebrated at a major Kremlin banquet, with medals and high praise for its important work – an event that was recalled by one of the proud security men present as showing that 'the KGB was again returning to its rightful place at the heart of Soviet society'.[72] The following December, Moscow played host to a week-long festival of movies and documentaries about 'Chekist heroes'. Among the biggest cinema hits of 1968 was *The Shield and the Sword*, a spy movie in four parts, which apparently inspired thousands (including Vladimir Putin) to sign up for a career in the security organs. By this time, a series of novels – several of which were subsequently made into hit movies – centred on heroic KGB exploits against Western intelligence was also becoming hugely popular with readers. Interestingly, one of the authors of these novels was a former KGB head of counter-intelligence, Oleg Gribanov, writing under the pseudonym Oleg Shmelev.[73]

Also in December 1965, KGB Chairman Semichastny wrote a report to the Central Committee that fulminated against all manner of liberal cultural themes, attacking new film and theatre productions which, he claimed, offered negative portrayals of officialdom and thus undermined authority.

Mikhail Romm's pioneering 1965 film *Ordinary Fascism* – ostensibly about the horrors of Nazism, but with clear parallels to the Stalin cult in places – was also castigated. Most bluntly, Semichastny opined that it was 'hard to find a justification for why we tolerate the politically harmful journal *Novy mir*'.[74]

Change and continuity

The first steps of the new leadership were clearly intended both to legitimise Khrushchev's removal and to provide reassurance that there was no cause for alarm. On 17 October, a *Pravda* editorial took the first matter in hand. Without naming names – which was hardly necessary – it declared that 'hare-brained scheming, hasty decisions and actions, rule by fiat, bragging and bluster, and unwillingness to take into account what science and practical experience have worked out' were all alien to Marxism-Leninism, adding that a task as serious as the construction of communism could not tolerate one-man decision making. Significantly, the editorial closed by reaffirming the importance of the resolutions of the Twentieth, Twenty-First and Twenty-Second Party Congresses, and restating party opposition to cults of personality, in this case making implicit reference not just to the Stalin cult, but also to that of Khrushchev.[75]

Brezhnev's first big outing as party leader came on 19 October, as he welcomed cosmonauts Komarov, Feoktistov and Egorov back to Moscow. Banners and portraits adorned the buildings of the capital once again and large crowds came to meet the latest returning heroes at the customary rally. After congratulating the cosmonauts and making the requisite statements about the Soviet people's love of the party and the dangers of capitalist war-mongering, Brezhnev segued into something approaching a 'mission statement' for the new leadership team. Although he spoke only briefly and quite vaguely, he took much the same line as Malenkov had in his speech at Stalin's funeral, emphasising that raising living standards was now a key goal and insisting that 'our Party wants all Soviet people to live a better, more secure and more cultured life with each passing year'.[76] The distinct vision of socialist modernity that Khrushchev had sought to establish was now blurring into a more overtly capitalistic focus on mass consumption as testament to regime legitimacy.[77] Indeed, many citizens would remember the two decades that followed as the best years of the Soviet system, since the Brezhnev era delivered not just more goods in the shops, but also better wages, more extensive welfare provision and more free time.[78]

The anniversary of the revolution on 7 November 1964 came to serve as a kind of coronation for Leonid Brezhnev. A host of leading figures from allied regimes and fraternal parties headed to Moscow, including Che Guevara from Cuba, Kim Il-sung from North Korea and Zhou Enlai from China, as well as Hungarian leader János Kádár, East Germany's Walter Ulbricht and Poland's Władysław Gomułka. Brezhnev said all the things that any Soviet leader would say on such occasions, boasting of great achievements since 1917 and telling of how 'glorious October' had shaped the course of global history. Again, he emphasised the importance of raising consumption levels, naming items – refrigerators, television sets, bicycles and clothes – which he announced would soon become better in quality and more widely available, and he pointed to recent moves to raise wages and strengthen the country's pension provisions, also promising greater investment in public infrastructure such as schools, healthcare and childcare.

Aware that his continued support for peaceful co-existence with the West – which he made clear was not predicated on Soviet ideological compromise, but on the desire to avoid ruinous nuclear war – was not what Chinese comrades wanted to hear, Brezhnev also restated Soviet support for 'the reunification of Taiwan with China'. Concluding his remarks, Brezhnev recognised that the Twentieth Party Congress had laid the foundations for the restoration of genuinely Leninist norms in the life of the party, adding that the October plenum of 1964 (at which Khrushchev was removed) had been an important landmark in ensuring that the resolutions of the Twentieth Party Congress were carried out in practice.

It was announced in November 1964 that the unpopular restrictions on the size of peasants' private plots, which had been introduced by Khrushchev in 1955, were now being lifted. Most of the country was shifted from a six-day to a five-day working week, bringing more leisure time for millions of citizens. In August 1965, *Pravda* acknowledged that recent anti-religious efforts had failed to bear fruit and a gentler tone was now to be taken. Construction of new apartments not only continued, but speeded up.

Car production, too, was now made a higher priority, with a clear goal of making private ownership of a vehicle a realistic aspiration for citizens.[79] When his first congress as party leader came around in March 1966, the central point of Brezhnev's keynote speech was again his bid to achieve a substantial rise in efforts to satisfy the people's material and cultural desires. From the outset, then, Brezhnev seized upon increased consumption for Soviet citizens as the primary way in which to distinguish his own rule from that of Khrushchev.[80] On the foreign policy front, he would soon begin ramping up Soviet rhetoric condemning the Americans' rapidly escalating war in Vietnam, as well as working to mobilise global opinion and sending increasing amounts of military aid to the Vietnamese.

Before long, the new leadership team had its first great triumph in the space race. Following the first three-person mission in October 1964, on 18 March 1965 cosmonauts Pavel Belyaev and Alexei Leonov became the latest to go into orbit. What made their mission so significant was that Leonov undertook the first ever space walk, exiting the Voskhod capsule through an airlock and spending around twelve minutes floating free in space, attached to the ship by a length of cord. Live television pictures of Leonov dangling in space quickly became iconic, and international acclaim again followed for the latest success. But the trip more than once came close to tragedy. First, Leonov's space suit inflated badly while outside the craft, and he was only just able to make it back in through the airlock after much struggling. Following that, a systems malfunction led to the air inside the craft becoming overly enriched with oxygen, meaning that the pair would almost certainly be burned alive at the merest hint of a spark. Lastly, another malfunction then meant Leonov and Belyaev also had to undertake a manual re-entry into the atmosphere. They eventually landed off target, in remote forests, where they had to wait overnight in sub-zero temperatures for the rescue teams to find them.[81]

Back on the ground, from the second half of the 1960s villagers across the USSR gained a much more concrete sense of things improving materially.[82] By that time, though, a long-term wave of mass migration (which followed earlier waves in the late tsarist period and during Stalinist industrialisation) was seeing around 1.5 million people departing the countryside for towns every year.[83] Those leaving for urban centres were overwhelmingly the young and talented – the very people on whom any hope of a prosperous future for the village relied. In 1967, one writer in *Literaturnaya gazeta* bemoaned the outflow of such people from rural areas, describing how a particular village in the Smolensk region had just one man and no women aged between twenty and thirty years, while another village had not hosted a single wedding in six years. Of the ninety-three milkmaids on one collective farm, the article reported, just one had completed secondary education; the author went on to add that almost all young people who did complete secondary education left the village, never to return.[84]

Like his predecessor, Brezhnev early on made his own bid to turn around the failing Soviet countryside. More investment in extending rural infrastructure and mechanisation of farm work soon followed. The prices that the state paid to collective farms for the produce that they handed over were also raised. From January 1965, pension provision was extended to Soviet villagers (almost a full decade after being introduced for urban residents), covering welfare not just for old age, but also for illness and loss of a family breadwinner, with additional material support for the poorest families and for disabled citizens soon to follow. A substantial proportion of collective farms' existing debts were cancelled. Maternity allowances for collective farm women were also codified at this point, granting fifty-six days both before and after delivery. August 1965 saw a new decree providing rural children with free transport to take them to school. The following year, new legislation guaranteed collective farm members a minimum wage for their work for the first time. This helped to improve the lot of rural women in particular, since they were the ones who did the vast majority of unskilled or unmechanised jobs, which typically paid the lowest wages.[85] No less important, 1965 also saw the end of a fundamental unfairness that had persisted right through the Khrushchev years and had explicitly marked peasants out as second-class citizens in the USSR. In granting collective farmers access to internal passports that year, the Soviet authorities were finally also giving them the right to work and rent accommodation away from their home village, without first having to obtain permission. Naturally, this did not much help the problem of rural population decline, but it did open new possibilities for tens of millions to change their lives.

Economic reform also suggested a new willingness to look pragmatically at important problems that the country faced. A number of leading economists had for some time been quietly advocating far-reaching changes, but with little impact.[86] Kosygin now took the matter on. A substantial drive to expand foreign trade ensued, and imported technology was increasingly sought out to lift strategic sectors – like the oil industry – in order to make them more competitive globally. The USSR was soon becoming a major energy provider to Europe and beyond, as more and more rich deposits of oil and gas were found and exploited. Similarly, a deal was signed with the Italian automobile maker Fiat in August 1966 to build a huge new car plant inside the Soviet Union, with Soviet workers there being trained in the very latest car production methods. In September 1965, the *sovnarkhozy* (regional economic councils) that Khrushchev had introduced were formally abandoned. No less significant, from 1965 a new research institute was set up to study consumer behaviour, the better to meet popular demand in the shops.[87] Taken together, these measures constituted an attempt to tackle at least some of the fundamental problems afflicting the Soviet economy: improving productivity, becoming more responsive to buyers' wants and needs and raising the sometimes abysmal quality of goods that were produced. As Kosygin framed it for the public, building the material base for communism, raising people's welfare and strengthening the country militarily all depended on the success of economic reform.[88]

Commonly known as the Kosygin reforms, changes to the structure of the economic system were also announced in autumn 1965. Previously, enterprises had been given tightly defined orders from the centre and rewarded primarily for fulfilment of numerical plan targets. This had contributed to problems with the quality of goods (since it was quantity that counted most) and had made factories reluctant to assimilate new technologies and respond to changing demand (since any such adaptation necessarily slowed down production for a time). Now, enterprises were to be given increased autonomy to shape their own trading arrangements. They began to study consumers' wants and needs more carefully, and an enterprise's success was to be measured (and its managers, in particular, rewarded) not with reference to total items produced, but by items actually sold, by how much any given factory earned relative to what it spent on wages and materials, by how effectively it adopted new products and more. Beginning with an initial 26,000 major enterprises in 1966, the plan was to roll the new system out everywhere in due course, transforming the future of the Soviet economy.[89] The early results seemed promising, and the five-year plan between 1966 and 1970 would prove one of the country's most successful yet; but the politics behind the reform proved tricky. There was still no real allowance made for even small-scale private enterprise, but the growing attention paid to market forces and the reduced influence for central planning bodies were problematic ideologically, especially once the initial burst of dynamism from the new leadership team slowed and a more conservative course began to emerge.

There was also an important new message being sent out to Soviet officialdom. After providing another thinly veiled critique of Khrushchev's leadership style, the ideological journal *Partiinaya zhizn* (*Party Life*) acknowledged that underperforming officials had to be replaced, but then went on to condemn attempts to 'pass off frequent changes in cadres as a sign of constant attention towards them', adding that, in fact, 'such instances testify to exactly the opposite'.[90] What this indicated, in particular, was a rejection of Khrushchev's 1961 decision to establish fixed-term limits for officials and the start of what would become known as the 'stability of cadres' principle. This was to be a hallmark of the Brezhnev years, and one that not only earned the new leadership the enduring loyalty of officials and bureaucrats throughout the country, but also created long-term conditions in which corruption flourished at all levels, social mobility slowed dramatically and political stagnation steadily took hold, as legions of (mostly) old men remained in post, enjoying the perks and prestige on offer until they died.

As Zhou Enlai's presence in Moscow for the 7 November celebrations in 1964 suggested, one of the early tasks of the new leadership was to find out whether fences might now be mended with China. The open polemics were reined in, and the initial signs coming from Beijing seemed positive. On 19 October, *Pravda* had published a communiqué from the Chinese leadership, offering congratulations to Brezhnev and Kosygin on their new posts, celebrating Soviet achievements and wishing future successes, adding 'may the communist parties of China and the Soviet union unite on the basis of Marxism-Leninism and proletarian internationalism'. All the big guns of the Chinese leadership had their names affixed, including Mao Zedong, Zhou Enlai and Liu Shaoqi.[91] Certainly, removing Khrushchev was a vital precondition for rapprochement; but it had not changed the fundamental point that Beijing remained unwilling to countenance either any notion of Soviet seniority within the socialist camp or any hint of Chinese ideological impropriety. In short, return to the status quo ante between the two communist giants was contingent upon a complete Soviet climbdown on practically all aspects of the schism.[92] Few in the Kremlin felt that was a price worth paying. Although already on the verge of retirement, Mikoyan in particular was steadfastly opposed to any Soviet compromise of this nature.

However unlikely the chances of reconciliation already were, Minister of Defence Rodion Malinovsky killed them stone dead at the evening reception following Brezhnev's 7 November speech. With Malinovsky somewhat the worse for drink, he first offended the US ambassador with some strongly worded remarks about his country. Soon after that, the Chinese delegation, headed by Zhou, came over to Malinovsky to express its agreement. Malinovsky replied by suggesting a toast to Sino-Soviet friendship, before adding 'Now that we've kicked out our Nikita, why don't you do the same to your Mao Zedong? Then we'll all get along just fine.' Stunned at this horrendously indiscreet behaviour, and well aware that Mao was perennially on the lookout for any hint of collusion with the USSR among his comrades, Zhou left the reception at once and the Chinese delegation headed home soon after.[93] There was to be no coming back from this. In January 1965, Kosygin went to Beijing for talks, but left without making any progress, once he had refused to disavow previous Soviet condemnation of Chinese behaviour.[94] In June 1965, Shelepin (perhaps the key individual seeking rapprochement) proposed drawing up a new friendship agreement between the two countries. But the idea was flatly rejected by Beijing, with the Chinese leadership insisting that the CPSU was now a bourgeois party and China's number one enemy.[95]

Over the next couple of years, relations between the two countries deteriorated even further. At first the Soviet leadership tried to take the high ground, choosing not to retaliate in kind against endless Chinese polemics and accusations. With the bloodbath of Mao's Cultural Revolution getting under way, in August 1966 the Soviet embassy in Beijing was besieged by protesters for days on end. With regular border infringements from China and increasingly shrill domestic propaganda aimed at the USSR (which still included claims on Soviet territory), the leaders in Moscow sensed war approaching.[96] When a small party of Chinese visitors to Lenin's mausoleum clashed with Moscow police in January 1967, the situation grew tenser still. Back in Beijing, the Soviet embassy was again besieged for more than two weeks, with diplomats' families having to be exfiltrated (with some considerable difficulty and intimidation). Loudspeakers erected outside the embassy blared attacks on the USSR, and protesters at one stage broke into the embassy grounds and tried to set the building on fire. That summer, China also carried out its first successful hydrogen bomb test. Unsurprisingly, on the Soviet side of the shared border, a major military build-up was gathering pace.[97]

Relations with China were not the only tricky question facing the new leadership. Plenty of observers inside and outside the USSR were soon trying to work out what the changes in the Kremlin meant in regard to Stalin. Here, the signals were decidedly mixed. As noted above, both *Pravda* and Brezhnev had quickly reaffirmed that the party line approved at the Twentieth and Twenty-Second Party Congresses remained valid, though they had also tweaked the meaning somewhat, shifting focus away from the Stalin cult specifically to cults more broadly. Even so, with Khrushchev gone and Mikoyan soon to follow him out the door, there was no longer any notable voice among the very top-level elite with anything like an anti-Stalin political agenda.

The line on Stalin had not yet changed entirely, however. A full month after Khrushchev's removal, on 18 November 1964, a newspaper article appeared, commemorating what would have been the seventy-fifth birthday of Stanislav Kosior, whose groundless arrest and execution Khrushchev had discussed in the Secret Speech. Describing him as an 'outstanding figure of the Communist Party and Soviet state', the piece outlined his achievements and contributions. It then told readers that 'S.V. Kosior shared the fate of many disciples of Lenin. He fell victim to arbitrary rule in the years of the Stalin cult.' The article cast his resistance to 'heavy-handed' rule in a clearly positive light, making it plain that his repression had been baseless, and that Stalin had been to blame.[98] Before much longer, though, the subject of Stalinist repressions would be off limits.

The Stalin question was mostly a source of debate behind the scenes. Fedor Burlatsky described an encounter in February 1965, in which Brezhnev had him look over a draft speech that had been sent from Shelepin for the upcoming celebrations to mark the twentieth anniversary of the victory over

Nazi Germany. According to Burlatsky, the draft was 'nothing less than a demand in the spirit of open neo-Stalinism for a complete reconsideration of all Party policy under Khrushchev'. Among the points that Shelepin was proposing were a restoration of Stalin's 'good name', renunciation of the Third Party Programme, abrogation of the policy of peaceful co-existence, a re-establishment of warm relations with Mao and again a denunciation of Tito's Yugoslavia. Apparently, Brezhnev did not grasp the enormity of what the draft said, but his cautious nature and wish to avoid controversy made it possible for Burlatsky to talk him out of supporting Shelepin's speech. The eventual report that Brezhnev gave to mark the anniversary mentioned Stalin only once and presented no substantial change of direction.[99]

Another potential fork in the road presented itself as the Twenty-Third Party Congress approached, with both pro- and anti-Stalin forces expecting important developments. In February 1966, a petition was sent to Brezhnev expressing fears that the congress would be used to rehabilitate Stalin. Twenty-five luminaries, from the worlds of science and culture in particular, affixed their names, including Igor Tamm, Petr Kapitsa and Andrei Sakharov, as well as Konstantin Paustovsky, Mikhail Romm and Maya Plisetskaya. Arbatov wrote of 'serious battles' being fought off stage, with political advisers especially pushing to retain the previous line on peaceful co-existence with the West and to ensure that the congress in spring 1966 was not seized on as a chance to reverse the policy lines established at the Twentieth and Twenty-Second Congresses. This proved possible, according to Arbatov, because Brezhnev was prepared to listen to expert advisers when they warned of the incalculable damage to Soviet standing that would surely follow any re-embrace of Stalin.[100] Before long, though, hardline members of the elite set to work weeding out such liberal-minded apparatchiks in their midst.[101] Ultimately, Brezhnev settled on a compromise position: making clear that the past should no longer be rubbished and accepting that serious mistakes and grievous crimes had occurred.

Even so, signs of changing positions on Stalinism were there to see for those who looked. The decision was taken to drop the Khrushchev-era title 'first secretary' and revert to the 'general secretary' branding of the Stalin years, while the 'Presidium' was similarly switched back to the 'Politburo' at the Twenty-Third Congress (to loud applause from delegates), with Khrushchev's new rules on term limits for officials also formally abandoned. When long-term Stalin ally Kliment Voroshilov died in 1969, he was buried with great fanfare. The following year, a bust was finally placed on Stalin's previously unmarked grave in the Kremlin wall. Already slowed to a trickle, the process of rehabilitating victims of Stalinist repression had essentially stopped, and would not start again until the late 1980s.

While the examples outlined above clearly constituted worrying indicators, they did not really represent a full-fledged return to Stalinism and its fundamental indifference to the plight of the masses. In the early morning of 26 April 1966, a powerful earthquake hit Uzbekistan, with its epicentre right underneath the capital Tashkent. The death toll was not especially high for a major urban area, but damage to the built environment was extensive, with around 3 million square metres of buildings lost and most of the city centre reduced to rubble. It left perhaps 70,000 families without shelter and destroyed hospitals, gas mains and schools. The city was turned into a giant tent camp, as powerful aftershocks went on for days.[102] Fairly quickly, though, and in sharp contrast to the regime's response when earthquakes had hit Turkmenistan and Tajikistan in 1948 and 1949, respectively, the disaster became a vehicle to show compassion and fraternity. Brezhnev and Kosygin immediately flew to the city, promising that rebuilding was a top priority and that the 'Soviet family' would rally round.

Among others, the poet Andrei Voznesensky also flew in right away, giving performances for the city's residents and writing about the situation on the ground for the country's newspapers, mobilising readers to do what they could to help. Many of the local children were packed off to summer camps and schools elsewhere around the USSR to get them away from danger. The key facet of aid to Tashkent, though, was the massive rebuilding effort that was soon dubbed 'the construction project of the century'. The Komsomol, in particular, mobilised tens of thousands of its members from Ukraine, Lithuania, Russia, Georgia and elsewhere to head across country to start rebuilding the Uzbek capital.[103] Progress was not without its problems – including some hasty city planning that was decidedly unsympathetic to local customs and needs; but it was rapid.[104] Within weeks, new buildings were springing up, and by the time most of the construction teams left around the end of 1967, Tashkent was a city transformed.

Alongside the new focus on stability and raising living standards, the predominant emotional and philosophical tone of the coming era had also been struck within a few months of the change in the Kremlin, with the twentieth anniversary of Victory Day in May 1965. The need to prepare for a potential new war (against an ally from the previous one) had seen Stalin fairly quickly call a halt to the mass glorification of Soviet victory in the Great Patriotic War.[105] This shifted somewhat under Khrushchev, as the war again became a setting for key movies like *Ballad of a Soldier* and *The Cranes Are Flying*, along with popular novels like Konstantin Simonov's *The Living and the Dead*. New memorials were also erected, and iconic sites such as Leningrad's Piskarevskoe cemetery and the Stalingrad memorial complex were either opened or else went into construction, with the anniversary of Victory Day on 9 May again an occasion for organised public celebration around the country.

While the twentieth anniversary of the victory did not mark an entirely new departure regarding war commemoration, it certainly did represent a significant gear change. For the first time since 1948, 9 May was again declared a public holiday (and would remain so thereafter). On the anniversary, theatres staged plays about the war; the media filled with tales of heroism for the motherland; parades, concerts and speeches celebrating veterans filled the country's public spaces, as people remembered those lost and celebrated a victory hard won. The pantheon of war heroes and forms of heroism steadily expanded, new symbols and discourses of commemoration were codified, and every republic, town, factory and school had a plethora of its own heroes to celebrate.[106] It is worth remembering in this context that veterans – both male and female – were to be found throughout Soviet society (as were war orphans and widows), and most were not yet old: in 1965, some were still in their thirties. In short, this was a past that was very much still alive, and it resonated powerfully.

All this was followed in October 1966 by a stream of events commemorating the twenty-fifth anniversary of the Battle of Moscow and then by a grandiose public ceremony for the reinterment in the centre of the capital of an unknown soldier in December 1966. Then there was the ceremonial lighting of an eternal flame at the new resting place of the Unknown Soldier in May 1967 – symbolically lit from the memorial at Leningrad's Field of

Mars, where many heroes of the 1917 revolution were interred. Still in charge of the country's television output at the time, Nikolai Mesyatsev recalled floods of letters from viewers deeply moved by the coverage they watched when such events were screened.[107] War commemoration was becoming an emotional resource that was ever more systematically tapped by the authorities. Millions of young people undertook hikes around battle sites, held meetings with veterans, lovingly created exhibitions and worked to identify human remains that they unearthed. All manner of museums and new memorials sprang up across the country, while television shows and newspaper columns were filled with tales of heroic deeds in the service of the motherland. Importantly, this was to be a broadly inclusive sphere of commemoration, with families, schools, towns and republics encouraged to show pride in their own heroes, as practically the whole country was woven into the celebratory narrative.[108]

The focus on glorification of the victory in war was, in many senses, ideal for Leonid Brezhnev, especially. Unlike some key rivals, he had seen active service on several fronts (albeit as a political commissar) and was able to stake out a prime place for himself within the new cult. Indeed, unlike his predecessor, Brezhnev made the war years a central plot line of his own personal story, with medals, anecdotes and later (ghost-written) memoirs all establishing his credentials. This also helped drive up the institutional prestige and lobbying power of the military establishment, which found that Brezhnev offered a far more sympathetic ear to its requests than Khrushchev had. Similarly, veterans' groups grew rapidly and became increasingly prominent, successfully putting forward their case for better welfare provision and positioning themselves as models of patriotism (and in many cases also 'manliness') for the country's youth to emulate.[109]

Many commentators have posited that this emerging war cult became a new legitimating myth for the Soviet system: as expectations of building a utopian communist future dulled, so the authorities implicitly shifted the centre of the regime's claim to legitimacy to credit won for the defeat of Nazism. After all, the war victory was one of the few points around which Soviet society was (with the exception of those areas annexed in the course of the victory) practically unified in its acclaim. Glorification of the defeat of Nazism also intertwined with that of the October 1917 Revolution, though, and the former was still presented as having been rooted in the latter. More broadly, war commemoration became a vessel in which all kinds of different emotions and motivations could co-exist: nostalgia for the Stalin years, local and all-union patriotism and internationalist anti-fascism and more besides. We might also think of the new war cult as a surrogate not just for declining ideological enthusiasm, but also for the Stalin cult in particular, in that it afforded a deeply emotional and grassroots-level interaction with regime 'greatness' that even the space victories had not quite reached.

More broadly still, the war cult reflected the start of a shift away from a predominant Khrushchev-era focus on modernity and progress into the future, and towards celebration of a glorious past. Nonetheless, it would be easy to overstate the scope of change that followed in the immediate aftermath of Khrushchev's removal from power. The preceding decade had clearly left a deep imprint on the country – in political, social and cultural affairs – that would be almost impossible to expunge fully, even if the new leadership team had set its mind on such a thing. Nonetheless, it would not be too long before the first real harbingers of resurgent regime conservatism appeared.

10

'DIFFERENT, BUT NOT AN ENEMY'

On 8 September 1965, KGB officers seized the noted literary critic Andrei Sinyavsky at a bus stop in central Moscow. Four days later, his friend Yuli Daniel was arrested at the airport as he returned to the capital from a trip to Novosibirsk. Both men had suspected for some time that trouble was coming. For several years, they had been writing and smuggling abroad satirical literary works under the pseudonyms Abram Tertz (Sinyavsky) and Nikolai Arzhak (Daniel), and for almost as long the KGB had been working hard to uncover the true identities of Tertz and Arzhak. Catching and then punishing the pair, however, would prove to be the start of a much longer saga. As one observer of the Soviet dissident movement would point out a few years later: 'Hundreds of lines could be drawn connecting individual acts of protest . . . and most of them would converge on the trial of Sinyavsky and Daniel.'[1] More widely, the case would prove a critical marker in the new Brezhnev regime's increasing conservatism.

An emerging heterodoxy

Although for many observers it was one of the defining moments of the Brezhnev era, the movement that emerged in the wake of the Sinyavsky and Daniel affair was unmistakably rooted in the developments of the preceding decade. Perhaps the most important thing in this context was the emergence of samizdat literature: a phenomenon that one authority on the subject has described as 'the infrastructure of independent thought in the USSR'.[2] Samizdat became the principal means by which many citizens began to evade the regime's vast censorship apparatus. By inserting multiple carbon papers into one's typewriter – these having become increasingly available to buy, thanks to rising consumerism – and then hitting the keys hard as one typed, it was possible to produce as many as nine or ten physical copies (albeit flimsy and faint) of any given document. These could then be passed on to friends and acquaintances, who might each type up another set of copies and distribute them to new people, repeating the same process again and again. Although distinctly low-tech, this was a crucial format for independent communication that was almost limitless in terms of its potential scale, and another information source over which the authorities always struggled to exert control.

Even under Stalin, there had been occasional instances of friends sharing illicit literature among themselves; but it was really from the mid- to late 1950s that the samizdat phenomenon began to emerge in a substantial way. Much of the early samizdat in circulation centred on literary works by proscribed domestic writers like Ivan Bunin and Marina Tsvetaeva (*Dr Zhivago* soon joined these ranks) or foreign authors like George Orwell and Arthur Koestler. The self-publishing phenomenon then entered its next phase in 1959, after a Muscovite named Alexander Ginzburg compiled a collection of unpublished works by new writers, called *Sintaksis* (*Syntaxis*). This was the first known instance of literature produced specifically for samizdat, rather than simply appearing there once regular avenues for publication were closed.[3] The importance of this lay in the fact that self-censorship – vital if one entertained hopes for publication – was typically no less swingeing than that imposed by the official censor, *Glavlit*. Having no aspirations for official publication naturally undercut self-censorship.

By the end of 1960, Ginzburg had already put out three volumes of *Sintaksis*. In their contents these tended not to be outright oppositional – some of the material was not explicitly political at all – but nonetheless still fell short of being ideologically acceptable to officialdom. As he prepared a fourth volume in 1961, Ginzburg was arrested.

Regardless of Ginzburg's arrest, new samizdat journals kept cropping up. After *Sintaksis* there quickly followed *Bumerang* (*Boomerang*), *Feniks* (*Phoenix*) and *Sfinksy* (*Sphinxes*), each adding to the flow of uncensored literature in circulation. In late 1964, the historian and party member Roy Medvedev began compiling one of the most enduring of all samizdat periodicals, known abroad as *Political Diary* (though it never had an official title inside the USSR) and consisting mainly of material such as extracts from camp memoirs or leaked accounts of events like Khrushchev's removal. The readership of Medvedev's journal was kept deliberately small, but it included numerous reform-minded members of the top party apparatus, as well as some of the country's scientific and cultural elite.[4]

There is little we can say for sure about the size of the readership of samizdat. One former student claimed that in the early 1960s there were more people carrying samizdat than textbooks in the main courtyard of Moscow State University.[5] Similarly, Vasily Aksenov recalled that 'all of young Moscow was talking about *Sintaksis*' in 1960.[6] Even in the capital, though, by no means everyone (or even all intellectuals) was reading samizdat, and in the provinces it could be much harder to find. As scholars have since pointed out, Cold War-era claims that samizdat became the only place where one could find truly 'honest' literature in the USSR were a major oversimplification.[7] Nonetheless, samizdat was a medium through which countless important works – from gulag memoirs (such as Varlam Shalamov's *Kolyma Tales* and Evgeniya Ginzburg's *Into the Whirlwind*) to novels, cultural criticism, treatises and much more – emerged for Soviet audiences, along with a plethora of rather less-lofty items, covering everything from football to pornography. All this was important because it helped open up a non-official public sphere, where issues of all kinds could be explored without direct 'supervision'.

Soon, another young Muscovite named Andrei Amalrik began using his connections with foreigners – in large part developed through organising unofficial art exhibitions – to have samizdat works smuggled abroad, in the process opening up the Soviet authorities' domestic actions to far greater international scrutiny. By the time Amalrik was arrested on trumped-up charges of parasitism in 1965, there was no stopping the steady flow of unsanctioned literature from reaching the outside world. From there, much of it was broadcast back to Soviet listeners by the likes of Radio Liberty and the BBC.

Another notable development, which paralleled the emerging samizdat scene in its 'do it yourself' ethic, was the Bard Movement. What might in the West be called singer-songwriters, 'Bards' typically sang or spoke their own poetry and accompanied themselves on guitar. In this context, they have sometimes been categorised alongside fellow 'guitar poets' elsewhere, such as Bob Dylan and Pete Seeger in the US, Georges Brassens in France and Victor

Jara in Chile.[8] In deliberate contrast to the pomp and polish of 'official' Soviet music by performers like Iosif Kobzon, they tended to be rough and ready in their approach to both singing and playing guitar, prioritising 'authenticity' and 'sincerity' over mastery of technique.[9] Only a few Bards ever positioned themselves explicitly as protest singers; but they were virtually all notable for writing and singing about sides of Soviet life that were deemed by officialdom to be unsuitable for the public sphere, such as labour camps, people killed in the war, criminal subculture, drunkenness and despair.

With regular concert halls and clubs mostly closed to them since they remained outside the official cultural establishment, Bards were largely confined to playing their gigs in friends' packed apartments. Vladimir Vysotsky, for example, was by the mid-1960s a regular performer at Andrei Sinyavsky's Moscow home. In time, both Bulat Okudzhava (whose poetry had appeared in the samizdat journal *Sintaksis*) and Vysotsky, in particular, gained major popularity and even a degree of official recognition, though others like Alexander Galich and Yuli Kim were forever subject to restrictions and persecution for their more overtly critical songs and views.[10] Many of those who attended or hosted these unofficial concerts came from among the capital's non-conformist cultural intelligentsia – also the milieu from which samizdat flowed most copiously. Furthermore, thanks to the growing ownership of cassette recorders, the songs that Bards played were sometimes also captured on tape and thus passed from person to person in a phenomenon that became known as *magnitizdat* (essentially, samizdat on tape).

One of the most significant developments to emerge from this non-conformist milieu was a series of open-air poetry readings in central Moscow. Things first began in July 1958, when a statue dedicated to the popular revolutionary-era poet Vladimir Mayakovsky was unveiled in the city square named in his honour. The celebrations included a line-up of officially approved speakers reciting both Mayakovsky's poetry and their own. As the scheduled events wound down, others then began to give impromptu readings around the base of the statue. Having enjoyed themselves, many agreed to return a week later, and soon these unofficial recitals were becoming a regular fixture of Saturday and Sunday evenings. One early participant recalled that the readings were 'the only place in the country where real freedom of speech existed', adding that most attendees still hoped and believed that some kind of communist renewal was possible now that Stalin was gone.[11] Nonetheless, the authorities remained apprehensive, especially since the events were so public in nature. Thanks to police intimidation and threats to expel participants from their places of work or study, the first series of readings at Mayakovsky Square was quietly brought to a close.

Then, in the summer of 1960, Vladimir Bukovsky and Vladimir Osipov – neither of whom had been involved in the initial sessions – decided to restart the unofficial poetry recitals at Mayakovsky Square. As he described it years later, Bukovsky saw this as a means by which to bring together all manner of non-conformists from across Moscow and beyond.[12] Osipov was apparently rather more radical in intent, seeking to emulate the Petőfi Circle that had played a major role in transforming cultural ferment into outright rebellion in Hungary during 1956.

Soon, the readings were up and running again. Typically at weekends, perhaps a few hundred attendees would gather in the square in the evening, usually staying until after midnight. Those wishing to do so simply got up to read and a cluster of people would form around them to listen. Many read their own work, but some also read poems by the likes of Mayakovsky, Pasternak and Akhmatova. Others were there solely to listen. Occasional visitors came from as far away as Leningrad and Kiev to attend the readings. Various of the initial samizdat poetry journals that appeared in the early 1960s were intimately connected to the gatherings in Mayakovsky Square: their compilers and typists would be among the participants, and the poems they contained may already have been read out dozens of times around the base of the statue. For some attendees, these poetry meetings became the single most important thing in the world.[13] One session in the middle of April 1961 – timed to commemorate the anniversary of Mayakovsky's suicide – drew a particularly large crowd, since it coincided with the public celebrations of Gagarin's space flight. The bigger the public gathering, though, the more uneasy the authorities became, and this particular evening ended in chaos, as aggressive policing turned the event into a 'gigantic fist-fight' according to Bukovsky.[14]

The visible policing of these poetry readings mostly involved the militia and Komsomol volunteer patrols, though the KGB naturally also had people circulating within the crowds. First came a softer approach by the authorities, with Moscow Komsomol officials offering to provide the organisers with their own venue in which to perform (which would have both pulled the readings away from public space and ensured Komsomol 'supervision', since that was the price to be paid for its patronage). When those involved refused to be co-opted in such a way, the approach hardened. Participants were covertly photographed and detained for questioning by police as they passed through nearby metro stations on their way to the square. In the square itself, police and Komsomol patrols engaged in all manner of provocations, starting fights with attendees and detaining people on flimsy pretexts, such as public swearing. Readers, in particular, had to be protected from the police, usually by audience members forming a human chain around them as they read. Once their performance was over, people helped get readers safely away from watching police, sometimes changing their clothes or providing decoys, distractions and escorts that ensured they could make it to the bus or metro without being grabbed. One regular reader, Alisa Gadasina, recalled that she even carried brass knuckles in her pocket in case she was subjected to police attack as she left the square.[15] Having already received several threatening warnings as the ringleader, Bukovsky was abducted one night as he headed home, bundled into a waiting car and driven to an abandoned building, where he was beaten for several hours before being warned that he would be killed if he went to the square again.[16]

Away from the public meetings, many participants also gathered at each other's apartments around the capital for informal 'salons' (a conscious appropriation of pre-revolutionary intelligentsia terminology), where talk about politics and culture naturally proved rather more open. One reader, Apollon Shukht, said that Osipov, in particular, began going to all the different salons, in order to seek out fellow oppositional types.[17] Though few attendees knew of it at the time, in the summer of 1961 Osipov and a handful of others began talking about a plot to assassinate Khrushchev. Friends persuaded them to abandon the idea before it progressed beyond talk, but the KGB got wind of it anyway (some later suggested the seed had in fact been sown by a KGB agent) and a slew of arrests followed. Osipov and some others were jailed, and not long after that Bukovsky was confined to a psychiatric institution. The poetry readings were once again over, but the bid to bring together non-conformists and critics had already borne fruit.

337

On 29 November 1963, an important new affair began with a short piece in the newspaper *Vecherny Leningrad* (*Evening Leningrad*). In it, the future winner of the Nobel Prize for Literature, Joseph Brodsky, was denounced as a 'dissolute and cynical parasite' and his poetry branded 'pornography'. Twenty-three years old at the time, and scraping a meagre living mostly through occasional translating work, Brodsky had not yet found any real fame, though he had already acquired some highly regarded admirers, including the legendary Leningrad poet Anna Akhmatova. The principal author of the denunciation, Yakov Lerner, had for some time made it his business to hassle Brodsky and a number of Leningrad's other bohemian intellectuals. For his part, Brodsky had already received a couple of orders to find regular employment or else face the consequences, and he was temporarily detained after several of his poems were published in Ginzburg's samizdat collection *Sintaksis*. Reflecting on events many years later, he suggested that by November 1963 his KGB file had simply grown too thick not to be acted upon.[18]

Once Lerner's denunciation appeared in the newspaper, it was straight away obvious to the young poet that a legal case against him was imminent. In a false step that could easily have proven ruinous, he checked himself into a psychiatric hospital during December 1963, in a misguided bid to be declared unfit for trial. Quickly realising the error he had made, Brodsky immediately begged friends to help get him back out of the hospital. Once released, he flitted from place to place as he waited for the situation to blow over. Then, on returning to Leningrad, he was arrested on the street in the middle of February 1964 and charged with parasitism. In what was to prove a critical move, his friend and mentor Akhmatova made contact with the journalist Frida Vigdorova to enlist her help in the ensuing fight for Brodsky's freedom. Vigdorova had already exposed shortcomings in a number of cases where individuals had been unjustly persecuted. Most notably, she had helped get the samizdat activist Andrei Amalrik reinstated at university after he was expelled in 1961, and she had also campaigned to get Boris Pasternak's lover Olga Ivinskaya and her daughter freed when they were jailed shortly after his death.[19]

As the trial opened on 18 February, the judge made her feelings clear from the outset, when she peremptorily ordered Brodsky to stand up straight. She then opened proceedings with a threat to have him thrown out of court if he did not answer questions properly. For his part, Brodsky asserted himself stoutly, refusing to apologise or to acknowledge any wrongdoing. Remarkably, his defence lawyer was no less robust, insisting in her opening statement that he had committed no crime, that he was not a parasite and that it was illegal for the authorities to hold him in custody. Ominously, though, the judge soon prorogued the hearing so that Brodsky could be sent for psychiatric evaluation and a decision on whether he was fit to be sentenced. The days he then spent in Leningrad's Pryazhka psychiatric hospital he later recalled as the hardest time of his entire life, and included being subjected to agonising sulphur injections and witnessing staff brutality towards his fellow patients.[20] On his first evening there, the man in the cot next to Brodsky's slit his wrists and bled to death.

Fortunately, doctors concluded that although he had various signs of mental illness, Brodsky was fit to face the law, and the court proceedings reconvened. The extent to which the whole affair was genuinely centred on Brodsky's employment status could be adduced from the fact that much of the trial was taken up with accusations about the content of his 'degenerate' poetry. Moreover, the similarity to other political trials in the USSR – with the verdict decided well in advance – can be gauged from the sign that hung on the courtroom door: 'Trial of the Parasite Brodsky'.[21] As before, the judge had no interest in acknowledging that his writing and translating efforts constituted real work. The proceedings were not just unfair, though: they were also shambolic at times. Several of the poems slated to be used as evidence for the prosecution, for example, had to be dropped because they turned out not to have been written by Brodsky. A number of stooges, designated as 'representatives of the public', were invited to speak, but it was soon apparent that none of them actually knew the accused or his poetry in any substantial way: one voiced baseless suspicions about why Brodsky had not served his military conscription; others expressed moral indignation at his poetry, but could not cite any offending lines specifically. The judge also counted as evidence of Brodsky's wrongdoing the letters of apparently outraged citizens that were sent to *Vecherny Leningrad* after he was denounced there by Lerner.

Even in the face of clear intimidation to toe the line, though, the first literary expert summoned to speak testified to the high quality of both

Brodsky's poetry and his translations, making it clear that the young man worked hard at his craft and lived very modestly. The second similarly described him as exceptionally gifted, with a bright future ahead of him as a writer. In his final remarks to the court, Brodsky insisted that he was not a parasite, but a poet – and one who would in future bring glory to his country. The judge saw things differently, however, and sentenced him to the maximum punishment available for parasitism: five years' exile from Leningrad, to be spent labouring on a collective farm in the far north of Russia.

Present in court throughout, Vigdorova wrote up copious notes as the trial progressed and, after the suspicious judge ordered her to stop writing, she later recorded events from memory at the end of each day. Not long after the trial was over, she released her transcript of proceedings into samizdat, and everyone could then see the shambles that she had witnessed. Subsequent KGB monitoring reports showed that Yevtushenko privately branded the trial 'fascistic', the writers Kornei Chukovsky and Samuil Marshak and the composer Dmitry Shostakovich all expressed outrage and promised to petition the highest authorities in Brodsky's defence.[22] Within a few months, Vigdorova's transcript had also made it abroad, where it began to garner international attention – BBC radio even broadcast a dramatisation of the trial in late 1964. In the sense that the previously unknown poet now attracted considerable attention abroad (his first volume of poetry would be published in the US while he was still in internal exile), all this was to a considerable extent the making of Brodsky's career.

The wider significance of the case lay partly in the fact that both Brodsky and his defenders had refused to submit. Importantly, friends and supporters also did not turn their backs on Brodsky, but instead sent warm clothes, chocolate, jam and writing materials to him in exile. The production and circulation of the trial transcript was another vital point of note, since it subjected the authorities' actions to outside scrutiny, and the process was duly replicated at numerous subsequent trials. A last matter to draw attention to was that the international response, in particular, had an impact – most notably including a personal letter of protest from French writer (and famous communist) Jean-Paul Sartre. With the country's highest judicial authorities seemingly embarrassed by the record of the abysmal court case, the whole affair was eventually reviewed and Brodsky was ultimately released from internal exile in September 1965. Vigdorova, however, had died of cancer the previous month (Brodsky would always keep a photograph of her on his desk thereafter). Andrei Sinyavsky and Yuli Daniel had also been arrested two weeks earlier.

Two writers on trial

The KGB's attempt to identify the mysterious writers Tertz and Arzhak had taken so long – Tertz (Sinyavsky) had started to send work abroad in 1956 and Arzhak (Daniel) in 1957 – that some questioned whether they really were writing from inside the USSR. In fact, Sinyavsky was present during a meeting at his own workplace, the Gorky Institute of World Literature, when an unsuspecting colleague had confidently asserted that Tertz was probably not Soviet at all. Having made lists of those with the necessary connections to smuggle work abroad, commissioned expert analyses of writing styles, intercepted mail, rifled through luggage at airports and spied on any number of suspects, the KGB had eventually settled on Yuli Daniel as one of the two perpetrators (actually, this was not a very closely guarded secret in the somewhat garrulous Daniel's wide social circle). Monitoring Daniel then led them to Sinyavsky, and by May 1964 the KGB had little doubt who both culprits really were. From then on, they worked to build a case against the pair, eavesdropping from the flat next door to Daniel's, following both of them in the street and listening in on their telephone calls.[23]

Sensing a crackdown beginning, news of the arrest of Sinyavsky and Daniel immediately caused alarm among the creative intelligentsia of the capital. Solzhenitsyn wrote that all of Moscow immediately began destroying or hiding samizdat.[24] Sinyavsky's close friend Igor Golomstock certainly did: he spent the whole night burning papers and secreting manuscripts.[25] In fact, during the few days between the arrest of Sinyavsky and of Daniel, the KGB had also swooped to seize Solzhenitsyn's hidden archive – an event which he later called 'the greatest misfortune in all my forty-seven years'.[26] Partly as a result of that seizure, Raisa Orlova and Lev Kopelev then carried out an emergency purge of the illicit manuscripts in their own apartment.[27]

Before October 1965 was out, the French newspaper *Le Monde* had started to draw international attention to the Sinyavsky and Daniel affair, followed not long after by the *Washington Post* and *The Times*. In November, members of International PEN wrote to Soviet Writers' Union boss Alexei Surkov to express their disquiet at the arrests, as did a group of prominent Australian writers. Members of the Nobel Prize committee (who, after much lobbying from Moscow, had recently awarded the Nobel Prize for Literature to Soviet establishment darling Mikhail Sholokhov) wrote to Culture Minister Furtseva, warning her of the damage being done to the Soviet Union's reputation abroad. When Sholokhov then spoke up against Sinyavsky and Daniel – implying that they ought to have been shot for their treachery – seventeen other Nobel laureates condemned him in an open letter. Collective letters of protest also came in to Moscow from Mexico, France, Italy, Chile, the Philippines and Japan, among others. One letter from India – where the USSR had long worked hard to build its soft power – featured 170 signatories from across the cultural establishment.[28]

One of the most important events of the Sinyavsky and Daniel affair took place more than a month before the case even reached trial. As Igor Golomstock spread the word of Sinyavsky's arrest, he ran into the mathematician Alexander Esenin-Volpin and told him the news. Volpin was the illegitimate son of the legendary poet Sergei Esenin (though his father had committed suicide while Volpin was still a baby) and had already undergone several spells of forced confinement in psychiatric units as a 'troublemaker'. Undaunted by this, Volpin remained a remarkable maverick. As one of those who first met him around this time recalled it, he 'seemed like a man from another planet, from a different century, with a different brain'.[29] In particular, he had for some time been arguing to friends that the Soviet Union had perfectly good laws and valuable safeguards against regime abuses, but that the authorities ignored these at will because the public let them. In short, he insisted that if citizens took Soviet laws seriously, the authorities would also be forced to do so.

Few took Volpin's line of thinking seriously until he successfully gained entry to the closed trial of Vladimir Osipov in 1961 (following his arrest for involvement in the aborted plot to kill Khrushchev) by waving a copy of the criminal code at the guards and showing them that he was legally entitled to enter. Vladimir Bukovsky later wrote that 'this absurd incident, with the comical Alik Volpin brandishing his criminal code like a magic wand to melt the doors of the court, was the beginning of our civil rights movement'.[30] What Volpin wanted when he heard of the arrest of Sinyavsky and Daniel was to make use of the constitutional right of Soviet citizens' to freedom of assembly.

Unlike some others, Volpin showed little interest in questions of artistic freedom in the case of Sinyavsky and Daniel. What he wanted was for the letter of the law to be observed, and there was no article of the criminal code that formally made it illegal to send literature abroad. After haggling for some time over how to respond, he and three others decided on a public 'meeting' (Volpin insisted that it should not be called a demonstration) at Moscow's Pushkin Square on 5 December, Constitution Day in the Soviet calendar. The quartet made up placards and leaflets and drafted a 'civic appeal', calling on people to join them and declaring that regime illegalities in previous years had 'cost the lives and freedom of millions of Soviet citizens. The bloody past demands that we are vigilant in the present.' Long before 5 December arrived, people all over the capital knew about the planned event. Moscow correspondents of Western newspapers were also aware, as were the Soviet authorities. Two of those who had been distributing the leaflets – Bukovsky and Vladimir Batshev – were seized on the streets at the start of December and locked up. Another participant named Yuliya Vishnevskaya – still a teenager at the time – was also apprehended and confined to a psychiatric unit shortly before the scheduled meeting. Sensibly, Volpin exited the capital, travelling to Georgia and only returning on the eve of the big day (and even then he did not risk spending the night at his own home).[31]

Knowing the likelihood of his being apprehended, Volpin and his wife Viktoriya spent much of 5 December travelling to and fro on Moscow's metro system in a bid to shake off potential KGB tails. Then they borrowed a wheelchair-type contraption from a friend, and Viktoriya managed to wheel her husband right up to the square undetected by the armies of KGB agents, police and others on patrol.[32] In all, there were about fifty people at the base of the Pushkin monument and perhaps as many as two hundred onlookers. One of those onlookers, Lyudmila Alexeyeva, recalled recognising various people she had seen before at Bulat Okudzhava concerts and exhibitions of foreign art.[33] A little while after 18:00, Volpin and the others unfurled placards that read 'We demand *glasnost* in the trial of Sinyavsky and Daniel' and 'Respect the constitution', along with calls for Bukovsky and Vishnevskaya to be released. KGB agents and foreign journalists alike instantly snapped away with their cameras, but it took only about thirty seconds for the signs to be ripped out of the protesters' hands and participants to be bundled into waiting cars. Even so, news of the protest made the front page of the *New York Times* and the calls for *glasnost* (openness) in the upcoming trial were then echoed by high-profile writers and thinkers abroad, including Norman Mailer, Italo Calvino, Doris Lessing, Bertrand Russell, Günter Grass and W.H. Auden, and broadcast back to Soviet audiences by the likes of Radio Liberty.

Like numerous others entangled in the Sinyavsky and Daniel affair, Mariya Rozanova and Larisa Bogoraz refused to accede to the old way of doing things. In years gone by, plenty of spouses had seen little option but to divorce and disown their husbands once they were branded enemies; but these women – the wives of Sinyavsky and Daniel, respectively – did no such thing. In fact, Daniel and Bogoraz had effectively separated as a couple some time previously, but she nonetheless stuck by him doggedly after his arrest. In mid-December 1965, she wrote to Brezhnev (and to the chief prosecutor and the editors of *Pravda* and *Izvestiya*) in her husband's defence, insisting that there was nothing anti-Soviet in his writing, that it was wholly unacceptable for writers to be jailed for their work and that the KGB and other officials were improperly declaring the guilt of the accused men before their trial. Citing the Universal Declaration of Human Rights, to which the Soviet regime was a signatory, she ended by demanding that both her husband and Sinyavsky be set free. Rozanova was little less assertive in her own letter to officials later that month, as she sketched a lineage of repression from 1937, through the Doctors' Plot, to her own husband's arrest. She reminded them that the Soviet constitution promised freedom both of speech and of the printed word, complained that investigators had threatened her during questioning and expressed concern about the kinds of pressure that were being applied to her husband. She ended the letter by all but daring the authorities to arrest her as well.[34]

Seeking to shape public opinion, on 13 January 1966 *Izvestiya* carried a lengthy and bitter attack on both Sinyavsky and Daniel and their supporters abroad. The latter were depicted as unscrupulous cold warriors seeking to undermine the USSR, but the two Soviet writers fared much worse. Frequently veering into hyperbole, the press castigated their 'hatred of our system and foul mockery of what is dearest to our motherland and people' and called their works 'shots fired in the back of a people fighting for peace on Earth and for universal happiness'.[35] Five days later, *Izvestiya* followed up with a number of letters from suitably outraged members of the public. One correspondent from Baku asserted that the people of Azerbaijan 'brand them with shame and contempt', while another from Voronezh called Sinyavsky and Daniel 'moral monsters' and demanded they be severely punished.[36] The Stalinist overtones were pretty clear.

The trial eventually began on 10 February and lasted for four days. Although declared open to the public, there was as usual little chance for supporters of the accused to enter. Instead, they stood outside every day in the cold, as did a number of curious foreign journalists. The pair were tried under article 70 of the criminal code (an updated version of the notorious article 58), for anti-Soviet agitation and propaganda, on the basis that they had sought to undermine the Soviet system by slandering it through their works. This was the first time ever that the Soviet regime had explicitly prosecuted writers for the content of their writing. The judge and the lead prosecutor repeatedly insisted on reading the words and thoughts of literary characters as the true words and thoughts of their authors. Daniel, in particular, railed against this spurious conception, reminding the court that even Sholokhov had written characters who criticised Soviet power.

In regard to Daniel, the authorities' attention during the trial centred mostly on his satirical story 'This is Moscow Speaking', in which, for a single day, the Soviet regime declares it legal for citizens to murder anyone over sixteen years of age – an event that ends in a mass score-settling with the country's leadership. Of the works that Sinyavsky had sent abroad, perhaps the most notable was an essay on the state of Soviet culture, entitled 'On Socialist Realism'. Sinyavsky's critique of Socialist Realism as a literary genre was nuanced and compelling (a Western account called it 'one of the most significant pieces of writing to come out of contemporary Russia'), rather than overtly hostile politically.[37] Once published abroad, several of the Tertz and Arzhak works had drawn considerable acclaim, with Tertz's work being translated into an impressive twenty-four languages. To the accusation that the very idea of a day of open murders was a disgraceful slander against the Soviet system, Daniel countered that it was so obviously a fantastical scenario that it could not possibly be taken seriously. Like Sinyavsky after him, he insisted that he had sent his work abroad not to help the country's enemies, but because he knew the works in question could never be published at home.

When his turn came, Sinyavsky was no less forthright, declaring from the beginning that he was not a political writer and that artistic work does not necessarily express one's political views. Both judge and prosecutor fired questions at him about everything from his depictions of Lenin to the design of the dust jacket for one overseas edition of his work (the judge speculated that the juxtaposition of black and red was supposed to show some kind of darkness in the Soviet system – Sinyavsky bluntly responded that he had no input whatsoever into questions of cover design). As with Daniel's 'day of open murders', passages of Sinyavsky's story *Lyubimov* (in which members of the security organs discuss attaching filters to the bottom of people's toilets, in order to catch any manuscripts that are flushed away) were cited as a clear libel of the Soviet system. Further 'evidence' of Sinyavsky's anti-Soviet purposes included citations of Western reviews that spoke of his work 'exposing the reality of the Soviet system'. Without any hint of irony (since they were about to jail him), it was even deemed slanderous that one of his stories ended with an author being imprisoned. In his final statement, Sinyavsky launched a powerful diatribe against the whole affair, likening interacting with the prosecution case to beating his head against a brick wall. He was, he insisted, different, but not an enemy of Soviet power.[38]

Like Vigdorova in the Brodsky trial, Bogoraz, Rozanova and Golomstock (who had been summoned as a witness) took extensive notes on proceedings as they happened, smuggling these out to waiting acquaintances during the breaks. When he was eventually called upon to give evidence, Golomstock repeatedly refused to respond to a host of questions designed to incriminate Sinyavsky. As a result, he soon found himself fired from his work, had scheduled publications pulped and then in May 1966 was handed a six-month sentence of his own for refusing to give evidence.

Sinyavsky was jailed for seven years and Daniel for five. The announcement was met with applause in the courtroom, and within days Writers'

Union officials were lining up to attack Sinyavsky for 'entering their ranks by deception'. At his (former) place of work, the Gorky Institute of World Literature, a series of meetings was held to declare support for the verdict and to condemn Sinyavsky. Present at one of those meetings, Svetlana Alliluyeva (Stalin's daughter) recalled that enormous pressure was put on Sinyavsky's former colleagues to turn on him publicly. In her own account, Alliluyeva recorded that this was one of only two occasions when she spoke up at a party meeting – to protest the witch hunt taking place in the institute against those who did not wish to condemn Sinyavsky. For this she was branded 'politically naïve'.[39]

Media coverage around the trial was predictably shrill and manipulative. *Pravda* told readers that the pair had described Soviet people as idiots, murderers and informers. On 22 February, the same newspaper also insisted that the pair were in the pay of foreign intelligence agencies, reassuring readers that 'Soviet artists are completely free in their work, their choice of subject and form of composition'.[40] Such attempts at mobilising popular indignation seemingly had some impact. Lyudmila Alexeyeva, for example, recalled attending a public meeting about the case along with Larisa Bogoraz soon after the trial had ended, when the latter confronted a speaker from the KGB who claimed that Sinyavsky and Daniel had been working for Soviet enemies. Announcing to the packed room that she was Daniel's wife, Bogoraz stood up to defend the two authors and to denounce their conviction. The response was hissing and heckling from the crowds around them, with shouts that the two guilty men should have been shot and an angry mob drawing around Alexeyeva and Bogoraz, before a friendly face helped to spirit them out of the hall.[41]

The Sinyavsky and Daniel case clearly set alarm bells ringing for some, however. Forty Soviet writers signed an appeal protesting about the length of the sentences that had been handed down. When asked during the course of several public lectures in early 1966 for his thoughts on the convictions, Lev Kopelev each time insisted that the verdicts were unfair. He also collected signatures for a letter to the upcoming Twenty-Third Party Congress, calling for the release of the two authors.[42] Soon enough, Kopelev was disciplined by both the party and the Writers' Union, and he was no longer allowed to give public lectures.

A movement takes shape

Andrei Sinyavsky and Yuli Daniel would not emerge from captivity until the 1970s, but their imprisonment in February 1966 continued directly and indirectly to generate further protests for years to come. One key facet of the fallout from their trial developed right next to the courthouse. Before the verdict on the final day, friends of the accused men and the foreign journalists covering the story stopped standing separately in the cold outside and began to talk to one another. This would prove the start of a connection that was absolutely critical for Soviet dissidents down the years. The gain for them was twofold. First, their complaints about regime abuses now made global news quickly; and second, they attained a degree of protection by virtue of the fact that people outside the USSR now knew their names and cared about their fates. This foreign dynamic also came to carry real meaning for a regime that was more concerned about its international reputation than was widely understood at the time. When communist newspapers in Great Britain (*Daily Worker*), France (*L'Humanité*) and Italy (*L'Unita*) broke ranks and refused to express support for the verdict against Sinyavsky and Daniel, it was a real blow for Moscow.

Famous names like Saul Bellow, Alberto Moravia and André Breton added their voices to the public calls for leniency. Graham Greene went so far as to request that his publishing royalties earned in the Soviet Union be signed over to the wives of the two writers, but authorities refused.[43] This charitable impulse was also replicated inside the USSR. Bogoraz and Rozanova were soon stunned to find strangers knocking on their door with offers of money, food, books and warm clothes for them and their imprisoned husbands. Such donations kept pouring in long after the two families' needs had been catered for, so they were then directed instead towards fellow political prisoners whom the two writers had met in the camps. Aside from the immediate material succour it provided to those detained, this was also a means of asserting the existence of a supportive community, of showing that those taking risks with their freedom might find support if and when they hit trouble.[44] In time, this ad hoc giving would morph into an enduring (albeit underground) charitable organisation, known as the Russian Social Fund for Persecuted Persons and their Families, that was administered by

Alexander Ginzburg and funded in large part out of Alexander Solzhenitsyn's foreign literary earnings.

The physicist Andrei Sakharov later likened this period in which the Soviet human rights movement began emerging to a kind of proto-Prague Spring, in the sense that he and others in his circle felt buoyed to act by this surge of liberal-minded political activism. But the authorities soon cracked down hard.[45] Only days after the end of Sinyavsky and Daniel's trial, the historian Alexander Nekrich was caught in the crosshairs after a public discussion of his book *June 22, 1941* turned openly anti-Stalinist and saw participants voice fears of an upcoming rehabilitation of Stalin.[46] The work soon faced official condemnation and was quietly removed from libraries and bookshops, with Nekrich subsequently expelled from the party.

The following month, another troublesome author was dealt with in no less decisive style. After publishing the novel *Ward 7* in the West, about his spell of psychiatric confinement between 1963 and 1964, Valery Tarsis was unexpectedly granted permission to give a cycle of lectures in the UK. Once across the border, he was stripped of his Soviet citizenship and thereafter subjected to a barrage of media attacks that branded him mentally unwell and desperate for attention and money. By the end of 1966, the authorities had also introduced a new article to the criminal code to aid their fight against dissenters. Far looser terminology now criminalised 'slanders' against the Soviet system, and another new decree gave fresh grounds for arrest and conviction by reframing protest as a public order issue, using laws on matters like disrupting traffic and blocking public footpaths. Alarmed at the deliberate vagueness of the measures – taken as a sure sign that the idea was to employ them arbitrarily against any and all protest – a host of prominent figures put their names to petitions against their introduction, but to no avail.

Regardless of toughening regime responses, the public meeting that Volpin had organised in December 1965 proved to be only the first of its kind.[47] Now, 5 December was marked annually at Pushkin Square, in honour not of Sinyavsky and Daniel specifically, but to mourn both the abused Soviet constitution and the fate of political prisoners alive and dead. Having discovered an invitation (subsequently found to have been composed by Volpin) left in his mailbox, in December 1966 Andrei Sakharov decided to join what would be his first public act of protest. On arrival, he found a few dozen others at the square, plus Western journalists and Soviet police. On the stroke of 18:00 about half of those in attendance removed their hats as a mark of respect (Sakharov assumed the half who did not must have been KGB) and observed a minute's silence, before peacefully going their separate ways.[48] Although uneventful, this short and dignified protest not only made a clear point, but also attracted global attention.

In the letters that he sent to Bogoraz from the Mordovia camp, Yuli Daniel repeatedly mentioned a fellow inmate named Anatoly Marchenko – a labourer from Siberia who had, by the mid-1960s, and before he even turned thirty, already spent the best part of a decade imprisoned. He had first been wrongly jailed as a result of a gang fight in Kazakhstan; later, after his release, he had been caught trying to cross the Soviet border with Iran. When Marchenko's next release eventually came around, at the end of 1966, Bogoraz and others collected him from Mordovia and brought him to Moscow. As Marchenko later recalled, this time he left the camps with a burning desire to chronicle what he had seen there, knowing full well that there had as yet been no decisive rebuttal of Khrushchev's claim that there were no longer any political prisoners inside the USSR.

Soon after his release, Marchenko was hard at work in the town of Alexandrov, with Bogoraz alongside helping to turn his experiences in the camps into a manuscript. Then, for three days in October 1967, Bogoraz, Alexeyeva and a few others came together and typed day and night, producing what would become *My Testimony*. When this ground-breaking account eventually appeared – in samizdat only inside the USSR, but a publishing sensation in large parts of the world – it carried a visceral power that few other works on the Soviet penal system have ever matched. At the outset, Marchenko declared that 'today's Soviet camps for political prisoners are just as horrific as in Stalin's time. A few things are better, a few things are worse,' adding that he was prepared to answer for the content of his work at a public trial when the inevitable accusations of slander arose.[49] Over the pages that followed, he described everything from prisoners' squabbles, protests and acts of self-harm through to the guards' callous methods of exerting control. As he predicted, before even a year had passed, Marchenko was again behind barbed wire.

In a variation on the theme of Vigdorova's transcript of the 1964 Brodsky trial, Alexander Ginzburg had spent a large part of 1966 compiling a whole dossier on the Sinyavsky and Daniel case. By the time this was completed, in November, it included translations of reports from foreign newspapers, copies of protest letters and excerpts from trial proceedings. To demonstrate that he had nothing to hide, Ginzburg sent one of the original five type-written copies directly to the KGB, with his name and address affixed. Another copy quickly found its way to France, from where it spread across the world, becoming known in English as *The White Book*. Almost immediately, Ginzburg came under concerted KGB pressure to make an official statement renouncing the volume, but he refused.

On 17 January 1967, the KGB launched a series of synchronised house searches at the apartments of Ginzburg, Yuri Galanskov, Alexei Dobrovolsky and Vera Lashkova. Within days, all four had been arrested. Ginzburg and Galanskov were the principal targets – the former for *The White Book* and the latter (who had been a regular participant in the Mayakovsky Square readings) for editing a samizdat collection of suppressed literature called *Feniks-66* (*Phoenix-66*). On 18 January, Galanskov and Ginzburg were smeared at length in the press, branded as idle, immoral and driven by a desire only for dollars and acceptance in the West, while their samizdat publications were labelled 'anthologies of slanderous materials'.[50] On 22 January, around forty friends of the accused held another public meeting at Pushkin Square, quickly leading to new arrests. Ginzburg's mother, in particular, made the point in writing that all her son had done was compile documents on an officially open trial, insisting that there was no justification whatsoever for his arrest. On 11 February, Andrei Sakharov wrote to the party leadership calling for the case against the four to be abandoned. After this he was demoted at work and his salary almost halved.[51] More petitions on behalf of the accused followed, including a November 1967 open letter demanding that the forthcoming trial be genuinely open to the public, signed by the likes of Larisa Bogoraz, Igor Golomstock, Petro Grigorenko, Yuli Kim and Oskar Rabin.

On 8 January 1968, the 'Trial of the Four' finally opened in Moscow, with the courthouse again packed with hand-picked 'representatives of the public', and the defendants' friends and family mostly locked outside. Ginzburg and Galanskov admitted that they had produced *The White Book* and *Feniks-66*, respectively, but both refused to acknowledge their behaviour as anti-Soviet.

In her closing speech, Galanskov's lawyer, Dina Kaminskaya, all but mocked the evidence put forward and insisted that none of the charges against her client had been proven. In his own closing statement on 12 January 1968, Galanskov declared that the state's accusations were 'totally unfounded and had no connection with reality'. Ginzburg, too, railed against the whole process, and when he was warned by the judge over his criticism of the KGB, he simply asserted that he already knew he was about to be convicted and that 'no honest man will condemn me'. A few hours later, the judge decided that the charges against all four had been proven in full.[52] Almost five years into his jail term, Galanskov died at the Mordovia camp (where he and Ginzburg were imprisoned alongside Yuli Daniel) from medical neglect through untreated stomach ulcers.

Beyond Moscow

Although it was the dissenters in Moscow who would attract most of the international attention, the second half of the 1960s also saw signs of non-Russian national sentiment becoming more pronounced in places. In both Kazakhstan and Uzbekistan there were early indicators among the student body of discontent at perceived Russification, with occasional leaflets and letters discovered calling on people to rise up.[53] In Tatarstan, there was a growing sense of frustration among Muslim intellectuals in particular, angry at the paucity of local-language movies and radio broadcasts.[54] There were growing signs of restlessness returning to the Baltic states, too. In 1967, for example, the KGB in Vilnius reported on students celebrating 'Lithuanian independence day' in February and proliferating signs of resentment towards Russians, Komsomol activists and others.[55]

One of the era's most interesting manifestations of non-Russian national sentiment came in Yerevan in April 1965. Here, Soviet and Armenian patriotism had for some time proved broadly compatible, with celebrated Armenians such as Mikoyan, the composer Aram Khachaturian and the war hero Marshal Ivan Bagramyan all firmly established in the pantheon of Soviet heroes. Even so, Moscow's refusal to consider the transfer of Nagorno-Karabakh from Azeri to Armenian control aroused some resentment, and by the 1960s locals, including many within the leading ranks of the Armenian

Communist Party, were increasingly eager for some official commemoration of the genocide that had seen around a million people killed by Ottoman forces between 1915 and 1917. Unlike the Armenian diaspora around the globe, the Soviet regime had never formally marked the specific significance of 24 April 1915, when the genocide had begun in earnest. Nonetheless, in the celebrations of Soviet Armenia's fortieth anniversary, in 1961, Khrushchev remarked in Yerevan that the coming of Soviet power had 'saved the Armenian people from annihilation at the hands of the Ottoman Empire'. When the fiftieth anniversary of the genocide's commencement came around, there was considerable public pressure for meaningful commemoration. There was also a simmering sense of injustice in Yerevan that more was not being done by Moscow to pressure Turkey into returning historically Armenian lands seized by the Ottoman Empire many years earlier (of his 1962 visit to Armenia, Vasily Grossman noted 'the longing of every Armenian for the lands of Kars and Van').[56]

Broadly sympathetic to public feeling on both issues, party bosses in Yerevan advised Moscow that although such national sentiment had not yet become anti-Soviet, it may well do so if the grievances remained unaddressed.[57] In early 1965, permission was duly granted for the erection of a commemorative obelisk and for a small memorial gathering for members of the Armenian political and cultural elite to mark the upcoming anniversary, though this hardly sated the wider public appetite for recognition. When the anniversary came on 24 April 1965, thousands of people thronged the streets of Yerevan in an unsanctioned rally and even forced their way into the private memorial event. Some of the assembled dignitaries inside actually applauded the protesters who intruded on their meeting, and the option of clearing crowds off the streets by force was immediately eschewed by Armenian officialdom. Protesters cited Lenin's own remarks on the need for a revision of Armenia's borders, and they declared their pride in the transformation of their republic since the revolution, making it plain that their own nationalism was not hostile to Soviet power.[58] Thereafter, Moscow agreed to sanction annual commemorative ceremonies for 24 April, as well as a much more extensive memorial complex that included a huge statue of Mother Armenia – on the very plinth in Yerevan where Stalin's monument had once stood.

At this stage, Ukraine provided perhaps the most significant example of changing trends. There were still a few nationalists in the west of Ukraine especially who displayed overtly anti-communist tendencies more typical of the 1930s and 1940s. In Kiev especially, though, by the mid-1960s there had emerged a new type of Ukrainian nationalist, whose beliefs and methods were much closer to those of the broadly liberal-minded Moscow dissidents. Actually, as the era developed, personal connections between Moscow and Kiev dissenters proliferated. Visiting the Mordovia camp complex in March 1966, Larisa Bogoraz made the acquaintance of Nina Strokata, as both stood waiting at the barbed wire fence to see their spouses. Strokata's husband, Sviatoslav Karavansky, was in prison for Ukrainian nationalist activity. The two wives chatted and subsequently returned to Moscow together, where Strokata informed Bogoraz's circle about on-going struggles in Ukraine, and bonds of friendship and co-operation began to form.[59] Another early Ukrainian dissident, Leonid Plyushch, was soon making regular trips between Kiev and the Soviet capital, translating Ukrainian samizdat into Russian (and vice versa). Some visitors to Ukrainian political prisoners in Russian camps also began staying the night at Moscow dissidents' apartments, as the rail route to both of the major destinations for political prisoners (Perm and Mordovia) took them through the capital.

The new Ukrainian nationalism was primarily concerned not with ethnicity, but with protection of local cultural traditions and language against seemingly inexorable Russification. Perhaps more than any other republic, Ukraine had made considerable gains in prestige and infrastructure under Khrushchev. Numerous authors and works previously banned on the grounds of bourgeois nationalism – most notably Volodymyr Sosiura's poem 'Love Ukraine' – re-emerged in print, as cultural restrictions eased somewhat. Nonetheless, the spread of the Russian language inside Ukraine continued apace, and fears of Russification by stealth persisted, not least since large numbers of Russians continued to settle inside the republic's towns and cities. It remained a consistent theme of regime discourse that Russian culture was the ideal for other Soviet peoples to emulate. As a 1964 samizdat piece by Ivan Svitlichny and Evhen Sverstyuk warned readers: 'We should not deceive ourselves about the immortality of a nation . . . its life depends directly on our willingness to stand up for ourselves.'[60]

Students in some of Ukraine's top universities were pushing for more teaching to be done in Ukrainian than in Russian, and for more study of Ukraine's past. Here, samizdat began to fill some important gaps in the official record. Leonid Plyushch recalled that the first samizdat he read in the early 1960s was an account of the terror famine of 1932–33 in Ukraine – information about which had for years been kept secret from the population.[61] One of the most powerful Ukrainian samizdat texts of the time was Ivan Dziuba's 1965 essay *Internationalism or Russification?* In it, Dziuba fulminated against the notion that Russian culture was the most advanced and that it was therefore only right that Ukrainian literature, art and more occupy a secondary status, even inside Ukraine. Asserting that 'our culture is being deliberately held back and impoverished', Dziuba wrote of talented Ukrainian writers, composers, painters and directors all facing endless obstacles and demonisation if they tried to do anything distinctively 'Ukrainian' in their art. Ukraine's scientists, he rightly pointed out, had to publish in Russian if they wanted their work to be noticed, meaning that same work was thereafter regarded as 'Russian', thus perpetuating the notion of Russian superiority. Then again, great works of world literature might be translated into Russian by regime publishing houses, but hardly ever into Ukrainian – meaning that the Russian language was often the only avenue by which to access important global culture. While Russian music, theatre and dance were all largely free to explore their native folklore and ancient customs, he argued, Ukrainians could not do so without arousing accusations of nationalism. Similarly, he asked whether there was any other country in the world where the people had such limited awareness of their great writers and scholars down the centuries, since their plays were not performed and their artworks were held in storage, rather than being on public display.[62] There was no chance of Dziuba's essay being published officially, of course, but it circulated widely in samizdat and became a clarion call that compellingly pinpointed systemic unfairness.

Formed in 1960, initially under the aegis of the Kiev Komsomol, the Club of Creative Youth was a key site that drew together hundreds of the Ukrainian capital's young intellectuals and artists and – not entirely unlike the readings at Mayakovsky Square in Moscow – generated a creative atmosphere that soon felt rebellious, even though many of the participants were fundamentally reformist communists in political outlook. They revived old Ukrainian folk traditions, such as carolling (going from house to house singing songs) and studied historic peasant life and culture.[63] Many of those who did not already know it, put concerted effort into mastering the Ukrainian language and speaking it in public. All this proved sufficiently popular that analogous groups soon sprang up in several other Ukrainian cities. Many people were also giving up their free time to join in with drives to preserve local architecture and other symbols of Ukraine's endangered cultural and religious heritage. As time passed, they pushed a little more at the limits of acceptable national sentiment, such as holding events commemorating Ukrainian artists and writers repressed or banned under Soviet power.

From 1960 onwards, one of the staple fixtures in the calendar for the Club of Creative Youth was 22 May: the anniversary of the date on which the remains of Taras Shevchenko – Ukraine's great national writer, who had been jailed by the imperial Russian authorities in 1841, partly for his insistence on writing in Ukrainian – were transferred from St Petersburg back to Kiev. That day, people sang folk songs, laid flowers and read poems at monuments to Shevchenko in Kiev and elsewhere across Ukraine. The Taras Shevchenko lauded by these young intellectuals, it should be said, was far more 'Ukrainian' than the image of him that was put about by Moscow officialdom: the former envisioned him primarily as a steadfast defender of Ukraine, while the latter presented him as a loyal friend of Russia. Official concerns over the annual 'pilgrimages' to Shevchenko monuments had already been rising for some time when, in May 1964, things reached snapping point. Then, students defied orders from officials and marked the anniversary of his remains being returned from Russia to Ukraine by holding a torchlit parade that ended in a confrontation between hundreds of youths and local police.[64]

The year 1965 ultimately saw the Club of Creative Youth closed down and a host of Ukrainian intellectuals arrested, many of them participants in its activities.[65] Nonetheless, in his samizdat chronicle of this wave of repression (written while incarcerated at Mordovia), Valentyn Moroz confidently asserted that 'the arrests of 1965 did not slow down but speeded up the Ukrainian renaissance'.[66] Scheduled to give a few introductory words at the opening of a Kiev movie premiere in September 1965, Dziuba instead turned the event into a political protest at the recent arrests and ultimately had to be dragged from the stage by the cinema manager. Soon he and Ivan Svitlichny were both in jail. When the trials of those arrested came around in March 1966, friends and supporters gathered outside (in some cases cheering the defendants and throwing flowers) and transcripts of defendants' speeches and testimonies were again produced and released into samizdat. As in Moscow, public collections raised money and gathered goods to help those condemned.[67] Although not yet a truly major social force among the Ukrainian population, the nationalists' appeal was clearly growing. For that reason, the authorities now came down ever harder on organised Ukrainian nationalism, ultimately jailing almost all its key figures before the end of the 1960s.

While Ukrainian dissenters in Kiev were largely seeking greater cultural autonomy, peoples elsewhere were still demanding the right to return home from Stalin-imposed exile. Even though the charges of treason that had underpinned the wartime deportations of multiple national groups (Kalmyks, Chechens and others) were quashed soon after Stalin's death, not quite all of them had been allowed to return to the lands from which they had been expelled. The roughly 140,000 Crimean Tatars who had survived the brutal deportation – their pre-war population had stood at almost 220,000 – organised themselves as a tight-knit national community and campaigned hard from the mid-1950s onwards to be granted the right to return to Crimea from their places of exile across Uzbekistan and Siberia.

Inspired by the belief that the Twentieth Party Congress indicated that their historic injustice would soon be rectified, Crimean Tatars had begun to send a slew of letters, petitions and delegations to Moscow – declaring their loyalty to Soviet power and pointing to their victimhood under the cult of personality. The result of all this campaigning, though, proved negligible, and by the mid-1960s a younger generation of activists had begun taking a more forthright approach, writing samizdat chronicles of their sufferings as a people, overtly embracing their native cultural traditions and holding public meetings to commemorate the anniversary of their expulsion from Crimea. The petitions that they continued to send were no longer so characterised by fawning declarations of loyalty, and some even began to use the word 'genocide' to describe the fate of their people.[68]

When they sent a petition to the Twenty-Third Party Congress in spring 1966, calling for their right to return home, there were almost as many signatures on it as there were adult Crimean Tatars. In June 1967, a delegation was met by several top regime officials, including the KGB chairman and chief prosecutor, and the prospects for resolution seemed promising. But the party decree that followed in September only annulled the charges against the Crimean Tatars, without granting them any explicit right to return to Crimea. Over a thousand families returned anyway, but the vast majority were denied residence permits and were soon ejected once again. The official reasons for denying them permission to return home were essentially fictional – primarily that there were no jobs or land for them there.[69] Importantly, Crimea had by this stage become the USSR's 'premier resort region', much favoured as a holiday spot by ordinary citizens and top elites alike (with many of the homes from which the Crimean Tatars had been ejected since occupied by incoming Russians and Ukrainians). The land that the Crimean Tatars wanted to return to, then, had become too valuable to be readily handed back.[70]

An attempt to hold a public demonstration in the Uzbek city of Chirchik in April 1968 drew thousands of activists chanting 'our home is Crimea'. But it culminated in police wading into protesters with batons and firing water cannon, and ended with around three hundred arrests. Thanks in large part to connections forged with the Moscow dissident Petro Grigorenko, news of this violence soon reached the Soviet capital and then the outside world. In May 1968, the Crimean Tatars took an even bolder step, as around eight hundred of them headed to Moscow to protest outside the party's Central Committee headquarters. Aware of the plan, the KGB and police managed to detain many of the would-be protestors on the streets and in their hotels on the eve of the protest; they were herded onto buses and ultimately sent back to Uzbekistan, though, perhaps seventy did manage to hold the planned demonstration on 18 May.[71] Then, in June 1968, the new KGB chairman, Yuri Andropov, warned his Central Committee colleagues that Crimean Tatars and Grigorenko were preparing to send an appeal to the UN with 250,000 signatures attached.[72] Before long, Grigorenko would be confined to a psychiatric unit, where he remained for the next five years. The struggle ultimately went on until Mikhail Gorbachev finally granted permission for the Tatars to return en masse to Crimea in 1989.

While the Crimean Tatars were fighting for the right to return to a homeland inside the USSR, others were seeking to leave the country entirely. The Volga Germans, whose roots in Russia dated back to the eighteenth century, had also been deported under Stalin (mostly to Kazakhstan). In the mid-1960s, they began to campaign not to return to their former homes, but for the right to emigrate to West Germany. Much more prominent internationally, though, would be the Jewish refusenik movement, which attracted huge global attention during the 1970s but was already starting to get under way in the second half of the 1960s. While the most extreme anti-Semitism of the late 1940s and early 1950s was largely ended after Stalin's death, Soviet Jews continued to face considerable discrimination. As one scholar has noted, the key change in attitude came not from Soviet officialdom, but from Soviet Jews, who gained new self-confidence in the post-Stalin years and were more willing to assert their rights.[73]

By the mid-1960s, crowds of many thousands gathered publicly at synagogues in Kiev, Odessa and Moscow to mark Yom Kippur. Jewish samizdat also flourished, and there was a growing degree of co-operation between activists in the main cities where Soviet Jews resided – namely, Moscow, Leningrad, Riga, Kiev and Odessa.[74] Keen to refute accusations of regime anti-Semitism, the Soviet press intermittently carried articles boasting of the successes enjoyed by Jewish writers, musicians and scientists in the USSR, and of the apparently rich Jewish cultural life on offer there. At the same time, however, officials from Khrushchev down were also apt to view as somehow backward and suspicious those Jews who sought to immerse themselves in specifically Jewish – rather than broader Soviet – culture.[75]

Unofficial quotas still existed to limit the number of Jews in some of the most prestigious higher education institutions and professions. Similarly, there was never a shortage of ordinary citizens or officials who were unashamed to use derogatory slurs and nicknames or otherwise suppress Jewish achievements. While working at the newspaper *Moskovskii komsomolets* (*Moscow Komsomol Member*), for example, Anatoly Gladilin recalled an editor remarking meaningfully one day that his column 'had a lot of Jewish surnames in it'.[76] The continuing prevalence of offensive stereotypes in popular culture, and of internal passports which still identified Jews as such (rather than as Russians, Ukrainians or some other Soviet nationality), ensured that many felt a considerable sense of 'otherness'. Working synagogues and rabbis could be especially hard to find, as was food produced in accordance with Jewish dietary laws.[77] There were also deeply worrying portents on occasion, such as a mysterious fire that burned down a synagogue at Malakhovka in 1959. Most notoriously, a 1963 book called *Judaism Without Embellishment*, published under the auspices of the Ukrainian Academy of Sciences, displayed clearly anti-Semitic overtones, including claims about global Jewish conspiracies to undermine the Soviet regime. Both at home and abroad, the outcry was such that the central authorities had to distance themselves from the offending work.

The initial post-Khrushchev period actually saw an increased willingness to allow Soviet Jews to emigrate, but the figures remained little more than a trickle. Only about 1,450 were granted permission to leave for Israel across the whole decade from 1954 to 1964, while the total for 1965 was almost 900 and then just over 2,000 in 1966.[78] This seemingly promising interlude was not to last, though, as political authorities seemingly grew alarmed at the prospect of unwittingly facilitating rising Jewish activism. A letter from KGB Chairman Semichastny to the party Central Committee in January 1966 described a recent event at Moscow's Central House of Writers, during which an official commemoration of Jewish authors repressed during the Stalin years had moved well beyond the bounds of officially acceptable comment to include what he described as 'demagogic' and 'ideologically immature' remarks. As before, there was implicit blame attached to the Israeli embassy, which was noted to have been 'propagandising' at the event in question – making clear the authorities' basic assumption that practically any manifestation of discontent inside the USSR was a product not of Soviet conditions, but of Western subversion and the Cold War struggle.[79]

A key turning point came with the Six Day War of June 1967, a moment described by some as the 'end of the thaw' for Soviet Jews.[80] With Moscow volubly backing Israel's Arab neighbours in the conflict (including press coverage likening Israeli expansion to the Nazis' quest for *Lebensraum*), diplomatic relations with Tel Aviv were again broken off. Jews inside the Soviet Union also felt increasingly embattled as media attacks on Israel frequently veered into dog-whistle anti-Semitism. Natan Sharansky recalled that even though his own sense of Jewish identity at the time was mostly limited to being on the receiving end of anti-Semitic prejudice, Soviet support for Israel's enemies, and the popular anti-Semitism it facilitated, caused him to feel that Israel was both 'fighting for its life and our dignity'.[81] Israel's unexpected victory then became a huge source of pride for many Soviet Jews, not least since one of the most common anti-Semitic tropes in the USSR centred on the groundless notion that Jews had 'hidden' from the action during the Second World War. When, in June 1967, the Soviet authorities cut off the already small flow of Soviet Jews allowed to leave for Israel, there was much domestic and international consternation and an authentic movement for emigration soon began to take shape.

While the various struggles outlined in the present chapter did not necessarily represent the predominant issues of the day for the majority of Soviet citizens during the 1950s and 1960s, they would in time grow particularly important. Dissident struggles would eventually become a feature of superpower diplomacy, and discourse on the observance of human rights would emerge as a key battleground of the 'moral Cold War'. Similarly, nationalities questions proved to be among the most explosive of all issues, as the entire Soviet system headed for collapse under Mikhail Gorbachev. The events of the Soviet Sixties clearly played an important part in the pre-history of the non-Russian national mobilisations of the Gorbachev years. It was only really from the end of the 1960s that a recognisable dissident movement emerged inside the USSR, but the formative events and trends that would shape that movement were very much rooted in the Sixties era. Furthermore, both the way in which dissenters conducted themselves and the way in which the authorities responded offer real insights into what had and had not changed inside the USSR since Stalin.

II

THE END OF THE SOVIET SIXTIES

On 7 November 1967, the Soviet Union marked the fiftieth anniversary of the revolution in suitably grandiose style. For months already, television and radio had been broadcasting shows about the great deeds of the previous half-century, while mountains of books were published, public talks were held and exhibitions organised to honour heroics performed in the name of communism and the motherland. Workers put in extra shifts to present 'labour gifts' – meaning output over and above plan targets – in everything from steel and coal to eggs and milk. A series of massive construction projects was hurriedly brought to completion in time to mark the big day, including the world's biggest hotel (the Rossiya, in Moscow), the world's tallest building (the Ostankino television tower) and the world's largest hydroelectric dam (Bratsk). As always, when the day finally came, Politburo members and assorted other dignitaries watched and waved from the Lenin mausoleum, as a seemingly endless parade of soldiers and military hardware went past, followed by communist youth, athletes, children, workers and more over the course of several hours.

Such events were, of course, orchestrated from above, but there was nonetheless also some considerable pride and enjoyment among the millions participating in festivities around the country. Having already made raising living standards his central focus, the fiftieth anniversary gave Brezhnev the ideal opportunity to showcase the new approach. There was an increase in the minimum wage, the annual holiday allowance grew from twelve to fifteen days, taxes were cut for the lowest earners and pensions were raised. Consumer goods and clothing were also imported as never before, in order to ensure that shops were well stocked for the occasion.[1]

In some senses, the Soviet regime was only just reaching the peak of its powers. Its military strength was finally approaching parity with the US, and the economy seemed to be picking up again thanks to Kosygin's reforms. The average wage had risen by almost 50 per cent across the 1960s, and by about 300 per cent for collective farmers specifically. There were also submerged signs of trouble ahead, however. Sociological surveys showed that young people, in particular, were less and less enthused by Marxism-Leninism.[2] A 1965 report on Ukraine, for example, had expressed worries about 'nihilism and apoliticism' among students there, adding that some were becoming indifferent to socialism and to the country's revolutionary past.[3] KGB research in 1967–68 found a great deal of apathy and open scepticism towards the party leadership and Komsomol among students, with one recent commentator suggesting that by then 'the very word communist had already been discredited among Soviet youth'.[4] Studying at Moscow State University around this time, William Taubman wrote that the students he lived among were basically loyal, but none of them were really expecting the arrival of full communism in the USSR.[5]

Discourse on subjects like egalitarianism and gender equality had begun to fade again, as hierarchies of privilege and a focus on pro-natalism strengthened. There was also a growing atmosphere of militarism on the Soviet domestic scene, as the cult of the Second World War intensified, and the Komsomol, in particular, rooted narratives of citizenship and heroism ever more clearly in a context of combat. The political authorities focused their minds more and more on protecting what the revolution had already won and on celebrating past glories. All this would bring a kind of stability – which was much prized by many citizens, weary after years of upheaval and uncertainty – but came at the cost of the vibrancy and optimism that had characterised much of the previous decade and a half. Reform of almost any kind was slipping down the agenda.

With the events of 1968 right at its centre, the period between 1966 and 1969 saw the emergence of a much more distinctly post-Khrushchev version of the Soviet system. What would in time become known – not entirely fairly – as the 'era of stagnation' was starting to get under way. Living standards continued to improve steadily, but problems like alcoholism, political disengagement and corruption were growing more and more substantial.

Brezhnev still spoke about plans for the construction of full communism even as late as the anniversary celebrations in November 1967, but it would not be long before rhetoric switched instead to heralding the achievement of 'developed socialism'. This was an entirely confected stage of socio-economic development, with no basis at all in Marxist theory, propounded mainly as a means of sidestepping the impending failure to meet the timetable for reaching utopia that had been set out by Khrushchev.

Deaths, endings and new directions

Few facets of the Soviet Sixties had resounded quite like the embrace of Cuba. The imagery of the exotic island and its culture, as well as the energy and romanticism of its revolution, had quickly become iconic. Even after the missile crisis had sapped public enthusiasm somewhat, Castro's visit to the USSR in summer 1963 still saw huge and excited crowds turn out to greet him, as well as renewed pronouncements of eternal Soviet-Cuban friendship. Before the decade was out, though, this attachment was fading noticeably on both sides. It was telling in this respect that Castro chose not to attend the November 1967 anniversary celebrations in Moscow. The Cubans were increasingly tiring of a partner they deemed too conservative and too cynical, while many Soviet citizens had begun to look on the 'island of freedom' as a drain on their own country's resources. The attitude of the Soviet leadership towards Havana also cooled steadily, as Castro sought to pursue a more activist and independent agenda in global affairs. Moscow instead prioritised relationships with the likes of India and Algeria, and sometimes built economic ties with regimes – like the Rightist military dictatorship in Brazil – to which Cuba objected.[6]

Relations with China were still deteriorating at a worrying rate as the Sixties era came to a close. Soviet forces guarding the border were almost trebled in 1967.[7] Then, in March 1969, apparently in the wake of a Chinese ambush, Soviet and Chinese troops opened fire on one another at Damansky Island (Zhenbao) in the Ussuri river, leaving 31 Soviet dead and an estimated 150 Chinese killed, and seemingly threatening all-out war.[8] With patience in the Kremlin finally exhausted, thinly veiled threats of a pre-emptive Soviet nuclear attack on China followed. At this sobering prospect,

Beijing grew less overtly hostile and relations began to stabilise somewhat – though it would be many years yet before they genuinely improved – as Zhou Enlai and Alexei Kosygin finally met that September, with both sides making clear that they did not want war.[9] Before long, though, Soviet nightmares were coming true, as Beijing and Washington began to find common ground against Moscow.

In contrast to the on-going strains with Cuba and China, relations between the superpowers were mostly entering a rather more productive era as the end of the decade approached. While the global struggle for supremacy continued, and accusations still flew between them over matters like the Vietnam War, the volatile Soviet diplomacy of the Khrushchev years was becoming a thing of the past. When the US backed Israel and the Soviet Union took the Arab side in the Six Day War, plenty of heated rhetoric naturally ensued; but the superpowers also co-operated in seeking to bring their respective partners to peace talks. In fact, it was during this crisis that Kosygin, KGB chief Andropov and Foreign Minister Gromyko raced direct from a Politburo meeting to use the much-vaunted 'hotline' between Moscow and Washington, only to discover that the line was not a telephone after all, but four young women, a KGB general and a teletype machine. As the three men waited, the women encoded and sent the message, then decoded and translated the reply, with the KGB general keeping an eye on them as they worked.[10]

Substantial progress was also being made in moving forward the global arms control agenda when, after the Partial Test Ban Treaty, the two countries took the lead in negotiating and signing first the 1967 Outer Space Treaty (which precluded the use of space for nuclear weapons purposes) and then the Nuclear Non-Proliferation Treaty in 1968. The Strategic Arms Limitation Talks then began in 1969, marking the start of a decade-long period known as 'détente', when the USA and USSR more consistently sought to reduce tensions and to increase trust and mutual co-operation.

By that time, the USA had one additional citizen, whose arrival on the other side of the Atlantic stunned the whole world. As Stalin's daughter and last direct descendant, Svetlana was quite clear that her father had done monstrous things in power (though she still blamed Beria's influence for some of his crimes), and she had long since switched to using her late mother's maiden name, Alliluyeva, in recognition of this fact. She was largely pitied and left to her own devices by Khrushchev, and was grateful to be forgotten. Even so, those who encountered her described how she seemed to be perpetually running from her past. Igor Golomstock – who met Svetlana socially through Andrei Sinyavsky, a colleague of hers at the Gorky Institute of World Literature – wrote that she 'exuded such powerful waves of gloom that it gave me the creeps'.[11]

In December 1963, Svetlana first met an Indian communist named Brajesh Singh while they were both being treated at a Moscow hospital for the elite. Singh was already in declining health, but the pair soon became inseparable. Soviet officials were far from enthusiastic about the idea of Stalin's daughter being romantically involved with a foreigner, however, and refused to let the pair marry. When Svetlana begged for permission to accompany Singh back to India, as he approached death in autumn 1966, that request was also refused. She was, however, allowed to return his ashes to India after he died in the USSR that October. On 19 December 1966, she headed to Delhi for what was supposed to be a thirty-day trip. She would not return to the USSR, where her young children remained, for almost twenty years.

Once in India, she quickly grew resentful at finding her movements tightly monitored and controlled from the Soviet embassy. As she privately began to consider the idea of defection, she also realised that Indian relations with the USSR were such that they could never allow her to claim asylum there. Her attention therefore turned to other routes out. As she was finally due to leave, having long overstayed her initial visa, on the night of 6 March 1967 she sneaked out of the Soviet embassy compound in Delhi and turned up soon after at the American embassy. Understandably wary of a hoax, and needing some time to verify her identity, officials there eventually accepted that she was indeed Stalin's daughter and quickly spirited her out of the country.[12] Naturally, the defection became a huge news story across the globe, with the Soviet media furiously insisting that Svetlana was mentally unbalanced and a traitor to her country, betraying the acute sense of embarrassment and anger that her defection had caused in Moscow.

A number of totemic names of the 'thaw' era cultural scene were also exiting the stage. In the early 1960s, one veteran Western journalist noted the importance of what he called a 'generation of survivors' in the Khrushchev-era literary sphere, who were 'occupying themselves with the rectification of past wrongs', as well as reshaping public discourse across various fields.[13] The list of names he cited consisted of Konstantin Paustovsky, Anna Akhmatova, Ilya Ehrenburg, Alexander Tvardovsky and Konstantin Simonov.

Akhmatova, who had suffered terribly under Stalin, but was published again under Khrushchev and was even allowed to travel to the UK in 1965 for an international celebration of her work, died in March 1966. Paustovsky's excoriating attack on 'Drozdovs' (meaning callous and corrupt officials) in late 1956 had marked perhaps the height of ferment around Dudintsev's explosive novel *Not by Bread Alone*. He had since protested volubly at multiple signs of re-Stalinisation (and the Soviet authorities had in turn lobbied hard to prevent him winning the Nobel Prize for Literature in 1965 for his beautiful memoir *The Story of a Life*), before dying at the age of seventy-six in summer 1968.

Ilya Ehrenburg's novella *The Thaw* had given the Khrushchev era its most enduring epithet, and the writer himself had consistently propounded a liberal-minded internationalism that not only got him into hot water at times, but also helped shape the cultural ethos of the era. Sick with cancer, he suffered a heart attack and died soon after, in August 1967, but not before he had refused to succumb to heavy pressure from above to put his name to a public condemnation of Israel following the Six Day War (an act that neatly mirrored an earlier refusal to sign letters condemning the 'doctor poisoners' in early 1953). Thousands turned out for Ehrenburg's funeral at the start of September 1967, though no representative from Soviet officialdom deigned to attend, and the proceedings almost ended in a riot, as large crowds were turned away by police.[14]

Alexander Tvardovsky lived on until 1971, but as one of the USSR's most influential cultural figures his career was effectively over before the 1960s ended. The Central Committee Department of Culture was attacking Tvardovsky more openly for his continued support of Solzhenitsyn.[15] Just as he had refused to join the public attacks on Pasternak in 1958, so Tvardovsky resisted again a decade later, when leading cultural figures were corralled into expressing support for the invasion of Czechoslovakia. *Novy mir* did formally endorse the ensuing occupation (something Solzhenitsyn later described as the day that marked the 'spiritual death' of the journal in his mind), but that decision was taken in Tvardovsky's absence.[16] This proved possible because his previous editorial board had already been torn apart and reconstituted by higher authorities. The tightening restrictions on what *Novy mir* was able to publish had anyway reached the point by 1968 that Tvardovsky questioned whether he ought to ask Brezhnev either to loosen censorship or just close down the journal, since he now had to gather three editions' worth of material to get enough past the censor to fill a single volume.[17] His misery at watching the enforced decline of his beloved journal ended when he was finally sacked as editor in February 1970.

Having only found fame in late 1962, Alexander Solzhenitsyn's career as an officially endorsed author was already entering its death throes by the mid-1960s. After months in which hopes for publication of his novel *The First Circle* had intermittently risen and then fallen, it was eventually rejected once and for all after Khrushchev's removal. By that time, the KGB was increasingly convinced of the author's hostility towards Soviet power, and he was under surveillance around the clock – as well as being the subject of frequent discussions in the Politburo and attacks in the media. When Solzhenitsyn sent parts of his other great work in progress – *Cancer Ward* – to *Novy mir* in 1966, Tvardovsky had declared 'if we don't print this, I see no reason for our existence'.[18] The final decision would not belong to him, though, and plans to commence publication were cancelled, never to be revived.

Infuriated at the increasing restrictions being placed upon him, Solzhenitsyn first made sure that copies of his manuscripts made it out of the country; then in 1967 he sent an explosive letter of complaint to the upcoming Fourth Writers' Congress, demanding an end to censorship and insisting that it was both illegal and deeply damaging to Soviet culture. However, barring a few remaining allies, the cultural establishment was by now turning decisively against him. Serving as ringleader for the ensuing attacks, Mikhail Sholokhov refused to remain a member of the same organisation as Solzhenitsyn and demanded his expulsion from the Writers' Union – a fate that would effectively mean professional death inside the USSR. When both *The First Circle* and *Cancer Ward* appeared to tremendous acclaim in the West during 1968 (and soon after in samizdat form inside the USSR), Solzhenitsyn was indeed expelled from the Writers' Union. Largely on the back of these two works, in

1970 Solzhenitsyn would follow Sholokhov as the USSR's next winner of the Nobel Prize for Literature, though by that time he was becoming just as famous for his dissident activity as for his writing.

The dissident milieu in which Solzhenitsyn was becoming established during the late 1960s also reached a critical milestone with the founding of the samizdat journal *Chronicle of Current Events*. First appearing in April 1968, and influenced by the Crimean Tatars' samizdat publications, the *Chronicle* would somehow survive into the early 1980s, producing more than sixty editions filled with reports on Soviet political trials, hidden persecution of minorities, accounts from inside psychiatric prisons and more. Of course, its contributors and information networks were relentlessly hounded, as the KGB vainly sought to silence it. Edited by a promising young poet named Natalya Gorbanevskaya, and with the wording of the Universal Declaration of Human Rights printed on the front cover of each edition, the *Chronicle* not only brought to light regime abuses from all over the USSR, but also played a big role in shaping the emerging discourse on human rights (rather than just observance of Soviet laws), as ideas of reform communism steadily lost traction among regime critics.

Making a rather bigger international splash that same year was Andrei Sakharov's seminal samizdat essay 'Reflections on Progress, Peaceful Co-Existence and Intellectual Freedom'. Where many earlier dissenters had criticised from distinctly liberal-communist or neo-Bolshevik positions, Sakharov's final emergence as a dissident came with a political liberalism that proved much more palatable abroad. Rather than a strident polemic, his essay was a 'clarion call to moderation, reason, and evolutionary change' directed towards both the ruling authorities and fellow citizens of the USSR.[19] He wrote of a global future in which both socialist and capitalist camps would work together to overcome threats to all humanity – most notably nuclear war – predicting an eventual convergence of the two systems as both acknowledged and assimilated the respective strengths of the other.

After a visiting Dutch academic managed to transmit the text of the entire essay over the telephone, it appeared in the Amsterdam newspaper *Het Parool* at the start of July 1968, quickly spreading around the world thereafter. Soon, Sakharov's boss – under direct orders from the KGB – was pressing him to disown the work publicly. He refused to do so and his security clearance was revoked, effectively ending his distinguished career as a world-leading physicist and making him, like Solzhenitsyn, a full-time dissident and high-profile thorn in the side of the Soviet authorities for years to come.

Solzhenitsyn's dissident activity and his major publications provided enduring fame and respect in the West, but he also bequeathed a less widely acknowledged cultural legacy at home. One scholar of Russian literature has even argued that 'the most permanent legacy that Solzhenitsyn left behind for later Soviet public culture was contained in the modest shape of two peasant sketches . . . "Matryona's House" and "Zakhar the Pouch" '.[20] These short stories (published in 1963 and 1965, respectively) were notable early examples – if not exactly originators – of an emerging literary genre that would sweep all before it from the late 1960s onwards, embodying the shifting cultural ethos of the time. Occasional stories that described the hardships of peasant life had already been published since the end of the Stalin years. *Novy mir* had been one of the first journals to carry such work, but as the 1960s progressed, the rural theme steadily morphed from a liberal-minded one into something more closely linked with a growing Russian nationalist sentiment that was distinguished by its conservatism – and even authoritarianism, in some cases.[21]

Solzhenitsyn's two short stories were an important moment in the blossoming of a literature that celebrated peasant traditions and the timeless Russian village apparently disappearing from sight. Known as Village Prose, the genre consciously rejected the great embrace of urban modernity and internationalism that had been characteristic of much of the preceding decade's cultural output. 'Matryona's House', in particular, centres on the unbending decency and kindness of the ageing and uneducated peasant lady Matryona in the face of a grasping and deceitful world around her. That the story culminates with Matryona being killed when hit by a train – a long-standing and widely understood symbol of advancing modernity in Russian literature – offers a clear sense of what the author believed was happening in his country. Similarly, while one of Yevtushenko's most famous poems of the Sixties era celebrated the construction of the gargantuan new Bratsk hydroelectric dam, among the biggest literary works of the subsequent period was Valentin Rasputin's *Farewell to Matyora* (1976) – a lament for an ancient

Russian village and its way of life about to be lost forever, as it waits to be flooded for the same dam project that Yevtushenko had glorified.

Until recently, the village had typically been framed as a site of backwardness in need of transformation (and many new urban dwellers tried to hide their rural roots for fear of mockery as 'bumpkins'). But now it was increasingly presented in Village Prose literature as a site where 'true' Russian values and ways resided, distinct from – but also threatened by – the new urban modernity. The peasant's closeness to nature, his simplicity, community values and stoicism were presented as facets of village life to be cherished and protected. Taking root within all this was a wider ethos of neo-traditionalism, of turning towards older ways and ideas. Discourse on family life more and more explicitly re-emphasised the idea of domestic duty as central to a woman's social and familial roles, as sharpening concerns about the declining birth rate (especially among the Slavic population) prompted an intensified regime pro-natalism.[22] Not unrelatedly, in 1968 *Literaturnaya gazeta* published a piece by Boris Urlanis entitled 'Save the Men', which effectively argued that the modern vision of emancipated Soviet womanhood was having a deleterious effect on Soviet men, and that political priority now ought to be given to tackling the multifarious crises affecting men (including galloping alcoholism and rising suicide rates) by returning social affairs to how they were in 'simpler times'.[23]

Key Village Prose writers Valentin Rasputin and Vladimir Soloukhin published their breakthrough works around the end of the 1960s (*Money for Maria* and *Black Boards*, respectively), to be followed by myriad other novels and essays about villagers being forcibly and painfully uprooted from their native land in the name of 'progress', or about the urban world imposing its order on rural people it could barely comprehend. Other works centred upon urbanites making voyages of rediscovery to 'home' villages that they or their parents had abandoned years before, and reconnecting with a wholesome and timeless way of life, which contrasted sharply with the unceasing bedlam, bureaucracy and soullessness of the modern city.[24] In Russia especially, stories like these were published in vast quantities and eagerly lapped up across the 'long 1970s' to come. They were also supplemented by the work of Russian nationalist thinkers like Viktor Chalmaev, whose writings propounded the notion that Soviet greatness was really just a modern manifestation of historic

371

Russian greatness, linking together historic deeds like the Battle of Poltava and the Battle of Stalingrad, and heroes like Dmitry Donskoi and Alexander Matrosov.

In theory, many of the messages and themes that ran through Village Prose literature, such as a deeply parochial view of the world and the place of religious faith in peasant life (Soloukhin was even a relatively open monarchist), should have been politically unacceptable. In reality, Village Prose writers took care not to go much beyond the boundaries of tolerated criticism, typically only hinting at their grievances over matters like collectivisation and anti-religious drives.[25] No less important, by this stage the Russian nationalist sentiment that such works often played to existed not just outside the formal structures of Soviet power, but increasingly also inside them.[26] Typically anti-Western in outlook, as well as hostile towards 'pampered' intellectuals, there was considerable common ground between the worldview of Russia's new Village Prose writers and that of elements within the Soviet political elites. Not unlike the swelling cult of the Great Patriotic War, with which Village Prose dovetailed at times, officialdom's growing tolerance for, and even tacit encouragement of, Russian nationalism arguably served as another surrogate for the declining power of communism to mobilise the masses, in the Soviet regime's Russian heartlands at least.[27]

More than ever before, by the second half of the 1960s the cultural impetus was to embrace the past and 'tradition': not just that of the revolutionary era, but also of pre-revolutionary Russia. A new golden era was beginning for the folksy Palekh arts and crafts, with paintings, lacquer boxes and more depicting old-fashioned scenes of Russian idyll and folklore done in the Orthodox style being produced and bought in ever growing numbers, while the Palekh village choir performed on television in nineteenth-century costume.[28] Hugely popular historical novels by the likes of Valentin Pikul offered depictions of the tsarist past that fuelled nostalgia for its 'normality' and for Russian 'greatness'.[29] The big hit in Soviet cinemas during 1966–67 was a lavish production of Tolstoy's 1860s epic *War and Peace*. It was telling of the support for the movie that its director, Sergei Bondarchuk, was given access to the holdings of fifty-eight museums and collections for purposes of historical accuracy, while thousands of ordinary citizens sent in their own family artefacts to use as props.[30] Less widely viewed inside the USSR, but acclaimed by foreign critics especially – and still today regularly featuring in film-makers' lists of the best movies of all time – Tarkovsky's 1966 master-piece *Andrei Rublev* focused on a medieval icon painter, whose works had helped embed Christianity in the Russian lands.

By the end of the 1960s, there was a major exhibition of traditional Russian folk arts, replete with ringing church bells, at Moscow's Manezh gallery, while the new 'Golden Ring' tourist route showcased all manner of ancient sites associated with either the Church or the tsarist past in Suzdal, Kostroma and Sergiev Posad, among others.[31] Similarly, domestic tourists flocked in ever growing numbers to historic towns of the Russian northwest, such as Novgorod and Pskov, to see their famed wooden churches and preserved villages, where traditional Russian folk crafts, songs and customs all flourished again with official encouragement.[32] Although this was to prove an arena in which Russian nationalism blossomed, it was by no means only conservatives and nationalists who were eager to reconnect with Russia's pre-revolutionary heritage. Igor Golomstock, for example, recalled that in the early 1960s he and Andrei Sinyavsky used to spend holidays driving around the Russian north, exploring its remote churches and looking for icons.[33]

In much the same vein, this period also saw the founding of what would soon become one of the country's largest public organisations, the All-Russian Society for the Protection of Historical and Cultural Monuments (VOOPIK). By the mid-1960s, Soviet power had seen countless old churches and monas-teries destroyed with barely an afterthought. Coming in the wake of May 1966 legislation aimed at preserving what remained of Russia's beautiful pre-revolutionary wooden architecture, along with a doubling of the state budget for preservation and renovation activity, VOOPIK very soon had a staff of 1,500 overseeing work on preserving old monuments and architec-ture, as well as literature and folk art. Like the war cult, this was a regime-backed phenomenon that clearly enjoyed mass public engagement. Within a year of its founding, around 7 million people were dedicating their spare time and energy to preserving exactly the kinds of structures and symbols that the authorities had for so long been leaving to ruination, or else actively destroying.

By the mid-1960s, there were also warnings within Soviet officialdom that Khrushchev's clampdown on religion had produced the opposite effect to that intended, with observance going up rather than down.[34] One 1969 report from Belorussia noted a significant rise in the number of young people there (including many Komsomol members) attending baptisms, adding that 'this kind of mass participation did not happen before'.[35] By 1968, the KGB in Dnepropetrovsk was also complaining of a sharp rise in religiosity among youth, including collecting religious artefacts, taping sermons from the radio and reading religious materials.[36] Similarly, when Ilya Ehrenburg travelled to the Russian city of Ufa in 1967 he found that the number of Muslims there going to the mosque for Friday prayers had climbed considerably since his last visit.[37] This broad revival of interest in religion was apparently developing among exactly the kind of educated and urban citizens who had until recently been increasingly inclined towards secularism.

While not widespread, there were also some important signs of distinctly right-wing political views emerging in some quarters. In 1965, an official from the Moscow City Komsomol named Valery Skurlatov produced what he called a 'statute of customs', which has been fairly widely viewed as neo-fascistic in its xenophobia, anti-Semitism and militarism.[38] The following year, the KGB reported that it had uncovered a neo-Nazi youth group of about fifty members on the island of Sakhalin. According to the KGB, the group had a fascist hymn, drank toasts to Hitler on his birthday and was making plans to expel Koreans from the island (and had actually set fire to a Korean family's house on Hitler's birthday).[39] Also uncovered by the KGB in late 1966, a group calling itself 'The All-Russian Social Christian Union for the People's Liberation' had twenty-eight full members and thirty more candidate members. Its overtly nationalistic propaganda materials promised an eventual Orthodox theocracy to follow armed revolution, decrying communism as anti-Russian and a threat to Christianity.[40]

The increased latitude that was now being offered for celebration of Russian (rather than Soviet) national sentiment tended not to apply so readily in the non-Russian republics. Ukrainians, for example, started their own Ukrainian Society for the Preservation of Historical and Cultural Monuments, which soon had over 2 million members. This society, though, found its actions much more tightly restricted, with its volunteers mostly only allowed to protect revolutionary monuments, as the Moscow authorities were rapidly growing wary of public interest in studying peasant dress, dance, art and customs outside of

Russia.[41] When the celebrated Ukrainian writer Oles Honchar published the novel *Cathedral*, which centres on attempts to save a sixteenth-century Cossack church from destruction, it proved widely popular in Ukraine, but was soon banned on grounds of nationalism, with existing copies pulped and its most vocal supporters coming under sustained attack.

Ukrainians were by no means the only national group that came out of the period more acutely attuned to questions of their own history and culture. In 1966, the Kyrgyz author Chingiz Aitmatov wrote of how compatriots who had embraced the promise of the revolution in the 1920s were by the 1960s increasingly alarmed at how much of their native culture had since been destroyed in its aftermath.[42] Many Lithuanians also went through a pronounced rediscovery of folk themes and historical culture that turned away from Soviet modernism.[43] As in Ukraine, the KGB complained in 1969 that local studies activities there were exerting a negative influence, by promoting 'local patriotism, not socialist internationalism', though in fact they differed little from what such groups were doing with official sanction inside Russia.[44]

Just as there was a growing tendency for public culture to look backwards and inwards, rather than forwards and outwards, as the end of the decade approached the best days of the Soviet space race were also starting to recede into the past. By the mid-1960s, the programme's lynchpin, Sergei Korolev, had for some time been accumulating health problems stemming from both his years in the gulag and his punishing work schedule. He had suffered a heart attack in 1964, but was very quickly back working up to eighteen hours a day and overseeing even the smallest details of the space programme. Still trying to work from his hospital bed, Korolev underwent a routine operation in January 1966. Exacerbated by his declining physical strength, the operation (performed by the minister of health, a practising surgeon) went tragically wrong, as Korolev began to bleed profusely and never awoke from the anaesthetic. Granted a state funeral on 18 January, his ashes were carried by members of the cosmonaut team, before being placed in the Kremlin wall by Brezhnev and Kosygin. Death at least meant that the secrecy surrounding his identity was finally lifted, and Korolev was publicly feted as one of the great Soviet heroes. For the space programme, though, his passing was both a harbinger of and a catalyst for darker times ahead.

Already concerned that the Americans were pulling ahead, Gagarin and five fellow cosmonauts had written to Brezhnev in October 1965 to complain about the declining state of the Soviet space programme. Even before Korolev's death, Kamanin wrote in his diary on 4 January 1966 of a profound sense of pessimism among the cosmonaut team. Following the unexpected passing of Korolev, his deputy, Vasily Mishin, took control, but quickly found that he could not conduct the orchestra as effectively as his predecessor had done: he found himself fighting more and more often with the cosmonauts under his command and struggling to persuade his political masters to keep the funding flowing at its previous level. In summer 1967, Kamanin noted in his diary that Mishin 'has no authority, no talent, and actually demotivates his subordinates'.[45]

The Soviet Union had by the mid-1960s unofficially joined the race for a manned mission to the moon. Alarmed at the cost, Khrushchev had initially demurred when Korolev tried to persuade him to take on the US in the race to be first, changing his mind only in summer 1964. By then, keeping up with the Americans was becoming harder and harder, especially after handing them a major head start. Testing on the new Soyuz craft – built specifically for the moon mission – found over 2,000 faults in 1966. One launch that autumn saw the ship's self-destruct mechanism activated as it headed off course towards China, and another resulted in a launchpad explosion at Tyuratam that killed one person, but could easily have claimed many more lives, as people desperately fled the scene and dived into bunkers.[46] With Politburo members keen to boast of new successes as the fiftieth anniversary of the revolution approached, Mishin was under real pressure. Then, on 23 April 1967, Vladimir Komarov went into space for a second time. The plan was for his Soyuz-1 craft to dock in space with Soyuz-2, which was due to launch the following day.

Having only commenced work on a moon landing programme several years after the US effort had begun, Komarov's mission was part of a scramble to make up lost ground. Struggling with technological problems from the outset though, he was eventually directed to return to Earth ahead of schedule and the launch of Soyuz-2 was postponed. As he attempted a manual re-entry, the capsule's main parachute failed to deploy and the reserve immediately tangled up, leaving the cosmonaut to plummet to his death. When Komarov's remains were eventually located, recorded Kamanin, they consisted only of 'a lump about 30cm in diameter and 80cm in length'.[47] Valentina Ponomareva later asserted unequivocally that the flight had been sent up prematurely 'precisely because there was an urge to show the world a great space achievement for the fiftieth anniversary of the October Revolution', adding her opinion that the mission would never have been allowed to proceed had Korolev still been alive.[48] The repercussions of the tragedy rumbled on for months, as the remaining cosmonauts pushed hard for Mishin to be blamed in the official inquiry that followed. Hopes of a 1968 moon landing lay in tatters.

While the death of Korolev was surely the most damaging in terms of its strategic impact on the Soviet space programme, and Komarov's passing was undoubtedly deeply traumatic, the most symbolically powerful blow came at the end of March 1968. Yuri Gagarin had lobbied long and hard for permission to fly to space again, though the authorities were naturally wary of taking risks with the safety of such a celebrated figure.[49] Even so, that lobbying showed signs of having paid off when he was named as the standby for Komarov's fateful 1967 mission. The ensuing tragedy meant that the idea of Gagarin ever going into space again was decisively rejected. Nonetheless, in March 1968 he was at least allowed to return to flying as a pilot, albeit starting with a spell alongside an experienced co-pilot. After two weeks of flying together regularly, on 27 March Gagarin and his co-pilot took off again from a Moscow airfield, but soon lost contact with ground control. In challenging conditions, the pair had smashed into the ground and both had been killed instantly.

The sudden death of perhaps the most iconic figure of the age was an unmistakably epochal moment. A formal statement from the Politburo and Council of Ministers spoke of his passing 'causing deep pain' in the hearts of millions across the world. Little information was ever made public about exactly what had caused the crash, prompting all manner of rumours and conspiracy theories. Seemingly, Gagarin's own father did not believe that his death had been an accident, suspecting that his son's former closeness to Khrushchev was at the heart of the matter, though there is as yet little evidence to suggest any cause other than a plane malfunction.[50] In what was surely the grandest event of its kind since Stalin's passing back in 1953, Yuri

Gagarin's funeral on 30 March 1968 was held with full military honours and with fellow cosmonauts and foreign diplomats in attendance, as Brezhnev, Kosygin and other members of the top leadership escorted his ashes to their resting place in the Kremlin wall.

Prague Spring

Even as they deposited Gagarin's remains at the end of March 1968, Brezhnev and Kosygin were increasingly focused on affairs taking place in neighbouring Czechoslovakia, a country that had previously been viewed by many as the Soviet Union's 'best friend' in the socialist camp. Only a few days earlier, the pair had been in Dresden with party leaders from Bulgaria, East Germany, Poland, Hungary and Czechoslovakia. The experience had proved a chastening one for the Czechoslovak delegation. Although less aggressive in tone than some of those present, Brezhnev told Alexander Dubček that the Politburo had already spent dozens of hours analysing events in his country and warned that 'we cannot remain indifferent to developments in Czechoslovakia'. In fact, the Soviet leadership had already begun to envision a worst-case scenario, in which Czechoslovakia went over to the capitalist camp and the Warsaw Pact collapsed.[51]

As with Khrushchev and Hungary a dozen years previously, Brezhnev had inadvertently played a critical role in facilitating the events that now troubled him. Facing rising public discontent and splits within the ruling Communist Party of Czechoslovakia, in December 1967 the arch-Stalinist Antonín Novotný had invited Brezhnev to Prague in a bid to bolster his grip on power with a show of Soviet support. Once there, though, Brezhnev spent a day and a half personally interviewing Novotný's colleagues to ascertain their views on the situation in the country. The results were not good for Novotný, as Brezhnev came away judging him as both 'not having the slightest clue about the true state of affairs in the country' and 'incapable of co-operating with his comrades'. Instead of saving Novotný, Brezhnev cut him adrift, telling the rest of the Czechoslovak leadership 'this is your affair'.[52] By 5 January 1968, the reform-minded Slovak Alexander Dubček had replaced Novotný as Czechoslovak Communist Party boss. Having lived for a considerable number of years in the USSR, and having fought in the resistance during the war, this hardly seemed a risky appointment. The initial assessment of Dubček that was provided by the Soviet ambassador in Prague presented him as a 'staunch friend of the Soviet Union'.

From the start, though, Dubček was convinced that the only way to tackle the growing public discontent and stagnation that had helped undo his predecessor was through substantive reform. He quickly got to work on this: pushing out the most notorious Stalinist hardliners from the Czechoslovak leadership, beginning to liberalise public discourse and rehabilitating many victims of political repression. Soon to be known across the world as 'socialism with a human face', from an early stage Dubček's experiment with liberalisation not only aroused great hopes among reform-minded communists everywhere, but also caused growing alarm among party bosses in Berlin, Warsaw, Sofia and Moscow. As always, inside the Kremlin they conflated the unsettling events in Czechoslovakia with the machinations of the Cold War enemy. KGB documents were soon speaking of the West taking a new approach in its efforts at subversion – one that now foregrounded a phony rhetoric about 'improving' socialism.[53]

The meeting in Dresden on 23 March had been intended to bully Dubček into moving his liberalisation programme into reverse gear. In fact, it achieved the opposite result, as popular support for reform inside Czechoslovakia hardened against outside attempts at intimidation. In April, the Czechoslovak leadership published its Action Programme, outlining what were comfortably the most fundamental reforms the communist bloc had ever witnessed: these included tolerance for new public associations, more private enterprise, a more independent foreign policy line and better legal protection of citizens' rights and freedoms. The process of exposing and removing party officials linked to past repressions also gathered pace, sparking concern in Moscow, as loyal allies grew thinner on the ground inside Czechoslovakia. Soon, long-standing restrictions on freedom to practise religion and to enter or leave the country were being eased. By summer, there were also voices within the Czechoslovak military hierarchy calling for the country's withdrawal from the Warsaw Pact, and some urged the government to demand the return of land claimed by the Soviet Union (and added to Ukraine) at the end of the war.

Over the course of spring and early summer, the Soviet ambassador in Prague, Stepan Chervonenko, filed a series of increasingly concerned reports about events there. KGB Chairman Yuri Andropov – who had coincidentally been ambassador to Hungary during the crisis in 1956 and was forever mindful of parallels between the two – was similarly notable for his tough stance. As party boss in Ukraine, Petro Shelest was especially concerned at signs of ferment spilling across his republic's border with Czechoslovakia. Hardliner Alexander Shelepin also warned about the growing influence of Czechoslovak reforms among the Soviet student body and the liberal intelligentsia.[54] Politburo members were continually infuriated by a steady flow of materials in the Czechoslovak media that they considered openly anti-Soviet. Brezhnev, in particular, took offence at the personal mockery he was subjected to on television screens and in print there.[55] Having been present at the liberation of Prague back in 1945, he also felt personally affronted at the seeming 'ingratitude' being shown towards the USSR. The basic assumption in the Kremlin was that Dubček was being manipulated by subversive radicals within his own team, with the resulting reforms steadily but intentionally empowering enemies of socialism inside Czechoslovakia. As viewed from the Kremlin, these enemies – with the US and West Germany calling the shots off stage – would soon be in a position to launch a decisive counter-revolution to pull Czechoslovakia from the socialist camp entirely, undermining the whole bloc's strategic position in the process.

Already by spring 1968, the Soviet media were warning of America ramping up its efforts to stir trouble in the communist camp. In April, a Central Committee plenum demanded greater effort in inculcating 'ideological firmness' and opposition to bourgeois influences among Soviet citizens, as censorship tightened even further.[56] However, Soviet authorities had little chance of fully insulating their own society from events taking place inside Czechoslovakia. Key Czechoslovak texts like the 'Two Thousand Words' manifesto (among the most strident of the reformists' declarations) soon appeared in samizdat and featured in broadcasts by stations like Radio Liberty and the BBC. Czechoslovak newspapers were on sale inside the USSR until June 1968, parts of western Ukraine picked up Czechoslovak television signals and thousands of Czechoslovak students were studying in Soviet universities. A report by the party leadership in Moldavia told that letters and appeals were being sent from Czechoslovakia to local citizens, seeking to persuade them that the reform programme there was neither anti-socialist nor anti-Soviet.[57] Soviet tour guides complained about Czechoslovak visitors attempting to propagandise the reforms taking place back home as they met people inside the USSR.[58] Similarly, well into the summer of 1968, thousands of Soviet tourists were still heading to Czechoslovakia every month, with the political reforms and changed public atmosphere on the streets practically unmissable to visitors.[59]

In the middle of May 1968, one Czechoslovak foreign correspondent based in Moscow wrote home describing shifting attitudes among the Soviet public. At the start of the year, he said, some were openly enthusiastic about Dubček's reform programme, but continual attacks in the media had seen more and more Soviet citizens expressing outright concern and opposition.[60] This picture was not true for absolutely everyone in the Soviet Union, of course. For those basically loyal to communism, but liberal-minded in their political views, the first half of 1968 was a hugely invigorating time, and one that seemed pregnant with possibilities. Sakharov, for example, recalled that when Soviet liberals looked to Czechoslovakia's reform programme 'everything we wanted seemed to be coming true'.[61]

One KGB informant's report from Odessa outlined two basic attitudes among students there. There were some who resented the Czechoslovaks' 'ingratitude' to the USSR and wanted decisive action taken, but they were few in number. The rest, it said, were watching events with great interest and 'benevolent curiosity', admiring the way that students there had made themselves into an important social force, and finding little that was objectionable in the Czechoslovaks' 'excesses' that were decried in the Soviet press.[62] Already in mid-May, Shelest was warning Moscow that Ukrainian regions bordering Czechoslovakia were seeing individuals (here he referred specifically to 'nationalists, Zionists, religious and other anti-Soviet elements') using the situation next door to 'express openly hostile, anti-Soviet sentiments'. He also cautioned that intelligence services from the US, UK and West Germany were smuggling ever more harmful literature across Soviet borders.[63]

Wary that the Baltic republics might again be especially susceptible to unrest, on 30 April 1968 the Estonian Communist Party, KGB and Ministry for the Defence of Public Order finalised a detailed plan of measures to be taken in the event of mass disorders in Tallinn (similar documents presumably also existed for Riga and Vilnius at least). The first priority was to despatch troops, KGB officers and police to protect the buildings and personnel of the Estonian Communist Party Central Committee, Council of Ministers and Presidium of the Supreme Soviet, as well as to secure telegraph offices, city and inter-city telephone exchanges, post offices, the radio station, television centre, railways and airport.[64] Volunteer patrols made up of 'the most author-itative workers' were to be established at twenty key factories and plants throughout the city and 'reliable people' were to join any crowds that gath-ered, in order to inform authorities of changing moods and rumours, warn of any terrorist intentions, and identify and (where possible) isolate ringleaders. Clearly, authorities were wary of what might possibly lie ahead.

Already long unhappy at the political laxness to be found in more free-thinking corners of the country, like Akademgorodok, party officials also cracked down there. Two events in early 1968 saw the authorities' patience snap. The first was a collective letter in February, protesting against the Ginzburg and Galanskov trial, that was signed by forty-six Akademgorodok scientists and students (later appearing in the *New York Times*). The second, in March, was a 'festival of Bards', held without seeking the permission of the party or Komsomol. Not only did the festival include a performance by the outspoken regime critic Alexander Galich – in fact, this was Galich's only official performance ever in the USSR, since he was pretty much an open dissident – but it also awarded him first prize for best performer.[65] Soon enough, a large round of sackings and expulsions from the party followed at Akademgorodok, as the new political orthodoxy was more stringently imposed.[66]

In the Politburo, the likes of Shelest and Andropov were delivering ever starker warnings that the window for action was closing. They demanded invasion, on the grounds that 'the threat to the great cause of socialism does not give us the right to behave in any other way'.[67] By summer 1968, virtually only Brezhnev was still not committed to a military response. His concerns centred mainly on the volatile international fallout that an invasion would surely provoke. When another meeting of Warsaw Pact leaders was called at short notice in mid-July, Dubček stayed away, heightening suspicions about his loyalties. The remainder met without him, and the East German, Polish and Bulgarian delegations openly and vigorously supported invasion. The message being conveyed to Prague increasingly resembled an ultimatum:

fraternal regimes had both a right and a duty to prevent counter-revolution in Czechoslovakia. This threat was then made more tangible by a series of Warsaw Pact military manoeuvres (long scheduled for September 1968, but brought forward in a naked bid to intimidate) carried out around Czechoslovakia's borders. The KGB also worked hard to sow disinformation and doubt among the public inside Czechoslovakia, though with little obvious success. On-going in the background for months already, Soviet military preparations for invasion moved into top gear in July.[68]

The two sides met for five days of last-ditch talks on the Czechoslovak-Soviet border, at Čierna nad Tisau at the end of July. Held in a cramped railwaymen's club, the negotiations were extremely difficult. Brezhnev fell ill with stress at one point, becoming jittery and shaky as his reliance on sleeping pills grew, and holding talks with Dubček while still in his pyjamas.[69] Nonetheless, the Soviet leader left convinced that he had secured concrete promises of imminent action to rein in the Czechoslovak reforms. Dubček, though, would later insist that he had given no such guarantees. At a separate meeting in Bratislava on 3 August, a pre-arranged letter was discreetly handed to Petro Shelest in the toilets, signed by five of the remaining pro-Soviet members of the Czechoslovak leadership. It insisted that 'the very existence of socialism in our country is under threat' and asked for the Soviet Union to assist 'with all means at your disposal'.[70]

Steadily fading throughout, Brezhnev's faith in Dubček's ability to right the situation in Czechoslovakia finally ran out. In a last telephone call between the two on 13 August, Brezhnev accused him of outright deceit and warned 'it is impossible to overstate, Sasha, how irritated I am by what you're doing now'.[71] A Politburo meeting lasting from 15 to 17 August saw the decision to invade approved unanimously. The day after, the news was passed on to almost 650 high-ranking party functionaries across the USSR, ordering officials everywhere to start giving 'serious attention to explanatory and mass political work among all segments of the Soviet public'. The message to be presented was that intervention was the USSR's 'internationalist duty' and a mark of fraternal solidarity to help the Czechoslovak people overcome a looming Rightist coup in their country.[72]

At 01:00 on 21 August, Operation Danube swung into action. Perhaps 350,000 Soviet troops, alongside smaller contingents from Bulgaria, Poland

and Hungary, poured into Czechoslovakia from the east, south and north. USSR Defence Minister Andrei Grechko warned his Czechoslovak counterpart that there would be merciless retribution if Soviet forces came under attack, and officials in Prague duly directed troops to remain in their barracks, in order to forestall the kind of hopeless carnage seen in Hungary. Even so, over 120 Czechoslovak citizens were killed in the chaotic events that followed. Seemingly believing that they would be greeted as friends, the invading forces were soon dismayed to encounter locals blocking roads, spitting at tanks and screaming in protest as they raced past. By 09:00, though, Soviet troops had entered the party's Central Committee building in Prague and seized Dubček and a handful of his closest collaborators, dragging them off to Moscow.

After the invasion

The protests of Czechoslovak citizens were overwhelmingly peaceful, but nonetheless vociferous. Almost from their very arrival, Soviet tanks were daubed with swastikas, likening their invasion to that of the Nazis three decades previously. Before long, walls and roads were covered in graffiti like 'Russians go home', 'Russian brothers – our enemies' and 'Lenin died on 21 August'.[73] For some considerable time afterwards, many Czechs and Slovaks refused even to talk to Soviet visitors they encountered, branding them 'occupiers' or worse.[74] This burning resentment was still very much in evidence during March 1969, when the Czechoslovak and Soviet ice hockey teams met at the world championships in Sweden, with both sides in with a chance of claiming the title. An intensely bad-tempered clash ended in a narrow victory for the Czechoslovak team, and within minutes crowds of jubilant supporters poured into town squares back home. The ensuing celebrations morphed into violence, as Soviet war memorials were defaced and diplomatic vehicles burned, while the Prague offices of the Soviet airline Aeroflot were ransacked. Moscow took an especially dim view of all this, threatening to put soldiers back on Czechoslovak streets right away if further disturbances were to occur. In fact, these events proved a convenient excuse for the USSR to redouble its clampdown, removing the last of Dubček's remaining allies from office and reversing more reforms.[75]

The invasion of Czechoslovakia also exacerbated divides within the communist world, with the Chinese, Romanian and Yugoslav regimes all publicly condemning it. In Bucharest especially, a defiant Nicolae Ceaușescu won great public acclaim by denouncing Soviet aggression. The USSR would also never recover the prestige it now lost with the West European Left. The French Communist Party announced its 'surprise and reprobation' at the intervention, and the politburo of the Italian Communist Party expressed both its incomprehension and its 'grave dissent'.[76] Condemnation also came from allied communist parties in Great Britain, Norway, Ireland and the Netherlands, among others. Further afield, the picture looked little better. Indian Prime Minister Indira Gandhi was somewhat restrained in registering her disapproval (stating only that every country had the right to live without outside interference), but a large faction of the Indian Communist Party branded the invasion 'an act of imperialist aggression'.[77] At the UN, a draft resolution condemning the invasion enjoyed widespread sympathy, but was predictably killed off by the Soviet veto. For the most part, though, the major Western powers signalled their opposition to the invasion, but took things no further, since they did not wish to abandon the progress being made in improving their own relations with the USSR.

The party and Komsomol organs had a clear narrative on events to present, and they immediately swung into action to get members in line, churning out newspaper articles and holding myriad lectures and talks. On 21 August alone – the very day of the invasion – the Moscow branch of the Communist Party held over 9,000 meetings (with around 885,000 people in attendance) at factories, universities, building sites and more.[78] The Soviet press reported unanimous support among the population, but such claims were first and foremost a bid to shape popular opinion, rather than an accurate reflection of the public mood. Of course, many citizens readily accepted the official narratives on Soviet fraternal aid to protect socialism in Czechoslovakia. A student in Moscow at the time, David Gurevich recalled sardonically that 'Plain folks . . . just rooted for our glorious tank forces the way they rooted for our ice hockey team.'[79] Similarly, Anatoly Marchenko (who was jailed on unrelated charges just as events in Czechoslovakia reached their peak) wrote that most of his fellow prisoners were either indifferent to the invasion or else openly critical of the Czechoslovaks.[80] Some felt that, regardless of all other considerations, too much Soviet blood had been spilt in liberating Czechoslovakia from Nazi occupation for that country now to be allowed to slip into the enemy camp. After the Soviet collapse, Mikhail Gorbachev would admit that although he had hoped the reforms would lead to political renewal in Czechoslovakia, he, like many other citizens, had come to the conclusion by summer 1968 that intervention was necessary 'to stop Western powers' subversion' there.[81]

Although the response was not as visceral as after the attack on Hungary in 1956, there is plenty of evidence to demonstrate that not everyone supported the invasion. The Ukrainian KGB soon registered hundreds of statements opposed to the invasion, and many instances of anti-Soviet leaflets and graffiti. Some likened it to tsarist imperialism, others to fascism or the US bombardment of Vietnam, insisting that the USSR should learn from Czechoslovakia, not to invade it.[82] Lithuanian KGB records show critical leaflets found scattered in the streets, with people complaining that the Soviet Union had forever lost its authority in the eyes of communists across the world and predicting revolution inside the USSR within a decade.[83] A party meeting at the Central Children's Library in Moscow saw one of the staff there brand the invasion 'fascism'; elsewhere, someone insisted that the introduction of armed forces into Czechoslovakia was 'a testament to our defeat on the ideological front'.[84] A report from KGB Chairman Andropov also noted hostile leaflets and graffiti discovered on walls at Akademgorodok.[85] Leaflets found at the Shevchenko University in Kiev the same month called on students to copy their brethren in France, Yugoslavia and Czechoslovakia and join the struggle to rein in elite privilege and bureaucratic power and to push for greater freedom of speech.[86]

Many in the USSR's creative and scientific intelligentsia veered between fury and despair at the invasion, with plenty of them later describing feelings of great personal shame and of having reached a kind of spiritual breaking point, though only a very small minority ever moved into sustained opposition. Yakov Alpert, for example, described being 'sickened to know that Soviet troops held the Czechoslovakian people at gunpoint', coming to the conclusion that the USSR had become a fascist country.[87] Holidaying together at Koktebel in Crimea, Vasily Aksenov and Yevgeny Yevtushenko heard news of the invasion over the radio, and both immediately hit the vodka to drown their despair.

Yevtushenko wrote that his own tears were those of a crestfallen idealist, while Aksenov's were tears of hatred. Others at their resort, though, remained unmoved, and the scene nearly ended in a brawl as a drunken Aksenov began to tell people around him that they were all slaves.[88] Aksenov would later describe the invasion bluntly as the point at which 'all of our hopes had been murdered'.[89]

On 25 August, behind the Kremlin walls, Dubček was still being berated by members of the Soviet leadership and threatened with the absorption of Czechoslovakia into the Soviet Union if he did not undo his reforms once back in Prague. Shortly before noon that same day, three women and five men approached the Kremlin from different directions, making their way through the usual crowds on Red Square. As their paths converged at the old Executioner's Place by St Basil's Cathedral, Larisa Bogoraz, Pavel Litvinov, Natalya Gorbanevskaya, Vadim Delone (Delaunay), Tanya Baeva, Viktor Fainberg, Vladimir Dremlyuga and Konstantin Babitsky sat down on the ground. As the clock began to strike twelve, Gorbanevskaya pulled out a handful of placards from inside her baby's pram. She then held up a small Czechoslovak flag; Bogoraz had a sign reading 'Hands Off the CzSSR' (Czechoslovak Socialist Republic) and Litvinov clutched one that read 'For Your Freedom and Ours'. Dremlyuga later called the moment in question 'a few minutes of pure freedom and joy'.[90]

Actually, both Gorbanevskaya and Baeva later recalled that it took only seconds for perhaps ten KGB people to come racing through the throng on Red Square and descend on the group, seizing the banners and beating Litvinov and Fainberg, in particular. In her account, Baeva described voices from the gathering crowd calling the protesters 'anti-Soviet', 'scum' and 'dirty yids'. Indeed, subsequent KGB reports claimed that the group was removed from the scene a few minutes later (once a suitable vehicle had been commandeered) for their own good, before the offended Soviet masses got to them. Gorbanevskaya – who could not be bundled away quite so brusquely as the others, since she had a baby and a pram with her – recalled instead that the hostile shouts purportedly emanating from outraged onlookers were actually an unsuccessful attempt by undercover KGB agents to whip up anger against the protesters. Either way, all eight were soon forced into nearby vehicles and driven away. As the car she was in pulled away, Gorbanevskaya shouted 'long live free Czechoslovakia' through the open window. For this the driver punched her in the mouth.[91]

Very soon, news of the Red Square protest was being reported by both Reuters and the BBC. Baeva somehow convinced her interrogators that she was only there by chance, and was let go after a few hours; Gorbanevskaya was spared criminal charges on account of her having two young children at home. The six others were put on trial, officially on the grounds that they had disrupted the passage of traffic and deliberately spread lies about the Soviet system (since their banners implied a Soviet invasion). By 5 September, long before the case actually reached court, KGB Chairman Andropov was 'proposing' that both Litvinov and Bogoraz be exiled to 'a remote area' (which is exactly what the courts decided, in due course).[92] Fainberg would be absent from the trial. Accounts suggest that the beating he took while being arrested (including the loss of several teeth) meant that the authorities did not want him to be seen in public.[93] He was sent instead to the Serbsky Institute, and was from there despatched to the notorious Leningrad Special Psychiatric Hospital, only being released four years later.

Knowing full well that the outcome was hardly in the balance, Bogoraz insisted on defending herself at trial. In court, she said she had felt compelled to act, since 'it was important to me that my "no" had been heard'. Litvinov, too, declared that he felt obliged as a Soviet citizen to 'express my disagreement with a mistake of the grossest kind committed by our government'.[94] For Bogoraz, in particular, sentenced to four years' exile in the small Siberian town of Chuna, conditions were to prove practically ruinous to her health. Although not charged alongside the other protesters, Gorbanevskaya was subsequently sent to the Serbsky Institute for psychiatric evaluation, where she was found to be 'not responsible' for her actions; but was released into the care of her mother. Once her first-hand account of the Red Square protest appeared in samizdat, and then also in the West a few months later, the Serbsky diagnosis was activated and she, too, was despatched to a psychiatric hospital in 1969.

The tightening-up that followed August 1968 inside the USSR was both wide-ranging and enduring. The ideological journal *Kommunist* targeted what it called 'political immaturity' among the scientific community and demanded an 'ideological tempering of the intelligentsia' while Soviet enemies were on the attack.[95] Mikhail Gorbachev recalled the post-invasion crackdown as 'a frontal assault against all forms of free thinking'.[96] Of the results in the cultural sphere, Vasily Aksenov said years later that 'everyone was shocked by this, by the extent of the crackdown. It was as if we all had a collective breakdown.'[97] Even some months before the invasion, reform-minded journalists and editors in the USSR had been steadily removed from their posts.[98] In the film industry, a new decree made studio bosses personally liable for movies made under their purview, stifling further the work of directors and writers.[99] Vladimir Voinovich wrote of a September 1968 Central Committee directive to editors and censors across the country to cancel all publications by writers known to have protested in defence of others, with offending books pulped and withdrawn from libraries.[100] Some among the liberal intelligentsia began to speak quietly of a new Soviet 'fascism', characterised by anti-intellectualism, ramped-up patriotism, demands for 'order' and celebration of 'Russianness'.[101] Boris Kagarlitsky wrote simply that 'on the morning of 21 August 1968, the entire ideology of Soviet liberalism collapsed in a few minutes, and all the hopes aroused by the Twentieth Congress fell to the ground.'[102]

Brezhnev consolidates power

In May 1968, as the Prague Spring still rumbled on, the Czechoslovak journalist Ján Riško noticed rumours among his fellow foreign correspondents in Moscow that Brezhnev might soon be removed from power by a group within the Soviet leadership that was seeking to 'run all domestic and international affairs much more firmly'.[103] Although these rumours ultimately proved incorrect, they do help to demonstrate that this was still a time when Brezhnev's political supremacy was not yet undisputed. While the wrangling at the top was not openly volatile, Brezhnev was, according to one source who saw developments at first hand, 'from the first day focused on strengthening his authority'.[104] Like Khrushchev and Stalin, not only did he appoint plenty of his 'own' people to key posts, but Brezhnev also proved effective at winning the enduring loyalty of others among the elite. In sharp contrast to Khrushchev's last years in power, he spoke to colleagues respectfully and took care to chat regularly with officials in the regions and non-Russian republics, spending hours every day on the telephone, building ties with those not already part of his 'clan' (which was known as 'the Dnepropetrovsk mafia', because many of them had been associated with him since his time in the Ukrainian city).[105]

As chairman of the Council of Ministers, Alexei Kosygin was in some senses the most obvious of the potential rivals to Brezhnev. Nikolai Baibakov, who worked under every leader from Stalin to Yeltsin, years later judged Kosygin the strongest and most erudite of all the top state figures he encountered, describing him as simple and restrained in his personal conduct and a deep thinker who had at his fingertips great knowledge of industry, finance and planning.[106] Similarly, Viktor Sukhodrev wrote that Kosygin was 'clearly on a higher intellectual plane than other Soviet leaders'.[107]

Because Brezhnev would take a few years to find his feet as a global statesman, that left Kosygin to play the lead international role at first, undertaking high-profile visits to the UK, France, Vietnam, the USA and North Korea, among others. Perhaps most notably, it was Kosygin who took personal control when the Soviet Union stepped in as mediator to help end a series of escalating border clashes between India and Pakistan in 1965. Bringing Pakistani President Ayub Khan and Indian Prime Minister Lal Bahadur Shastri to Tashkent for talks during January 1966, Kosygin continually shuttled between the two bitter enemies until they were prepared first to talk to one another directly, and then to agree terms to end their dispute. In the process, he won considerable global attention and acclaim. This was indeed a major feat of diplomacy that did both Kosygin and the USSR great credit, though it was ultimately somewhat overshadowed by the fact that Shastri suddenly died (of natural causes) on the final night of the talks in Tashkent, soon after leaving the gala dinner that had been held to celebrate the agreement.

Kosygin was never really 'defeated' in the post-Khrushchev power struggle – since he remained Soviet prime minister until his death in 1980 – but he was increasingly sidelined by a jealous Brezhnev. While he was still head of Soviet television and radio, Nikolai Mesyatsev recalled being unofficially warned by intermediaries that Brezhnev was growing irritated at how much news coverage Kosygin was receiving during a 1967 visit to the UK. The message was soon acted upon and his media profile dropped.[108] Every time Kosygin went abroad, the newspapers knew that they also had to report heavily on whatever Brezhnev was doing at the same time, regardless of how mundane it might be.[109] Before long, Kosygin's role in foreign affairs was also considerably reduced, as Brezhnev became more active in that sphere himself.

Crucially, Kosygin had never assembled the kind of client network that could prove essential in a Soviet leadership struggle. On the contrary, he was quickly and deliberately surrounded by Brezhnev loyalists: at one stage he had five deputies under him who were all 'Brezhnev men'.[110] He was thus fairly easily neutralised as a potential threat. Baibakov recalled seeing Kosygin emerge from Politburo meetings 'literally shaking with indignation' about decisions that were being taken, but lacking the support to act.[111] Most importantly, his 1965 economic reform – which Kosygin was hugely committed to – was quietly strangled. Led by Mikhail Suslov, but seemingly with Brezhnev in the background, other Politburo members steadily withdrew their previous support for its phased implementation, and the ambitious scope of Kosygin's attempts at driving long-term economic change was steadily watered down. Once events in Czechoslovakia had convinced most in the Kremlin of the danger posed by practically any reform at all, Kosygin's plan was finished.[112] For at least one liberal-minded regime insider, this was a key moment at which it became clear that a different era was really under way.[113]

Since Brezhnev was typically courteous and collegial within the Politburo, and was inclined to let colleagues oversee their respective fiefdoms largely as they saw fit, most were soon content to work under him.[114] Mikhail Suslov, in particular, had the kind of status that could have made him a potential rival, but he proved entirely willing to remain squarely behind Brezhnev until his death in 1982. Nikolai Podgorny (described witheringly by one observer as a man of 'big ambition but little ammunition') took Mikoyan's vacated post as chairman of the Supreme Soviet. This officially made him the most powerful after Brezhnev and Kosygin, but in reality put him in a job that had little real influence or prospect for advancement.[115] In a move that would be used more than once by Brezhnev's clique, Podgorny's position was then weakened when his most important ally was attacked and later demoted. As Ukrainian party boss, Petro Shelest held the biggest job outside Moscow; and, as Khrushchev's own rise to power had shown, his power base could make him an influential player in any leadership challenge. By autumn 1965, though, Shelest was coming in for concerted criticism within the leadership over an apparent failure to tackle rising Ukrainian nationalism.[116] Russian nationalists like Shelepin also accused him and his team of trying to carve out special benefits for Ukraine at the expense of other Soviet republics. As both Shelest's patron and his predecessor in Kiev, Podgorny was also an implicit target in these attacks. Like Kosygin, he would remain in post for years to come, but without the allies or influence to challenge Brezhnev.

For all that Kosygin was the best-qualified alternative to Brezhnev, the most dangerous rival was surely Alexander Shelepin. In fact, it was Shelepin whom the Czechoslovak journalist Ján Riško had named as the likely challenger to Brezhnev in May 1968. He had already served as head of the Komsomol and as KGB chairman, before being moved in 1962 to head up Khrushchev's new Party-State Control Commission – a 'super-ministry' with the power to intervene in myriad aspects of party and state work, ensuring that decrees were being implemented on the ground, tackling corruption and appointing personnel to key posts, and more. According to Rada Khrushcheva, her father had viewed Shelepin as a future second-in-command, and maybe even a successor, once he had acquired more experience at the top level of party leadership.[117] Brezhnev's circle had thus eyed Shelepin warily even before Khrushchev's removal from power. They were also aware of whispers after October 1964 insisting that Brezhnev was a temporary 'compromise' figure, to be brushed aside by Shelepin and his team of 'Young Turks' when the time was right.[118]

Shelepin has been widely understood as the leading neo-Stalinist candidate: politically very conservative, deeply anti-Western and with a strong Russian nationalist streak. In sharp contrast to Brezhnev, he also took a hard line against corruption and was no supporter of the material privilege that most other members of the elite enjoyed immensely. Unlike some others at the top, he also had the courage of his convictions – standing alone in his opinion when he disagreed with the majority.[119] Where Shelepin differed most from Kosygin as a rival to be wary of was in the size and strength of his client network.

He did not have Brezhnev's personal charm (a highly effective part of his skillset for much of his career), but Shelepin did inspire considerable loyalty among those close to him, and many with whom he had worked at the Komsomol in the 1950s were thereafter promoted upwards in his slipstream.

Along with presiding KGB Chairman Vladimir Semichastny, members of this 'Komsomol clique' around Shelepin included the minster of internal affairs (Vadim Tikunov), the head of the State Committee for Television and Radio (Nikolai Mesyatsev), the head of TASS (Dmitry Goryunov) and the head of the Komsomol (Sergei Pavlov), as well as a plethora of other high-ranking party and state figures (and KGB officials in particular) in the regions and non-Russian republics. One biographer asserts that there were friends of Shelepin 'everywhere'.[120] These were typically men considerably younger and better educated than the generation of officials (including the likes of Brezhnev, Suslov, Kosygin and Podgorny) who had been born around the start of the twentieth century and who reached political maturity in the 1920s and 1930s.

Although he had supported Shelepin's elevation to full Politburo member in November 1964 – a reward for his active participation in the removal of Khrushchev – Brezhnev was soon working at getting Shelepin out of his powerful Party-State Control Commission job, and he was not short of support in this. Georgy Arbatov, for example, described how those who feared a return to full-fledged Stalinism gathered around Brezhnev in order to stop Shelepin.[121] Again, Brezhnev did not openly target the man, but instead weakened the ground on which he stood. In December 1965, as he ostensibly spoke in praise of the work of Shelepin's Party-State Control Commission, Brezhnev promoted a number of changes supposedly intended to streamline and enhance its work, but which ultimately parcelled out key functions to other organisations and steadily reduced Shelepin's powers as its chairman. In summer 1966, the Brezhnev and Shelepin cliques engaged in an arm wrestle over the vacant post of minister of internal affairs, with both keen to see their own man in charge. Brezhnev was able to convince a majority within the Politburo to back his (unqualified) candidate, Nikolai Shchelokov, by tapping into their concern at the extent of Shelepin's rising influence.

What remains unclear is whether any kind of concrete plan for taking power ever came together among Shelepin's team. There are suggestions that it did, but not a great deal in the way of hard evidence. In his memoirs, Mikoyan claimed that at an unspecified point in 1967 – by which time he was already retired from active political life – someone from 'Shelepin's group' approached him with an invitation to support an imminent struggle against Brezhnev. The group apparently wanted the venerable Mikoyan to speak at an upcoming meeting with initial criticism of Brezhnev, whereupon other plotters would take the lead. Deeply disappointed with Brezhnev as he already was, Mikoyan nonetheless had serious concerns about Shelepin's Russian chauvinism and refused any involvement.[122]

Arguably the key moment in the struggle to stop Shelepin came when he was deprived of his most loyal and powerful supporter. As both the failed (1957) and the successful (1964) coup attempts had shown, the co-operation of the security organs could help make or break any designs on taking power. In May 1967, while Shelepin was absent through illness, KGB Chairman Semichastny was unexpectedly summoned from the Lubyanka to a Politburo meeting. With most of those present signed up to the plan in advance, Brezhnev opened the meeting by insisting that, as KGB chairman, Semichastny had to carry the can for Stalin's daughter's recent defection to the West (permission for her trip to India had actually been approved by Mikoyan and Kosygin). Then, Suslov, Kosygin, Podgorny and the rest all voted in favour of Brezhnev's proposal and Semichastny's career at the KGB was over in an instant. To keep him away from Moscow and Shelepin, Semichastny was then appointed to a new job as deputy chair of the Ukrainian Council of Ministers, in Kiev. Dozens of other Shelepin associates soon followed, facing sharp career demotions or ambassadorial postings abroad. It would take a few more years before Shelepin was himself excluded from the Politburo – after which he saw out his days as a great pariah, avoided by all – but his star would only grow dimmer and his political isolation deeper from the end of the 1960s.

Kosygin and Shelepin represented very different routes that the Soviet Union could conceivably have taken. The stability and system decay that followed in the years after Khrushchev's removal, then, were by no means inevitable. However, although his dominance within the Soviet leadership was firmly established by the end of the 1960s, Brezhnev's best days as a political actor were rapidly running out. The stress surrounding events in Czechoslovakia in particular had seen him become increasingly reliant on tranquilisers – a problem that would in time grow especially acute. He had anyway suffered at least two heart attacks, seemingly from a combination of overwork and heavy smoking, even before coming to power. Once he was established as the boss, his work ethic waned notably. Nikolai Baibakov, for example, recalled one personal meeting in which he presented Brezhnev with detailed economic plans, only for the general secretary to grow visibly bored and depressed, placing his hands heavily on his knees and saying that he wanted to go hunting instead (which they duly did).[123] Similarly, Ambassador Anatoly Dobrynin wrote that when he called on Brezhnev during his visits to Moscow and asked him for any instructions on future dealings with the US leadership, he got the reply: 'What instructions do you need? You know better than I how to deal with the Americans.'[124] Before the mid-point of the 1970s had been reached, Brezhnev's health was in obvious decline: his attention wandered ever more quickly, he struggled at times to walk unaided, he slurred and became heavily reliant on notes when speaking (all of which would spawn countless jokes at his expense).

As with the period immediately after Stalin's death, it took a while for the longer-term direction of travel to reveal itself following Khrushchev's ouster, but that process was clearly approaching completion by the end of the 1960s. Events surrounding the Prague Spring were both a cause and a reflection of increasingly reactionary attitudes at the top of the Soviet regime, and this left an indelible impression on the balance of power within the Politburo, on economic and cultural affairs, and much more besides.[125] In addition to the deleterious impact that it had on the lives and hopes of millions of Czechs and Slovaks, snuffing out reformism next door also meant killing much of the remaining dynamism, optimism and romanticism that had helped characterise the previous fifteen years inside the USSR, marking the end of the 'Soviet Sixties'.

EPILOGUE

Running roughly from the invasion of Czechoslovakia in 1968 through to the accession to power of Mikhail Gorbachev in 1985, the Soviet Union's 'long 1970s' was a period largely in keeping with the broader picture of how that decade played out across much of the globe: a time of deepening political conservatism and dissipating idealism. Nonetheless, living standards were mostly rising, Soviet military strength was growing and overt signs of significant discontent remained few. Some reform-minded individuals, like the historian Yuri Afanasev, would later speak of the long 1970s as almost twenty years 'lost', but others have recalled instead a kind of Soviet golden age of stability, status and relative prosperity.[1] The notion of the period between 1968 and 1985 as an era of 'stagnation' – a term used by Gorbachev in particular, as he sought to put clear water between his own rule and that of Brezhnev – was for years widespread, but is now increasingly being rejected or else finessed by historians, as new research on the period accumulates. The picture starting to emerge is one of an age in which especially social and cultural developments cannot be adequately encapsulated with simplistic notions like 'decline' and 'inertia'.[2] Doubtless, there are exciting new findings to come.

At least a handful of accounts have, for a variety of reasons, presented the Soviet Sixties as having effectively marked the beginning of the end for the communist regime.[3] One recent scholar, for example, has written (with specific reference to the Secret Speech) that Khrushchev 'discredited the regime, its values, and the idea of communism'.[4] Coming from a very different angle, a foreign visitor to Moscow at the end of the 1950s, marvelling at the new atmosphere in the country, commented 'one can only wonder what the Soviet Union will be like when the young generation of today becomes the ruling generation of tomorrow'.[5] Certainly, there are fascinating linkages to be explored in the way that events and themes covered in this book shaped the people who would support and lead the reforms of the late 1980s that ultimately (albeit accidentally) killed off the Soviet regime. A host of those key reformists experienced the Soviet Sixties as their formative period, when they began careers in the party, in journalism, academia and more. Plenty of them spoke quite openly in the late 1980s about seeing themselves as 'Children of the Twentieth Party Congress', taking that era-defining moment of revived idealism as a touchstone for their subsequent careers and lives. The death throes of the Soviet Sixties could also be instructive in this sense. Mikhail Gorbachev spoke years later of making a working visit to Czechoslovakia in 1969, where he unexpectedly witnessed the extent of post-invasion public animosity towards the Soviet Union – a moment which, he recalled, prompted his own reappraisal of the invasion and became for him 'a major impulse towards critical thinking'.[6]

Ties between the Soviet Sixties and the events that culminated in the Soviet collapse are by no means restricted to a few crucial individuals, however. The (relative) liberalisation of nationalities policy after Stalin not just eased accumulating tensions somewhat, but also facilitated an engagement with questions of national culture and tradition that only grew over time. This was, of course, one of the absolutely central issues around which the Soviet Union eventually fell apart. Similarly, from the mid-1950s onwards, rising standards of living – in terms of housing, leisure, goods in the shops and more – were increasingly understood as something that citizens had a right to expect from Soviet power. This notion naturally proved problematic once the economy began to seize up and then head towards collapse by the late 1980s. Intractable division within the ruling Communist Party – broadly, between hardline and more moderate communists – would also prove a central feature of the regime's final disintegration, and this was another divide that had some considerable basis in the events of the Soviet Sixties, as those in favour of and those opposed to reform clashed on questions of culture, foreign policy, ideology and much more. Ecological concerns would also occupy a prominent place in the socio-political tumult of the Gorbachev years, and we see here that not only was this an area in which considerable damage had been done during the earlier period, but it was also one in which the earliest stages of public mobilisation could be observed.

One of the most fascinating dynamics of the Sixties era is that of roads that could easily have been taken, but ultimately were not. These included the failed coup in 1957, the USSR's stillborn drive for computerisation and the abortive attempt by Kosygin to breathe new life into the Soviet economy during the mid-1960s. Each of these had the potential to reshape subsequent Soviet history quite dramatically. Indeed, there exists a school of thought which suggests that Leonid Brezhnev might well have been a markedly more reform-minded leader were it not for the Prague Spring, which shaped and defined his rule from a fairly early moment.[7]

Many important legacies of the Soviet Sixties have naturally persisted into the present day. Despite their planned life expectancy of around twenty-five years when first built, the distinctive five-storey *khrushchevki* (Khrushchev houses) can still be found inhabited right across the former Soviet space. Movies like *Carnival Night* and books like *Dr Zhivago* now stand squarely among the all-time classics in Russia and beyond. There is also still considerable pride in the great victories of the era, like the launch of Sputnik and Yuri Gagarin's pioneering space flight, as well as myriad reminders in the form of statues, museums, street names and more. The cult of the Great Patriotic War that emerged in the mid-1960s – in which commemoration of the eventual victory over Nazism was increasingly made to serve wider purposes of regime legitimacy – similarly remains as strong as ever inside Russia at least, though its memorials are being removed across some other parts of the former Soviet space, and surviving veterans are now dwindling in number.

Some aspects of life in the Soviet Sixties had changed little from the Stalin era. The attitude of the authorities towards those with 'unacceptable' political views remained pretty implacable (baseless political repression was condemned, not political repression per se); a vast wealth of information about both the past and present remained hidden from ordinary citizens; and the economy was mostly still inefficient, unresponsive to public demand and impervious to reform. Even in spite of extensive regime efforts to the contrary, many people did not change their views on Stalin, on religion, alcohol, the developing world, equality of the sexes and many other things besides. Of course, the interests of the party and its representatives still swept all before them, and avenues for legitimate expression of disagreement remained seriously limited.

There was also plenty that did change, however. Political struggles among members of the elite now ended in demotion or disgrace for the losers, rather than physical destruction. The threat of sanctions for disobedience remained powerful and real, but the place of rewards for compliance and support was also growing more important to the Soviet social order. Architectural styles, fashions, the range of items available to buy in shops, attitudes towards sex, and the boundaries of what was and was not permissible in literature, cinema and more were all changing. Mass disorders in Kaunas, Tbilisi, Temirtau, Novocherkassk and elsewhere – all within the space of only a few years – told primarily not only of local circumstances, but also of a wider change in atmosphere and expectation, as the Soviet system evolved away from unfettered Stalinism. Such developments as the proliferating points of contact with the outside world and changing consumer appetites were also a vital feature of the age (and they continued into the long 1970s and beyond). These generated new socio-political challenges and realities, such as the growth of Western cultural influence and the declining ability of the regime to control the flow of information and ideas entering the country.

In broad terms, the Soviet experience of 'the Sixties' had a considerable amount in common with the way that events played out elsewhere. Changing (and contested) cultural trends, internationalism, social and political upheaval, faith in modernity and optimism for the future were all important dynamics of the age in many different countries. Nonetheless, there were also fundamental ways in which the USSR stood apart. Though much reduced in scale from the Stalin years, both the use and the threat of political repression must still occupy a prominent place in our understanding of the age. Similarly, the continuing drive to police and to re-forge citizens' behaviours and beliefs was largely without parallel beyond the communist world in the extent to which it penetrated into everyday life. Perhaps most importantly for the more liberal-minded citizens inside the USSR, the conservative turn that followed the end of the Sixties was both sharper and more prolonged than tended to be the case elsewhere. Even so, from Moscow to Central Asia and the Western border of Ukraine, the USSR was a country permanently transformed by the time the Soviet Sixties came to an end.

NOTES

Introduction

1. S. Khrushchev ed., *Memoirs of Nikita Khrushchev*, Vol. 2, University Park, PA: Penn State University Press, 2006, p. 147.
2. A. Stevenson, *Friends and Enemies: What I learned in Russia*, New York: Harper, 1959, p. xxi.
3. See J. Fürst, *Stalin's Last Generation: Soviet post-war youth and the emergence of mature socialism*, Oxford: Oxford University Press, 2010; C. McCallum, *The Fate of the New Man: Representing and reconstructing masculinity in Soviet visual culture, 1945–1965*, Ithaca, NY: Cornell University Press, 2018; Y. Gorlizki and O. Khlevniuk, *Substate Dictatorship: Networks, loyalty and institutional change in the Soviet Union*, New Haven, CT, and London: Yale University Press, 2020.
4. V. Aksenov, *Zenitsa oka: Vmesto memuarov*, Moskva: Vagrius, 2005, p. 435.
5. A. Gladilin, *Ulitsa generalov: Popytka memuarov*, Moskva: Vagrius, 2008, p. 84.
6. O. Kalugin, *Spy Master: My thirty-two years in intelligence and espionage against the West*, New York: Basic Books, 2009, p. 21.
7. A. Marwick, *The Sixties: Cultural revolution in Britain, France, Italy and the United States, 1958–1974*, Oxford: Oxford University Press, 1998, p. 3.
8. C. Jian et al. eds, *The Routledge Handbook of the Global Sixties: Between protest and nation building*, Abingdon: Routledge, 2018; A. Gorsuch and D. Koenker, 'Introduction: The socialist 1960s in global perspective', in A. Gorsuch and D. Koenker eds, *The Socialist Sixties: Crossing borders in the Second World*, Bloomington, IN: Indiana University Press, 2013.
9. On this phenomenon in the USA, see J. Varon et al., 'Time is an ocean: The past and future of the sixties', *The Sixties*, Vol. 1, No. 1, 2008; S. Hall, 'Framing the American 1960s: A historiographical review', *European Journal of American Culture*, Vol. 31, No. 1, 2012.
10. A. Yurchak, *Everything Was Forever until It Was No More*, Princeton, NJ: Princeton University Press, 2005.

Chapter I

1. W. Risch, *The Ukrainian West: Culture and the fate of empire in Soviet Lviv*, Cambridge, MA: Harvard University Press, 2011, p. 36.
2. A. Senn, 'The Sovietization of the Baltic states', *Annals of the American Academy of Political and Social Sciences*, Vol. 317, 1958, p. 125.
3. T. Tannberg, *Politika Moskvy v respublikakh Baltii v poslevoennye gody (1944–1956)*, Moskva: Rosspen, 2010.

4. R. Dale, 'Divided we stand: Cities, social unity and post-war reconstruction in Soviet Russia, 1945–1953', *Contemporary European History*, Vol. 24, No. 4, 2015.

5. P. Shelest, *Da ne sudimy budete: Dnevniki i vospominaniya chlena politburo TsK KPSS*, Moskva: Tsentrpoligraf, 2016, p. 107.

6. P. Stronski, *Tashkent: Forging a Soviet city, 1930–1966*, Pittsburgh, PA: University of Pittsburgh Press, 2010.

7. Fürst, *Stalin's Last Generation*.

8. V. Okpysh ed., *Tovarishch Komsomol: Dokumenty s"ezdov komsomola, plenumov, biuro i sekretariata TsK VLKSM, 1918–1968*, Moskva: Molodaya gvardiya, 1969.

9. E. Zubkova, *Obshchestvo i reformy, 1945–64*, Moskva: Rossiya molodaya, 1993, p. 47.

10. F. Chuev ed., *Molotov Remembers: Inside Kremlin politics*, Chicago, IL: Ivan R. Dee, 1993, p. 367.

11. L. Petrushevskaya, *The Girl from the Metropol Hotel: Growing up in communist Russia*, London: Penguin, 2017, p. 59.

12. D. Filtzer, 'The standard of living of Soviet industrial workers in the immediate postwar period, 1945–1948', *Europe-Asia Studies*, Vol. 51, No. 6, 1999.

13. Yu. Orlov, *Dangerous Thoughts: Memoirs of a Russian life*, New York: W. Morrow, 1991, p. 91.

14. J. Steinbeck, *A Russian Journal*, London: Penguin, 2001, p. 115.

15. A. Gallyamova, *Tatarskaya ASSR v period postStalinizma, 1945–1985*, Kazan: Tatarskoe knizhnoe izdatel'stvo, 2015, p. 292.

16. M. Edele, 'Veterans and the village: The impact of Red Army demobilisation on Soviet urbanisation, 1945–1955', *Russian History*, Vol. 36, 2009.

17. M. Nakachi, *Replacing the Dead: The politics of reproduction in the postwar Soviet Union*, Oxford: Oxford University Press, 2021.

18. E. Fraser, *Military Masculinity and Postwar Recovery in the Soviet Union*, Toronto: University of Toronto Press, 2019.

19. L. Denisova, 'The daily life of Russian peasant women', in M. Ilic ed., *The Palgrave Handbook of Women and Gender in Twentieth Century Russia and the Soviet Union*, London: Palgrave, 2018, p. 156.

20. D. Brown, *Soviet Russian Literature since Stalin*, Cambridge: Cambridge University Press, 1978, p. 3.

21. E. Korneichuk, 'Soviet art under government control', in A. Rosenfield and N. Dodge eds. *Nonconformist Art: The Soviet experience, 1956–1986*, London: Thames and Hudson, 1995, p. 38.

22. K. Roth-Ey, *Moscow Prime Time: How the Soviet Union built the media empire that lost the Cold War*, Ithaca, NY: Cornell University Press, 2011, pp. 28–29.

23. R. Stites, *Russian Popular Culture*, Cambridge: Cambridge University Press, 1992, p. 118.

24. J. Fürst, 'The importance of being stylish', in J. Fürst ed., *Late Stalinist Russia: Society between reconstruction and reinvention*, London: Routledge, 2006.

25. A. Adzhubei, *Ya byl zyatem Khrushcheva*, Moskva: Algoritm, 2014.

26. A. Pyzhikov, 'Sovetskoe poslevoennoe obshchestvo i predposylki khrush-chevskikh reform', *Voprosy Istorii*, No. 2, 2002.

27. R. Dale, 'Rats and resentment: The demobilization of the Red Army in postwar Leningrad, 1945–1950', *Journal of Contemporary History*, Vol. 45, No. 1, 2010.

28. Y. Gorlizki, 'Theft under Stalin: A property rights analysis', *Economic History Review*, Vol. 69, No. 1, 2016.

29. D. Shepilov, *The Kremlin's Scholar: A memoir of Soviet politics under Stalin and Khrushchev*, New Haven, CT, and London: Yale University Press, 2007, p. 143.
30. S. Barnes, *Death and Redemption: The gulag and the shaping of Soviet society*, Princeton, NJ: Princeton University Press, 2011.
31. O. Mertelsmann, 'Soviet mass violence in Estonia revisited', *Journal of Genocide Research*, Vol. 11, Nos 2–3, 2009.
32. A. Weiner, 'The making of a dominant myth: The Second World War and the construction of political identities within the Soviet polity', *Russian Review*, Vol. 55, No. 4, 1996.
33. M. Plisetskaya, *I, Maya Plisetskaya*, New Haven, CT, and London: Yale University Press, 2001, p. 81.
34. O. Troyanovskii, *Cherez gody i rasstoyaniya: Istoriya odnoi sem'i*, Moskva: Vagrius, 1997, p. 172.
35. T. Johnston, 'Subversive tales?', in Fürst ed., *Late Stalinist Russia*.
36. H. Salisbury, *Moscow Journal: The end of Stalin*, Chicago, IL: University of Chicago Press, 1961, p. 15.
37. J. Brodsky, *Less than One: Selected essays*, London: Penguin, 1992, p. 8.
38. Orlov, *Dangerous Thoughts*, p. 111.
39. O. Leibovich, *V gorode M: Ocherki politicheskoi povsednevnosti sovetskoi provintsii*, Moskva: Rosspen, 2008, p. 182.
40. D. Brandenberger, 'Stalin's last crime? Recent scholarship on postwar Soviet anti-Semitism and the Doctors' Plot', *Kritika*, Vol. 6, No. 1, 2005.
41. See C. Hooper, 'A darker big deal', in Fürst ed., *Late Stalinist Russia*.
42. J. Heinzen, *The Art of the Bribe: Corruption, politics and everyday life in the Soviet Union, 1943–1953*, New Haven, CT, and London: Yale University Press, 2017.
43. N. Lebina, *Povsednevnost' epokhi kosmosa i kukuruzy: Destruktsiya bol'shogo stilya: Leningrad, 1950–1960-e gody*, Sank Peterburg: Pobeda, 2015, pp. 30–37.
44. G. Arbatov, *The System: An insider's life in Soviet politics*, New York: Random House, 1992.
45. J. Brooks, *Thank You, Comrade Stalin! Soviet public culture from revolution to Cold War*, Princeton, NJ: Princeton University Press, 2001.
46. B. Tromly, 'The Leningrad Affair and Soviet patronage politics, 1949–1950', *Europe-Asia Studies*, Vol. 56, No. 5, 2004.
47. Y. Gorlizki and O. Khlevniuk, *Cold Peace: Stalin and the Soviet ruling circle, 1945–1953*, Oxford: Oxford University Press, 2004.
48. Y. Gorlizki, 'Stalin's cabinet: The Politburo and decision-making in the post-war years', *Europe-Asia Studies*, Vol. 53, No. 2, 2001.
49. M. Zezina, 'Shokovaya terapiya: Ot 1953 goda k 1956 godu', *Otechestvennaya istoriya*, No. 2, 1995, p. 122.
50. E. Ginzburg, *Within the Whirlwind*, London: Collins and Harvill Press, 1981, p. 383.
51. Shepilov, *The Kremlin's Scholar*, p. 1.
52. S. Tranum ed., *Life at the Edge of Empire: Oral histories of Soviet Kyrgyzstan*, Bishkek: Createspace, 2009, p. 154.
53. Ginzburg, *Within the Whirlwind*, p. 356.
54. Shelest, *Da ne sudimy budete*, p. 116.
55. Adzhubei, *Ya byl zyatem Khrushcheva*, p. 74.
56. A. Voznesenskii, *Na virtual'nom vetru*, Moskva: Vagrius, 1998, p. 30.
57. Yu. Aksyutin, *Khrushchevskaya 'ottepel'' i obshchestvennye nastroeniya v SSSR v 1953–1964 gg.*, Moskva: Rosspen, 2010, p. 32.

58. K. Stajner, *Seven Thousand Days in Siberia*, London: Canongate, 1988, p. 359.
59. I. Golomstock, *A Ransomed Dissident: A life in art under the Soviets*, London: I.B. Tauris, 2018, p. 33.
60. O. Rabin, *Tri zhizni*, Paris: Tret'ya volna, 1986, p. 34.
61. V. Naumov, 'N.S. Khrushchev i reabilitatsiya zhertv massovykh politicheskikh represii', *Voprosy istorii*, No. 4, 1997, p. 29.
62. L. Bohri, 'Rollback, liberation, containment or inaction?', *Journal of Cold War Studies*, Vol. 1, No. 3, 1999, p. 89.
63. Y. Yevtushenko, *A Precocious Autobiography*, London: Collins, 1963.
64. J. Rubenstein, *The Last Days of Stalin*, New Haven, CT, and London: Yale University Press, 2016, p. 105.
65. Zh. Medvedev, 'Zagadka smerti Stalina', *Voprosy istorii*, No. 1, 2000.
66. N. Mukhitdinov, *Gody, provedennye v Kremle*, Tashkent: Izdatel'stvo narodnogo nasledia imeni Abdully Kadyri, 1994, p. 87.
67. W. Hayter, *The Kremlin and the Embassy*, London: Hodder & Stoughton, 1966.
68. C. Bohlen, *Witness to History, 1926–1969*, London: Weidenfeld and Nicolson, 1973, p. 372.
69. S. Alliluyeva, *Twenty Letters to a Friend: A memoir*, London: Harper, 1967.
70. A. Artizov et al. eds, *Reabilitatsiya: kak eto bylo, dokumenty prezidiuma TsK KPSS i drugie materialy Mart 1953-Fevral' 1956*, Moskva: Mezhdunarodnyi fond 'Demokratiya', 2003.
71. R. Pikhoya, *Moskva, kreml', vlast'*, Moskva: AST, 2007, p. 229.
72. N. Lebina, 'Antimiry: Printsipy konstruirovaniya anomalii', in E. Yarska-Smirnova and P. Romanov eds, *Sovetskaya sotsial'naya politika: Stseny i deistvuyushchie litsa, 1940–1985*, Moskva: Tsentr sotsial'noi politiki i gendernykh issledovanii, 2008, p. 251.
73. Shepilov, *The Kremlin's Scholar*, p. 262.
74. M. Dobson, *Khrushchev's Cold Summer: Gulag returnees, crime and the fate of reform after Stalin*, Ithaca, NY, and London: Cornell University Press, 2009, p. 38.
75. http://www.sovlit.net/conversationswithaksyonov/
76. Leibovich, *V gorode M*, p. 263.
77. M. Dobson, '"Show the bandit-enemies no mercy!": Amnesty, criminality and public response in 1953', in P. Jones ed., *The Dilemmas of De-Stalinization: Negotiating social change in the Khrushchev era*, Abingdon: Routledge, 2006.
78. M. Altshuler, *Religion and Jewish Identity in the Soviet Union, 1941–64*, Lebanon, NH: Brandeis University Press, 2012.
79. A. Pyzhikov, 'Problema kul'ta lichnosti v gody khrushchevskoi ottepeli', *Voprosy istorii*, No. 4, 2003, p. 47.
80. Aksyutin, *Khrushchevskaya 'ottepel'*, p. 45.
81. Rubenstein, *The Last Days of Stalin*, pp. 99–100.
82. Salisbury, *Moscow Journal*, p. 368.
83. Pikhoya, *Moskva, kreml', vlast'*, p. 232.
84. V. Naumov and Yu. Sigachev eds, *Lavrentii Beria, 1953: Stenogramma iul'skogo plenuma TsK KPSS i drugie dokumenty*, Moskva: Mezhdunarodnyi fond 'Demokratiya', 1999.
85. T. Blauvelt, 'Patronage and betrayal in the post-Stalin succession: The case of Kruglov and Serov', *Communist and Post-Communist Studies*, Vol. 41, 2008.
86. M. Loader, 'Beria and Khrushchev: The power struggle over nationality policy and the case of Latvia', *Europe-Asia Studies*, Vol. 68, No. 10, 2016.

87. M. Florin, 'What is Russia to us? Making sense of Stalinism, colonialism and Soviet modernity in Kyrgyzstan, 1956–1965', *Ab Imperio*, No. 3, 2016.
88. S. Yekelchyk, *Ukraine: Birth of a modern nation*, Oxford: Oxford University Press, 2007, p. 159.
89. Naumov and Sigachev eds, *Lavrentii Beria, 1953*, pp. 46–52.
90. Loader, 'Beria and Khrushchev'.
91. A. Weiner and A. Rahi-Tamm, 'Getting to know you: The Soviet surveillance system, 1953–1957', *Kritika*, Vol. 13, No. 1, 2012, p. 37.
92. M. Kramer, 'The early post-Stalin succession struggle and upheavals in East-Central Europe: Internal-external linkages in Soviet policy making (part 1)', *Journal of Cold War Studies*, Vol. 1, No. 1, 1999.
93. M. Kramer, 'The early post-Stalin succession struggle and upheavals in East-Central Europe: Internal-external linkages in Soviet policy making (part 3)', *Journal of Cold War Studies*, Vol. 1, No. 3, 1999.
94. A. Mikoyan, *Tak bylo: Razmyshleniya o minuvshem*, Moskva: Vagrius, 1999, p. 584.
95. A. Malenkov, *O moem otse Georgii Malenkove*, Moskva: 'Tekhnoekos', 1992, p. 59.
96. Pikhoya, *Moskva, kreml', vlast'*.
97. M. Kramer, 'The early post-Stalin succession struggle and upheavals in East-Central Europe: Internal-external linkages in Soviet policy making (part 2)', *Journal of Cold War Studies*, Vol. 1, No. 2, 1999.
98. A. Knight, *Beria: Stalin's first lieutenant*, Princeton, NJ: Princeton University Press, 1993, p. 193.
99. W. Taubman, *Khrushchev: The man and his era*, London: Free Press, 2003, p. 250.
100. Blauvelt, 'Patronage and betrayal'.
101. Naumov and Sigachev eds, *Lavrentii Beria, 1953*, pp. 64–66.
102. V. Khaustov ed. *Delo Beriya: Prigovor obzhalovaniyu ne podlezhit*, Moskva: Mezhdunarodnyi fond 'Demokratiya', 2012.
103. Yu. Emel'yanov, *Khrushchev: 'ottepel'' ili . . .*, Moskva: Akademicheskii proekt, 2018, p. 252.
104. K. Goff, *Nested Nationalism: Making and unmaking nations in the Soviet Caucasus*, Ithaca, NY: Cornell University Press, 2020, p. 100.
105. N. Baibakov, *Ot Stalina do El'tsina*, Moskva: GazOil Press, 1998, p. 122.
106. https://digitalarchive.wilsoncenter.org/document/111921
107. Artizov et al. eds, *Reabilitatsiya*, p. 8.
108. E. Zubkova, *Russia after the War: Hopes, illusions and disappointments, 1945–1957*, Armonk, NY: M.E. Sharpe, 1998, p. 182.
109. A. Chernyaev, *Moya zhizn' i moe vremya*, Moskva: Mezhdunarodnye otnosheniya, 1995, p. 219.

Chapter 2

1. E. Zubkova 'The rivalry with Malenkov', in W. Taubman et al. eds, *Nikita Khrushchev*, New Haven, CT, and London: Yale University Press, 2000, p. 75.
2. L. Volin, 'The Malenkov-Khrushchev new economic policy', *Journal of Political Economy*, Vol. 62, No. 3, 1954, p. 188.
3. K. Ironside, *A Full-Value Ruble: The promise of prosperity in the postwar Soviet Union*, Cambridge, MA: Harvard University Press, 2021, p. 34.

4. Aksyutin, *Khrushchevskaya 'ottepel''*, p. 97.

5. N. Mitrokhin, 'The rise of political clans', in J. Smith and M. Ilic eds, *Khrushchev in the Kremlin: Policy and government in the Soviet Union, 1953–1964*, London: Routledge, 2011, p. 30.

6. Chuev ed., *Molotov Remembers*, p. 359.

7. N. Mitrokhin, 'Back-office Mikhaila Suslova ili kem i kak proizvodilas' ideologiya brezhnevskogo vremeni', *Cahiers du monde russe*, Vol. 54, Nos 3/4, 2013.

8. A. Dobrynin, *In Confidence: Moscow's ambassador to six Cold War presidents*, Seattle, WA: University of Washington Press, 2001, p. 21.

9. Adzhubei, *Ya byl zyatem Khrushcheva*, p. 115.

10. F. Kovacevic, '"An ominous talent": Oleg Gribanov and KGB counterintelligence', *International Journal of Intelligence and CounterIntelligence*, 2022.

11. A. Knight, *The KGB: Police and politics in the Soviet Union*, London: HarperCollins, 1988.

12. Blauvelt, 'Patronage and betrayal'.

13. N. Petrov, *Ivan Serov: Pervyi predsedatel' KGB*, Moskva: Materik, 2005, p. 338.

14. A. Vas'kin, *Povsednevnaya zhizn' sovetskoi stolitsy pri Khrushcheve i Brezhneve*, Moskva: Molodaya gvardiya, 2017.

15. M. Kalb, *The Year I Was Peter the Great*, Washington, DC: Brookings Institution Press, 2017, p. 111.

16. Golomstock, *A Ransomed Dissident*, p. 39.

17. M. Gorbachev, *Memoirs*, London: Doubleday, 1995, p. 59.

18. S. Reid, 'This is tomorrow!', in Gorsuch and Koenker eds, *The Socialist Sixties*, p. 37.

19. Lebina, *Povsednevnost' epokhi kosmosa i kukuruzy*.

20. Vas'kin, *Povsednevnaya zhizn'*, p. 230.

21. J. Smith, *Works in Progress: Plans and realities on Soviet farms, 1930–1963*, New Haven, CT, and London: Yale University Press, 2014, p. 180.

22. V. Shestakov, 'XX s''ezd KPSS', in A. Senyavskii ed., *XX s''ezd KPSS v kontekste rossiiskoi istorii*, Moskva: Institut rossiiskoi istorii, 2012, p. 139.

23. Aksyutin, *Khrushchevskaya 'ottepel'*, p. 109.

24. T. Capote, *The Muses Are Heard: An account*, New York: Random House, 1956.

25. E. Mozejko ed., *Vasily Pavlovich Aksenov: A writer in quest of himself*, Bloomington, IN: Slavica, 1986, p. 17.

26. E. Gilburd, *To See Paris and Die: The Soviet lives of Western culture*, Cambridge, MA: Harvard University Press, 2018.

27. Vas'kin, *Povsednevnaya zhizn'*, p. 425.

28. P. Shakarian, 'An Armenian reformer in Khrushchev's Kremlin: Anastas Mikoyan and the politics of difference in the USSR, 1953–64', Ohio State University, 2021.

29. N. Tomilina ed., *Nikita Khrushchev: Dva tsveta vremeni*, tom 2: *Dokumenty iz lichnogo fonda N.S. Khrushcheva*, Moskva: Mezhdunarodnyi fond 'Demokratiya', 2009, p. 521.

30. L. Alexeyeva and P. Goldberg, *Thaw Generation: Coming of age in the post-Stalin era*, London: Little, Brown and Company, 1990, p. 83.

31. R. Orlova and L. Kopelev, *My zhili v Moskve, 1956–1980*, Moskva: Kniga, 1990, p. 20.

32. O. Vainshtein, 'Orange jackets and pea green pants: The fashion of *stilyagi* in Soviet postwar culture', *Fashion Theory*, Vol. 22, No. 2, 2018.

33. *Komsomol'skaya pravda*, 5.10.1958.

34. Salisbury, *Moscow Journal*, p. 419.

35. N. Lebina, *Muzhchina i zhenshchina: Telo, moda, kul'tura SSSR – ottepel'*, Moskva: Novoe literaturnoe obozrenie, 2018, p. 35.

36. *Pravda*, 08.03.1954.

37. *Current Digest of Soviet Press*, Vol. 7, No. 2, 1954, pp. 30–31.

38. *Pravda*, 04.09.1962.

39. *Partiinaya zhizn'*, No. 19, 1967, p. 11.

40. M. Ilic, *Soviet Women: Everyday lives*, London: Routledge, 2020, p. 8.

41. A. Jacobs, 'Love, marry, cook', in A. Lakhtikova et al. eds, *Seasoned Socialism: Gender and food in late Soviet everyday life*, Bloomington, IN: Indiana University Press, 2019.

42. D. Leinarte, *Family and the State in Soviet Lithuania: Gender, law and society*, London: Bloomsbury, 2021, p. 21.

43. D. Filtzer, *Soviet Workers and De-Stalinization: The consolidation of the modern system of Soviet production relations, 1953–1964*, Cambridge: Cambridge University Press, 1992.

44. D. Khasbulatova, *Rossiiskaya gendernaya politika v XX stoletii: Mify i realii*, Izdatel'stvo Ivanovo gos. universitet, 2005, p. 245.

45. Nakachi, *Replacing the Dead*.

46. L. Attwood, 'Celebrating the "frail-figured welder": Gender confusion in women's magazines of the Khrushchev era', *Slavonica*, Vol. 8, No. 2, 2002, p. 168.

47. M. Goldovskaya, *Woman with a Movie Camera: My life as a Russian filmmaker*, Austin, TX: University of Texas Press, 2006, p. 45.

48. S. Reid, 'Masters of the earth: Gender and destalinisation in Soviet reformist painting of the Khrushchev era', *Gender and History*, Vol. 11, No. 2, 1999, p. 277.

49. N. Baranskaya, *A Week Like Any Other: Novellas and stories*, Seattle, WA: Seal Press, 1989.

50. McCallum, *The Fate of the New Man*.

51. M. Dumančić, *Men Out of Focus: The Soviet masculinity crisis in the long sixties*, Toronto: University of Toronto Press, 2021.

52. Lebina, *Muzhchina i zhenshchina*.

53. Nakachi, *Replacing the Dead*.

54. ibid.

55. A. Randall, '"Abortion will deprive you of happiness!": Soviet reproductive politics in the post-Stalin era', *Journal of Women's History*, Vol. 23, No. 3, 2011.

56. A. Williams, 'Materials for maternity: The abortion procedure, communist morality and urbanisation in Soviet Russia, 1944–1968', University of Leeds, 2023.

57. Nakachi, *Replacing the Dead*; L. Denisova, *Rural Women in the Soviet Union and Post-Soviet Russia*, London: Routledge, 2010, p. 181.

58. V. Kozlov and S. Mironenko eds, *58-10: Nadzornye proizvodstva prokuratury SSSR po delam ob antisovetskoi agitatsii i propagande*, Moskva: Mezhdunarodnyi fond 'Demokratiya', 1999.

59. J. Hardy, 'Gulag tourism: Khrushchev's "show" prisons in the Cold War context, 1954–59', *Russian Review*, Vol. 71, No. 1, 2012.

60. A. Solzhenitsyn, *The Gulag Archipelago*, Vol. 3: *An experiment in literary investigation*, London: Harper & Row, 1978, p. 427.

61. B. Vail', *Osobo opasnyi*, London: Overseas Publication Interchange, 1980.
62. R. Pimenov, *Vospominaniya*, Moskva: Panorama, 1996, p. 103.
63. Hardy, 'Gulag tourism', p. 53.
64. M. Elie and J. Hardy, 'Letting the beasts out of the cage: Parole in the post-Stalin gulag, 1953–73', *Europe-Asia Studies*, Vol. 67, No. 4, 2015.
65. GARF, f. 9401, op. 2, d. 492, l. 144.
66. J. Hardy, *The Gulag after Stalin: Redefining punishment in Khrushchev's Soviet Union, 1953–1964*, Ithaca, NY: Cornell University Press, 2016.
67. Dobson, *Khrushchev's Cold Summer*.
68. B. Firsov, *Raznomyslie v SSSR 1940–1960-e gody*, Sankt Peterburg: Izdatel'stvo Evropeiskogo universiteta, 2008, p. 251.
69. S. Mikoyan, 'Aleksei Snegov v bor'be za "destalinizatsiyu"', *Voprosy istorii*, No. 4, 2006.
70. Mikoyan, *Tak bylo*, p. 589.
71. A. Beda, *Sovetskaya politicheskaya kul'tura cherez prizmu MVD, 1946–1958*, Moskva: Mosgorarkhiv, 2002, p. 46.
72. H. Berman, *Soviet Criminal Law and Procedure*, Cambridge, MA: Harvard University Press, 1972.
73. N. Adler, 'Life in the "Big Zone": The fate of returnees in the aftermath of Stalinist repression', *Europe-Asia Studies*, Vol. 51, No. 1, 1999, p. 10.
74. Petrov, *Ivan Serov*.
75. Firsov, *Raznomyslie v SSSR*, pp. 250–52.
76. S. Cohen and K. vanden Heuvel eds, *Voices of Glasnost: Interviews with Gorbachev's reformers*, New York: Norton, 1990, p. 232.
77. Dobson, *Khrushchev's Cold Summer*, p. 52.
78. Artizov et al. eds, *Reabilitatsiya*.
79. Dobson, *Khrushchev's Cold Summer*, p. 78.
80. S. Cohen, *The Victims Return: Survivors of the gulag after Stalin*, London: I.B. Tauries, 2011.
81. http://www.sovlit.net/conversationswithaksyonov/
82. N. Adler, *Keeping Faith with the Party: Communist believers return from the gulag*, Bloomington, IN: Indiana University Press, 2012.
83. A. Weiner, 'The empires pay a visit: Gulag returnees, East European rebellions, and Soviet frontier politics', *Journal of Modern History*, Vol. 78, No. 2, 2006; S. Dudoignon, 'From revival to mutation: The religious personnel of Islam in Tajikistan from de-Stalinization to independence', *Central Asian Survey*, Vol. 30, No. 1, 2011.
84. I. Ramanava, 'The amnesty and rehabilitation of victims of Stalinist repression in Belarus', in K. McDermott and M. Stibbe eds, *De-Stalinising Eastern Europe: Rehabilitation of Stalin's victims after 1953*, Basingstoke: Palgrave, 2015, p. 223.
85. Vas'kin, *Povsednevnaya zhizn'*, p. 25.
86. Brown, *Soviet Russian Literature since Stalin*, p. 67.
87. A. Barenberg, 'From prisoners to citizens?', in D. Kozlov and E. Gilburd eds, *The Thaw: Soviet society and culture during the 1950s and 1960s*, Toronto: University of Toronto Press, 2013, p. 184.
88. ibid.
89. Dobson, *Khrushchev's Cold Summer*.
90. V. Kozlov, *Neizvestnyi SSSR: Protivostoyanie naroda i vlasti, 1953–1985*, Moskva: Olma-Press, 2006, p. 70.

91. Stajner, *Seven Thousand Days in Siberia*.
92. Solzhenitsyn, *Gulag Archipelago*, Vol. 3, p. 285.
93. S. Barnes, ' "In a manner befitting Soviet citizens": An uprising in the post-Stalin Gulag', *Slavic Review*, Vol. 64, No. 4, 2005, p. 830.
94. ibid., p. 848.
95. Tomilina ed., *Nikita Khrushchev*, tom 2, pp. 51–54.
96. S. Pavlov, 'Na smenu pridut drugie', in Yu. Aksyutin ed., *Nikita Khrushchev: Materialy k biografii*, Moskva: Izdatel'stvo politicheskoi literatury, 1989, p. 202.
97. O. Gerasimova, *'Ottepel'', 'Zamorozki' i studenty Moskovskogo universiteta*, Moskva: AIRO, 2015, p. 257.
98. B. Tromly, *Making the Soviet Intelligentsia: Universities and intellectual life under Stalin and Khrushchev*, Cambridge: Cambridge University Press, 2014, p. 178.
99. Aksyutin, *Khrushchevskaya 'ottepel'*, p. 89.
100. V. Kozlov, *Mass Uprisings in the USSR: Protest and rebellion in the post-Stalin years*, New York: M.E. Sharpe, 2002, p. 27.
101. Petrushevskaya, *The Girl from the Metropol Hotel*, p. 142.
102. NARB, f. 63p, op. 22, d. 10, ll. 1–34.
103. M. Pohl, 'Women and girls in the Virgin Lands', in M. Ilic et al. eds, *Women in the Khrushchev Era*, Basingstoke: Palgrave, 2004, p. 68.
104. L. Brezhnev, *Virgin Lands: Two years in Kazakhstan, 1954–1955*, Oxford: Pergamon, 1979.
105. V. Tomilina, 'Kampaniya po osvoeniyu tselennykh i zalezhnykh zemel' v 1954–59 gg.', *Voprosy istorii*, No. 9, 2009.
106. Pavlov, 'Na smenu pridut drugie', p. 202.
107. L. Mlechin, *Kak Brezhnev smenil Khrushcheva*, Moskva: ZAO Tsentrpoligraf, 2014, p. 75.
108. Pohl, 'Women and girls in the Virgin Lands'.
109. M. Pohl, 'From White Grave to Tselinograd to Astana', in Kozlov and Gilburd eds, *The Thaw*.
110. Kozlov, *Mass Uprisings in the USSR*.
111. M. Pohl, 'From White Grave to Tselinograd to Astana', p. 277.
112. Kozlov, *Mass Uprisings in the USSR*.
113. Pohl, 'From White Grave to Tselinograd to Astana', pp. 295–96.
114. M. Zezina, *Sovetskaya khudozhestvennaya intelligentsiya i vlast' v 1950e – 1960e gody*, Moskva: Dialog MGU, 1999, p. 119.
115. I. Ehrenburg et al., 'Three Soviet artists on the present needs of Soviet art', *Soviet Studies*, Vol. 5, No. 4, 1954, p. 415.
116. ibid., p. 427.
117. ibid., p. 443.
118. *Izvestiya*, 09.06.1954.
119. L. Skorino, 'A critic of Pomerantsev', *Soviet Studies*, Vol. 6, No. 1, 1954.
120. *Komsomol'skaya pravda*, 17.03.1954.
121. *Pravda*, 25.05.1954.
122. F. Barghoorn, 'Soviet cultural diplomacy since Stalin', *Russian Review*, Vol. 17, No. 1, 1958, p. 45.
123. A. Fursenko and T. Naftali, *Khrushchev's Cold War: The inside story of an American adversary*, New York: Norton, 2007, p. 41.
124. S. Rajak, 'New evidence from the former Yugoslav archives', *Bulletin of the Cold War International History Project*, Nos 12/13, 2001.

125. Aksyutin, *Khrushchevskaya 'ottepel'*, p. 140.
126. Khrushchev ed., *Memoirs of Nikita Khrushchev*, Vol. 3.
127. Taubman, *Khrushchev*, p. 263.
128. Aksyutin, *Khrushchevskaya 'ottepel'*, p. 112.
129. Chuev ed., *Molotov Remembers*, p. 332.
130. Troyanovskii, *Cherez gody i rasstoyaniya*, p. 170.
131. Aksyutin, *Khrushchevskaya 'ottepel'*, pp. 154–65.
132. *Pravda*, 05.03.1954.
133. A. Fursenko ed., *Prezidium TsK KPSS 1954–1964: Chernovye protokol'nye zapisi zasedanii: stenogrammy*, Moskva: Rosspen, 2004.
134. Naumov, 'N.S. Khrushchev i reabilitatsiya'.
135. Pyzhikov, 'Problema kul'ta lichnosti'.
136. K. Aimermakher ed., *Doklad N.S. Khrushcheva o kul'te lichnosti Stalina na XX s''ezde: Dokumenty*, Moskva: Rosspen, 2002.

Chapter 3

1. M. Smith, 'Faded red paradise: Welfare and the Soviet city after 1953', *Contemporary European History*, Vol. 24, No. 4, 2015.
2. A. Igolkin, 'XX s''ezd KPSS i izmeneniya v toplivo-energeticheskoi politike', in Senyavskii ed., *XX s''ezd KPSS*.
3. Mikoyan, *Tak bylo*, p. 595.
4. Artizov et al. eds, *Reabilitatsiya*, p. 11.
5. Mikoyan, *Tak bylo*, p. 592.
6. Aimermakher ed., *Doklad N.S. Khrushcheva*, pp. 185–223.
7. ibid., pp. 223–29.
8. Fursenko ed., *Prezidium TsK KPSS, 1954–1964*.
9. Aimermakher ed., *Doklad N.S. Khrushcheva*, pp. 234–37.
10. Gorlizki and Khlevniuk, *Substate Dictatorship*, p. 130.
11. Kh. Sabanchiev, 'Sekretnyi doklad N.S. Khrushcheva na XX s''ezde KPSS i sud'by repressirovannykh narodov', *Voprosy istorii*, No. 7, 2016.
12. Aimermakher ed., *Doklad N.S. Khrushcheva*, 'Arkheograficheskoe predislovie', pp. 41–48.
13. P. Jones, *Myth, Memory, Trauma: Rethinking the Stalinist past in the Soviet Union, 1953–79*, New Haven, CT, and London: Yale University Press, 2013, p. 34.
14. Baibakov, *Ot Stalina do El'tsina*, p. 116.
15. A. Parry, 'The Twentieth Congress: Stalin's "Second Funeral"', *American Slavic and East European Review*, Vol. 15, No. 4, 1956.
16. Chuev ed., *Molotov Remembers*, p. 351.
17. F. Burlatskii, 'Khrushchev: Shtrikhi k politicheskomu portretu', in Aksyutin ed., *Nikita Khrushchev*, p. 10.
18. Adzhubei, *Ya byl zyatem Khrushcheva*, p. 135.
19. Khrushchev ed., *Memoirs of Nikita Khrushchev*, Vol. 2.
20. Senyavskii ed., *XX s''ezd KPSS*.
21. A. Senyavskii, 'XX s''ezd KPSS na vesakh istorii', in Senyavskii ed., *XX s''ezd*, p. 11.
22. Jones, *Myth, Memory, Trauma*; Dobson, *Khrushchev's Cold Summer*.
23. Chuev ed., *Molotov Remembers*, p. 350.
24. J. Rettie, 'How Khrushchev leaked his Secret Speech to the world', *History Workshop Journal*, Vol. 62, No. 1, 2006.

25. Aimermakher ed., *Doklad N.S. Khrushcheva*, p. 623.
26. M. Prozumenshchikov, ' "Sekretnyi" doklad N.S. Khrushcheva', in Aimermakher ed., *Doklad N.S. Khrushcheva*, pp. 17–40.
27. ibid., p. 27.
28. L. Luthi, *The Sino-Soviet Split: Cold War in the communist world*, Princeton, NJ: Princeton University Press, 2008.
29. Aimermakher ed., *Doklad N.S. Khrushcheva*, pp. 664–740.
30. T. Blauvelt, 'Status shift and ethnic mobilisation in the March 1956 events in Georgia', *Europe-Asia Studies*, Vol. 61, No. 4, 2009.
31. O. Khlevnyuk, 'Patronazh Moskvy i gruzinskii natsionalizm nakanune sobytii 1956', *Voprosy istorii*, No. 12, 2003.
32. L. Avalishvili, 'The March 1956 events in Georgia', in T. Blauvelt and J. Smith eds, *Georgia after Stalin: Nationalism and Soviet power*, London: Routledge, 2015, p. 35.
33. Blauvelt, 'Status shift', p. 662.
34. Aimermakher ed., *Doklad N.S. Khrushcheva*.
35. Avalishvili, 'The March 1956 events in Georgia'.
36. Kozlov, *Mass Uprisings in the USSR*.
37. MIA, f. 96, op. 16, d. 416, ll. 4–6.
38. MIA, f. 96, op. 16, d. 419, ll. 13–17.
39. Avalishvili, 'The March 1956 events in Georgia'.
40. T. Blauvelt, 'Resistance, discourse and nationalism', in Blauvelt and Smith eds, *Georgia after Stalin*.
41. Kozlov and Mironenko eds, *58-10*, p. 293.
42. L. Lur'e and I. Malyarova eds, *1956 god: Seredina veka*, Sankt Peterburg: Neva, 2007, p. 170.
43. Pikhoya, *Moskva, kreml', vlast'*, p. 307.
44. Dobson, *Khrushchev's Cold Summer*.
45. Gorbachev, *Memoirs*, p. 61.
46. K. Loewenstein, 'Re-emergence of public opinion in the Soviet Union: Khrushchev and responses to the Secret Speech', *Europe-Asia Studies*, Vol. 58, No. 8, 2006.
47. A. Pyzhikov, *Khrushchevskaya 'ottepel' '*, Moskva: Olma Press, 2002, p. 44.
48. Arbatov, *The System*, p. 108.
49. Zezina, 'Shokovaya terapiya', p. 129.
50. A. Novikov ed., 'Pervaya reaktsiya na kritiku 'kul'ta lichnosti' I.V. Stalina. Po itogam vystuplenii A.M. Pankratova v Leningrade v marte 1956 goda', *Voprosy istorii*, No. 8, 2006.
51. RGANI, f. 5, op. 30, d. 139, l. 5.
52. Aimermakher ed., *Doklad N.S. Khrushcheva*.
53. C. Hooper, 'What can and cannot be said: Between the Stalinist past and new Soviet future', *Slavonic and East European Review*, Vol. 86, No. 2, 2008, p. 315.
54. Yu. Aksyutin, 'Otkliki na XX s''ezd v strane i za rubezhom', in Senyavskii ed., *XX s''ezd KPSS*, p. 49.
55. A. Pyzhikov, 'Istoki dissidenstva', *Svobodnaya mysl'*, No. 12, 2003.
56. F. Burlatsky, *Khrushchev and the First Russian Spring*, London: Weidenfeld and Nicolson, 1988, p. 13.
57. Tromly, *Making the Soviet Intelligentsia*, p. 136.
58. B. Tromly, 'Soviet patriotism and its discontents among higher education students in Khrushchev-era Russia and Ukraine', *Nationalities Papers*, Vol. 37, No. 3, 2009, p. 305.

59. S. Huxtable, 'Making news Soviet: Rethinking journalistic professionalism after Stalin', *Contemporary European History*, Vol. 27, No. 1, 2018.
60. V. Pimonov ed., *Govoryat 'osobo opasnye'*, Moskva: Detektiv-press, 1999, p. 20.
61. V. Ronkin, *Na smenu dekabryam prikhodyat yanvari . . .*, Moskva: Obshchestvo 'Memorial', 2003, p. 25.
62. L. Silina, *Nastroeniya sovetskogo studenchestva, 1945–1964*, Moskva: Russkii mir, 2004, p. 108.
63. Iu. Aksiutin, 'Popular responses to Khrushchev', in Taubman et al. eds, *Nikita Khrushchev*.
64. Tromly, *Making the Soviet Intelligentsia*.
65. MIA, f. 96, op. 16, d. 436, ll. 28–390.
66. RGANI, f. 5, op. 31, d. 189, ll. 1–2.
67. Pyzhikov, 'Istoki dissidenstva'.
68. RGANI, f. 5, op. 33, d. 4, ll. 41–46.
69. Sabanchiev, 'Sekretntyi doklad'.
70. Kozlov, *Mass Uprisings in the USSR*.
71. Artizov et al. eds, *Reabilitatsiya*.
72. Mikoyan, *Tak bylo*, p. 596.
73. Mikoyan, 'Aleksei Snegov v borbe za "destalinizatsiyu"'.
74. A. Artizov and Yu. Sigachev, 'Vvedenie', in Artizov et al. eds, *Reabilitatsiya*.
75. Aimermakher ed., *Doklad N.S. Khrushcheva*.
76. *Pravda*, 28.03.1956.
77. G. Kuzovkin 'Partiino-komsomol'skie presledovaniya', in L. Eremina and E. Zhemkova eds, *Korni travy: Sbornik statei molodykh istorikov*, Moskva: Zven'ya, 1996, p. 90.
78. RGANI, f. 89, op. 6, d. 2, ll. 1–15.
79. *Izvestiya*, 25.11.1956.
80. S. Reid, 'Modernising Socialist Realism in the Khrushchev thaw', in Jones ed., *The Dilemmas of De-Stalinization*. p. 214.
81. Goldovskaya, *Woman with a Movie Camera*, p. 39.
82. Roth-Ey, *Moscow Prime Time*, p. 26.
83. Dumančić, *Men Out of Focus*, p. 10.
84. N. Zorkaya, *The Illustrated History of Soviet Cinema*, New York: Hippocrene Books, 1989, p. 209.
85. A. Anemone, 'Tatiana Samoilova and the search for a new Soviet woman', in M. Rojavina ed., *Women in Soviet Film: The thaw and post-thaw periods*, London: Routledge, 2017, p. 13.
86. Goldovskaya, *Woman with a Movie Camera*, p. 31.
87. D. Brown, *Soviet Russian Literature since Stalin*, p. 229.
88. *Trud*, 31.10.1956.
89. D. Kozlov, *The Readers of Novyi Mir: Coming to terms with the Stalinist past*, Cambridge, MA: Harvard University Press, 2013, p. 89.
90. ibid., p. 96.
91. Pimenov, *Vospominaniya*, p. 33.
92. D. Kozlov, 'Naming the social evil', in Jones ed., *The Dilemmas of De-Stalinization*, p. 80.
93. V. Zubok, *Zhivago's Children: The last Russian intelligentsia*, Cambridge, MA, and London: Harvard University Press, 2009, p. 76.
94. K. Loewenstein, '*Obshchestvennost'* as key to understanding Soviet writers of the 1950s: *Moskovskii literator*, October 1956–March 1957', *Journal of Contemporary History*, Vol. 44, No. 3, 2009.

95. E. Gilburd, 'Picasso in thaw culture', *Cahiers du monde russe*, Vol. 47, Nos 1/2, 2006.
96. A. Naiman, 'Picasso in Russia 2.0', *Moscow News*, 15 June 2010.
97. S. Reid, 'Picasso, the *Thaw* and the "New Realism" in Soviet Art', Symposium *Revoir Picasso*, 2015, p. 3.
98. Gilburd, 'Picasso in thaw culture', p. 68.
99. *Izvestiya*, 02.12.1956.
100. *Literaturnaya gazeta*, 15.12.1956.
101. K. Chukovskii, *Dnevnik, 1930–1969*, Moskva: Sovremennyi pisatel', 1994, p. 245.

Chapter 4

1. Kramer, 'The early post-Stalin succession struggle and upheavals in East-Central Europe (part 1)'.
2. Cs. Békés et al. eds, *The 1956 Hungarian Revolution: A history in documents*, Budapest: Central European University Press, 2002, pp. 178–82.
3. V. Chebrikov et al. eds, *Istoriya sovetskikh organov gosudarstevennoi bezopasnosti: Uchebnik*, Moskva, 1977, p. 491.
4. Y. Malashenko, 'The Special Corps', in J. Györkei and M. Horváth eds, *1956: Soviet Military Intervention in Hungary*, Budapest: Central European University Press, 1998, p. 267.
5. M. Kramer, 'The Soviet Union and the 1956 crises in Hungary and Poland: Reassessments and new findings', *Journal of Contemporary History*, Vol. 33, No. 2, 1998.
6. Györkei and Horváth eds, *1956: Soviet Military Intervention in Hungary*, p. 187.
7. Tromly, *Making the Soviet Intelligentsia*.
8. V. Iofe, *Granitsy smysla: stat'i, vystupleniya, esse*, Sankt Peterburg: Obshchestvo 'Memorial', 2002, p. 119.
9. Anon. 'Vlast' i intelligentsiya: "Delo" molodykh istorikov (1957–58)', *Voprosy istorii*, No. 004, 1994, p. 111.
10. K. Smith, *Moscow 1956: The silenced spring*, Cambridge, MA: Harvard University Press, 2017.
11. Ronkin, *Na smenu dekabryam*, p. 88.
12. Yu. Burtin ed., 'Studencheskoe brozhenie v SSSR (konets 1956)', *Voprosy istorii*, No. 1, 1997, p. 16.
13. Zh. Kydralina, 'Politicheskie nastroeniya v Kazakhstane v 1945–1985 gg.', *Voprosy istorii*, No. 8, 2008, p. 66.
14. RGANI, f. 5, op. 30, d. 141, ll. 54–56.
15. Silina, *Nastroeniya sovetskogo studenchestva*, p. 147.
16. GARF, f. 9401, op. 2, d. 482, l. 25; GARF, f. 8131, op. 32, d. 77481, ll. 1–3.
17. Ronkin, *Na smenu dekabryam*, p. 167.
18. V. Kozlov ed., *Kramola: Inakomyslie v SSSR pri Khrushcheve i Brezhneve, 1953–1982*, Moskva: Materik, 2005, p. 322.
19. GARF, f. 8131, op. 31, d. 73957, l. 45.
20. Pimenov, *Vospominaniya*, p. 73.
21. I. Casu and M. Sandle, 'Discontent and uncertainty in the borderlands: Soviet Moldavia and the Secret Speech, 1956–57', *Europe-Asia Studies*, Vol. 66, No. 4, 2014.
22. Weiner, 'The empires pay a visit'.

23. Petrov, *Ivan Serov*, p. 169.
24. GARF, f. 9402, op. 2, d. 492, l. 121.
25. Weiner and Rahi-Tamm, 'Getting to know you'.
26. F. Bobkov, *KGB i vlast'*, Moskva: Veteran MP, 1995, p. 144.
27. G. Kuzovkin, 'Partiino-Komsomol'skie presledovaniya', in Eremina and Zhemkova eds, *Korni travy*.
28. R. Hornsby, *Protest, Reform and Repression in Khrushchev's Soviet Union*, Cambridge: Cambridge University Press, 2013.
29. Chebrikov et al. eds, *Istoriya sovetskikh organov gosudarstvennoi bezopasnosti*, p. 509.
30. GARF, f. 8131, op. 31, d. 80330, ll. 1–2.
31. RGANI, f. 89, op. 6, d. 6, l. 1.
32. Firsov, *Raznomyslie v SSSR*, p. 261.
33. *Istochnik*, No. 6, 1995, p. 153.
34. GARF, f. 8131, op. 32, d. 5080, l. 7.
35. E. Papovyan, 'Primenenie stat'i 58-10 UK RSFSR v 1957–1958', in Eremina and Zhemkova eds, *Korni travy*.
36. GARF, f. 8131, op. 32, d. 5080, l. 19.
37. Hornsby, *Protest, Reform and Repression*.
38. Kozlov, *Neizvestny SSSR*.
39. E. Papovyan and A. Papovyan, 'Uchastie verkhovnogo suda', in Eremina and Zhemkova eds, *Korni travy*.
40. GARF, f. 8131, op. 32, d. 5080, l. 64.
41. *Pravda*, 19.01.1957.
42. RGANI, f. 5, op. 30, d. 189, ll. 29–32.
43. Aksyutin, *Khrushchevskaya 'ottepel''*, pp. 268–69.
44. Chernyaev, *Moya zhizn' i moe vremya*, p. 223.
45. Zubok, *Zhivago's Children*.
46. Taubman, *Khrushchev*, pp. 308–09.
47. Mikoyan, *Tak bylo*, p. 597.
48. Hayter, *The Kremlin and the Embassy*, p. 42.
49. Taubman, *Khrushchev*, p. 306.
50. P. Naumov, 'Vvedenie', in N. Kovaleva et al. eds, *Molotov, Malenkov, Kaganovich: Stenogramma iyun'skogo plenuma TsK KPSS i drugie dokumenty*, Moskva: Mezhdunarodnyi fond 'Demokratiya', 1998, p. 14.
51. Kovaleva et al. eds, *Molotov, Malenkov, Kaganovich*.
52. Mlechin, *Kak Brezhnev smenil Khrushcheva*, p. 88.
53. Kovaleva et al. eds, *Molotov, Malenkov, Kaganovich*.
54. ibid.
55. Postanovlenie plenuma TsK KPSS ob antipartiinoi gruppe Malenkova, G.M., Kaganovicha, L.M., Molotova, V.M., 29.06.1957.
56. GARF, f. 8131, op. 31, d. 85762, l. 13.
57. Dobson, *Khrushchev's Cold Summer*, p. 191.
58. Aksyutin, *Khrushchevskaya 'ottepel''*, pp. 282–89.
59. Y. Alpert, *Making Waves: Stories from my life*, New Haven, CT, and London: Yale University Press, 2000, p. 6.
60. P. Messina, *Soviet Communal Living: An oral history of the kommunalka*, Basingstoke: Palgrave, 2011.
61. Brodsky, *Less than One*, p. 455.
62. See LVA, f. 201, op. 1, d. 1117, l. 52.
63. V. Voinovich, *The Anti-Soviet Soviet Union*, New York: Harcourt, 1985, p. 104.

64. NARB, f. 63p, op. 19, d. 9, ll. 60–63.
65. RGANI, f. 5, op. 37, d. 65, ll. 1–65.
66. M. Smith, *Property of Communists: The urban housing programme from Stalin to Khrushchev*, Ithaca, NY: Cornell University Press, 2010, p. 26.
67. Lebina, *Povsednevnost' epokhi kosmosa i kukuruzy*.
68. See N. Melvin, *Soviet Power and the Countryside: Policy innovation and institutional decay*, New York: Palgrave, 2003.
69. M. Amirkhanova, 'Naselenie dagestanskogo sela v 50-e–60-e gg.', *Voprosy istorii*, No. 3, 2009.
70. J. Smith, *Works in Progress*, p. 196.
71. S. Harris, *Communism on Tomorrow Street: Mass housing and everyday life after Stalin*, Baltimore, MD: Johns Hopkins University Press, 2013, p. 72.
72. S. Reid, 'Khrushchev modern: Agency and modernization in the Soviet home', *Cahiers du monde russe*, Vol. 47, No. 1, 2006.
73. M. Smith, 'Khrushchev's promise to eliminate the urban housing shortage', in M. Ilic and J. Smith eds, *Soviet State and Society under Nikita Khrushchev*, London: Routledge, 2009.
74. Smith, *Property of Communists*.
75. Filtzer, *Soviet Workers and De-Stalinization*, p. 164.
76. Smith, *Property of Communists*.
77. Messina, *Soviet Communal Living*, p. 65.
78. Gallyamova, *Tatarskaya ASSR v period PostStalinizma*, p. 167.
79. J. Conterio, 'Our Black Sea coast: The sovietization of the Black Sea littoral under Khrushchev and the problem of overdevelopment', *Kritika*, Vol. 19, No. 2, 2018.
80. A. Prishchepa and D. Bycherov, 'Istoriya issledovaniya i osveniya Yamal'skogo regiona studencheskimi stroitel'nymi otryadami SSSR (1950–1970-e gg.)', *Voprosy istorii*, No. 3, 2021.
81. P. Grebenyuk, 'Sotsial'naya sfera Magadanskoi oblasti v 1958–65 gg.', *Voprosy istorii*, No. 7, 2021, p. 208.
82. E. Iarskaia-Smirnova and P. Romanov, 'Heroes and spongers', in M. Rasell and E. Iarskaia-Smirnova eds, *Disability in Eastern Europe and the Former Soviet Union: History, policy and everyday life*, London: Routledge, 2014.
83. C. Shaw, *Deaf in the USSR: Marginality, community, and Soviet identity, 1917–1991*, Ithaca, NY: Cornell University Press, 2017.
84. G. Tsipursky, *Socialist Fun: Youth, consumption and state-sponsored popular culture in the Soviet Union, 1945–1970*, Pittsburgh, PA: University of Pittsburgh Press, 2016.
85. Vas'kin, *Povsednevnaya zhizn'*.
86. A. Kozlov, *Kozel na sakse, i tak vsyu zhizn'*, Moskva: Vagrius, 1998, p. 158
87. S. Reid, 'Cold War in the kitchen: Gender and the destalinization of consumer taste in the Soviet Union under Khrushchev', *Slavic Review*, Vol. 61, No. 2, 2002, p. 212.
88. Filtzer, *Soviet Workers and De-Stalinization*.
89. A. Kalinovsky, 'Tractors, power lines, and the welfare state: The contradictions of Soviet development in post-World War II Tajikistan', *Asiatische Studien*, Vol. 69, No. 3, 2015.
90. S. Oushakine, 'Against the cult of things: On Soviet productivism, storage economy, and commodities with no destination', *Russian Review*, Vol. 73, No. 2, 2014, p. 209.

91. ibid.
92. D. Koenker, 'The smile behind the sales counter: Soviet shop assistants on the road to full communism', *Journal of Social History*, Vol. 54, No. 3, 2021.
93. N. Chernyshova, *Soviet Consumer Culture in the Brezhnev Era*, London: Routledge, 2013, p. 4.
94. M. Voslensky, *Nomenklatura: The Soviet ruling class,* New York: Doubleday, 1984.
95. Ironside, *A Full-Value Ruble*.
96. D. Bartlett, *Fashion East: The spectre that haunted socialism*, Cambridge, MA: MIT Press, 2010.
97. Tromly, *Making the Soviet Intelligentsia*, p. 175.
98. Mukhitdinov, *Gody provedennye v Kremle*.
99. A. Lakhtikova, 'Sated people', in A. Lakhtikova et al. eds, *Seasoned Socialism*.
100. Arbatov, *The System*, p. 84.
101. Koenker, 'The smile behind the sales counter'.
102. S. Lovell, 'Soviet Exurbia', in D. Crowley and S. Reid eds, *Socialist Spaces: Sites of everyday life in the Eastern Bloc*, Oxford: Berg, 2002.
103. Chernyshova, *Soviet Consumer Culture*.
104. *Nedelya*, 09.09.1962.
105. Bartlett, *Fashion East*, p. 184.
106. H. Salisbury, *To Moscow and Beyond: A reporter's narrative*, London: Michael Joseph, 1960, p. 15.
107. L. Zakharova, 'Dior in Moscow', in D. Crowley and S. Reid eds, *Pleasures in Socialism: Leisure and luxury in the eastern bloc*, Evanston, IL: Northwestern University Press, 2010.
108. Bartlett, *Fashion East*, p. 192.
109. K. Roth-Ey, 'Finding a home for television in the USSR, 1950–1970', *Slavic Review*, Vol. 66, No. 2, 2007, p. 282.
110. C. Evans, *Between Truth and Time: A history of Soviet central television*, New Haven, CT, and London: Yale University Press, 2016.
111. S. Lovell, *Russia in the Microphone Age: A history of Soviet radio, 1919–1970*, Oxford: Oxford University Press, 2015, p. 157.
112. RGANI, f. 5, op. 30, d. 141, ll. 17–18.
113. A. Podrabinek, *Dissidenty: 'Mezhdu tyurmoi i svobodoi'*, Moskva: AST, 2015, p. 13.
114. G. Sosin, *Sparks of Liberty: An insider's memoir of Radio Liberty*, University Park, PA: Penn State University Press, 1999, p. xiv.
115. Lovell, *Russia in the Microphone Age*, p. 169.
116. P. Koivunen, *Performing Peace and Friendship: The World Youth Festivals and Soviet cultural diplomacy*, London: De Gruyter, 2022.
117. P. Koivunen, 'The 1957 Youth Festival', in Ilic and Smith eds, *Soviet State and Society*.
118. Koivunen, *Performing Peace and Friendship*.
119. NARK, f. 779, op. 33, d. 18, ll. 1–16.
120. Zubok, *Zhivago's Children*, p. 103.
121. S. Belfrage, *A Room in Moscow*, London: Reynal, 1958, pp. 13–14.
122. V. Semichastnyi, *Bespokoinoe serdtse*, Moskva: Vagrius, 2002, p. 68.
123. Rabin, *Tri Zhizni*, p. 38.
124. Belfrage, *A Room in Moscow*, p. 14.
125. Koivunen, *Performing Peace and Friendship*.

126. Gerasimova, '*Ottepel*'', '*Zamorozki*' *i studenty Moskovskogo universiteta*, p. 393.
127. *Literaturnaya gazeta*, 08.08.1957.
128. Koivunen, *Performing Peace and Friendship*.
129. Kozlov, *Kozel na sakse*, p. 106.
130. Vas'kin, *Povsednevnaya zhizn'*, p. 31.
131. L. Plyushch, *History's Carnival: A dissident's autobiography*, London: Collins and Harvill Press, 1979, p. 15.
132. K. Roth-Ey, 'Loose girls on the loose', in Ilic et al. eds, *Women in the Khrushchev Era*.
133. *Komsomol'skaya pravda*, 11.08.1957.

Chapter 5

1. P. Vail' and A. Genis, *60-e: Mir sovetskogo cheloveka*, Moskva: AST, 2013, p. 100.
2. M. Rogacheva, *The Private World of Soviet Scientists from Stalin to Gorbachev*, Cambridge: Cambridge University Press, 2017, p. 42.
3. https://digitalarchive.wilsoncenter.org/document/165445
4. A. Siddiqi, *Sputnik and the Soviet Space Challenge*, Gainesville, FL: University Press of Florida, 2000, p. 151.
5. ibid., p. 161.
6. A. Siddiqi, 'Korolev, Sputnik, and the international geophysical year', in R. Lanius ed., *Reconsidering Sputnik: Forty years since the Soviet satellite*, London: Routledge, 2000.
7. S. Khrushchev, 'The first earth satellite', in Lanius ed., *Reconsidering Sputnik*, p. 270.
8. *Pravda*, 09.10.1957.
9. P. Dickson, *Sputnik: The shock of the century*, Lincoln, NE: University of Nebraska Press, 2019.
10. *Trud*, 08.10.1957.
11. Ya. Golovanov, *Korolev: Fakty i mify*, Moskva: Nauka, 1994, p. 544.
12. S. Gerovitch ed., *Voices of the Soviet Space Program: Cosmonauts, soldiers, and engineers who took the USSR into space*, Basingstoke: Palgrave, 2014, p. 50.
13. Golovanov, *Korolev*, p. 586.
14. T. Rupprecht, 'Socialist high modernity and global stagnation: A shared history of Brazil and the Soviet Union during the Cold War', *Journal of Global History*, Vol. 6, No. 3, 2011.
15. L. Siegelbaum, 'Sputnik goes to Brussels: The exhibition of a Soviet technological wonder', *Journal of Contemporary History*, Vol. 47, No. 1, 2012.
16. Golovanov, *Korolev*, p. 544.
17. O. Turkina, *Soviet Space Dogs*, London: Fuel, 2014.
18. ibid., p. 178.
19. G. Kornienko, *Kholodnaya voina: Svidetel'stvo ee uchastnika*, Moskva: Olma Press, 2001.
20. L. Barker and R. Skotak, 'Klushantsev: Russia's wizard of *fantastika*', in A. Banerjee ed., *Russian Science Fiction Literature and Cinema*, Boston: Academic Studies Press, 2018.
21. I. Csicsery-Ronay Jr, 'Towards the last fairytale', in Banerjee ed., *Russian Science Fiction Literature and Cinema*, p. 240.
22. M. Froggatt, 'Science in propaganda and popular culture in the USSR under Khrushchev (1953–1964)', University of Oxford, 2006.

23. S. Schmid, 'Celebrating tomorrow today: The peaceful atom on display in the Soviet Union', *Social Studies of Science*, Vol. 36, No. 3, 2006.
24. M. Dumančić, *Men Out of Focus*.
25. C. Kelly, 'Thank you for the wonderful book: Soviet child readers and the management of children's reading, 1950–1975', *Kritika*, Vol. 6, No. 4, 2005, p. 717.
26. E. Zhidkova, 'Praktiki i razresheniya semeinykh konfliktov', in Yarska-Smirnova and Romanov eds, *Sovetskaya sotsial'naya politika*.
27. TsDOOSO, f. 2186, op. 1, d. 82, l. 19.
28. B. Grushin, *Chetyre zhizni Rossii v zerkale oprosov obshchestvennogo mneniya*, Moskva: Progress-Traditsiya, 2001.
29. RGASPI, f. 1, op. 31, d. 144, l. 1.
30. S. Harris, 'Dawn of the Soviet jet age: Aeroflot passengers and aviation culture under Nikita Khrushchev', *Kritika*, Vol. 21, No. 3, 2020.
31. W. Taubman, Khrushchev: the Man and his era.
32. A. Hale-Dorrell, 'Industrial farming, industrial food: Transnational influences on Soviet convenience food in the Khrushchev era', *Soviet and Post-Soviet Review*, Vol. 42, No. 2, 2015.
33. A. Bronovitskaya, N. Malinin and Y. Palmin, *Moscow: A guide to Soviet modernist architecture, 1955–1991*, London: Artguide, 2019, p. 9.
34. A. Sillitoe, *The Road to Volgograd*, New York: Knopf, 1964, p. 14.
35. See S. Bittner, *The Many Lives of Khrushchev's Thaw: Experience and memory in Moscow's Arbat*, Ithaca, NY: Cornell University Press, 2008.
36. Interview with Zaslavskaya, in Cohen and vanden Heuvel eds, *Voices of Glasnost*, p. 116.
37. N. Pushkareva and A. Zhidchenko, 'Women scholars of Akademgorodok: Everyday life in a Soviet university town during the thaw', *Russian Review*, Vol. 81, No. 2, 2022.
38. K. Tatarchenko, 'A house with the window to the West: The Akademgorodok Computer Center (1958–1993)', Princeton University, 2013.
39. A. Novikov ed., 'Sovetskaya intelligentsiya, Lubyanka, i Staraya Ploshchad' v 1960-x – 1980-x godakh', *Voprosy istorii*, No. 9, 2005.
40. E. Pollock, 'From *partiinost'* to *nauchnost'* and not quite back again: Revisiting the lessons of the Lysenko affair', *Slavic Review*, Vol. 68, No. 1, 2009.
41. Gerasimova, *'Ottepel'', 'Zamorozki' i studenty Moskovskogo universiteta*.
42. S. Gerovitch, 'InterNyet: Why the Soviet Union did not build a nationwide computer network', *History and Technology*, Vol. 24, No. 4, 2008.
43. ibid.
44. Interview with Evgeny Velikhov, in Cohen and vanden Heuvel eds, *Voices of Glasnost*, p. 159.
45. Siddiqi, *Sputnik and the Soviet Space Challenge*.
46. D. Holloway, *The Soviet Union and the Arms Race*, New Haven, CT, and London: Yale University Press, 1983.
47. R. Sagdeev, *The Making of a Soviet Scientist*, New York: Wiley, 1994, p. 54.
48. A. Sakharov, *Memoirs*, New York: Knopf, 1990, p. 174.
49. ibid., p. 172.
50. ibid., p. 215.
51. P. Josephson, *Red Atom: Russia's nuclear power program from Stalin to today*, Pittsburgh, PA: University of Pittsburgh Press, 2005, p. 3.
52. P. Josephson, 'Atomic-powered communism: Nuclear culture in the postwar USSR', *Slavic Review*, Vol. 55, No. 2, 1996.

53. Josephson, *Red Atom*, p. 20.
54. ibid., p. 147.
55. S. Guth, 'Oasis of the future: The nuclear city of Shevchenko/Aqtau, 1959–2019', *Jahrbücher für Geschichte Osteuropas*, Vol. 16, No. 1, 2018.
56. Josephson, *Red Atom*.
57. L. Coumel, 'A failed environmental turn? Khrushchev's thaw and nature protection in Soviet Russia', *Soviet and Post-Soviet Review*, Vol. 40, No. 2, 2013.
58. N. Breyfogle, 'At the watershed: 1968 and the beginnings of Lake Baikal environmentalism', *Slavonic and East European Review*, Vol. 93, No. 1, 2015.
59. P. Josephson, *An Environmental History of Russia*, Cambridge: Cambridge University Press, 2013, p. 177.
60. Gallyamova, *Tatarskaya ASSR v period postStalinizma*, p. 230.
61. Josephson, *Red Atom*.
62. K. Brown, *Plutopia: Nuclear families, atomic cities, and the great Soviet and American plutonium disasters*, Oxford: Oxford University Press, 2015.
63. ibid.
64. ibid.
65. ibid.
66. Gerovitch ed., *Voices of the Soviet Space Program*, 'Construction Engineer Sergey Safro', p. 31.
67. Siddiqi, *Sputnik and the Soviet Space Challenge*, p. 263.
68. S. Gerovitch, *Soviet Space Mythologies: Public images, private memories and the making of a cultural identity*, Pittsburgh, PA: University of Pittsburgh Press, 2015, p. 75.
69. ibid., p. 57.
70. See http://www.astronautix.com/k/kamanindiaries.html
71. A. Jenks, *The Cosmonaut Who Couldn't Stop Smiling: The life and legend of Yuri Gagarin*, DeKalb, IL: Northern Illinois University Press, 2011.
72. S. Walker, *Beyond*, London: William Collins, 2021.
73. Jenks, *The Cosmonaut Who Couldn't Stop Smiling*, pp. 134–135.
74. *Pravda*, 13.04.1961.
75. Gerovitch, *Soviet Space Mythologies*, p. 129.
76. B. Pastukhov, *Druzei moikh prekrasnye cherty*, Moskva: Molodaya gvardiya, 2012, p. 78.
77. M. Schwartz, 'A dream come true', in E. Maurer et al. eds, *Soviet Space Culture: Cosmic enthusiasm in socialist societies*, London: Palgrave, 2011, p. 233.
78. Kalugin, *Spy Master*, p. 50.
79. Vas'kin, *Povsednevnaya zhizn'*, p. 417.
80. Fraser, *Military Masculinity*.
81. Jenks, *The Cosmonaut Who Couldn't Stop Smiling*.
82. A. Siddiqi, 'From cosmic enthusiasm to nostalgia for the future', in Maurer et al. eds, *Soviet Space Culture*, p. 285.
83. *Pravda* 25.04.1961.
84. http://www.astronautix.com/k/kamanindiaries.html
85. L. Kohonen, *Picturing the Cosmos: A visual history of early Soviet space endeavour*, Bristol: Intellect, 2017.
86. M. Ruthers, 'Children and the cosmos', in Maurer et al. eds, *Soviet Space Culture*, p. 208.
87. Siddiqi, *Sputnik and the Soviet Space Challenge*, p. 352.
88. Gerovitch, *Soviet Space Mythologies*.

89. Gerovitch ed., *Voices of the Soviet Space Program*, 'Second Backup: Valentina Ponomareva'.
90. http://www.astronautix.com/k/kamanindiaries.html
91. Siddiqi, *Sputnik and the Soviet Space Challenge*, p. 353
92. *Pravda*, 16.06.1963.
93. R. Sylvester, '"You are our pride and our glory!" Emotions, generation and the legacy of revolution in women's letters to Valentina Tereshkova', *Russian Review*, Vol. 78, No. 3, 2019.
94. Fraser, *Military Masculinity*, p. 166.
95. See R. Sylvester, 'Let's find out where the cosmonaut school is', in Maurer et al. eds, *Soviet Space Culture*.
96. http://www.astronautix.com/k/kamanindiaries.html May 1968
97. Gerovitch, *Soviet Space Mythologies*, p. 14.
98. Gerovitch ed., *Voices of the Soviet Space Program*, 'Second Backup: Valentina Tereshkova', p. 228.

Chapter 6

1. D. Engerman, 'The Second World's Third World', *Kritika*, Vol. 12, No. 1, 2011.
2. Stevenson, *Friends and Enemies*, p. 6.
3. Mikoyan, *Tak bylo*, p. 60.
4. J. Thompson and S. Thompson, *The Kremlinologist: Llewellyn E. Thompson, America's man in Cold War Moscow*, Baltimore, MD: Johns Hopkins University Press, 2018, p. 186.
5. Rabin, *Tri zhizni*, p. 41.
6. P. Carlson, *'K' Blows Top*, New York: Public Affairs, 2009, p. xii.
7. R. Magnusdottir, *Enemy Number One: The United States of America in Soviet ideology and propaganda, 1945–1959*, Oxford: Oxford University Press, 2018.
8. V. Sukhodrev, *Yazyk moi – drug moi: Ot Khrushcheva do Gorbacheva*, Moskva: Olimp, 1999, p. 105.
9. ibid., p. 74.
10. Pikhoya, *Moskva, kreml', vlast'*, p. 406.
11. Fursenko and Naftali, *Khrushchev's Cold War*, p. 266.
12. Thompson and Thompson, *The Kremlinologist*, p. 217.
13. Mikoyan, *Tak bylo*, p. 605.
14. A. Skutnev, '"Doktrina Khrushcheva" protiv "doktrina Eisenkhauera" (vesna-leto 1960 g.)', *Voprosy istorii*, No. 3, 2008.
15. Sukhodrev, *Yazyk moi – drug moi*.
16. A. Iandolo, 'Beyond the shoe: Rethinking Khrushchev at the fifteenth session of the United Nations General Assembly', *Diplomatic History*, Vol. 41, No. 1, 2017.
17. ibid.
18. Sukhodrev, *Yazyk moi – drug moi*, p. 126.
19. J. Haslam, *Near and Distant Neighbours: A new history of Soviet intelligence*, Oxford: Oxford University Press, 2015, p. 188.
20. H. Harrison, *Driving the Soviets up the Wall: Soviet–East German relations, 1953–61*, Princeton, NJ: Princeton University Press, 2003.
21. Kornienko, *Kholodnaya voina*, p. 92.
22. Harrison, *Driving the Soviets up the Wall*, p. 139.
23. Kornienko, *Kholodnaya voina*, p. 101.
24. L. Crump, *Warsaw Pact Reconsidered: International relations in Eastern Europe, 1955–69*, London: Routledge, 2017; P. Muehlenbeck and N. Telepneva eds,

Warsaw Pact Intervention in the Third World: Aid and influence in the Cold War, London: Bloomsbury, 2018.

25. T. Krasovitskaya ed., *'Vozvratit' domoi druz'yami SSSR': Obuchenie inostrantsev v Sovetskom Soyuze, 1956–1965*, Moskva: Rosspen, 2013, p. 55.

26. Zh. Shen and Y. Xia, *Mao and the Sino-Soviet Partnership, 1945–1959*, New York: Lexington, 2017.

27. O. Westad, *The Cold War: A world history*, London: Allen Lane, 2017, p. 237.

28. Khrushchev ed., *Memoirs of Nikita Khrushchev*, Vol. 3, p. 441.

29. N. Mesyatsev, *Gorizonty i labirinty moei zhizni*, Moskva: Vagrius, 2005, p. 383.

30. Luthi, *The Sino-Soviet Split*, p. 50.

31. Emel'yanov, *Khrushchev*, p. 478.

32. Crump, *Warsaw Pact Reconsidered*, p. 59.

33. *Kommunist*, No. 1, 1961.

34. M. Eby, 'Global Tashkent: Transnational visions of a Soviet city in the postcolonial world, 1953–1966', *Ab Imperio*, No. 4, 2021, p. 239.

35. A. Hale-Dorrell, *Corn Crusade: Khrushchev's farming revolution in the post-Stalin Soviet Union*, Oxford: Oxford University Press, 2018, p. 48.

36. Mukhitdinov, *Gody, provedennye v Kremle*, p. 154.

37. V. Mastny, 'The Soviet Union's partnership with India', *Journal of Cold War Studies*, Vol. 12, No. 3, 2010.

38. Rupprecht, 'Socialist high modernity'.

39. C. Katsakioris, 'Soviet lessons for Arab modernisation: Soviet educational aid to Arab countries after 1956', *Journal of Modern European History*, Vol. 8, No. 1, 2010, p. 91.

40. E. Banks, 'Sewing machines for socialism? Gifts of development and disagreement between the Soviet and Mozambican women's committees, 1963–87', *Comparative Studies of South Asia, Africa and the Middle East*, Vol. 41, No. 1, 2021; R. Hornsby, 'The post-Stalin Komsomol and the Soviet fight for Third World youth', *Cold War History*, Vol. 16, No. 1, 2016.

41. Krasovitskaya ed., *'Vozvratit' domoi druz'yami SSSR'*, pp. 530-552.

42. Y. Zoubir, 'The United States, the Soviet Union, and the decolonisation of the Maghreb, 1945–62', *Middle Eastern Studies*, Vol. 31, No. 1, 1995.

43. Katsakioris, 'Soviet lessons for Arab modernisation'.

44. K. Roth-Ey, 'How do you listen to Radio Moscow? Moscow broadcasters, "Third World" listeners, and the space of the airwaves in the Cold War', *Slavonic and East European Review*, Vol. 98, No. 4, 2020.

45. V. Zubok, 'Spy vs spy: The KGB vs the CIA, 1960–62', *Bulletin of the Cold War International History Project*, No. 4, 1994.

46. O. Sanchez-Sibony, *Red Globalization: The political economy of the Soviet Cold War from Stalin to Khrushchev*, Cambridge: Cambridge University Press, 2017.

47. K. Brutents, *Tridtsat' let na Staroi Ploshchadi*, Moskva: Mezdunarodnye otnosheniya, 1998.

48. A. Kalinovsky, 'Not some British colony in Africa: The politics of decolonization and modernization in Soviet Central Asia, 1955–1964', *Ab Imperio*, No. 2, 2013.

49. Mukhitdinov, *Gody, provedennye v Kremle*, p. 163.

50. A. Kalinovsky, *Laboratory of Socialist Development: Cold War politics and decolonization in Soviet Tajikistan*, Ithaca, NY, and London: Cornell University Press, 2018.

51. Eby, 'Global Tashkent'.
52. R. Cucciola, 'Sharaf Rashidov and the international dimensions of Soviet Uzbekistan', *Central Asian Survey*, Vol. 39, No. 2, 2020.
53. C. Varga-Harris, 'Between national tradition and Western modernization: Soviet woman and representations of socialist gender equality as a third way for developing countries, 1956–1964', *Slavic Review*, Vol. 78, No. 3, 2019.
54. R. Yordanov, *The Soviet Union and the Horn of Africa during the Cold War*, Lanham, MD: Lexington Books, 2016.
55. A. Iandolo, 'The rise and fall of the Soviet model of development in West Africa, 1957–64', *Cold War History*, Vol. 12, No. 4, 2012.
56. A. Iandolo, 'Imbalance of power: The Soviet Union and the Congo crisis, 1960–61', *Journal of Cold War Studies*, Vol. 16, No. 2, 2014.
57. S. Mazov, *A Distant Front in the Cold War: The USSR in West Africa and the Congo, 1956–1964*, Redwood City, CA: Stanford University Press, 2010.
58. S. Mazov, 'Soviet aid to the Gizenga government in the former Belgian Congo (1960–61) as reflected in Russian archives', *Cold War History*, Vol. 7, No. 3, 2007.
59. Khrushchev ed., *Memoirs of Nikita Khrushchev*, Vol. 3, p. 879.
60. Iandolo, 'Imbalance of power'.
61. S. Nayudu, 'When the elephant swallowed the hedgehog: The Prague Spring and Indo-Soviet relations, 1968', *Cold War International History Project* Working Paper, 83, 2017.
62. Sanchez-Sibony, *Red Globalization*, p. 21.
63. ibid., p. 147.
64. Mazov, *A Distant Front in the Cold War*, p. 222.
65. Banks, 'Sewing machines for socialism?'
66. S. Mazov, 'Sovetskii soyuz i zapadnaya Afrika v 1956–64 gody', *Novaya i noveishaya istoriya*, No. 2, 2007.
67. S. Mikoyan, *The Soviet Cuban Missile Crisis: Castro, Mikoyan, Kennedy, Khrushchev, and the Missiles of November*, Redwood City, CA: Stanford University Press, 2012.
68. J. Goncalves, 'Sputnik premiers in Havana', in Gorsuch and Koenker eds, *The Socialist Sixties*.
69. A. Gorsuch, ' "Cuba, My Love": The romance of revolutionary Cuba in the Soviet sixties', *American Historical Review*, Vol. 120, No. 2, 2015.
70. Vail' and Genis, *60-e: Mir sovetskogo cheloveka*, p. 70.
71. Gorsuch, ' "Cuba, My Love" '.
72. RGASPI, f. 6, op. 14, d. 1, l. 4.
73. See Gorsuch, ' "Cuba, My Love" '.
74. Adzhubei, *Ya byl zyatem Khrushcheva*, p. 235.
75. A. Shevchenko, *Breaking with Moscow*, New York: Knopf, 1985, p. 176.
76. R. Hornsby, 'The enemy within? The Komsomol and foreign youth inside the post-Stalin Soviet Union', *Past and Present*, Vol. 232, No. 1, 2016.
77. LYA, f. 1-k, op. 3, d. 623, l. 54.
78. I. Orlov and A. Popov, *Russo touristo: sovetskii vyezdnoi turizm, 1955–1991*, p. 109.
79. A. Gorsuch, *All This Is Your World: Soviet tourism at home and abroad after Stalin*, Oxford: Oxford University Press, 2011.
80. R. Applebaum, 'The Friendship Project: Socialist internationalism in the Soviet Union and Czechoslovakia in the 1950s and 60s', *Slavic Review*, Vol. 74, No. 3, 2015.

81. A. Gorsuch, 'Time travellers: Soviet tourists to Eastern Europe', in A. Gorsuch and D. Koenker eds, *Turizm: The Russian and East European tourist under capitalism and socialism*, Ithaca, NY: Cornell University Press, 2006.

82. TsDAGO, f. 7, op. 17, d. 607, l. 78.

83. S. Zhuk, *Rock and Roll in the Rocket City: The West, identity and ideology in Soviet Dnipropetrovsk, 1960–1985*, Baltimore, MD: Johns Hopkins University Press, 2010.

84. Krasovitskaya ed., '*Vozvratit' domoi druz'yami SSSR*', pp. 157–58.

85. ibid., p. 258.

86. ibid., p. 538.

87. TsDAGO, f. 7, op. 20, d. 50, l. 5.

88. See T. Rupprecht, *Soviet Internationalism after Stalin: Interaction and exchange between the USSR and Latin America*, Cambridge: Cambridge University Press, 2015.

89. J. Alexander and J. McGregor, 'African soldiers in the USSR: Oral histories of ZAPU intelligence cadres' Soviet training, 1964–1979', *Journal of Southern African Studies*, Vol. 43, No. 1, 2017.

90. D. Gurevich, *From Lenin to Lennon: A memoir of Russia in the sixties*, London: Harcourt, 1991, p. 111.

91. Krasovitskaya ed., '*Vozvratit' domoi druz'yami SSSR*', p. 581.

92. C. Katsakioris, 'Burden or allies? Third World students and internationalist duty through Soviet eyes', *Kritika*, Vol. 18, No. 3, 2017.

93. R. Hornsby, 'Engineering friendship? Komsomol work with students from the developing world inside the USSR in the 1950s and 1960s', *Social History*, Vol. 48, No. 1, 2023.

94. J. Hessler, 'Death of an African student in Moscow: Race, politics, and the Cold War', *Cahiers du monde russe*, Vol. 47, Nos 1/2, 2006.

95. Krasovitskaya ed., '*Vozvratit' domoi druz'yami SSSR*', p. 378.

96. H. Salisbury, *A New Russia?*, New York: Harper & Row, 1962, p. 21.

97. Yurchak, *Everything was Forever*.

98. S. Sherry, 'Better something than nothing: The editors and translators of *Inostrannaia literatura* as censorial agents', *Slavonic and East European Review*, Vol. 91, No. 4, 2013.

99. Gilburd, *To See Paris and Die*, p. 145.

100. Orlova and Kopelev, *My zhili v Moskve*.

101. R. De Luca, 'Tarkovsky screens Hemingway: Andrei Tarkovsky's first student film, *The Killers* (1956)', *Studies in Russian and Soviet Cinema*, Vol. 13, No. 2, 2019.

102. Vail and Genis, *60-e: Mir sovetskogo cheloveka*, p. 81.

103. Gilburd, *To See Paris and Die*, p. 119.

104. S. Zhuk, 'Hollywood's insidious charms: The impact of American cinema and television in the Soviet Union during the Cold War', *Cold War History*, Vol. 14, No. 4, 2014.

105. Lebina, *Muzhchina i zhenshchina*, p. 37.

106. Lebina, *Povsednevnost' epokhi kosmosa i kukuruzy*, p. 318.

107. Vas'kin, *Povsednevnaya zhizn'*, p. 373.

108. D. Muzafari, *Sunshine Girl: My journey from the Soviet Orient to the Western world*, London: Amazon, 2020, p. 93.

109. N. Cliff, *Moscow Nights: The Van Cliburn story*, New York: Harper, 2016.

110. Turkina, *Soviet Space Dogs*.

111. F. Starr, *Red and Hot: The fate of jazz in the Soviet Union, 1917–1980*, Oxford: Oxford University Press, 1993.

112. W. Taubman, *The View from the Lenin Hills: An American student's report on Soviet youth in ferment*, London: Hamish Hamilton, 1968, p. 70.

113. J. Fürst, *Flowers through the Concrete: Explorations in Soviet Hippieland*, Oxford: Oxford University Press, 2021, p. 55.

114. Zhuk, *Rock and Roll in the Rocket City*.

115. ibid., p. 13.

116. Gurevich, *From Lenin to Lennon*, p. 128.

117. A. Troitsky, *Back in the USSR: The true story of rock in Russia*, London: Omnibus Press, 1987, p. 15.

Chapter 7

1. Salisbury, *To Moscow and Beyond*, p. 12.

2. Bobkov, *KGB i vlast'*, p. 174.

3. J. Elkner, 'The changing face of repression under Khrushchev', in Ilic and Smith eds, *Soviet State and Society*.

4. J. Fedor, *Russia and the Cult of State Security: The Chekist tradition, from Lenin to Putin*, London: Routledge, 2013.

5. ibid.

6. *Nedelya*, 01.09.62.

7. Y. Gorlizki, 'Policing post-Stalin society: The militia and public order under Khrushchev', *Cahiers du monde russe*, Vol. 44, Nos 2/3, 2003.

8. L. Shelley, *Policing Soviet Society: The evolution of state control*, London: Routledge, 1996.

9. ERAF, f. 1, op. 191, d. 16, ll. 1–13.

10. Semichastnyi, *Bespokoinoe serdtse*, p. 208.

11. Vail', *Osobo opasnyi*, p. 189.

12. Chebrikov et al. eds, *Istoriya sovetskikh organov gosudarstvennoi bezopasnosti*.

13. LYA, f. 1-k, op. 18, d. 92, ll. 10–20.

14. https://www.kgbdocuments.eu/documents/the-selection-training-teaching-and-use-of-agents-a-paper-written-by-head-of-the-second-department-of-the-second-board-of-the-kgb-of-the-lssr/

15. https://digitalarchive.wilsoncenter.org/document/110403

16. V. Mitrokhin, *KGB Lexicon: The Soviet intelligence officer's handbook*, London: Routledge, 2002, p. 329.

17. E. Cohn, 'A Soviet theory of broken windows: Prophylactic policing and the KGB's struggle with political unrest in the Baltic republics', *Kritika*, Vol. 19, No. 4, 2018.

18. O. Kharkhordin, *The Collective and the Individual in Russia: A study of practices*, Berkeley, CA: University of California Press, 1999.

19. Chebrikov et al. eds, *Istoriya sovetskikh organov gosudarstvennoi bezopasnosti*, p. 564.

20. Haslam, *Near and Distant Neighbours*, p. 178

21. C. Andrew and V. Mitrokhin, *The Mitrokhin Archive: The KGB in Europe and the West*, London: Penguin, 2015, p. 227

22. Kovacevic, '"An ominous talent"'.

23. Andrew and Mitrokhin, *The Mitrokhin Archive*.

24. Kalugin, *Spy Master*, p. 52.

25. Zubok, 'Spy vs spy'.

26. https://www.kgbdocuments.eu/assets/documents/2102e_97k.pdf

27. https://digitalarchive.wilsoncenter.org/document/119632

28. S. Plokhy, *The Man with the Poison Gun*, London: Oneworld, 2016.

29. J. Delaney Grossman, 'Khrushchev's anti-religious policy and the campaign of 1954', *Soviet Studies*, Vol. 24, No. 3, 1973.

30. M. Shkarovskii, 'Russkaya pravoslavnaya tserkov' v 1958–1964 godakh', *Voprosy istorii*, No. 2, 1999.

31. A. Stone, ' "Overcoming peasant backwardness": The Khrushchev anti-religious campaign and the rural Soviet Union', *Russian Review*, Vol. 67, No. 2, 2008.

32. V. Smolkin, *A Sacred Space Is Never Empty: A history of Soviet atheism*, Princeton, NJ, and Oxford: Princeton University Press, 2018, p. 78.

33. Yu. Geras'kin, 'K voprosu o podderzhke russkoi pravoslavnoi tserkvi naseleniem v period "khrushchevskikh gonenii" ', *Otechestvennaya istoriya*, No. 4, 2007.

34. N. Davis, 'The number of Orthodox churches before and after the Khrushchev anti-religious drive', *Slavic Review*, Vol. 50, No. 3, 1991, p. 614.

35. E. Tasar, *Soviet and Muslim: The institutionalization of Islam in Central Asia*, Oxford: Oxford University Press, 2017, p. 54.

36. Altshuler, *Religion and Jewish Identity*.

37. M. Dobson, 'Child sacrifice in the Soviet press: Sectarianism and the "sectarian" in the post-Stalin Years', *Russian Review*, Vol. 73, No. 2, 2014.

38. T. Vagramenko, 'KGB "evangelism": Agents and Jehovah's Witnesses in Soviet Ukraine', *Kritika*, Vol. 22, No. 4, 2021.

39. Kozlov and Mironenko eds, *58-10*.

40. L. Alexeyeva, *Soviet Dissent: Contemporary movements for national, religious and human rights*, Middletown, CT: Wesleyan University Press, 1985, p. 204.

41. E. Tasar, 'The official madrasas of Soviet Uzbekistan', *Journal of Economic and Social History of the Orient*, Vol. 59, No. 1, 2016.

42. Z. Yusufjovna-Abman, 'State feminism in Soviet Central Asia', in M. Ilic ed., *The Palgrave Handbook of Women and Gender*, p. 300.

43. Tasar, *Soviet and Muslim*.

44. ibid.

45. Smolkin, *A Sacred Space Is Never Empty*.

46. TsAOPIM, f. 635, op. 1, d. 2543, ll. 6–8.

47. M. Dobson, 'The social scientists meets the "believer": Discussions of God, the afterlife, and communism in the mid-1960s', *Slavic Review*, Vol. 74, No. 1, 2015.

48. Geras'kin, 'K voprosu o podderzhke russkoi tserkvi naseleniem'.

49. V. Smolkin-Rothrock, 'The ticket to the Soviet soul: Science, religion, and the spiritual crisis of late Soviet atheism', *Russian Review*, Vol. 73, No. 2, 2014.

50. Plisetskaya, *I, Maya*, p. 183.

51. Lebina, *Muzhchina i zhenshchina*.

52. Vail' and Genis, *60-e: Mir sovetskogo cheloveka*, p. 303.

53. Tranum ed., *Life at the Edge of Empire*.

54. Yusufjovna-Abman, 'State feminism in Soviet Central Asia', p. 304.

55. Tasar, *Soviet and Muslim*, p. 27.

56. R. MacColl, *Just Back from Russia: 77 days inside the Soviet Union*, London: Daily Express Publication, 1955, p. 87.

57. Brodsky, *Less than One*, p. 92.

58. S. White, *Russia Goes Dry: Alcohol, state and society*, Cambridge: Cambridge University Press, 1995, p. 35.

59. Lebina, *Povsednevnost' epokhi kosmosa i kukuruzy*.

60. G. Karpova, 'Vypem za rodinu!', in Yarska-Smirnova and Romanov eds, *Sovetskaya sotsial'naya politika*.

61. D. Petrov ed. *Istoria glazami Krokodila XX vek: Sobitiya, 1957–1979*, Moskva: XX senchuri krokokdil, 2015.

62. Lebina, *Povsednevnost' epokhi kosmosa i kukuruzy*.

63. Grebenyuk, 'Sotsial'naya sfera Magadanskoi oblasti', p. 212.

64. A. Livschiz, 'De-Stalinizing Soviet childhood', in Jones ed., *The Dilemmas of De-Stalinization*.

65. Gurevich, *From Lenin to Lennon*, p. 47.

66. TsDOOSO, f. 61, op. 14, d. 210, ll. 1–3.

67. B. LaPierre, 'Making hooliganism on a mass scale: The campaign against petty hooliganism in the Soviet Union, 1956–1964', *Cahiers du monde russe*, Vol. 47, Nos 1/2, 2006, p. 352.

68. B. LaPierre, *Hooligans in Khrushchev's Russia: Defining, policing and producing deviance during the thaw*, Madison, WI, and London: University of Wisconsin Press, 2012.

69. C. Varga-Harris, *Stories of House and Home: Soviet apartment life during the Khrushchev years*, Ithaca, NY: Cornell University Press, 2015, p. 129.

70. D. Field, *Private Life and Communist Morality in Khrushchev's Russia*, New York: Peter Lang, 2007.

71. M. Ilic, 'What did women want', in Ilic and Smith eds, *Soviet State and Society*.

72. Plyushch, *History's Carnival*, p. 14.

73. LaPierre, *Hooligans in Khrushchev's Russia*.

74. S. Fitzpatrick, 'Social parasites: How tramps, idle youths and busy entrepreneurs impeded the Soviet march to communism', *Cahiers du monde russe*, Vol. 47, Nos 1/2, 2006.

75. E. Zubkova ed., 'Na "krayu" sovetskogo obshchestva: Marginal'nye gruppy naseleniya i gosudarstvennaya politika, 1940–1960e gody', *Russkaya istoriya*, No. 5, 2009, p. 21.

76. A. Amalrik, *Involuntary Journey to Siberia*, London: Harcourt, 1970, p. 133.

77. *Komsomol'skaya pravda*, 29.08.1962.

78. A. Ledeneva, *Russia's Economy of Favours: Blat, networking and informal exchange*, Cambridge: Cambridge University Press, 1998, p. 3; Yurchak, *Everything was Forever*.

79. S. Hearne, 'Selling sex under socialism: Prostitution in the postwar USSR', *European Review of History*, Vol. 29, No. 2, 2022.

80. ERAF, f. 5, op. 50, d. 8, ll. 19–21.

81. ERAF, f. 5, op. 50, d. 8, ll. 42–43.

82. ERAF, f. 1, op. 286, d. 8, ll. 1–147.

83. Vas'kin, *Povsednevnaya zhizn'*, p. 287.

84. Yu. Feofanov and D. Barry, *Politics and Justice in Russia: Major trials of the post-Stalin years*, London: Routledge, 1996.

85. Y. Gorlizki, 'Scandal in Riazan: Networks of trust and the social dynamics of deception', *Kritika*, Vol. 14, No. 2, 2013.

86. Voslensky, *Nomenklatura*, p. 192.

87. Gorlizki and Khlevniuk, *Substate Dictatorship*.

88. Tomilina ed., *Nikita Khrushchev*, tom 2, p. 521.

89. A. Edgar, 'Marriage, modernity, and the friendship of nations: Interethnic intimacy in post-war Central Asia in comparative perspective', *Central Asian Survey*, Vol. 26, No. 4, 2007.

90. J. Sahadeo, *Voices from the Soviet Edge: Southern migrants in Leningrad and Moscow*, Ithaca, NY: Cornell University Press, 2019.

91. S. Kirmse, 'Internationalist nation builders: Youth under Brezhnev in the Soviet south', *Europe-Asia Studies*, Vol. 74, No. 7, 2022.

92. N. Kibita, 'Controlling resources in the Ukrainian SSR during the sovnarkhoz reform (1957–65): Testing the idea of decentralisation', *Europe-Asia Studies*, Vol. 65, No. 6, 2013.

93. Yekelchyk, *Ukraine*, p. 174.

94. S. Grybkauskas, *Governing the Soviet Union's National Republics: The second secretaries of the Communist Party*, London: Routledge, 2020.

95. T. Lloyd, 'Congo on the Dnipro: Third Worldism and the nationalization of Soviet internationalism in Ukraine', *Kritika*, Vol. 22, No. 4, 2021.

96. Z. Saktaganova, 'Natsional'naya politika v Kazakhstane v 1953–65 gg.', *Voprosy istorii*, No. 9, 2021.

97. Gallyamova, *Tatarskaya ASSR v period postStalinizma*, p. 358.

98. M. Lehmann, 'Apricot socialism: The national past, the Soviet project, and the imagining of community in late Soviet Armenia', *Slavic Review*, Vol. 74, No. 1, 2015.

99. Goff, *Nested Nationalism*.

100. LYA, f. 1-k, op. 3, d. 619, l. 114.

101. T. Remeikis, *Opposition to Soviet Rule in Lithuania, 1945–1980*, Chicago, IL: Institute of Lithuanian Studies, 1980, p. 37.

102. V. Davoliute, *The Making and Breaking of Soviet Lithuania*, London: Routledge, 2013, p. 88.

103. N. Dodkhudoyev, *Tajikistan: Land of sunshine*, London: Soviet Booklets, 1959, p. 6.

104. N. Chernyshova, 'De-Stalinisation and industrialisation in the Soviet borderlands: Beria's attempted national reform in Soviet Belarus', *Europe-Asia Studies*, Vol. 73, No. 2, 2021.

105. Florin, 'What is Russia to us?'

106. S. Grybkauskas, *Moscow and the Non-Russian Republics in the Soviet Union: Nomenklatura, intelligentsia and centre-periphery relations*, London: Routledge, 2021.

107. J. Smith, 'The battle for language: Opposition to Khrushchev's education reform in the Soviet republics', *Slavic Review*, Vol. 76, No. 4, 2017.

108. J. Smith, *Red Nations: The nationalities experience in the USSR*, Cambridge: Cambridge University Press, 2013, p. 211.

109. Loader, 'Beria and Khrushchev'.

110. Gorlizki and Khlevniuk, *Substate Dictatorship*, p. 172.

111. M. Loader, 'Restricting Russians: Language and immigration laws in Soviet Latvia, 1956–1959', *Nationalities Papers*, Vol. 45, No. 6, 2017, p. 1002.

112. S. Grybkauskas, 'Economic strategies and immigration in the Soviet Union's western borderlands: Lithuania, Latvia and Belorussia in the 1950s and 1960s', *Europe-Asia Studies*, Vol. 74, No. 3, 2022, p. 482.

113. Loader, 'Restricting Russians', p. 1097.

114. Loader, 'Beria and Khrushchev', p. 1785.

115. J. Hasanli, *Khrushchev's Thaw and National Identity in Soviet Azerbaijan, 1954–1959*, New York: Lexington, 2014, p. 65.

116. ibid., p. 198.

117. W. Prigge, 'The Latvian purges of 1959: A revision study', *Journal of Baltic Studies*, Vol. 35, No. 3, 2004, p. 217.

118. M. Loader, 'A Stalinist purge in the Khrushchev era? The Latvian Communist Party purge, 1959–1963', *Slavonic and East European Review*, Vol. 96, No. 2, 2018.

119. R. Abduvalieva, *Chingiz Aitmatov: The glorious path of an Eurasian writer*, London: New Generation Publishing, 2020, p. 40.

120. S. Keller, 'The puzzle of the manual harvest in Uzbekistan: Economics, statistics and labour in the Khrushchev era', *Central Asian Survey*, Vol. 34, No. 3, 2015, p. 303.

121. Salisbury, *A New Russia?*, p. 7.

122. Kalinovsky, 'Tractors, power lines and the welfare state'.

123. Kalinovsky, *Laboratory of Socialist Development*.

124. A. Kalinovsky and I. Scarborough, 'The oil lamp and the electric light', *Kritika*, Vol. 22, No. 1, 2021.

125. T. Rashidov, 'Soviet boarding schools as a forge of national professionals and intellectuals in Soviet Tajikistan in the 1950s and 1960s', *Central Asian Survey*, Vol. 38, No. 4, 2019.

126. Roth-Ey, *Moscow Prime Time*.

127. Plisetskaya, *I, Maya Plisetskaya*, p. 202.

128. D. Caute, *The Dancer Defects: The struggle for cultural supremacy during the Cold War*, Oxford: Oxford University Press, 2003.

129. P. Finn and P. Couvée, *The Zhivago Affair: The Kremlin, the CIA and the battle over a forbidden book*, London: Harvill Secker, 2014, p. 99.

130. Brown, *Soviet Russian Literature since Stalin*, p. 262.

131. V. Afiani and N. Tomilina eds, *'A za mnoyu shum pogoni . . .' Boris Pasternak i vlast': Dokumenty, 1956–1972*, Moskva: Rosspen, 2001, p. 63.

132. Finn and Couvée, *The Zhivago Affair*, p. 156.

133. *Pravda*, 29.10.1958.

134. Afiani and Tomilina eds, 'A za mnoyu shum pogoni', p. 156.

135. Chukovskii, *Dnevnik*.

136. Voinovich, *The Anti-Soviet Soviet Union*, p. 216.

137. *Pravda*, 29.10.58.

138. Semichastnyi, *Bespokoinoe serdtse*, p. 72.

139. Zubok, *Zhivago's Children*.

140. RGANI, f. 5, op. 36, d. 119, l. 64; Afiani and Tomilina eds, *'A za mnoyu shum pogoni'*.

141. Mlechin, *Kak Brezhnev smenil Khrushcheva*, p. 213.

142. https://newrepublic.com/article/63633/beatniks-and-bolsheviks

143. Vail' and Genis, *60-e: Mir sovetskogo cheloveka*.

144. Yevtushenko, *A Precocious Autobiography*, pp. 98–101.

145. E. Evtushenko, *Volchii pasport*, Moskva: Vagrius, 1998, p. 13.

146. Yevtushenko, *Precocious Autobiography*, p. 120.

147. Brown, *Soviet Russian Literature since Stalin*.

148. V. Aksenov, *Colleagues*, London: Putnam, 1962, pp. 12, 25.

149. Zezina, *Sovetskaya khudozhestvennaya intelligentsiya i vlast'*.

150. G. Amalrik, *Memories of a Tatar Childhood*, London: Hutchinson, 1979, p. 139.

151. M. Scammell, 'Art as politics and politics in art', in Rosenfield and Dodge eds, *Nonconformist Art: The Soviet experience*.

152. Voinovich, *The Anti-Soviet Soviet Union*, p. 220.

153. A. Popoff, *Vasily Grossman and the Soviet Century*, New Haven, CT, and London: Yale University Press, 2020, p. 282.

154. ibid.
155. J. Kavanagh, *Rudolf Nureyev: The life*, London: Penguin, 2019.
156. R. Nureyev, *An Autobiography with Pictures*, London: Hodder, 1962, p. 13.
157. Kavanagh, *Rudolf Nureyev*.
158. Plisetskaya, *I, Maya Plisetskaya*, p. 240.
159. Field, *Private Life and Communist Morality*.
160. Hearne, 'Selling sex under socialism'.
161. A. Werth, *Russia: Hopes and fears*, London: Penguin, 1969, p. 110.
162. E. Cohn, *The High Title of a Communist: Postwar party discipline and the values of the Soviet regime*, DeKalb, IL: Northern Illinois University Press, 2015.
163. S. Hearne, 'Sanitising sex in the USSR: State approaches to sexual health in the Brezhnev era', *Europe-Asia Studies*, Vol. 74, No. 10, 2022.
164. D. Field, 'Irreconcilable differences: Divorce and conceptions of private life in the Khrushchev era', *Russian Review*, Vol. 57, No. 4, 1998, p. 599.
165. Werth, *Russia*, p. 115.
166. R. Alexander, 'Sex education and the depiction of homosexuality under Khrushchev', in M. Ilic ed., *The Palgrave Handbook of Women and Gender*, p. 358.
167. R. Alexander, 'The queer life of Lieutenant Petrenko: The KGB and male homosexuality in the Ukrainian SSR of the 1960s', *Europe-Asia Studies*, 2022.
168. D. Healey, *Russian Homophobia from Stalin to Sochi*, London: Bloomsbury Academic, 2017.
169. ibid.
170. ibid.
171. Field, *Private Life and Communist Morality*, p. 41; Leinarte, *Family and the State in Soviet Lithuania*.
172. I. Kon, *The Sexual Revolution in Russia*, London: Simon and Schuster, 1995.
173. Lebina, *Muzhchina i zhenshchina*, p. 43.
174. Denisova, *Rural Women in the Soviet Union*, p. 86.
175. Muzafari, *Sunshine Girl*.
176. Williams, 'Materials for maternity'.
177. Nakachi, *Replacing the Dead*, p. 202.
178. Kon, *The Sexual Revolution in Russia*.

Chapter 8

1. A. Fokin, *'Kommunizm ne za gorami': Obrazy budushchego u vlasti i naseleniya SSSR na rubezhe 1950–1960-x godov*, Moskva: Rosspen, 2017, p. 25.
2. ibid., p. 147.
3. Khrushchev ed., *Memoirs of Nikita Khrushchev*, Vol. 3, p. 179.
4. Pikhoya, *Moskva, kreml', vlast'*, p. 399.
5. A. Titov, 'The 1961 party programme and the fate of Khrushchev's reforms', in Ilic and Smith eds. *Soviet State and Society*, p. 17.
6. Fokin, *'Kommunism ne za gorami'*, p. 75.
7. Chernyaev, *Moya zhizn' i moe vremya*, p. 258.
8. Bobkov, *KGB i vlast'*, p. 259.
9. Mikoyan, *Tak bylo*, p. 613.
10. https://carnegieendowment.org/2017/03/29/formation-and-evolution-of-soviet-union-s-oil-and-gas-dependence-pub-68443
11. Titov, 'The 1961 party programme', p. 13.

12. N. Tomilina ed., *Boi s 'ten'yu' Stalina: Dokumenty i materialy ob istorii XXII s"ezda KPSS i vtorogo etapa destalinizatsii*, Moskva: RGNF, 2015.

13. L. Gruliow ed., *Current Soviet Policies*, Vol. IV, New York: Praeger, 1962.

14. V. Adamsky and Yu. Smirnov, 'Moscow's biggest bomb: The 50-megaton test of October 1961', *Bulletin of the Cold War International History Project*, No. 4, 1994, p. 19.

15. ibid., p. 21.

16. Chuev ed., *Molotov Remembers*, p. 367.

17. Tomilina ed., *Boi s 'ten'yu' Stalina*.

18. V. Grossman, *An Armenian Sketchbook*, London: MacLehose Press, 2013, p. 30.

19. M. Scammell, *Solzhenitsyn: A biography*, London: Hutchinson, 1985.

20. ibid.

21. Orlova and Kopelev, *My zhili v Moskve*, p. 79.

22. V. Lakshin, *Solzhenitsyn, Tvardovsky and Novy mir*, Cambridge, MA: MIT Press, 1980, p. 2.

23. Khrushchev ed., *Memoirs of Nikita Khrushchev*, Vol. 2, p. 553.

24. Evtushenko, *Volchii pasport*, p. 242.

25. R. Romanova ed., *Aleksandr Tvardovskii: Trudy i dni*, Moskva: Voldei, 2006, p. 580.

26. P. Jones, 'The thaw goes international', in Gorsuch and Koenker eds, *The Socialist Sixties*.

27. Kozlov, *The Readers of Novy Mir*, p. 224.

28. M. Dobson, 'Contesting the paradigms of de-Stalinization: Readers' responses to *One Day in the Life of Ivan Denisovich*', *Slavic Review*, Vol. 64, No. 3, 2005.

29. Chukovskii, *Dnevnik*, p. 328.

30. V. Kozlov, *Massovye besporyadki v SSSR pri Khrushchev i Brezhneve, 1953–1980 gg*, Novosibirsk: Sibirskii Khronograf, 1999.

31. ibid.

32. RGASPI, f. 17, op. 91, d. 1498, l. 3.

33. A. Graziosi and O. Khlevnyuk eds, *Regional'naya politika N.S. Khrushcheva*, Moskva: Rosspen, 2009, pp. 428–30.

34. RGANI, f. 5, op. 31, d. 198, l. 5.

35. Ironside, *A Full-Value Ruble*.

36. O. Popova, 'Spetsifika mental'nosti sovetskikh grazhdan 1960 gg. cherez prizmu prodovol'stvennogo defitsita', *Voprosy istorii*, No. 11, 2018, p. 130.

37. Graziosi and Khlevnyuk eds, *Regional'naya politika*, pp. 445–46.

38. Kozlov, *Neizvestnyi SSSR*, p. 275.

39. Shelest, *Da ne sudimy budete*, p. 165.

40. RGANI, f. 89, op. 6, d. 14, l. 3.

41. RGANI, f. 89, op. 51, d. 2.

42. A. Skorik and V. Bondarev, 'Novocherkassk, 1962', *Voprosy istorii*, No. 7, 2012.

43. S. Baron, *Bloody Saturday in the Soviet Union: Novocherkassk, 1962*, Redwood City, CA: Stanford University Press, 2001.

44. A. Shubin et al., 'Make way for the working class! The Russian workers' uprising in Novocherkassk, 1962', The Anarchist Library website, https://theanarchistlibrary.org/library/various-authors-make-way-for-the-working-class

45. Semichastnyi, *Bespokoinoe serdtse*, p. 348.

46. Mikoyan, *Tak bylo*, p. 610.

47. Skorik and Bondarev, 'Novocherkassk, 1962'.

48. Shubin et al. 'Make way for the working class'.

49. Baron, *Bloody Saturday in the Soviet Union*.
50. RGANI, f. 89, op. 6, d. 16, ll. 1–10.
51. A. Solzhenitsyn, *The Oak and the Calf*, London: Collins, 1980.
52. Shelest, *Da ne sudimy budete*, p. 191.
53. Khrushchev ed., *Memoirs of Nikita Khrushchev*, Vol. 3, p. 318.
54. S. Mikoyan, *The Soviet Cuban Missile Crisis*, p. 106.
55. A. Kokoshin, 'Karibskii krizis 1962 g. i ego uroki', *Voprosy istorii*, No. 9, 2015.
56. S. Plokhy, *Nuclear Folly*, London: Allen Lane, 2021.
57. Mikoyan, *The Soviet Cuban Missile Crisis*, p. 131.
58. Khrushchev ed., *Memoirs of Nikita Khrushchev*, Vol. 3, p. 333.
59. Thompson and Thompson, *The Kremlinologist*, p. 302.
60. Taubman, *Khrushchev*.
61. Kornienko, *Kholodnaya voina*, p. 145.
62. Andrew and Mitrokhin, *The Mitrokhin Archive*, p. 237.
63. Dobrynin, *In Confidence*, p. 96.
64. Fursenko and Naftali, *Khrushchev's Cold War*.
65. Plokhy, *Nuclear Folly*.
66. Mikoyan, *The Soviet Cuban Missile Crisis*.
67. Khrushchev ed., *Memoirs of Nikita Khrushchev*, Vol. 3, p. 352.
68. See D. Johnson and D. Tierney eds, *Failing to Win: Perceptions of victory and defeat in international politics*, Cambridge, MA: Harvard University Press, 2006.
69. D. Raleigh ed., *Russia's Sputnik Generation: Soviet Baby Boomers talk about their lives*, Bloomington, IN: Indiana University Press, 2006, p. 76.
70. Troyanovskii, *Cherez gody i rasstoyaniya*, p. 259.
71. Semichastnyi, *Bespokoinoe serdtse*, p. 208.
72. Kalugin, *Spy Master*, p. 58.
73. Arbatov, *The System*, p. 74.
74. J. Friedman, *Shadow Cold War: The Sino-Soviet competition for the Third World*, Chapel Hill, NC: University of North Carolina Press, 2015.
75. Luthi, *The Sino-Soviet Split*.
76. *Izvestiya*, 22.08.1963.
77. C. Stanciu, 'Autonomy and ideology: Brezhnev, Ceausescu and the world communist movement', *Contemporary European History*, Vol. 23, No. 1, 2014.
78. RGANI, f. 5, op. 30, d. 424, l. 82.
79. GARF, f. 8131, op. 31, d. 96151, ll. 1–3.
80. Luthi, *The Sino-Soviet Split*.
81. Khrushchev ed., *Memoirs of Nikita Khrushchev*, Vol. 3, p. 479.
82. P. Johnson ed., *Khrushchev and the Arts: The politics of Soviet culture, 1962–1964*, Cambridge, MA: MIT Press, 1965, p. 1.
83. Reid, 'Modernising Socialist Realism in the Khrushchev thaw'.
84. Gilburd, *To See Paris and Die*.
85. Adzhubei, *Ya byl zyatem Khrushcheva*, p. 178.
86. Vas'kin, *Povsednevnaya zhizn'*, p. 499.
87. S. Reid, 'In the name of the people: The Manege affair revisited', *Kritika*, Vol. 6, No. 4, 2005.
88. Johnson ed., *Khrushchev and the Arts*, pp. 101–05.
89. A. Vaksberg, 'Something unknown about Neizvestny: Interview with Ernst Neizvestnyi by Arkadii Vaksberg', *Russian Politics and Law*, Vol. 37, No. 1, 1999.
90. Khrushchev ed., *Memoirs of Nikita Khrushchev*, Vol. 2, p. 559.
91. Chukovskii, *Dnevnik*, p. 331.

92. V. Afiani ed., *Kul'tura i vlast' ot Stalina do Gorbacheva: Apparat TsK KPSS i kul'tura 1958–1964*, Moskva: Rosspen, 2005.
93. Kozlov, *The Readers of Novy Mir*, p. 182.
94. Evtushenko, *Volchii pasport*, p. 252.
95. J. Woll, *Real Images: Soviet cinema and the thaw*, London: I.B. Tauris, 1999, p. 110.
96. Emel'yanov, *Khrushchev*, p. 584.
97. Voznesensky, *Na virtual'nom vetru*, pp. 79–81.
98. E. Johnson, 'Nikita Khrushchev, Andrei Voznesensky, and the cold spring of 1963: Documenting the end of the post-Stalin thaw', *World Literature Today*, Vol. 75, No. 1, 2001.
99. K. Kustanovich, *The Artist and the Tyrant: Vassily Aksenov's works in the Brezhnev era*, Columbus, OH: Slavica, 1992, p. 28.
100. A. Voznesenskii, in Aksyutin ed., *Nikita Khrushchev*, p. 130.
101. Gladilin, *Ulitsa generalov*, p. 104.
102. Zubok, *Zhivago's Children*, p. 217.
103. E. Afanas'eva ed., *Ideologicheskie komissii TsK KPSS, 1958–1964: Dokumenty*, Moskva: Rosspen, 1998.
104. Zezina, *Sovetskaya khudozhestvennaya intelligentsiya i vlast'*, p. 318.
105. Afiani ed., *Kul'tura i vlast'*.
106. E. Hutchinson, 'Ivan Denisovich on trial: Soviet writers, Russian identity, and Solzhenitsyn's failed bid for the 1964 Lenin Prize', *Kritika*, Vol. 22, No. 1, 2021.
107. ibid., p. 100.

Chapter 9

1. *Pravda*, 13.10.1964.
2. LaPierre, *Hooligans in Khrushchev's Russia*.
3. Hardy, *The Gulag after Stalin*.
4. Elie and Hardy, 'Letting the beasts out of the cage'.
5. A. Marchenko, *My Testimony*, London: Penguin, 1969.
6. Knight, *The KGB*.
7. *Pravda*, 24.05.1959.
8. S. Bloch and P. Reddaway, *Russia's Political Hospitals*, London: First Futura, 1978, p. 152.
9. Hornsby, *Protest, Reform and Repression*.
10. Bloch and Reddaway, *Russia's Political Hospitals*, p. 107.
11. Hornsby, *Protest, Reform and Repression*, p. 242.
12. V. Tarsis, *Ward 7: An autobiographical novel*, London: Dutton, 1965.
13. V. Bukovsky, *To Build a Castle: My life as a dissenter*, London: André Deutsch, 1978.
14. Leeds Russian Archive, Terlecka Collection, *International Association on the Political Use of Psychiatry: A list of victims*, 1985, p. 11.
15. Bloch and Reddaway, *Russia's Political Hospitals*.
16. Arbatov, *The System*, p. 108.
17. Kozlov ed., *Kramola*.
18. GARF, f. 8131, op. 33, d. 96712, l. 19.
19. Pikhoya, *Moskva, kreml', vlast'*, p. 462.
20. Aksyutin, *Nikita Khrushchev*.
21. Alexeyeva and Goldberg, *Thaw Generation*, p. 105.

22. Sakharov, *Memoirs*, p. 234.

23. W. Taubman, Khrushchev: the Man and his era p. 616.

24. Semichastnyi, *Bespokoinoe serdtse*, p. 343.

25. A. Sushkov, *Prezidium TsK KPSS v 1957–1964 gg.*, Ekaterinburg: RAN, 2009.

26. *Pravda*, 17.04.1964.

27. Taubman, *Khrushchev*.

28. ibid., p. 479.

29. ibid., p. 614.

30. Mesyatsev, *Gorizonty i labirinty moei zhizni*, p. 415.

31. A. Aleksandrov-Agentov, *Ot Kollontai do Gorbacheva*, Moskva: Mezhdunarodnye otnosheniya, 1994, p. 70.

32. N. Egorychev, *Soldat, politik, diplomat: Vospominaniya ob ochen' raznom*, Moskva: Tsentrpoligraf, 2017, p. 137.

33. Sushkov, *Prezidium TsK KPSS*, p. 234.

34. Shelest, *Da ne sudimy budete*, pp. 211–16.

35. W. Tompson, 'The fall of Nikita Khrushchev', *Soviet Studies*, Vol. 45, No. 6, 1991, p. 1104.

36. Shelest, *Da ne sudimy budete*.

37. Mesyatsev, *Gorizonty i labirinty moei zhizni*, p. 444.

38. Egorychev, *Soldat, politik, diplomat*, p. 150.

39. ibid., p. 158.

40. Shelest, *Da ne sudimy budete*, p. 217. Because her father (Khrushchev's son) Leonid had been killed during the war, Yuliya had been raised from a young age by her grandparents and so was, to all intents and purposes, Khrushchev's daughter, rather than his granddaughter.

41. A. Artizov ed., *Nikita Khrushchev, 1964: Stenogrammy plenuma TsK KPSS i drugie dokumenty*, Moskva: Materik, 2007, p. 10.

42. Semichastnyi, *Bespokoinoe serdtse*, p. 360.

43. Mesyatsev, *Gorizonty i labirinty moei zhizni*, p. 451.

44. Artizov, ed., *Nikita Khrushchev, 1964*, pp. 217–26.

45. S. Khrushchev, *Khrushchev on Khrushchev: An inside account of the man and his era by his son, Sergei Khrushchev*, London: Little, Brown and Company, 1990, p. 154.

46. Mikoyan, *Tak bylo*, p. 616.

47. RGASPI, f. m-1, op. 31, d. 126, ll. 1–6.

48. P. Grebenyuk, 'Rukovodyashchie kadry i izmeneniya v obshchestvenno-politicheskoi sfere na severo-vostoke SSSR v 1958–1964 gg', *Voprosy istorii*, No. 8, 2021.

49. RGANI, f. 89, op. 6, d. 28, l. 2.

50. Solzhenitsyn, *The Oak and the Calf*, p. 88.

51. Cohen and vanden Heuvel eds, *Voices of Glasnost*, p. 183.

52. ibid., p. 289.

53. Mikoyan, *Tak bylo*, p. 627.

54. Marchenko, *My Testimony*, p. 261.

55. Adzhubei, *Ya byl zyatem Khrushcheva*, p. 325.

56. Voznesnskii, *Na virtual'nom vetru*, p. 86.

57. D. Bonavia, *Fat Sasha and the Urban Guerrilla*, London: Hamish Hamilton, 1973, pp. 6–7.

58. *Pravda*, 14.09.1971.

59. *Pravda*, 16.10.1964.

60. Aleksandrov-Agentov, *Ot Kollontai do Gorbacheva*, p. 119.

61. Chuev ed., *Molotov Remembers*, p. 372.

62. Mlechin, *Kak Brezhnev smenil Khrushcheva*, p. 70.
63. Hayter, *The Kremlin and the Embassy*, p. 115.
64. Mikoyan, *Tak bylo*, p. 627.
65. S. Schattenberg, 'Trust, care, and familiarity in the Politburo: Brezhnev's scenario of power', *Kritika*, Vol. 16, No. 4, 2015.
66. Arbatov, *The System*, p. 135.
67. Troyanovskii, *Cherez gody i rasstoyaniya*, p. 205.
68. W. Chamberlain, 'The trend after Khrushchev: Immobilism', *Russian Review*, Vol. 25, No. 1, 1966, p. 3.
69. *Pravda*, 17.11.1964.
70. Pikhoya, *Moskva, kreml', vlast'*, p. 496.
71. B. Schwarz, *Music and Musical Life in Soviet Russia*, Bloomington, IN: Indiana University Press, 1983, p. 440.
72. Jones, *Myth, Memory, Trauma*, p. 216.
73. Kalugin, *Spy Master*, p. 66.
74. Kovacevic, '"An ominous talent"'.
75. Novikov ed., 'Sovetskaya intelligentsiya', p. 12.
76. *Pravda*, 17.10.1964.
77. *Pravda*, 20.10.1964.
78. See Reid 'This is tomorrow!', in Gorsuch and Koenker eds, *The Socialist Sixties*.
79. Chernyshova, *Soviet Consumer Culture*, p. 47.
80. L. Siegelbaum, *Cars for Comrades: The life of the Soviet automobile*, Ithaca, NY: Cornell University Press, 2008.
81. Chernyshova, *Soviet Consumer Culture*.
82. Siddiqi, *Sputnik and the Soviet Space Challenge*.
83. Denisova, *Rural Women in the Soviet Union*.
84. L. Siegelbaum, 'People on the move', in D. Fainberg and A. Kalinovsky eds, *Reconsidering Stagnation in the Brezhnev Era: Ideology and exchange*, London: Lexington, 2016, p. 46.
85. *Literaturnaya gazeta*, 27.12.1967.
86. Denisova, *Rural Women in the Soviet Union*.
87. P. Hanson, *The Rise and Fall of the Soviet Economy: An economic history of the USSR from 1945*, Harlow: Pearson, 2003, p. 100.
88. Oushakine, 'Against the cult of things'.
89. *Izvestiya*, 28.09.1965.
90. Hanson, *The Rise and Fall of the Soviet Economy*.
91. *Partiinaya zhizn'*, No. 20, 1964.
92. *Pravda*, 19.10.1964.
93. Luthi, *The Sino-Soviet Split*.
94. Arbatov, *The System*, p. 114. Arbatov's account was relayed to him by Yuri Andropov, who was standing next to Malinovsky during the events in question.
95. ibid., p. 118.
96. Mikoyan, *Tak bylo*, p. 621.
97. S. Radchenko, *Two Suns in the Heavens: The Sino-Soviet struggle for supremacy, 1962–1967*, Redwood City, CA: Stanford University Press, 2009, p. 180.
98. ibid.
99. *Pravda*, 18.11.1964.
100. Burlatsky, *Khrushchev and the First Russian Spring*, pp. 213–17.
101. Arbatov, *The System*, pp. 128–30.

102. Mitrokhin, ' "Back office" Mikhaila Suslova'.
103. Stronski, *Tashkent*.
104. TsDAGO, f. 7, op. 20, d. 135, l. 55.
105. N. Raab, 'The Tashkent earthquake of 1966: The advantages and disadvantages of a natural tragedy', *Jahrbücher für Geschichte Osteuropas*, Vol. 62, No. 2, 2014.
106. L. Kirschenbaum, *The Legacy of the Siege of Leningrad, 1941–1995: Myth, memories, and monuments,* Cambridge: Cambridge University Press, 2009.
107. M. Edele, *Soviet Veterans of the Second World War: A popular movement in an authoritarian society, 1941–1991*, Oxford: Oxford University Press, 2009, p. 9.
108. Mesyatsev, *Gorizonty i labirinty moei zhizni*.
109. R. Hornsby, 'Soviet youth on the march: The all-union tours of military glory, 1965–87', *Journal of Contemporary History*, Vol. 52, No. 2, 2016.
110. Edele, *Soviet Veterans of the Second World War*.

Chapter 10

1. F. Feldbrugge, *Samizdat and Political Dissent in the Soviet Union*, Leiden: Sijthoff, 1975, p. 2.
2. V. Igrunov, 'Vvedenie', in A. Daniel ed., *Antologiya samizdata: Nepodtsenzurnaya literatura v SSSR, 1950-e – 1980-e*, tom 1, kniga 1, Moskva: Mezhdunarodnyi Institut Gumanitarno-Politicheskikh Issledovanii, 2005, p. 10.
3. A. Daniel, 'Istoki i smysl sovetskogo samizdata', in Daniel ed., *Antologiya samizdata*, tom 1, kniga 1, p. 19.
4. S. Cohen ed., *An End to Silence: Uncensored opinion in the Soviet Union*, New York: Norton, 1984.
5. L. Polikovskaya ed., *'My predchustvie . . . predtecha': Ploshchad' Mayakovskogo, 1958–1965,* Moskva: Obshchestvo 'Memorial', 1997.
6. Aksenov, *Zenitsa oka*, p. 200.
7. A. Komaromi, 'The material existence of Soviet samizdat', *Slavic Review*, Vol. 63, No. 3, 2004.
8. R. Djagalov, 'Guitar poetry, democratic socialism . . .', in Gorsuch and Koenker eds, *The Socialist Sixties*.
9. R. Platonov, *Singing the Self: Guitar poetry, community and identity in the post-Stalin period*, Evanston, IL: Northwestern University Press, 2012.
10. ibid.
11. Polikovskaya ed., *'My predchuvstvie . . . predtecha'*.
12. Bukovsky, *To Build a Castle*.
13. Polikovskaya ed., *'My predchuvstvie . . . predtecha'*, p. 65.
14. Bukovsky, *To Build a Castle*.
15. Polikovskaya ed., *'My predchuvstvie . . . predtecha'*.
16. Bukovsky, *To Build a Castle*.
17. Polikovskaya ed., *'My predchuvstvie . . . predtecha'*.
18. S. Volkov ed., *Conversations with Joseph Brodsky*, New York: The Free Press, 1998.
19. A. Raskina, 'Frida Vigdorova's transcript of Joseph Brodsky's trial: Myths and reality', *Journal of Modern Russian History and Historiography*, Vol. 7, 2014.
20. L. Losev, *Iosif Brodskii: Opyt literaturnoi biografii*, Moskva: Molodaya gvardiya, 2006, p. 88.
21. R. Burford, 'Getting the bugs out of socialist legality: The case of Joseph Brodsky', *American Journal of Comparative Law*, Vol. 22, No. 3, 1974, p. 469.

22. RGANI, f. 5, op. 30, d. 454, l. 98.
23. https://digitalarchive.wilsoncenter.org/document/110342
24. Solzhenitsyn, *The Oak and the Calf*, p. 108.
25. Golomstock, *A Ransomed Dissident*, p. 87.
26. Solzhenitsyn, *The Oak and the Calf*, p. 103.
27. Orlova and Kopelev, *My zhili v Moskve*, p. 116.
28. A. Ginzburg ed., *Belaya kniga po delu A. Sinyavskogo i Yu. Danielya*, München: Posev, 1967.
29. A. Daniel ed., *Pyatoe dekabrya 1965 goda v vospominaniyakh uchastnikov sobytii, materialakh samizdata, dokumentakh partiinykh i komsomol'skikh organizatsii, v zapiskakh KGB v TsK KPSS*, Moskva: Obshchestvo 'Memorial', 1995.
30. Bukovsky, *To Build a Castle*, p. 131.
31. Daniel ed., *Pyatoe dekabrya 1965 goda*.
32. ibid.
33. Alexeyeva and Goldberg, *Thaw Generation*.
34. Ginzburg ed., *Belaya kniga*.
35. *Izvestiya*, 13.01.1966.
36. *Izvestiya*, 18.01.1966.
37. https://www.dissentmagazine.org/wp-content/files_mf/1410896620On_Socialist_Realism_Winter_1960.pdf
38. Ginzburg ed., *Belaya kniga*.
39. S. Alliluyeva, *Only One Year*, New York: Harper Collins, 1969, p. 171.
40. *Pravda*, 22.02.1966.
41. Alexeyeva and Goldberg, *Thaw Generation*, p. 154.
42. Orlova and Kopelev, *My zhili v Moskve*, p. 203.
43. D. Caute, *Politics and the Novel during the Cold War*, London: Routledge, 2009, p. 225.
44. See B. Walker, 'Pollution and purification in the Moscow human rights networks of the 1960s and 1970s', *Slavic Review*, Vol. 68, No. 2, 2009.
45. Sakharov, *Memoirs*, p. 287.
46. B. Kagarlitsky, *The Thinking Reed: Intellectuals and the Soviet state, 1917 to the present*, London: Verso, 1988, p. 190.
47. V. Bredikhin ed., *Lubyanka i Staraya Ploshchad': Sekretnye dokumenty TsK KPSS i KGB o repressiyakh 1937–1990 gg. v SSSR*, Moskva: Posev, 2005.
48. Sakharov, *Memoirs*, p. 273.
49. Marchenko, *My Testimony*, pp. 20–21.
50. *Komsomol'skaya pravda*, 18.01.1968.
51. Sakharov, *Memoirs*, p. 274.
52. P. Litvinov and P. Reddaway eds, *The Trial of the Four*, London: Viking, 1972.
53. Pikhoya, *Moskva, kreml', vlast'*, p. 509.
54. Gallyamova, *Tatarskaya ASSR v period postStalinizma*, p. 594.
55. https://www.kgbdocuments.eu/assets/documents/2007e_32k.pdf
56. Grossman, *An Armenian Sketchbook*, p. 39.
57. Lehmann, 'Apricot socialism'.
58. A. Saparov, 'Renegotiating the boundaries of the permitted: The national(ist) revival in Soviet Armenia and Moscow's response', *Europe-Asia Studies*, Vol. 70, No. 6, 2018.
59. Alexeyeva and Goldberg, *Thaw Generation*, pp. 139–40.
60. http://museum.khpg.org/en/index.php?id=1127288239
61. Plyushch, *History's Carnival*, p. 40.

62. I. Dziuba, *Internationalism or Russification: A study in the Soviet nationalities problem*, London: Weidenfeld and Nicolson, 1968.

63. S. Yekelchyk, 'The early 1960s as a cultural space: A microhistory of Ukraine's generation of cultural rebels', *Nationalities Papers*, Vol. 43, No. 1, 2015.

64. B. Tromly, 'An unlikely national revival: Soviet higher learning and the Ukrainian "Sixtiers", 1953–65', *Russian Review*, Vol. 68, No. 4, 2009.

65. Shelest, *Da ne sudimy budete*, p. 263.

66. V. Moroz, *Report from the Beria Reserve: The protest writings of Valentyn Moroz*, Toronto: Peter Martin, 1974, p. 91.

67. Alexeyeva, *Soviet Dissent*, pp. 36–37.

68. ibid., p. 141.

69. Bobkov, *KGB i vlast'*, p. 300.

70. B. Williams, 'The hidden ethnic cleansing of Muslims in the Soviet Union: The exile and repatriation of Crimean Tatars', *Journal of Contemporary History*, Vol. 37, No. 3, 2002.

71. P. Grigorenko, *Memoirs*, New York: Norton, 1982, p. 355.

72. Bredikhin ed., *Lubyanka i Staraya Ploshchad'*, pp. 52–53.

73. Altshuler, *Religion and Jewish Identity*, p. 101.

74. B. Pinkus, *The Jews of the Soviet Union: The history of a national minority*, Cambridge: Cambridge University Press, 1990, p. 317.

75. G. Estraikh, 'Birobidzhan in Khrushchev's thaw: The Soviet and Western outlook', *Journal of Modern Jewish Studies*, Vol. 18, No. 1, 2019.

76. Gladilin, *Ulitsa generalov*, p. 79.

77. Salisbury, *To Moscow and Beyond*, p. 71.

78. Pinkus, *The Jews of the Soviet Union*, p. 252.

79. B. Morozov, *Documents on Jewish Emigration*, London: Routledge, 1999, p. 57.

80. Estraikh, 'Birobidzhan in Khrushchev's thaw', p. 2.

81. N. Sharansky, *Fear No Evil*, New York: Penguin, 1988, p. xiv.

Chapter II

1. S. Schattenberg, *Brezhnev: The making of a statesman*, London: I.B. Tauris, 2021.

2. Grushin, *Chetyre zhizni Rossii*.

3. Novikov ed., 'Sovetskaya intelligentsiya', p. 6.

4. S. Zhuk, *KGB Operations against the US and Canada in Soviet Ukraine, 1953–1991*, London: Routledge, 2022, p. 198.

5. Taubman, *The View from the Lenin Hills*, p. 183.

6. Gorsuch, '"Cuba, My Love"', p. 259.

7. https://digitalarchive.wilsoncenter.org/document/110403

8. D. Ryabushkin, 'Ostrov Damanskii. 2 marta 1969 goda', *Voprosy istorii*, No. 5, 2004.

9. Radchenko, *Two Suns in the Heavens*.

10. Sukhodrev, *Yazyk moi – drug moi*, p. 208.

11. Golomstock, *A Ransomed Dissident*, p. 132.

12. Alliluyeva, *Only One Year*.

13. Salisbury, *A New Russia?*, p. 34.

14. J. Rubenstein, *Tangled Loyalties: The life and times of Ilya Ehrenburg*, Tuscaloosa, AL: University of Alabama Press, 1996, p. 395.

15. Romanova ed., *Aleksandr Tvardovskii*.

16. Solzhenitsyn, *The Oak and the Calf*, p. 230.

17. Chukovskii, *Dnevnik*, p. 451.

18. Scammell, *Solzhenitsyn: A Biography*, p. 566.
19. J. Bergman, *Meeting the Demands of Reason: The life and thought of Andrei Sakharov*, Ithaca, NY: Cornell University Press, 2009, p. 141.
20. D. Peterson, 'Samovar life: Russian nurture and Russian nature in the rural prose of Valentin Rasputin', *Russian Review*, Vol. 53, No. 1, 1994, p. 84.
21. G. Hosking, 'The Russian peasant rediscovered: "Village prose" of the 1960s', *Slavic Review*, Vol. 32, No. 4, 1973.
22. Nakachi, *Replacing the Dead*.
23. Dumančić, *Men Out of Focus*.
24. Peterson, 'Samovar life'.
25. K. Parthe, *Russian Village Prose: The radiant past*, Princeton, NJ: Princeton University Press, 1992.
26. N. Mitrokhin, *Russkaya partiya: Dvizhenie russkikh natsionalistov v SSSR, 1953–85 gody*, Moskva: Novoe literaturnoe obozrenie, 2003.
27. Y. Brudny, *Reinventing Russia: Russian nationalism and the Soviet state, 1955–1991*, Cambridge, MA: Harvard University Press, 1999.
28. A. Jenks, 'Palekh and the forging of a Russian nation in the Brezhnev era', *Cahiers du monde russe*, Vol. 44, No. 4, 2003.
29. D. Kozlov, 'The historical turn in late Soviet culture: Retrospectivism, factography, doubt, 1953–91', *Kritika*, Vol. 2, No. 3, 2001.
30. Zorkaya, *The Illustrated History of Soviet Cinema*, p. 261.
31. S. Pattle, 'Forging the golden ring: Tourist development and heritage preservation in the late Soviet Union', *Slavonic and East European Review*, Vol. 96, No. 2, 2018.
32. V. Donovan, *Chronicles in Stone: Preservation, patriotism and identity in northwest Russia*, Ithaca, NY: Cornell University Press, 2019.
33. Golomstock, *A Ransomed Dissident*.
34. Smolkin, *A Sacred Space Is Never Empty*, p. 81.
35. NARB, f. 63p, op. 37, d. 39, l. 14.
36. S. Zhuk, 'Popular religiosity in the "closed city" of Soviet Ukraine: Cultural consumption and religion during late socialism, 1959–84', *Russian History*, Vol. 40, No. 2, 2013, p. 184.
37. Werth, *Russia*, p. 200.
38. Mitrokhin, *Russkaya partiya*, p. 294.
39. RGASPI, f. 1s, op. 1s, d. 542, ll. 38–42.
40. Mitrokhin, *Russkaya partiya*, p. 230.
41. K. Farmer, *Ukrainian Nationalism in the Post-Stalin Era: Myths, symbols, and ideology in Soviet nationalities policy*, London: Martinus Nijhoff, 1980, p. 80.
42. A. Igmen, *Speaking Soviet with an Accent: Culture and power in Kyrgyzstan*, Pittsburgh, PA: University of Pittsburgh Press, 2012, p. 37.
43. Davoliute, *The Making and Breaking of Soviet Lithuania*, p. 120.
44. https://www.kgbdocuments.eu/documents/the-certificate-of-the-3rd-branch-of-the-2nd-department-of-the-kgb-of-the-lssr-on-work-with-agents-as-of-1-july-1969/
45. http://www.astronautix.com/k/kamanindiaries.html
46. A. Siddiqi, *The Soviet Space Race with Apollo*, Gainesville, FL: University Press of Florida, 2000, p. 569.
47. http://www.astronautix.com/k/kamanindiaries.html
48. Gerovitch ed., *Voices of the Soviet Space Program*, 'Second Backup: Valentina Ponomareva', p. 229.

49. Siddiqi, *The Soviet Space Race with Apollo*, p. 627.
50. Jenks, *The Cosmonaut Who Couldn't Stop Smiling*, pp. 246–60.
51. G. Bischof et al. eds, *The Prague Spring and the Warsaw Pact Invasion of Czechoslovakia in 1968*, London: Lexington, 2010, p. 6.
52. J. Navratil ed., *The Prague Spring 1968: A National Security Archive documents reader*, Budapest: Central European University Press, 1998, pp. 7–20.
53. O. Pavlenko, 'Sovetskie informatsionno-analiticheskie i operativnye materialy', in N. Tomilina ed., *'Prazhskaya vesna' i mezhdunarodnyi krizis 1968 goda: Dokumenty*, Moskva: Mezhdunarodnyi fond 'Demokratiya', 2010.
54. Pikhoya, *Moskva, kreml', vlast'*, pp. 530–32.
55. Schattenberg, *Brezhnev*.
56. O. Lavinskaya, 'Tsenzura v SSSR', in Tomilina ed., *'Prazhskaya vesna'*.
57. M. Kramer, 'Soviet Moldavia and the 1968 Czechoslovak crisis: A report on the political "spill-over"', *Bulletin of the Cold War International History Project*, No. 11, 1998.
58. R. Applebaum, 'A test of friendship', in Gorsuch and Koenker, *The Socialist Sixties*, pp. 213–32.
59. RGASPI, f. m-1, op. 30, d. 430, l. 9.
60. Navratil ed., *The Prague Spring 1968*, p. 145.
61. Sakharov, *Memoirs*, p. 281.
62. https://digitalarchive.wilsoncenter.org/document/115979
63. M. Kramer, 'Ukraine and the Soviet-Czechoslovak crisis of 1968 (part 2)', *Bulletin of the Cold War International History Project*, Nos 14/15, 2003.
64. ERAF, f. 1, op. 5, d. 108, ll. 1–4.
65. S. Chuprinin, *Ottepel': Sobytiya, mart 1953–avgust 1968 goda*, Moskva: Novoe literaturnoe obozrenie, 2020.
66. P. Josephson, *New Atlantis Revisited: Akademgorodok, the Siberian city of science*, Princeton, NJ: Princeton University Press, 1997, p. 297.
67. Kramer, 'Ukraine and the Soviet-Czechoslovak crisis', p. 320.
68. Bischof et al. eds, *The Prague Spring*, p. 14.
69. Schattenberg, *Brezhnev*, p. 276.
70. Navratil ed., *The Prague Spring 1968,* pp. 324–25.
71. M. Prozumenshikov, 'Politburo decision making', in Bischof et al. eds, *The Prague Spring*, p. 124.
72. Navratil ed., *The Prague Spring 1968*, p. 414.
73. TsDAGO, f. 7, op. 20, dd. 81–99.
74. R. Hornsby, 'Strengthening friendship and fraternal solidarity: Soviet youth tourism to Eastern Europe under Khrushchev and Brezhnev', *Europe-Asia Studies*, Vol. 71, No. 9, 2019.
75. O. Tuma et al., 'The (inter communist) Cold War on ice: Soviet-Czechoslovak ice hockey politics, 1967–1969', *Cold War International History Project* Working Paper, 69, 2014.
76. M. Bracke, *Which Socialism? Whose Détente? West European communism and the Czechoslovak crisis of 1968*, Budapest: Central European University Press, 2007.
77. Nayudu, 'When the elephant swallowed the hedgehog'.
78. N. Tomilina ed., *Chekhoslovatskii krizis 1967–69 gg. v dokumentakh TsK KPSS*, Moskva: Rosspen, 2010, pp. 866–70.
79. Gurevich, *From Lenin to Lennon*, p. 93.
80. A. Marchenko, *To Live Like Everyone*, London: I.B. Tauris, 1989, pp. 127, 172.

81. M. Gorbachev and Z. Mlynar, *Conversations with Gorbachev: On perestroika, the Prague Spring, and the crossroads of socialism*, New York: Columbia University Press, 2012, p. 6.
82. Z. Wojnowski, *The Near Abroad: Socialist Eastern Europe and Soviet patriotism in Ukraine, 1956–85*, Toronto: University of Toronto Press, 2017, p. 128.
83. LYA, f. k-1, op. 15, d. 4120, ll. 9–11.
84. Tomilina et al. eds, *Chekhoslovatskii krizis, 1967–69 gg.*, p. 866.
85. https://digitalarchive.wilsoncenter.org/document/115979
86. https://digitalarchive.wilsoncenter.org/document/112462
87. Alpert, *Making Waves*, p. 143.
88. Evtushenko, *Volchii pasport*, p. 299.
89. http://www.sovlit.net/conversationswithaksyonov/
90. J. Pazderka, *The Soviet Invasion of Czechoslovakia in 1968: The Russian perspective*, London: Lexington, 2019, p. 163.
91. N. Gorbanevskaya, *Red Square at Noon*, London: André Deutsch, 1972, pp. 33–34.
92. https://digitalarchive.wilsoncenter.org/document/188128
93. Gorbanevskaya, *Red Square at Noon*.
94. ibid.
95. *Kommunist*, 18.12.1968.
96. Gorbachev and Mlynar, *Conversations with Gorbachev*, p. 65.
97. http://www.sovlit.net/conversationswithaksyonov/
98. Huxtable, 'Making news Soviet', p. 81.
99. Dumančić, *Men Out of Focus*.
100. Voinovich, *The Anti-Soviet Soviet Union*, p. 160.
101. H. Salisbury, 'Introduction', in Gorbanevskaya, *Red Square at Noon*, p. 8.
102. Kagarlistky, *The Thinking Reed*, p. 200.
103. Navratil ed., *The Prague Spring 1968*, p. 145.
104. Egorychev, *Soldat, politik, diplomat*, p. 174.
105. Schattenburg, 'Trust, care, and familiarity in the Politburo'.
106. Baibakov, *Ot Stalina do El'tsina*, p. 155.
107. Sukhodrev, *Yazyk moi – drug moi*, p. 190.
108. Mesyatsev, *Gorizonty i labirinty moei zhizni*, p. 497.
109. Sukhodrev, *Yazyk moi – drug moi*, p. 255.
110. Schattenberg, *Brezhnev*.
111. Baibakov, *Ot Stalina do Yel'tsina*, p. 159.
112. A. Bezbordov, 'Vliyanie voenno-promyshlennogo kompleksa SSSR', in Tomilina ed., *Prazhskaya vesna*.
113. Cohen and vanden Heuvel eds, *Voices of Glasnost*, p. 78.
114. Schattenberg, 'Trust, care and familiarity in the Politburo'.
115. Aleksandrov-Agentov, *Ot Kollontai do Gorbacheva*, p. 261.
116. Shelest, *Da ne sudimy budete*, p. 263.
117. L. Mlechin, *Shelepin*, Moskva: Molodaya gvardiya, 2009.
118. Voslensky, *Nomenklatura*, p. 259.
119. Bobkov, *KGB i vlast'*, p. 177.
120. Mlechin, *Shelepin*, p. 344.
121. Arbatov, *The System*, p. 120.
122. Mikoyan, *Tak bylo*, p. 629.
123. Baibakov, *Ot Stalina do El'tsina*, p. 176.
124. Dobrynin, *In Confidence*, p. 131.
125. Pikhoya, *Moskva, kreml', vlast'*, p. 518.

Epilogue

1. Interview with Yuri Afanasev, in Cohen and vanden Heuvel eds, *Voices of Glasnost*, p. 98; Tranum ed., *Life at the Edge of Empire*, p. 174.
2. Fürst, *Flowers through the Concrete*; Chernyshova, *Soviet Consumer Culture*; Fainberg and Kalinovsky eds, *Reconsidering Stagnation*.
3. A. Yemshit, 'Nachalo destalinizatsii ili 'khrushchevskaya ottepel'': Mesto i rol' v sovetskoi istorii', *Voprosy istorii*, No. 10, 2020.
4. Senyavskii, 'XX s"ezd KPSS na vesakh istorii', in Senyavskii ed., *XX s"ezd KPSS*, p. 27.
5. M. Hindus, *House Without a Roof: Russia after forty-three years of revolution*, London: Gollancz, 1962, p. 427.
6. Gorbachev and Mlynar, *Conversations with Gorbachev*, p. 42.
7. Pavlenko, 'Sovetskie informatsionno-analiticheskie i operativnye materialy', in Tomilina ed., '*Prazhskaya vesna*'.

SELECT BIBLIOGRAPHY

Archival materials

ERAF (Tallinn/Tartu) – National Archives of Estonia
GARF (Moscow) – State Archive of the Russian Federation
LVA (Riga) – Latvian State Archive
LYA (Vilnius) – Lithuanian Special Archives
MIA (Tbilisi) – Ministry of Internal Affairs (Georgia) Archive
NARB (Minsk) – National Archive of the Republic of Belarus
NARK (Petrozavodsk) – National Archive of the Republic of Karelia
RGANI (Moscow) – Russian State Archive of Contemporary History
RGASPI (Moscow) – Russian State Archive of Socio-Political History
TsAOPIM (Moscow) – Central Archive of Socio-Political History of Moscow
TsDAGO (Kyiv) – Central State Archive of Public Organisations of Ukraine
TsDOOSO (Ekaterinburg) – Centre of Documentation of Public Organisations of
Sverdlovsk Oblast

Memoirs and document collections

Adzhubei, A. *Ya byl zyatem Khrushcheva*, Moskva: Algoritm, 2014
Afanas'eva, E. ed. *Ideologicheskie komissii TsK KPSS, 1958–1964: Dokumenty*, Moskva:
Rosspen, 1998
Afiani, A. and Tomilina, N. *'A za mnoyu shum pogoni . . .' Boris Pasternak i vlast':
Dokumenty, 1956–1972*, Moskva: Rosspen, 2001
Aimermakher, K. ed. *Doklad N.S. Khrushcheva o kul'te lichnosti Stalina na XX s'ezde:
Dokumenty*, Moskva: Rosspen, 2002
Aksenov, V. *Zenitsa oka: Vmesto memuarov*, Moskva: Vagrius, 2005
Aksyutin, Yu. ed. *Nikita Khrushchev: Materialy k biografii*, Moskva: Izdatel'stvo poli-
ticheskoi literatury, 1989
Aleksandrov-Agentov, A. *Ot Kollontai do Gorbacheva*, Moskva: Mezhdunarodnye
otnosheniya, 1994
Alexeyeva, L. and Goldberg, P. *Thaw Generation: Coming of age in the post-Stalin era*,
London: Little, Brown and Company, 1990
Alliluyeva, S. *Twenty Letters to a Friend: A memoir*, London: Harper, 1967
Alliluyeva, S. *Only One Year*, New York: Harper Collins, 1969
Alpert, Y. *Making Waves: Stories from my life*, New Haven, CT, and London: Yale
University Press, 2000
Amalrik, A. *Involuntary Journey to Siberia*, London: Harcourt, 1970
Amalrik, G. *Memories of a Tatar Childhood*, London: Hutchinson, 1979

Arbatov, G. *The System: An insider's life in Soviet politics*, New York: Random House, 1992

Artizov, A. ed. *Nikita Khrushchev, 1964: Stenogrammy plenuma TsK KPSS i drugie dokumenty*, Moskva: Materik, 2007

Artizov, A. et al. eds. *Reabilitatsiya: kak eto bylo, dokumenty prezidiuma TsK KPSS i drugie materialy Mart 1953-Fevral' 1956*, Moskva: Mezhdunarodnyi fond 'Demokratiya', 2003

Baibakov, N. *Ot Stalina do El'tsina*, Moskva: GazOil Press, 1998

Békés, Cs. et al. eds. *The 1956 Hungarian Revolution: A history in documents*, Budapest: Central European University Press, 2002

Belfrage, S. *A Room in Moscow*, London: Reynal, 1958

Bobkov, F. *KGB i vlast'*, Moskva: Veteran MP, 1995

Bohlen, C. *Witness to History, 1926–1969*, London: Weidenfeld and Nicolson, 1973

Bonavia, D. *Fat Sasha and the Urban Guerrilla*, London: Hamish Hamilton, 1973

Bredikhin, V. *Lubyanka i Staraya Ploshchad': Sekretnye dokumenty TsK KPSS i KGB o repressiyakh 1937–1990 gg. v SSSR*, Moskva: Posev, 2005

Brezhnev, L. *Virgin Lands: Two years in Kazakhstan, 1954–1955*, Oxford: Pergamon, 1979

Brodsky, J. *Less than One: Selected essays*, London: Penguin, 1992

Brutents, K. *Tridtsat' let na Staroi Ploshchadi*, Moskva: Mezdunarodnye otnosheniya, 1998

Bukovsky, V. *To Build a Castle: My life as a dissenter*, London: André Deutsch, 1978

Burlatsky, F. *Khrushchev and the First Russian Spring*, London: Weidenfeld and Nicolson, 1988

Burtin, Yu. ed. 'Studencheskoe brozhenie v SSSR (konets 1956)', *Voprosy istorii*, No. 1, 1997

Capote, T. *The Muses Are Heard: An account*, New York: Random House, 1956

Chebrikov et al. eds. *Istoriya sovetskikh organov gosudarstevennoi bezopasnosti: Uchebnik*, Moskva, 1977

Chernyaev, A. *Moya zhizn' i moe vremya*, Moskva: Mezhdunarodnye otnosheniya, 1995

Chuev, F. ed. *Molotov Remembers: Inside Kremlin politics*, Chicago, IL: Ivan R. Dee, 1993

Chukovskii, K. *Dnevnik, 1930–1969*, Moskva: Sovremennyi pisatel', 1994

Cohen, S. and vanden Heuvel, K. eds. *Voices of Glasnost: Interviews with Gorbachev's reformers*, New York: Norton, 1990

Daniel, A. ed. *Pyatoe dekabrya 1965 goda v vospominaniyakh uchastnikov sobytii, materialakh samizdata, dokumentakh partiinykh i komsomol'skikh organizatsii, v zapiskakh KGB v TsK KPSS*, Moskva: Obshchestvo 'Memorial', 1995

Daniel, A. ed., *Antologiya samizdata: Nepodtsenzurnaya literatura v SSSR, 1950-e – 1980-e*, tom 1, kniga 1, Moskva: Mezhdunarodnyi Institut Gumanitarno-Politicheskikh Issledovanii, 2005

Dobrynin, A. *In Confidence: Moscow's ambassador to six Cold War presidents*, Seattle, WA: University of Washington Press, 2001

Egorychev, N. *Soldat, politik, diplomat: Vospominaniya ob ochen' raznom*, Moskva: Tsentrpoligraf, 2017

Evtushenko, E. *Volchii pasport*, Moskva: Vagrius, 1998

Feklisov, A. *Za okeanom i na ostrove: zapiski razvedchika*, Moskva: DEM, 1994

Fitzpatrick, S. *A Spy in the Archives: A memoir of Cold War Russia*, London: I.B. Tauris, 2014

Fursenko, A. ed. *Prezidium TsK KPSS 1954–1964: Chernovye protokol'nye zapisi zasedanii: stenogrammy*, Moskva: Rosspen, 2004

Gerovitch, S. ed. *Voices of the Soviet Space Program: Cosmonauts, soldiers, and engineers who took the USSR into space*, Basingstoke: Palgrave, 2014

Ginzburg, A. ed. *Belaya kniga po delu A. Sinyavskogo i Yu. Danielya*, München: Posev, 1967

Ginzburg, E. *Within the Whirlwind*, London: Collins and Harvill Press, 1981

Gladilin, A. *Ulitsa generalov: Popytka memuarov*, Moskva: Vagrius, 2008

Goldovskaya, M. *Woman with a Movie Camera: My life as a Russian filmmaker*, Austin, TX: University of Texas Press, 2006

Golomstock, I. *A Ransomed Dissident: A life in art under the Soviets*, London: I.B. Tauris, 2018

Gorbachev, M. *Memoirs*, London: Doubleday, 1995

Gorbachev, M. and Mlynar, Z. *Conversations with Gorbachev: On perestroika, the Prague Spring, and the crossroads of socialism*, New York: Columbia University Press, 2012

Gorbanevskaya, N. *Red Square at Noon*, London: André Deutsch, 1972

Graziosi, A. and Khlevnyuk, O. eds, *Regional'naya politika N.S. Khrushcheva*, Moskva: Rosspen, 2009

Grigorenko, P. *Memoirs*, New York: Norton, 1982

Grossman, V. *An Armenian Sketchbook*, London: MacLehose Press, 2013

Grushin, B. *Chetyre zhizni Rossii v zerkale oprosov obshchestvennogo mneniya*, Moskva: Progress-Traditsiya, 2001

Grybkauskas, S. 'Anti-Soviet protests and the localism of the Baltic republics' *nomenklatura*: Explaining the interaction', *Journal of Baltic Studies*, Vol. 49, No. 4, 2018

Gurevich, D. *From Lenin to Lennon: A memoir of Russia in the sixties*, London: Harcourt, 1991

Györkei, J. and Horváth, M. eds. *1956: Soviet Military Intervention in Hungary*, Budapest: Central European University Press, 1998

Hansson, C. and Liden, K. eds. *Moscow Women: Thirteen interviews*, London: Allison & Busby, 1984

Hayter, W. *The Kremlin and the Embassy*, London: Hodder & Stoughton, 1966

Hindus, M. *House Without a Roof: Russia after forty-three years of revolution*, London: Gollancz, 1962

Ilic, M. *Life Stories of Soviet Women: The interwar generation*, London: Routledge, 2013

Johnson, P. ed. *Khrushchev and the Arts: The politics of Soviet culture, 1962–1964*, Cambridge, MA: MIT Press, 1965

Kalb, M. *The Year I Was Peter the Great*, Washington, DC: Brookings Institution Press, 2017

Kalugin, O. *Spy Master: My thirty-two years in intelligence and espionage against the West*, New York: Basic Books, 2009

Khaustov, V. ed. *Delo Beriya: Prigovor obzhalovaniyu ne podlezhit*, Moskva: Mezhdunarodnyi fond 'Demokratiya', 2012

Khrushchev, S. *Khrushchev on Khrushchev: An inside account of the man and his era by his son, Sergei Khrushchev*, London: Little, Brown and Company, 1990

Khrushchev, S. ed. *Memoirs of Nikita Khrushchev*, vols. 2 and 3, University Park, PA: Penn State University Press, 2006

Kornienko, G. *Kholodnaya voina: Svidetel'stvo ee uchastnika*, Moskva: Olma Press, 2001

Kovaleva, N. ed. *Molotov, Malenkov, Kaganovich: Stenogramma iyun'skogo plenuma TsK KPSS i drugie dokumenty*, Moskva: Mezhdunarodnyi fond 'Demokratiya', 1998

Kozlov, A. *Kozel na sakse, i tak vsyu zhizn'*, Moskva: Vagrius, 1998

Kozlov, V. ed. *Kramola: Inakomyslie v SSSR pri Khrushcheve i Brezhneve, 1953–1982*, Moskva: Materik, 2005

Kozlov, V. and Mironenko, S. eds. *58-10: Nadzornye proizvodstva prokuratury SSSR po delam ob antisovetskoi agitatsii i propagande*, Moskva: Mezhdunarodnyi fond 'Demokratiya', 1999

Krasovitskaya, T. ed. *'Vozvratit' domoi druz'yami SSSR': Obuchenie inostrantsev v Sovetskom Soyuze, 1956–1965*, Moskva: Rosspen, 2013

Leibovich, O. *V gorode M: Ocherki politicheskoi povsednevnosti sovetskoi provintsii*, Moskva: Rosspen, 2008

Litvinov, P. and Reddaway, P. eds. *The Trial of the Four*, London: Viking, 1972

Lur'e, L. and Malyarova, I. eds. *1956 god: Seredina veka*, Sankt Peterburg: Neva, 2007

MacColl, R. *Just Back from Russia: 77 days inside the Soviet Union*, London: Daily Express Publication, 1955

Malenkov, A. *O moem otse Georgii Malenkove*, Moskva: 'Tekhnoekos', 1992

Marchenko, A. *My Testimony*, London: Penguin, 1969

Marchenko, A. *To Live Like Everyone*, London: I.B. Tauris, 1989

Messina, P. *Soviet Communal Living: An oral history of the kommunalka*, Basingstoke: Palgrave, 2011

Mesyatsev, N. *Gorizonty i labirinty moei zhizni*, Moskva: Vagrius, 2005

Mikoyan, A. *Tak bylo: Razmyshleniya o minuvshem*, Moskva: Vagrius, 1999

Mikoyan, S. 'Aleksei Snegov v bor'be za "destalinizatsiyu"', *Voprosy istorii*, No. 4, 2006

Mikoyan, S. *The Soviet Cuban Missile Crisis: Castro, Mikoyan, Kennedy, Khrushchev, and the Missiles of November*, Redwood City, CA: Stanford University Press, 2012

Mitrokhin, V. *KGB Lexicon: The Soviet intelligence officer's handbook*, London: Routledge, 2002

Morozov, B. *Documents on Jewish Emigration*, London: Routledge, 1999

Mukhitdinov, N. *Gody, provedennye v Kremle*, Tashkent: Izdatel'stvo narodnogo naslediya imeni Abdully Kadyri, 1994

Muzafari, D. *Sunshine Girl: My journey from the Soviet Orient to the Western world*, London: Amazon, 2020

Naumov, V. and Sigachev, Yu. eds. *Lavrentii Beria, 1953: Stenogramma iul'skogo plenuma TsK KPSS i drugie dokumenty*, Moskva: Mezhdunarodnyi fond 'Demokratiya', 1999

Navratil, J. ed. *The Prague Spring 1968: A National Security Archive documents reader*, Budapest: Central European University Press, 1998

Nureyev, R. *An Autobiography with Pictures*, London: Hodder, 1962

Okpysh, V. ed. *Tovarishch Komsomol: Dokumenty s"ezdov komsomola, plenumov, biuro i sekretariata TsK VLKSM, 1918–1968*, Moskva: Molodaya gvardiya, 1969

Orlov, Yu. *Dangerous Thoughts: Memoirs of a Russian life*, New York: W. Morrow, 1991

Orlova, R. and Kopelev, L. *My zhili v Moskve, 1956–1980*, Moskva: Kniga, 1990

Pastukhov, B. *Druzei moikh prekrasnye cherty*, Moskva: Molodaya gvardiya, 2012

Pazderka, J. *The Soviet Invasion of Czechoslovakia in 1968: The Russian perspective*, London: Lexington, 2019

Petrov, D. ed. *Istoria glazami Krokodila XX vek: Sobitiya, 1957–1979*, Moskva: XX senchuri krokokdil, 2015

Petrushevskaya, L. *The Girl from the Metropol Hotel: Growing up in communist Russia*, London: Penguin, 2017

Pimenov, R. *Vospominaniya*, Moskva: Panorama, 1996

Pimonov, V. *Govoryat 'osobo opasnye'*, Moskva: Detektiv-press, 1999

Plisetskaya, M. *I, Maya Plisetskaya*, New Haven, CT, and London: Yale University Press, 2001

Plyushch, L. *History's Carnival: A dissident's autobiography*, London: Collins and Harvill Press, 1979

Podrabinek, A. *Dissidenty: 'Mezhdu tyurmoi i svobodoi'*, Moskva: AST, 2015

Polikovskaya, L. ed. *'My predchustvie . . . predtecha': Ploshchad' Mayakovskogo, 1958–1965,* Moskva: Obshchestvo 'Memorial', 1997

Rabin, O. *Tri zhizni*, Paris: Tret'ya volna, 1986

Raleigh, D. ed. *Russia's Sputnik Generation: Soviet Baby Boomers talk about their lives*, Bloomington, IN: Indiana University Press, 2006

Reddaway, P. ed. *Uncensored Russia: Protest and dissent in the Soviet Union*, New York: American Heritage Press, 1972

Reddaway, P. *The Dissidents: A memoir of working with the resistance in Russia, 1960–1990*, Washington: Brookings Institution Press, 2020

Rettie, J. 'How Khrushchev leaked his Secret Speech to the world', *History Workshop Journal*, Vol. 62, No. 1, 2006

Romanova, R. ed., *Aleksandr Tvardovskii: Trudy i dni*, Moskva: Voldei, 2006

Ronkin, V. *Na smenu dekabryam prikhodyat yanvari . . .*, Moskva: Obshchestvo 'Memorial', 2003

Sagdeev, R. *The Making of a Soviet Scientist*, New York: Wiley, 1994

Sakharov, A. *Memoirs*, New York: Knopf, 1990

Salisbury, H. *To Moscow and Beyond: A reporter's narrative*, London: Michael Joseph, 1960

Salisbury, H. *Moscow Journal: The end of Stalin*, Chicago, IL: University of Chicago Press, 1961

Salisbury, H. *A New Russia?*, New York: Harper & Row, 1962

Semichastnyi, V. *Bespokoinoe serdtse*, Moskva: Vagrius, 2002

Sharansky, N. *Fear No Evil*, New York: Penguin, 1988

Shelest, P. *Da ne sudimy budete: Dnevniki i vospominaniya chlena politburo TsK KPSS*, Moskva: Tsentrpoligraf, 2016

Shepilov, D. *The Kremlin's Scholar: A memoir of Soviet politics under Stalin and Khrushchev*, New Haven, CT, and London: Yale University Press, 2007

Shevchenko, A. *Breaking with Moscow*, New York: Knopf, 1985

Shubin, A., Tarasov, A., Siuda, P. and Firth, W. (trans.), 'Make way for the working class: The Russian workers' uprising in Novocherkassk, 1962', The Anarchist Library website, https://theanarchistlibrary.org/library/various-authors-make-way-for-the-working-class

Sillitoe, A. *The Road to Volgograd*, New York: Knopf, 1964

Solzhenitsyn, A. *The Gulag Archipelago*, Vol. 3: *An experiment in literary investigation*, London: Harper & Row, 1978

Solzhenitsyn, A. *The Oak and the Calf*, London: Collins, 1980

Sosin, G. *Sparks of Liberty: An insider's memoir of Radio Liberty*, University Park, PA: Penn State University Press, 1999

Stajner, K. *Seven Thousand Days in Siberia*, London: Canongate, 1988

Steinbeck, J. *A Russian Journal*, London: Penguin, 2001

Stevenson, A. *Friends and Enemies: What I learned in Russia*, New York: Harper, 1959

Sukhodrev, V. *Yazyk moi – drug moi: Ot Khrushcheva do Gorbacheva*, Moskva: Olimp, 1999

Taubman, W. *The View from the Lenin Hills: An American student's report on Soviet youth in ferment*, London: Hamish Hamilton, 1968

Thompson, J. and Thompson, S. *The Kremlinologist: Llewellyn E. Thompson, America's man in Cold War Moscow*, Baltimore, MD: Johns Hopkins University Press, 2018

Tomilina, N. ed. *Nikita Khrushchev: Dva tsveta vremeni*, tom 2: *Dokumenty iz lichnogo fonda N.S. Khrushcheva*, Moskva: Mezhdunarodnyi fond 'Demokratiya', 2009

Tomilina, N. ed. *Chekhoslovatskii krizis 1967–69 gg. v dokumentakh TsK KPSS*, Moskva: Rosspen, 2010

Tomilina, N. ed. *'Prazhskaya vesna' i mezhdunarodnyi krizis 1968 goda: Dokumenty*, Moskva: Mezhdunarodnyi fond 'Demokratiya', 2010

Tomilina, N. ed. *Boi s 'ten'yu' Stalina: Dokumenty i materialy ob istorii XXII s"ezda KPSS i vtorogo etapa destalinizatsii*, Moskva: RGNF, 2015

Tranum, S. ed. *Life at the Edge of Empire: Oral histories of Soviet Kyrgyzstan*, Bishkek: Createspace, 2009

Troyanovskii, O. *Cherez gody i rasstoyaniya: Istoriya odnoi sem'i*, Moskva: Vagrius, 1997

Vail', B. *Osobo opasnyi*, London: Overseas Publication Interchange, 1980

Vaksberg, A. 'Something unknown about Neizvestny: Interview with Ernst Neizvestnyi by Arkadii Vaksberg', *Russian Politics and Law*, Vol. 37, No. 1, 1999

Voinovich, V. *The Anti-Soviet Soviet Union*, New York: Harcourt, 1985

Volkov, S. ed. *Conversations with Joseph Brodsky*, New York: The Free Press, 1998

Voslensky, M. *Nomenklatura: The Soviet ruling class,* New York: Doubleday, 1984

Voznesenskii, A. *Na virtual'nom vetru*, Moskva: Vagrius, 1998

Werth, A. *Russia: Hopes and fears*, London: Penguin, 1969

Yevtushenko, Y. *A Precocious Autobiography*, London: Collins, 1963

Secondary literature

Abashin, S. *Sovetskii kishlak: Mezhdu kolonializmom i modernizatsiei*, Moskva: Novoe literaturnoe obozrenie, 2015

Abduvalieva, R. *Chingiz Aitmatov: The glorious path of an Eurasian writer*, London: New Generation Publishing, 2020

Adamsky, V. and Smirnov, Yu. 'Moscow's biggest bomb: The 50-megaton test of October 1961', *Bulletin of the Cold War International History Project*, No. 4, 1994

Adler, N. 'Life in the "Big Zone": The fate of returnees in the aftermath of Stalinist repression', *Europe-Asia Studies*, Vol. 51, No. 1, 1999

Adler, N. *Keeping Faith with the Party: Communist believers return from the gulag*, Bloomington, IN: Indiana University Press, 2012

Afiani, V. ed. *Kul'tura i vlast' ot Stalina do Gorbacheva: Apparat TsK KPSS i kul'tura 1958–1964*, Moskva: Rosspen, 2005

Aksenov, V. *Colleagues*, London: Putnam, 1962

Aksyutin, Yu. *Khrushchevskaya 'ottepel'' i obshchestvennye nastroeniya v SSSR v 1953–1964 gg.*, Moskva: Rosspen, 2010

Alexander, J. and McGregor, J. 'African soldiers in the USSR: Oral histories of ZAPU intelligence cadres' Soviet training, 1964–1979', *Journal of Southern African Studies*, Vol. 43, No. 1, 2017

Alexander, R. *Regulating Homosexuality in Soviet Russia, 1956–1991*, Manchester: Manchester University Press, 2021

Alexander, R. 'The queer life of Lieutenant Petrenko: The KGB and male homosexuality in the Ukrainian SSR of the 1960s', *Europe-Asia Studies*, 2022.

Alexeyeva, L. *Soviet Dissent: Contemporary movements for national, religious and human rights*, Middletown, CT: Wesleyan University Press, 1985

Altshuler, M. *Religion and Jewish Identity in the Soviet Union, 1941–64*, Lebanon, NH: Brandeis University Press, 2012

Amirkhanova, M. 'Naselenie dagestanskogo sela v 50-e–60-e gg.', *Voprosy istorii*, No. 3, 2009

Andrew, C. and Mitrokhin, V. *The Mitrokhin Archive II: The KGB and the world*, London: Penguin, 2005

Andrew, C. and Mitrokhin, V. *The Mitrokhin Archive: The KGB in Europe and the West*, London: Penguin, 2015

Anon. 'Vlast' i intelligentsiya: "delo molodykh istorikov (1957–58)', *Voprosy istorii*, No. 004, 1994

Applebaum, R. 'The Friendship Project: Socialist internationalism in the Soviet Union and Czechoslovakia in the 1950s and 60s', *Slavic Review*, Vol. 74, No. 3, 2015

Attwood, L. 'Celebrating the "frail-figured welder": Gender confusion in women's magazines of the Khrushchev era', *Slavonica*, Vol. 8, No. 2, 2002

Banerjee, A. ed. *Russian Science Fiction Literature and Cinema*, Boston: Academic Studies Press, 2018

Banks, E. 'Sewing machines for socialism? Gifts of development and disagreement between the Soviet and Mozambican women's committees, 1963–87', *Comparative Studies of South Asia, Africa and the Middle East*, Vol. 41, No. 1, 2021

Baranskaya, N. *A Week Like Any Other: Novellas and stories*, Seattle, WA: Seal Press, 1989

Barghoorn, F. 'Soviet cultural diplomacy since Stalin', *Russian Review*, Vol. 17, No. 1, 1958

Barnes, S. ' "In a manner befitting Soviet citizens": An uprising in the post-Stalin Gulag', *Slavic Review*, Vol. 64, No. 4, 2005

Barnes, S. *Death and Redemption: The gulag and the shaping of Soviet society*, Princeton, NJ: Princeton University Press, 2011

Baron, S. *Bloody Saturday in the Soviet Union: Novocherkassk, 1962*, Redwood City, CA: Stanford University Press, 2001

Bartlett, D. *Fashion East: The spectre that haunted socialism*, Cambridge, MA: MIT Press, 2010

Bartos, A. *Kosmos: A portrait of the Russian space age*, Princeton, NJ: Princeton Architectural Press, 2001

Beda, A. *Sovetskaya politicheskaya kul'tura cherez prizmu MVD, 1946–1958*, Moskva: Mosgorarkhiv, 2002

Bergman, J. *Meeting the Demands of Reason: The life and thought of Andrei Sakharov*, Ithaca, NY: Cornell University Press, 2009

Berman, H. *Soviet Criminal Law and Procedure*, Cambridge, MA: Harvard University Press, 1972

Bezborodov, A. ed. *Istoriya kommunisticheskoi partii Sovetskogo Soyuza*, Moskva: Rosspen, 2013

Bischof, G. ed. *The Prague Spring and the Warsaw Pact Invasion of Czechoslovakia in 1968*, London: Lexington, 2010

Bittner, S. *The Many Lives of Khrushchev's Thaw: Experience and memory in Moscow's Arbat*, Ithaca, NY: Cornell University Press, 2008

Blauvelt, T. 'Patronage and betrayal in the post-Stalin succession: The case of Kruglov and Serov', *Communist and Post-Communist Studies*, Vol. 41, 2008

Blauvelt, T. 'Status shift and ethnic mobilisation in the March 1956 events in Georgia', *Europe-Asia Studies*, Vol. 61, No. 4, 2009

Blauvelt, T. and Smith, J. eds. *Georgia after Stalin: Nationalism and Soviet power*, London: Routledge, 2015

Bloch, S. and Reddaway, P. *Russia's Political Hospitals*, London: First Futura, 1978

Bohri, L. 'Rollback, liberation, containment or inaction?', *Journal of Cold War Studies*, Vol. 1, No. 3, 1999

Boobbyer, P. *Conscience, Dissent and Reform in Soviet Russia*, London: Routledge, 2005

Boym, S. *Common Places: Mythologies of everyday life in Russia*, Cambridge, MA, and London: Harvard University Press, 1994

Bracke, M. *Which Socialism? Whose Détente? West European communism and the Czechoslovak crisis of 1968*, Budapest: Central European University Press, 2007

Brandenberger, D. 'Stalin's last crime? Recent scholarship on postwar Soviet anti-Semitism and the Doctors' Plot', *Kritika*, Vol. 6, No. 1, 2005

Breyfogle, N. 'At the watershed: 1968 and the beginnings of Lake Baikal environmentalism', *Slavonic and East European Review*, Vol. 93, No. 1, 2015

Bronovitskaya, A. et al. *Moscow: A guide to Soviet modernist architecture, 1955–1991*, London: Artguide, 2019

Brooks, J. *Thank You, Comrade Stalin! Soviet public culture from revolution to Cold War*, Princeton, NJ: Princeton University Press, 2001

Brown, D. *Soviet Russian Literature since Stalin*, Cambridge: Cambridge University Press, 1978

Brown, K. *Plutopia: Nuclear families, atomic cities, and the great Soviet and American plutonium disasters*, Oxford: Oxford University Press, 2015

Brudny, Y. *Reinventing Russia: Russian nationalism and the Soviet state, 1955–1991*, Cambridge, MA: Harvard University Press, 1999

Brunstedt, J. 'Building a pan-Soviet past: The Soviet war cult and the turn away from ethnic particularism', *Soviet and Post-Soviet Review*, Vol. 38, No. 2, 2011

Brusilovskaya, L. *Kul'tura povsednevnosti v epokhu 'ottepeli': Metamorfozy stilya*, Moskva: URAO, 2001

Burford, R. 'Getting the bugs out of socialist legality: The case of Joseph Brodsky', *American Journal of Comparative Law*, Vol. 22, No. 3, 1974

Carlson, P. *'K' Blows Top*, New York: Public Affairs, 2009

Casu, I. and Sandle, M. 'Discontent and uncertainty in the borderlands: Soviet Moldavia and the Secret Speech, 1956–57', *Europe-Asia Studies*, Vol. 66, No. 4, 2014

Caute, D. *The Dancer Defects: The struggle for cultural supremacy during the Cold War*, Oxford: Oxford University Press, 2003

Caute, D. *Politics and the Novel during the Cold War*, London: Routledge, 2009

Chamberlain, W. 'The trend after Khrushchev: Immobilism', *Russian Review*, Vol. 25, No. 1, 1966

Chernyshova, N. *Soviet Consumer Culture in the Brezhnev Era*, London: Routledge, 2013

Chernyshova, N. 'De-Stalinisation and industrialisation in the Soviet borderlands: Beria's attempted national reform in Soviet Belarus', *Europe-Asia Studies*, Vol. 73, No. 2, 2021

Chuprinin, S. *Ottepel': Sobytiya, mart 1953–avgust 1968 goda*, Moskva: Novoe literaturnoe obozrenie, 2020

Cliff, N. *Moscow Nights: The Van Cliburn story*, New York: Harper, 2016

Cohen, S. ed. *An End to Silence: Uncensored opinion in the Soviet Union*, New York: Norton, 1984

Cohen, S. *The Victims Return: Survivors of the gulag after Stalin*, London: I.B. Tauris, 2011

Cohn, E. *The High Title of a Communist: Postwar party discipline and the values of the Soviet regime*, DeKalb, IL: Northern Illinois University Press, 2015

Cohn, E. 'Coercion, re-education and the prophylactic chat: *Profilaktika* and the KGB's struggle with unrest in the republic of Lithuania', *Russian Review*, Vol. 76, No. 2, 2017

Cohn, E. 'A Soviet theory of broken windows: Prophylactic policing and the KGB's struggle with political unrest in the Baltic republics', *Kritika*, Vol. 19, No. 4, 2018

Conterio, J. 'Our Black Sea coast: The sovietization of the Black Sea littoral under Khrushchev and the problem of overdevelopment', *Kritika*, Vol. 19, No. 2, 2018

Coumel, L. 'A failed environmental turn? Khrushchev's thaw and nature protection in Soviet Russia', *Soviet and Post-Soviet Review*, Vol. 40, No. 2, 2013

Crowley, D. and Reid, S. eds. *Socialist Spaces: Sites of everyday life in the Eastern Bloc*, Oxford: Berg, 2002

Crowley, D. and Reid, S. eds. *Pleasures in Socialism: Leisure and luxury in the eastern bloc*, Evanston, IL: Northwestern University Press, 2010

Crump, L. *Warsaw Pact Reconsidered: International relations in Eastern Europe, 1955–69*, London: Routledge, 2017

Cucciola, R. 'Sharaf Rashidov and the international dimensions of Soviet Uzbekistan', *Central Asian Survey*, Vol. 39, No. 2, 2020

Dale, R. 'Rats and resentment: The demobilization of the Red Army in postwar Leningrad, 1945–1950', *Journal of Contemporary History*, Vol. 45, No. 1, 2010

Dale, R. 'Divided we stand: Cities, social unity and post-war reconstruction in Soviet Russia, 1945–1953', *Contemporary European History*, Vol. 24, No. 4, 2015

Davies, S. 'From Iron Curtain to Velvet Curtain? Peter Brooks' *Hamlet* and the origins of British–Soviet cultural relations during the Cold War', *Contemporary European History*, Vol. 27, No. 4, 2018

Davis, N. 'The number of Orthodox churches before and after the Khrushchev anti-religious drive', *Slavic Review*, Vol. 50, No. 3, 1991

Davoliute, V. *The Making and Breaking of Soviet Lithuania*, London: Routledge, 2013

De Luca, R. 'Tarkovsky screens Hemingway: Andrei Tarkovsky's first student film, *The Killers* (1956)', *Studies in Russian and Soviet Cinema*, Vol. 13, No. 2, 2019

Delaney Grossman, J. 'Khrushchev's anti-religious policy and the campaign of 1954', *Soviet Studies*, Vol. 24, No. 3, 1973

Denisova, L. *Rural Women in the Soviet Union and Post-Soviet Russia*, London: Routledge, 2010

Dickson, P. *Sputnik: The shock of the century*, Lincoln, NE: University of Nebraska Press, 2019

Dobson, M. 'Contesting the paradigms of de-Stalinization: Readers' responses to *One Day in the Life of Ivan Denisovich*', *Slavic Review*, Vol. 64, No. 3, 2005

Dobson, M. *Khrushchev's Cold Summer: Gulag returnees, crime and the fate of reform after Stalin*, Ithaca, NY, and London: Cornell University Press, 2009

Dobson, M. 'Child sacrifice in the Soviet press: Sectarianism and the "sectarian" in the post-Stalin Years', *Russian Review*, Vol. 73, No. 2, 2014

Dobson, M. 'The social scientists meets the "believer": Discussions of God, the afterlife, and communism in the mid-1960s', *Slavic Review*, Vol. 74, No. 1, 2015

Dodkhudoyev, N. *Tajikistan: Land of sunshine*, London: Soviet Booklets, 1959

Donovan, V. '"How well do you know your *krai*?" The *Kraevedenie* revival and patriotic politics in late Khrushchev-era Russia', *Slavic Review*, Vol. 74, No. 3, 2015

Donovan, V. *Chronicles in Stone: Preservation, patriotism and identity in northwest Russia*, Ithaca, NY: Cornell University Press, 2019

Dudoignon, S. 'From revival to mutation: The religious personnel of Islam in Tajikistan from de-Stalinization to independence', *Central Asian Survey*, Vol. 30, No. 1, 2011

Dumančić, M. *Men Out of Focus: The Soviet masculinity crisis in the long sixties*, Toronto: University of Toronto Press, 2021

Dziuba, I. *Internationalism or Russification: A study in the Soviet nationalities problem*, London: Weidenfeld and Nicolson, 1968

Eby, M. 'Global Tashkent: Transnational visions of a Soviet city in the postcolonial world, 1953–1966', *Ab Imperio*, No. 4, 2021

Edele, M. *Soviet Veterans of the Second World War: A popular movement in an authoritarian society, 1941–1991*, Oxford: Oxford University Press, 2009

Edele, M. 'Veterans and the village: The impact of Red Army demobilisation on Soviet urbanisation, 1945–1955', *Russian History*, Vol. 36, 2009

Edgar, A. 'Marriage, modernity, and the friendship of nations: Interethnic intimacy in post-war Central Asia in comparative perspective', *Central Asian Survey*, Vol. 26, No. 4, 2007

Ehrenburg, I., Khachaturian, A. and Pomerantsev, V. 'Three Soviet artists on the present needs of Soviet art', *Soviet Studies*, Vol. 5, No. 4, 1954

Elie, M. and Hardy, J. 'Letting the beasts out of the cage: Parole in the post-Stalin gulag, 1953–73', *Europe-Asia Studies*, Vol. 67, No. 4, 2015

Emel'yanov, Yu. *Khrushchev: 'ottepel'' ili . . .*, Moskva: Akademicheskii proekt, 2018

Emshit, A. 'Nachalo destalinizatsii ili 'khrushchevskaya ottepel'': Mesto i rol' v sovetskoi istorii', *Voprosy istorii*, No. 10, 2020

Engerman, D. 'The Second World's Third World', *Kritika*, Vol. 12, No. 1, 2011

Engerman, D. 'Learning from the East: Soviet experts and India in the era of competitive co-existence', *Comparative Studies of South Asia, Africa, and the Middle East*, Vol. 33, No. 2, 2013

Eremina, L. and Zhemkova, E. eds. *Korni travy: Sbornik statei molodykh istorikov*, Moskva: Zven'ya, 1996

Estraikh, G. 'Birobidzhan in Khrushchev's thaw: The Soviet and Western outlook', *Journal of Modern Jewish Studies*, Vol. 18, No. 1, 2019

Evans, C. *Between Truth and Time: A history of Soviet central television*, New Haven, CT, and London: Yale University Press, 2016

Fainberg, D. and Kalinovsky, A. eds. *Reconsidering Stagnation in the Brezhnev Era: Ideology and exchange*, London: Lexington, 2016

Farmer, K. *Ukrainian Nationalism in the Post-Stalin Era: Myths, symbols, and ideology in Soviet nationalities policy*, London: Martinus Nijhoff, 1980

Fedor, J. *Russia and the Cult of State Security: The Chekist tradition, from Lenin to Putin*, London: Routledge, 2013

Feldbrugge, F. *Samizdat and Political Dissent in the Soviet Union*, Leiden: Sijthoff, 1975

Feofanov, Yu. and Barry, D. *Politics and Justice in Russia: Major trials of the post-Stalin years*, London: Routledge, 1996

Field, D. 'Irreconcilable differences: Divorce and conceptions of private life in the Khrushchev era', *Russian Review*, Vol. 57, No. 4, 1998

Field, D. *Private Life and Communist Morality in Khrushchev's Russia*, New York: Peter Lang, 2007

Filtzer, D. *Soviet Workers and De-Stalinization: The consolidation of the modern system of Soviet production relations, 1953–1964*, Cambridge: Cambridge University Press, 1992

Filtzer, D. 'The standard of living of Soviet industrial workers in the immediate postwar period, 1945–1948', *Europe-Asia Studies*, Vol. 51, No. 6, 1999

Finn, P. and Couvée, P. *The Zhivago Affair: The Kremlin, the CIA and the battle over a forbidden book*, London: Harvill Secker, 2014

Firsov, B. *Raznomyslie v SSSR 1940–1960-e gody*, Sankt Peterburg: Izdatel'stvo Evropeiskogo universiteta, 2008

Fitzpatrick, S. 'Social parasites: How tramps, idle youths and busy entrepreneurs impeded the Soviet march to communism', *Cahiers du monde russe*, Vol. 47, Nos 1/2, 2006

Florin, M. 'What is Russia to us? Making sense of Stalinism, colonialism and Soviet modernity in Kyrgyzstan, 1956–1965', *Ab Imperio*, No. 3, 2016

Fokin, A. 'Kommunizm ne za gorami': Obrazy budushchego u vlasti i naseleniya SSSR na rubezhe 1950–1960-x godov*, Moskva: Rosspen, 2017

Fraser, E. *Military Masculinity and Postwar Recovery in the Soviet Union*, Toronto: University of Toronto Press, 2019

Friedman, J. *Shadow Cold War: The Sino-Soviet competition for the Third World*, Chapel Hill, NC: University of North Carolina Press, 2015

Fursenko, A. and Naftali, T. *Khrushchev's Cold War: The inside story of an American adversary*, New York: Norton, 2007

Fürst, J. ed. *Late Stalinist Russia: Society between reconstruction and reinvention*, London: Routledge, 2006

Fürst, J. *Stalin's Last Generation: Soviet post-war youth and the emergence of mature socialism*, Oxford: Oxford University Press, 2010

Fürst, J. *Flowers through the Concrete: Explorations in Soviet Hippieland*, Oxford: Oxford University Press, 2021

Galas, M. 'Podgotovka k liberalizatsii politicheskogo (gosudarstvennogo) rezhima SSSR vo vtoroi polovine 1950-x – 1964 gg. (po dokumentam RGASPI), *Voprosy istorii*, No. 10, 2020

Gallyamova, A. *Tatarskaya ASSR v period postStalinizma, 1945–1985*, Kazan: Tatarskoe knizhnoe izdatel'stvo, 2015

Gerasimova, O. 'Ottepel'', 'Zamorozki' i studenty Moskovskogo universiteta*, Moskva: AIRO, 2015

Geras'kin, Yu. 'K voprosu o podderzhke russkoi pravoslavnoi tserkvi naseleniem v period "khrushchevskikh gonenii"', *Otechestvennaya istoriya*, No. 4, 2007

Gerovitch, S. 'InterNyet: Why the Soviet Union did not build a nationwide computer network', *History and Technology*, Vol. 24, No. 4, 2008

Gerovitch, S. *Soviet Space Mythologies: Public images, private memories and the making of a cultural identity*, Pittsburgh, PA: University of Pittsburgh Press, 2015

Gilburd, E. 'Picasso in thaw culture', *Cahiers du monde russe*, Vol. 47. Nos 1/2, 2006

Gilburd, E. *To See Paris and Die: The Soviet lives of Western culture*, Cambridge, MA: Harvard University Press, 2018

Goff, K. '"Why not love our language and our culture?": National rights and citizenship in Khrushchev's Soviet Union', *Nationalities Papers*, Vol. 43, No. 1, 2015

Goff, K. *Nested Nationalism: Making and unmaking nations in the Soviet Caucasus*, Ithaca, NY: Cornell University Press, 2020

Golovanov, Ya. *Korolev: Fakty i mify*, Moskva: Nauka, 1994

Gorlizki, Y. 'Stalin's cabinet: The Politburo and decision-making in the post-war years', *Europe-Asia Studies*, Vol. 53, No. 2, 2001

Gorlizki, Y. 'Policing post-Stalin society: The militia and public order under Khrushchev', *Cahiers du monde russe*, Vol. 44, Nos 2/3, 2003

Gorlizki, Y. 'Too much trust: Regional party leaders and local political networks under Brezhnev', *Slavic Review*, Vol. 69, No. 3, 2010

Gorlizki, Y. 'Scandal in Riazan: Networks of trust and the social dynamics of deception', *Kritika*, Vol. 14, No. 2, 2013

Gorlizki, Y. 'Structures of trust after Stalin', *Slavonic and East European Review*, Vol. 91, No. 1, 2013

Gorlizki, Y. 'Theft under Stalin: A property rights analysis', *Economic History Review*, Vol. 69, No. 1, 2016

Gorlizki, Y. and Khlevniuk, O. *Cold Peace: Stalin and the Soviet ruling circle, 1945–1953*, Oxford: Oxford University Press, 2004

Gorlizki, Y. and Khlevniuk, O. *Substate Dictatorship: Networks, loyalty and institutional change in the Soviet Union*, New Haven, CT, and London: Yale University Press, 2020

Gorsuch, A. *All This Is Your World: Soviet tourism at home and abroad after Stalin*, Oxford: Oxford University Press, 2011

Gorsuch, A. '"Cuba, My Love": The romance of revolutionary Cuba in the Soviet sixties', *American Historical Review*, Vol. 120, No. 2, 2015

Gorsuch, A. and Koenker, D. eds. *Turizm: The Russian and East European tourist under capitalism and socialism*, Ithaca, NY: Cornell University Press, 2006

Gorsuch, A. and Koenker, D. *The Socialist Sixties: Crossing borders in the Second World*, Bloomington, IN: Indiana University Press, 2013

Grebenyuk, P. 'Sotsial'naya sfera Magadanskoi oblasti v 1958–65 gg.', *Voprosy istorii*, No. 7, 2021

Grebenyuk, P. 'Rukovodyashchie kadry i izmeneniya v obshchestvenno-politicheskoi sfere na severo-vostoke SSSR v 1958–1964 gg', *Voprosy istorii*, No. 8, 2021

Gruliow, L. ed. *Current Soviet Policies*, Vol. IV, New York: Praeger, 1962

Grybkauskas, S. *Governing the Soviet Union's National Republics: The second secretaries of the Communist Party*, London: Routledge, 2020

Grybkauskas, S. *Moscow and the Non-Russian Republics in the Soviet Union: Nomenklatura, intelligentsia and centre-periphery relations*, London: Routledge, 2021

Grybkauskas, S. 'Economic strategies and immigration in the Soviet Union's western borderlands: Lithuania, Latvia and Belorussia in the 1950s and 1960s', *Europe-Asia Studies*, Vol. 74, No. 3, 2022

Guillory, S. 'Culture clash in the socialist paradise: Soviet patronage and African students' urbanity in the Soviet Union, 1960–1965', *Diplomatic History*, Vol. 38, No. 2, 2014

Guth, S. 'Oasis of the future: The nuclear city of Shevchenko/Aqtau, 1959–2019', *Jahrbücher für Geschichte Osteuropas*, Vol. 16, No. 1, 2018

Hale-Dorrell, A. 'Industrial farming, industrial food: Transnational influences on Soviet convenience food in the Khrushchev era', *Soviet and Post-Soviet Review*, Vol. 42, No. 2, 2015

Hale-Dorrell, A. *Corn Crusade: Khrushchev's farming revolution in the post-Stalin Soviet Union*, Oxford: Oxford University Press, 2018

Hall, S., 'Framing the American 1960s: A historiographical review', *European Journal of American Culture*, Vol. 31, No. 1, 2012

Hanson, P. *The Rise and Fall of the Soviet Economy: An economic history of the USSR from 1945*, Harlow: Pearson, 2003

Hardy, J. 'Gulag tourism: Khrushchev's "show" prisons in the Cold War context, 1954–59', *Russian Review*, Vol. 71, No. 1, 2012

Hardy, J. *The Gulag after Stalin: Redefining punishment in Khrushchev's Soviet Union, 1953–1964*, Ithaca, NY: Cornell University Press, 2016

Harris, S. *Communism on Tomorrow Street: Mass housing and everyday life after Stalin*, Baltimore, MD: Johns Hopkins University Press, 2013

Harris, S. 'Dawn of the Soviet jet age: Aeroflot passengers and aviation culture under Nikita Khrushchev', *Kritika*, Vol. 21, No. 3, 2020

Harrison, H. *Driving the Soviets up the Wall: Soviet–East German relations, 1953–61*, Princeton, NJ: Princeton University Press, 2003

Hasanli, J. *Khrushchev's Thaw and National Identity in Soviet Azerbaijan, 1954–1959*, New York: Lexington, 2014

Haslam, J. *Near and Distant Neighbours: A new history of Soviet intelligence*, Oxford: Oxford University Press, 2015

Healey, D. *Russian Homophobia from Stalin to Sochi*, London: Bloomsbury Academic, 2017

Hearne, S. 'Sanitising sex in the USSR: State approaches to sexual health in the Brezhnev era', *Europe-Asia Studies*, Vol. 74, No. 10, 2022

Hearne, S. 'Selling sex under socialism: Prostitution in the postwar USSR', *European Review of History*, Vol. 29, No. 2, 2022

Heinzen, J. *The Art of the Bribe: Corruption, politics and everyday life in the Soviet Union, 1943–1953*, New Haven, CT, and London: Yale University Press, 2017

Heinzen, J. 'Soviet entrepreneurs in the late socialist shadow economy: The case of the Kyrgyz Affair', *Slavic Review*, Vol. 79, No. 3, 2020

Hessler, J. 'Death of an African student in Moscow: Race, politics, and the Cold War', *Cahiers du monde russe*, Vol. 47, Nos 1/2, 2006

Holloway, D. *The Soviet Union and the Arms Race*, New Haven, CT, and London: Yale University Press, 1983

Hooper, C. 'What can and cannot be said: Between the Stalinist past and new Soviet future', *Slavonic and East European Review*, Vol. 86, No. 2, 2008

Hornsby, R. *Protest, Reform and Repression in Khrushchev's Soviet Union*, Cambridge: Cambridge University Press, 2013

Hornsby, R. 'The enemy within? The Komsomol and foreign youth inside the post-Stalin Soviet Union', *Past and Present*, Vol. 232, No. 1, 2016

Hornsby, R. 'The post-Stalin Komsomol and the Soviet fight for Third World youth', *Cold War History*, Vol. 16, No. 1, 2016

Hornsby, R. 'Soviet youth on the march: The all-union tours of military glory, 1965–87', *Journal of Contemporary History*, Vol. 52, No. 2, 2016

Hornsby, R. 'Strengthening friendship and fraternal solidarity: Soviet youth tourism to Eastern Europe under Khrushchev and Brezhnev', *Europe-Asia Studies*, Vol. 71, No. 9, 2019

Hornsby, R. 'Engineering friendship? Komsomol work with students from the developing world inside the USSR in the 1950s and 1960s', *Social History*, Vol. 48, No. 1, 2023

Hosking, G. 'The Russian peasant rediscovered: "Village prose" of the 1960s', *Slavic Review*, Vol. 32, No. 4, 1973

Hutchinson, E. 'Ivan Denisovich on trial: Soviet writers, Russian identity, and Solzhenitsyn's failed bid for the 1964 Lenin Prize', *Kritika*, Vol. 22, No. 1, 2021

Huxtable, S. 'In search of the Soviet reader: The Kosygin reforms, sociology, and changing concepts of Soviet society, 1964–1970', *Cahiers du monde russe*, Vol. 54, Nos 3/4, 2013

Huxtable, S. 'Making news Soviet: Rethinking journalistic professionalism after Stalin', *Contemporary European History*, Vol. 27, No. 1, 2018

Huxtable, S. *News from Moscow: Soviet journalism and the limits of postwar reform*, Oxford: Oxford University Press, 2022

Iandolo, A. 'The rise and fall of the Soviet model of development in West Africa, 1957–64', *Cold War History*, Vol. 12, No. 4, 2012

Iandolo, A. 'Imbalance of power: The Soviet Union and the Congo crisis, 1960–61', *Journal of Cold War Studies*, Vol. 16, No. 2, 2014

Iandolo, A. 'Beyond the shoe: Rethinking Khrushchev at the fifteenth session of the United Nations General Assembly', *Diplomatic History*, Vol. 41, No. 1, 2017

Iandolo, A. *Arrested Development: The Soviet Union in Ghana, Guinea and Mali, 1955–1968*, Ithaca, NY: Cornell University Press, 2022

Igmen, A. *Speaking Soviet with an Accent: Culture and power in Kyrgyzstan*, Pittsburgh, PA: University of Pittsburgh Press, 2012

Ilic, M. ed. *The Palgrave Handbook of Women and Gender in Twentieth Century Russia and the Soviet Union*, London: Palgrave, 2018

Ilic, M. *Soviet Women: Everyday lives*, London: Routledge, 2020

Ilic, M. et al. eds. *Women in the Khrushchev Era*, Basingstoke: Palgrave, 2004

Ilic, M. and Smith, J. eds. *Soviet State and Society under Nikita Khrushchev*, London: Routledge, 2009

Iofe, V. *Granitsy smysla: stat'i, vystupleniya, esse*, Sankt Peterburg: Obshchestvo 'Memorial', 2002

Ironside, K. 'Between fiscal, ideological and social dilemmas: The Soviet "bachelor tax" and post-war tax reform, 1941–1962', *Europe-Asia Studies*, Vol. 69, No. 6, 2017

Ironside, K. *A Full-Value Ruble: The promise of prosperity in the postwar Soviet Union*, Cambridge, MA: Harvard University Press, 2021

Jenks, A. 'Palekh and the forging of a Russian nation in the Brezhnev era', *Cahiers du monde russe*, Vol. 44, No. 4, 2003

Jenks, A. *The Cosmonaut Who Couldn't Stop Smiling: The life and legend of Yuri Gagarin*, DeKalb, IL: Northern Illinois University Press, 2011

Jian, C. et al. eds. *The Routledge Handbook of the Global Sixties: Between protest and nation building*, Abingdon: Routledge, 2018

Johnson, D. and Tierney, D. *Failing to Win: Perceptions of victory and defeat in international politics*, Cambridge, MA: Harvard University Press, 2006

Johnson, E. 'Nikita Khrushchev, Andrei Voznesensky, and the cold spring of 1963: Documenting the end of the post-Stalin thaw', *World Literature Today*, Vol. 75, No. 1, 2001

Jones, P. ed. *The Dilemmas of De-Stalinization: Negotiating cultural and social change in the Khrushchev era*, London: Routledge, 2005

Jones, P. *Myth, Memory, Trauma: Rethinking the Stalinist past in the Soviet Union, 1953–79*, New Haven, CT, and London: Yale University Press, 2013

Josephson, P. 'Atomic-powered communism: nuclear culture in the postwar USSR', *Slavic Review*, Vol. 55, No. 2, 1996

Josephson, P. *New Atlantis Revisited: Akademgorodok, the Siberian city of science*, Princeton, NJ: Princeton University Press, 1997

Josephson, P. *Red Atom: Russia's nuclear power program from Stalin to today*, Pittsburgh, PA: University of Pittsburgh Press, 2005

Josephson, P. *An Environmental History of Russia*, Cambridge: Cambridge University Press, 2013

Kagarlitsky, B. *The Thinking Reed: Intellectuals and the Soviet state, 1917 to the present*, London: Verso, 1988

Kalinovsky, A. 'Not some British colony in Africa: The politics of decolonization and modernization in Soviet Central Asia, 1955–1964', *Ab Imperio*, No. 2, 2013

Kalinovsky, A. 'Tractors, power lines, and the welfare state: The contradictions of Soviet development in post-World War II Tajikistan', *Asiatische Studien*, Vol. 69, No. 3, 2015

Kalinovsky, A. *Laboratory of Socialist Development: Cold War politics and decolonization in Soviet Tajikistan*, Ithaca, NY, and London: Cornell University Press, 2018

Kalinovsky, A. and Scarborough, I. 'The oil lamp and the electric light', *Kritika*, Vol. 22, No. 1, 2021

Kamp, M. 'The Soviet legacy and women's rights in Central Asia', *Current History*, Vol. 115, No. 783, 2016

Katsakioris, C. 'Soviet lessons for Arab modernisation: Soviet educational aid to Arab countries after 1956', *Journal of Modern European History*, Vol. 8, No. 1, 2010

Katsakioris, C. 'Burden or allies? Third World students and internationalist duty through Soviet eyes', *Kritika*, Vol. 18, No. 3, 2017

Katsakioris, C. 'The Lumumba University in Moscow: Higher education for a Soviet-Third World alliance, 1960–1991', *Journal of Global History*, Vol. 14, No. 2, 2019

Kavanagh, J. *Rudolf Nureyev: The life*, London: Penguin, 2019

Kazakova, O. ed. *Estetika 'ottepeli': Novoe v arkhitekture, iskusstve, kul'ture*, Moskva: Rosspen, 2013

Keller, S. 'The puzzle of the manual harvest in Uzbekistan: Economics, statistics and labour in the Khrushchev era', *Central Asian Survey*, Vol. 34, No. 3, 2015

Kelly, C. 'Thank you for the wonderful book: Soviet child readers and the management of children's reading, 1950–1975', *Kritika*, Vol. 6, No. 4, 2005

Khalid, A. *Central Asia: A new history from the imperial conquests to the present*, Princeton, NJ: Princeton University Press, 2021

Khandozhko, R. 'Dissidence behind the nuclear shield? The Obninsk atomic research centre and the infrastructure of dissent in the late Soviet Union', *Jahrbücher für Geschichte Osteuropas*, Vol. 66, No. 1, 2018

Kharkhordin, O. *The Collective and the Individual in Russia: A study of practices*, Berkeley, CA: University of California Press, 1999

Khasbulatova, D. *Rossiiskaya gendernaya politika v XX stoletii: Mify i realii*, Izdatel'stvo Ivanovo gos. universitet, 2005

Khlevnyuk, O. 'Patronazh Moskvy i gruzinskii natsionalizm nakanune sobytii 1956', *Voprosy istorii*, No. 12, 2003

Kibita, N. 'Controlling resources in the Ukrainian SSR during the sovnarkhoz reform (1957–65): Testing the idea of decentralisation', *Europe-Asia Studies*, Vol. 65, No. 6, 2013

Kirmse, S. 'Internationalist nation builders: Youth under Brezhnev in the Soviet south', *Europe-Asia Studies*, Vol. 74, No. 7, 2022

Kirschenbaum, L. *The Legacy of the Siege of Leningrad, 1941–1995: Myth, memories, and monuments,* Cambridge: Cambridge University Press, 2009

Klumbyte, N. and Sharafutdinova, G. eds. *Soviet Society in the Era of Late Socialism, 1964–1985,* London: Lexington, 2014

Knight, A. *The KGB: Police and politics in the Soviet Union*, London: HarperCollins, 1988

Knight, A. *Beria: Stalin's first lieutenant*, Princeton, NJ: Princeton University Press, 1993

Koenker, D. *Club Red: Vacation travel and the Soviet dream*, Ithaca, NY: Cornell University Press, 2013

Koenker, D. 'The smile behind the sales counter: Soviet shop assistants on the road to full communism', *Journal of Social History*, Vol. 54, No. 3, 2021

Koenker, D. and Bamberger, B. 'Tips, bonuses or bribes: The immoral economy of service work in the Soviet 1960s', *Russian Review*, Vol. 79, No. 2, 2020

Kohonen, L. *Picturing the Cosmos: A visual history of early Soviet space endeavour,* Bristol: Intellect, 2017

Koivunen, P. *Performing Peace and Friendship: The World Youth Festivals and Soviet cultural diplomacy*, London: De Gruyter, 2022

Kokoshin, A. 'Karibskii krizis 1962 g. i ego uroki', *Voprosy istorii*, No. 9, 2015

Komaromi, A. 'The material existence of Soviet samizdat', *Slavic Review*, Vol. 63, No. 3, 2004

Kon, I. *The Sexual Revolution in Russia*, London: Simon and Schuster, 1995

Konyshev, D. 'Vremya "ottepeli" 1953–1964 gg. kak epokha dvortsovykh perevorotov', *Voprosy istorii*, No. 2, 2017

Kovacevic, F. ' "An ominous talent": Oleg Gribanov and KGB counterintelligence', *International Journal of Intelligence and CounterIntelligence*, 2022.

Kozlov, D. 'The historical turn in late Soviet culture: Retrospectivism, factography, doubt, 1953–91', *Kritika*, Vol. 2, No. 3, 2001

Kozlov, D. *The Readers of Novyi Mir: Coming to terms with the Stalinist past*, Cambridge, MA: Harvard University Press, 2013

Kozlov, D. 'Pod vidom preodoleniya kul'ta lichnosti: Nerealizovannaya reforma prepodovaniya istorii v shkole (1956–1957)', *Ab Imprio*, No. 2, 2017

Kozlov, D. 'Sotsializatsiya sovetskoi molodezhi perioda "ottepeli": Variant al'ternativnykh identichnosti (na primere Arkhangel'skoi oblasti)', *Laboratorium*, No. 2, 2012

Kozlov, D. and Gilburd, E. eds. *The Thaw: Soviet society and culture during the 1950s and 1960s*, Toronto: University of Toronto Press, 2013

Kozlov, V. *Massovye besporyadki v SSSR pri Khrushchev i Brezhneve, 1953–1980 gg,* Novosibirsk: Sibirskii Khronograf, 1999

Kozlov, V. *Mass Uprisings in the USSR: Protest and rebellion in the post-Stalin years*, New York: M.E. Sharpe, 2002

Kozlov, V. *Neizvestnyi SSSR: Protivostoyanie naroda i vlasti, 1953–1985*, Moskva: Olma-Press, 2006

Kozovoi, A. 'Dissonant voices: Soviet youth mobilization and the Cuban missile crisis', *Journal of Cold War Studies*, Vol. 16, No. 3, 2014

Kramer, M. ed., 'Soviet Moldavia and the 1968 Czechoslovak crisis: A report on the political "spill-over"', *Bulletin of the Cold War International History Project*, No. 11, 1998

Kramer, M. 'The Soviet Union and the 1956 crises in Hungary and Poland: Reassessments and new findings', *Journal of Contemporary History*, Vol. 33, No. 2, 1998

Kramer, M. 'The early post-Stalin succession struggle and upheavals in East-Central Europe: internal-external linkages in Soviet policy making (part 1)', *Journal of Cold War Studies*, Vol. 1, No. 1, 1999

Kramer, M. 'The early post-Stalin succession struggle and upheavals in East-Central Europe: Internal-external linkages in Soviet policy making (part 2)', *Journal of Cold War Studies*, Vol. 1, No. 2, 1999

Kramer, M. 'The early post-Stalin succession struggle and upheavals in East-Central Europe: Internal-external linkages in Soviet policy making (part 3)', *Journal of Cold War Studies*, Vol. 1, No. 3, 1999

Kramer, M. 'Ukraine and the Soviet-Czechoslovak crisis of 1968 (part 2)', *Bulletin of the Cold War International History Project*, Nos 14/15, 2003

Kustanovich, K. *The Artist and the Tyrant: Vassily Aksenov's works in the Brezhnev era*, Columbus, OH: Slavica, 1992

Kydralina, Zh. 'Politicheskie nastroeniya v Kazakhstane v 1945–1985 gg.', *Voprosy istorii*, No. 8, 2008

Lakhtikova et al. eds. *Seasoned Socialism: Gender and food in late Soviet everyday life*, Bloomington, IN: Indiana University Press, 2019

Lakshin, V. *Solzhenitsyn, Tvardovsky and Novy mir*, Cambridge, MA: MIT Press, 1980

Lanius, R. ed. *Reconsidering Sputnik: Forty years since the Soviet satellite*, London: Routledge, 2000

LaPierre, B. 'Making hooliganism on a mass scale: The campaign against petty hooliganism in the Soviet Union, 1956–1964', *Cahiers du monde russe*, Vol. 47, Nos 1/2, 2006

LaPierre, B. *Hooligans in Khrushchev's Russia: Defining, policing and producing deviance during the thaw*, Madison, WI, and London: University of Wisconsin Press, 2012

Lebina, N. *Povsednevnost' epokhi kosmosa i kukuruzy: Destruktsiya bol'shogo stilya: Leningrad, 1950–1960-e gody*, Sank Peterburg: Pobeda, 2015

Lebina, N. *Muzhchina i zhenshchina: Telo, moda, kul'tura SSSR – ottepel'*, Moskva: Novoe literaturnoe obozrenie, 2018

Ledeneva, A. *Russia's Economy of Favours: Blat, networking and informal exchange*, Cambridge: Cambridge University Press, 1998

Lehmann, M. 'Apricot socialism: The national past, the Soviet project, and the imagining of community in late Soviet Armenia', *Slavic Review*, Vol. 74, No. 1, 2015

Leinarte, D. *Family and the State in Soviet Lithuania: Gender, law and society*, London: Bloomsbury, 2021

Li, D. and Xia, Y. 'Competing for leadership: Split or détente in the Sino-Soviet bloc, 1959–61', *International History Review*, Vol. 30, No. 3, 2008

Lloyd, T. 'Congo on the Dnipro: Third Worldism and the nationalization of Soviet internationalism in Ukraine', *Kritika*, Vol. 22, No. 4, 2021

Loader, M. 'Beria and Khrushchev: The power struggle over nationality policy and the case of Latvia', *Europe-Asia Studies*, Vol. 68, No. 10, 2016

Loader, M. 'Restricting Russians: Language and immigration laws in Soviet Latvia, 1956–1959', *Nationalities Papers*, Vol. 45, No. 6, 2017

Loader, M. 'A Stalinist purge in the Khrushchev era? The Latvian Communist Party purge, 1959–1963', *Slavonic and East European Review*, Vol. 96, No. 2, 2018

Loewenstein, K. 'Re-emergence of public opinion in the Soviet Union: Khrushchev and responses to the Secret Speech', *Europe-Asia Studies*, Vol. 58, No. 8, 2006

Loewenstein, K. '*Obshchestvennost'* as key to understanding Soviet writers of the 1950s: *Moskovskii literator*, October 1956–March 1957', *Journal of Contemporary History*, Vol. 44, No. 3, 2009

Losev, L. *Iosif Brodskii: Opyt literaturnoi biografii*, Moskva: Molodaya gvardiya, 2006

Lovell, S. *Russia in the Microphone Age: A history of Soviet radio, 1919–1970*, Oxford: Oxford University Press, 2015

Luthi, L. *The Sino-Soviet Split: Cold War in the communist world*, Princeton, NJ: Princeton University Press, 2008

Magnusdottir, R. *Enemy Number One: The United States of America in Soviet ideology and propaganda, 1945–1959*, Oxford: Oxford University Press, 2018

Marwick, A. *The Sixties: Cultural revolution in Britain, France, Italy and the United States, 1958–1974*, Oxford: Oxford University Press, 1998

Maslova, I. 'Russkaya pravoslavnaya tserkov' i KGB (1960–1980-e gody)', *Voprosy istorii*, No. 12, 2005

Mastny, V. 'The Soviet Union's partnership with India', *Journal of Cold War Studies*, Vol. 12, No. 3, 2010

Matusevich, M. 'Journeys of hope: African diaspora and the Soviet society', *African Diaspora*, Vol. 1, No. 1, 2008

Maurer, E. et al. eds. *Soviet Space Culture: Cosmic enthusiasm in socialist societies*, London: Palgrave, 2011

Mazov, S. 'Sovetskii soyuz i zapadnaya Afrika v 1956–64 gody', *Novaya i noveishaya istoriya*, No. 2, 2007

Mazov, S. 'Soviet aid to the Gizenga government in the former Belgian Congo (1960–61) as reflected in Russian archives', *Cold War History*, Vol. 7, No. 3, 2007

Mazov, S. *A Distant Front in the Cold War: The USSR in West Africa and the Congo, 1956–1964*, Redwood City, CA: Stanford University Press, 2010

McCallum, C. *The Fate of the New Man: Representing and reconstructing masculinity in Soviet visual culture, 1945–1965*, Ithaca, NY: Cornell University Press, 2018

McCallum, C. 'A beautiful dream, facing both the future and the past: De-Stalinization, visual culture and the fortieth anniversary of the October Revolution', *Revolutionary Russia*, Vol. 33, No. 1, 2020

McDermott, K. and Stibbe, M. eds. *De-Stalinising Eastern Europe: Rehabilitation of Stalin's victims after 1953*, Basingstoke: Palgrave, 2015

McDermott, K. and Stibbe, M. eds. *Eastern Europe in 1968: Responses to the Prague Spring and Warsaw Pact invasion*, Basingstoke: Palgrave, 2018

Medvedev, Zh. 'Zagadka smerti Stalina', *Voprosy istorii*, No. 1, 2000

Melvin, N. *Soviet Power and the Countryside: Policy innovation and institutional decay*, New York: Palgrave, 2003

Mertelsmann, O. 'Soviet mass violence in Estonia revisited', *Journal of Genocide Research*, Vol. 11, Nos 2–3, 2009

Miller, B. 'The new Soviet *narkoman*: Drugs and youth in post-Stalinist Russia', *Region*, Vol. 4, No. 1, 2015

Mitrokhin, N. *Russkaya partiya: Dvizhenie russkikh natsionalistov v SSSR, 1953–85 gody*, Moskva: Novoe literaturnoe obozrenie, 2003

Mitrokhin, N. 'Back-office Mikhaila Suslova ili kem i kak proizvodilas' ideologiya brezhnevskogo vremeni', *Cahiers du monde russe*, Vol. 54, Nos 3/4, 2013

Mlechin, L. *Shelepin*, Moskva: Molodaya gvardiya, 2009

Mlechin, L. *Kak Brezhnev smenil Khrushcheva*, Moskva: ZAO Tsentrpoligraf, 2014

Moroz, P. *Report from the Beria Reserve: The protest writings of Valentyn Moroz*, Toronto: Peter Martin, 1974

Mozejko, E. ed. *Vasily Pavlovich Aksenov: A writer in quest of himself*, Bloomington, IN: Slavica, 1986

Muehlenbeck, P. and Telepneva, N. eds, *Warsaw Pact Intervention in the Third World: Aid and influence in the Cold War*, London: Bloomsbury, 2018

Naiman, A. 'Picasso in Russia 2.0', *Moscow News*, 15 June 2010

Nakachi, M. *Replacing the Dead: The politics of reproduction in the postwar Soviet Union*, Oxford: Oxford University Press, 2021

Naumov, V. 'N.S. Khrushchev i reabilitatsiya zhertv massovykh politicheskikh represii', *Voprosy istorii*, No. 4, 1997

Nayudu, S. 'When the elephant swallowed the hedgehog: The Prague Spring and Indo-Soviet relations, 1968', *Cold War International History Project* Working Paper, 83, 2017

Novikov, A. ed. 'Sovetskaya intelligentsiya, Lubyanka, i Staraya Ploshchad' v 1960-x – 1980-x godakh', *Voprosy istorii*, No. 9, 2005

Novikov, A. ed. 'Pervaya reaktsiya na kritiku 'kul'ta lichnosti' I.V. Stalina. Po itogam vystuplenii A.M. Pankratova v Leningrade v marte 1956 goda', *Voprosy istorii*, No. 8, 2006

Orlov, I. and Popov, A. *Russo Touristo: Sovetskii vyezdnoi turizm, 1955–1991*, Moskva: Izdatel'skii dom VShE, 2016

Oushakine, S. 'Against the cult of things: On Soviet productivism, storage economy, and commodities with no destination', *Russian Review*, Vol. 73, No. 2, 2014

Parry, A. 'The Twentieth Congress: Stalin's "Second Funeral"', *American Slavic and East European Review*, Vol. 15, No. 4, 1956

Parthe, K. *Russian Village Prose: The radiant past*, Princeton, NJ: Princeton University Press, 1992

Pattle, S. 'Forging the golden ring: Tourist development and heritage preservation in the late Soviet Union', *Slavonic and East European Review*, Vol. 96, No. 2, 2018

Peterson, D. 'Samovar life: Russian nurture and Russian nature in the rural prose of Valentin Rasputin', *Russian Review*, Vol. 53, No. 1, 1994

Petrov, N. *Ivan Serov: Pervyi predsedatel' KGB*, Moskva: Materik, 2005

Pikhoya, R. *Moskva, kreml', vlast'*, Moskva: AST, 2007

Pinkus, B. *The Jews of the Soviet Union: The history of a national minority*, Cambridge: Cambridge University Press, 1990

Platonov, R. *Singing the Self: Guitar poetry, community and identity in the post-Stalin period*, Evanston, IL: Northwestern University Press, 2012

Plokhy, S. *The Man with the Poison Gun*, London: Oneworld, 2016

Plokhy, S. *Nuclear Folly*, London: Allen Lane, 2021

Pollock, E. 'From *partiinost'* to *nauchnost'* and not quite back again: Revisiting the lessons of the Lysenko affair', *Slavic Review*, Vol. 68, No. 1, 2009

Popoff, A. *Vasily Grossman and the Soviet Century*, New Haven, CT, and London: Yale University Press, 2020

Popova, O. 'Spetsifika mental'nosti sovetskikh grazhdan 1960 gg. cherez prizmu prodovol'stvennogo defitsita', *Voprosy istorii*, No. 11, 2018

Prigge, W. 'The Latvian purges of 1959: A revision study', *Journal of Baltic Studies*, Vol. 35, No. 3, 2004

Prishchepa, A. and Bycherov, D. 'Istoriya issledovaniya i osveniya Yamal'skogo regiona studencheskimi stroitel'nymi otryadami SSSR (1950–1970-e gg.)', *Voprosy istorii*, No. 3, 2021

Pushkareva, N. and Zhidchenko, A. 'Women scholars of Akademgorodok: Everyday life in a Soviet university town during the thaw', *Russian Review*, Vol. 81, No. 2, 2022

Pyzhikov, A. *Opyt modernizatsii sovetskogo obshchestva v 1953–64 godakh: Obshchestvenno-politicheskii aspekt*, Moskva: Gamma, 1998

Pyzhikov, A. *Khrushchevskaya 'ottepel''*, Moskva: Olma Press, 2002

Pyzhikov, A. 'Sovetskoe poslevoennoe obshchestvo i predposylki khrushchevskikh reform', *Voprosy Istorii*, No. 2, 2002

Pyzhkov, A. 'Istoki dissidenstva', *Svobodnaya mysl'*, No. 12, 2003

Pyzhikov, A. 'Problema kul'ta lichnosti v gody khrushchevskoi ottepeli', *Voprosy istorii*, No. 4, 2003

Raab, N. 'The Tashkent earthquake of 1966: The advantages and disadvantages of a natural tragedy', *Jahrbücher für Geschichte Osteuropas*, Vol. 62, No. 2, 2014

Radchenko, S. *Two Suns in the Heavens: The Sino-Soviet struggle for supremacy, 1962–1967*, Redwood City, CA: Stanford University Press, 2009

Rajak, S. 'New evidence from the former Yugoslav archives', *Bulletin of the Cold War International History Project*, Nos 12/13, 2001

Randall, A. '"Abortion will deprive you of happiness!": Soviet reproductive politics in the post-Stalin era', *Journal of Women's History*, Vol. 23, No. 3, 2011

Rasell, M. and Iarskaia-Smirnova, E. eds. *Disability in Eastern Europe and the Former Soviet Union: History, policy and everyday life*, London: Routledge, 2014

Rashidov, T. 'Soviet boarding schools as a forge of national professionals and intellectuals in Soviet Tajikistan in the 1950s and 1960s', *Central Asian Survey*, Vol. 38, No. 4, 2019

Raskina, A. 'Frida Vigdorova's transcript of Joseph Brodsky's trial: Myths and reality', *Journal of Modern Russian History and Historiography*, Vol. 7, 2014

Razzakov, F. *Sovetskoe detstvo*, Moskva: Algoritm, 2014

Reid, S. 'Masters of the earth: Gender and destalinisation in Soviet reformist painting of the Khrushchev era', *Gender and History*, Vol. 11, No. 2, 1999

Reid, S. 'Cold War in the kitchen: Gender and the destalinization of consumer taste in the Soviet Union under Khrushchev', *Slavic Review*, Vol. 61, No. 2, 2002

Reid, S. 'In the name of the people: The Manege affair revisited', *Kritika*, Vol. 6, No. 4, 2005

Reid, S. 'Khrushchev modern: Agency and modernization in the Soviet home', *Cahiers du monde russe*, Vol. 47, No. 1, 2006

Reid, S. 'Picasso, the *Thaw* and the "New Realism" in Soviet Art', Symposium *Revoir Picasso*, 2015

Remeikis, T. *Opposition to Soviet Rule in Lithuania, 1945–1980*, Chicago, IL: Institute of Lithuanian Studies, 1980

Risch, W. *The Ukrainian West: Culture and the fate of empire in Soviet Lviv*, Cambridge, MA: Harvard University Press, 2011

Rogacheva, M. *The Private World of Soviet Scientists from Stalin to Gorbachev*, Cambridge: Cambridge University Press, 2017

Rojavina, M. ed. *Women in Soviet Film: The thaw and post-thaw periods*, London: Routledge, 2017

Rosenfield, A. and Dodge, N. eds. *Nonconformist Art: The Soviet experience, 1956–1986*, London: Thames and Hudson, 1995

Roth-Ey, K. 'Finding a home for television in the USSR, 1950–1970', *Slavic Review*, Vol. 66, No. 2, 2007

Roth-Ey, K. *Moscow Prime Time: How the Soviet Union built the media empire that lost the Cold War*, Ithaca, NY: Cornell University Press, 2011

Roth-Ey, K. 'How do you listen to Radio Moscow? Moscow broadcasters, "Third World" listeners, and the space of the airwaves in the Cold War', *Slavonic and East European Review*, Vol. 98, No. 4, 2020

Roth-Ey, K. 'Listening out, listening for, listening in: Cold War radio broadcasting and the late Soviet audience', *Russian Review*, Vol. 7, No. 4, 2020

Rubenstein, J. *Tangled Loyalties: The life and times of Ilya Ehrenburg*, Tuscaloosa, AL: University of Alabama Press, 1996

Rubenstein, J. *The Last Days of Stalin*, New Haven, CT, and London: Yale University Press, 2016

Rupprecht, T. 'Socialist high modernity and global stagnation: A shared history of Brazil and the Soviet Union during the Cold War', *Journal of Global History*, Vol. 6, No. 3, 2011

Rupprecht, T. *Soviet Internationalism after Stalin: Interaction and exchange between the USSR and Latin America*, Cambridge: Cambridge University Press, 2015

Ryabakova, E. 'Zhenshchiny i zhenskii byt v SSSR 1950–1960-x gg. v sovetskoi i sovremennoi rossiisskoi istoriografii', *Vestnik Rossiiskogo universiteta druzhby narodov*, Vol. 16, No. 4, 2017

Ryabushkin, D. 'Ostrov Damanskii. 2 marta 1969 goda', *Voprosy istorii*, No. 5, 2004

Sabanchiev, Kh. 'Sekretnyi doklad N.S. Khrushcheva na XX s"ezde KPSS i sud'by repressirovannykh narodov', *Voprosy istorii*, No. 7, 2016

Sahadeo, J. *Voices from the Soviet Edge: Southern migrants in Leningrad and Moscow*, Ithaca, NY: Cornell University Press, 2019

Saktaganova, Z. 'Natsional'naya politika v Kazakhstane v 1953–65 gg.', *Voprosy istorii*, No. 9, 2021

Sanchez-Sibony, O. *Red Globalization: The political economy of the Soviet Cold War from Stalin to Khrushchev*, Cambridge: Cambridge University Press, 2017

Saparov, A. 'Renegotiating the boundaries of the permitted: The national(ist) revival in Soviet Armenia and Moscow's response', *Europe-Asia Studies*, Vol. 70, No. 6, 2018

Scammell, M. *Solzhenitsyn: A biography*, London: Hutchinson, 1985

Schattenberg, S. 'Trust, care, and familiarity in the Politburo: Brezhnev's scenario of power', *Kritika*, Vol. 16, No. 4, 2015

Schattenberg, S. *Brezhnev: The making of a statesman*, London: I.B. Tauris, 2021

Schmid, S. 'Celebrating tomorrow today: The peaceful atom on display in the Soviet Union', *Social Studies of Science*, Vol. 36, No. 3, 2006

Schwarz, B. *Music and Musical Life in Soviet Russia*, Bloomington, IN: Indiana University Press, 1983

Senn, A. 'The Sovietization of the Baltic states', *Annals of the American Academy of Political and Social Sciences*, Vol. 317, 1958

Senyavskii, A. ed. *XX s''ezd KPSS v kontekste rossiiskoi istorii*, Moskva: Institut rossi-iskoi istorii, 2012

Shaw, C. *Deaf in the USSR: Marginality, community, and Soviet identity, 1917–1991*, Ithaca, NY: Cornell University Press, 2017

Shelley, L. *Policing Soviet Society: The evolution of state control*, London: Routledge, 1996

Shen, Z. and Xia, Y. *Mao and the Sino-Soviet Partnership, 1945–1959*, New York: Lexington, 2017

Sherry, S. 'Better something than nothing: The editors and translators of *Inostrannaia literatura* as censorial agents', *Slavonic and East European Review*, Vol. 91, No. 4, 2013

Shkarovskii, M. 'Russkaya pravoslavnaya tserkov' v 1958–1964 godakh', *Voprosy istorii*, No. 2, 1999

Shlapentokh, V. *Public and Private Life of the Soviet People: Changing values in post-Stalin Russia*, Oxford: Oxford University Press, 1989

Siddiqi, A. *The Soviet Space Race with Apollo*, Gainesville, FL: University Press of Florida, 2000

Siddiqi, A. *Sputnik and the Soviet Space Challenge*, Gainesville, FL: University Press of Florida, 2000

Siddiqi, A. *The Red Rockets' Glare: Spaceflight and the Soviet imagination, 1857–1957*, Cambridge: Cambridge University Press, 2014

Siegelbaum, L. ed. *Borders of Socialism: Private spheres of Soviet Russia*, Basingstoke: Palgrave, 2006

Siegelbaum, L. *Cars for Comrades: The life of the Soviet automobile*, Ithaca, NY: Cornell University Press, 2008

Siegelbaum, L. 'Sputnik goes to Brussels: The exhibition of a Soviet technological wonder', *Journal of Contemporary History*, Vol. 47, No. 1, 2012

Silina, L. *Nastroeniya sovetskogo studenchestva, 1945–1964*, Moskva: Russkii mir, 2004

Skorik, A. and Bondarev, V. 'Novocherkassk, 1962', *Voprosy istorii*, No. 7, 2012

Skorino, L. 'A critic of Pomerantsev', *Soviet Studies*, Vol. 6, No. 1, 1954

Skutnev, A. ' "Doktrina Khrushcheva" protiv "doktrina Eisenkhauera" (vesna-leto 1960 g.)', *Voprosy istorii*, No. 3, 2008

Smith, J. *Red Nations: The nationalities experience in the USSR*, Cambridge: Cambridge University Press, 2013

Smith, J. *Works in Progress: Plans and realities on Soviet farms, 1930–1963*, New Haven, CT, and London: Yale University Press, 2014

Smith, J. 'The battle for language: Opposition to Khrushchev's education reform in the Soviet republics', *Slavic Review*, Vol. 76, No. 4, 2017

Smith, J. and Ilic, M. eds. *Khrushchev in the Kremlin: Policy and government in the Soviet Union, 1953–1964*, London: Routledge, 2011

Smith, K. 'A new generation of political prisoners: "Anti-Soviet" students, 1956–57', *The Soviet and Post-Soviet Review*, Vol. 32, Nos 2–3, 2005

Smith, K. *Moscow 1956: The silenced spring*, Cambridge, MA: Harvard University Press, 2017

Smith, M. *Property of Communists: The urban housing programme from Stalin to Khrushchev*, Ithaca, NY: Cornell University Press, 2010

Smith, M. 'Social rights in the Soviet dictatorship: The constitutional right to welfare from Stalin to Brezhnev', *Humanity*, Vol. 3, No. 3, 2012

Smith, M. 'Faded red paradise: Welfare and the Soviet city after 1953', *Contemporary European History*, Vol. 24, No. 4, 2015

Smolkin, V. *A Sacred Space Is Never Empty: A history of Soviet atheism*, Princeton, NJ, and Oxford: Princeton University Press, 2018

Smolkin-Rothrock, V. 'The ticket to the Soviet soul: Science, religion, and the spiritual crisis of late Soviet atheism', *Russian Review*, Vol. 73, No. 2, 2014

Stanciu, C. 'Autonomy and ideology: Brezhnev, Ceausescu and the world communist movement', *Contemporary European History*, Vol. 23, No. 1, 2014

Starr, F. *Red and Hot: The fate of jazz in the Soviet Union, 1917–1980*, Oxford: Oxford University Press, 1993

Stites, R. *Russian Popular Culture*, Cambridge: Cambridge University Press, 1992

Stone, A. '"Overcoming peasant backwardness": The Khrushchev anti-religious campaign and the rural Soviet Union', *Russian Review*, Vol. 67, No. 2, 2008

Stronski, P. *Tashkent: Forging a Soviet city, 1930–1966*, Pittsburgh, PA: University of Pittsburgh Press, 2010

Sushkov, A. *Prezidium TsK KPSS v 1957–1964 gg.*, Ekaterinburg: RAN, 2009

Swain, G. 'Before national communism: Joining the Latvian Komsomol under Stalin', *Europe-Asia Studies*, Vol. 64, No. 7, 2012

Sylvester, R. '"You are our pride and our glory!" Emotions, generation and the legacy of revolution in women's letters to Valentina Tereshkova', *Russian Review*, Vol. 78, No. 3, 2019

Tannberg, T. *Politika Moskvy v respublikakh Baltii v poslevoennye gody (1944–1956)*, Moskva: Rosspen, 2010

Tarsis, V. *Ward 7: An autobiographical novel*, London: Dutton, 1965

Tasar, E. 'The official madrasas of Soviet Uzbekistan', *Journal of Economic and Social History of the Orient*, Vol. 59, No. 1, 2016

Tasar, E. *Soviet and Muslim: The institutionalization of Islam in Central Asia*, Oxford: Oxford University Press, 2017

Taubman, W. *Khrushchev: The man and his era*, London: Free Press, 2003

Taubman, W. et al. eds. *Nikita Khrushchev*, New Haven, CT, and London: Yale University Press, 2000

Telepneva, N. 'Saving Ghana's revolution: The demise of Kwame Nkrumah and the evolution of Soviet policy in Africa, 1966–1972', *Journal of Cold War Studies*, Vol. 20, No. 4, 2018

Tismaneanu, V. ed. *Promises of 1968: Crises, illusion, and utopia*, Budapest: Central European University Press, 2011

Tomilina, V. 'Kampaniya po osvoeniyu tselennykh i zalezhnykh zemel' v 1954–59 gg.', *Voprosy istorii*, No. 9, 2009

Tompson, W. 'The fall of Nikita Khrushchev', *Soviet Studies*, Vol. 45, No. 6, 1991

Tromly, B. 'The Leningrad Affair and Soviet patronage politics, 1949–1950', *Europe-Asia Studies*, Vol. 56, No. 5, 2004

Tromly, B. 'Soviet patriotism and its discontents among higher education students in Khrushchev-era Russia and Ukraine', *Nationalities Papers*, Vol. 37, No. 3, 2009

Tromly, B. 'An unlikely national revival: Soviet higher learning and the Ukrainian "Sixtiers", 1953–65', *Russian Review*, Vol. 68, No. 4, 2009

Tromly, B. *Making the Soviet Intelligentsia: Universities and intellectual life under Stalin and Khrushchev*, Cambridge: Cambridge University Press, 2014

Troitsky, A. *Back in the USSR: The true story of rock in Russia*, London: Omnibus Press, 1987

Tsipursky, G. 'Conformism and agency: Model young communists and the Komsomol press in the later Khrushchev years, 1961–64', *Europe-Asia Studies*, Vol. 65, No. 7, 2013

Tsipursky, G. *Socialist Fun: Youth, consumption and state-sponsored popular culture in the Soviet Union, 1945–1970*, Pittsburgh, PA: University of Pittsburgh Press, 2016

Tuma, O. et al. 'The (inter communist) Cold War on ice: Soviet-Czechoslovak ice hockey politics, 1967–1969', *Cold War International History Project* Working Paper, 69, 2014

Turkina, O. *Soviet Space Dogs*, London: Fuel, 2014

Vagramenko, T. 'KGB "evangelism": Agents and Jehovah's Witnesses in Soviet Ukraine', *Kritika*, Vol. 22, No. 4, 2021

463

Vail', P. and Genis, A. *60-e: Mir sovetskogo cheloveka*, Moskva: AST, 2013

Vainshtein, O. 'Orange jackets and pea green pants: The fashion of *stilyagi* in Soviet postwar culture', *Fashion Theory*, Vol. 22, No. 2, 2018

Varga-Harris, C. 'Homemaking and the aesthetic and moral perimeters of the Soviet home during the Khrushchev era', *Journal of Social History*, Vol. 41, No. 3, 2008

Varga-Harris, C. *Stories of House and Home: Soviet apartment life during the Khrushchev years*, Ithaca, NY: Cornell University Press, 2015

Varga-Harris, C. 'Between national tradition and Western modernization: Soviet woman and representations of socialist gender equality as a third way for developing countries, 1956–1964', *Slavic Review*, Vol. 78, No. 3, 2019

Varon, J. et al. 'Time is an ocean: The past and future of the sixties', *The Sixties*, Vol. 1, No. 1, 2008

Vas'kin, A. *Povsednevnaya zhizn' sovetskoi stolitsy pri Khrushcheve i Brezhneve*, Moskva: Molodaya gvardiya, 2017

Volin, L. 'The Malenkov-Khrushchev new economic policy', *Journal of Political Economy*, Vol. 62, No. 3, 1954

Walker, B. 'Pollution and purification in the Moscow human rights networks of the 1960s and 1970s', *Slavic Review*, Vol. 68, No. 2, 2009

Walker, S. *Beyond*, London: William Collins, 2021

Weiner, A. 'The making of a dominant myth: The Second World War and the construction of political identities within the Soviet polity', *Russian Review*, Vol. 55, No. 4, 1996

Weiner, A. 'Déjà vu all over again: Prague spring, Romanian summer and Soviet autumn on the Soviet western frontier', *Contemporary European History*, Vol. 15, No. 2, 2006

Weiner, A. 'The empires pay a visit: Gulag returnees, East European rebellions, and Soviet frontier politics', *Journal of Modern History*, Vol. 78, No. 2, 2006

Weiner, A. and Rahi-Tamm, A. 'Getting to know you: the Soviet surveillance system, 1953–1957', *Kritika*, Vol. 13, No. 1, 2012

Westad, O. *The Cold War: A world history*, London: Allen Lane, 2017

White, S. *Russia Goes Dry: Alcohol, state and society*, Cambridge: Cambridge University Press, 1995

Williams, B. 'The hidden ethnic cleansing of Muslims in the Soviet Union: The exile and repatriation of Crimean Tatars', *Journal of Contemporary History*, Vol. 37, No. 3, 2002

Williams, K. 'The Russian view(s) of the Prague Spring', *Journal of Cold War Studies*, Vol. 14, No. 2, 2012

Wojnowski, Z. 'De-Stalinization and Soviet patriotism: Ukrainian reactions to East European unrest in 1956', *Kritika*, Vol. 13, No. 4, 2012

Wojnowski, Z. 'De-Stalinization and the failure of Soviet identity building in Kazakhstan', *Journal of Contemporary History*, Vol. 52, No. 4, 2016

Wojnowski, Z. *The Near Abroad: Socialist Eastern Europe and Soviet patriotism in Ukraine, 1956–85*, Toronto: University of Toronto Press, 2017

Woll, J. *Real Images: Soviet cinema and the thaw*, London: I.B. Tauris, 1999

Yarska-Smirnova, A. and Romanov, P. eds. *Sovetskaya sotsial'naya politika: Stseny i deistvuyushchie litsa, 1940–1985*, Moskva: Tsentr sotsial'noi politiki i gendernykh issledovanii, 2008

Yekelchyk, S. *Ukraine: Birth of a modern nation*, Oxford: Oxford University Press, 2007

Yekelchyk, S. 'The early 1960s as a cultural space: A microhistory of Ukraine's generation of cultural rebels', *Nationalities Papers*, Vol. 43, No. 1, 2015

Yordanov, R. *The Soviet Union and the Horn of Africa during the Cold War*, Lanham, MD: Lexington Books, 2016

Yudin, K. 'Ot stalinskoi diktatury k khrushchevskoi modernizatsii', *Voprosy istorii*, No. 12, 2016

Yurchak, A. *Everything Was Forever until It Was No More*, Princeton, NJ: Princeton University Press, 2005

Zezina, M. 'Shokovaya terapiya: Ot 1953 goda k 1956 godu', *Otechestvennaya istoriya*, No. 2, 1995

Zezina, M. *Sovetskaya khudozhestvennaya intelligentsiya i vlast' v 1950e – 1960e gody*, Moskva: Dialog MGU, 1999

Zhuk, S. *Rock and Roll in the Rocket City: The West, identity and ideology in Soviet Dniepropetrovsk, 1960–1985*, Baltimore, MD: Johns Hopkins University Press, 2010

Zhuk, S. 'Popular religiosity in the "closed city" of Soviet Ukraine: Cultural consumption and religion during late socialism, 1959–84', *Russian History*, Vol. 40, No. 2, 2013

Zhuk, S. 'Hollywood's insidious charms: The impact of American cinema and television in the Soviet Union during the Cold War', *Cold War History*, Vol. 14, No. 4, 2014

Zhuk, S. *KGB Operations against the US and Canada in Soviet Ukraine, 1953–1991*, London: Routledge, 2022

Zorkaya, N. *The Illustrated History of Soviet Cinema*, New York: Hippocrene Books, 1989

Zoubir, Y. 'The United States, the Soviet Union, and the decolonisation of the Maghreb, 1945–62', *Middle Eastern Studies*, Vol. 31, No. 1, 1995

Zubkova, E. *Obshchestvo i reformy, 1945–64*, Moskva: Rossiya molodaya, 1993

Zubkova, E. *Russia after the War: Hopes, illusions and disappointments, 1945–1957*, Armonk, NY: M.E. Sharpe, 1998

Zubkova, E. 'Na "krayu" sovetskogo obshchestva: Marginal'nye gruppy naseleniya i gosudarstvennaya politika, 1940–1960e gody', *Russkaya istoriya*, No. 5, 2009

Zubok, V. 'Spy vs spy: The KGB vs the CIA, 1960–62', *Bulletin of the Cold War International History Project*, No. 4, 1994

Zubok, V. *A Failed Empire: The Soviet Union and the Cold War from Stalin to Gorbachev*, Chapel Hill, NC: University of North Carolina Press, 2009

Zubok, V. *Zhivago's Children: The last Russian intelligentsia*, Cambridge, MA, and London: Harvard University Press, 2009

Unpublished PhD theses

Froggatt, M. 'Science in propaganda and popular culture in the USSR under Khrushchev (1953–1964)', University of Oxford, 2006

Shakarian, P. 'An Armenian reformer in Khrushchev's Kremlin: Anastas Mikoyan and the politics of difference in the USSR, 1953–64', Ohio State University, 2021

Tatarchenko, K. 'A house with the window to the West: The Akademgorodok Computer Center (1958–1993)', Princeton University, 2013

Williams, A. 'Materials for maternity: The abortion procedure, communist morality and urbanisation in Soviet Russia, 1944–1968', University of Leeds, 2023

INDEX